USA

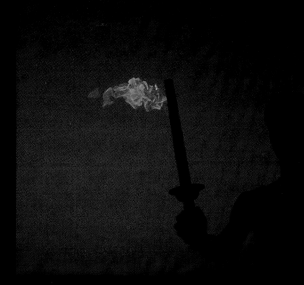

(ALLSPORT / VANDYSTADT)

"Everybody should have a dream.

Everybody should work toward that dream. And if you believe hard enough, whether it be in the Olympic Games, or be in the business world, or the music world or the educational world, it all comes down to one thing.

One day we can all stand on the top of the victory stand, and one day we can watch our flag rise above all others to the crescendo of our national anthem, and one day, you can say, on this day, 'I am a champion.'"

Jesse Owens

COMMEMORATIVE PUBLICATIONS
SALT LAKE CITY, UTAH

ATHENS TO ATLANTA

100 YEARS OF GLORY

publisher
Mikko Laitinen
Commemorative Publications
P.O. Box 21038
Salt Lake City, Utah 84121

corporate manager
Judd L. Parr

managing editor
Lisa H. Albertson

text
Lee Benson
Doug Robinson, Dee Benson

USOC editor
Frank Zang

USOC associate editor
C. Robert Paul

printing
Banta ISG Bushman Press, Inc.
Provo, Utah

binding
Prizma Industries, Inc.
Salt Lake City

duotones and color separations
Pre Press Services, Inc.
Salt Lake City

typesetting
Linda Vrieze
Salt Lake City

computer input
Teresa Jones
Salt Lake City

production thanks to
 PageMaker FreeHand PhotoStyler ALDUS® Adobe

publisher's thanks
Atlanta Committee for the Olympic Games, Atlanta Chamber of Commerce, Alexandra Le Clef Mandl - IOC Olympic Museum, Karen Goddy, Shiirley Ito and Michael Salmon - Amateur Athletic Federation of Los Angeles, Stephanie Mullen - Allsport, Noteworthy Books - Marketing Agency Servicing Public and School Libraries and Bookstores, Len Corbosiero, Tarja Laitinen, Sharon Parr, Eric Linder

photographers
Allsport / Los Angeles — Shaun Botterill, Simon Bruty, David Cannon, Richard Clarkson, Chris Cole, Tim Defrisco, Tony Duffy, Jim Gund, Mike Hewitt, David Leah, Ken Levine, Bob Martin, James Meehan, Gray Mortimore, Joe Patronite, Mike Powell, Steve Powell, Pascal Rondeau, Billy Stickland, Rick Stewart

Allsport / Vandystandt

Allsport / Letikuva Oy

Olympic Poster Photography Credits: Amsterdam 1928, p.92, Barcelona 1992, p.226 — courtesy of Amateur Athletic Foundation of Los Angeles; Los Angeles 1984, p.204 — Allsport; All Others, p. 20, 28, 36, 44, 52, 62, 74, 82, 102, 112, 124, 132, 142, 152, 162, 170, 180, 188, 196, 216 — International Olympic Committee.

Photo Credits: p.16 - Allsport / Rondeau; p.17 - Allsport / Gund; p.150-151 - Allsport / Stickland.

Olympic spirit through a child's eyes. (Allsport / M. Powell)

Published under license from the U.S. Olympic Committee by:

 Commemorative Publications
P.O. Box 21038
Salt Lake City, Utah 84121
(801) 278-6260

You can lead a horse to water... (ALLSPORT / MARTIN)

FIELD OF DREAMS

Balancing Act (ALLSPORT / BRUTY)

Photo Op: Barcelona by night.
(ALLSPORT / VANDYSTADT)

u.s. olympic committee

Home of the U.S. Olympic Committee. (ALLSPORT / DEFRISCO)

The United States Olympic Committee, a streamlined organization of 71-member organizations, is the moving force for support of sports in the United States that are on the program of the Olympic and/or Pan American Games, or those wishing to be included.

The USOC is recognized by the International Olympic Committee as the sole agency in the United States whose mission involves training, entering and underwriting the full expenses for the United States teams in the Olympic and Pan American Games. It is the guardian of the Olympic movement in the U.S.

The USOC also supports the bid of U.S. cities to hose the winter and summer Olympic Games, or the winter and summer Pan American Games, and after reviewing all the candidates, votes on and may endorse one city per event as the U.S. bid city. The USOC endorsed Atlanta as the host for the 1996 Olympic Games, while Salt Lake City is the U.S. candidate city for the 2002 Olympic Winter Games. The USOC also selects the cities which will host its own U.S. Olympic Festival and approves the U.S. trial sites for the Olympic and Pan American Games team selections.

Another responsibility of the USOC is the promotion and support of physical fitness and public participation in athletic activities by encouraging developmental programs in the various sports and providing new programs.

America is unique in the Olympic world to the extent that the nation's Olympic effort is propelled by its individual citizens, and by major support from the corporate community. The USOC is one of only a few National Olympic Committees in the world that does not receive continuous support from the federal government.

Therefore the USA's Olympic teams are truly representative of the free enterprise system, and the USOC is proud to say, "America doesn't send athletes to the Olympic Games, Americans do." More than 80 percent of the USOC fund-raising activities are spent for support of the athletes and National Governing Bodies (NGBs).

The U.S. Olympic effort is sustained through the generosity of more than a million individual Americans and U.S. corporations. The mission of the USOC Development Division is to secure the funds necessary to maximize the opportunity for U.S. athletes to perform at the highest level and compete successfully in Olympic competition.

The USOC surpassed its fundraising goal for the 1989-92 quadrennium, reaching $308 million in revenue. For the current quadrennium leading to the Centennial Olympic Games in Atlanta, the USOC has established an operating budget of $388 million. Many different marketing and fundraising programs are used to meet the needs of U.S. athletes to finance their training and preparation for competition.

The U.S. Olympic Committee's Program Areas encompass seven divisions that work together toward the common goal of enhancing athlete development. Despite this shared sense of purpose, each division offers very specialized, distinct services to the NGBs and other member organizations. The seven Program Areas are:

- Athlete Support
- Coaching Development and Education
- Drug Control
- Grants and Insurance Administration
- Olympic Training Centers
- Sports Medicine
- Sport Science and Technology

During the four-year period leading up to the 1996 Olympic Games in Atlanta, the USOC will award close to 10,000 grants in direct aid to athletes, totalling $26 million. The USOC administers five types of athlete grants—

basic, special assistance, tuition, Olympic Job Opportunities and Operation Gold. Athlete support also comes in the form of the Career and Education Assistance program and through an alumni relations division.

The athletes also have an important voice in the U.S. Olympic Movement through the Athletes Advisory Council. All governance councils of the USOC and the NGBs have at least 20 percent membership and voting power held by recent or active athletes representing each sport.

The USOC currently maintains and operates Olympic Training Centers in Colorado Springs, Colo., and Lake Placid, N.Y., with a third complex being built in San Diego. In all the OTCs serve more than 15,000 athletes each year. For athletes selected by their respective NGBs, the USOC offers the athletes free room and board, training facilities, sports medicine care, sport science testing and analysis, local transportation and recreational facilities.

The Colorado Springs complex, which originally opened in 1977, is the headquarters for all the Olympic Training Center programs, as well as the USOC's administrative offices and home of several sport NGBs. The OTC opened in the fall of 1993 the first phase of a $12.88 million construction and renovation project that upgraded the facilities. A state-of-the-art aquatics center and a multipurpose gymnasium are showcase facilities on the OTC campus. Other outstanding facilities include a swimming flume, the world's third largest Olympic Shooting Center and a nearby world-class velodrome.

The Lake Placid OTC opened in November of 1982, and primarily serves athletes who participate in the Olympic winter sports. The newest shining jewel in the OTC collection, the ARCO Training Center, is under construction in San Diego as the USOC's first warm-weather complex. The USOC also supports the U.S. Olympic Education Center at Northern Michigan University in Marquette.

Through these facilities, the USOC's sports medicine division offers a clinical services program which is charged with providing a total health care package for all athletes in residence at the Olympic Training Centers, as well as those athletes at the U.S. Olympic Festivals and USOC-sponsored international competitions. The USOC Sport Science and Technology Division also aids in the athletes' performances through sports biomechanics, sports physiology, sport psychology, computer science and engineering technology.

In addition to entering and underwriting the full expenses of U.S. teams at the Olympic, Pan American and World University Games, the USOC also operates the U.S. Olympic Festival, which has become the nation's premier multisport event, involving more than 3,000 athletes in 37 winter and summer sports. Dating back to 1978, the Festival is held during non-Olympic summers in cities throughout the U.S. with St. Louis serving as the host city in 1994 and Denver in 1995.

Another annual event is the gathering of the U.S. Olympic Committee's "family" for the United States Olympic Congress, which is a convention that focuses directly on the Olympic Movement. The event is scheduled to be held in Nashville in 1994, Atlanta in 1995 and Indianapolis in 1996.

FOR MORE INFORMATION:
U.S. Olympic Committee
One Olympic Plaza
Colorado Springs, Colorado 80909
719 / 578-4529

USOC MEMBER ORGANIZATIONS

Olympic/Pan American Games Sport Organizations

National Archery Association
U.S. Badminton Association
USA Baseball
USA Basketball
U.S. Biathlon Association
U.S. Bobsled and Skeleton Federation
USA Bowling
USA Boxing
American Canoe Association
U.S. Cycling Federation
United States Diving, Inc.
American Horse Shows Association
U.S. Fencing Association
U.S. Field Hockey Association
U.S. Figure Skating Association
USA Gymnastics
USA Hockey
United States Judo, Inc.
U.S. Luge Association
U.S. Modern Pentathlon Association
American Amateur Racquetball Association
U.S. Amateur Confederation of Roller Skating

U.S. Rowing Association
U.S. Sailing Association
National Rifle Association
U.S. Skiing
U.S. Soccer Federation
Amateur Softball Association
U.S. International Speedskating Association
U.S. Swimming, Inc.
U.S. Synchronized Swimming, Inc.
USA Table Tennis
U.S. Taekwondo Union
U.S. Team Handball Federation
U.S. Tennis Association
USA Track & Field
U.S. Volleyball Association
United States Water Polo
U.S. Weightlifting Federation
USA Wrestling

Affiliated Sports Organizations

U.S. Curling Association
U.S. Orienteering Federation
United States Sports Acrobatics Federation
U.S. Squash Racquets Association
American Trampoline and Tumbling Association
Triathlon Federation USA
Underwater Society of America
American Water Ski Association

Community-Based Multisport Organizations

Amateur Athletic Union
American Alliance for Health, Physical Education, Recreation and Dance
Boys and Girls Clubs of America
Catholic Youth Organization
Jewish Community Centers Association
National Exploring Division, Boy Scouts of America
National Association of Police Athletic Leagues
National Congress of State Games
U.S. National Senior Sport Organization
YMCA of the USA
YWCA of the USA

Education-Based Multisport Organizations

National Association of Intercollegiate Athletics
National Collegiate Athletic Association
National Federation of State High School Associations
National Junior College Athletic Association

Armed Forces

U.S. Armed Forces Sports

Disabled In Sports

American Athletic Association for the Deaf
United States Cerebral Palsy Athletic Association
Dwarf Athletic Association of America
National Handicapped Sports
National Wheelchair Athletic Association
Special Olympics International
U.S. Association for Blind Athletes

THE ROAD...

...TO ATLANTA

SERVING IT UP SOUTHERN STYLE

Is there any doubt that Atlanta will throw one great Olympic Games in 1996? Think of it. It's Southern Hospitality and the Olympic Centennial all in one big mix.

And Atlanta couldn't be happier. When it was announced that they had won the bid, Atlantans not only threw a big celebration, complete with fireworks and a band, but they threw another a year later. And this was six years before the Olympics would come to their city.

It was just such enthusiasm and energy that enabled Atlanta to wrest the Games away from bigger, more favored bidders in the first place. Certainly, the odds were stacked against Atlanta from the beginning.

For starters, an American city had hosted the Olympics in 1984, only 12 years earlier, and the Winter Olympics had been in North America both in 1980 (Lake Placid) and 1988 (Calgary). Of the previous 23 Olympic Games, more than half of them (13) had been held in Europe.

What's more, by modern standards, Atlanta was a late entry in the race for '96. The campaign didn't begin until 1987 and then with just nine volunteers led by Atlanta attorney Billy Payne.

But then Atlanta beat Minneapolis-St. Paul and a dozen other cities for the U.S. bid, and the enthusiasm began to grow. Here was a chance, Atlantans believed, to pump $5.1 billion into the state's economy over the next six years, plus add 80,000 jobs and worldwide exposure.

Still, Atlanta was not the most well-heeled bid. Athens spent $30 million on its Olympic bid; Atlanta $7.1 million.

Athens was a big favorite to win the bid, if only for sentimental reasons. The Olympics of 1996 will mark the 100th year since the modern Olympics began in Athens. The return to Athens for the centennial celebration seemed too much to pass up. The other favorite was Melbourne, at least partly because the Olympics hadn't been held in the Southern Hemisphere since 1956.

In the end, political turmoil and instability, not to mention air pollution and traffic congestion, hurt Athens' bid. Meanwhile, Atlanta used a combination of charm, style, organization, enthusiasm and technology to win the bid. Atlantans went beyond the usual practice of lavishing IOC members with the red carpet treatment. A $1 million three-dimensional interactive computer program, created for the Atlanta bid committee by Georgia Tech, allowed a viewer to seemingly fly through Atlanta and view it and its Olympic facilities from any angle on the screen. Almost 70 IOC members, who visited

Atlanta, were fascinated and impressed.

The results of the final IOC vote in Japan stunned everyone. Atlanta beat runnerup Athens 51-35 on the fifth of five ballots, with Toronto third and Melbourne fourth.

"I am absolutely amazed," said Michael Lomax, chairman of the Fulton County Commission. "I can't believe Atlanta has gone from a place nobody thought had a chance to really get those Games."

Thousands of people watched the IOC's announcement on TV in progressive city and with very friendly people. It's what's known as southern hospitality."

Thus, Atlanta will join St. Louis (1904) and Los Angeles (1932, 1984) as the only U.S. cities ever to host the Summer Olympics. By the time the '96 Games arrive, Atlanta will have built an 85,000-seat Olympic Stadium, an aquatic center, a velodrome, a tennis center and other facilities. The crown jewel will be the Olympic Stadium, a $209 billion project that the Atlanta Committee for the Olympic Games (ACOG) will of the Olympic Center in downtown Atlanta.

The bulk of the events will be staged at venues either in the Olympic Ring in the heart of the city or at the Olympic Park at Stone Mountain, 15 miles east of downtown. In addition, there will be yachting and beach volleyball in Savannah, Ga., whitewater slalom events on the Ocoee River in Tennessee, and women's softball in Columbus, Ga. Preliminary round soccer matches will be held in Alabama, Florida and Washington, D.C., while the finals will be held in

More than eight million tickets will be sold and two million visitors are expected to fill the 73,000 hotel rooms within a 90-minute radius of the Olympic Center in downtown Atlanta.

Atlanta. When the winner was announced, there was a cry of joy and disbelief. Fireworks and balloons were released into the morning sky. Strangers hugged; a band played the Olympic anthem. Crowds gathered six deep around vending carts to buy Olympic T-shirts and hats.

"I think what helped us win the Games was that people were very surprised by Atlanta and what a great place it is," says Bob Brennan, Atlanta's Olympic press chief. "This is the first time the Olympic Games have been held in the Eastern U.S. or in the South. Most people know little about the South beyond what they saw in Gone With the Wind. They're finding Atlanta is a modern, reconfigure for the Atlanta Braves baseball team and present as a gift to the city of Atlanta at the conclusion of the Games.

The total budget for the Games is $1.573 billion while the estimated revenues are $1.589 billion. Both represent all-time highs, and that's just the start of the Atlanta superlatives. Virtually everything about the Atlanta Games is projected to be bigger than anything in its wake. As many as 200 countries, the largest number by far, may enter teams, represented by more than 15,000 athletes, coaches and team officials. More than eight million tickets will be sold and two million visitors are expected to fill the 73,000 hotel rooms within a 90-minute radius Athens, Ga.

Enthusiasm for the Olympics has revived Atlanta and, perhaps not coincidentally, sent the city's sporting endeavors on something of a roll. Since the city won the Olympic bid, the Atlanta Braves have gone to the World Series twice; a native son, Evander Holyfield, has claimed the world heavyweight boxing title twice; Georgia Tech has won a share of the national football championship; and the National Football League chose Atlanta as the site for the 1994 Super Bowl. Count all the above as a harbinger of good things to come in '96.

ABOVE / *Atlanta's skyline.*
(ALLSPORT / LEVINE)

1896

April 6-15, 1896

13 Nations

311 Athletes

9 Sports

11 USA golds

ATHENS

A REVIVAL OF THE FITTEST

Inspired by the ancients, revived by a Frenchman, funded by a merchant, and received with open arms by the Greeks, the Olympic Games made their comeback in Athens on the 6th of April 1896. It was a most improbable comeback, given that 1,503 years had passed since the 293rd and final edition of the original Olympic era was held in 393 A.D. Those Games were the last before Emperor Theodosis II banned all non-Christian events in the Roman Empire.

Since the first Olympic Games, staged in 776 B.C. in Olympia, were convened to honor the Greek God Zeus — and indeed, since Greek mythology holds that Zeus himself was the first medal winner in a wrestling match with Kronos, his father — the Olympic Games qualified as non-Christian.

So that was that and for 15 centuries the world let the Olympics lie in antiquity. They might be lying there yet if not for a French Baron named Pierre de Coubertin, a son of an artist, a graduate of St. Cyr (France's West Point), a student of history, and a would-be athlete who was somewhat hampered in that area by his 5-foot-3 inch, 100-pound frame.

The Baron became obsessed with reviving the Olympic movement. Being a Frenchman and, more exactly, a Parisian, his notion was to have the Games make their grand re-entrance in Paris. He chose the year 1900 for the occasion.

He presented this timetable to a world athletics congress he convened in Paris in 1894. Seventy-eight delegates from

TOP / *The host city of Athens gave medals only to the first- and second-place finishers. But it was a silver medal for the winner and a bronze one for the runner-up.* (ALLSPORT)

RIGHT / *Athens had the job of host but no suitable stadium and no funds for reconstruction. Greek philanthropist Georgios Averoff solved that problem. Wealthy and an architect, he designed and helped finance the reconstruction of the Panathenaic Stadium.* (ALLSPORT)

The Athens Olympics were rudimentary in many regards. There were no events for women. Swimming was held in the Bay of Zea, where water temperatures were 55 degrees. As for the competitors, they were a curious mix.

T 155289

TOP (LEFT) / *Rope climbing saw its debut as an Olympic event in Athens. It was discontinued in 1932.* (IOC)

TOP (RIGHT) / *While the rings have moved indoors, they're considered the ultimate display of strength.* (IOC)

MIDDLE / *The four freestyle events were held in the open water where swimmers were at the mercy of 55-degree water and rough waves. In his second race and second victory, 18-year-old Alfred Hajos applied knowledge to experience and smeared his body with a layer of grease to protect himself from the cold.* (IOC)

BOTTOM / *The crouch start was an American innovation that intrigued the European crowd. Thomas Burke (second from left) used it convincingly, winning the 100-meter dash in 12 seconds flat.* (IOC)

OPPOSITE (TOP) / *Twenty-year-old Robert Garrett entered the discus throw on a whim and won.* (IOC)

OPPOSITE (BOTTOM) / *He trailed for 23 miles and the hometown fans saw little hope in claiming the marathon title as their own. But Spiridon Louis became an instant hero when he entered the stadium first, salvaging the pride of the Greeks with a victory in the most important of events.* (ALLSPORT)

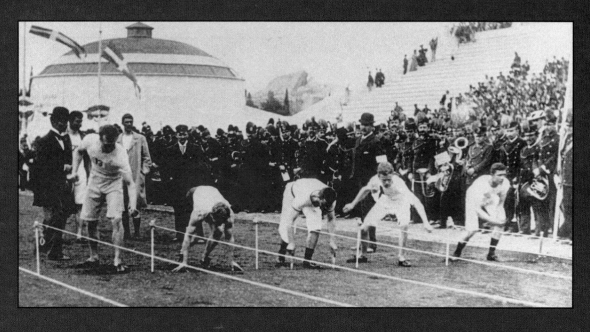

some 34 countries were so taken by Coubertin's idea that they decided that A) They couldn't wait six years and B) The Olympic flame should be revived where it expired.

The first Olympic Games of the modern era would be held in Athens, Greece, in 1896.

The Greeks, who had already made several, albeit unsuccessful, attempts at reviving one of the best ideas they ever had, were immediately enthusiastic. Their enthusiasm didn't transfer to their pocketbooks, however, and when public funding to build the facilities — chiefly the restoration of the Panathenaic Stadium, white marble columns and all — stalled, philanthropists were required to save the cause. The chief benefactors turned out to be Evangelios Zappas, a leader of earlier Olympic revival movements, and Georgious Averoff, a Greek merchant who pledged one million drachma, or about $200,000, to whip the stadium back into splendor.

More than 100,000 Grecians welcomed the return of the Games on Sunday, Apr, 6, 1896 — some 80,000 of them filling the Olympic Stadium while another 20,000, at least, lined the surrounding hills. King George opened the Games, welcoming 311 athletes from 13 countries.

The Athens Olympics were rudimentary in many regards. There were no events for women. Swimming was held in the Bay of Zea, where water temperatures were 55 degrees. The stadium track was a narrow oblong 330 yards in circumference, making turning difficult for the runners. As for the competitors, they were a curious mix. Some were seasoned athletes. Others entered events by happenstance. Robert Garrett of Baltimore fit both categories. He came to Athens to enter the shot put, which he won. Then, when discovering that the discus the Greeks used was much lighter than the ones he'd used back home, he entered the discus on a whim, and won.

Track and field, cycling, fencing, gymnastics, shooting, swimming, tennis, weightlifting, and wrestling were the sports of Athens. Greeks dominated, winning 47 medals, well ahead of France's 11 medals, Germany's 15, and the United States' 19. The U.S. did win 11 gold medals, however, compared to Greece's 10, and dominated the

signature track and field venue with nine of 12 wins there.

More than a little home-country disgruntlement was brewing when the final event, the marathon, took place. The idea for this long distance run had been suggested by French historian Michael Breal, who knew well the legend of Pheidippides, the professional runner sent to Athens in 449 B.C. to deliver important news of a victory by the Grecian army over the Persians at the Battle of Marathon. Upon his arrival, Pheidippides reportedly called out, "Rejoice, we conquer!," and then dropped dead.

Except for the death part, the Olympic "marathon" would reenact Pheidippides' run as closely as possible. It would begin in the city of Marathon and end in Athens, 40 kilometers (approximately 23 miles) away. The Greeks, naturally, were anxious that one of their own would follow in the footsteps of Pheidippides. The domination of the Americans in the running events only added to their anxiety.

Seventeen entrants started out from the Marathon Bridge, including Edwin Flack of Australia and American Arthur Blake, the one-two finishers in the 1,500-meter run. When these two took the early lead, all of Greece went into mourning. But Flack and Blake would discover the folly of starting too fast and leave the lead to Spiridon Louis, a short, spindly, postal messenger from Maroussi, Greece, whose entrance two hours and fifty-eight minutes later into the Panathenaic Stadium was met with the equal of any pandemonium that would follow in the next 100 years of hometown heroes winning Olympic medals.

King George embraced Louis, who was given an antique vase, a golden cup, a laurel wreath, and a horse and cart. Forty years later, Spiridon would be summoned to the Berlin Games of 1936 to deliver a laurel wreath from the sacred grove of Olympia to Adolf Hitler.

All was well that ended well. The movement had been blessed. By Zeus perhaps. Or at least his spirit. Climaxed by Spiridon Louis' run into history as the stadium chanted "Elleen!" "Elleen!" ("A Greek!" "A Greek!"), there was no argument that an encore was decidedly in order for the first Olympic Games of the modern era.

james b. connolly

Better Late Than Never

The first man to win an Olympic championship in 1,503 years almost missed the track meet.

James B. Connolly, a maverick either well ahead of his time, or well behind it, depending on your point of view, caught the Olympic spirit as soon as he read in a magazine in 1895 that the ancient Games of Olympia were to be revived the next year in the city where they expired in 393 A.D. — Athens, Greece. A sophomore at Harvard at the time, Connolly immediately went to his track coach and his professors and informed them of his intent.

To which they replied, "huh?"

"Games at Athens? What Games? What Athens?" they said to Connolly, according to his memoirs.

Worse, they refused to give him time off from his schoolwork to participate.

None of this sat particularly well with Connolly, a champion triple jumper — or "hop, step and jumper" as his specialty was known at the time. So he quit Harvard, or they quit on him, and the Olympics had their first protest even before the Games had officially begun.

Connolly was the first American athlete to announce his intent to compete in Athens and drummed up the support of the Suffolk Athletic Club in South Boston. Their deal was this: He'd wear their emblem — a stag's head done in gold — while he competed … and they'd wish him well. They'd have gladly given him some money and equipment, but they didn't have any.

Nonplussed, Connolly made his travel plans and soon enough was united with the other American athletes who, in due course, had also decided Athens and the first Olympic Games added up to an adventure they couldn't resist. There were 10 track and field athletes in all: Connolly from the Suffolk A.C., five athletes — Tom Burke, Arthur Blake, Tom Curtis, Ellery Clarke and Bill Hort — from the Boston Athletic Club, and four athletes — Herb Jamieson, Frank Lane, Al Tyler and Bob Garrett — from the track team at Princeton, where the coach and professors obviously adopted a more liberal point of view than Harvard.

The team, such as it was, left New York Harbor en masse on Mar. 9, 1896, embarking on a 17-day boat-and-train voyage that, they reckoned, would get them in Athens some 12 days before the official start of the Games — enough time to get rid of boat-and-train lag and to sufficiently train and acclimatize.

They traveled to Gibraltar by boat and then made their way to Naples by train before setting off for Greece. All went well enough until Naples, 12 days out, when a pickpocket stole Connolly's wallet. The Naples police were equally as unimpressed with where Connolly was going as his Harvard professors and they insisted that he stay in their city until they concluded their investigation. Finally, a frustrated Connolly had to bolt from the police station and run for the train to Brindisi, which was leaving the platform with only nine members of the American team on board. Connolly just made the train, grabbing the outstretched hands of Arthur Blake and Tom Burke, who pulled him in at the last second.

"I never ran faster in my life, not even in spiked shoes," wrote Connolly.

It was a good thing he caught that

train, considering the news that was about to greet the U.S. Olympians five days later when they arrived in Athens at 9 p.m. the night of Mar. 25 ... Or so they thought.

When they checked into their hotel they noticed they were in the midst of a massive city-wide celebration. They inquired if Athens was always like this at night. It was then that they were told that Athens wasn't always like this — only on the eve of the start of the Olympic Games.

It turned out that the Greeks were still using the Greek Orthodox Calendar in 1896, and when they said the first Olympic Games of the modern era would begin on April 6th, they meant *their* April 6th.

America, and most of the rest of the world that was on the Western Roman calendar, lagged 12 days behind the Greek calendar. The Americans had arrived on Apr. 5, according to Greece reckoning, and not Mar. 25.

As the members of the Boston A.C. athletes grilled the college kids from Princeton about not knowing of such things, Connolly realized that he had approximately 12 hours — not 12 days — to get ready to compete.

He decided going to bed was worthless.

Connolly's event was the first to be decided the next morning, thus ensuring that the winner of the hop, step and jump would be the first Olympic champion since a boxer from Armenia named Barasdates was awarded an olive wreath as the last champion prior to the cancellation of the ancient Games in 393 A.D.

The Greeks had not taken this revival casually. Eighty-thousand people filled the stadium the morning of March 26/April 6. King George I of Greece declared the Games open to not only the capacity crowd inside the stadium, but to the 20,000 who lined the grassy hills and knolls outside.

Quite taken by the scene, even if he hadn't gotten any sleep, Connolly readied himself to jump. He was the last of 12 contestants. The rules were slightly different than he was used to in the States — calling for more of a hop, hop and jump than a hop, step and jump — but by now he was getting used to adjusting quickly. His first jump felt good and was accompanied by a loud cheer from the stands. Leading that cheer was the crew of the United States Navy ship *Liberty*, which had just docked in the harbor.

"I came quite awake then," wrote Connolly, who, by now completely inspired, went on to completely dominate the competition, winning by three feet and three inches. His top jump of 44 feet, 11 3/4 inches was far from his career best — indeed, the next year he would break the world triple jump record by becoming the first human to clear 49 feet — but under the circumstances it was a fête for celebration.

"I was the first Olympic victor in more than 1,500 years," wrote Connolly. "It was a moment in a young fellow's life."

The U.S. team went on to win nine of the 12 track and field events in Athens before Connolly bid Athens adieu and made his way back across Europe, not leaving for home from Paris until he was down to his last three dollars.

He got back to South Boston in the dead of night, alone, with no brass band to greet him. His possessions included an Olympic diploma in a shoe box, a gold cup given to him by Prince George, a bust of a Greek god whose name he wasn't sure of, an olive wreath from the sacred grove of Zeus in old Olympia, and 20 yards of silk for his mother to make a dress.

And also the championship medal, the first of the modern era.

As time went on, and as the modern Olympics found their niche as worldwide sporting festivals without parallel, Connolly's stature rose

Connolly realized that he had approximately 12 hours — not 12 days — to get ready to compete.

accordingly. So it was that 53 years later — after he had become an accomplished journalist and writer, with some 25 books and 200 short stories to his credit; after a distinguished career writing for some of America's leading magazines such as *Colliers*; after serving his county in the Spanish-American war and earning a citation for bravery at San Juan Hill — James B. Connolly was invited back to Harvard. During the commencement ceremonies for the Class of '49, they brought him up to the stage. There, they gave him his block "H" ... and told him they were sorry. π

ABOVE / *James Brendan Connolly forsaked his education at Harvard to compete in the hop, step and jump — today's triple jump — in Athens. With his jump of 44-11 3/4, he also leaped into the Olympic annals as the first champion of the modern Olympic Games.* [ALLSPORT]

M A R A

LEFT / *Although no race in the ancient Greek Olympics was longer than 5,000 meters, Olympic organizers were inspired enough by the story of Pheidippides and the Battle of the Marathon to propose a long-distance race in the first modern Olympics in 1896. Since 1896, one of the most formidable foes of the marathon has been the heat. Little has that changed for today's marathoners. In Barcelona, with a field of runners battling temperature and humidity, Hwang Young-Cho would break away at the 25-mile mark to give South Korea its first Olympic marathon championship since 1936.*
(ALLSPORT / M. POWELL)

T   H   O   N

1900

May 20 - October 28, 1900

22 Nations

1330 Athletes (11 women)

17 Sports

21 USA golds

PARIS

The Olympic movement, anxious to establish itself internationally after its grand debut in Athens, moved outside Greece for the first time in the 2,000-plus year history of the Games. And soon wondered why.

The Games of 1900 came to a Paris engulfed in political and social turmoil. The home of Baron Pierre de Coubertin, the father of the modern Olympics, didn't know what to do with the Baron's invention, or where to put it. Or, for that matter, what to do with the Baron. Truly a zealot now that he was flushed by the success of Athens, Coubertin's aspirations for Paris were lofty and grand. He envisioned coupling the Olympics with the Universal Exposition scheduled for Paris during the summer of 1900. He planned to reconstruct the temples, statues, gymnasiums and stadiums of ancient Greece — an Olympic Park as it were — and hold all the competitions there. The program would include all the sports seen at Olympia along with several new additions.

Little did the organizers of Paris' Universal Exposition realize that what Coubertin was suggesting would become standard procedure for Olympic Games of the future. In 1900, all they realized was that they considered Coubertin a pest. Through political machinations and maneuverings they succeeded in not only shelving Coubertin's grandiose plans for a sporting exhibition, but also in shelving the Baron. He was replaced by Daniel Merillon, a more willing participant in the Exposition's plans to hold "exhibitions

TOP / *With three Wimbledon titles under her belt, Charlotte Cooper of Great Britain handily won the first women's Olympic tennis competition in Paris.* (IOC)

RIGHT / *The yachting events in 1900 were unique to the Olympic program (that is, they didn't survive past Paris) and were divided into seven classes based on weight. The French and English shared three victories apiece while a Swiss sailed to victory in the 1-2 ton class.* (IOC)

UNDER *EXPOSURE*

There was little mention of the Games in the press, local or worldwide, and as far as anyone knew, Pierre de Coubertin's name was not mentioned at all. His prediction months ahead of the event, that "we have made a hash of our work," proved to be prophetic.

of physical exercises and sports" as part of the Expo. A small part. These exhibitions — a part of what Expo organizers called "International Championships" — wound up being spread out over a period of five months (from the 20th of May to the 28th of October) and were mostly devoid of spectators, press coverage, and any mention of the word "Olympic."

Indeed, many of 1900's winners had no idea they were Olympic champions until many years later, and some not at all. Michael Théato, a Frenchman who won the marathon, only knew that he'd finished first in a hot, very confusing footrace. Not until 12 years later did Théato find out it was the Olympic marathon he had won.

That marathon also underscored the Parisian Games' lack of organization. The course wound through the winding, narrow streets of Paris and was not well marked. One contestant, Arthur Newton of the United States, thought he was in the lead for the last half of the race when no other runners passed him. But he had gotten lost and taken the wrong route. When he finally crossed the finish line he found, to his surprise, four runners already there resting.

The golf competition produced the first woman champion of the Olympic movement. Peggy Abbott of the United States was visiting Paris that summer with her mother. Since both were members of the Chicago Golf Club and avid golfers, they decided to enter an "international golf tournament" at Compiègne. Peggy won the nine-hole event with a score of 47 and her mother finished seventh. Both would go to their graves not realizing they had competed in the Olympics. In that regard, they were just like the seven-year-old French boy who was drafted into duty as a coxswain for

TOP / *Running in 102 degree heat on a confusing course — only eight of the 19 starters finished — made for a heated controversy in the marathon where the first two finishers were French. Emile Champion, taking a refreshment, finished second to streetwise Michel Théato, a 23-year-old bakery deliveryman.* (IOC)

ABOVE / *Diving wasn't a part of the Olympic program yet, though Paris did host an obstacle race and underwater swimming event. The venue was the river Seine and swimmers got more than a little help from the current.* (IOC)

Dutch rowers François Brandt and Roelof Klein in the two-man-with-cox rowing competition. No sooner had the Dutchmen won than their lightweight teammate jumped out of the boat and disappeared into the streets of Paris, little realizing he was not only an Olympic champion but would remain the youngest winner in Olympic history.

Twenty-two nations and 1,330 official competitors wound up participating in Paris. The vast majority — 884 in all — came from France. The competition venues, such as they were, stretched from one end of Paris to the other. Swimming events were held in the Seine, hampered by boats, waves, heat and garbage. The track and field competitions were held on the grass turf of the Racing Club de France in the Bois de Boulogne. Jumpers had to dig their own pits, runners had to compete on an uneven 500-meter grass track, and throwers had to contend with numerous tree branches that stopped many of their best efforts. Spectators were rare, and rarer yet when javelins began flying through the trees.

As they did in Athens in 1896, U.S. athletes dominated the track and field events, winning 17 of 23 gold medals — even if they didn't actually receive them — while increasing their all-time Olympic total to 26 firsts in 35 events.

There was little mention of the Games in the press, local or worldwide, and as far as anyone knew, Coubertin's name was not mentioned at all. His prediction months ahead of the event, that "we have made a hash of our work," proved to be prophetic. As Coubertin and his fellow Parisians would discover firsthand 24 years later when the Olympics returned to Paris with the Games of the VIIIth Olympiad, the encore would look all the better because of the unfortunate example of 1900.

alvin kraenzlein
&
meyer prinstein

Never On Sunday

Judging by the way Alvin Kraenzlein was holding his jaw, Meyer Prinstein was not happy about the way the Olympic long jump finals of 1900 had turned out. The two were teammates but who could tell? Their hosts, the French, were curious: Did the Americans always celebrate winning a competition with a fistfight?

Actually, it wasn't much of a fistfight. The rest of the 55-man strong United States Olympic Team quickly broke it up, and, besides, Kraenzlein wasn't a willing participant. He wasn't the angry one. It was Prinstein — outraged that Kraenzlein had competed on Sunday — who had the chip on his shoulder.

This was not a religious issue. Prinstein was Jewish and by point of fact recognized Saturday, not Sunday, as his Sabbath Day. If anyone had had a sacred problem with competing on the Sabbath it would have been Kraenzlein, a Christian. The issue was that the French had scheduled the long jump finals for Sunday and Prinstein's supervisors, from the Syracuse University, would not allow him to compete. But Kraenzlein wasn't a Syracuse man. He represented the University of Pennsylvania, an institution with a more liberal bent. They told Kraenzlein to decide for himself if he wanted to compete on the Christian Sabbath Day.

Kraenzlein decided he wanted to compete — and he won. His winning jump of 23 feet, six and 3/4 inches was one centimeter, or just less than a half-inch, better than the jump Prinstein had managed in the preliminary rounds held the day before. Thus Kraenzlein was the champion and Prinstein a most unhappy silver medalist.

So unhappy that Prinstein confronted Kraenzlein and suggested that they have a jump-off, just the two of them, *mano à mano*, the next day.

When Kraenzlein said no thanks, Prinstein slugged him.

Both athletes, of course, could blame the French for putting them in such a position in the first place. Scheduling was not a long suit of the second Olympic Games held in Paris, and the long jump proved it.

The long jump finals, as well as a number of other track and field final events, had originally been scheduled for Saturday, July 14. When Kraenzlein and Prinstein and the rest of the American Olympic team set sail for Europe, that was their understanding. But in the meantime, the French organizers realized that July 14 was Bastille Day, the Republic's most revered holiday, and it was feared attendance would be severely reduced as a result. Without consulting any of the foreign delegations, the French bumped the finals to the next day, July 15, a Sunday.

At the time, Sunday competition in the United States was universally taboo. But since this track meet was in Paris, on the other side of the Atlantic Ocean, it was left up to the various U.S. clubs and colleges that together made up the collective U.S. Olympic team to individually sort out their own consciences. The majority of the schools, including Yale, Princeton, Chicago, Michigan and Syracuse, refused to participate. A few, including Georgetown and Penn, left it up to their athletes, as did the New York Athletic Club.

Thus was a Kraenzlein-Prinstein showdown prevented in the finals.

To say such a showdown was eagerly anticipated by the masses would be to do more justice to the sparse Paris crowds than is deserved.

But the athletes and coaches of the American team were rather disappointed that such a duel couldn't take place. They knew that Kraenzlein and Prinstein were the two best long jumpers in America, and had spent the last few years building up a world-class rivalry. Less than three months before they came to Paris they had engaged in a thrilling long jump showdown in Philadelphia, where Prinstein, competing on Kraenzlein's home Penn turf, had jumped 24 feet, 7 1/4 inches to not only defeat Kraenzlein but add three inches to the previous world record, which had been held, of course, by Alvin Kraenzlein.

On Bastille Day, in Paris's long jump pre-liminaries, Prinstein kept his edge on Kraenzlein by reg-istering the day's best jump at a distance of 23 feet, 6 1/4 inches. It was more than a foot behind his world record, but, considering the circumstances, an eye-popping leap nonetheless. The jumping conditions in Paris were on a par with the organ-ization. The field events were held in a park at the Croix-Catelan, where the jumpers had to dig their own pit and were forbidden from jumping off anything but the natural grassy surface.

On Saturday night, Prinstein was feeling very good about his chances of being the second Olympic long jump champion of the modern era. Not only had he established a mark that would be hard to beat the next day by those who decided to jump on Sunday — mostly Europeans, so he thought — but he was sure his chief rival, Kraenzlein, would not be jumping either.

But Kraenzlein had other ideas,

and, with Prinstein's mark in the dirt providing something concrete for him to aim at, he wound up equaling that mark, and another centimeter besides.

Kraenzlein, at 23, two years older than Prinstein, was nothing if not a competitor. Part of his sluggish start in the long jump competition on Saturday he could blame on his concurrent participation that day in the 110-meter hurdles, where he set an Olympic record of 15.4 seconds despite the grassy track. Kraenzlein was a hurdler ahead of his time. Instead of hurdling by tucking up both legs over the hurdle, as was custom-ary, Kraenzlein ex-tended his lead leg and tucked up only his trailing leg. It was a style that, with time, would be adopted by

every hurdler in the world.

The Penn man would also win the 60-meter dash in Paris as well as the 200-meter hurdles, which, despite the mushy track, would include a world-record clocking of 25.4 seconds. He did all of this medal winning in three days — the 110-meter hurdles on Saturday, the long jump and 60-meter dash on Sunday, and the 200-meter hurdles on Monday. Becoming the first winner of four Olympic gold medals in the same Games was taxing, almost nonstop, work.

Prinstein was also a busy trackman in Paris. Besides the long jump, he

entered the triple jump, which, fortunately for him, was held on Monday. He consoled himself by handily taking that title with an Olympic record of 47 feet, 5 3/4 inches. His jump was almost two feet farther than the jump registered by the silver medalist James Connolly, who had won the inaugural Olympic triple jump four years earlier in Athens.

Prinstein brooded over his long jump loss for four long years before getting to avenge his defeat by winning the Olympic gold medal in St. Louis in 1904 (where he also won the triple jump). He won yet again in the Intercalated Games in Athens in 1906. As for Kraenzlein, he was perfectly content to rest on his Parisien laurels. After setting a world record in the low hurdles (23.6) later that year that would last for 25 years, he retired from competition shortly

Prinstein confronted Kraenzlein and suggested that they have a jump-off. When Kraenzlein said no thanks, Prinstein slugged him.

thereafter and became a coach. After Paris, he never competed on Sunday again. π

FOOTBALL

LEFT / *When soccer was introduced as an Olympic event in 1900, the field was comprised of only three teams. Today, the field is limited to 16 teams which must qualify in pre-Olympic tournaments. The 1992 Games featured the first-ever under-23 Olympic competition for men. Women's soccer joins the Olympic program for the first time in 1996 with no age restrictions.*
(ALLSPORT / CANNON)

1904

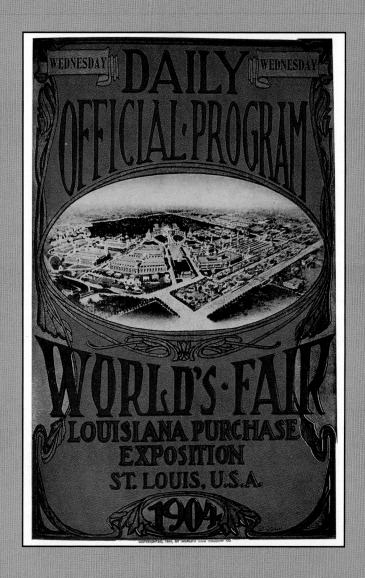

July 1 - November 23, 1904

12 Nations

687 Athletes (525 Americans)

14 Sports

80 USA golds

ST. LOUIS

For its third act of the modern era the Olympics came to America, and if the movement thought it had seen it all in Athens and Paris, well, it hadn't.

Determined to do things their way, the Americans did just that. As in Paris four years earlier, the Games were tied to a World's Fair — in this case the World's Fair & Louisiana Purchase Exposition — but whereas the Parisians treated sport as a kind of petulant stepchild, in St. Louis, sport was given one of the rings of the circus all to itself. A total of 390 sporting events wound up being held in St. Louis from July through November of 1904, although the International Olympic Committee would officially sanction just 88 of them. It was in St. Louis that basketball was seen for the first time in the Olympic Games, although only as a demonstration sport since it was just 13 years since the game's invention and since America was the only country that had any familiarity with it whatsoever. Other made-in-America creations such as baseball and lacrosse, the plunge-for-distance (included in the swimming program, where the suspense was to see if those who went down would come back up) and a form of water polo that the Germans, after their team dropped out of the draw, disgustedly described as "softball in the water," were St. Louis exhibitions.

St. Louis was also where boxing, a sport considered too barbaric by the Europeans, made its Olympic debut, albeit only with Americans boxing

TOP / *Two women put on the gloves to demonstrate the new Olympic sport of boxing, an event completely dominated by the U.S. — since only the Americans participated.* (IOC)

RIGHT / *To be sure, the odds were distinctly in the Americans' favor due to their sheer number — 525 out of 617 athletes were from the U.S. — but in swimming, foreign competitors won four of the six events where more than one nation was represented.* (IOC)

THE THIRD ACT

Several made-in-America creations debuted as demonstration and medal sports including a form of water polo that the Germans disgustedly described as "softball in the water."

RIGHT / *Six-foot, six-inch, 250-pound Ralph Rose accumulated five Olympic medals from 1904 to 1912. In St. Louis, he won gold, silver and bronze in the shot put, discus and hammer throw, respectively. In London, he snagged another gold in the shot. And, in Stockholm, he added his third gold with a win in the discontinued event of the two-handed shot put.* (ALLSPORT)

Americans.

If all this was a bit too much too soon for the movement, it seemed to manifest itself in the no-shows from Europe. Few foreigners bothered to come. For one thing, the Russo-Japanese War was going on, requiring Great Britain's attention, among others. As for the almost non-existent presence of Frenchmen — including a number of world record-holders in track and field — it may have had something to do with St. Louis' concurrent celebration of the 100th Anniversary of the Louisiana Purchase, Thomas Jefferson's 1803 deal of the century that doubled the size of the United States in exchange for a $15 million cashier's check sent to the French government. One hundred years wasn't enough time to get over the worst real estate blunder of all-time.

Among the French no-shows was Pierre de Coubertin, the father of the modern Olympics, who stayed in Paris

and got updates.

It should also be added that St. Louis was the Olympics where black men first officially competed. Two Zulu tribesmen from Africa, in town as part of the Boer War exhibit at the World's Fair, participated in the marathon, and George Poage of Milwaukee, third in the 400-meter hurdles final, was the first black to win a medal.

Of the 12 nations and 617 athletes who participated, 525 were Americans and 41 were from Canada. Still, perhaps the most impressive performances of the Games was delivered by a 35-year-old Irishman named Thomas Kiely who won the all-arounder competition. The all-arounder was the forerunner to the decathlon, which wouldn't make its debut until 1912, and featured 10 events in one day. Great Britain had recruited Kiely to represent the Commonwealth, offering free round-trip passage if he agreed. He did not. He paid his own

passage and won Ireland's first-ever Olympic medal.

Americans dominated most of the events held at the huge track — a third of a mile in circumference with 220-yard straightaways — located on the campus of Washington University. Archie Hahn, the "Milwaukee Meteor," won the sprints, James Davies Lightbody won the middle distances, Ray Ewry won the standing jumps and yet another Yank, Harry Hillman, was yet another triple winner with gold medals at 400 meters and both hurdles races.

In water polo, the U.S. won all three medals; in soccer, the silver and bronze. One U.S. boxer, Oliver Kirk, won two titles, the bantamweight and featherweight. In all, the United States won 80 gold medals, 85 silver medals and 81 bronze medals for a grand total of 246 medals of all colors. Germany came next with five gold medals and 15 overall. Neighbors Cuba and Canada

RIGHT / *The cycling program in the 1904 Games — which allowed professionals to compete — was all red, white and blue with no foreign participants. The Americans won all 21 medals, including an impressive four-gold performance by Marcus Hurley .* (IOC)

BELOW / *In the two-hand lift, heavyweight Perikles Kakousis of Greece blew away the American field with a winning lift of 111.7 kg — about 245 pounds and almost 60 pounds more than anyone else.* (IOC)

placed third and fourth with 11 and six medals, respectively.

St. Louis may have left the Olympic movement more than a little bewildered after the varied stage it presented in 1904, but it also left little doubt that the Games could be staged as a major event and, as President Theodore Roosevelt's involvement and rapt attention suggested, could attract the attention of an entire nation. If nothing else, the brash Americans threw a whale of a party in 1904, and they didn't apologize for throwing it, either.

thomas hicks

THE MARATHON MAN

Fred Lorz appeared to be in good shape. Excellent shape, considering the circumstances. He had just negotiated the meanest, orneriest, nastiest marathon course anyone could think of, and now, as they were dusting off the Francis Trophy prior to the victory ceremony, he was having the pleasure of not only meeting Alice Roosevelt, the daughter of the President, but having his picture taken with her. Alice was insistent. Who wouldn't want her picture taken with a man who had just run 24 miles in oppressive 90-degree heat, with more than a little bit of humidity thrown in for good measure, over dusty, hilly, uneven roads as dozens of "official" lead vehicles kicked up mountains of dust — and yet, he looked like he'd just climbed out of the cab of a truck? Fred Lorz seemed too good to be true.

Just as this triumphant scene was reaching its climax, it was discovered that Fred Lorz WAS too good to be true. Fifteen minutes after his suave, controlled run into the Olympic Stadium on the grounds of St. Louis'

Washington University, the next marathon man came onto the track. Thomas Hicks of Cambridge, Mass., looked like you'd expect a person to look after an afternoon run in a dust storm during a heatwave. He was hardly moving, listing badly to his side, and, it appeared, barely coherent. He ran with his attendants close by, ready to prop him back up if he fell. When he crossed the finish line he did fall, right there in front of Alice Roosevelt, who shifted her gaze and looked at this Lorz fellow standing beside her with new wonder. And she wasn't alone.

The judges and officials who had accompanied Hicks rushed Lorz, the so-called winner, their fists and voices raised. They were sure he hadn't run the whole race. They were sure he was an imposter.

Lorz managed his best smile and told them, "You're right."

Still smiling, he explained that it was a prank, a practical joke. As a matter of face, he was just about to come clean with them when Hicks made his rather dramatic appearance into the stadium. He was going to tell them that he had run the first three

miles of the race in fine shape, but then he developed a cramp that caused him to pull off to the side. When a truck driver offered him a ride, he accepted. When the truck broke down about 15 miles later, however, and Lorz got back on his feet, he decided, well, why not run the remaining four or so miles into the stadium?

The officials were not amused. Appalled was a better description. Lorz was summarily dismissed not only from the stadium, but from running altogether, for the rest of his life, by order of the Amateur Athletic Union of the United States of America.

Now it was Hicks's turn for the glory, the fuss, and the photograph with the President's daughter — except for one problem. Hicks wasn't up to it. He wandered around the finish area in something of a stupor before being rushed off to bed.

It had been a good race for Hicks through the first 15 miles, as he took the lead and held it. But then he began to show signs of collapse. Accompanied by a personal trainer, Hugh McGrath of the Charlesbank Gymnasium of Boston, Hicks was

given assistance through the rest of the race. At the 17-mile point, he was given a grain of sulphate strychnine and the white of one egg. Three miles later, as his color again faded, he was given another dose of strychnine, two more eggs, and a sip of French brandy. His body was also sponged by hot water heated on the radiator of one of the nearby automobiles.

One more shot of brandy and two more eggs got him to the stadium, where he scarcely lifted his feet while covering the final 440 yards. He had lost eight pounds during the race — and he only weighed 133 pounds to begin with.

At that, Hicks wasn't in the worst shape of the 31 runners who had entered the St. Louis marathon on the afternoon of Aug. 30, 1904. Seventeen of them didn't finish, including William Garcia of San Francisco, who collapsed midway through the race with severe stomach cramps. Garcia was rushed to the hospital where it was discovered the dust from the automobiles had ripped apart his stomach lining. They guessed he would have died if unattended for one more hour.

The dust, heat, humidity, uneven terrain, and the seven hills that dotted the course took their toll on the rest of the field in varying degrees. One runner who might have survived all of these natural disasters added another of his own choosing, which proved to be his downfall. Felix Carvajal of Cuba took a detour into a farmer's field to eat some green apples. He immediately got a stomach ache that slowed him until the pains subsided.

As it was, Carvajal finished fourth, thereby completing one of the most eventful Olympic journeys ever taken, before or since. A mailman in Cuba, Carvajal raised money to travel to the St. Louis Olympics by staging running exhibitions in his hometown of Havana. He traveled by steamer to New Orleans, where he lost all the money he'd raised in a crap game. Undaunted, he hitchhiked to St. Louis, where he showed up at the starting line wearing street shoes and a pair of long work trousers. He was prepared to run that way until the start of the race was held up long enough for Martin Sheridan, a weightman on the U.S. team, to find a pair of scissors and cut his trousers off above the knee.

Other runners took other detours. The race featured the first two blacks to participate in the Olympic Games — two Kaffir tribesmen from Zululand, South Africa, named Lentauw and Yamasani. Both were in St. Louis as part of the Boer War exhibit at the Louisiana Purchase Exposition. Of the two, Lentauw had the most running talent. He finished ninth despite being chased well off course early in the race by two dogs. Yamasani also finished, placing

12th.

Albert Corey, a Frenchman living in America, finished second, some six minutes behind Hicks but in considerably better shape. Third was Arthur Newton of New York, the fifth-place finisher four years previous in the 1900 Games when he got lost in the streets of Paris and came to the finish line thinking he was the winner.

Once the winner, Hicks, came around and ate a dinner consisting of "an enormous amount of food," he accepted the Francis Trophy as the winner of the race and expressed his great satisfaction at having both finished and triumphed. "I would rather have won this race than be President of the United States," he told reporters. After that he announced his retirement from running.

As for Lorz, with time his practical joke became much more palatable. His lifetime ban was commuted to just a little over six months and by the next April he would win the 1905 Boston Marathon, running all the way from start to finish. ∎

Three miles later, as his color faded, Hicks was given another dose of strychnine, two more eggs, and a sip of French brandy.

ABOVE / *With a little help from friends, a dazed Thomas Hicks made it to the marathon finish line in 3:28:63. After St. Louis, that kind of helping hand would disqualify competitors as Dorando Pietri of Italy found out in 1908.* (IOC)

STEEPLE

CHASE

(Allsport)

1 9 0 6

April 22 - May 2, 1906

20 Nations

884 Athletes

ATHENS

Javelin throwers losing their spears in the trees of a Paris park in 1900? Pygmies throwing the 56-pound weight in St. Louis in 1904? World's Fairs relegating the Games to months-long sideshows alongside farm exhibits and lemonade stands? By 1906, Pierre de Coubertin's modern Olympic movement needed resuscitation even if the next Olympiad was only half completed. If the Greeks hadn't come to the rescue, again, the second coming of the Olympic Games might have been buried under the St. Louis Arch. Zeus, Hercules, Athena, Hermes and the rest of the gods of Olympia were just going to have to understand the momentary change in format.

Ten years after the original, the sequel came to Athens and its marble-encased Panathenean Stadium. Here, finally, was a win-win situation for the movement. Greece wanted the Games, and the Games wanted Greece. That they couldn't be officially called the Olympics — and indeed, to this day they are referred to only as the Intercalated (or inserted) Games; a mere asterisk between the third Olympics in St. Louis and the fourth Olympics in London — didn't matter in 1906 and hasn't mattered since.

They certainly looked official enough. For the first time since 1896, spectators were again an integral part of the events as 884 athletes from 20 nations attended. And for the first time ever, many of the national teams were officially sanctioned by their countries — as was the case with the team from the United States.

The Greeks had been anxious for another Olympics ever since the successful revival they pulled off in 1896.

TOP / *At the Intercalated Games, the Germans, despite partisan support, toppled the Greeks in the tug-of-war event.* (IOC)

RIGHT / *And, one, two, three ... A gymnastics team event in the early days of the Games.* (IOC)

OFFICIALLY UNOFFICIAL

Greece wanted the Games, and the Games wanted Greece. That they couldn't be officially called the Olympics didn't matter in 1906 and hasn't mattered since. They certainly looked official enough.

Indeed, during the course of those '96 Games there was a serious lobbying effort, both from Greeks and others (most notably the Americans), to establish Athens as the permanent site of the modern Olympic Games. At the closing banquet of the '96 Games, the King of Greece suggested to Coubertin that he either approve such an idea or resign his position. As quick on his feet as any athlete had been in the 10 days previous, Coubertin pretended not to understand the King's message and answered with a gushing acknowledgment of the terrific job Athens had done in hosting the inaugural Olympic Games. Not long after, Coubertin kept the offensive by suggesting that Athens host interim Games every two years between Olympiads. Such were the circumstances that brought about the first Athenian Games. There might have been a second and a third and on and on, but political unrest in Greece in 1910 demanded an interruption that effectively proved to be a cancellation.

Tennis, soccer, rowing and an expanded gymnastics program were among events that were added to Athens' original schedule of 1896. It was still track and field that commandeered the stage, however. As in 1896, and again in 1900 and 1904, athletes from the United

States dominated. But not without increasing difficulty. Paul Pilgrim, who won at 400 and 800 meters, was among the most decorated U.S. winners as well as one of the least expected. He was not on the official roster sanctioned by the new United States Olympic Committee and was allowed to accompany the team only if he paid his own way.

On the voyage across the Atlantic aboard the S.S. *Barbarossa*, Pilgrim wondered if he'd made the right choice. A severe storm sent a huge wave crashing over the deck, almost drowning several passengers and injuring a number of U.S. athletes. Among them was James Mitchell, the heavy favorite to win the 14-pound "stone throw" event, who suffered a dislocated shoulder and was forced to withdraw from the competition.

Mitchell's misery, as it turned out, was a gift to Greece. The host nation, anxious for a triumph in the field events after being shut out in 1896, got its only gold medal in that area when native son George Georgantas won the stone throw.

The Greeks were even more anxious for a marathon winner who could duplicate the feeling Spiridon Louis gave them when he won the inaugural Olympic marathon in 1896. Incentives were high. If a Greek won the 1906

marathon, he would receive a free loaf of bread and three free cups of coffee every day for a year, a free luncheon for six every week for a year, a statue of Hermes (the "messenger of the gods"), and free shaves for the rest of his life.

Alas, it was not to be. The top Greek, John Alepous, placed fifth, well behind winner William John Sherring, a Canadian who had come to Athens two months early, gotten a job as a railway station porter, trained every other day, and dropped from 135 pounds to 112 pounds in the process. The 80-degree heat that greeted the marathon runners did not bother the acclimatized Sherring, who won by seven minutes. In addition to his gold medal, Sherring wound up getting $4,000 from his hometown of Hamilton, Ontario, and the Greeks gave him two consolation prizes — a statue of Athena ("the goddess of wisdom and warfare") and, presumably to fatten him back up, a lamb.

As in '96, the Games were supported enthusiastically by the Greek public as well as by their royalty. The Crown Prince presided daily in the stadium. Among the sights he saw was Peter O'Connor of Ireland, officially a member of Great Britain's Olympic team and the winner of the triple jump, leap off the peristyle after receiving his award and climb to

the top of the flagpole, where he took down the Union Jack that had been raised and replaced it with an Irish flag.

Politics had come to the Games, but so had stability. No sooner had O'Connor dropped to earth than the International Olympic Committee, with Coubertin in firm control, announced that in two years hence in London, the capital of Great Britain, the Games of the IVth Olympiad would be held.

ABOVE / Paul Pilgrim wasn't a favorite in the 400-meter race. In fact, he wasn't even a part of the first official U.S. Olympic Team sent to Athens, but he paid his own way and beat Wyndham Halswelle of Great Britain in a time of 53.2. Halswelle (**RIGHT**) would win the race two years later in London, but it would be a hollow victory at that. (IOC)

OPPOSITE (TOP) / Spectators line the dock to get a bird's-eye view of the 1906 swimming competition. (IOC)

(**BOTTOM**) / Four out of the five 16-man naval rowing boat teams hailed from Greece, but Italy managed to squeeze in a third-place showing in the one-time appearance of this event. (IOC)

ABOVE / Fernand Gonder of France easily clears the bar at 3.25 meters (10-8) and goes on to win the pole vault event with a final height of 11-5 3/4, four inches better than the next competitor but well under his 12-3 1/2 world record. (IOC)

ray ewry

Standing Ovation

He had polio as a child. He couldn't jump out of bed, let alone over his head. His first coaches were his doctors, who encouraged him to exercise his legs enough that perhaps, miracle of miracles, he could one day get out of his wheelchair.

In 1883, when he was 10 years old, Raymond Ewry was not in good shape.

By the turn of the century, he was one of the world's best athletes. And by the time he was through appearing in his fourth Olympic Games — in the London Games of 1908 — Raymond Ewry just might have become, as one newspaper account said, "the greatest jumper who ever lived."

Certainly, his credentials qualify him as the greatest standing jumper who ever lived. When he retired in 1910, Ewry retired his Olympic records along with him. To this day, no Olympian has jumped higher from a standing start than Ewry's best of 5-foot-5. Neither has anyone jumped farther from a standing start than Ewry's bests of 11 feet, 4 7/8 inches in the long jump and 34 feet, 8 1/2 inches in the triple jump.

Of course, it is also true that no one has tried. At least not in the Olympics. Not long after Ewry's retirement, the standing jumps were discontinued from the Olympic program. Unless or until a standing jump revolution occurs, Ewry's records are destined to stand forever.

The polio survivor from Lafayette, Indiana, won 10 gold medals in all, eight in the official Olympic Games of 1900, 1904 and 1908 and another two in the Intercalated Games in Athens in 1906. He never placed second. In nearly a century of Olympic Games since, no other single athlete has so dominated his events or accumulated as many gold medals (distance runner Paavo Nurmi's nine gold medals rank second on the all-time list, sprinter Carl Lewis' eight rank third, "officially" tying with Ewry).

Ewry's only competition was himself. His Olympic records were also world records and, to keep himself occupied, he kept chasing them.

So it was that he came to the Athens Games of 1906 and, after making sure of the standing high jump title with an opening jump of five feet, 1 1/4 inches, he asked the Greek officials to raise the bar to 5-5 1/2 — a half-inch beyond the world record he'd set in Paris six years previous.

The date was May 1, 1906, and, as the nine other finalists from six nations looked on with keen interest, the 6-foot-3 Ewry took three cracks at the unprecedented height. They watched a style that was flawless, with no wasted motion — the form of one who had once been confined to a wheelchair and knew the propriety of efficient movement. Ewry would crouch low, like a baseball catcher but with one leg, the outside one, extended forward. Sideways to the bar, he would look upward at it, careful to estimate the trajectory his ellipse would have to take. When he would spring, it was all at once, the lead leg going over first, the back leg following in the classic scissors style of the day, the same used by running high jumpers.

To be sure, running high jumpers watched Ewry with keen interest as well. A form that — at its 5-5 best —

would have placed second in the 1896 Athens Games *running* high jump as well as seventh in the 1900 Paris Games was worth watching. In Athens, in 1906, where just five of 24 contestants survived into the finals and a jump of 5-foot-10 proved to be the winner, the flat-footed Ewry could have been especially competitive.

He just brushed the bar on each of his world-record attempts in Athens, having to content himself, in the end, with his margin of victory over his good friend, Martin Sheridan of New York, and Leon DuPont of Belgium, who tied for second place at four feet, 7 1/8 inches — more than a half-foot behind Ewry.

He followed his high jump performance with an even more decisive victory in the standing long jump, winning by eight inches over fellow Americans Sheridan and Lawson Robertson, and by 13 inches over DuPont.

After the American sweep in that event, the sight of three American flags rising at once up the flagpole inspired this account the next morning in the Athens newspaper *Estia*:

"The Stadium was covered yesterday by the Star Spangled Banner, the flag of the Americans, having been hoisted three times, thanks to the invincible and fearful athletes whom the new world sent to us ... Greece, as well as the other nations taking part in these games, are also enthusiastic about these victories. The speed with which the new world rises up in the horizon could not but shake the Stadium of Athens with its athletics triumphs. The Americans came here with all the ambitions of the new world."

Thus had Ray Ewry — a champion from the new world — left his mark on the new Olympic movement. Indeed, this onetime college football player at Purdue University — where he also captained the track team while earning bachelor's and graduate degrees in mechanical engineering — was more a part of the Games' modern beginnings than any single athlete. When they held one, he was there.

It was for a very good reason that he did not compete in the first

Olympic Games of the modern era in Athens in 1896 — since the standing jumps were not a part of the program. But he picked up the pace after that. Every summer that the Olympics were scheduled his routine was the same. He would check the schedule and ask his supervisors at the New York City Water Dept., where he worked as a hydraulics engineer, for the time off; and then, in the company of the New York Athletic Club, of which he was a member in good standing, he would make his way to the Games.

His inaugural Olympic experience in Paris not only yielded the 5-foot-5 high jump record but also the most memorable afternoon in standing jump history. All three events were held on the same day, July 16, 1900, and Ewry won all three handily. After winning the high jump by five inches, he won the triple jump by over two feet and the long jump by three inches. He'd left the competition flat-footed.

In St. Louis in 1904 he was just as dominating, winning the high jump by six inches, the triple jump by nearly a foot and a half and the long jump by eight inches (while setting a world record of 11 feet, 4 7/8 inches). In 1906, after the triple jump had been eliminated from the Olympics, he again won convincingly. It was only in London in 1908, when he was 34 years old, that anyone came significantly close to Ewry. He won the high jump by an inch and the long jump by four inches.

He retired after that. He thought

about going to Stockholm in 1912 — to try for 12 medals in '12 — but one day during a workout at the New York Athletic Club, as recounted by Dick Schaap in his book about the Olympic Games, Ewry's friend and fellow Olympian, Martin Sheridan, casually said, "Ray, you're getting to be an old man. You ought to quit."

So he did. The Olympics went to Stockholm without him — where, as it turned out, the standing jumps were included for the last time. No one threatened Ray Ewry's records there. Like their owner, they went out on top. π

They watched a style that was flawless, with no wasted motion — the form of one who had once been confined to a wheelchair and knew the propriety of efficient movement.

ABOVE / *First in the standing high jump: 1900, 1904, 1906, 1908. First in the standing long jump: 1900, 1904, 1906, 1908. First in the standing triple jump: 1900, 1904. Ray Ewry was outstanding in his field, collecting 10 gold medals (two unofficial medals from the 1906 Games in Athens). Had he competed in Stockholm, odds are he would have held all 12 of the Olympic standing jump titles. The standing jumps were discontinued as Olympic events after 1912.* (ALLSPORT)

RIGHT / *In 1984, American Mike Conley was considered a favorite to win the triple jump. Instead, he finished second behind teammate Al Joyner. In 1988, Conley failed to make the team. But in 1992, he rebounded to qualify for the Olympics, giving him a chance to fulfill a dream of Olympic gold. With a leap of 58-11 1/2, the dream was realized. His wind-aided mark of 59-7 1/2 gave him a gold medal while Conley's best legal jump of 57-9 1/2 was an Olympic record.*
(ALLSPORT / VANDYSTADT)

T R I P L E

J U M P

1908

April 27 - October 31, 1908

22 Nations

2,035 Athletes (36 women)

21 Sports

23 USA golds

LONDON

The London Games of 1908 were the Olympics of debuts. There was the first actual awarding of gold medals. There was the standardizing of the marathon distance. There was the introduction of figure skating, the first winter sport to appear in an Olympics. And there was the introduction of women's gymnastics as a demonstration event.

Unfortunately, international refereeing didn't also make its debut.

It was the one downside of London in the summer of '08. Arguing. Plenty of arguing. The IOC, assuming that since Great Britain was the most accomplished sporting nation on earth — with its well-established All-England Tennis Championships at Wimbledon, its Henley Royal Regatta, its Derby, and its Football Association Cup Final — decided to employ an exclusively British jury of judges, referees and officials to regulate the venues and interpret the rules.

It was a recipe for chaos. As British victories mounted on the scoreboard — the final tally showed Great Britain with 145 medals, 98 ahead of the second-place United States team — the cries of unfavorable treatment mounted. Enough official complaints were registered — by the French, the Canadians, the Swedes, and especially by the United States — that the most lasting legacy of the Games of 1908 is a 60-page book that the British Olympic Association, a most civilized organization, published at the conclusion of the London Olympics. Its title: *Replies to Criticism of the Olympic Games*.

TOP / *Marathoner Dorando Pietri inspired a song entitled "Dorando," written by a budding young songwriter named Irving Berlin.* (IOC)

RIGHT / *Frenchmen Maurice Schilles and André Auffray, who incredibly had never before ridden together, won the 2000-meter tandem race in London. The event was discontinued after the 1972 Games in Munich.* (IOC)

WHAT'S HAPPENED TO CIVILIZATION?

The IOC decided to employ an exclusively British jury of judges, referees and officials to regulate the venues and interpret the rules. It was a recipe for chaos.

But while London put an end forever to home-country officiating — in subsequent Olympics, non-partial international judges became a staple of the Games — it also put on the map a number of enduring Olympic traditions, not the least of which was the idea of awarding medals and expanding the program to include a wider variety of events.

In all, the 21 official and unofficial sports — including polo and motorboat racing on the Thames — that were included on London's master agenda attracted a record number of nations (22) and a record number of participants (2,035). Many of these sports could conveniently be seen in one location — at the just-completed Olympic Stadium built in conjunction with the Franco-British Exposition at Shepherd's Bush. Besides the usual track and field facilities, the stadium featured a cycling track, a soccer pitch, a platform for wrestling and gymnastics, and a 100-meter long swimming pool situated squarely in the middle of the stadium floor.

One of London's innovations — the standardizing of the marathon distance — was completely inadvertent. The course started at Windsor Castle outside of London, with the starting line directly

underneath the castle's windows so the royal children of King Edward VII and Queen Alexandra could watch. After a 26-mile route to the Olympic Stadium, the organizers added a partial lap of the Shepherd's Bush track, 385 yards to be exact, so the runners could finish in front of the King and Queen's royal box. Every marathon run since the Olympic marathon of July 24, 1908, has been at a distance of 26 miles, 385 yards.

Appropriately enough, those last 385 yards turned out to be quite significant. An Italian named Dorando Pietri entered the stadium first, well ahead of the crowd of runners trailing behind him. But it was an inordinately hot day, even for London in July, and Dorando was dazed and disoriented. As he entered the stadium, he initially turned left instead of right. The British officials lining the track pointed him in the proper direction, but after just a few steps going the right way, Dorando collapsed on the track. The officials rushed to him, but Dorando, fearing disqualification if he accepted aid, managed, despite his stupor, to wave

them away. He got up and went a few more steps and collapsed again. This time the officials picked him up without protest. This process continued — Dorando would collapse, the officials would pick him up — until the next runner, John Hayes of the United States, came into the stadium. The pro-British crowd — which is to say anti-American — was soon whipped into a frenzy as Hayes steadily gained on the staggering Dorando. Finally, the British officials picked Dorando up, carried him across the line, and ordered the Italian flag run up the flagpole. The flag hit the top just as Hayes crossed the finish line.

In sharp contrast to any number of unsuccessful protests filed before it, the protest filed immediately by the United States, on Hayes' behalf, was upheld. But that didn't stop Dorando Pietri from getting a golden cup from Queen Alexandra the next day and from becoming an international celebrity.

The Olympic Stadium was filled to its 68,000 capacity for the running of the marathon, the concluding event of the

London Games. Held in conjunction with the Franco-British Exposition, the Olympics had lasted a full six months, from April through October. As the competitions, and the controversies, had progressed, so had the public's interest. A pontifical and prolific British press also added to the intrigue. And Britain's overall domination — in boxing, for example, British athletes won every gold medal and all but one of the silver medals — produced a groundswell of public pride. Slowly but surely over the hot course of the summer of 1908, Londoners had come to realize the home island advantage the Olympics had bestowed upon them was a significant weapon indeed.

ABOVE / *Running strong, alone and in the lead, Dorando Pietri met with exhaustion at the finish line. Disqualified for being helped across the line, Pietri lost the marathon title to American John Hayes, a 22-year-old sporting goods manager at Bloomingdale's in New York City.* (IOC)

400
FIASCO

A curious thing happened to J.C. Carpenter, an American from Cornell University, just as he was about to break the tape and win the 400-meter final in London's Olympic Stadium. He looked up ... and a British official was cutting the tape before he got there.

Carpenter was none too pleased with this development. But, at that, he was faring better than his two countrymen in the race: John Taylor, who had been wrestled off the track by yet another British official, and W.C. Robbins, who was herded away from the finish line. As race finishes go, this one was not following the normal procedure. And for the three Americans, it would get worse.

These were the Olympic Games of 1908, the fourth of the modern era and the first to be held in London, the capital of the Commonwealth. For several days now, the track and field events had been going on in the searing summer heat at Shepherd's Bush. Even for July in England, the weather was uncommonly warm, as

was the general atmosphere surrounding the Games. From the start, it seemed, there was a conspiracy to have the British hosts and their visitors — those from their former colonies especially — at each other's throats.

To get things started on the wrong foot, there had been the unfortunate flag mixup at the Opening Ceremonies. King Edward had been there, and Queen Alexandria, and the Grenadier Guards had played, and 2,000 doves were released into the air as a symbol of peace and brotherhood. But when the American athletes marched into the stadium and looked up at the flags surrounding the top of the stadium representing the 22 nations entered in the London Games — they couldn't find theirs waving in the breeze. The British said they were terribly sorry, they couldn't seem to find an Old Glory anywhere. The Americans, in turn, came to the part of the march where they were expected to dip their flag in front of the king — and said they were sorry, too. Weight man Martin Sheridan, a veteran of two Olympic Games and a man who knew a snub when he saw

one, happened to be also carrying his own American flag. "This flag dips to no earthly king," he said. His statement not only contributed to a certain "them" versus "us" mentality for the Games that were to follow, but also established an American no-dip tradition that would endure through every Olympic opening ceremony parade to follow.

By the time several more days had passed — and Carpenter, Taylor and Robbins were getting ready to lap the Shepherd's Bush track in the 400 final — there had been much more contention of this sort. The International Olympic Committee had put the British in charge of officiating and judging all of the competitions and the Brit's practice of holding the draws for heats in secret did not meet with favor by the rest of the nations, the Americans, in particular. Neither was the host nation's habit of openly coaching with megaphones a practice that was warmly received.

From England's point of view, two habits of the American's were wearing very thin, very fast, too: First, they were winning just about everything they entered and second, they cheered

lustily every time they did.

Prior to July 23rd — the date of the 400 final — Americans on the track alone had won gold medals in the 800-meter run, the 1,500-meter run, the 400-meter hurdles, the high jump, pole vault, long jump, shot put, discus, hammer throw, standing high jump, standing long jump and Greek discus throw (which was won by Sheridan). Despite competing on their home turf, British athletes had won just four gold medals — in the steeplechase, the triple jump, the 5-mile run and the 3-mile team run. For them, one of the brightest moments during the Games had come during the running of the 100-meter dash, when Reginald Walker of South Africa became the first non-American to ever win at that distance, using an Olympic record 10.8 clocking to nudge James Rector of the U.S. at the tape.

British-U.S. sentiment had reached something of a climax in the 1,500 final, where Great Britain's Harold Wilson, the world record-holder, lost to Mel Sheppard, an 800-meter specialist who wasn't suppos-ed to be able to last for 1,500 meters. Worse yet for the home crowd, Sheppard was an Irish-American.

By the time the 400-meter final came along, tensions were strained, to say the least.

Two heats had been run to determine the 400's four finalists — the aforementioned Carpenter, Robbins and Taylor from America as well as Lieutenant Wyndham Halswelle from Great Britain. Halswelle was a Scot whose credentials included winning four races in the 1906 Scottish Championships — at distances of 100, 220, 440 and 800 yards — all in the same afternoon. In the preliminary heats here, he had run a 48.4 400 to shatter the existing Olympic record of 49.2. He was as big a favorite as Great Britain had in 1908 — and the crowd in Shepherd's

Bush knew it.

Before the race ever started, there was local concern that the three Yanks would conspire against the lone Brit, teaming against him to impeded his progress and deny him his crown. Several newspaper articles said so in print.

Amid this backdrop, the four started out. Taylor dropped back quickly, the victim of his own quick start. Robbins ran to the front and opened a 12-yard lead by the halfway point. Carpenter and Halswelle reeled him in, however, and passed him as they came to the final turn. Carpenter

If the Revolutionary War hadn't already been fought, there's a good chance it would have started then and there, on a late July afternoon on the Shepherd's Bush track.

went by first and moved to the outside, with Halswelle close behind. As Halswelle moved to pass Carpenter, also on the outside, the American moved even farther out. Thinking the move was intentional, the British official standing nearest cried out "foul!" "foul!" and began chasing Carpenter down the track. Over the P.A. system, the track announcer also called out "foul!" as yet another British official moved to the finish line and cut the tape in front of a fast-finishing — not to mention stunned — Carpenter.

A considerable flap/row emerged as U.S. officials rushed to the track in protest after the British officially ruled a "no race." If the Revolutionary War hadn't already been fought, there's a good chance it would have started then and there, on a late July afternoon on the Shepherd's Bush

track.

The Amateur Athletic Association (AAA) of Great Britain convened the next day at the Garden Club on the grounds of the Franco-British Exhibition to decide what to do next. As noted in the Official Report of the 1908 Games, present at the meeting were Mr. Duxfield, vice president of the AAA; Sir Lees-Knowles, Mr. G.S. Roberton, Mr. E.W. Parry and Dr. M.J. Bulger of the British Olympic Council; Mr. Percy Fisher, Mr. David Scott Duncan and Mr. Pennycook of the Scottish Amateur Athletic Association; and, finally, Mr. W.J. Basan and Mr. E.H. Pelling of the London Athletic Club.

Out of this partial, very-British body came the ruling: Mr. J.C. Carpenter was guilty of obstructing Lt. Halswelle's progress and the race would be rerun the next day — without Mr. J.C. Carpenter.

When the Americans heard the decision, they protested the British ruling by refusing to enter either Robbins or Taylor in the rescheduled final. Halswelle came to the track the next afternoon and, in the first and only "walk-over" in Olympic history, jogged unchallenged to the gold medal.

In the next Olympic Games in Stockholm, Sweden — and in all Games thereafter — the International Olympic Committee changed its rules and required that the supervision and officiating of events be done by international groups and not by the host country. ∎

DON'T I KNOW YOU?

Avery Brundage brought Olympic credentials to the presidency of the IOC. (ALLSPORT)

Most Olympians do not stop excelling when their Olympic careers have come to an end, using the Games as a springboard to more success and, in some cases, considerably more recognition. Here's a sampling of famous Americans who once wore the red, white and blue in Olympic battle, and went on to fame in other pursuits:

GERTRUDE EDERLE: In the Paris Games of 1924, Ederle was a 19-year-old member of the U.S. swimming team who distinguished herself with one gold medal and two bronze medals. Two years later, Ederle silenced all critics who said women weren't equipped for feats of endurance when she became the first woman to swim the English Channel. Her time of 14 hours, 31 minutes, bettered by two hours the fastest crossing by a man.

GEORGE S. PATTON, JR.: A lieutenant in the U.S. Army in 1912, Patton represented the United States in the modern pentathlon as that sport made its debut that year in the Stockholm Games. Patton finished fifth in the competition, placing behind four Swedish soldiers. The young 26-year-old officer placed seventh in swimming: sixth in riding: fourth in fencing: and third in running. He'd have won the gold medal with a finish of seventh or better in the fifth and final event, shooting. But he placed 21st in a field of 32. In World War II, Patton, known as "Old Blood and Guts," became a famous general, commanding the Seventh Army in the invasion of Sicily and the Third Army in the Battle of the Bulge.

BEN SPOCK: Spock won a gold medal in rowing in the Paris Olympics of 1924 as part of an eight-man crew from Yale University, where he was an undergrad. He later went to medical school and became Dr.

Benjamin Spock, author of the best-selling book, *The Common Sense Guide to Baby & Child Care*, and one of the most respected child care authorities in the world.

ALFRED GILBERT: In 1908, Gilbert represented the United States in the London Games as a pole vaulter, winning the gold medal with a vault of 12 feet, 2 inches. A Yale University student with a penchant for inventions, Gilbert later invented the Erector Set, one of the most popular toys in the world.

AVERY BRUNDAGE: As a U.S. Olympian in 1912, Brundage competed in both the pentathlon, where he finished sixth, and the decathlon, where he did not place. Forty years later, in 1952, Brundage was elected president of the International Olympic Committee, a position he held for the next 20 years. π

1992 rhythmic gymnast champion Alexandra Timoshenko of the Unified Team.
(Allsport / Vandystadt)

Winner of six gold medals in Barcelona, Unified Team gymnast Vitaly Scherbo. (Allsport / Vandystadt)

1988 all-around champion Elena Shoushounova of the USSR. (Allsport / Bruty)

Guo Linyao of China brings home a Barcelona bronze in the parallel bars.
(Allsport / Vandystadt)

LEFT / *Shouts of joy: Algeria's first Olympic gold. Hassiba Boulmerka, 1992.* (ALLSPORT / VANDYSTADT)

RIGHT / *Free throw: Soviets celebrate after upsetting the heavily favored U.S. team, 1988.* (ALLSPORT / BRUTY)

LEFT / *Tears of joy: Sweet victory for Korea's team handball squad, 1988 .* (ALLSPORT / RONDEAU)

RIGHT / *"Down under" they don't celebrate sittin' down, 1992.* (ALLSPORT / VANDYSTADT)

LEFT / *Winning style? Daichi Suzuki, 1988.* (ALLSPORT / BRUTY)

RIGHT / *Jumping for joy: Steve Lundquist, 1984.* (ALLSPORT / DUFFY)

Hard fall (Allsport / Duffy)

Injured Angolan (Allsport / M. Powell)

A slight miscalculation (Allsport / Clarkson)

KO'ed (Allsport / Duffy)

With Dad's help (Allsport / Mortimore)

The "too-high" hurdles (Allsport / Meehan)

1912

May 5 - July 22, 1912

27 Nations

2,547 Athletes

13 Sports

25 USA golds

STOCKHOLM

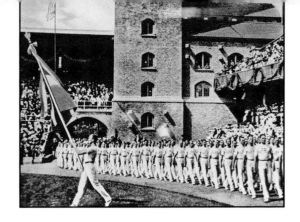

The Olympics took a break from problems in 1912. Whatever challenges and difficulties the Games would face before, and after, they avoided during a cool and trouble-free Swedish summer. The Games of 1912 followed Stockholm's Law: Everything that could go right, did.

They began with an Opening Ceremonies presided over by Sweden's King Gustav and ended in the same stadium where the local organizers hosted a banquet and invited all of the athletes, team leaders, and officials to join the King. What transpired in between was one of the most smoothly efficient Olympics ever presented as Stockholm proved to be a breeding ground for both sport and the Olympic movement in the 20th century. Its track and field stadium, built specially for the Games, set a new world standard with its well-defined throwing circles and jumping pits and cinder track. Its gymnastics and wrestling tournaments included more contestants and more innovations than ever before. Its association football (soccer) tournament, including teams from most European nations, was generally hailed as the event that turned on the continent masses to the sport. Its swimming and diving events included women for the first time. And its equestrian competition, held in the track stadium after an overnight transformation, was hailed as the best of its kind in history.

Just as important, the Stockholm Games introduced three athletes whose performances and deportment went beyond mere athleticism. Thus were the

THE STUFF OF LEGENDS

Stockholm introduced the first true legends of the modern games. What Hannes Kolehmainen would do for distance running, Duke Kahanamoku would do for swimming and Jim Thorpe would do for athletics.

TOP / *The Finnish team makes its entrance at the 1912 Stockholm Olympics.* (ALLSPORT)

RIGHT / *Estonian Martin Klein, competing for Russia, wrestled Alfred Asikainen for 11 hours under the hot sun before pinning the Finn. Exhausted, the Estonian defaulted the final, settling for the silver in the middleweight Greco-Roman class.* (ALLSPORT)

first true legends of the modern Games created. Legends who would inspire thousands of sportsmen around the world to become like them. To become the next Hannes Kolehmainen, or the next Duke Kahanamoku, or — and this was the most impractical goal of all — the next Jim Thorpe, would become the stuff of dreams for the youth of the world.

Kolehmainen was a 22-year-old Finnish vegetarian, Kahanamoku a 22-year-old son of Hawaiian royalty, and Thorpe a 24-year-old American Indian from the Carlisle Institute for Indians in Carlisle, Pa. What Kolehmainen would do for distance running, Kahanamoku would do for swimming and Thorpe would do for athletics.

With the 5,000- and 10,000-meter runs on the Olympic program for the first time in Stockholm, Kolehmainen first won the 10,000 by nearly a minute, and then, in the inaugural 5,000-meter race, broke the tape in one of the most thrilling races in Olympic history, then and now. After running neck and neck through the 3.1-mile race, the Finn nipped France's Jean Bouin in a photo-finish before anyone had thought of the necessity for a photo-finish. Bouin was given a time of 14:36.7 to Kolehmainen's 14:36.6 — a world record by a tenth of a second that would stand for the next 15 years and inspire a nation of young Finnish runners to take a run at it.

Kahanamoku, given his Christian

name of Duke because the Duke of Edinburgh was visiting the royal Hawaiian palace in Honolulu when he was born, set a world record in the 100-meter freestyle swimming race and, beyond that, set an Olympic standard for style and class that would be emulated by generations of swimmers — including a young Johnny Weissmuller, who would eventually take his place at the head of the swimming world.

Both Kolehmainen and Kahanamoku would add to their legends in additional

TOP / *Military revolver teams were discontinued from the Olympic shooting program in 1920. Here, one of the Swedish pistol teams shows the right stuff. The Swedes captured a gold in the 30-meter event and a silver at 50 meters.* (ALLSPORT)

ABOVE / *The Norwegians captured gold in the team free exercises and apparatus event, which made its one-time appearance in Stockholm.* (ALLSPORT)

Olympics, whereas Thorpe would be enshrined forever in Olympic annals solely for his Stockholm "double." The American Indian, whose native name was "Bright Path," won both the five-event pentathlon (since discontinued) and 10-event decathlon in world-record style. In his spare time, he also placed fourth in the open division high jump and seventh in the long jump.

Thorpe returned a conquering hero to America, where he left amateur track and field and became a star professional football and baseball player. His Olympic medals were forfeited the next January when it was discovered he had once played baseball for $25 a week and was thus considered, in the eyes of the IOC, a "professional." Hugo Wieslander, the Swedish athlete who finished second to Thorpe, refused to accept the vacated gold medal, however, and a fight to reinstate Thorpe's name in the official Olympic record ensued. That fight would not be won until 70 years later, 30 years after Thorpe's death in 1953, when the IOC returned his name to the record book and sent his family his medals.

Athletes from the United States dominated the track and field events in Stockholm, headed by 100- and 200-meter winner Ralph Craig, who trained incessantly on the specially constructed cork track aboard the oceanliner *Finland* that not only transported the U.S. team from New York to Stockholm but acted as the team's hotel once it was docked. Also well-tuned were Americans James "Ted" Meredith, Mel Sheppard and Ira Davenport, the one-two-three finishers in the 800-meter run — a race that rivaled the 5,000 for drama. Just eight-tenths of a second separated the first six finishers, with Meredith, an 18-year-old schoolboy, winning by 18 inches. The first four runners, including Melville Brock of Canada, bettered the existing world record. Also of note was the silver medalist in the 10,000 meter run, Louis Tewanima, a schoolmate of Jim Thorpe's at the Carlisle Institute for Indians.

But dominating as Carlisle and the United States were on the track, it was Sweden that topped the overall medals chart with 65 (to 61 for the U.S.). The Swedes excelled especially in women's gymnastics, diving, and the equestrian events — to say nothing of the job they did as hosts.

RIGHT / *Twenty-two-year-old Hannes Kolehmainen (#122), a vegetarian bricklayer, started the trend of great Finnish runners in Stockholm, where the 5,000- and 10,000-meter races were introduced. He won both races and collected his third gold eight years later in Antwerp in the marathon. American Louis Tewanima, trailing the mighty Finn, won the silver in the 10,000 meters.* (IOC)

BELOW / *The Brits entered two teams in the eight-oared shell with coxswain and won both the silver and gold in Stockholm, which featured four rowing events.* (IOC)

Top / *After seven false starts, Ralph Craig hit the tape first in 10.8 seconds. It was an American sweep in 100 meters with Alvah Meyer and Donald Lippincott finishing second and third, respectively.* (IOC)

Above / *A Danish treat: Demonstration of team exercises in Stockholm.* (Allsport)

Right / *A Russian gymnast warms up on the parallel bars as his teammate looks on in Stockholm.* (IOC)

alma richards

ON A WING OF A PRAYER

Far away from but not long off the farms of southern Utah where he grew up, Alma Richards watched as the Swedish officials raised the high jump bar to six feet, four inches. Somehow, some way, it had come to this: Either he jumped higher than he had ever jumped before or he relinquished the Olympic championship to a German he had never seen before.

These were the Games of the Vth Olympiad, held in the grand new Olympic stadium built in Stockholm from the ground up by Sweden's finest architects. A year ago, neither the stadium nor Richards were in anything approaching the shape they were in today. A lot had happened in a hurry. For his part, Richards considered his latest challenge, situated above that bar at the end of the high jump runway, and decided he needed some help. He took off the floppy felt cap he wore as good luck charm, walked to the edge of the track and, in full view of the capacity crowd of 22,000, knelt down to pray.

"God," said the 22-year-old Mormon boy, "give me strength. And if it's right that I should win, give me strength to do my best to set a good example all the days of my life."

With that, he moved back toward the task at hand.

By now he had everyone's attention. That included the other high jump finalist, Hans Liesche of Berlin, Germany, as well as those finalists who had just recently been eliminated from the competition. Among them were George Horine of Stanford University, the current world record-holder who had been done in either by the Olympic pressure and by the flu, or both, and would place third, and two more Americans, Egon Erickson and Jim Thorpe, who would place in a tie for fourth. The day before, Thorpe had won the pentathlon competition and in another five days he would win the decathlon, earning distinction, as declared by King Gustav of Sweden, as the "world's greatest athlete." But for now he had been relegated to the position of spectator by the German and by his American teammate, who was wiping the grass stains from his knees as he adjusted the floppy cap back on his head.

There was no question that Alma Richards, or "Dick" as he came to be known on the oceanliner, the *Finland*, that had carried the U.S. Olympic Team from New York to Stockholm, had gotten to the Olympics in a more unconventional way than the others. A year before, he hadn't known the Olympics existed. Four years before that, he hadn't known track and field existed.

He had dropped out of school after the eighth grade, opting instead for the wide open ranges around his hometown of Parowan, a southern Utah outpost settled by the Mormons. Richards was big for his age. He was almost to his full 6-foot-4, 205-pound size when he left school and climbed aboard his horse to chase rabbits. It wouldn't be until four years had passed that he would decide, at the age of 20 and after the urgings of a college professor who promised him it would expand his horizons, to go back to school.

Impressed by his size, Richards was soon drafted by the track coach at his new boarding school to join the track team. He did, and just three months

after being introduced to the many running, throwing and jumping events involved in his new sport, he scored enough points all by himself in the 1911 Utah high school championships to enable little Murdock Academy of Beaver, Utah, to win the state title over all the big schools in Salt Lake City.

As a high school sophomore he enrolled at Brigham Young Academy in Provo, where the college track coach happened across Richards one day playing basketball. Watching Richards jump prompted the coach — who assumed Richards was in college — to lure the young athlete over to the high jump pit. When he went over the bar at 5 feet, 11 inches in his basketball suit, Coach E.L. "Timpanogos" Roberts decided he had just personally witnessed the most naturally gifted high jumper in the world. It became Roberts' obsession to groom his find for the Olympic Games a year hence in Stockholm. He explained to him about the Olympics and worked with him throughout the winter. In the late spring, he gave Richards a copy of Rudyard Kipling's poem, "If," and put him on a train bound for Chicago, site of one of three U.S. Olympic Trials.

Richards won that Chicago competition with a jump of six feet, three inches. He still almost didn't make the team. When the selection committee convened in New York to review the results of the three concurrent trials — held in Chicago, Los Angeles and San Francisco — they agreed that since none of them had ever heard of this Richards fellow, his jump must have been either mismeasured or a fluke. They were about to dismiss him when one member of the committee, the famous football coach Amos Alonzo Stagg, cleared his voice and said they were wrong. Maybe it was true, this fellow Richards was a complete unknown, said Stagg, the football coach at University of Chicago, but he had personally seen him clear 6-3 and he had done it with ease. By way of compromise, Richards was added to the U.S. team, but in the category of a "supplemental member."

Supplemental or not, when the

Finland shoved off from New York Harbor, Alma "Dick" Richards was on board. The crossing was not entirely tranquil for him. His farm roots were not hidden by the change of venue, nor was his anonymity, and he soon became the butt of numerous country

bumpkin jokes during the voyage.

But as the high jump bar in Stockholm moved up, and Richards moved with it, the mood of his teammates turned to camaraderie. Erickson, Thorpe and Horine, the world record-holder, gathered around the high jump standard as Richards, his praying finished, gathered himself for his first try at 193 centimeters, the metric equivalent to six feet, four inches. "Go Dick," they implored, using the nickname they had derived from Richards' last name.

At all the heights prior to this one, Richards had qualified only with his third and final jump. In sharp contrast, Liesche, the German and a most stylish jumper, had qualified at every height with his first jump. There was no doubt who was the gold medal

favorite between these two.

Richards jumped first. Right after his prayer.

"I felt as if the whole world was lifted off my shoulders," he would write in his memoirs. "My confidence returned completely."

He cleared the bar easily, by more than an inch.

Psychologically speaking, Liesche was now on shaky ground. And it got shakier as his first jump was interrupted by a great roar from the crowd. He looked over to the finish line and saw three Americans, Tad Meredith, Mel Sheppard and Ira Davenport, finish in that order in a stirring end to the 800-meter race. In the process, they relinquished Hans Braun, the pre-race favorite and Liesche's friend and teammate, to sixth place.

Liesche missed badly on his first jump, and again on his second. He tried to compose himself for his third and final try, but again, the bar clanged to the ground as Richards, the new Olympic champion with a new Olympic record, was mobbed by his teammates.

The triumph sent Richards on to other heights. Upon his return home, he got an academic scholarship to Cornell University, where he set numerous collegiate national high jump marks. Later he got a law degree at Southern Cal, but before that he branched into other track and field events, eventually becoming, like his teammate Thorpe, a decathlete. He won the 1915 national AAU decathlon championship with times and distances that came close to Thorpe's winning numbers in Stockholm. His goal to replace Thorpe as the "world's greatest athlete" in the next Olympics in 1916 were dashed by world war. But as a soldier competing in the American Expeditionary Force Track & Field Championships at the Olympic Stadium outside Paris in 1919, he would enter six events and score more points than any other soldier. As he accepted his various medals from General John J. "Blackjack" Pershing, the General told him, "You, sir, are the greatest athlete in the Armed Forces of the United States." ⚡

TWISTED FATE

ust as fate would have it, the decathlon and Jim Thorpe made concurrent debuts in the 1912 Olympic Games. Never has an event been so blessed.

So dominating was the American Indian's performance, and so widespread was the sympathy for his cause after he was stripped of his gold medal, that forevermore the winner of the Olympic decathlon and the phrase "World's Greatest Athlete" would be synonymous.

The 24-year-old Thorpe was in a league of his own over the two days in Stockholm when the 10-event decathlon made its first appearance in the Games. Among the 29 competitors, he finished first in five of the events (long jump, shot put, high jump, hurdles and discus), second in two (100-meter and 1,500-meter runs) and third in three (400-meter run, pole vault and javelin). He set a world record that would stand for 16 years. More significantly, his times and distances were sufficient to place in the top 10 in the next 44 years of Olympic decathlons. Not until the Rome Games in 1960 would Jim Thorpe -- circa 1912, when he used a bamboo pole for the pole vault; when his head had to follow his feet over the bar in the high jump; when sprinters used no starting blocks; when discus throwers didn't start with their backs to the target; and when the track wasn't foam rubber but cinders -- have been kept out of the top 10.

When Sweden's King Gustav awarded Thorpe his trophies in Stockholm and said, "Sir, you are the greatest athlete in the world," he knew what he was talking about.

Thorpe's status was short-lived in the eyes of the International Olympic Committee, which, upon learning that he had once made $25 a week playing baseball in America, disqualified him, on the grounds that he was a professional, the following January and ordered his gold medal be given to Hugo Wieslander of Sweden, the man who finished second to Thorpe, some 500 points in arrears. Still in awe six months later, Wieslander refused to take the medal, a stance he stayed with all his life.

The public never did side with the IOC. As Thorpe moved on to more athletic success back home in the United States as a professional football and baseball player, protests and appeals were filed and re-filed. Finally, in the fall of 1982, some 70 years after the Stockholm Games and nearly 30 years after Thorpe's death, the IOC reversed its decision. Jim Thorpe's gold medal was returned to his children and his name was again placed at the top of the 1912 decathlon finishers. The world's greatest athlete was a winner, on and off the track. π

ABOVE / *What Jim Thorpe would never know: what people would never forget.* (ALLSPORT / USOC)

OVERCOMING OBSTACLES

Some obstacles are more scenic than others.
(ALLSPORT / MARTIN)

American Gail Devers overcame Graves' disease and a tough 100-meter field in Barcelona, but the final hurdle proved to be her undoing. (ALLSPORT / M. POWELL)

Modern pentathlete James Haley and horse rise to the challenge. (ALLSPORT / MORTIMORE)

Roger Kingdom won the 110-meter hurdles in L.A. and Seoul.
(ALLSPORT / DUFFY)

RIGHT/ *Women's swimming was introduced as an Olympic event in Stockholm and the Americans have been a powerhouse ever since. One of the most dominating swimmers in American history was Tracy Caulkins (pictured). From 1978-84, Caulkins set five world records and more than 60 American records. In Los Angeles, she was finally able to add an Olympic title to her illustrious career. In fact, she earned three golds, in the 200-meter individual medley, 400-meter individual medley, and as a member of the 4x100-medley relay team.* (ALLSPORT / DUFFY)

S   W   I   M

M I N G

1920

April 20 - September 12, 1920

29 Nations

2,607 Athletes

21 Sports

41 USA golds

ANTWERP

LET THE GAMES BEGIN (AGAIN)

In light of the war that had been inflicted on the world from 1914 through 1918:

• The Games of the VIth Olympiad were canceled, occasioning the first interruption of the Olympics of the modern era.

• The International Olympic Committee's headquarters were moved to the neutral confines of Lausanne, Switzerland, the site of president Pierre de Coubertin's new home.

• And when the Games were resumed in 1920 they were not resumed in Berlin, where they had been scheduled for 1916, but in a land victimized by the war.

So it was that the VIIth Olympic Games came to Antwerp, Belgium, in the spring of 1920, barely 20 months since the end of the conflict. The world was digging out from the ravages of war and no one, the IOC reasoned, personified that effort better than the Belgians, who were proving to be as gallant in recovery as they had been in captivity.

A stadium sprang up almost overnight to host the track and field events and the Opening and Closing Ceremonies. The stadium's 30,000 seating capacity proved to be more than adequate, as the average price of admission, around 30 cents, was beyond the reach of the majority of postwar Belgians. As the Games wore on — they lasted from April 20 through September 12 — school children were allowed in free of charge.

King Albert of Belgium and his wife, Queen Elizabeth, were there to open the Games and Cardinal Mercier was there to bless the festival and hold a Requiem Mass for the war dead — among them many champions from the Stockholm Games of 1912.

TOP / *Antwerp, site of the Games of the VIIth Olympiad.* (ALLSPORT)

RIGHT / *Albert Hill of Great Britain wins the classic middle distance double 800 and 1,500 meters.* (ALLSPORT)

The world was digging out from the ravages of war and no one, the IOC reasoned, personified that effort better than the Belgians.

The vast majority of the competing athletes in Antwerp were war veterans — some still carrying their burdens of battle. The most inspirational of these veterans was Joseph Guillemot of France, a soldier whose lungs had been badly poisoned by mustard gas and was not expected to be able to mount much of a threat as a distance runner. But in his first race, the 5,000 meters, Guillemot not only won with a strong kick at the finish, but the person he passed down the stretch was a 23-year-old Finn named Paavo Nurmi. It would be Nurmi's only loss in Antwerp, alongside three gold medals (one of which came in the 10,000-meter run, when he avenged his defeat and relegated Guillemot to the silver medal) — and, indeed, the only loss the Flying Finn would suffer to someone other than a Finn in an Olympic career that would span three Olympiads and include nine gold medals and three silver medals.

Nurmi's teammate and idol, Hannes Kolehmainen, put the finishing touches to his two-Olympic career with a gold medal in the marathon, his fourth gold medal overall. In all, the Finns won 11 gold medals in track and field, and all but held their own with the Americans, whose most-watched performer was Charley Paddock, dubbed the "World's Fastest Human" after winning the 100 meters. Swimmer Duke Kahanamoku of Honolulu dominated the pool in Antwerp just as he had dominated the pool eight years earlier in Stockholm, winning the freestyle races at 100 and 800 meters.

Eddie Eagan, a boxer for the U.S. team, won the light heavyweight gold medal. Twelve years later, at the Lake Placid Winter Games of 1932, Eagan would make history by winning a gold medal as part of the winning U.S. four-man bobsled team, thus becoming the first person to win gold medals in both the summer and winter Olympic Games.

Albert Hill, at 36 considered well past his prime, carried Great Britain's colors to wins at both 800 and 1,500 meters.

The host Belgians saw countryman Henry George win cycling gold in the 50-kilometer track event and saw its national team win the soccer championship, albeit in bizarre fashion. After the Belgians took a 2-0 lead in the title match against Czechoslovakia, the Czech team grew so irritated with what it considered biased refereeing that it walked off the pitch. Belgium was declared the winner by forfeit.

Controversy also arose when several members of the U.S. team moved out of accommodations provided by the Belgian Organizing Committee. These accommodations were located in various schools throughout the city, where the athletes slept eight to a classroom on cots. Many of the American field event

competitors found the cots too small to provide a good night's sleep. When Dan Ahearn, a triple jumper who had moved to quarters with roomier cots, couldn't be found one night after curfew, the U.S. Olympic Committee suspended him from the team. That decision would have stood if not for a unified effort from many of Ahearn's teammates, who said they would not compete if Ahearn wasn't reinstated. He was, and finished sixth in his event.

Austere as its conditions were, Antwerp was rich in giving birth to a number of innovations that would become Olympic traditions. It was at Antwerp that the Olympic flag with its five colored rings — a gift from the city of Antwerp — made its debut. So did the Olympic motto of *Citius, Altius, Fortius*, a Greek phrase meaning, literally, Faster, Higher, Braver (although the commonly accepted translation became Swifter, Higher, Stronger). And it was at Antwerp that the athlete's oath was first taken. Victor Bion, a Belgian fencer, took the oath on behalf of the 2,607 athletes representing 29 nations, repeating these words that have since become a staple of the Opening Ceremonies: "In the name of all the competitors I promise

that we shall take part in these Olympic Games, respecting and abiding by the rules which govern them, in the true spirit of sportsmanship, for the glory of sport and the honour of our teams." Bion went on to win a silver medal in team epee.

After the competitors had obeyed their oath, for the most part, and the Games came to a peaceful close,

Coubertin assembled the IOC along with Belgian officials and royalty in the Antwerp Town Hall for a meeting. In his speech he said, in part, "These festivals are, above all, the festivals of human unity." The Olympics hadn't managed to stop a war from tearing apart the world. But it had managed to help bring part of that world back together. The world was digging out from the ravages of war and no one, the IOC reasoned, personified that effort better than the Belgians.

TOP / *The last time the tug of war was to be an Olympic event, Great Britain powered its way to a gold medal.* (ALLSPORT)

LEFT / *Pointing the way to victory for Finland's Hannes Kolehmainen. Kolehmainen would win the gold medal by the narrowest margin in Olympic marathon history.* (IOC)

jack kelly

HE WORE A KELLY GREEN HAT

Tightly gripping the oars as he sat astride his shell in the still water of a canal in Antwerp, Belgium, Jack Kelly had no idea how this race was going to turn out. Neither, for that matter, did he have any idea of the terrific things that lay ahead for him in his storybook life — that his son, Jack Jr., would become a four-time Olympic rower; that his daughter, Grace, would become America's favorite movie star and then marry into royalty and he would become Prince Rainier's father-in-law; that his construction business back home in Philadelphia would turn him into a millionaire and that 20 years later he would personally nominate Franklin D. Roosevelt as the next President of the United States.

As he awaited the start of the 1920 Olympic single sculls rowing final, Jack Kelly knew only this: He was not terribly fond of the British.

Just weeks earlier, he had been snubbed out of the annual Henley Royal Regatta race held on the River Thames in England. Prior to the 1920 event, the Henley's organizers had

sent word to Kelly and his club, the Vesper Boat Club of Philadelphia, that they would not be welcome. The reasons weren't entirely clear. There had been an incident between Vesper and the Henley Regatta people years earlier, in 1905, when, after the Vesper's eight-man crew won their event, charges of violations of the amateur laws of the day were leveled. That might have had something to do with it. And there was some aspersion that Kelly, who once made his living as a bricklayer, wasn't welcome because he had worked with his hands — and Henley wasn't keen on people who worked with their hands.

Whatever the reason, Kelly didn't row in the famed Diamond Sculls race at Henley and it ate at him because if you were a tennis player, you played Wimbledon; a baseball player, the World Series; and if you were a rower, you rowed the Diamond Sculls on the Thames at Henley. It further ate at Kelly, who was generally regarded as America's finest oarsman after two straight national single sculls championships, because he thought that not only could he row at Henley, he could win there as well.

Coming to Europe three weeks later to row in the Olympics was a consolation prize at best. The Olympics had 24 years of tradition, Henley triple that. The Olympics immortalized discus throwers, not rowers.

But as the boats lined up for the final, Kelly's spirits brightened. Because there, in the boat next to him, sat one Jack Beresford, a good man of the Commonwealth. It was Beresford, as a matter of fact, who had won the Diamond Sculls at Henley, further establishing his reputation as the best single sculls rower in the world.

Antwerp wasn't Henley-on-Thames, and the main canal that connected Antwerp and Brussels — site of the Olympic rowing events — wasn't the Thames, but it was going to have to do. In the vengeance department, this was what 29-year-old Jack Kelly had been served.

In America — especially on his home course on the Schuylkill River in Philadelphia — Kelly had a reputation for being quite, well, confident. One often-told story was about the Schuylkill referee who

warned Kelly, notoriously a fast starter, to hold his position before the gun was fired. When the gun went off, the rest of the shells went off with it. But not Kelly, who sat stationary in his boat and, looking at the referee, said, "Is it all right to go now?" When the referee said, "Of course, you darned fool," Kelly started — and won the race.

But against Beresford in the race for the Olympic gold medal, Kelly would not hesitate. He started quickly, with the gun, as did the British champion, and, as they moved ahead of the field, they matched oar for oar down the 2,000 meters of canal water. It was unusually stiff competition for Kelly — who, during one stretch of his superlative career, would win 124 races in a row in the United States — and he might not have summoned every ounce of strength he needed to cross the finish line first …

… but he kept thinking of Henley …

… of being snubbed …

… by the British …

… and with one especially strong push at the finish he nosed ahead for the victory — by one second.

In every single sculls Olympic final before Antwerp, and in every single sculls Olympic final through the Barcelona Games of 1992 — there would not be a closer finish.

Flushed by the thrill of victory, Kelly was able to come back after just a 30-minute rest and become the first and only person to win gold medals in both the single sculls and double sculls in the same Olympics. He teamed with his cousin, Paul Costello, to dominate the field, winning by 9.6 seconds over a team from Italy while negotiating the same 2,000-meter course.

Kelly wore his trademark kelly green hat to the victory podium, after which he took off the hat and sent it to King George of England.

In the next Olympic Games at Paris in 1924, rowing down the River Seine,

Kelly again teamed with his cousin to win the double sculls over a home-river French pair, although he declined to enter the singles, this time won by Beresford. His three gold medals in three tries remain the single most successful run by a U.S. rower in the history of the Games.

Kelly retired from rowing not long afterward as he and his wife gave birth to their famous children and Jack turned his ambitions to other fronts. His construction business helped build 20th century Philadelphia and so, for that matter, did Kelly. He became a politician, narrowly losing a race for mayor of Philadelphia in 1935 and a bid for the U.S. Senate in 1936. But in 1940 he was the man the Democratic Party chose to stand at the podium at the Democratic National Convention in Philadelphia to nominate Franklin D. Roosevelt for a third term as President of the United States.

The son of a poor Irish immigrant who worked in the mills all his life, Kelly and his family came to emblemize the American dream. He saw all his daughter's films and, after she married the Prince of Monaco, he got the royal treatment in Monte Carlo. He stayed at the Palace, he got instant credit at the casino, they reserved the best spot for him on the beach. His was not an uneventful life.

Rowing remained a lifetime love. After his son, Jack Jr., got old enough — Jack Sr. decided seven was about right — Kelly took him to the Schuylkill and put him in a boat. He tutored him tirelessly. As the son began to show promise, Kelly bought the Vesper Boat Club and its entire fleet of boats. Training gear would never be a problem.

Some sons might have rebelled at such drive and determination from a father. Jack Jr. wasn't one of them. He was his father all over again, rowing in a different era. Like Jack Sr., Jack Jr. became the best single sculls rower in America, winning national championships four times, in 1946, 1948, 1950 and 1952. In 1947, he won the Sullivan Award as America's top amateur athlete, and in 1949, he became the first U.S. rower to win the European sculling championship.

Jack Jr. competed in four Olympic Games, although a combination of injuries, illness and plain bad luck prevented him from duplicating his father's gold medals. He won a bronze medal in the single sculls in his last Games, in Melbourne in 1956.

But at the Henley Royal Regatta, it was a different story. Jack Jr. went to the famous race in 1947, the second generation welcomed where the first generation wasn't. He advanced easily through all the rounds and, in the final of the Diamond Sculls, he beat Carl Fronsdal of Norway by eight full lengths …

… and he wore a kelly green hat while he did it. π

ABOVE / *American Jack Kelly won the single sculls and, 30 minutes later, he capped his day's performance with a win in the double sculls.* (ALLSPORT)

DIVING

Silhouette in the sky (ALLSPORT / BRUTY)

1924

May 4 - July 27, 1924

45 Nations

3,092 Athletes

17 Sports

45 USA golds

PARIS

For some reason, Pierre de Coubertin had a hard time melding ideals with reality in his hometown. By the time 1924 came along, the Olympic movement he resuscitated had picked up considerable steam. Athens had staged two largely successful Olympics, London had managed, despite introducing bickering as an Olympic event, one progressive go in 1908; and the 1912 and 1920 Games at Stockholm and Antwerp, respectively, had been steps in the right direction. Even St. Louis, in 1904, had tried (if not with terrific success) to present the Olympics as a headline event. It was only in Paris, in 1900, that the Games of Zeus had borne little resemblance to the ideals of international brotherhood and marquee status that Coubertin had in mind.

More than a little rankled, Coubertin used his influence as president of the IOC — a commission that was about to expire — to secure another Parisian try in 1924. Amsterdam had originally been selected, but such was the Father of the Olympics' influence, that 24 years after its first, futile effort, when Coubertin himself was pushed off the stage, Paris again hosted the world's athletes.

Not that there wasn't some drama and doubt before the Games arrived, however. Any hopes Coubertin entertained about smooth sailing were dashed in 1923 by the twin daggers of a slumping French economy and the flooding of the Seine, the river that intersects Paris. So dire was Paris' plight that the IOC alerted Los Angeles, a city prospering in the midst of America's Roaring '20s, that the Games of '24

TOP / *Opening shot: The Comte de Clary, president of the Free Pistol Association, presides in Paris.* (IOC)

RIGHT / *American Johnny Weissmuller (center) set an Olympic record of 5:04.2 in the 400-meter freestyle. Weissmuller also captured the gold in the 100-meter freestyle. In years to come, he would go on to become Hollywood's first Tarzan.* (ALLSPORT)

IF AT FIRST YOU DON'T SUCCEED...

The turnout to Paris was unprecedented. It was in Paris that the underground art of scalping made its Olympic debut. So keen was the interest for the Opening Ceremonies that "speculators" more than tripled their original investments.

ABOVE / *Ville Ritola leads countryman Eero Berg in the 10,000 meters. Finnish runners dominated the distance events throughout the early Olympics.* (ALLSPORT)

would be moved there (Amsterdam's turn in the rotation had already been bumped to 1928).

But Paris rebounded in time, shoring up (quite literally) in time to send a wire to Los Angeles that moved that city's turn to 1932 — by which time, ironically, Los Angeles would be in an economic downturn of its own.

The turnout to Paris was unprecedented. With the World War now six years distant, 44 nations — 15 more than at Antwerp — sent teams, totaling 3,092 competitors. Spectator interest, aided by Paris' central location and easy accessibility, reached new heights. It was in Paris that the underground art of scalping — selling tickets for more than their face value — made its Olympic debut. So keen was the interest for the Opening Ceremonies on May 4 in the Colombes Stadium, where French President Gaston Doumergue opened the Games, that "speculators" more than tripled their original investments.

It was in Paris that the United States first laid serious claim as the most dominant sporting nation on earth. Whereas in earlier Olympiads Americans shined mostly in track and field, in Paris they took the lead in almost every venue. They won a majority of medals in every sport except cycling and gymnastics; and, at that, American Frank Kriz won a gymnastics gold medal for the first U.S. gold since 1904.

Most glamorous of the Americans was 20-year-old Johnny Weissmuller, later to be Tarzan in the movies, who won three gold medals in swimming and added a bronze in water polo. In winning the 100-meter freestyle race, Weissmuller became heir apparent to the great Hawaiian champion, Duke Kahanamoku, the 100's winner in 1912 and 1920. Thirty-four years old in 1924, Kahanamoku finished second to Weissmuller.

Many other Americans made their competitive marks in Paris in the summer of '24, but none more dramatically than Robert LeGendre, who set a world record in the long jump despite failing to qualify for the U.S. long jump team. Competing in the pentathlon — a mini-decathlon comprising the long jump, javelin, discus, and 200- and 1,500-meter runs — LeGendre jumped 25 feet, 5 3/4 inches, three inches beyond the world mark and a full foot farther than William De Hart Hubbard of the U.S., the official long

jump champion.

Among the more anonymous U.S. gold-medalists was the No. 7 rower in the shell that won the eight-oared shell with coxswain. His name: Ben Spock. Twenty-one years later, as Dr. Benjamin Spock, the gold-medal rower would write the internationally acclaimed best-seller *The Common Sense Book of Baby and Child Care.*

Wide-ranging as the American's exploits were in Paris, none came close to attracting the attention accorded Paavo Nurmi, the Flying Finn, who used Paris to ensconce himself as an Olympic legend. The reclusive Finnish distance runner won four gold medals and would no doubt have won a fifth if Finnish officials hadn't kept him out of the 10,000-meter run, where another Finn, Vilho "Ville" Ritola, was the victor. Other Finnish runners won the marathon and the steeplechase and Finns also won in the pentathlon and the javelin, giving the nation of three million a total of 10 gold medals in track and field, just two behind the 12 won by U.S. athletes.

France's proudest moment came in the cycling competition when Armand Blanchonnet won the road race by an astonishing 10 minutes — the most lopsided breakaway in Olympic history, before or after.

Despite the superlative performances in Paris — eight world records and 25 Olympic records were set on the track and in the pool — the climate wasn't always favorable. As the events stretched on from May 4 through July 27, temperatures continued to rise and so did unbridled "partisan" spectating. The summer of '24 was one of the hottest in Parisien history, with temperatures

reaching as high as 113 degrees, and Parisians often treated foreigners with heated contempt. Particularly foreigners who won. The most unpleasant incident occurred in the rugby final, when the team from the United States beat the team from France. A riot broke out in the stands and at least one American supporter was rushed to the hospital.

Still, on balance, Paris had decidedly continued the Olympics' rise on the world consciousness chart. All things considered, Coubertin got his wish. There was ticket scalping, hometown partisanship, bickering, more fan interest than ever before, and a bona fide superstar in Paavo Nurmi. Twenty-eight years into the era of the Modern Games, the Olympics had arrived in Paris.

TOP / *Jackson Scholz edges past a leaping Charles Paddock in the 200-meter race. American sprinters finished in four of the top five positions.* (ALLSPORT)

ABOVE / *The Americans and Romanians battle for position in this rugby match. The American squad surprised hometown favorite France to win what would become the last Olympic gold medal in rugby.* (IOC)

harold abrahams
&
eric liddell

CHARIOTS
OF
REALITY

The Paris Olympics of 1924 gave them their gold medals — although they came in the mail a month late, bearing insufficient postage. It was Hollywood that came along more than 60 years later and gave them fame.

So elegantly produced was the Hugh Hudson film "Chariots of Fire," which won the 1981 Oscar for Best Picture, that Harold Abrahams and Eric Liddell became household names some six decades after their careers, after each had passed on.

Also because of the beauty of the production, the fact that the movie was largely a distortion of facts was either ignored or in large part forgiven.

The important parts were true: Abrahams did win the 100-meter sprint at the Stade Colombes at 7:05 p.m. on July 7, 1924, and, four days later, Liddell did win the 400-meter final in the same stadium. Further, Abrahams was indeed a Cambridge-educated, soon-to-be-lawyer of Jewish descent while Liddell was indeed a devout Christian from Scotland, the son of missionaries, who declined a position in the Olympic 100-meter draw because the heats were to be run on Sunday.

What wasn't true:

A) British steeplechaser Evelyn Montague, who finished sixth in Paris, was not a close friend and Cambridge classmate of Abrahams'. Montague went to Oxford and was only a casual acquaintance.

B) Abrahams did not run around the Trinity College courtyard at Cambridge before the clock struck 12 times. By point of fact, this fête was performed years later by David Burghley, a British gold-medal hurdler in the 1928 Games at Amsterdam who would later become a member of Parliament and also a participant in the Olympic Games in Los Angeles in 1932.

C) A character styled after Burghley did not save the day for Liddell by giving him his spot in the 400 after Liddell discovered on the eve of the Paris Games that the 100's heats were to be run on the Sabbath. Not only was this character fictitious, but Liddell knew of the Sunday schedule some six months before the Games began.

D) And Abrahams and Liddell did not meet in the British Amateur Athletic Association 100-yard dash championship the year previous, where a win by Liddell inspired Abrahams to double his efforts for revenge at the Olympic Games. A showdown between Abrahams and Liddell had indeed been eagerly anticipated at that 1923 meeting of the AAA, but Abrahams withdrew because of an ear infection, leaving Liddell to win the race in a new British Commonwealth record of 9.7 seconds.

Abrahams, while hardly the persecution of anti-Semitism as suggested by Hollywood, was indeed an intense, win-oriented, highly-confident athlete with dogged determination that caused him to hire the great coach, Sam Mussabini. The son of a Lithuanian Jew who moved to London and became a wealthy financier, Harold went to all the best schools and was relentless in his pursuit to become the first European to win the Olympic 100-meter sprint.

In real life, Liddell was as the movie portrayed him — an unstylish, transformed rugby player who relied more on heart and determination than natural talent and coordination. It was

true, as the movie showed, that Liddell was knocked down during the 440-yard finals at a meet between England, Ireland and Scotland, and still got up and won, making up a 20-yard deficit in the process. It was also true that on the Sabbath Day when the 100-meter heats were run in Paris, Liddell found his way to a Scottish-speaking church and preached a sermon.

In Paris, the movie concentrates chiefly on Abraham's upset win in the 100, where he sets an Olympic record while defeating pre-race favorites Jackson Scholz and world record-holder and defending Olympic champion Charley Paddock of the United States, and on Liddell's win in the 400 meters, where, arms flailing, head back, he, too, sets an Olympic record while easily finishing five yards in front of Horatio Fitch of the U.S. and Guy Butler of Great Britain.

Not featured is the only sprint show-down Abrahams and Liddell ever had — when they met in the 200-meter final.

Liddell won the battle of the Britons, but not exactly with cinematic drama. Liddell placed third with a time of 21.9, behind both Scholz and Paddock. Abrahams came in a distant sixth, or last, with a 22.3 clocking. The movie does show Abrahams' defeat in the 200, but only to suggest that it added another reason for his determination to win the 100. In reality, the 100 had already been decided, in Abrahams' favor, two days before.

Just prior to his win in the 400, Liddell did indeed receive an inspirational handwritten note as he was warming up. And the note did say, "He who honors me, I will honor." But the note was not written by Scholz, as Hollywood version suggested, but by an unidentified fan, presumably a Christian, who knew of Liddell's convictions and sent the word from the stands.

After Paris, neither Abrahams or Liddell would compete in another Olympic Games. Liddell returned home briefly to Scotland, where a parade in his honor was held along the Edinburgh High Street and he was afforded a hero's welcome. After that he rejoined his missionary parents in China. He died in 1945, at the age of 43, in a Japanese World War II internment camp from a brain tumor.

Abrahams returned to London, where he lived the rest of his life. He married a stage star, opera singer Sybil Evers, in 1935, long after his running days were over. He became a radio commentator for BBC, a lawyer, a writer, and, for many years, the president of the British AAA. He died in 1978 in London at the age of 79.

One of Abrahams' writing projects was entitled *The Olympic Games Book*. In it, he gives a first-person account of his impressions of those Paris Games of 1924.

Of Eric Liddell, he wrote:

"A performance which made a particular impression upon me was Eric Liddell's 400 meters in the Olympic record time of 47.6 sec. Liddell turned to the 400 meters mainly because he was not willing to run in the 100 meters, which was on a Sunday. Eric broke every possible rule of style, with his head right back, knees well up and arms all over the place. But, my goodness, what spiritual power!"

And of his own performance, he said:

"My good fortune in the 100 meters is, I believe, sufficiently far away to make it possible to refer to it without seeming self-satisfied. The truth of the matter is that until twenty-four hours before the final I never thought I had any real chance of defeating the four American sprinters headed by Charley Paddock ... my best luck of all — if there is such a thing as luck — is I had been dead stale at the championships a fortnight previously and I was not the favourite. I had everything to win, but little to lose.

"I am still amazed," wrote Abrahams in conclusion, "at the enormous difference to my life that ten seconds or so on the evening of July 7th, 1924, made."

He had no idea.

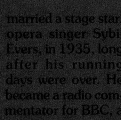

Liddell was as the movie portrayed him — an unstylish, transformed rugby player who relied more on heart and determination than natural talent and coordination.

ABOVE / *Due to his religious convictions, Great Britain's Eric Liddell decided he could not compete in the Olympic 100-meter finals, which was to be held on Sunday. Instead, he concentrated on the 200 and 400 meters. This strategy paid off as Liddell tied the Olympic record of 47.6 and won the gold in the 400 meters.* (ALLSPORT)

GREAT RACES

ABOVE / *Although the Americans were favored, Brit Harold Abrahams (#419) snatched the 100-meter victory in an Olympic record 10.6 in 1924.* (ALLSPORT)

BELOW / *In 1956, the British 4x100-meter relay had a slight lead going into the final leg, but Australia's anchor was the 100-meter champion Betty Cuthbert. Australia won the race by a half yard.* (ALLSPORT)

OPPOSITE (TOP) / *In 1928 women were allowed to compete in track and field. The first event was the 100 meters, which was won by 16-year-old American Elizabeth Robinson.* (ALLSPORT)

(BOTTOM) / *This 80-meter hurdle race in 1948 finished with both Fanny Blankers-Koen and Maureen Gardner equaling the Olympic record of 11.2. After a short but nervous wait, the results were posted: Blankers-Koen winner.* (ALLSPORT)

TOUR DE FORCES

Greg Louganis — off the board
(ALLSPORT / DUFFY)

In most sports and most events, winning is a universal experience in the Olympic Games, with gold medals making a tour of the world. There have been exceptions, however; isolated cases where one country has settled in ... and stayed put.

Perhaps the most notable streak in Olympic history occurred from 1912 through 1968 in the pole vault, a 56-year, 13-Olympic Games' period during which every winner came from the United States. The streak is all the more curious considering the universal participation in the pole vault throughout the U.S. domination — and the fact that since a German athlete broke the string in 1972, the United States hasn't won since.

In springboard diving — another sport with a wide range of participating nations — the United States put together a streak almost the equal of the 56-year pole vault skein. From 1920-68, covering 48 years and 11 Olympic Games, U.S. divers captured the event. After a Soviet diver won in 1972, the U.S. resumed its streak, winning in every Olympics since with the exception of the boycotted 1980 Games.

Hurdling has been another American stronghold. U.S. men's hurdlers have won 18 of the 23 gold medals awarded in the 110-meter high hurdles and 17 of the 22 awarded in the 400-meter inter-mediate hurdles. The longest winning streak occurred from the 1932-72 Games at 110 meters, as U.S. hurdlers captured nine straight gold medals in a 40-year span.

In fencing and field hockey, teams from Hungary and India have put together sizeable streaks. Hungary's men's sabre team won 44 straight matches and eight straight Olympic gold medals from 1924-60, while India's men's field hockey team put together a 30-match winning streak from 1928-60, winning six gold medals before losing the 1960 final.

In men's basketball, the United States won its first 62 games from 1936 until the controversial gold-medal loss to the Soviet Union in 1972. Overall, the U.S. is 91-2 in Olympic history, with 10 gold medals in the dozen Olympics it has entered.

For sheer dominance, no streaks can touch those produced by the United States' men in the 4x100-meter track relay or the former Soviet Union women in team gymnastics. Discounting boycotts, each is undefeated in Olympic history. In the 4x100-meter relay, the U.S. has won every Olympic final, eight in all, since the event began in 1960 — with the exception of 1980, when the United States did not participate. In women's team gymnastics, the former Soviet Union won 10 golds in a row, from 1952-92, with the exception of the 1984 Games, when it did not participate. Since the Soviet Union disbanded after the 1992 Games, its perfect record is destined to stand forever. π

ROADSIDE ATTRACTIONS

Asia's attractions: Bhudda and bikes. (ALLSPORT / CANNON)

Future cyclists of Korea? (ALLSPORT / RONDEAU)

The road less traveled. (ALLSPORT / M. POWELL)

1928

May 17 - August 12, 1928

46 Nations

3,014 Athletes

14 Sports

22 USA golds

AMSTERDAM

Buoyed by the success of the Paris Games four years previous, the Olympics came to Amsterdam healthier than they'd ever been. Ironically, Pierre de Coubertin, their modern founder, wasn't healthy at all. For the first time since St. Louis in 1904, the aging and infirm Coubertin, by now retired as president of the International Olympic Committee, did not attend the four-year festival in person. He sent his regards and his regrets, however, and had them read at the Opening Ceremonies. "I should be wise to take the present opportunity of bidding you farewell," he said. "I beg to thank those who have followed me and helped me to fight a forty-year war, not often easy and not always cleanly fought."

But by 1928, a war that had been won.

No longer was the Olympic movement on shaky ground. No longer were there persistent rumors every four years that the current Games would be "the last." No longer was it called a frivolous exercise that could not stand on its own. A record 46 nations sent Olympic teams to The Netherlands, totaling 3,014 athletes, and sophistication was higher than ever. The United States track team, for instance, arrived with a contingent of 11 coaches, four managers and six trainers. (Ironically, it would be the U.S.'s worst showing on the track to that date in Olympic history as only one runner, Raymond Barbuti at 400 meters, would win an individual gold medal. The team did fare better in the field events, winning five of the eight gold medals available).

WOMEN ON TRACK

Women's appearance on the Amsterdam track was met with more than a little resistance. When the women did appear, it was under the stipulation that they wear shorts that came within 12 centimeters — about four inches — of the knee.

TOP / *"The Flying Finn" in a moment of rest after yet another Olympic gold medal. Between 1920 and 1928 Paavo Nurmi won nine gold medals.* (ALLSPORT)

RIGHT / *The Canadians revenged their loss in the 100 meters by beating the U.S. team in the 4x100-meter relay in a world record 48.4.* (ALLSPORT)

Amsterdam marked the first-ever Olympic track and field competition for women. Included on the program were the discus, the high jump, the 100- and 200-meter sprints, the 4x100-meter relay and the 800-meter run. Women hadn't been allowed at all in the ancient Greek Games, and had been admitted only slowly in the modern Games, competing, prior to 1928, in tennis, golf, archery, figure skating, yachting, swimming, diving and fencing. Their appearance on the Amsterdam track — the first to be standardized at 400 meters in circumference — was met with more than a little resistance, most notably from Coubertin himself and from Pope Pius XI, who roundly condemned the decision from the Vatican. When the women did appear, it was under the stipulation that they wear shorts that came within 12 centimeters (about four inches) of the knee.

For all the commotion, all went well enough until the 800-meter run, when Lina Radke, the victor from Germany, headed a field of struggling, exhausted runners that lay sprawled in various stage of collapse just beyond the finish line. Immediately there were outcries that women were not physically equipped to run such a long and exhausting distance. Despite protests from a number of sources, including the women runners,

that all they lacked was experience in training for such an event, the IOC, led by its new president Comte de Baillet-Latour of Belgium, banned women from participating in any races beyond half a lap — a ban that would stand for 32 years. It wouldn't be until the Rome Games of 1960 that the 800 would make its Olympic reappearance.

The most famous of the first women track and field Olympians turned out to be pretty 18-year-old Ethel Catherwood, "The Saskatoon Lily" from Saskatoon, Canada. After taking the gold medal with

a jump of 5 feet, 2 and 1/2 inches, Catherwood returned in glory to Saskatoon, where the provincial government gave her a trust fund of $3,000, although not as an aid for continued training, but to help her in her piano studies.

It was in Amsterdam that Finland's Paavo Nurmi added the last of his dozen Olympic medals, albeit just one gold. The famous Flying Finn was by far the most recognizable face in Amsterdam — a fact that forced the entire Finnish team, on its way to participate in the Opening Ceremonies, to enter the Olympic Stadium by climbing over a back wall in order to avoid the crowds waiting in front. Nurmi lost to his rival and countryman, Ville Ritola, in the 5,000-meter run after relegating Ritola — whose personal Olympic haul wasn't exactly immodest with five gold medals

ABOVE / *David Lord Burghley was one the most colorful characters in the 1928 Games, winning the 400-meter hurdles in an Olympic record 53.4.* (ALLSPORT)

CENTER / *Capturing both the attention of the crowd and the gold medal, Canada's Ethel Catherwood "The Saskatoon Lily" smiles for photographers. She would later marry fellow high jumper and gold-medal winner Harold Osborn.* (IOC)

and three silvers — to second place at 10,000 meters. In the 3,000-meter steeplechase, despite suffering from the exhaustion of the 5,000 the day before, Nurmi finished second in what would be his final Olympic race.

The most electrifying performer in Amsterdam was Percy Williams, a 19-year-old black Canadian from Vancouver who had hitchhiked across Canada to participate in that country's Olympic trials. He won both the 100- and 200-meter sprint titles in those trials and, with the rest of the world thrown in for good measure, duplicated that feat in Amsterdam. His counterpart in the water was Johnny Weissmuller, who, as he had four years previous in Paris, won gold in the 100-meter freestyle and the 4x200-meter freestyle relay.

For the first time since 1912, the Amsterdam Games saw the Olympic re-emergence of Germany, finally off probation for its aggressiveness in the first world war. As if to make up for lost time, the Germans responded by winning 10 gold medals and 31 overall, second only to the United States' totals of 22 gold medals and 31 overall. Alas, Germany's participation would extend only for two more Olympic Games until another "aggression" would ban it from the 1948 Games in London.

It was at Amsterdam, too, where David Lord Burghley of England, one of the most colorful characters in Olympic history, won the 400-meter hurdles; where the custom of torch-lighting was introduced; and where India entered its first Olympic field hockey team. In front

of a capacity crowd of 40,000, India beat the host Dutch by a 3-0 margin in the final, starting a consecutive gold medal streak that would extend until the Rome Games of 1960. As the women 800-meter runners would tell you, that would be a long time.

TOP / *A lunge for the tape provides the margin of victory for American Ray Barbuti over Canada's James Ball in the 400 meters in Amsterdam.* (ALLSPORT)

ABOVE / *Canadian Percy Williams arrived the underdog and left Amsterdam as the double Olympic sprint champion. He won the 100 meters in 10.8 and the 200 meters in 21.8.* (ALLSPORT)

paavo nurmi

BORN TO WIN

In three Olympic Games, Paavo Nurmi already had nine gold medals. As the 5,000-meter final was about to begin in Amsterdam's Olympic Stadium, there was no reason to suspect No. 10 wasn't just another Olympic- or world-record away.

He was the quintessential Flying Finn. Not to mention the Phantom Finn, the Phenomenal Finn, and the greatest distance runner anyone had ever seen. In the Amsterdam Games of 1928, any suspicions that, at 31, Nurmi might be getting old, for a distance runner, had been laid to rest five days earlier when he won the 10,000-meter final with a stirring burst that carried him to an Olympic record and a six-tenths of a second victory over his countryman, Vilho "Ville" Ritola.

Finishing second to Nurmi was nothing new for Ritola, a man who might have been called the world's greatest distance runner himself if not for the unfortunate timing of his birth with Paavo Nurmi's. The 10,000 marked the fifth time Ritola had looked up at an Olympic finish line and seen nothing but ... Nurmi. Four

years earlier, in the Paris Olympics of 1924, Ritola had finished behind Nurmi in the 5,000-meter final and the cross-country final as well as in two team races that were won by Finland. As the Amsterdam Games began it had been more of the same — and it appeared it would be always so as Nurmi, never one for chitchat, refused to shake Ritola's hand as they warmed down. Even for the reclusive Nurmi, his exit from the track that day was cold. He refused all interviews and waved off photographers who rushed in to take his picture as he left for the locker room.

His win in the 10,000 only enhanced Nurmi's reputation as a stoical, no-nonsense runner who hated to lose. It was a reputation that had begun quickly in the 1920 Olympic Games in Antwerp, where Nurmi burst into the world's Olympic consciousness by losing his first race, the 5,000-meter final. A Frenchman named Joseph Guillemot had lagged just behind Nurmi's shoulder throughout that inaugural race, only to sprint away in the final 30 yards and win by four-tenths of a second. Thoroughly disgusted with himself, Nurmi brushed aside the photo-

graphers that day too; then, three days later, he avenged his defeat as he came from behind to beat Guillemot by 1.6 seconds in the 10,000-meter run.

He would not lose again. He added two cross-country triumphs before he was finished with the Antwerp Games and then, in the Paris Games of 1924, he cemented his reputation with five gold medals in five finals. At that, it was the gold medal he *didn't* get that most firmly confirmed his seeming invincibility as well as his single-minded determination. It was in the 10,000-meter run. For whatever reasons, Finland's Olympic officials decided not to enter Nurmi in that event, leaving Ritola, who was making his Olympic debut, a free rein. Ritola took full advantage, setting a world record with a time of 30 minutes and 23 seconds. Meanwhile, Nurmi was on the training track, wearing a full sweatsuit while pounding out lap after lap to let off his steam. A number of journalists sat on the fence surrounding the track and timed his run — which, as it turned out, was exactly 10,000 meters. After Nurmi finished, the journalists compared their stopwatches and none had

exceeded 30 minutes.

For further effect, two months later, while competing in a track meet in Finland, Nurmi won a 10,000-meter race in 30 minutes and six seconds, breaking Ritola's world record while establishing one of his own that would last for the next 12 years.

The final chapter in Nurmi's 10,000 Revenge had been written here, in Amsterdam, as he relegated Ritola to his usual silver-medal finish. The race was as exciting as you could ask for, moving no less than General Douglas MacArthur, the head of the U.S. Olympic Committee and future World War II hero, to move from his box seat to the finish line for the final lap and exult, "It's worth crossing the ocean just to see this." But thrilling as the stretch run was, in the end it was Nurmi's race, as always. The world was in its normal orbit.

Nine straight wins in nine Olympic races over the past eight years. He was indominability defined. Nobody beat Nurmi. This was a man who, capitalizing on his fame after the Paris Games, went to America for a barnstorming "cross-country" tour in the winter of 1925. American track fans flocked to see him. Baseball had Ruth. Football had Nagurski. Boxing had Dempsey. Running (and the Olympics) had Nurmi. In months of racing from coast to coast, Nurmi set world records at every indoor distance and lost only once, when he dropped down to the half-mile and took second to Alan Helffrich, the American record-holder.

Nurmi's career was a clinic in meteoric rises. He grew up dirt poor in Turku, Finland, 100 miles north of Helsinki, where he took up serious running after his father died when he was 12. An introvert, he ran with just himself as company, chasing, and

often catching, the mail trains as they steamed into Turku. After Hannes Kolehmainen won three gold medals at the Olympics in 1912, Nurmi's running had new drive and direction. He wanted to be the next Hannes.

He would be tireless in pursuing his Olympic dreams. It was Nurmi who introduced steady pacing to a sport that had traditionally relied on gut instincts. He strapped a stopwatch to his wrist and checked it continually. With time, he stopped competing against humans entirely until the last lap of races, competing only against his watch. When he won the 1,500-meter gold medal in 1924, setting an Olympic record in the process, Nurmi calculated he would run the first 1,000 meters in 2:30. His time at

1,000 meters was 2:30.1. The word was, Nurmi was disappointed.

He would set some 29 world records in his career, and that was just the records set at the universally accepted outdoor distances. One of his most enduring records — it would last for nearly 20 years — was the 11 miles, 1,648 yards he ran in one hour, a distance just 12 yards short of 12 miles and the exact five-minute-per-mile average that had been Nurmi's projected pace.

Such was the mechanical man/legend who came to the 5,000 final in Amsterdam for his encore encounter with Ville Ritola, his faithful sidekick, at his side.

Lap after lap the two Finns stayed side by side, leaving the pack — except for Edvin Wide of Sweden, another longtime rival — well behind.

On the gun lap Nurmi and Ritola nudged ahead of Wide, setting up yet another close finish. But around the final curve, as the entire stadium expected just the opposite to happen, Ritola moved into a higher gear and the great Nurmi did not. Ritola accelerated down the final straightaway, towing Nurmi behind him. As a stunned stadium looked on, Ritola breasted the tape two seconds ahead of his nemesis.

For months and years afterward, speculation raged that Nurmi had purposely let up on the final curve, allowing the countryman who had never beaten him to finally feel the winner's tape across his chest. Did he or didn't he? Only Nurmi knew for sure. And, true to form, it would be a subject he would never address.

After a flap over appearance fee disqualified him from the next Olympic Games in Los Angeles in

His win in the 10,000 only enhanced Nurmi's reputation as a stoical, no-nonsense runner who hated to lose.

1932, Nurmi, by now 35, retired to Finland where he made a fortune in real estate and kept as much as possible from public view. He wasn't seen on a track again until the 1952 Olympic Games in Helsinki. At the age of 55, he ran into the stadium during the Opening Ceremonies carrying the Olympic torch. So dramatic was his unannounced entrance, so unmistakable was his stride, so entrenched was his Olympic reputation, that the athletes of the world, just as Douglas MacArthur had done 24 years earlier, sprang out of their seats and ran to the side of the track, there to get a better look at this legendary runner. ◊

ABOVE / *Finland's Ville Ritola finally broke the winning streak of countryman Paavo Nurmi in the 5,000 meters in Amsterdam.* (ALLSPORT)

FAMILY TRADITIONS

A 90's kind of mascot: Atlanta's Whatizit.
(ALLSPORT / GUND)

The traditions that make up the heart and soul of the Olympic Games did not all come together at once. Little by little, assorted ceremonies, oaths, mottos and slogans have been added. A roll call of some of the most well-known Olympic traditions includes:

1896: The Olympic Hymn, composed by Spyros Samaras of Greece, makes its debut. So does the parade of athletes, post-event flag-raising ceremonies in honor of the home nation of the victor, and the opening of the Games by the head of state. Greece's King George I opened the Games of 1896, saying: "I declare the opening of the first international Olympic Games in Athens."

1908: Winners are given "gold" medals for the first time (in reality they aren't made of gold, but of gilt). Also,

the "unofficial motto" of the Olympic Games makes its appearance: "The most important thing in the Olympic Games is not to win but to take part, just as the most important thing in life is not the triumph but the struggle. The essential thing is not to have conquered but to have fought well."

1913: While on a trip to Delphi, Pierre de Coubertin, the founder of the modern Olympic movement, sees an emblem of five interlocking rings which he adopts as the Olympic logo.

1920: At the start of the Antwerp Games, Victor Boin, a Belgian fencer, is the first athlete to take the Olympic oath, declaring: "In the name of all the competitors I promise that we shall take part in these Olympic Games, respecting and abiding by the rules which govern them, in the true spirit of sportsmanship, for the glory of sport and the honor of our teams." It is also at Antwerp that the Olympic flag, with the five colored rings, is

adopted, and where the official Olympic motto of "Citius, Altius, Fortius" makes its debut. The literal translation from Greek to English is "Faster, Higher, Braver," although the commonly accepted meaning will become "Swifter, Higher, Stronger."

1932: Los Angeles unveils the first official Olympic Village in the suburb of Baldwin Hills.

1936: Berlin introduces the Olympic Flame. A torch is lit in the ancient city of Olympia, Greece, and carried to Berlin, where Fritz Shilgen is the inaugural Olympic torchbearer.

1956: The first "en masse" closing ceremony takes place, with athletes from all nations breaking rank as they enter the stadium.

1968: Olympic judges and officials take their first oath. π

A Seoul-ful gaze (Allsport / Vandystadt)

Dove of Peace (Allsport / M. Powell)

Barcelona 1992 (Allsport / Rondeau)

Flo-Jo's 1988 Olympic haul (Allsport / Duffy)

U.S. Olympic Team members in Barcelona (Allsport / Cole)

1984 Opening Ceremonies (Allsport / Duffy)

C A U T

SLIPPERY

I O N !

WHEN WET

1932

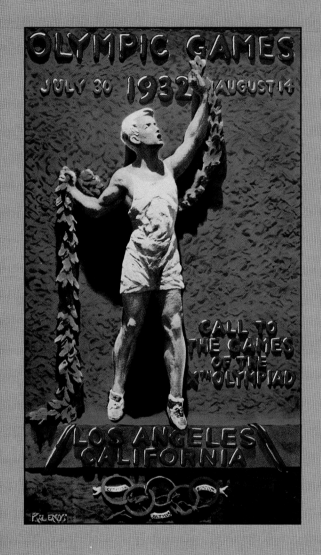

July 30 - August 14, 1932

37 Nations

1, 408 Athletes

14 Sports

41 USA golds

LOS ANGELES

HARD TIMES, GOOD TIMES

et down as they were, smack in the middle of the worst economic crisis America — and in most cases, the world — had ever known, the Los Angeles Olympic Games of 1932 not only provided a brief diversion from the decade-long Hard Times, they also turned a profit.

Granted, the profit was razor-thin. Almost negligible. But in 1932 anything that made even a little bit of money was an aberration. And for two weeks in July and August, as Los Angeles delivered perfect weather, excellent competitions, and more happy endings than a lot of people were used to seeing, the Games of '32 were just that — a Depression Era aberration.

They didn't start well. Twenty nations sent in their regrets at the last moment, unable to attend because of financial difficulties. Some teams that did come arrived on steamer ships, traveling a step above stowaway class. The Norwegian team came only after a Norwegian living in L.A. sprang for its expenses. Even America's hometown team was pared down. Four years earlier, the United States had sent 400 Roaring '20s athletes to Amsterdam in style. Now, after raising barely half of the $350,000 it needed to fund its Olympic Team, the United States was sending a squad of 340 to its own backyard.

Also, there were two major pre-Games controversies. One centered around the Olympic Village; the other around Paavo Nurmi's disqualification.

For the first time in Olympic history, all male athletes would be housed together in L.A. In the Baldwin Hills

ABOVE / *Los Angeles enjoyed a hometown advantage in diving as Americans swept both the men's and women's events in springboard and platform.* (ALLSPORT)

RIGHT / *In a controversial finish, Finland's Lauri Lehtinen edges American Ralph Hill. Although it appeared Lehtinen had interfered with Hill, no official protest was lodged.* (ALLSPORT)

They didn't start well. Twenty nations sent in their regrets at the last moment, unable to attend because of financial difficulties. Some teams that did come arrived on steamer ships, traveling a step above stowaway class.

suburb, some 550 wood-frame houses had been built on 331 acres to accommodate nearly 2,000 athletes and coaches. The resistance to such a living arrangement was nearly universal: Foes could not coexist as next-door neighbors; training secrets would be at jeopardy; cultures would clash.

As for Nurmi, the IOC's decision on the eve of the Games to disqualify the Flying Finn, already the winner of 12 medals and nine gold medals in three previous Olympics, because of evidence he padded his expense account while racing that spring in Europe, cast something of a pall on the party. How could the Olympics go on without Mr. Olympics?

Add to this atmosphere the depressing sight of another Mr. Olympics, 1912 decathlon winner Jim Thorpe, standing outside the Olympic Stadium's gates prior to the Opening Ceremonies, unable to afford the $3 admission, and Los Angeles had its work cut out.

But Thorpe's plight was noticed by several reporters, who got him a seat in the press box to watch the Hollywood-style Opening Ceremonies. Not far away sat Nurmi, in a suit and tie, as the Finnish team marched into the stadium on the track below. Now that everyone was settled, Charles Curtis, vice president of the United States — President Herbert Hoover felt it was more important to campaign for re-election — declared the Games open.

Who could have guessed that what

was about to unfold was an Olympics full of superlatives?

The competitions were superb. On the track, Olympic records were set in every event except the long jump. In the swimming pool, the Japanese men's team brought in oxygen masks and won every gold medal but one in blistering times. The lone non-Japanese winner was American swimmer Buster Crabbe, an $8-a-week clothing store stock clerk when the Games began. After Crabbe's win in the 400-meter freestyle he was signed to a movie contract and for the next thirty years alternated between being Tarzan, Flash Gordon and Buck Rogers.

Another L.A. first was the intro-

TOP / *Istvan Pelle of Hungary shows his winning form on the pommel horse. Pelle also won the gold in the floor exercise and silvers in the all-around and parallel bars.* (ALLSPORT)

ABOVE / *World record-holder Helene Madison was considered a sure bet to win the 100- and 200-meter freestyle. The American did not disappoint, winning the gold in both events and anchoring the world record-setting 4x100-meter freestyle relay team.* (ALLSPORT)

duction of the photo-electric timer. It made a dramatic debut in the 100-meter run, when the original scoreboard result that showed Ralph Metcalfe the winner was changed after a review of the film and the gold medal was awarded to Metcalfe's teammate, Eddie Tolan.

Perhaps the most memorable of the meet's performers was Mildred "Babe" Didriksen, who won gold medals in the hurdles and javelin and a silver medal in the high jump despite tying Jean Shiley at a new world record height of 5 feet, 5 1/4 inches. In a subsequent jump-off for the gold, Didriksen style was called illegal, although by the next year that style, the "western roll," became not only legal but universally adopted.

Besides the resounding success of the Olympic Village — an idea that would be enthusiastically adopted by every subsequent Olympics — another legacy of Los Angeles' first Olympic Games was the sportsmanlike behavior of the fans who flocked to the Olympic Stadium (later to be named the Los Angeles Memorial Coliseum) and other venues. William Henry, the stadium's public address announcer, set the tone when, after a controversial finish to the men's 5,000-meter run, the crowd burst into jeers and boos. They felt their countryman, Ralph Hill, had been intentionally bumped by Finland's Lauri Lehtinen, who edged Hill at the tape by inches.

"Ladies and gentlemen, remember these people are our guests!" said Henry, and the murmuring died down.

For his part, Hill graciously accepted his silver medal at the subsequent medal ceremony, refused to file a protest, congratulated Lehtinen openly, and declined the Finn's urging to join him on the top step of the peristyle.

By their conclusion, slightly more than one million spectators had taken a break from the Depression to watch these Games. The $2 million brought in from ticket revenue, plus the re-selling of the Olympic Village houses, allowed the local organizing committee to walk away with enough in the bank to organize the Southern California Committee for the Olympic Games, a group dedicated to one day getting the Olympics back to Southern California. Fifty-two years later, that goal was realized in the 1984 Los Angeles Olympic Games.

Top / *It took a world-record performance by American Babe Didriksen (right) to beat teammate Evelyne Hall in the 80-meter hurdles.* (Allsport)

Above / *Judges ruled that Babe Didriksen had illegally "dove" over the bar, clearing the way for fellow American Jean Shiley (pictured) to win the gold medal in a jump-off. Both women cleared the world record height of 5'5 1/4".* (Allsport)

buster crabbe

HOLLYWOOD SPLASH

Clarence "Buster" Crabbe looked to his immediate left and saw the good news. He had left the three Japanese swimmers in his wake. The bad news was farther over, in the first lane, where a Frenchman who should have self-destructed by now, hadn't.

Two hundred meters remained in the 400-meter freestyle final in the Olympic pool at the Los Angeles Games of 1932. In the stands was a capacity crowd of over 10,000, soaking in the sun, wearing shades, looking very Hollywood, and hoping something positive, such as an American winning, would happen in the water below them.

Now they were losing some hope. It was true, Crabbe, a 24-year-old Southern Cal law student, had put some distance between himself and the three Japanese swimmers in the race; and it was also true that the Japanese, who would win every other men's gold swimming medal at these Games, were the ones to keep an eye on. But that didn't make the Frenchman, Jean Taris, go away. Off to himself in lane one, almost unnoticed, Taris had churned to a three length lead at the halfway point. In 400-meter races, three length leads are not to be trifled with.

Crabbe had noticed Taris in the trial heats, and dismissed him as a short-range missile. In every race the Frenchman had swum well through 300 meters and then had run out of gas, barely qualifying for the next round.

But now, as Crabbe looked across the pool, the horrifying thought went through his mind, 'what if Taris had been blowing up on purpose to set him up?' As the race went past the 300-meter mark, that suspicion changed to sure knowledge, and Crabbe turned to everything he had left.

He forgot about the Japanese. He set his sights on Taris. He kept his head down, breathing only when absolutely necessary. He heard the crowd through the waves, its urgings increasing in volume. He didn't think he had a chance but all that cheering made him think maybe he did. This was his backyard, after all, and this was his pool, more or less. During the past six months, after the pool had been built next to the USC campus and not far from his student apartment, he had often climbed over the fence after hours and put in long training sessions.

Head down, arms flailing, he finally touched the end wall. Only then did he look up ... and over. There, in lane one, he saw the Frenchman's head bob, as good a sign as any that he'd just now touched the wall himself. Crabbe knew he'd done it. He'd won. By a tenth-of-a-second and an Olympic record as it turned out — 4:48.4 to 4:48.5. The Japanese finished third, fourth and fifth, four seconds slower.

"That one-tenth of a second changed my life," said Crabbe — and no one who saw him in the 192 motion pictures he would make in the next 20 years would accuse him of anything but an understatement.

These were the Hollywood Games and Clarence 'Buster' Crabbe's was the quintessential Hollywood Ending ... and Beginning.

A struggling law student who was working a Depression-era job for Depression-era $8-a-week wages at a

Los Angeles department store before the Games began, Crabbe was grabbed by the movies almost before he toweled off from his gold-medal swim. Paramount Pictures, in search of a jungle hero to compete with MGM's Tarzan, auditioned 20 Olympians for the job and whittled them down to one — Crabbe. For what they had in mind, he was perfect: 6-foot-1, 188-pounds, sculpted body, and, just like MGM's Tarzan, Johnny Weissmuller, an Olympic swimming champion.

The fact that Crabbe had never acted was irrelevant.

By March of the following year he was "Kaspa the Lion Man" in "King of the Jungle," and commanding $200-a-week wages. He soon enough made another jungle film, "Search for Beauty," and a serial star was born. In no particular order, he would go on to become Flash Gordon, a part he would hold through 40 episodes; Buck Rogers (12 feature films), Captain Gallant, Billy the Kid, Thunda the Jungle Man and any number of cowboys in Zane Grey Westerns. He was also Tarzan, once, as he followed in the footsteps of Weissmuller — the freestyle swimming champion of the 1924 and 1928 Olympic Games — quite directly.

With his win in Los Angeles, Crabbe had also filled the footsteps of another Olympic and American swimming champion, the legendary Duke Kahanamoku. It was Kahanamoku who had set the stage for Weissmuller, winning the 100-meter freestyle championship at the 1912 and 1920 Olympic Games. Too, it was Kahanamoku, a native Hawaiian, who had inspired Olympic aspirations in Crabbe, who was also raised in Hawaii. Like Kahanamoku, Crabbe learned to swim at a young age in the rough, open water of the Pacific Ocean; and like Kahanamoku, he was an avid surfer. Crabbe, who

was 1/32nd Polynesian himself, had been on the dock as a 16-year-old when a crowd gathered in Honolulu to send Kahanamoku off to the 1924 Olympic Games in Paris — where, as it turned out, the 20-year-old Weissmuller edged the 34-year-old Hawaiian for the 100-meter gold.

After waving good-bye and good luck to his idol, Crabbe had walked home that day from the Honolulu dock determined he would be on the next boat that went to the Olympic Games.

He made good on that determination. He made the U.S. swimming team for the 1928 Games in Amsterdam, where, despite getting sick on the ocean passage and losing

10 pounds, he won a bronze medal in the 1,500 freestyle and a bronze in the 400 freestyle. His appetite whetted, he determined to do even better when the Games would be held in U.S. water four years hence.

By the time of the '32 Games in L.A., Kahanamoku had retired, Weissmuller had become Tarzan, and Crabbe looked around to find himself the lone returnee from the U.S. team in Amsterdam. He also looked around to see a team of Japanese teenagers wearing oxygen masks, a team that would dominate just about everything in their path. Everything, as it turned out, except for himself and the Frenchman.

Operating in a swimming venue commanded by the Japanese, Crabbe was hardly the star of the Los Angeles Games. On the track, Babe Didriksen grabbed the headlines, and, in general, the biggest stir was created by the resident film stars of the Golden Era who made it a point to sit in the best seats and see the most glamorous events. The place to be was at Pickfair, the opulent mansion of Douglas Fairbanks and Mary Pickford, who, during the Games, regularly hosted Olympic officials and athletes to mix with Hollywood's social elite. Crabbe was not one of them. At least not yet. ◊

Crabbe was grabbed by the movies almost before he toweled off from his gold-medal swim. The fact that Crabbe had never acted was irrelevent.

ABOVE / A golden gathering: United States Olympic champions bask in the glory of their achievements. Sitting left to right: Mickey Riley — springboard diving; Georgia Coleman — springboard diving; Clarence Crabbe — 400-meter freestyle; and Helen Madison — 100- and 400-meter freestyle. (COURTESY OF AAF)

Mad Dash

What if ... there were electronic timing in 1932? (ALLSPORT)

For as long as anyone can remember, victory in the Olympic 100-meter dash has bestowed upon the winner the most fundamental and coveted of titles: World's Fastest Human.

The 100-meter dash was the first race of the modern Olympics in 1896, and the World's Fastest Human proved to be American Thomas Burke. Using a strange new crouch start, Burke won the race in 12.0 seconds. It wasn't until 1908 that anyone ran under 11 seconds in the Olympics — still a pedestrian time by today's standards.

Of course sprint times, now measured to 100th of a second by electronic starting blocks and electronic photo/timers at the finish, have since dropped dramatically. In 1968, James Hines, another American, recorded a time of 9.95 — a world record that stood 15 years.

Few sprinters have been able to hold onto the title of World's Fastest Human. Speed and power have long been believed to be a gift only for the young. By the time the next Olympics come around four years later, usually a younger man takes the title. Only two men have ever won two Olympic 100-meter dash titles.

However, now that the loosening of amateur rules has allowed athletes to earn money and stay in the sport longer, we're learning that sprinting may not belong entirely to the youngsters. Carl Lewis won the Olympic 100-meter dash in both 1984 and 1988, the latter in a world record of 9.93. In 1991, at the age of 30, he set a world record of 9.86.

The only other man to defend his Olympic title at 100 meters was the USA's Archibald Hahn, but at the time there were only two years between Olympics — 1904 and 1906.

Only four other men have managed to medal in the 100 more than once in the Olympics - America's Ralph Metcalfe (two silvers), Jamaica's Lennox Miller (silver and bronze), Russia's Valery Borzov (gold and bronze) and Great Britain's Linford Christie (silver and gold).

On rare occasions, it has been difficult to decide the World's Fastest Human, as was the case in the 1932 Olympics. Americans Eddie Tolan and Ralph Metcalfe ran dead even the last 20 meters of the race. According to Olympic historian David Wallechinsky, most observers believed the race had ended in a tie or that Metcalfe had won. Hours later, seven judges viewed a film of the race and determined that Tolan had *crossed* the finish line two inches ahead of Metcalfe. However, the race was so close that Metcalfe actually *reached* (but didn't cross) the finish line first. By today's rules of the first person to *reach* the line wins, Metcalfe would have been the winner.

Americans have dominated the 100-meter dash, winning 15 gold medals in the 22 Olympics in which they have participated and 35 of a potential 66 medals. π

IN MY WAKE

TOP / *Fighting the whitewater.* (ALLSPORT / RONDEAU)

RIGHT / *Exhausted celebration: Brit gold.* (ALLSPORT / CANNON)

MIDDLE LEFT / *Finn class: Seoul.* (ALLSPORT)

MIDDLE RIGHT / *Early morning workout.* (ALLSPORT / VANDYSTADT)

LEFT / *In 1932, a jump-off was needed to determine the women's Olympic high jump championship. American Jean Shiley captured the gold over teammate Babe Didriksen. In 1988, a jump-off was again needed to decide who would take home the gold. This jump-off would be between American Louise Ritter (pictured) and world-record holder Stefka Kostadinova of Bulgaria. Ritter was considered a long shot to medal, let alone capture the gold. But with an Olympic-record leap of 6-8, she produced one of the Games' most surprising upsets.* (ALLSPORT / M. POWELL)

1936

GERMANY
BERLIN·1936
1-16 AUGUST

OLYMPIC GAMES

August 1-16, 1936

49 Nations

4,066 Athletes

19 Sports

24 USA golds

BERLIN

ULTERIOR MOTIVES

In 1936, Adolf Hitler had a thing or two he wanted to prove to the world. Since the Olympic Games were scheduled for Berlin that summer, and since he was the Chancellor of Germany, he seized on the propaganda opportunity of a lifetime.

What the world saw as a sporting competition, Hitler saw as a chance to prove that Germany's blue-eyed, blond-haired Aryan race was superior in all aspects. Athletic superiority would be a nice starting point. Today, the venues. Tomorrow, the world.

Of course, no one knew the lengths Hitler would go to later on, when the horrors of Auschwitz and the invasion of innocent nations would turn the earth into a battleground never seen before or since. Part of the casualties of the war Hitler started would be the 1940 and the 1944 Olympic Games. The legacy of irony left by the Berlin Games of 1936 is that they were the beginning of an end, and not, as Hitler believed, merely the glorious beginning.

But, then, a lot of things Hitler believed proved to be unfounded. Beginning with this Aryan superiority notion. It took barely the first morning of the first day of the Olympic track and field competition for hard cold reality to run headlong into a Fuhrer's fantasies.

Hitler was in the chancellor's box that warm August morning as 70,000 Germans filed into the Olympic "Reichssportfeld." Those who passed the Fuhrer extended their arms and chanted "Sieg Heil!" Swastikas adorned the stadium, as did soldiers. The scene of a new, prosperous and strong Germany was set. Everything was in place. The world had been prepped. One example

TOP / The Nazi Party overshadows the usual pomp and circumstance at the Opening Ceremonies in Berlin. (ALLSPORT)

RIGHT / American Jesse Owens started a legacy with his haul of four Olympic gold medals. He set three Olympic records and one world record in Berlin. (ALLSPORT)

It took barely the first morning of the first day of the Olympic track and field competition for hard cold reality to run headlong into a Fuhrer's fantasies.

ABOVE (LEFT) / American springboard champion Dorothy Poynton-Hill (right) poses with teammate and silver medalist Velma Dunn and bronze medalist Kathe Kohler of Germany. At 21, Poynton-Hill collected her fourth diving medal in her third and last Olympics. (ALLSPORT)

ABOVE (RIGHT) / The Germans won their first track and field gold medal in the shot put. The honor went to Hans Woellke whose heave of 53-1 3/4 gave him an Olympic record. Pictured is teammate Hans Heinrich Sievert who didn't fare as well. (ALLSPORT)

LEFT / The one to watch: Kee Chung Sohn, a.k.a. Kitei Son (#382), educated the field on marathon racing and then the press after his victory on the plight of his captive country Korea. (ALLSPORT)

of Hitler's propaganda machine had been the massive worldwide bulletins that for months had been sent to 3,690 magazines and newspapers, more than 3,000 of them outside Germany. These bulletins, translated into 14 languages, proclaimed the glories of the new Germany and advanced the spectacular Olympic show about to unfold in Berlin.

As the Games began, Hitler could not have been more pleased. The winner of the first competition, the shot put, was Hans Woellke, a German policeman. He was followed by Sulo Barlund, a shirttail Aryan relative from Finland, and Gerhard Stock, another German. Hitler himself presided at the medal ceremony, shaking the victors' hands. The second set of winners also fit the Aryan recipe: Two Finns and a Swede had medaled in the 5,000-meter run.

But in the day's third competition, the high jump, the first two finishers were Cornelius Johnson and David Albritton, both from the United States and both black. This presented a problem for Hitler, who in his propaganda sheets had said, "The Americans ought to be ashamed of themselves for letting their medals be won by Negroes. I myself would never shake hands with one of them."

He left the stadium before the high jump medals ceremony began.

In many ways, the Berlin Olympics put Hitler in his place. Worldwide resentment at his anti-Semitism policies almost cost him the Games in the first place. And only after Hitler agreed that Germany would refrain from racial discrimination did the International Olympic Committee abide by its 1931 vote — conducted when Heinrich Bruning was Germany's chancellor — and hold the course for Berlin.

The most well-known exchange in that regard took place between Hitler and IOC president Henri de Baillet-Latour of Belgian. Angered by IOC demands that the German team include Jews, Hitler said to Baillet-Latour, "When you are invited to a friend's home, you don't tell him how to run it, do you?"

To which the Belgian replied: "Excuse me, Mr. Chancellor, when the five rings are raised over the stadium, it is no longer

ABOVE (LEFT) / *Olympian Lord Burghley and star of Amsterdam congratulates American Forrest Towns, winner of the 110-meter hurdles, and Italy's Trebisonda Valla, winner of the 80-meter hurdles.* (ALLSPORT)

ABOVE (RIGHT) / *Shuhei Nishida (pictured) and Sueo Oe of Japan refused a vault-off for second place. Instead, they had their medals cut in half, sharing half the silver and half the bronze.* (ALLSPORT)

Germany. It is the Olympics and we are masters there."

The IOC's no-nonsense approach helped persuade many nations not to boycott Berlin. In the United States, a boycott almost came about anyway. After months of debate, the Amateur Athletic Union voted by a bare 58-56 majority to send a team to Germany.

No event, or chain of events, marked Berlin as much as the accomplishments of one James Cleveland (Jesse) Owens, a black American and the grandson of slaves who won every event he entered — the 100- and 200-meter sprints, the long jump, and the 4x100-meter relay.

It was Owens' long jump triumph that defined the currents that continually undercut Hitler's well-laid ulterior designs. Owens had already won gold medals in the sprints and was the clear favorite in the long jump. When he arrived at the track, still in his warmups, he jogged down the runway and jumped into the pit. To his shock, the German officials measured the jump and counted it.

Shaken, Owens jumped a second time and fouled.

He was now one jump from either qualifying into the second round or being eliminated. It was then that Luz Long, a lanky, blue-eyed, blond-haired German, walked to Owens' side, offered his hand, and calmed down his American competitor. Luz told Owens that he personally didn't subscribe to the Aryan superiority theory, "even though I look the part," and, since Owens "could qualify with your eyes closed," suggested that he place his takeoff mark several inches behind the takeoff board.

Owens easily qualified on his third jump and proceeded to win the competition, four and a half inches ahead of the silver medalist — Luz Long.

"You can melt down all the medals and cups I have, and they wouldn't be a plating on the 24-carat friendship I felt for Luz Long at that moment," Owens wrote in his memoirs.

Berlin had other moments. Among them the first-ever Olympic basketball tournament (won by the U.S. men's team during a rainstorm on an outdoor tennis court); the first-ever torch relay from Olympia, Greece; and the first use of live television.

But mostly, Berlin 1936 marked the beginning of Hitler's stare-down with the world. In many ways, it would prove to be a harbinger of events to come.

ABOVE (LEFT) / *Consetta Anne Caruccio led the American gymnastics team to a fifth-place finish in the team combined exercises in Berlin.* (ALLSPORT)

ABOVE (RIGHT) / *Swiss gymnast Georges Miez scored a 18.666 in floor exercises, good enough to earn him the gold medal in 1936.* (ALLSPORT)

Above / *The Peruvian goalkeeper leaps high for a save against Austria. The 1936 match was marred with controversy and ultimately ordered to be replayed. Having won the match 4-2, Peru refused to replay the match and the entire Peruvian Olympic squad returned home.* (Allsport)

Right / *Decathlete Glenn Morris led an American sweep of the event and established a world record of 7,254 points.* (Allsport)

sohn kee chung

Bittersweet Victory

In the end, when his mighty marathon was finished, Sohn Kee Chung — a.k.a. Kitei Son — was a winner, but he felt like a loser. Tears of joy turned to tears of another kind right there on the Olympic victory stand. He was a man without his country, a man without his own name in the Olympic Games of 1936, and it was only in victory that he realized he was powerless to change it.

So Sohn Kee Chung returned home, retired from competitive running and lived in relative obscurity for years. If he couldn't run for his homeland, he wouldn't run at all.

Sohn was merely a pawn in the hands of the Japanese, and he knew it fully on the victory stand in Berlin. He was a pawn in a political game that had begun when Japan occupied Korea after winning the Russo-Japanese war of 1904-05. In 1910, two years before Sohn was born, the Japanese annexed Korea as its own. The events that would shape Sohn's entire life had begun.

The Japanese set about the task of erasing the Korean culture. They forced the Koreans to adopt the Japanese language and to change their names to Japanese pronunciations. Sohn Kee Chung became Kitei Son.

But Sohn had something that freed him from the Japanese, if only temporarily. He loved to run. "The Japanese could stop our musicians from playing our songs," he said. "They could stop our singers and silence our speakers. But they could not stop me from running."

His family's meager circumstances gave him reason to run. His father barely earned enough money to support four children and a wife. As a boy, Sohn ran two miles daily to buy bread for the family because the store near their home was too expensive. The family couldn't afford ice skates and bicycles, but that didn't stop Sohn from playing with the other children of his neighborhood. When his friends raced on their ice skates, he raced them on foot along the snowy banks of the Yalu River. When his friends raced their bikes, he raced them on foot.

But he ran alone for his own pleasure, too. He ran along the banks of the river, wearing rubber shoes tied to his feet with rope. "I had no concept of distance," he said. "I just ran as far as I could along the river."

Sohn's running began to gain notice in a society that prided itself in moving slowly. Koreans believed that walking a slow, dignified walk indicated stature in society.

Sohn's mother tried to dissuade him from running and to spend more energy on his studies. He entered grade-school races without telling her, but eventually news reached his mother of her son's talent. She watched a race herself, and when he won she gave him a new pair of socks as a reward.

"If you really like to run, do what you must," she told him. "But if you begin, you must endure all pains to succeed."

He began to win 5,000- and 10,000-meter races in school, and at the age of 19 he entered his first marathon. He not only won the race, but clocked a time of 2:29:34 — just off the world record of 2:29.01. Eventually, the course was declared short, but two years later, in 1935, Sohn ran another marathon, this time on an accurately measured course, and smashed the world record, running 2:26:42.

Still, Sohn's performances were suspect to the outside world because he had not competed abroad. The 1936 Olympics would be his chance to show the world.

The Japanese allowed Sohn to compete in the Olympics, but only if he represented Japan, just as Koreans Kim Eun Bae and Kwon Tae Ha had done in the 1932 Olympics. Sohn and Nam Sung Yong, both Koreans, took the top two spots in the Japanese Olympic marathon trials, but the Japanese were not eager to be represented by two Koreans in the Olympics and ordered another trials race to be held in Berlin.

Two months before the Olympics, they began a 12-day journey by boat and train to Berlin. Just 10 days before the Olympic marathon, the Japanese put their top four marathoners through an 18-mile trial race. One of the Japanese runners took a short cut — as instructed by his superiors, according to Sohn — but Sohn and Nam finished 1-2 anyway.

Sohn would run in the Olympics, but not as Sohn Kee Chung. He was furious to find his name on the official entry lists as Kitei Son, Japan. He tried to tell anyone who would listen of his true identity and nationality. He signed his name in Korean script and drew a small map of Korea next to it. But it was all in vain. His country had been virtually forgotten under Japanese rule.

On Aug. 9, on a record hot, 94-degree day, 56 runners from 27 countries toed the starting line. Among them was the pre-race favorite, Argentina's Juan Carlos Zabala, the defending Olympic champion and record holder. Sohn planned to follow Zabala's pace, but once the race began he changed his mind. "He ran a dreadful speed," recalls Sohn. "I thought, 'These are marathoners and they are running like it is a much shorter race. Is the information that I am the world's fastest marathoner false?'"

Sohn dropped into last place and began to reassess his goal of victory. He decided fifth place would be acceptable since Korea's best finish in an Olympic marathon had been sixth. But after just three miles the heat began to take its toll, and Sohn found himself in fifth place. At six miles he started to pick up the pace, but Great Britain's Ernie Harper, using hand signals, told him to slow down. He and Harper proceeded to run together and at 11 miles they moved into second and third place.

Meanwhile, Zabala charged on. At five miles his lead had been 45 seconds, and at nine miles it 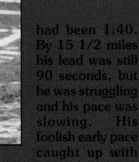 had been 1:40. By 15 1/2 miles his lead was still 90 seconds, but he was struggling and his pace was slowing. His foolish early pace caught up with him. At 17 miles, Sohn and Harper passed him. Zabala fell. He got up and tried to go on, but two miles later he quit.

Sohn began to pull away from Harper. He ran the last five miles alone, and when he entered the stadium he was greeted with a roar of 100,000 spectators that carried him over the last 100 meters in 12 seconds. "It was like I was flying," he would say.

Sohn won by more than two minutes in an Olympic record 2:29:19. Harper was second and Nam was third.

Sohn cried for joy, but then on the victory stand the Japanese flag was raised and the Japanese national anthem was played. Both Sohn and Nam lowered their heads as the flag was raised. "It was unendurable, humiliating torture," he says. "I hadn't run for Japan. I ran for myself and for my oppressed Korean people. I could not prevent myself from crying. I wished that I had never come to Berlin."

There was, at least, joy and pride at home. The children of Korea gathered in the streets and ran in imitation of Sohn. A Seoul newspaper printed a wire photo of Sohn on the victory stand, but covered the Japanese rising sun on his uniform with white paint (for this, the colonial government suspended publication of the newspaper for 10 months and fired 10 of the newspaper's employees).

Sohn was Korea's first Olympic champion, but few outside of Korea

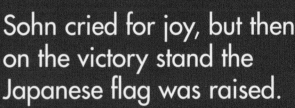

Sohn cried for joy, but then on the victory stand the Japanese flag was raised.

recognized him as such. For the five decades, the Olympic records continued to list him as Kitei Son, Japan. He tried to tell reporters the truth after his Olympic victory, but his interpreter was a Japanese, and his pleas went unheard.

Sohn vowed never to run for Japan again. Indeed, he never ran another marathon.

When South Korea courted an Olympic bid in the early 1980s, there was a renewal of interest in Sohn and his story and what he had meant to his country. It was Sohn, at the age of 76, who carried the Olympic torch around the track to open the 1988 Summer Games in Seoul. ∏

ABOVE / Sohn Kee Chung (Kitei Son) won the gold medal and set an Olympic record of 2:29:19.2 in the marathon. (ALLSPORT)

THE CALM...

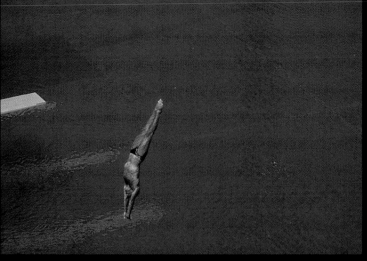

(ALLSPORT / VANDYSTADT)

(ALLSPORT / VANDYSTADT)

(ALLSPORT / DUFFY)

(ALLSPORT / BRUTY)

BEFORE THE STORM

OPPOSITE (LEFT TO RIGHT, TOP TO BOTTOM) / *Breathe deeply.* (ALLSPORT / VANDYSTADT)

Words of encouragement: Phoebe and Bela. (ALLSPORT / PATRONITE)

When you have set 36 world records, you are allowed to give advice. Vaulters Sergei Bubka (left) and Maxim Tarasov. (ALLSPORT / HEWITT)

Early morning practice for the U.S. women's swim team. (ALLSPORT / BRUTY)

Gwen Torrence in the blocks. (ALLSPORT / M. POWELL)

Swimmer Nelson Diebel takes time out to snap a few Kodak moments. (ALLSPORT / VANDYSTADT)

AMERICA'S MONOPOLY

Jesse Owens leaves a lasting impression. (ALLSPORT)

Ever since the initial modern Olympic Games were held in 1896, the long jump has been dominated by American athletes.

Of the 22 Olympic Games in which they have competed, Americans have won 20 gold medals. They have won 43 of a possible 66 medals in that time, sweeping the event four times. Their only two losses were by a total of 2 1/4 inches.

American long jumpers have been a part of two legendary Olympic performances. In 1968, Bob Beamon stunned the sports world by leaping 29-2 1/2 — nearly two feet beyond the world record. It was 12 years before the first 28-foot jump. Beamon's world record, which lasted 23 years, is considered the single greatest athletic feat ever in the Olympics.

On the other hand, one shouldn't overlook Jesse Owens' long jump performance in the 1936 Olympics Games, although it was nearly overshadowed by a demonstration of sportsmanship that produced one of the Olympics' fondest and most endearing memories. Owens, the world-record holder, was a strong favorite to win the Olympics, but his first two jumps in the trials were fouls. He was one foul — or one poor jump — away from elimination. Owens' chief rival, Luz Long, a blond German who was supposed to forge Hitler's theory of Aryan superiority, introduced himself in English to Owens, a black man. It was a gesture made all the more significant in the presence of Berlin and the Nazis, who thought blacks were an inferior race. Long didn't care. Indeed, he didn't believe in the Aryan theory and even joked about it with Owens.

Long suggested that Owens move his takeoff mark back several inches in front of the takeoff board, since any of his legal jumps would easily qualify for the final. Owens took the advice and qualified. In the finals, Owens won the gold and set an Olympic record that lasted 24 years. Long won the silver and was the first one to congratulate Owens.

Long was killed in World War II, but Owens, who continued to write Long's family, never forgot him and neither has the rest of the world. π

CATCHIN' SOME AIR

TOP / *Sun worshipper*

MIDDLE / *Reverse limbo*

BOTTOM / *Air time*

ABOVE / *Please don't touch!*

(ALL PHOTOS - ALLSPORT / VANDYSTADT)

1948

July 29 - August 14, 1948

59 Nations

4,099 Athletes

17 Sports

38 USA golds

LONDON

B y the time 1948 rolled around, the Olympics were getting used to starting and stopping. Three of the last eight Games had been halted by reason of world conflict, and a fourth — the 1936 Games in Berlin — had almost been substituted by a festival in Barcelona, although that plan had been foiled by the eruption of the Spanish Civil War.

If nothing else, however, the world wars were proving the resilience of the Olympic movement. They could interrupt them, but they couldn't stop them. Just as Antwerp, a city ravaged by the Germans in World War I, had emerged as a symbol of peaceful rebuilding when it staged the 1920 Olympics, now London, a city ravaged by the Germans in World War II, had emerged as the same kind of symbol. And just as in Antwerp, more nations and more athletes — 59 nations and 4,099 athletes — attended than ever before.

With rubble lying everywhere and food rationing still very much the order of the day, London featured an atmosphere of thank-goodness-we're-still-alive cooperation. Athletes were housed in the Royal Air Force barracks just outside of town or in school buildings in Richmond Park. There was little complaining. Wembley Stadium, primarily a soccer pitch, was altered to accommodate a temporary track and swimming pool. These were the austere Olympics. The total expenditure by the London Organizing Committee, headed by David Lord Burghley, the 400-meter hurdles gold medalist from 1928, was 600,000 British pounds, or about $1 million. When huge crowds, starved for sporting relief, attended the Games — regularly filling Wembley's 82,000 seats — the organizers, to their delight, discovered at the end of the Games that they had realized a small profit of around $25,000.

All this was in sharp contrast to the first London Olympics held at Shepherd's Bush in 1908 (the magnificent stadium built there had been a victim of the Blitzkrieg). Those Games had been

THE AUSTERE OLYMPICS

If nothing else, however, the world wars were proving the resilience of the Olympic movement. They could interrupt them, but they couldn't stop them.

TOP / *After a 12-year hiatus due to World War II, the Olympic Games resumed in London in 1948.* (ALLSPORT)

ABOVE / *Mel Patton lunges for the finish line just ahead of fellow American Norwood (Barney) Ewell to capture the gold in the 200 meters.* (ALLSPORT)

punctuated by bickering, dissatisfaction and, until the end, little public interest.

One thing that was the same 40 years later was the finish of the marathon. The famous 1908 race featured the race's leader, Dorando Pietri of Italy, staggering and collapsing on the stadium track as the eventual winner, John Hayes of the United States, came onto the track. The 1948 race saw Etienne Gailly, a Belgian who was a paratrooper during the war, play the part of Dorando. He entered the stadium in first place, but he was listing badly to the right and it soon became obvious to the 82,000 spectators that he was in trouble. After less than 100 yards another runner, an Argentinean fireman named Delfa Cabrera, entered the stadium. He was not listing and he was closing fast. Playing the part of Hayes, he went on to the gold medal as Gailly collapsed 60 yards short of the finish line. He was passed again by Thomas Richards of Great Britain, but, to the crowd's relief, got up in time to stagger across the line and win the bronze medal before collapsing for good.

London featured the Olympic debut of Emil Zatopoek, a 27-year-old Czecho-slavakian army lieutenant who, over the next three Olympiads, would become the next Nurmi. In winning the 10,000 meters, Zatopek so demoralized world record-holder Viljo Heine of Finland that Heine dropped out. The Czech runner, nicknamed "Emil the Terrible" by the British press, also came within 0.2 seconds of winning the 5,000. It was at London, too, that Robert Mathias, a 17-year-old schoolboy from California, won the decathlon, surviving a pouring rain and much older and experienced rivals

during a final day that lasted 12 hours.

But mostly, London featured Fanny Blankers-Koen, the first woman superstar of the Olympics. A mother of four from The Netherlands, Blankers-Koen won four gold medals, in the 100- and 200-meter sprints, the 80-meter hurdles and the 4x100-meter relay. Equally as alluring, although less publicized in light of Mrs. Blankers-Koen's accomplishments, was Frenchwoman Micheline Ostermeyer, a concert pianist who won gold medals in the discus and shot put and added a bronze medal in the high jump.

The most thrilling finish came in the 100-meter sprint, where Harrison Dillard of the United States was the unexpected gold medalist. Dillard was the world record-holder in the 110-meter hurdles but hit the lead hurdle and failed to make the U.S. team in that event at the qualifying trials. He came to London as just the U.S.'s No. 3 qualifier in the 100-meter dash, but in the final he used a strong finishing kick to edge teammate Norwood "Barney" Ewell in a photo-finish for the gold medal. Dillard might have gone on to become a double medal winner — there would be none on the track in London — but the 4x100 U.S. relay team, which crossed the finish line 20 yards ahead of the field, was disqualified for passing the baton outside the legal limit. The second place team, from Great Britain, was given the gold medal. The best example of the postwar no-bickering spirit present throughout the 1948 Games came when the U.S.'s disqualification was announced and the Brits were declared the winners. Instead of a loud cheer in Wembley Stadium, the crowd sat in silence.

More than anything else, Great Britain's team seemed to reflect the sentiment that World War II was still too near its finish — at least on their island. The Brits won just three gold medals, and were only 12th overall in the medal count, by far the worst home-country showing in the Games' history.

Still, the fun and Games were an unqualified hit in postwar England, where the most boffo event of all, as King George opened the Games of the XIVth Olympiad and 7,000 pigeons were released into the London sky, was the beginning.

RIGHT / *American weightlifter John Davis won gold medals decidedly in both 1948 and 1952.* (ALLSPORT)

BELOW / *An unlikely combination: A concert pianist by training, France's Micheline Ostermeyer won gold in both the shot put and the discus in London.* (ALLSPORT)

OPPOSITE (TOP) / *Failing to qualify for the 1948 Olympics in the 110-meter hurdles, world record-holder Harrison Dillard (left) got another chance qualifying third in the 100 meters. Not wasting the opportunity, the young American equaled the Olympic record of 10.3 and won the gold.* (ALLSPORT)

OPPOSITE (LEFT) / *He was only a teenager when American Bob Mathias won the first of two Olympic gold medals in the decathlon.* (ALLSPORT)

fanny blankers-koen

SUPER MOM

In many ways, Francina Blankers-Koen was a woman ahead of her time. Long before anyone had heard of women's lib and feminism — ideas she would later scorn — she managed to mingle the traditional roles of a housewife and mother with her athletic career.

It was a familiar sight around Amsterdam to see Fanny, as she was called, pushing her baby carriage to the track stadium to train. "The trouble (with most women athletes) is that they do not want to train hard enough," she said. But she herself could train just twice a week sometimes "between washing dishes and darning socks."

That notwithstanding, she was a dominating athlete. At the 1946 Dutch track and field championships, she won five events. Between races she hurried home to breast feed her five-month-old daughter.

"My wife is a real housewife," her husband, Jan, boasted. "She cooks, cleans and takes care of our children. She sews and knits their clothes."

Fanny even knitted between events during track meets.

Some didn't know what to make of Fanny. She was widely disapproved of in her native Holland for taking time away from her roles as a wife and mother and homemaker to pursue her athletic career. If she found that unsettling, she would be equally dismayed years later when she returned home to a massive heroine's welcome for her Olympic triumphs.

Of her youth, Fanny recalls, "My father said I never could walk when I was a child — just run." She grew to a full 5-foot-10, 145 pounds, with long legs, and when she was 17 she aspired to an Olympic gold medal. But in what sport?

"I've made up my mind to go in for sports," she told a Dutch swimming coach, "but I don't know which to pick — swimming or track and field." The coach recommended track and field, explaining that Holland already had plenty of top caliber swimmers. A year later Fanny qualified for the 1936 Olympics at the age of 18. She tied for sixth in the high jump and ran a leg on Holland's fifth-place 4x100-meter relay team.

Little did she know that she would have to wait a dozen years before she got another chance for an Olympic medal. The Olympic Games were canceled in '40 and '44 because of World War II. By the time the Olympics came around again, Fanny held six world records, for the 100-yard dash, 80-meter hurdles, high jump, long jump and two relays. She also had a family. She had married her coach, Jan Blankers, and given birth to two children, in 1941 and 1945. If that weren't enough, she was 30 years old — too old, many said, to win the Olympic sprints, never mind her records.

When World War II ended, Fanny resumed her training. Sometimes she took her children to the track in the basket of her bicycle and, while she practiced the high jump, they played in the sand pit beneath her. Sometimes she pushed her baby carriage to the stadium and parked it next to the track while she ran.

When Fanny and Jan left for the 1948 Olympic Games in London they left their children with her parents. Her father told Fanny, "Win, and I will dance around the kitchen table."

She entered four events at the

1948 Olympic Games in London. The first was the 100-meter dash. Too old to win a sprint? She won the final by a full three yards, clocking 11.9 on a muddy track. After the race, she took the microphone of a Dutch broadcaster and sent a message home: "Papa, dance now around the kitchen table!"

She found stiffer competition in the 80-meter hurdles, her next event. Her

results were posted. Fanny had won her second gold medal, with an Olympic-record time of 11.2.

Strangely, it was only now that Fanny began to wilt under the pressure. Before the semifinals of the 200-meter dash, she sat alone in the women's locker room and cried. Eventually, Jan gained admittance to see his wife. She told her husband she wanted to withdraw from the 200 and

railroad station to the town hall, where a reception was held in her honor. "All I've done is run fast," said Fanny. "I don't quite see why people should make so much fuss about that."

Fanny returned to the Olympic Games in 1952 at the age of 34, but blood poisoning, an upset stomach and a boil on her leg forced her to withdraw from three events. She entered the hurdles, but she tripped on the second barrier, staggered a few

She didn't even compete in her best events, the high jump and long jump, because Olympic rules limited her to three individual events.

chief rival was Maureen Gardner, a 19-year-old ballet instructor from Great Britain. In the semifinals, Gardner hit a hurdle and stumbled to the finish, barely qualifying for the final with a third-place finish. In the final, it was Fanny who had troubles. The starter's pistol didn't fire — and then it did. Fanny was a step behind Gardner at the start. She caught Gardner at the second hurdle, but at the fifth hurdle she took off too close to the barrier and hit the cross bar. She stumbled and, as Fanny would later say, "I staggered in like a drunkard."

She felt the finish tape strike her forehead, but she also saw Gardner and Australia's Shirley Strickland cross the finish line with her, and no one could be certain who had won. The three of them waited anxiously as the judges studied the finish-line photos. Then a band struck up God Save the King, and Fanny was sure that meant she had lost. What she didn't know was that the band was playing for the arrival of King George VI in the stadium. Moments later the

go home. "If you don't want to go on you must not," he told her. "But I'm afraid you will be sorry later if you don't run." Finally, he recalled memories of her parents and their two children, and she burst into tears. Fanny won her semifinal heat by six yards in an Olympic record of 24.3. The next day, on a muddy track, she won the final by seven yards — the biggest margin ever in the 200.

Fanny claimed another gold medal in the 400-meter relay, rallying her team from a five-yard deficit, from fourth place to first, on the anchor leg.

Of the nine events on the women's Olympic track and field schedule, she had won four of them, making her the only woman ever to claim four gold medals in one Olympics. Undoubtedly, she could have won more gold. She didn't even compete in her best events, the high jump and long jump, because Olympic rules limited her to three individual events.

Thousands of Fanny's countrymen honored her return to Amsterdam. She and her family were driven in an open horse-draw carriage from the

steps and then quit the race.

When she refused to quit the sport after that, she found herself the subject of another public debate. People demanded that she retire. A newspaper wrote, "An appeal to Fanny: Put away your spikes for good. The same Holland that demanded successes of you wants to keep the best memory."

Once again, Fanny didn't understand what all the fuss was about. She did not fully retire until she was 37.

In 1985, when the women's movement wanted to celebrate her as a heroine of feminist, she balked. "Oh, no, oh, no," she said. "I don't like the word. Feminists ... they want to work, they want the husband to do the housekeeping. I don't like that stuff ... Women can do a lot, of course, but it's still not the same as being a man." π

ABOVE / *Fanny Blankers-Koen of Holland dominated the track in London. She is the only woman to win four gold medals in track and field.* (ALLSPORT)

1 0 0

LEFT / *In an attempt to become the first woman to win the 100 meters/100 meter-hurdles double since Fanny Blankers-Koen did it in 1948, Gail Devers came up inches short. After winning the 100 meters and establishing herself as the fastest woman, few would have bet against the American sprinter winning a second gold. Coming to the last hurdle ahead of the field, she was unexpectedly too close to the hurdle. Result: Hit, sprawl, and a crawl to a fifth-place finish.* (ALLSPORT / DUFFY)

METERS

1952

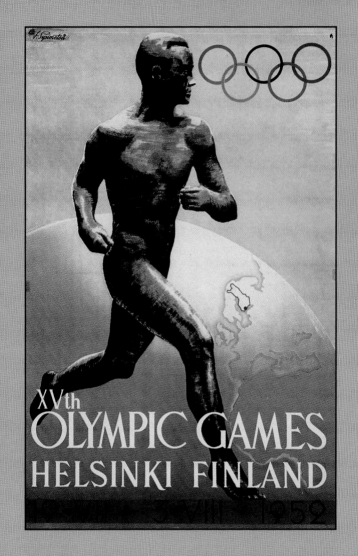

July 19 - August 3, 1952

69 Nations

4,925 Athletes

17 Sports

40 USA golds

HELSINKI

USSR RSVPs

T he Games of the XVth Olympiad in Helsinki, Finland, are memorable for two rather remarkable occurrences: For one thing, there was the inaugural entrance of the Soviet Union as a unified sports power the likes of which the Olympic movement had never before seen. For another, there was the extraordinary hospitality of the Finns.

These Games had been a long time coming to Helsinki. They had originally been awarded for 1940 but the world war caused what turned out to be a 12-year delay. When the first Finnish Olympics finally did arrive, when J. K. Paasikivi, the President of Finland, declared the Games open and the great Paavo Nurmi brought the Olympic torch into the 70,000-seat Olympic Stadium, the country was as ready as it could be.

For that reason, it was an odd and completely unexpected stage that proceeded to be set in the homeland of men who could outrun the reindeer. This was a country whose athletic reputation as the dictator of distance running was well established. Of the first seven 5,000- and 10,000-meter runs contested since the events made their Olympic debut in Stockholm in 1912, a Finn had won five of each. Of the past six Olympic marathons, Finns had won two of them. If the names didn't exactly roll off the tongue, they were nonetheless well known the world over — Gunnar Hockert, Lauri Lehtinen, Ville Ritola, Albi Stenroos, Hannes Kolehmainen, and of course the great Paavo Nurmi, whose Olympic legacy included a total of 12 medals, nine of them gold, and it might have been more if he hadn't been

Before their 40 years of self-imposed Olympic exile, the czarist-turned-communist country had one gold medal to its Olympic credit. In Helsinki, the Soviet Union chalked up 22 gold medals.

TOP / *In Helsinki, American Sammy Lee successfully defends his Olympic title in platform diving.* (ALLSPORT)

RIGHT / *Double take? Air Force sergeant Mal Whitfield (left) equaled his 1948 800-meter victory with another in Helsinki. He ran both races in an Olympic record of 1:49.2.* (ALLSPORT)

disqualified from the 1932 Olympics for accepting excessive expense money.

With 12 years of warmup time, it was not an uncommon belief as the 1952 Games approached that Finns would own the finish line.

But for whatever reason, it didn't happen. The Finns turned out to be the epitome of gracious hosts. Their motto was "You first." They were conspicuous in the distance events only by their absence on the winner's peristyles. Not one Finn won a race, or a medal, in any of the distances, or in any of the races, period.

Instead, the host nation took a back seat and let its visitors show off in what amounted to perhaps the most jingo-free Olympics in history. The Finns won just six gold medals overall, and three of them came at the mostly ignored canoe and kayak venue. The hero of the Games would be one Emil Zatopek of Czechoslovakia, a distance runner no less, who accomplished an unprecedented "triple" with wins at 5,000 meters, 10,000 meters, and the marathon. When Zatopek — whose wife, Dana, would win the women's javelin — punctuated his three-for-three sweep by winning the marathon on the last day of the competition, he was hoisted to the shoulders of the Jamaican sprint relay team, who jogged him around the Olympic Stadium as 70,000 Finns — to their credit — rose and stood in ovation.

The Finns also yielded the stage to the new entry from the Soviet Union and

OPPOSITE (TOP) / *One of the heros in Helsinki was Czechoslovakia's Emil Zatopek who became the first runner to win the 5,000 meters (pictured), 10,000 meters, and the marathon at the same Games. He set Olympic records in all three events.* (ALLSPORT)

(BOTTOM) / *Having never run a marathon before did not seem to bother Czechoslovakian Emil Zatopek, who unwittingly ran the distance in an Olympic record time of 2:23:03.2.* (ALLSPORT)

LEFT / *Raising his hands in celebration is Belgium's Andre Noyelle. Noyelle edged out countryman Robert Grondelaers to win the road race in 1952.* (ALLSPORT)

BELOW / *Parry O'Brien revolutionized shot putting with his new style — a style that led the American to a narrow victory and Olympic record. He would repeat as champion in 1956.* (ALLSPORT)

the other countries making up the Union of Soviet Socialist Republics. This combined team was the curiosity of Helsinki. The Russians hadn't entered an Olympics since 1912 and, at that, their Olympic past was mostly undistinguished. Before their 40 years of self-imposed Olympic exile, the czarist-turned-communist country had one gold medal to its Olympic credit.

All that was about to quickly change as the Games of '52 soon enough turned into a medals showdown between the United States and the USSR. In an unabashed preview of what was to come for the next 40 years — until the ultimate breakup of the USSR after the 1988 Games in Seoul— the ideologically opposed super powers opened their unique and special brand of fierce competition.

The United States managed to prevail in total medals, 76-71, and gold medals, 40-22, but this was obviously no clearcut decision. Everywhere one looked, the emotions of these USA-USSR showdowns were creating exciting and interesting finishes. In the Most Thrilling category — and, as far as the U.S. was concerned, Most Satisfying — the race

in the 3,000-meter steeplechase final between Horace Ashenfelter of the United States and Vladimir Kazantsev of the USSR qualified as best of show. A 27-year-old FBI agent from New Jersey, Ashenfelter's personal best time coming into the Olympics was 18 seconds slower than the world record, held by Kazantsev. But in the final, Ashenfelter took the lead early and never looked back. The G-Man — who pundits back in the States said should have been *following* the Russian — won in 8:45.4, shaving three seconds off Kazantsev's suddenly defunct world record.

Shrouded in mystery when the Games began, the Soviet athletes entertained athletes from many nations, including the United States, at their secluded compound outside the city. They served caviar, traded training techniques and, in the spirit of the Olympics, began to break down at least some of the barriers that had taken almost half-a-century to erect.

A total of 5,678 athletes from 69 nations — both figures representing record numbers — wound up participating in Helsinki as, for the first time since the end of the second World War, athletes from both sides of that

conflict competed side-by-side.

By the time the great Zatopek sprinted into the stadium and into the arms of the Jamaicans, there had been no political protests or, for that matter, any acts of unsportsmanlike behavior that amounted to any significance. That the Finns had set a gracious and neutral stage, there was no question.

eight oars w/ coxswain

THE GREAT EIGHT

The members of the U.S. Olympic eight-man rowing crew watched with more than a little wonder as they stood on the shores of the Meilahti Gulf outside of Helsinki, Finland. It was chilly for the 23rd of July. The wind was whipping up whitecaps on the Bay and spectators were hurrying to their cars. That wasn't what had the Americans' attention, however. They were looking at the water's edge, where the team from the Soviet Union — the team they had just beaten for the gold medal — was hoisting *their* shell over their shoulders to carry it to the boathouse.

"It's a privilege to lose to you. You're good," Slava Amiragov, the No. 5 man in the Soviet crew said as he passed Robert Detweiler, the captain of the U.S. crew and, at No. 5, Amiragov's counterpart.

After stowing their boat, the Soviets invited the Americans to their Olympic compound to sample some post-racing caviar, swap post-race stories, and perhaps tell them how they got to be so fast.

As Detweiler and his teammates made their back to the Olympic Village they could only marvel at what had been wrought in such a short amount of time. Here they were in Finland, Olympic champions, preparing to go to a party hosted by the Russians they just beat — and less than six months ago they had barely known each other, much less shared the same shell.

That the team that came to be known as the Great Eight came together at all had required something of a crisis. In the early spring of 1952, its members had reported for the start of the rowing season at the Naval Academy, where they were fellow Midshipmen. None had serious expectations at rowing for the varsity that season, since the varsity squad was pretty much intact from the year before.

Rusty Callow, Navy's coach, had other ideas, however. The year before, Callow's first at Navy, had ended in embarrassment or disaster or both, take your pick. The occasion had been the 1951 collegiate national championships on the Ohio River at Marietta, Ohio. For Navy, a school that always took a certain amount of pride in its proficiency at water sports, no day had ended darker than that day on the Ohio. A ferocious storm just as the racing began had swamped each of the Naval Academy's boats — Plebe, junior varsity, and varsity. The day was commonly referred to as "Little Pearl Harbor" and was capped by a headline in the next day's *Washington Post* that read: "Navy Loses Three Ships at Marietta."

Stewing on that outcome all winter long wore on Callow, a collegiate crew coach for the past 31 years who had won three national championships at the University of Washington and a number of Eastern Seaboard titles while with the University of Pennsylvania. When the next season rolled around, he decided to clean ship, so to speak. He dismissed every varsity rower and promoted six Plebes from his 1951 freshman eight-man team plus two members of the 1951 junior varsity to the varsity eight.

With exactly zero minutes of varsity experience to its credit, the new crew

had no idea how it might fare that season, and neither did Callow, although he had reason for some hope since the '51 Plebe crew had been undefeated until Marietta.

In the first race of the season, at Yale on Skimmer (or homecoming) Day, no less, the greenest eight-man crew in college rowing lined up on the historic Housatonic hoping it would at least be representative against an experienced Eli crew touted to be the Beast of the East that season. All they could do was put their heads down and row and pray and never look up.

So that is what they did. They didn't come up for air, or a look, until they'd crossed the finish line, where they were greeted by almost total silence. Soon enough they realized why. Behind them was the Yale boat. Way behind them. About 100 yards. Only when the Eli's crossed the line did the noise pick up, and it wasn't complimentary. The Middies picked their shell out of the water and carried it to the boathouse to a chorus of the most beautiful abuse they'd ever heard. As they walked, it dawned on them that unless the Yale crew had a bad day — a VERY bad day — they just might be on to something.

They came from all over the country. In the bow, seated at No. 1, was Frank Shakespeare from Delaware; behind him, in order, were Willie Fields from Georgia, Jim Dunbar from Indiana, Dick Murphy from New Jersey, Detweiler from Ohio, Henry Proctor from Oregon, Wayne Frye from Ohio, Ed Stevens from Michigan and, finally, in the coxswain's seat, the "ninth" member of the eight-man crew, Dave Manring from Ohio.

Callow worked them harder than ever after the opening win over Yale. Daily they would collect on the Severn River next to the Naval Academy campus in Annapolis, Maryland. Officers and Gentlemen and Rowers, in that order. Sometimes Callow, a civilian, would forget about the chow hour and have to be reprimanded by someone with a higher rank, but hour after hour they rowed on, preparing for whatever heights, and lengths, might await them.

It was soon proved that the Yale race was no fluke. The Navy boat stormed through its regular schedule in the East. The Middies won at all stops, including a romp at the midseason Adams Cup on the Charles River in Boston and a national championship on Lake Onondaga in Syracuse, where memories of "Little Pearl Harbor" the year before were quieted, if not dashed, with a record time — 15 minutes and eight seconds — for the three-mile course.

Fresh from that collegiate title they reported to the U.S. Olympic Trials at Lake Quinsigamond in Worcester, Mass., where it was more of the same. They let up a bit in the semifinals and barely beat a crew from Cal — the school that had provided the nation's Olympic champions in the 1948 Games in London — so in the finals they went back to their "Yale mentality" and beat boats from Princeton and Washington by more than 10 seconds, an eternity on a 2,000-meter course.

Thus did they earn their commissions to Helsinki, Finland, for the Games of the XVth Olympiad — the Games, as it turned out, that would welcome Russian athletes for the first time since Stockholm in 1912, and Soviet Union athletes for the first time ever.

The Soviet rowers did not impress the Navy eight at first. The Australians and the Germans and the British were of considerably more concern than the seemingly disjointed Russians, an odd collection of rowers of all shapes and sizes who curiously employed their coach — a 165-pound man — as their coxswain as well. Further, the Soviets did not feather their oars when they brought them back, a wind-resistance problem to be sure.

But as fate had it, the first race for the United States in the preliminary round was against the Soviets, and by the midway point all thoughts of Soviet incompetence had vanished for one very good reason ...

... the Soviet boat was even with them.

Only a furious push at the finish — with Manring screaming for 30-stroke revolutions — got the U.S. boat to the line first.

In the races to follow, the U.S. crew cruised into the finals, there to find, once again, the determined Soviets, who had survived their opening loss by winning every race since.

By now sufficiently impressed, and with the gold medal on the finish line, the Navy crew again returned to "Yale mentality." Heads bowed, they made their way through the rough waters of the Bay as determinedly as they possibly could. Again the Soviet shell

As they walked, it dawned on them that unless the Yale crew had a bad day — a VERY bad day — they just might be on to something. Six months later in Helsinki, that same crew became known as the Great Eight.

kept pace, but this time not as confidently. By the three-quarter point, a gap opened. By the finish line, it was a gap of over five seconds.

The exhausted U.S. rowers collapsed on the dock until it was time for their medals. After the playing of the Star Spangled Banner they broke with rowing tradition and, instead of the other way around, gave their jerseys to the Soviets. After which the Great Eight watched as their new friends from the Soviet Union took care of their shell. π

RIGHT / *Great Britain's Daley Thompson became the first decathlete to successfully defend his Olympic title since American Bob Mathias repeated in 1948 and 1952. Thompson would win his first gold in Moscow and second in Los Angeles. Despite easing up down the backstretch of the final event, the 1,500 meters, he equaled the world record of 8,798 points.*
(ALLSPORT / S. POWELL)

1956

November 22 - December 8, 1956
June 10-16, 1956 (Stockholm)
67 Nations
3,342 Athletes
17 Sports
32 USA golds

MELBOURNE

The first Down Under Games did not get off to a terrific start. Just as preparations were rounding into place and the final nail was being pounded into the last of Melbourne's Olympic facilities; just as the country was getting ready to take a bit of a walkabout and drain a pint at the local pub to toast the pending invasion; just as the late spring weather was turning particularly nice ... the world got ornery. On one front, the Israelis led a takeover of the Suez Canal. Egypt, Iraq and Lebanon quickly sent in their cancellation notices, refusing to take part if Israel was going to be there. On another front, Soviet troops invaded Hungary. Spain, Holland and Switzerland immediately dropped out to protest the Soviet aggression — although Hungary and the Soviet Union sent full teams. On still another front, the Republic of China sent word it wouldn't attend because the IOC had recognized Taiwan.

To climax this inauspicious start, as the Games opened on a warm Saturday in the 102,000-seat Melbourne Cricket Grounds, the official torch-bearer, a 19-year-old Aussie named Ron Clarke who would go on to become one of the great distance runners of all time, burned his right arm as he lit the cauldron.

But except for a water polo brawl caused by the untimely pairing of Hungary versus the Soviet Union, that's as star-crossed as the first Olympics

TOP / *A young Ron Clarke burned his arm while lighting the torch at the Opening Ceremonies. Clarke, who held the world record in the 10,000 meters at the time of the 1964, 1968 and 1972 Olympics, ironically only claimed a bronze in Tokyo.* (ALLSPORT)

RIGHT / *Betty Cuthbert of Australia edges past countrywoman Marlene Matthews (bronze) and Christa Stubnick of East Germany (silver) to win the gold in the 200 meters. Incredibly, the three repeated their respective finishes in the 100 meters.* (ALLSPORT)

NO WORRIES, MATE

As the world churned, the Aussies, in typical Down Under fashion, accepted the Games' inauspicious start, pumped up the pace and ended with an unforgettable farewell party.

staged south of the equator ever got. (The Hungarian team, which went on to win the gold medal, won that water polo match/fight 4-0, although it was terminated prematurely by the Swedish referee who called it a "boxing match under water." Since the majority of the 5,500 in attendance appeared to be very much on Hungary's side, Australian riot police were called in to escort the Soviet team from the pool).

For the most part, the Aussie Games, held from Nov. 22 through Dec. 8 to coincide with the Australian late spring, had no worries. Sixty-seven countries still attended, numbering 3,342 competitors, even though almost all of them, not counting New Zealand and Fiji, had to travel from eight to 18 hours to finally find Melbourne.

Far away from the traditional, and inherently biased, playing fields of Europe and America, a collection of Olympic "firsts" were registered by any number of nations taking advantage of Australia's neutral conditions. Norway, for example, collected its first-ever track and field gold medal when Egil Danielson won the javelin with a world-record throw, and in

the triple jump, when Vilhjalmur Einarsson took the silver medal by jumping a foot and a half farther than ever before, the nation of Iceland collected its first and only Olympic medal.

Too, Melbourne was the birthplace of stars. Twenty-year-old Al Oerter emerged from the United States to win the first of four consecutive gold medals he would win in the discus; U.S. sprinter Bobby Morrow, a 21-year-old Texan, won three gold track medals in the 100, 200 and 4x100 relay and Betty Cuthbert, an 18-year-old Aussie, matched him with three golds of her own in the same events. Distance runner Vladimir Kuts of the Soviet Union managed the difficult 5,000-meter/10,000-meter double and diver Pat McCormick of the United States managed the equally difficult platform/springboard double.

Hungary's athletes, personifying an underdog nation under siege, were sentimental favorites wherever they went. Their most inspirational moment came when 30-year-old Laszlo Papp, once an Olympic champion in the middleweight class but now considered over the hill, became the first man in Olympic history

to win three boxing golds by again capturing the light middleweight title. The courageousness of Papp's effort gained stature in later years as the man he beat — Jose Torres of the United States — went on to become the light heavyweight champion of the world.

Another notable upset occurred in the marathon, where 36-year-old Alain Mimoun, the silver medalist in both 1948 and 1952, finally got his gold medal, beating the great Czechoslovakian runner and his personal nemesis, Emil Zatopek, in the process. When Zatopek, slowed by cramps, finished sixth, Mimoun was at the finish line waiting to embrace the friend and rival who had relegated him to second-place status for eight long years.

With the exception of Cuthbert and

ABOVE / *Bobby Joe Morrow leads the American sweep of the 200 meters in an Olympic record of 20.6, claiming the double sprint title in Melbourne. Three days earlier, Morrow had sprinted against a nine m.p.h. headwind to a 10.5 100-meter victory.* (ALLSPORT)

only a few others, Australia's athletes stayed off the winner's peristyles until the swimming venue opened for business. Knowing the pool could very likely be their finest hour, the Aussies had saved swimming for last. Their timing proved to be perfect. In the water they were in their own hemisphere. They totaled 14 medals in all, eight gold, four silver and two bronze, to easily outdistance all other nations, including a U.S. team that had dominated the swimming events in Helsinki in 1952. Foremost of the Aussie swimmers was teenager Dawn Fraser, who set a world record while leading an Australian medals sweep in the women's 100-meter freestyle final.

Keeping equal pace with Melbourne's penchant for picking up momentum as the Games wore on was the romance of U.S. hammer thrower Harold Connolly and Czech discus thrower Olga Fikotova. After meeting on the practice fields, Connolly and Fikotova, in this order, fell in love, won gold medals in their respective disciplines, and, after the

Games, overcame Iron Curtain red tape and were married and settled in California.

The spirit of togetherness carried into Melbourne's Closing Ceremonies, where, for the first time, the custom of parading into the stadium nation by nation was discarded and the athletes broke rank and ran to the infield en

masse. The idea for such a departure from tradition was credited to a 17-year-old Taiwanese athlete, whose reasoning was that by the time the Olympic Games had run their course, the world wasn't divided any longer, but united. As the world's athletes ran hand in hand onto the grass of the Melbourne Cricket Grounds, singing "Goodbye Olympians" to the tune of "Waltzing Matilda," it appeared he was right.

Top (left) / *A young, 20-year-old American named Alfred Oerter would win the first of four consecutive discus gold medals in the Olympics, each time setting a new Olympic record.* (ALLSPORT).

Top (right) / *Vladimir Kuts of the Soviet Union managed the difficult distance double of 5,000 and 10,000 meters in Melbourne.* (ALLSPORT).

Center / *His gold medal in 1956 capped a 12-year Olympic boxing career for Hungary's Laszlo Papp. He became the first boxer to win three gold medals.* (ALLSPORT)

pat m'cormick

ONE TOUGH LADY

Four preliminary dives later, in the 1956 Melbourne Olympic Games, Pat McCormick found herself in an unusual position.

She wasn't winning.

She was in second place in the three-meter springboard event at the end of the first day of competition, and her chance for history was evaporating. McCormick had just two dives remaining in which to reassert her long stranglehold on diving, and then, regardless of the outcome, she would retire to become a full-time housewife and mother. That was the plan, she had said.

McCormick was seeking an unprecedented fourth gold medal in diving and hoping to repeat her performance four years earlier at the Helsinki Olympics. In the preliminary round, she hit her first three dives, but she missed her fourth dive badly, which left her in second place, 1.68 points behind teammate Paula Jean Myers.

Two more dives. In a way, McCormick had been training for this moment for eight years, beginning the

moment she finished fourth in the 1948 U.S. Olympic Trials and missed a berth on the Olympic team by less than one point.

"That's when I set my sights on winning two gold medals in two Olympics," she said. "I wanted to do something nobody else had ever done before ... I started training the very next day."

That was McCormick for you. If she hadn't always been the most polished diver in the world, she had been one of its toughest, most persistent and hardest working performers. But what else do you expect from a woman who grew up on Muscle Beach.

She says she can never remember a day that she wasn't playing and swimming in the ocean, usually while tagging along with her older brother. They liked to hang out at Muscle Beach, where weightlifters flexed their muscles. Pat and her brother worked out with the men and performed in weekend shows.

"Muscle Beach really helped me later as a diver because I became physically strong," says Pat. " ... My mother tried to get me to be more ladylike, but I was a tomboy."

When she was 11 she began to

compete in swimming and diving competitions, and by 16 she was the champion of Long Beach. She was strong and athletic and self-taught, but she was still a raw talent. In 1947, two significant things happened that changed her life. Aileen Allen, a coach at the Los Angeles Athletic Club, saw her diving and invited her to join the LAAC, where she would train with many of diving's stars and coaches.

"She couldn't point her toes and she couldn't straighten out her body," recalls Sammy Lee, a two-time Olympic champion who trained at the LAAC. "All she had was physical strength."

But that was to change quickly. That same year she also met Glenn McCormick. He had been a wrestler and gymnast at University of Southern California, but he used his gymnastics training to coach Pat on the diving board. They were a good team. He became one of diving's foremost diving coaches and she became the most decorated female diver in Olympic history. A year later they were married.

"I can't dive well when he isn't around," said Pat, who used to repeatedly touch her wedding ring

before each dive.

The new Mrs. McCormick improved dramatically. In 1947, she was a surprise runner-up in the platform at the national championships. In 1948, she was a close fourth in the Olympic Trials.

"That defeat was the greatest thing that ever happened to me because all of a sudden I knew I could win the Olympics," she recalls.

In 1949, she won her first national title, on platform. A year later, she swept the outdoor national championships, winning the one- and three-meter springboard and the platform. In 1951, she became the first diver ever to win all five national champion-ships (two indoors, three outdoor), and later won gold and silver medals in the Pan American Games.

Her coaches credited her meteoric rise to one thing: hard work. She pursued an exhausting training routine of 80 to 100 dives per day, six days per week, which added up to about 25,000 dives per year.

"She was physically strong, and that helped her get height, but more than that, she just outworked the other divers during that period," said Glenn.

Lee agrees. "She had a mental concentration and toughness that other women didn't seem to have."

Tough? During a medical exam of McCormick in 1950, a doctor discovered a six-inch healed over wound in her scalp; several scars at the base of her spine; blood welts across her collarbone from the impact of the water; lacerations of the feet and elbows; a healed cracked rib and broken finger; a loose jaw; and all her front teeth were chipped.

And her diving career was still six years away from completion.

"I've seen worse casualty cases, but only where a building caved in," the doctor told her.

In 1952, at the age of 22, McCormick went to her first Olympics. With Glenn in the stands at Helsinki,

she won the springboard, outscoring runner-up Madeleine Moreau of France 147.30 to 139.34. Her third dive — a 1 1/2 reverse somersault with a tuck — produced the highest score of the two-day event, an 18.92. Then she won her second gold medal in the platform, beating her young teammate, Myers, 79.37 to 71.63.

During the next four years, McCormick refused offers to turn pro and postponed plans for a family in her quest for another pair of gold medals.

But she didn't wait. Five months before the Olympic trials and eight months before the Melbourne Olympics of 1956 she gave birth to her first child. She continued to train during her pregnancy and even swam a half-mile daily up to two days before the birth to maintain her fitness. Again she won the platform and springboard at the Olympic trials.

This time her husband/coach would be more than a spectator at the Olympics. Glenn was selected as the Olympic coach. McCormick won her third gold by a rout in the springboard, beating runner-up Jeanne Stunyo of the U.S., 142.36 to 125.89.

Then came the platform event, and McCormick found herself in second place behind Myers with two dives to go. "Pat was steady because she did so many dives in practice," Glenn said once, "but she also was a competitor. This is a quality in a lot of champions, that they refuse to be beaten. Pat was

like that. If she got behind, she was almost impossible to beat."

McCormick knew she needed two exceptional dives to win. On her fifth dive, she hit a 2 1/2 front somersault, but Myers remained in first place. McCormick's final dive — a difficult full twisting 1 1/2 — was almost perfect, bringing her a score of 18.17 points. Myers had one more dive, but her feet came over on the entry and she scored only 15.87 points. McCormick had her fourth gold. She finished with 84.85 points, and her two teammates — Juno Irwin (81.64) and Myers (81.58) — gave the U.S. a medal sweep.

"That was my last competitive dive," McCormick said. "Now I plan to attend to the business of being a

She pursued an exhausting training routine of 80 to 100 dives per day, six days per week, which added up to about 25,000 dives per year.

housewife."

She raised a family, and one of her children, Kelly, eventually took up diving. "She (her mother) showed me her gold medals when I was a little girl," recalls Kelly. "I made a bet with her that someday I'd make an Olympic team and win."

Kelly won half the bet. She made the Olympic team twice, but there was no gold medal. She won a silver in 1984 and a bronze in '88, both of them in the springboard. For that matter, no female diver has ever been able to match McCormick's record of four Olympic diving championships. It took 32 years before a man (Greg Louganis) was able to equal McCormick's Olympic feat. Undoubtedly, McCormick's place in Olympic history is secure. π

ABOVE / In a rare moment of rest, Pat McCormick pauses for a pose. (ALLSPORT)

H₂O

(ALLSPORT / VANDYSTADT)

(ALLSPORT / DUFFY)

(ALLSPORT / BRUTY)

(ALLSPORT / BRUTY)

LOVE-STRUCK ROMEOS

Hal Connolly throws caution to the wind. (ALLSPORT)

Despite the pressure-cooker atmosphere of the Olympic Games, where focus and concentration are in keen demand, any number of romances have sprung up during the heat of the competition. Among the most famous:

ANTWERP, 1920: Richmond Landon, a high jumper from Yale, and Alice Lord, a diver from New York, met while traveling with the United States Olympic Team across the Atlantic Ocean on the sailing ship, the *Princess Matoika*. The setting wasn't ideal for a shipboard romance. The *Matoika* was a converted funeral ship and reeked of formaldehyde. Still, Landon and Lord found themselves spending much of the time ignoring the unpleasant odor and listening to

Duke Kahanamoku and his fellow Hawaiian swimmers strum their ukeleles on the deck. After participating in Antwerp — where Landon won the high jump gold medal — they returned home and were soon married.

MELBOURNE, 1956: United States hammer thrower Harold Connolly and Czechoslovakian discus thrower Olga Fikatova met on the practice fields of Melbourne while awaiting the start of their respective events. They soon became inseparable, attracting a good deal of international attention in the process. Their romance only accentuated their performances as both went on to win gold medals. Not long after the Games, Olga emigrated to Los Angeles and married Harold. They competed in several more Olympics together before divorcing

after 18 years in 1975.

MEXICO CITY, 1968: Gymnast Vera Caslavska of Czechoslovakia not only became the first woman to win four individual gold medals in a single Olympics in Mexico City -- she also became the first woman to get married *during* an Olympics when she and Czech 1,500-meter runner Josef Odlozil tied the knot. Caslavska, who also won three gold medals the previous Olympics in Tokyo, and Odlozil, who won a silver medal in the 1,500 meters in Tokyo and placed eighth in Mexico City, marched in the Opening Ceremonies on Oct. 12 as single people and in the Closing Ceremonies on Oct. 27 as a married couple. There were married the day before the Closing Ceremonies, barely 24 hours after Caslavska won her final gold medal. π

B R E A K   T I M E

1960

August 25 - September 11, 1960

84 Nations

5,348 Athletes

17 Sports

34 USA golds

ROME

Showing no hard feelings that it was in Rome that the ancient Olympics had been laid to rest, the Games of the XVIIth Olympiad returned to the Italian capital in the summer of 1960. It had been some 1,567 years since Theodosius, emperor of the Holy Roman Empire, had outlawed all non-Christian celebrations after the last of the ancient festivals was held in Rome in 393 A.D.

In some ways, nothing had changed. Any spectators who had managed to live 15 centuries could walk into the Basilica of Maxentius and again see a wrestling tournament, just like in the old days. Or they could walk into the Terme di Caracalla and again see gymnasts cavorting. To their credit, Rome's Olympic organizing committee had a sense of the past and used the ancient and glorious architecture of Rome to connect the Olympics of then with the Olympics of now.

Modern Italy was also well represented. The major events, including track and field and swimming, were held in Mussolini's palatial Foro Italico, and boxing was staged in the Palazzo dello Sport.

Rome's smooth transition from past to present was personalized perfectly in the boxing tournament. It was in boxing that the last recorded gold medal was won in the ancient games — by a man named Barasdates from Armenia. A lot of the slack left by more than 15 centuries of inactivity was immediately picked up when a man named Cassius Marcellus

TOP / *The Soviet Union's Larissa Latynina led a dominating Soviet Union gymnastics squad that captured 19 of the 20 available medals, including the top four finishers in the all-around. Between 1956 and 1964, Latynina won nine Olympic golds.* (ALLSPORT)

RIGHT / *To the world he is known as Muhammad Ali, but in Rome in 1960, the young 18-year-old boxer made his claim to fame simply known as Cassius Clay.* (ALLSPORT)

FLOAT LIKE A BUTTERFLY, STING LIKE A BEE

Rarely has there been a more fortuitous confluence than the 1960 blending of Cassius Clay, an Olympic gold medal, and videotape.

LEFT / *She overcame polio, double pneumonia, and scarlet fever as a child, and, in Rome, 20-year-old American Wilma Rudolph, a mother and college track star, dominated again, matching Betty Cuthbert's triple-gold haul four years earlier.*
(ALLSPORT)

BELOW / *Rafer Johnson, who capped his silver-medal performance in Melbourne's decathlon with a gold four years later in Rome, was chosen to light the torch at the Opening Ceremonies in Los Angeles 24 years later.*
(ALLSPORT)

gold medal, and videotape.

Also adding to Clay's stature was a decidedly lackluster performance by Americans on the track. For the first time in Olympic history, U.S. athletes were just part of the boys. Never had so many races been won by so many different nations. Peter Snell and Murray Halberg of New Zealand won at 800 and 5,000 meters, respectively. Herb Elliott of Australia won at 1,500 meters. Armin Hary of Germany won at 100 meters and Italy's Livio Berruti set off a national celebration by becoming the first non-North American 200-meter winner in Olympic history. Pyotr Bolotnikov of the Soviet Union won at 10,000 meters, Zdzislaw Kryszkowiak of Poland won the steeplechase, Abebe Bikila of Ethiopia became the first African to win an Olympic gold medal when he ran in bare feet and won the marathon, and in the 4x100-meter relay, the U.S. string of eight straight Olympic triumphs was halted when Germany prevailed.

No one epitomized the disappointment of the Americans more than Ray Norton, the world record-holder at 200 meters who was favored to win both

Clay from Louisville, Kentucky, won the light heavyweight gold medal in 1960.

Clay — later to become the world's most well-known athlete as Muhammad Ali — never stopped swinging, or talking. The 18-year-old "Louisville Lip" decisively beat 25-year-old, three-time European amateur champion Zvigniew Pietrzkowski of Poland in the championship bout. Before and after, he entertained the world's media with his lively banter, his colorful poetry, and his glowing speeches about America. Since it was also in 1960 that videotape made its Olympic debut — enabling delayed prime time television coverage the world over — whatever Clay said, the universe heard. Rarely has there been a more fortuitous confluence than the 1960 blending of Cassius Clay, an Olympic

PRECEDING PAGES / *One of the most dominating athletes ever, Romanian Iolanda Balas wins the first of two Olympic titles in the high jump. From 1956 to 1966, Balas would win an amazing 140 consecutive meets.*
(ALLSPORT)

sprints and instead finished sixth in both the 100 and 200. Norton was also a member of the 4x100-meter relay team that was disqualified for an illegal baton exchange.

The United States did get wins in both hurdles races and at 400 meters — as Otis Davis ran a 44.9 world record — and there were nothing but rave reviews for sprinter Wilma Rudoph, a polio victim as a child, who won three women's gold sprint medals and was dubbed "La Gazelle Noire" (the black gazelle) by an enamored Italian press.

The decathlon provided the most thrilling finish in Rome. For two days, Rafer Johnson of the United States and C.K. Yang of Taiwan — college teammates and friends at UCLA — battled neck-and-neck. Just 67 points separated them when they arrived at the final event, the 1,500-meter run. Yang's best time at that distance, 4:36, was 18 seconds faster than Johnson's 4:54, and he needed at least a 10-second margin to overtake his friend and win Taiwan's first-ever Olympic gold medal. With that carrot in place, Yang set out in front as the 1,500 began, and Johnson stayed just behind his shoulder. Yang ran a 4:48, Johnson a best-ever 4:49, and as they collapsed against each other on the track,

the American had his gold medal by a mere 58 points.

In sharp contrast to the stirring decathlon competition, there was the basketball tournament, won by a United States team that featured Jerry West, Oscar Robertson and Jerry Lucas and outscored its opponents by a 102-59 average.

Italian spectating started off slowly for the Games, but as the videotape, and the Italian athletes, rolled, the Olympic halls began to fill. Particularly popular was the boxing arena, where not only Clay held court, but a large contingent of home-grown pugilists. Six Italians made it into the 10 finals. The two who won gold, welterweight Giovanni Benvenuti and heavyweight Franco De Piccoli, would not have to worry about buying pasta in Rome for a long time to come.

In cycling, too, the Italians dominated, and in most other sports they used their homecourt advantage to hold their own. Their 36 medals, including 13 gold, were the most in Italian Olympic history and trailed only the totals of the United States (71 total, 34 gold) and the Soviet Union (103 total, 43 gold). It all added up to an unconditional success as a worthy encore after a layoff of more than 15 centuries — a point well emphasized at the Closing

Ceremonies, where, as the Olympic flame was being doused, 80,000 Italians lit newspaper torches, keeping the stadium aglow.

LEFT / *World record-holder Glenn Davis continued the U.S. domination in the 400-meter hurdles in Rome. Davis, who defended his Olympic title, led an American sweep of the event.* (ALLSPORT)

ABOVE / *The field was loaded with talent for the 1960 women's discus competition. Included in the field were two former Olympic champions as well as two future Olympic champions. Soviet Nina Ponomorava, who had won in 1952, rose to the challenge, winning with an Olympic record throw of 180-9.* (ALLSPORT)

RIGHT/ *Calvin Smith hands the baton to anchorman Carl Lewis in the 4x100-meter relay. The Americans, along with Sam Graddy and Ron Brown, set the only track and field world record at the 1984 Games.*
(ALLSPORT / DUFFY)

4 x 1 0 0

RELAY

abebe bikila

WHAT, NO SHOES?

The best pair of running shoes ever made were Abebe Bikila's feet. Durable. Strong. Flexible. And stable as the high plains of Africa from which they came.

At the 1960 Olympic Games, Bikila took his perfect feet to Rome for a nighttime run down 26.2 miles of no less a road than the Appian Way, also known as "the Queen of the Roads." The cobblestones were rough and uneven and visible only through the glow of hundreds of torches held by Italian soldiers who lined the marathon route. The temperature was so hot at the start it not only had the thousands of Italian spectators talking to themselves, but the runners besides. The pre-race favorites were New Zealand's Barry Magee, Denmark's Thyge Torgensen, Sergie Popov and Konstanin Vorobiev of the Soviet Union, and the much heralded Rhadi Ben Abdesselem from Morocco. No one outside of Ethiopia had ever heard of Abebe Bikila, the guy in the bare feet.

Bikila's family back in Mout,

Ethiopia, knew he was a runner, and they thought he was pretty good, and Abebe himself knew he was pretty good, and his fellow officers of the Imperial Bodyguards, whose job it was to protect the life of His Imperial Majesty Haile Selassie I, the Emperor of Ethiopia, knew all about Abebe's love affair with running. But Addis Ababa, Ethiopia's capital, was hardly the running capital of anywhere and the great African running dynasty was yet to be born. And Private Bikila, at the getting-up-there age of 28, had only run a grand total of two marathons in his life, a mere rookie, and he had yet to run anywhere outside Ethiopia.

What he had done was log countless miles of rugged-terrain running along the dirt roads and foothills of East Africa. An elevation of 8,100 feet isn't much for sea shells, date palms or beach volleyball, but it is unbeatable for developing a world class set of lungs. A few 20-mile fun runs in the mountains above Addis Ababa can do wonders for both a fuller appreciation for oxygen and the ability to get by with less of it.

Rome was hot the night of Sept.

9, 1960, and Rome was humid, and the route was rough. The Russians and the Danes and the Brits and the Russians didn't like it much as they laced up the latest running flats Adidas and Puma had to offer. Abebe liked the conditions just fine as he placed his bare black African toes on the starting line. This was nothing like home. It was a lot better.

And Abebe was no stranger to the Appian Way. Days earlier he and his coach, Onni Niskanen, had surveyed the entire course. The finish was at the historic Triumphal Arch of Constantine — the first non-stadium marathon finish in Olympic history. The Arch was an imposing and impressive sight to Abebe and his coach, but not nearly as imposing as another marker along the route: the obelisk of Axum, located at the beginning of an incline about a mile from the finish line. It was easy to see, and, what was more important to Abebe, the obelisk actually belonged to Ethiopia. It had been stolen from Axum (an ancient kingdom in northeastern Africa from which Ethiopia was formed) by invading Italian troops and carted

back to Rome.

It would be the perfect spot, the coach and the runner reasoned, for Abebe to make his move if anyone was still on his heels at 25 miles. The fact that in the entire world only Abebe and Onni and possibly His Majesty Haile Selassie I thought the 28-year-old palace guard had a ghost of a chance of winning bothered Abebe not at all. He told Onni after deciding to run without shoes, "let's make some history for Africa."

Bikila ran with the pack at first, anonymity intact, until four kilometers when he and runners from Belgium, Great Britain and the Moroccan, Ben Abdesselem, broke away. At 18 kilometers, the two Africans pulled away from the others. They ran mile

An elevation of 8,100 feet isn't much for sea shells, date palms or beach volleyball, but it is unbeatable for developing a world class set of lungs.

after mile at a 5-minute-per-mile pace, never looking at each other or at the thousands of spectators lining the ancient course. Neither runner showed signs of strain. At 22 miles they were still together, stride for stride, and people were starting to ask aloud, "who is Abebe Bikila, where is he from, and WHAT HAPPENED TO HIS SHOES?"

But of course the real racing geniuses, the ones who knew what marathon running was all about, were only waiting for Ben Abdesselem to make his move and blow away this upstart 5-foot-10-inch, 128-pound cop from Ethiopia.

Then they came to the obelisk of Axum — and the Ethiopian cop put

the race away. He churned up the incline like he was reclaiming the monument for Ethiopia and left a disbelieving Rhadi Ben Abdesselem in the shadows. He gained 200 yards on his fellow African in the last mile and after negotiating his way around an errant Roman motor scooter that entered the course 60 yards from the finish, he hit the tape at the Arch of Constantine as the first black African ever to win an Olympic gold medal. His time of 2:15:16.2 set a new world record.

It left all of Rome talking, "Who is this guy AND WHERE ARE HIS SHOES?"

Abebe's fame quickly spread in

Ethiopia and he received a promotion from private to sergeant in the Imperial Bodyguards. The Emperor also gave him a new Volkswagen.

In 1964 Bikila ran again, at the Tokyo Games, just 40 days after undergoing an appendectomy. He wasn't supposed to be able to run, let alone win, but he set another world record (2:12:11.2), this time with shoes on, and beat the runner-up by nearly four minutes, during which time the unassuming Ethiopian entertained the crowd of 75,000 in Japan's Olympic Stadium by doing his customary post-race sit-ups and push-ups on the infield grass.

Bikila had become the first person

ever to win back-to-back Olympic marathons. After Tokyo, he was promoted to lieutenant in the Imperial Bodyguards. He trained hard for the next Olympics in 1968 where he would no doubt again be the favorite. He was confident of a win in Mexico City's Addis Ababa-like altitude, but a bone fracture at 17 kilometers ended his quest for three in a row.

In 1969, while driving the Volkswagen given to him by the Emperor, Bikila collided with another car. The greatest marathon man of his time was paralyzed from the waist down. His next appearance at an Olympics was in the archery competition at the wheelchair games.

His bare feet never again felt the mountain trails of his homeland, but he saw it as God's will that he was allowed to run and win in two Olympic games.

His death came suddenly from a brain hemorrhage in 1973 at the age of 41. Sixty-five thousand people attended his funeral. ☞

ABOVE / *In only his third marathon, Ethiopia's barefooted Abebe Bikila became the first black African to win this Olympic event. He would repeat the feat in Tokyo, becoming the first person to win two Olympic marathons.* [AllSPORT]

1964

October 10-24, 1964

94 Nations

5,140 Athletes

19 Sports

36 USA golds

TOKYO

hey were called the "Happy Games" as the Olympics made their way to Asia for the first time in 1964. The Japanese had originally been awarded host status for the 1940 Games, to coincide with the nation's 2,600th birthday but withdrew in 1938 because of the Sino-Japanese war. Then, considering the outcome of World War II and the fact that Japan (like Germany) wasn't invited back when the Olympics made their post-war recovery in 1948 in London, there was some speculation that Japan would never get another chance. When it did, Tokyo's enthusiasm was matched only by its pocketbook. An estimated $3 billion was spent in city renewal in preparation for the Games and a record $60 million was budgeted for the Games themselves.

Determined to show the world that bygones could be bygones and destruction could be overcome, Japan personified that sentiment by having the torch lit during the Opening Ceremonies by Yoshinori Sakai, a resident of Hiroshima who was born 19 years earlier during the bombing that ended the war and leveled the city.

Appropriately enough, the theme of overcoming adversity carried over into the Olympic competition. Many of Tokyo's most intriguing stories were of athletes standing on top of winner's rostrums who had no business being there. Included were Australian swimmer Dawn Fraser, Ethiopian marathon runner Abebe Bikila, U.S. sprinter Bob Hayes, U.S. boxer Joe Frazier, and the Japanese women's volleyball team.

TOP / *Australian Dawn Fraser has good reason to smile, becoming the first Olympic swimmer to win the same event three consecutive times.* (ALLSPORT)

RIGHT / *Antonius Geesink's surprise victory in the open division prevented Japan from winning the gold in all of the divisions of the new Olympic sport of judo. The Dutchman relegated pre-match favorite Akio Kaminaga to the silver.* (ALLSPORT)

AGAINST ALL ODDS

Many of Tokyo's most intriguing stories were of athletes standing on top of winner's rostrums who had no business being there. Among them were Australian swimmer Dawn Fraser, who suffered serious injuries in a car accident seven months earlier, and Abebe Bikila, who had an appendectomy just 40 days before the marathon.

Fraser had suffered major injuries in a car accident that took the life of her mother seven months earlier. She was in a neck brace for six weeks after that accident and her training was severely restricted. Still, she persevered to win her third straight gold medal at 100 meters. Bikila, whose unexpected barefoot triumph in the marathon four years earlier in Rome made him the natural favorite, had to have an emergency appendectomy just 40 days before the Tokyo marathon and wasn't even expected to enter, let alone set a world-record time of 2:12:11 and become the first back-to-back marathon champion in Olympic history.

As for Hayes, a leg injury in June made him a question mark in the dashes,

LEFT / *Twenty-two-year old Vera Caslavska from Prague snatched the all-around title from 1960 star Larissa Latynina of the Soviet Union. Caslavska went on to defend her all-around title in Mexico City, ending her Olympic career with seven golds and four silvers.* (ALLSPORT)

ABOVE / *In 1964, America's Wyomia Tyus ran a 11.4 for the gold in the 100 meters. In Mexico City, she lowered her time to 11.0, established a world record and became the first sprinter, male or female, to win an (official) Olympic 100 meters twice in a row.* (ALLSPORT)

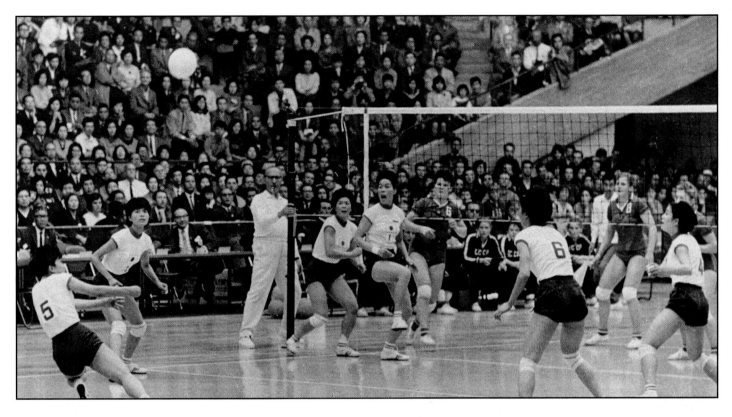

yet he tied the world record of 10.0 at 100 meters and in the 4x100-meter relay ran an 8.6 anchor leg to make up a three-meter deficit and rally the U.S. team to the gold medal and a world record of 39 seconds flat.

Frazier's story of perseverance didn't take a backseat to any of the above. A heavyweight boxer from Philadelphia who worked in a butcher's shop, Frazier had lost to 300-pound Buster Mathis in the U.S. trials and was sent to Tokyo only as Mathis' sparring partner. But when Mathis broke his index finger sparring with Frazier, it was Frazier who was entered as the U.S. representative in the Olympic tournament. Determined to make the most of his opportunity, Frazier shrugged off a broken finger of his own (he broke his left thumb in the semifinals against a Russian opponent), refused x-rays, said, "I got to get this gold medal. It's the only way I can get out of the slaughterhouse," and decisioned Hans Huber, a bus driver from Regensburg, Germany, in the championship bout. Six years later, Joe Frazier would become heavyweight champion of the world.

The Japanese women's volleyball team had trained religiously for four years in anticipation of that sport's Olympic debut (for both men and women) in Tokyo. Ten of the team's 12 members worked for the same company, a spinning mill near Osaka, and practiced together six hours a day, seven days a week, 51 weeks a year, while under the supervision of their company "overseer," the noted volleyball coach Hirofumi Daimatsu. By the time the Olympics rolled around, Daimatsu's was a team possessed, convinced no nation on earth could get the best of it on the court.

But then a major problem arose off the court when North Korea's Olympic team was banned from the Tokyo Games by the IOC for participating in unsanctioned games in Indonesia the year previous. This meant that North Korea's women's volleyball team was out of the draw, reducing the tournament to just five teams, one fewer than the minimum required by the Olympic charter. The tournament was saved when Japan sent one million yen to South Korea to cover the expenses of outfitting a women's team and sending it to Tokyo. The South Koreans didn't win a match and finished last. The Japanese didn't lose a match and breezed to the gold medal. Their final match, against the Soviet Union, was televised live and drew an 80 percent TV rating in Japan.

Overall, the Japanese received the highest of marks as hosts. Their toughest test for diplomacy came in the judo tournament. That sport, time-honored in Japan, also made its Olympic debut in Tokyo, and was enthusiastically received as gold medal after gold medal was taken by *nippon*. In the finals of the unlimited class, judo's most glamorous division, there was eager anticipation for Akio Kaminaga, the Japanese champion, to capture the gold medal. When Kaminaga was overcome, however, by a 6-foot-6, 267-pound giant Dutchman named Anton Geesink, an embarrassed silence engulfed the judo hall. Soon, however, the Japanese audience gathered itself and politely cheered the foreign conqueror.

So went the tranquil Games of '64, an Olympics practically devoid of protests, boycotts and controversy. At the Closing Ceremonies, as a huge "Sayonara" was lit on the scoreboard, Japan bowed, and the world bowed back.

ABOVE / *To the delight of the hometown fans, the Japanese women stormed to the first gold medal in women's volleyball.* (ALLSPORT)

billy mills

AGAINST THE ODDS, PART II

From the moment he crossed the finish line, the Billy Mills story read like a Hollywood script, which of course is exactly what it became. Nearly two decades after the fact, there was the movie, "Running Brave." Here was an instant legend. Here was a symbol for underdogs and the power of the human will and overcoming obstacles.

From childhood right to the finish line in Tokyo, the odds were against Billy Mills. He was 7/16 Sioux Indian. He was born and raised in poverty in a small village on the Oglala Sioux reservation in South Dakota, just one in a family of 15. His mom died when he was seven, his father died when he was 12 and the orphaned Mills was sent to a boarding school for Indians in Lawrence, Kansas.

He began running to train for boxing, but after losing more fights than he won he decided to stick with running where no one can hit you back. His running earned him an athletic scholarship to the University of Kansas. He took a degree in physical education, joined the Marines, became a lieutenant, and in 1962, two years before the defining moment of his life, he retired from running.

His running career had been relatively undistinguished. His best finish in the NCAA track championships was fifth. He struggled for acceptance at Kansas, where white society rejected him because of his Indian blood. His anger and frustration at such treatment grew into resentment and hostility. During his senior year, he quit the 10,000-meter race at the NCAA championships because his coach yelled at him to move to the front of the pack. Mills wanted to run from behind or not at all.

And so he retired. Or so he thought. His wife, Pat, a track fan, kept dragging him to watch meets, knowing that the watching would make him yearn to compete again. Mills returned to the sport with new resolve. In 1964 he made the Olympic team in both the 10,000 and the marathon (in which he would finish 14th). Still, the odds were stacked against him. Only one other American had ever medaled in the Olympic 10,000 — Lewis Tewanima, who, ironically, was also an Indian. What's more, the field at the '64 Olympics was loaded. It included New Zealand's Murray Halberg, the defending Olympic 5,000-meter champion, Russia's Pyotr Bolotnikov, the defending Olympic 10,000 champion, Australia's Ron Clarke, the 10,000 world-record holder and the pre-race favorite, and three future Olympic champions — Kenya's barefoot Naftali Temu, Tunisia's Mohamed Gammoudi and Ethiopia's Mamo Wolde. Some of them had run nearly a minute faster than Mills.

"The reporters from all over the world were always stopping these people and asking them questions, but no one asked me even one question," recalls Mills. "It was like I was invisible." Undaunted, Mills was confident. "I knew if I stayed up with the leaders and put on a good final kick I would win. What the reporters didn't know was that in my speed training a few days earlier I had run a 220 in 23.6."

As expected, Clarke took command of the race, which was run on a track that was still wet from a

morning rain. By surging every other lap he had dropped all but four runners halfway through the race. All who remained in contention, besides Clarke, were Gammoudi, Wolde, Kokichi Tsuburaya of Japan and Mills. They reached the 5,000-meter halfway mark in 14:06, which was only nine seconds slower than Mills' best time for that distance.

When Mills heard the split time, he was full of self doubts. "Ron Clarke nearly broke me at the 5,000-meter mark," recalls Mills. " ... I was thinking I couldn't continue at this pace. I had taken the lead at the 5,000, but I dropped right back to fourth and the leaders started pulling away from me. I thought that I might just as well let them go ... At one point I was going to go one more lap, take the lead and go one more (lap). That way if I did quit it would be while I was winning. I kept thinking that if I had to quit, I wasn't going to do it in front of where Pat was sitting; I'd do it at the other end of the field."

Lap by lap, Mills talked himself into sticking with Clarke. Four times during the race he seemed to fall from contention, dropping as much as 15 meters behind, but each time he rallied.

Tsuburaya was the first to lose contact. With 2 1/2 laps to go Wolde fell off the pace. The remaining trio pressed on, with Clarke in front, followed by Mills and then Gammoudi. Clarke seemed a sure winner. Gammoudi and Mills had never even broke 29 minutes and the pace was much stiffer than that. But then Mills saw something. "I was in second

place, and Clarke looked back. I saw him look back, and I thought, 'My gosh, he's worried.' It was just so clear in my mind: he ... was worried. From that point on I stayed with him."

Heading into the final lap, Mills pulled even with Clarke and even forged a slight lead, with Gammoudi close behind them, but there was another problem besides their burning fatigue: the track was congested with stragglers who had been lapped, forcing the leaders to thread their way up the track. As Clarke would later say, it was "like a dash for a train in a peak-hour crowd." It proved to be more than a mere nuisance. Coming out of the first turn and heading for the backstretch, Clarke found himself closing rapidly on one of the lapped runners, Temu.

"I had Clarke perfectly boxed in," recalls Mills. "When I ran Clarke into Temu's back, I was going to start my kick. ... Clarke saw that I had boxed him in, and he gave me a little nudge. I nudged him back, and then he leaned into me a little, and I leaned into him. Then he lifted me up and pushed me into the third lane. I thought I was going to fall, and my legs started to buckle. But I recovered and started to close back on Clarke's shoulder. Just then Gammoudi broke between Clarke and me, knocking Clarke to the inside and me to the outside."

Gammoudi bolted to a 10-meter lead over Clarke, with Mills another four meters back. Mills appeared to be out of the race.

"There were probably 75,000 screaming people in the stadium, but all I could hear was the throbbing of my heart," says Mills. I kept thinking, One more try. One more try."

Clarke caught Gammoudi and passed him at the top of the homestretch, but Gammoudi fought back and pulled even with him, while Mills sprinted to catch them. "We came off the last curve, and I could see the tape stretched across the finish line. Then I thought, I can win. I can win."

Threading his way through more stragglers, Mills unleashed his final sprint down the homestretch. He trailed by five meters with 80 meters to go, but halfway down the homestretch he was sure he would win. He passed Clarke and then he

Four times during the race he seemed to fall from contention, dropping as much as 15 meters behind, but each time Billy Mills rallied.

caught Gammoudi 20 meters from the finish. He felt the tape break across his chest, and then a Japanese official ran up to him and asked, "Who are you? Who are you." Mills panicked. "I thought, 'Oh, my gosh, do I have one more lap to go.' But the race was over, and I was being led off to a press conference."

Mills had set an American and Olympic record of 28:24.4, running 46 seconds faster than his previous personal record. He finished just .4 of a second ahead of Gammoudi. Clarke was third in 28:25.8.

Asked about Mills after the race, Clarke said, "I never heard of him." π

STRANGE BUT TRUE

The re-establishment of the Olympic Games in the mod-ern era has not been without its unconventional moments. Stranger things may have happened, but not a lot stranger:

In the 1956 Olympic marathon, held in Melbourne, Australia, there was a false start. After one of the competitors jumped the gun for the 26-mile, 385-yard run, all 46 runners were called back to the starting line and they tried it again.

The body of Pierre de Coubertin, the French Baron who founded the modern Olympic movement, was buried in his adopted hometown of Lausanne, Switzerland, upon his death in 1937. But, as per his request, his heart was removed, encased in a marble column, and buried amid the ruins of the ancient city of Olympia, Greece.

In the 1908 London Games, Forrest Smithson, a God-fearing hurdler from Portland, Oregon, ran in the Sunday 110-meter final while carrying a Bible in his right hand. He won in the world-record time of 15.0 seconds.

In the 1920 Games in Antwerp, Belgium, Oscar Swahn and his son, Alfred, helped Sweden win the silver medal in the running deer shooting event. Oscar was 72 years old at the time — the oldest medal winner in Olympic history. The father-and-son Swahn team competed in three Olympic Games together, in 1908, 1912 and 1920, and Alfred added a fourth appearance in 1924, when he was 45, and won a bronze medal. In all, the Swahns won 15 medals for Sweden and their mantelpiece — six golds, four silvers and five bronzes.

In the fast start-slow finish department, Jieudone Lamothe, a distance runner from Haiti, is without Olympic peer. In a 5,000-meter heat in the 1976 Games in Montreal, Lamothe led the field after the first lap. After that he slowed ... considerably. He finished in last place by some five minutes. His time of 18 minutes and 50 seconds is the slowest 5,000-meter time in Olympic history.

The persistence award belongs to Ivan Osiier of Denmark, a fencer who participated in seven Olympics, beginning with the 1908 Games in London. Osiier went on to compete in the 1912, 1920, 1924, 1928, 1932 and 1948 Games. Osiier wasn't in it for the glory. He won a silver medal in epee in 1912, and never came closer than sixth place in any event thereafter. π

ABOVE/ *Bible-toting hurdler, Forrest Smithson.* (ALLSPORT)

EYE OPENERS

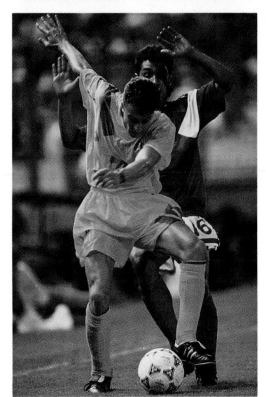

TOP LEFT / *Servin' it up: men's doubles table tennis.* (ALLSPORT / COLE)

TOP RIGHT / *Viva La France: men's team handball in Barcelona.* (ALLSPORT / VANDYSTADT)

MIDDLE LEFT / *Japan's answer to William Tell.* (ALLSPORT / CANNON)

MIDDLE RIGHT / *Battling Brits: field hockey.* (ALLSPORT / BOTTERILL)

BOTTOM LEFT / *Tough D: soccer in Barcelona.* (ALLSPORT / LEAH)

BOTTOM RIGHT / *Eye on the birdie: badminton.* (ALLSPORT)

1968

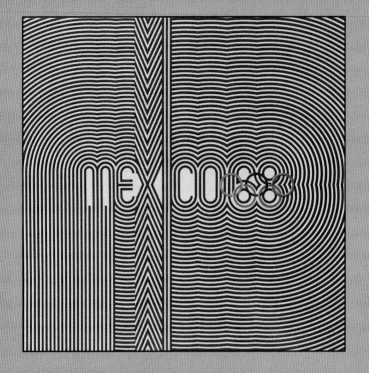

October 12-27, 1968
113 Nations
5,531 Athletes
19 Sports
45 USA golds

MEXICO CITY

ATTITUDE AND ALTITUDE

The Games of the XIXth Olympiad in Mexico City could be summed up in two words: Attitude and Altitude. One or the other made its mark on virtually all of the proceedings during the most rambunctious and turbulent of the modern Olympic Games.

The late '60s were a time of change and unrest throughout the world. In the United States, particularly, the atmosphere was volatile after the assassinations of Robert Kennedy and Dr. Martin Luther King and the country's controversial intervention in the Vietnam War. In Mexico, unrest over poverty almost stopped the Olympics before they began. Thousands of students organized protests aimed at directing the Olympic funds elsewhere. Their exuberance was stalled, if not entirely stilled, on the night of Oct. 2, 1968, when the Mexican army clashed with more than 10,000 demonstrators in downtown Mexico City, leaving 260 dead and another 1,200 injured.

That was 10 days before the Games were to begin.

Somehow, however, the 1968 Olympic Games opened on time and on cue on Oct. 12, ready and waiting to see if more protests were to come, and to see, finally, if Mexico's altitude of 7,347 feet — the highest by far in Olympic annals — really would play host to the most aberrational track meet in history.

The answer, to both questions, was yes.

Never before had an Olympics been

TOP / *Future world heavyweight champion George Foreman gives the "V" for victory in Mexico City.* (IOC)

RIGHT / *America's world record-setting 4x400-meter relay team raised their fists in sympathy of Tommie Smith and John Carlos, the first and third finishers of the 200-meter race who were dropped from the U.S. team for using the Olympic stage to protest the civil rights injustices in the U.S.* (ALLSPORT)

Never before had an Olympics been held at such an altitude. Never had there been a track and field meet the equal of Mexico City's. Records fell like gravity. Thin air was easy to slice through.

held at such a height. Physiologists had debated for years as to just what effect Mexico City's rare air would have on the Games, particularly in track and field. A number of nations wanted the Games moved because of the unfair advantages to be gained by athletes from similarly high elevations. Great Britain petitioned the IOC to limit the amount of time athletes could train at altitude — a noble idea but one hardly enforceable.

It turned out that the predictions were well founded. Never had there been a track and field meet the equal of Mexico City's. Records fell like gravity. In every race at 1,500 meters or less, both men's and women's, either a world record or an Olympic record was set. In all, 10 world running marks were established in the short races where the thin air was easy to slice through, in addition to another six Olympic records. In the field events, where the same principles of thin air applied, it was more of the same. Four world records were set and six Olympic records. Out of a total of 30 track and field events, only four ran their course without some kind of notation in the Olympic or world record books.

Foremost of the record-setters was long jumper Bob Beamon of the United States. On a perfect day for long jumping — humid, overcast, and the thinnest air a jumper could hope for — Beamon bettered the existing world record, co-held by Ralph Boston, by nearly two feet. In the 33 years prior to Beamon's jump, the long jump world record had increased by just eight and a half inches. In the span of one afternoon, the unknown American not only broke the 28-foot barrier, but with his leap of 29-2 1/2, the 29-foot barrier as well.

But just as it appeared the ugliness

TOP / *Kenya's Kip Keino Kipchoge secured an Olympic record and the largest margin of victory (20 meters) in Olympic 1500-meter history. He and other African runners dominated the distance events in the high altitude of Mexico City.* (ALLSPORT)

MIDDLE (LEFT) / *American Dick Fosbury "flopped" his way to a 1968 Olympic record of 7-4 1/2 and the gold medal. His unorthodox style revolutionized the sport of high jumping.* (ALLSPORT)

MIDDLE (RIGHT) / *Colette Besson of France took the 400-meter field and herself by complete surprise. Her previous best was 53.8. Her time in Mexico City, 52 seconds flat, equaled the Olympic record.* (ALLSPORT)

BOTTOM / *The pole vault event almost stymied Bill Toomey's efforts to win the gold in the decathlon. Only one miss away from elimination put the pressure on the 29-year-old American, who, in the end, cleared the bar at 13-9 1/2, a personal best.* (ALLSPORT)

that preceded Mexico City's Games would be diluted by these stunning developments on the track, the protests resumed. This time from within. After placing first and third in the 200-meter final, Tommie Smith and John Carlos of the United States took a message of black oppression to the medal peristyle with them. They mounted the stand wearing black socks, with their warmup pants rolled to their knees. They wore civil rights buttons and when the Star Spangled Banner was played, they bowed their heads and raised their clenched right fists to the sky. The two runners, who were teammates at San Jose State, were members of a group called Olympic Project for Human Rights. They were using the Olympic medium to draw attention to what they considered civil rights injustices against blacks in the United States.

Their irreverence carried over into the general atmosphere of the Games, and when the U.S. 4x400-meter relay team took the medal podium after setting yet another world record the last day of the track competition, Vince Matthews, Ronald Freeman, Larry James and Lee Evans also raised their fists, in sympathy of Smith and Carlos and their cause.

Somewhat overlooked among all of this podium positioning was the protest-less presence of 23-year-old American Wyomia Tyus. The defending 100-meter champion from Tokyo, Tyus defeated four other one-time world record-holders in Mexico City in the world-record time of 11.0 seconds to become the first person in history to win two straight Olympic sprint titles.

The protests also cast something of a shadow on what proved to be the curtain call of one Alfred Oerter of West Babylon, New York. Oerter used the Mexico City air to win his fourth and final consecutive gold medal in the discus. From 1956, when he won unexpectedly in Melbourne as a 20-year-old Olympic rookie, through 1968, when his triumph surprised no one, Oerter dominated his event like no man before or since. He retired after the '68 Games although he was just 32 years old. A dozen years later, he would try out for the 1980 U.S. Olympic Team. At the age of 44, he just missed a spot, finishing fourth.

Black athletes who definitely *didn't* protest in Mexico were those from the high altitudes of Africa. Every race from

1,500 meters and beyond — distance events that required increased lung capacity — went to African runners with the exception of the 5,000-meter run, and that winner, Mohammed Gammoudi of Tunisia, trained all summer at a high-altitude camp in the French Alps.

Somewhat lost in the commotion in and around the Olympic track stadium was the almost total domination of the U.S. swimmers. Of 102 possible medals, U.S. swimmers won 58 of them, including 23 gold medals. The only protests in the pool, and they were silent, came from the rest of the world. Also, it was in Mexico City that high jumper Dick Fosbury "flopped" his way to an Olympic record of 7 feet, 4 1/2 inches, and that George Foreman, a black boxer from Houston and future world champion, won the gold medal in the heavyweight division and celebrated by parading around the ring carrying a tiny American flag — a protest of the other protests.

In the end, the venue that suffered most from Mexico's high altitude was rowing, where no less than 16 oxygen resuscitations were required. As for Mexico City's "attitudes," it wouldn't be for several Olympics before stadiums stopped holding their collective breath when medal winners mounted the peristyle's steps.

TOP / *Running away from the rest of the field, Great Britain's David Hemery won the 400-meter hurdles race by an amazing eight yards lowering the world record to 48.12.* (ALLSPORT)

ABOVE / *Just two of the victims that the high altitude claimed at these Games.* (ALLSPORT)

bob beamon

A LEAP IN TIME

Of all the great athletic performances in the history of the world, there are a handful that separate themselves from the rest. Jacob held his own in an all-night wrestling match with an angel. The kid David beat the giant Goliath with only a rock and a sling. Babe Ruth called the shot. Jesse Owens outran a racehorse. But the most storied, most legendary, most talked about athletic performance of all time was a single leap in the mountains of Mexico.

Bob Beamon's long jump in the 1968 Olympic Games has been called the greatest single athletic performance in history. It was a leap so great that Beamon himself was crushed by the weight of it — first, as he collapsed on the runway upon realizing what he had done, and later as his career crumbled under the burden of it. As the mark endured and endured through the years its legend grew. It became an adjective. When someone performed a great athletic feat, it was called *Beamonesque*.

The man who performed this marvelous feat was a wiry, 6-foot-3, 157-pound black man from South Jamaica, New York. He graduated from a high school he once described as a jungle and was offered a contract to play professional basketball for the Harlem Magicians. Instead, he went to North Carolina A&T and eventually to the University of Texas-El Paso. He was suspended from the UTEP team the year of the Olympics for refusing to compete against BYU (in a protest against what he perceived as racist policies at that school), which left him without a coach for the four months leading up to the Olympics.

That notwithstanding, Beamon was the Olympic favorite. He had won 22 of 23 meets coming into the Games, and he came to Mexico City predicting a gold medal and a world record. Still, he was by no means a cinch. The competition included the three medalists from the 1964 Olympics — in order, Great Britain's Lynn Davies, America's Ralph Boston and Russia's Igor Ter-Ovanesyan. The latter two shared the world record of 27-4 3/4. What's more, Beamon could be unpredictable. He was prone to foul, at least partly because, unlike his rivals, he used no check marks on the runway to gauge his strides and approach on the runway.

Sure enough, in the Olympic preliminaries, Beamon fouled his first two attempts. If he fouled his third and final attempt, he wouldn't advance to the final. Beamon consulted with Boston, who had acted as his informal coach. Boston advised him to adjust his stride pattern on his approach, and Beamon, heeding the advice, qualified for the next afternoon's final.

The Olympic final began late in the afternoon under a dark, thickly clouded sky that had rained periodically throughout the day and threatened to do so again. The first three jumpers fouled. Beamon, fourth in the order, stepped onto the runway for his first attempt. "Come on, make this a good one," Boston told him in what proved to be a considerable understatement.

Beamon, with his 9.5 100-yard dash speed, charged down the runway. His left foot struck the takeoff board perfectly — at the very end of the board. The moment Beamon left the earth it was apparent that this was something special. Ordinarily, long jumpers fly through the air on a relatively flat trajectory, but Beamon soared to a startling height — five and

a half to six feet in the air, according to some observers. He hurtled through the air, his knees rising nearly to his chin, his eyes wide in an attitude of disbelief. He slammed into the sand, then bounded up immediately and landed again outside the pit.

"That's over 28 feet," Boston told Davies.

"With his first jump?" replied Davies. "No, it can't be."

Davies and Boston trotted to the pit for a closer look. Meet officials tried to measure the mark with a state-of-the-art electronic optical device, but the jump had exceeded its range. As officials slid the marker to the place where Beamon had broken the sand, it fell off the end of the rail short of the mark.

Finally, the officials had to use an old-fashioned tape to measure the jump. A couple of measurements were taken, and still, incredibly, the mark came up the same: 8.90 meters. The measurement was flashed on the scoreboard, but many observers couldn't convert meters into feet and inches. Track fans in the stands kept working out conversions but continually came up with an impossible figure of 29 feet-plus. Ter-Ovanesyan knew the metric system well, and he knew immediately what Beamon's jump meant. "Compared to this jump, the rest of us are as children," he told Davies. Beamon knew it was a record jump, but he also couldn't convert the metric system.

Eventually, the conversion was official: 29-2 1/2. It was more than Beamon could take. His legs gave way. He sank to the track sobbing in what doctors later called a cataplectic seizure and pressed his forehead to the track, holding up the start of the 400-meter dash final for several minutes. Overcome with tears and nausea, Beamon had to be helped up by his teammates.

Consider that in the previous 33 years since Jesse Owens' leap of 26-8 1/4, the world record had improved only 8 1/2 inches. With a single leap, Beamon improved it by nearly 2 feet — 21 3/4 inches to be precise. The first 28-foot jump was still 14 years away. Beamon had leaped right over it.

"I can't go on," Davies told Boston. "What is the point. We'll all look silly." Then he told Beamon, "You have

> "I can't go on," Davies told Boston. "What is the point. We'll all look silly." Then he told Beamon, "You have destroyed this event."

destroyed this event."

The contest resumed, but Davies was right. As Ter-Ovanesyan began his first jump it began to rain. He finished fourth. Davies finished only ninth. Boston was third. Germany's Klaus Beer was second with a leap of 26-10 1/2 — some 2 1/2 feet behind Beamon's mark. Beamon took only one other jump and then quit.

In the days and years that followed, some would try to belittle Beamon's mark, pointing to the undisputable ideal conditions. Beamon had an aiding wind of 2.0 meters per second — anything more would have rendered it wind-aided and therefore would have disallowed it for record purposes. And then there was the altitude of 7,347 feet where the thinner air (reportedly, 27 percent less atmospheric pressure and 23 percent less air density) was perfect for sprint and jump records, as these Games clearly proved. But the fact remains that the rest of the field, which included the two world record-holders, failed to break even 27 feet.

"Some people said I made a lucky jump in the Olympics," said Beamon. "After a while that kind of talk gets in your mind."

And so it did. Beamon, burdened with trying to live up to his own legend, never came within two feet of his record jump. He leaped 26 feet 11 inches in 1969. The following year, beset with injuries, he failed to reach 26 feet. He joined the pro track circuit in 1973 and eventually retired in '76.

Beamon's perfect jump brought him fame and legend, but little else. He later left track and pursued a career in coaching and youth work.

Many predicted that Beamon's mark would last forever, but it didn't. At the 1991 World Championships in Tokyo, 23 years after Mexico City, Mike Powell sailed 29 feet 4 1/2 inches. It was a world record, but it did nothing to erase the legend of Beamon's feat and his place in history.

As Beamon once told Sports Illustrated reporter William Oscar Johnson, "Mine was a jump way before its time."

BELOW / *Bob Beamon of the United States rose above the competition to turn in one of the greatest athletic performances in history. His gold medal-winning leap of 29-2 1/2 eclipsed the world record by an astonishing 21 3/4 inches.* (ALLSPORT)

LONG

LEFT / *Mike Powell secured his place in the history books in 1991 by breaking the record of Bob Beamon's legendary jump. Beamon's jump of 29-2 1/2 was the longest-standing record in track and field until Powell's jump of 29-4 1/2 in Tokyo. Powell has had the misfortune of competing in the same era as an another legend, Carl Lewis. He has taken a backseat to Lewis in the Olympic long jump in 1988 and 1992, winning silver medals in both Games.*
(ALLSPORT / BRUTY)

J U M P

1972

August 26 - September 11, 1972

122 Nations

7,830 Athletes

21 Sports

33 USA golds

MUNICH

A SHATTERED DREAM

The Olympic Games dedicated to peace, to international brotherhood; the very Games that in ancient Greece put wars on hold while the celebrations took place, were shattered at 4:25 a.m. on Sept. 5, 1972, when eight Palestinians, calling themselves the Black September Terrorists, broke into the Munich Olympic Village and took nine Israeli athletes hostage.

Less than 23 hours later, as the terrorists and their hostages attempted to board an airplane and escape Germany, a shootout between German sharpshooters and the terrorists left all nine hostages dead as well as five Palestinians and one policeman. The Games of dreams had instead yielded a nightmare.

The attack could have come anywhere and any year. As a bystander, Munich was as innocent as the Israelis. But just as Ford's Theatre will forever be linked with Lincoln, Munich will forever and inexorably be linked with Black September. Five days from a conclusion that would have been considered successful, if not entirely profitable, the Games of '72 became the Games of Tragedy.

On Aug. 26, the first Olympics to be staged on German soil since Hitler presided over the 1936 Games in Berlin opened with more than a little pomp and circumstance. Eighty thousand people jammed the new Olympic Stadium, just part of the state-of-the-art facilities paid

TOP / *Munich was the host to one of the darkest chapters of Olympic history. Palestinian terrorists stormed the Olympic Village and the Israeli dormitory. Eleven Israeli athletes were killed before it ended.* (ALLSPORT)

RIGHT / *Going into the final event of the pentathlon — the 200 meters — Great Britain's Mary Peters (left) leads by a slim margin. Had Peters ran the race 0.1 second slower, she would have lost the gold to West Germany's talented Heide Rosendahl.* (ALLSPORT)

They set out in quest of Olympic glory with grim determination. These would be the Games of superlative after superlative. But just as Ford's Theatre will forever be linked with Lincoln, Munich will forever and inexorably be linked with Black September.

for by Munich's Olympic budget of $600 million, a figure 10 times greater than Tokyo's "astonishing" budget of just eight years previous. The 122 nations in attendance and the 7,830 competitors were by far the most in Olympic history. They set out in quest of Olympic glory with grim determination. These would be the Games of superlative after superlative. Gymnast Olga Korbut of the Soviet Union would win a gold medal in floor exercise and spark a worldwide fad in her sport. So would Frank Shorter, a Yale graduate and a decided underdog, by winning the marathon. Valeri Borzov of the Soviet Union would dictate the sprints and become the World's Fastest Human. Ulrike Meyfarth, a 16-year-old German schoolgirl, would become the darling of the home country when she high-jumped six feet, 3 1/2 inches to set a world record that was just a half inch below her own height.

They would also be the Games of Dave Wottle, a runner from the United States in the Billy Mills "who's he?" tradition, who combined his honeymoon with his Olympic experience and won gold in the 800 meters while wearing a golf hat.

And for the superlatives of superlatives, they would be the Games of Lasse Viren and Mark Spitz.

A 23-year-old policeman from Finland, Viren dusted off Olympic memories of Nurmi and Vitola and Kolehmainen and the rest of the Flying Finns of bygone Olympics as he became only the fourth Olympian in history to win the 5,000- and 10,000-kilometer races in the same Games. Viren did it the hard way. Unlike previous double winners, he had to contend with a semifinal heat in the 5,000. That heat was held the day after his dramatic win in the 10,000 when he fell early in the race and not only got up to win, but to win in world-record time. Viren went on to survive the 5,000 heat and then the 5,000 final as well, winning that event in Olympic record time as the last mile was run in an unofficial 4:01.

Spitz set an Olympic record by winning seven gold medals in the same Games. For punctuation, he set a world record in each of the seven wins. His weren't the only pool breakthroughs. In all, 30 world records and 80 Olympic records were established in the fast lanes of Munich.

But if these were performances for the ages, there were also performances to be forgotten. In the men's basketball gold-medal game between the Soviets and the United States, a curious rules interpretation gave the Soviet team three tries at a game-winning shot. On the third try they got it right, winning 50-49 in the most controversial finish in basketball and Olympic history. The Americans

ABOVE / *American Rod Milburn, considered the favorite in the 110-meter hurdles, almost did not make the team. However, in Munich, he raced to the gold while equaling the world record of 13.24.* (ALLSPORT)

would not accept their silver medals afterward.

Others also had problems with outcomes and medal presentations. After losing the field hockey final to Germany, Pakistan's team members stormed the judges' table and poured water on the officials, after which they took the victory stand and refused to stand at attention during the playing of the German national anthem. All 11 members of the Pakistan team were banned from the Olympics for life by the IOC. With that penalty, they joined the same club as Vince Matthews and Wayne Collett, the one-two finishers in the 400-meter final who got their lifetime Olympic bans for talking to each other and refusing to stand at attention during the playing of the American anthem.

The fact that the above displays of questionable sportsmanship all occurred after the Sept. 5 terrorist attack only served to underscore the star-crossed skies Munich seemed to operate under, and the ornery atmosphere of outrage that prevailed to the finish. The Games had been interrupted for 24 hours after the massacre, to pay homage to the dead, and a memorial service was held in the Olympic Stadium where the Munich Opera House Orchestra played Beethoven's *Egmont Overture*. Some thought they should have been called off altogether, although Avery Brundage, in one of his last acts as IOC president, prevailed with the view that the Olympics should not yield to terrorists.

Two teams, from Norway and the Netherlands, did leave after the massacre, as did the medal-laden Spitz. An American Jew, Spitz had captured his seventh and last gold medal on Sept. 4 and was preparing to address an international news conference at 9 a.m. the next morning when news of the hostage-taking was released. Reasoning he would be an especially vulnerable target, Spitz agreed to only answer questions while seated and surrounded by U.S. swimming officials. After just a few questions, Spitz ended the press conference with "Let's get the hell out of here." Within hours he was on a plane to England.

ABOVE / *The winning long jump of 22-3 gave Heide Rosendahl one of three medals she was to win in Munich. Rosendahl collected another gold as part of West Germany's 4x400-meter relay team and a silver in the pentathlon.* (ALLSPORT)

OPPOSITE / *In one of the greatest performances in Olympic history, American swimmer Mark Spitz not only won an unprecedented seven gold medals in a single Olympic Games, but established world records in every event.* (ALLSPORT)

SEVEN WONDERS

When Mark Spitz arrived in Munich in 1972 he held six world records, he was the U.S. collegiate and national champion — and he was one scared swimmer.

In a career that had otherwise been characterized by phenomenal success, the only blip on the screen had been in the Olympics. In the Mexico City Games of 1968, Spitz had arrived a brash 18-year-old predicting, à la Joe Namath, an unprecedented haul of six gold medals. When his take included just two golds — and both of them came on relay teams — he left Mexico, if not totally beaten, thoroughly beaten up. The best he'd done individually was second in the 100-meter butterfly and third in the 100-meter freestyle. His ignominy reached its lowest point in his final race when

he finished last in his specialty, the 200-meter butterfly.

Thus he came to Munich four years later not looking as much the hunter as the hunted. It didn't help that his first race would be ... the 200 butterfly.

The California native did not look from side to side or into the stands as the 200 fly final approached on Aug. 28. He looked straight ahead and fidgeted nervously until the gun sounded and he was off, racing to exorcise the demons of Mexico. He swam with a fury, not letting up until he touched the wall and realized he was there first — in the world-record time of 2:00.70. The next finisher, teammate Gary Hall, was more than two seconds behind despite swimming a race that would have won every previous Olympic final by four seconds.

Spitz fairly leaped out of the water

and held his arms high in the classic Olympic victory salute. Now he could swim the rest of the Games with no monkey on his back. A little more than an hour later, he won his second gold medal, leading the U.S. 4x100-meter freestyle relay team to a world record.

By the time the Games were over, Mark Spitz would enter five more finals — in order, the 200-meter freestyle, the 100-meter butterfly, the 4x200-meter freestyle relay, the 100-meter freestyle and the 4x100-meter medley relay — and would claim five more gold medals, setting world records in all except the 4x100-meter freestyle relay. His seven gold medals would eclipse the previous single-Games high of five set by Italian fencer Nedo Nadi in 1920. When the water finally settled, the once frightened American swimmer had left quite a case for not entering an Olympics overconfident. π

teofilo stevenson

NOT FOR SALE

The crux of the whole matter was always this: How good was Teofilo Stevenson, the Cuban boxer? Sure, he could pummel the world's amateurs and dominate the Olympics like no heavyweight before him, but that never seemed to be enough. Sports fans and boxing aficionados always wanted to know the same thing: How would he do against the great professionals of his time — namely, Muhammad Ali, Joe Frazier and George Foreman.

But of course no one will ever know. Stevenson never wavered in his condemnation of prize fighting and his belief in amateurism, Cuba and his people. No million-dollar offer — and there were plenty of those — could change his mind.

But it was fun to imagine a Stevenson-Ali bout. The glowering, dark, handsome Cuban was 6-foot-3 1/2, and nearly 220 pounds, with long arms, broad shoulders and a thick chest. He brought speed, technique, power and movement to the ring.

Stevenson fought 12 Olympic bouts. Only the last two went the distance. He became the only man ever to win three Olympic gold medals in a single weight class, but, then, nearly all Olympic champions moved on to the professional ranks immediately and weren't eligible to defend their Olympic title. Not Stevenson. He fought his Olympic fights, refused another fortune from the American capitalists, sang the Cuban party line and then disappeared until the next Olympics or the next major international tournament.

"I have no stomach for (professional boxing)," he said. "With so many people in the world starving it is a shame to get $5 million to fight. I'm an amateur. I will always be an amateur. I am happy as I am."

He came to Munich in 1972, all of 20 years old, and methodically hammered his way through the field. It wasn't supposed to be so easy. A year earlier, Stevenson had lost to the USA's Duane Bobick in the semifinals of the Pan American Games.

"I know he's tall and strong, but the last time all he had was a good jab, no right hand," Bobick said before the Olympics. But Stevenson had spent the last 12 months developing a good right hand, working personally with his Moscow coach, Andrei Chervonenko. Now he carried a right for Castro's left.

After stopping Poland's Ludwik Denderys in one round, Stevenson met Bobick. Using the left jab and his new right, he pounded Bobick, forcing the fight to be stopped in the third round.

Stevenson took out Germany's Peter Hussing in 4 minutes and three seconds in his next bout and won the gold medal. "I have never been hit so hard in all my 212 bouts," said Hussing. "You just don't see his right hand. All of a sudden it is there on your chin."

Foreman, the 1968 Olympic heavyweight champion who would win the world professional heavyweight title in 1973, was similarly amazed by Stevenson. "He is a much more mature boxer than I was four years ago," he said.

By now, professional fight promoters were drooling down their chins. They offered Stevenson a

reported $1 million to $2 million to turn pro and/or to defect to the U.S.

"No, I will not leave Cuba for $1 million or for much more than that," he said. "What is a million dollars against eight million Cubans who love me? ... I will not trade the Cuban people for all the dollars in the world."

The offers persisted. Promoter Don King tried to lure Stevenson into the pro ranks. So did his rival, Bob Arum, who offered Stevenson $1 million to fight Leon Spinks. When that failed, Arum offered him $1 million to fight Ali, and to ease Stevenson's conscience, the money would be paid to the Cuban sports institute. But just as the deal appeared ready to close, the U.S. Treasury Department said it violated the American trade embargo against Cuba. End of deal.

Stevenson never would turn pro. "Professional boxing treats a fighter like a commodity to be bought and sold and discarded when he is no longer of use," said Stevenson. "I wouldn't exchange my piece of Cuba for all the money they could give me."

Fidel Castro, Cuba's dictator, loved it of course and praised Stevenson for not giving into pro boxing's "traffickers of bodies and of souls."

The Cuban government rewarded Stevenson. They gave him two homes, two cars and a job. He served as the boxing advisor for the country's sports institute, but Stevenson reportedly never made more than $400 a month. Even after his career ended, and Cuba and its revolution sank deeper and deeper into poverty and failure, one suspects the proud boxer never changed his mind.

Bob Surkein, who had served as head referee for the Olympics and refereed amateur fights for more than 30 years, was asked to rate Olympic boxers in the wake of the '72 Games. This was a man who had seen every Olympic heavyweight from 1948 to 1972.

"Stevenson is the best," he said. "Better than Foreman or Frazier, and as good as Ali, but Ali fought as a light

heavy in the Olympics. Stevenson has quick hands and he already moves almost as well as Ali — and he's bigger. He is a classic boxer, like all the Cubans. He has a strong jab and a punishing one. He turns his hand over as he punches so he makes contact with his palm down, with all four knuckles at once. He has a tremendous straight right . . ."

Stevenson himself told *Sports Illustrated*, "I have seen the professionals on television. For me, I think Muhammad Ali is the best. Even now, there are some I think I could beat ... Oscar Bonavena and Floyd Patterson. The others I am not so sure,

"What is a million dollars against eight million Cubans who love me? ... I will not trade the Cuban people for all the dollars in the world."

and I will never know. Maybe it would take time."

Stevenson returned to the Olympics in Montreal in 1976. In the past four years he had lost two fights, both to Igor Vysotsky of the Soviet Union. But Vysotsky, who knocked out Stevenson three months before the Olympics, was unable to compete in the Games because of eye injuries. Stevenson required a total of just 7 minutes and 22 seconds to dispatch his first three opponents. In the championship fight, Romania's Mircea

Simon avoided Stevenson, but in the third round Stevenson connected, and with 25 seconds left in the fight Simon's seconds threw in the towel.

At the age of 29, Stevenson went to Moscow for his third Olympics. Stevenson put on a listless, plodding, uninspired performance that actually drew whistles from the Soviet crowd. He stopped Solomon Ataga of Nigeria in the first round and Grzegorz Skrzecz late in the third round. But in the semifinals Hungary's István Lévai became the first man to go the distance with Stevenson in the Olympics by running around the ring for three rounds. The two rarely mixed it up, but Stevenson was declared the winner.

In the final Stevenson met Pyotr Zaev, a squat 5-foot-10, 191-pound Soviet. This time the challenger willingly mixed it up with the Cuban and still went the distance. Stevenson threw mostly jabs and rarely used his vaunted right hand, but he scored with an uppercut in the second round. Zaev landed several good rights to the head, and one of the five judges — from Nicaragua — actually voted for the Soviet. Stevenson won the decision and his third gold medal, but hardly in a convincing fashion.

As *Sports Illustrated*'s Ron Fimrite wrote, "In four tedious bouts, two of which actually went the distance, the dour Cuban expended about as much energy as the ordinary prizefighter does in conversation with Howard Cosell. And if Stevenson established anything it is that his once formidable gifts are on the decline. Either that or he is simply bored with the bum-of-the-month quadrennial campaign his amateur status has imposed on him."

Stevenson continued to produce unimpressive performances in the next few years. In 1984 he seemed to regain his old form just in time for the Los Angeles Olympics, but the Cubans joined the Soviet boycott and Stevenson stayed home. That was what any good Cuban would do.

1976

Montréal 1976

July 17 - August 1, 1976

92 Nations

6,189 Athletes

21 Sports

34 USA golds

MONTREAL

The burgeoning Olympic movement had almost collapsed under its own weight when it arrived at Montreal in the summer of 1976. Not only did the specter of the Munich massacre four years earlier haunt the return of the Games, but more than ever before the Olympics were trying to sort out who and what they were. Were they the world's policeman? Were they the world's moral conscience? Was every new host city expected to spare no expense and stage an extravaganza that would top the last extravaganza?

It was enough to provoke a nostalgic longing for the old days, when the Olympics tried to survive by tagging onto fairs and expositions and the questions were concerned with establishing, not defining, an identity.

Montreal's only consolation was that the ancient Olympic Games went through a similar crisis after the Romans took over — and the Romans, who finally shut down the ancient era, seemed to have even fewer answers than the Canadians did.

Suffice it to say that the Olympics had never had so much interest as in 1976. Interest from an international press that wondered if the Games should continue at all in the wake of Munich's terrorist tragedy. Interest from politicians who wondered if the Games should continue if the International Olympic Committee failed to screen its guest list and eliminate certain unpopular nations. And interest, literally, from any number of Montreal banks.

By the time Britain's Queen Elizabeth arrived at the Olympic Stadium to declare

IDENTITY CRISIS

The Olympics had never generated so much debate as in 1976 — what with riding in the wake of the Munich massacre and running a staggering 1.2 billion tab for the Games. It was enough to provoke a nostalgic longing for the days when the Olympics tried to survive by tagging onto fairs and exhibitions.

TOP / *Montreal's colorful Opening Ceremonies.* (ALLSPORT / MORLEY)

RIGHT / *Lasse Viren of Finland proved to be one of the most dominating distance runners in recent Olympic history, winning both the 5,000 and 10,000 meters for the second consecutive time in Montreal.* (ALLSPORT / DUFFY)

open the Games of the XXIth Olympiad — where the Queen, incidentally, followed in the royal footsteps of her father, George VI, and great grandfather, Edward VII, who declared open the London Games of 1948 and 1908, respectively — Montreal had spent a staggering $1.2 billion on its Games. Security alone, complete with overtime for 16,000 cops, cost $100 million. The stadium another $650 million, a sum

that, in itself, was $50 million more than Munich's total budget when it set the previous world-record expenditure four years earlier.

The only hope of Montreal taxpayers — who had originally been promised by their mayor that the Games "wouldn't cost a penny" — was that the world would be sufficiently wowed to at least justify part of such a debt. A hope that was dashed only 48 hours before the

Games were to begin. Just as Elizabeth was reviewing the performances of her father and grandfather to make sure she got it right, 24 nations — about a fourth of the invitees — pulled out of the Games in protest of the inclusion of New Zealand. The complaint was that New Zealand had sent a rugby team on tour of South Africa the year previous, a tour that was in violation of the international sports ban against South Africa for its

racial discriminatory apartheid policies. The 24 countries, from Africa and the Caribbean, said if New Zealand stayed, they wouldn't. They packed their bags and left.

To move matters from bad to worse, the team from the Republic of China (Taiwan) was denied entry into Canada because the Canadian government did not diplomatically recognize the Taiwanese government.

FAR LEFT (TOP) / *The Soviet Union's Tatyana Kazankina wins her specialty, the 1,500 meters — a win she would repeat in Moscow. Four days earlier, Kazankina had shaved over a second off the world record in the 800 meters.* (ALLSPORT / DUFFY)

FAR RIGHT (BOTTOM) / *Soviet triple jumper Viktor Saneyev found himself in select company after winning the gold. He is one of four track and field athletes to win the same Olympic championship three or more times.* (ALLSPORT / DUFFY)

LEFT / *The title of "Greatest Athlete" was bestowed on American decathlete Bruce Jenner who set the world record in Montreal.* (ALLSPORT / USOC)

Into this quagmire came ... the Games. Any more serious disruptions, and the movement could have been rendered comatose. But the tide turned just in time. Bickering and contention gave way to healthy racing, wrestling and contesting. Just when the Olympics needed it, brilliance saved the day.

Most brilliant among those athletes from the 88 nations that remained was a 14-year-old Romanian schoolgirl named Nadia Comaneci. Wearing a stoical expression and exhibiting a precision never before seen in women's gymnastics, Nadia became Montreal's signature athlete. Not only did she register the first perfect score, a 10, in official gymnastics competition, she registered the first seven perfect scores. So dominating was her performance that she completely overshadowed Olga Korbut, the darling of Munich, as well as all the other gymnasts.

The brilliance spread to the track,

LEFT / The East German women finished first in 11 of 13 events in Montreal. Kornelia Ender won four of those events, becoming the first woman swimmer to win four gold medals at a single Olympics. (ALLSPORT / DUFFY)

Garderud set a world steeplechase record, Hungary's Miklos Nemeth set a world javelin record, and in the boxing hall, future world professional champions abounded, the list including Sugar Ray Leonard and Leon and Michael Spinks, all of the American team. At that, the best of the group may have been Cuban heavyweight Teofilo Stevenson, the avowed "amateur" who beat his first three opponents in seven minutes and 22 seconds en route to the second of his three consecutive Olympic gold medals.

As the lights went out in its $650 million stadium on Aug. 1, it was agreed that Montreal, after a most unfortunate start, had been blessed with pleasant weather and memorable performances. Post-Montreal forecasts projected that the Olympic movement would, like Montreal's debt, carry on.

LEFT / American swimmer Shirley Babashoff won six silver medals in the 1972 and 1976 Olympics. (ALLSPORT / DUFFY)

where Cuba's Alberto Juantorena, he of the nine-foot stride, became the first man in Olympic history to win at both 800 and 1,500 meters — a double duplicated by Tatyana Kazankina of the Soviet Union in the women's 800 and 1,500. Equally impressive, and unprecedented, was Finland's Lasse Viren in winning the 5,000- and 10,000-meter runs, becoming the first person to pull off that difficult double in two successive Olympics.

World records fell by the droves in Montreal. Eighteen of them by a U.S. men's swimming team that won 12 of 13 gold medals and 10 of 11 silver medals — its dynasty invaded only by Great Britain breaststroker David Wilkie, who got the only non-Yank gold and silver medals. East Germany's women

swimmers were almost the equal of the American men, winning 10 out of 12 women's gold medals as 18-year-old Kornelia Ender won four gold medals — equaling U.S. swimmer John Naber in that department.

The superlatives went on and on. America's Bruce Jenner established personal bests in five of 10 events and set a world record in winning the decathlon. Sweden's Anders

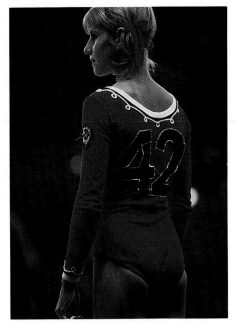

LEFT/ Olga Korbut, the darling of the Munich Games who captured the hearts of the fans as well as three gold medals, was overshadowed by 14-year-old Nadia Comaneci of Romania in Montreal. (ALLSPORT / DUFFY)

nadia comaneci

THE PERFECT "10"

The capacity crowd in the Montreal Forum was still settling into the Olympic arena's brand spanking new 16,000 seats when Nadia Comaneci moved to the uneven parallel bars and went through her first gyration, which was flawless.

Not a lot of people paid attention to the 14-year-old Romanian gymnast with the hard-to-pronounce name. When Olga Korbut, the darling of Munich, took her turn they would, of course, put down their hot dogs and their cold Cokes and get interested. But Korbut, competing with the Soviet team on the same rotation as the Romanian team, was, like them, a spectator right now, waiting for Comaneci to get finished.

Who was to know that over the course of the next 90 seconds, Nadia Comaneci of Romania, all 4-foot-11, 86 pounds of her, would change the face of her sport forever?

She pitched a perfect routine. From start to finish, she never wavered. Her steps and waves and flip-flops were impeccable and her dismount was like an Eagle landing on a lily pad. All the

while, her face wore such an expression of calm and expectation — as if she knew she did what she was told and she better be paid accordingly — that the judges were nonplussed. They had no choice. They went where no gymnastics judge had ever gone before. To the top of the scoring charts. They gave Nadia a 10, the first in Olympic history.

In the annals of Olympic drama, there had been a lot of innovative, show-stopping moves and moments. High jumper Dick Fosbury unveiling his flop in 1968. Hurdler Alvin Kraenzlein going over the hurdles with one leg extended in 1900. Abebe Bikila showing up without shoes for the marathon in 1960. But none had so dramatically grabbed the attention of his or her peers as this 14-year-old schoolgirl had on the night of July 19, 1976, in the Montreal Forum.

She also quickly grabbed the attention of the computer experts who had only days earlier completed the modifications that had produced the Forum's state-of-the-art gymnastics scoreboard. It was a scoreboard capable of doing everything — except register 10's. Since there had never

been a 10 in Olympic gymnastics history, or in any world-class gymnastics competition, why bother? The technicians would end up spending that night re-making their scoreboard so it would be perfect. Like Nadia.

As videotapes played and replayed Nadia's "10" on sportscasts around the world, Comaneci turned into Montreal's most recognizable face and biggest gate attraction. An "indebted" Montreal Olympic Organizing Committee looked on gratefully as Nadia diverted the publicity to something sporting — and also started paying some of the bills.

Outside the Forum for the second night of the women's gymnastics competition, $16 seats were re-selling for $100. The enthusiasm centered around the hope that if Nadia could be a 10 once, she could be a 10 again. Good thinking, as it turned out, since Comaneci was indeed just getting started. After scoring her initial 10 in the team compulsory competition, she came back in the all-around to score three more — two more on bars and another on the beam. The spirit was contagious. The Soviet Union's Nelli

Kim also got a 10, for her vault routine.

A few nights later, in the individual apparatus competition, Comaneci added three more 10's — another two on the uneven bars and one more on the beam. In all, she scored seven 10's en route to three gold medals (all-around, bars and beam), one silver medal (team competition) and one bronze medal (floor exercise).

She had done it all with a comportment that would have pleased the most hardened riverboat gambler. Her face, guarded by dark, brooding eyes, did not change expression, even in victory. Her waves to the adoring crowds were as practiced and controlled as the routines that made them necessary.

It was only in the obligatory press interviews that her youth spilled out. She hugged her favorite doll, an Eskimo, and said she was homesick. And as for her unprecedented 10's? With child-like innocence she said of course she deserved them. Why not? Her routines *had* been perfect.

Heaven knew she had practiced them enough. At the age of six she had been enrolled in a special gymnastics school in Romania, where exuberance for athletics — and for catching the Soviets — was unbounded during the regime of Nikolae Ceausescu. Nadia was "discovered" when she was five and attending kindergarten. As her coach, Bela Karolyi (later to tutor 1984 all-around Olympic champion Mary Lou Retton), relayed over and over again to the world press in Montreal, he first saw Nadia and a friend on the school playground during recess, pretending to be

gymnasts. Karolyi knew the right moves when he saw the right moves, even if they were unrefined. He rushed to the playground — but recess was over and the children had gone back to class. Inside the school Karolyi went from class to class, asking, "Who loves gymnastics here?" Finally he came to Nadia and her friend's class, where they answered back, "We!" "We!"

The next year, Nadia placed 13th in her first competition. Karolyi bought her a doll — the Eskimo — and told her she must never finish 13th again. She didn't. Coming into the Montreal Olympics she was unbeaten in eight years. She had won the junior championship of Romania when she was nine, the national championship when she was 11, and the European championship when she was 13. Maybe the world hadn't heard of Nadia Comaneci when she came to Montreal for the Olympics of 1976. But she had heard of the world. "I am here to do my job," the daughter of a Romanian mechanic announced upon her arrival.

Her skill level may not have been any better — or even the equal of — the well-conditioned, much-practiced gymnasts from the Soviet Union. The team from the USSR included no less than Lyudmilla Tourischeva, the five-time European champion whose reign had been halted by Nadia, and Korbut, the double gold-medal winner four years previous in Munich whose enthusiastic, light demeanor was in sharp contrast to Comaneci's darkness.

But it was her fearlessness that set Nadia apart. She showed no fright as she sailed through her routines, oblivious to any dangers or the possibility of unfortunate consequences. She was equally oblivious to the capacity crowds and the television cameras and all the pressure they might otherwise have generated.

In later years, that fearlessness would manifest itself in other, equally significant, ways. In 1989, just days after her 28th birthday, Romania's most famous Olympian crawled in the

They had no choice. They went where no gymnastics judge had ever gone before. To the top of the scoring charts.

middle of the night on her hands and knees through mud and ice to escape across the border into Hungary. From there she made her way to New York and a life of freedom. π

EDWIN MOSES

THE HUNTED MAN

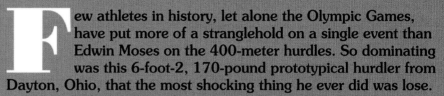

Few athletes in history, let alone the Olympic Games, have put more of a stranglehold on a single event than Edwin Moses on the 400-meter hurdles. So dominating was this 6-foot-2, 170-pound prototypical hurdler from Dayton, Ohio, that the most shocking thing he ever did was lose.

When Andre Phillips of the United States nudged past Moses, his longtime nemesis, and carried El Hadj Dia Ba of Senegal along in his wake, relegating Moses to a bronze medal in the Seoul Games of 1988, Phillips was speechless, as was the world. This was "Man Bites Dog" news. This was the greyhounds at the track finally catching the electronic rabbit.

The defeat was only the third in 11 years for Moses, and a first in the Olympics. Ever since he strode onto the scene with his supposed-to-be-impossible, 13-steps-between-hurdles style in Montreal in 1976, he had been as much an Olympic fixture as the flame.

His victory by eight meters in Montreal in world-record time (47.64) was the biggest margin in Olympic history, even though Moses had barely been introduced to the hurdles the previous spring.

He was a no-show at the next Games in Moscow because of political reasons outside his control, and he had to be content with the realization that his world-record clocking (by now 47.13) was almost two seconds better than the Moscow winner. At Los Angeles in 1984 he came back in a big way, first by reciting the Athlete's Oath and next by beating Danny Harris to the tape.

That win was yet another in a string of 122 straight wins that stretched nearly 10 full years from August 1977 to June 1987, when Harris finally caught his mentor in a meet in Madrid. Three weeks later, in the U.S. National Championships, Moses and Harris met again, and Moses won.

If it seemed this physics major from Morehouse University in Atlanta had nothing left to prove after that, it didn't stop Moses from preparing for the Seoul Games, where, at the age of 33, his quest was to not only become the first three-time gold medalist in his specialty, but the oldest as well.

He ran his fastest Olympic time ever in Seoul, a 47.56, but the 29-year-old Phillips, a man who had chased Moses for nearly 10 years, ran 47.19. In a curious kind of way, it was a fitting tribute to the greatest hurdler of them all. He got the best out of himself, and, ultimately, he also got the best out of those chasing him. π

LEFT / *No other man in the history of hurdling has dominated an event as Edwin Moses has. He did not lose a single race from August 1977 until June 1987. His streak ended at 107 victories by fellow American Danny Harris.* (ALLSPORT / DUFFY)

1980

July 19 - August 13, 1980

81 Nations

5,512 Athletes

21 Sports

USA did not compete

MOSCOW

POLITICAL PAWNS

I t could be said — perhaps facetiously, perhaps not — that the most significant event of the Games of the XXIIth Olympiad was a shooting competition that took place seven months before the Opening Ceremonies were held in Moscow's Lenin Stadium.

When the armies of the Soviet Union answered a "request" on Dec. 28, 1979, and crossed the Russian border into Afghanistan to become an active participant in that country's civil uprising, the Games of Moscow also crossed a border — from international sporting event to the frontier of political statement.

The request for the Red Army's help came ostensibly from Afghanistan leader Babrak Karmal, who had been installed just the day previous, to assist in quelling an uprising of Muslim rebels. The Soviet Union's quick response, and just as quick trigger fingers, sent shock waves throughout the world. In the West, there was outrage. Jimmy Carter, the President of the United States, expressed America's opposition to the Soviets' offensiveness by ordering a U.S. boycott of that summer's Moscow Olympics. He urged every other free nation to do the same. Sixty-one did. And others that didn't — choosing instead to demo-cratically allow their athletes to make up their own minds — wound up sending teams at less than full speed.

Thus Moscow was left with the lowest number of participating nations since the Helsinki Games of 1952. Full or partial teams from 81 nations came. And Afghanistan was one of them.

The Western boycott only further fueled the Soviet Union's desire to use the Moscow Games as a kind of propaganda nonpareil: Welcome to the

TOP / *Releasing the pigeons at the Opening Ceremonies has been a part of Olympic tradition since 1948.* (ALLSPORT / DUFFY)

RIGHT / *Red sky in Moscow's Red Square.* (ALLSPORT / DUFFY)

The Western boycott only further fueled the Soviet Union's desire to use the Moscow Games as a kind of propaganda nonpareil: Welcome to the capital of communism. Prepare to be wowed … and please stay with the tour guide.

capital of communism. Prepare to be wowed ... and please stay with the tour guide.

When a fleet of army jets — spared from the Afghan front — flew over Lenin Stadium in the early morning hours of July 19th to seed the gloomy gray clouds hovering over Moscow, it was the first of many signs that, with a budget of $9 billion, the Soviets weren't about to put their worst foot forward. By the time 100,000 spectators had filed into the stadium later that afternoon to watch Soviet basketball star Sergei Belov light the torch in the Opening Ceremonies, and to watch thousands of soldiers perform card stunts with a precision never before seen in card stunt history, the sun was shining brightly.

Many American athletes, in addition to athletes from other boycotting nations, were upset about being used as political

pawns and not getting their fair shot in the Moscow sun. Their only consolation came when stories began filtering out of the USSR about playing fields that were perhaps not exactly level. Soviet fans were vocal not just to show support for their hometown favorites but to make certain their disdain for the opposition — West or East — was not lost in any

translations.

More disconcerting were the reports of repeated and numerous arguments over questionable officiating, a Moscow art that reached its peak in

TOP / *Vladimir Salnikov won three gold medals, but none was bigger than the 1,500-meter freestyle in which he became the first swimmer to break the 15-minute barrier. Eight years later, in Seoul (pictured), he would win the 1,500 meters again.* (ALLSPORT / M. POWELL)

CENTER / *Barbara Krause cruised to victory while lowering her own world record in the 100-meter freestyle to 54.79. The East German squad repeated its Montreal streak, again winning 11 of 13 events.* (ALLSPORT / DUFFY)

the men's triple jump. As the competition wound to its final round four athletes had emerged as the class of the field. The group included two Soviets, Jaak Uudmae and the legendary but aging Viktor Saneyev, winner of the last three Olympic triple jump gold medals; as well as two "Westerners," João Carlos de Oliveira of Brazil and Ian Campbell of Australia.

Jump after jump in the finals, Oliveira and Campbell landed in the 17-meter area of the sand only to look back and see the official raising a red flag to indicate a foul. Once, when Campbell rushed out of the pit to argue he looked back to see his mark already being raked clean, rendering any subsequent tribunal, fair or otherwise, moot. On Oliveira's fourth jump it appeared he was close, if not beyond, Saneyev's 12-year-old world record of 17.39 meters. But, again, he looked back and saw the "red" flag.

In the end, Oliveira and Campbell received nine red flags in 12 jumps. Uudmae wound up with the gold; Saneyev, in his swan song, won the silver. Oliveira got the bronze medal. Campbell placed fifth.

In the final medal count, the Soviet Union won 195 of the 630 medals awarded and 80 of the 127 gold medals. East Germany won 126 and 47,

respectively. Add in seven other Soviet Bloc nations and the final totals were 321 total medals and 161 gold medals for the Soviets and their allies; 136 and 49 for all other nations.

In light of those totals, it is ironic that the most memorable event of the Moscow Games came in the men's 1,500-meter run, when Steve Ovett and

Sebastian Coe of Great Britain joined with Jurgen Straub of East Germany to produce what was dubbed as the "race of the century." In a stirring last lap, both Coe, the winner, and Straub edged past Ovett as they placed one, two, three, in that order, and snapped Ovett's three-year string of 45 straight wins at that distance.

The boycotted Olympics held in the heart of communism had been curious in more ways than one.

ABOVE / *Oarsmen ready themselves for the start of the double sculls.* (ALLSPORT / DUFFY)

CENTER / *The questionable raising of the red flag stirred controversy in the triple jump. In the end, Soviet Jaak Uudmae won the gold medal over teammate and sentimental favorite Viktor Saneyev, the winner of the last three Olympic triple jump golds.* (ALLSPORT / DUFFY)

Sebastian Coe & Steve Ovett

RACE OF THE CENTURY

When against all odds Mother Nature somehow produces two of the greatest middle-distance runners in history at nearly the same time, there ought to be a law that they race each other. But Sebastian Coe and Steve Ovett continually avoided each other at the height of their considerable powers from the late 70s and early 80s. When one was racing in Lausanne, the other was in Viareggio. When one was in Budapest, the other was in London. And so it went. On those occasions when they did compete in the same city and the same meet, they ran in separate races — say, Coe in the 800 and Ovett in the 1,500.

In this manner, together but separately, Coe and Ovett pushed the middle distances to unheard of speeds, collecting 15 outdoor world records and victory after victory, but rarely against each other. Thus, they robbed the sport of a great spectacle. It finally took the grandeur of the Olympic Games to force them to race each other in 1980 — the Battle of the Great Britons, it was billed —

arguably the greatest showdown ever on the Olympic track.

Coe and Ovett were both from England, and both possessed that rare combination of a sprinter's speed and a cross-country runner's stamina. But there the similarities end. Ovett was big by a miler's standards, 6-foot, 154 pounds; Coe was small and deer-like, at 5-9 3/4, 119 pounds. Coe was affable, open, gentlemanly and bound for a career in politics; Ovett was moody, remote, outspoken and aloof. Not only did Coe and Ovett avoid each other on the track, they avoided each other period. They reportedly were not on speaking terms.

Less than a year apart in age, they arrived on the international track scene at roughly the same time. From 1979 through 1981, Coe set nine world records, at 800 meters, 1,000 meters, 1,500 meters and the mile. From 1978 through 1983, Ovett set six of them, in the 1,500, mile and two-mile, but never while running against his rival. It was a game of dare; see 'em and raise 'em. In 1981, for instance, Coe set a world record in the mile of 3:48.53 in Weltklasse. Two days later, Ovett broke Coe's record in Koblenz with a time of 3:48.40.

Two days later, Coe broke Ovett's record with a run of 3:47.33 in Belgium.

Coe and Ovett met once in 1978 in the 800-meter run at the European Championships. Germany's Olaf Beyer won the race, with Ovett second and Coe third, but this was really before the great British duo had reached their peak form. Ovett had already been an unbeatable force in the mile for two years, but it wasn't until 1979 that Coe really arrived. In a span of 41 days, he set three world records — 3:49.0 for the mile, 3:32.1 for the 1,500 and 1:42.33 for the 800. Meanwhile, Ovett narrowly missed two world records himself that year, running a 3:49.6 mile and a 3:32.2 in the 1,500 meters. Both Coe and Ovett finished the season unbeaten.

In 1980, they carefully avoided each other again. On July 1, Ovett and Coe both competed in the Bislett Games in Oslo, but not against each other. Sebastian and his father/coach Peter had planned to make one record attempt before the Olympics, but with Ovett committed to the mile they decided to try for the world record at 1,000 meters. Coe beat the record by

a half-second, running 2:13.40. Less than an hour later he watched as Ovett broke his world record in the mile by .2, running 3:48.8.

Two weeks later — and just nine days before the Olympics — Ovett returned to Oslo and tied Coe's record of 3:32.1 at 1,500 meters.

The stage was set for Moscow. Coe and Ovett would finally meet in what was billed as the race(s) of the century. This was no race against the clock; it was man against man.

The American-led boycott of the 1980 Moscow Olympics drained the Games of many top athletes, but it did nothing to diminish the luster of the 800 and the 1,500, where the Battle of Britons would take place. Everyone else in those races seemed to be mere extras on the set.

The 800 was first, and as is often the case in Olympic races, the pace was slow and cautious. A tight pack of runners cruised the first lap in a pedestrian 54.8 seconds. Coe, who had been jostled at the start and dropped to the back of the pack out of harm's way, was running wide, in seventh place, while Ovett was badly boxed in the inside lane, surrounded on all sides by bodies. This was Coe's opportunity to make a sustained drive for home — there was no way Ovett could escape to give chase — but Coe stayed where he was. It was a lost opportunity and a tactical error he would always regret.

Russia's Nikolai Kirov made the first move. He accelerated down the backstretch, followed by Brazil's Agberto Guimaraes. Ovett shoved, pushed and forearmed his way out of the box and pursued Kirov, as the pack began to string out, still Coe did not make a decisive move. Ovett took the lead and was pulling away as they swept out of the last turn. Coe had moved to fourth by now, but he trailed by 10 meters. He had moved too late. He caught the fading Guimaraes and then Kirov, but Ovett, running the last lap in 50 seconds flat, was a clear winner with a time of 1:45.4, a half-second ahead of Coe.

"I threw it away over the last lap," said Coe. He bravely faced the press and told them, "I chose this day of all days to run the worst race of my life. I cannot even explain why … The

1,500 … is going to be the race of my life. I must win it."

That seemed much to ask. Coe had concentrated on the 800 so far in his career. The Olympic final was only his eighth 1,500-meter race in four years, and he had never met Ovett at that distance. Ovett, on the other hand, had won a record 45 consecutive 1,500/mile races since 1977.

"Losing the 800 was a terrible disappointment," said Coe. "If I hadn't had the 1,500 coming up, I'd have been tortured with recriminations. But the 1,500 was there. There was no choice. I had to make myself ready for it."

This time Coe was determined to be more aggressive and to place

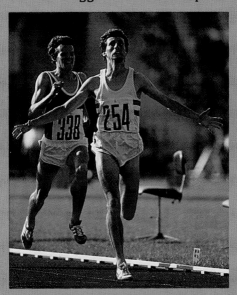

himself in a better position from which to strike. Again, the 1,500, like the 800, was a cautious affair, but this time Coe ran from the front. Germany's Jurgen Straub and Coe covered the first lap in a tedious 61.6, with Ovett two meters back in sixth.

As they neared 800 meters, Straub was still in the lead, with Coe on his shoulder. Now Ovett moved to Coe's shoulder. "Seb was up in a controlling position," Peter said. "I felt a fair race was on."

With a little more than 700 meters to go, Straub accelerated, and Coe and Ovett tucked in behind him. It was just what Coe wanted. "When Jurgen nailed his sail to the mast it allowed me to do what I do best," said Coe. "I found a rhythm, a lane of my own."

Looking on, Peter also was elated

with the Straub's move. "No one in the world can sustain that speed as Seb can," he said.

They covered the next lap in 54.1. One lap to go. Who would move first and when? 250 meters to go, then 200 meters, and still no one made a move. Straub was four meters ahead of Coe and six ahead of Ovett. Heading into the last turn, Coe swung wide and passed him. As the trio moved into the home stretch together, Ovett was running on Coe's shoulder in perfect striking position, but Coe had left himself another gear. He accelerated again and began to pull away. Ovett pressed to go faster, pulled even with Straub and then faltered. Coe, covering the last 800 in 1:48.5 and the last 400 in 52.1, finished with a time of 3:38.4, .4 ahead of Straub and .6 ahead of Ovett. When he reached the finish line, Coe spread his arms wide as if to receive victory. His face broke into a dramatic grimace that was a mixture of disbelief, joy and relief. He went to his knees and touched his head to the track, then bounced up and sidestepped a security guard to take a victory lap.

"I was so high after the 800 that I couldn't get up again," said Ovett.

Afterward, Coe and Ovett discussed their mutual relief and agreed to have a couple of drinks together. But they would continue to dodge each other on the track in coming years. They met again in the 1984 Olympics, but Ovett was struggling with his health at the time and it was not the matchup it had been in '80. Coe repeated his Moscow performance — a silver in the 800 and a gold and Olympic record in the 1,500, but nothing would top his showdown with Ovett in Moscow. When someone asked Coe why he had looked up at the sky while on the medal stand following the Moscow 1,500, he said, "Perhaps somebody, somewhere, loves me after all." π

RIGHT / *First introduced as an Olympic event in 1980, women's field hockey has typically been dominated by Commonwealth nations. In 1984, the American squad took the bronze, but the retirement of all but three of its members left a young team to defend its 1984 success. Above, the Americans managed a tie, 2-2, against Great Britain in Seoul.*
(ALLSPORT / STICKLAND)

FIELD

HOCKEY

1984

Los Angeles 1984 Olympic Games

July 28 - August 12, 1984

140 Nations

7,078 Athletes

21 Sports

83 USA golds

LOS ANGELES

In serious need of resuscitation in 1984, the Olympic Games came to Los Angeles and proceeded to produce a Hollywood ending.

The Olympic movement was staggering. The downward spiral began in 1968 with racial protests on the Mexico City victory peristyles. It continued in 1972 in Munich the day nine Israeli athletes were murdered by Palestinian terrorists. It carried on in 1976 when Montreal was plagued first by an African boycott and then by record debts. It got worse in 1980 when more than half of the world's IOC-recognized countries elected not to participate in Moscow — and Moscow spent a record $9 billion to host the 81 nations that did come.

Into this mix came L.A., the city of Angels but also the city supposedly without a heart; the city that defied definition; the city that wore shades, yawned at its movie stars and wouldn't ask for its own autograph; the city of smog, urban racial tension and four-hour freeway commutes; and the city that voted by almost a 5-to-1 margin *not* to use any local taxes to put on the Olympic Games.

No one knew quite what to make of this marriage the IOC and the LAOOC (Los Angeles Olympic Organizing Committee) had put together.

But as is often the case with impossible challenges, they tend to attract the attention of people wanting to prove that they aren't impossible. Out of this impossible challenge came just the U-turn the Olympics was looking for. While the

911 HOLLYWOOD STYLE

TOP / *Los Angeles lights up for the Closing Ceremonies.* (ALLSPORT)

RIGHT / *It was a banner day for the American 4x100-meter freestyle relay team. The foursome — Christopher Cavanaugh, Michael Heath, Matt Biondi and Rowdy Gaines — set a world record of 3:19.03 and added yet another gold to America's poolside haul of 21 gold medals in swimming.* (ALLSPORT)

Los Angeles did what it does best. It turned the Olympics into a party. The world came and did lunch. It was just the U-turn the Olympics was looking for.

Games of the XXIIIth Olympiad couldn't be called the most competitive in the modern era — indeed, the domination of Team U.S.A. bordered on shameless — and while they couldn't be called free of social conflict either — the Soviet Union and 13 other Soviet Bloc nations were conspicuous only by their boycott — they could be called the most hassle-free, incident-free and debt-free Games since the Olympic movement was reborn.

Los Angeles did what it does best. It turned the Olympics into a party. The world came and they did lunch. A record 7,078 athletes from 140 nations participated in 16 days of glory and profit and almost no smog. The freeways — improbably blessed for a fortnight by cooperative locals who suspended as much of their business travel as possible and who told their relatives from Wisconsin to wait until later to visit Disneyland — ran like NASA liftoffs. Inner-city racial tension went from a simmer to capitalistic melting-pot as thousands of homes within walking-distance of the L.A. Memorial Coliseum turned their yards into parking lots.

The Games operated on a $500 million budget — about a 20th of

TOP / *Running in what would become the fastest Olympic 5,000-meter final, Said Aouita of Morocco (622) sprinted past Markus Riffel of Switzerland to a 13:05.59 victory. That time was still more than four seconds off the world record held by David Moorcroft of Great Britain.* (ALLSPORT)

ABOVE / *American Evelyn Ashford's smooth strides carried her to an Olympic gold and the Olympic record in the 100 meters.* (ALLSPORT / DUFFY)

LEFT / *Coming out of retirement, America's Valerie Brisco-Hooks became the first woman to win the 200/400-meter double. Brisco returned to the Olympic track four years later in Seoul (pictured) to run the third leg in the 4x400-meter relay. The U.S. took the silver.* (ALLSPORT / M. POWELL)

Moscow's bottom line — and thanks in large part to $140 million in corporate sponsorships and $225 million in television rights fees, realized a profit of some $225 million. Peter Ueberroth, the organizing committee's leader, became so revered that Major League baseball, always on the look for a miracle, asked him to be its next commissioner.

Athletes from around the world were honored. Great Britain's Sebastian Coe won the last of his Olympic gold medals in the 1,500-meter run, setting an Olympic record in the process; 37-year-old Portugal marathoner Carlos Lopes won one for the old guys, West German swimmer Michael (The Albatross) Gross was indomitable, Morocco got its first-ever woman's medal (Nawal El Moutawakel in the 400-meter hurdles) and first-ever men's gold medal (Said Aouita in the 5,000-meter run), and the first gold medal of the Games, won by Chinese shooter Xu Haifong, set off dancing in the streets of Beijing as China resumed Olympic participation for the first time since 1952.

But mostly the names of L.A.'s Games were American. Of the 514 medals awarded, over a third (174) went to U.S. athletes. And in the gold medal category, more than half (83) of the 223 awarded were accompanied by the playing of the Star Spangled Banner.

Motivated by home turf, home crowds, California sunshine, and fueled by energy built up over eight long years after being boycotted out of Moscow in 1980, America shined. Carl Lewis became the first man to win four gold track and field medals since Jesse Owens, capturing, like Owens, the 100- and 200-meter sprints, the long jump, and anchoring the U.S. men's 4x100-meter relay team. Michael Jordan and Cheryl Miller led the last of America's great all-

amateur basketball teams to easy gold-medal triumphs. In winning the all-around, Mary Lou Retton won America's first Olympic women's individual gymnastics gold medal. Valerie Brisco-Hooks became the first woman Olympian to win at 200 and 400 meters. The list went on and on. The boxing team won nine of the 12 gold medals awarded, and that didn't include future heavyweight world champion Evander Holyfield who was disqualified for a late knockout punch and had to settle for a bronze medal. The U.S. swimmers won 21 of 34 gold medals.

Still, the world didn't seem to mind, at least not the world that attended. The '84 Olympics ended with a raucous Closing Ceremonies that saw the traditional mingling of the athletes turn into something approaching an all-night beach bash. The last memory of L.A. is of the Australians unfurling their huge national banner on the grass floor of the

Coliseum and using it as a trampoline to bounce the world's athletes to the sky while the public address announcer bellowed "PLEASE LEAVE THE COLISEUM." There are worse ways to end the Games.

TOP / *Setting his second world record and capturing his second gold medal, Germany's Michael Gross gets off to a quick start in the 100-meter butterfly.* (ALLSPORT)

ABOVE / *The world record-holder in the 100- and 200-meter butterfly races, American Mary T. Meagher dominated the competition and seized gold in both events.* (ALLSPORT / DUFFY)

OPPOSITE / *Considered by many to be the greatest diver in history, American Greg Louganis was the first person in 56 years to win both diving events, a feat he repeated in 1988.* (ALLSPORT)

TOP (LEFT) / *Peter Vidmar became the first American to win an individual gold in men's gymnastics in 52 years.* (ALLSPORT / S. POWELL)

TOP (MIDDLE) / *Twenty-seven-year old Koji Gushiken of Japan came from behind to nip leaders Peter Vidmar and Li Ning in the battle for the all-around title.* (ALLSPORT / S. POWELL)

TOP (RIGHT) / *Mary Lou Retton jumps for joy in the floor exercise event, but it was her perfect vault that gave the American cause to celebrate. She edged Ecaterina Szabo of Romania, 79.175 to 79.125, to capture the coveted all-around title.* (ALLSPORT / S. POWELL)

LEFT / *She was the youngest person to ever win a track and field gold medal in the Olympics. The event was the high jump, the place Munich, and the athlete 16-year-old Ulrike Meyfarth who stood 6 feet and 1/2 inches. Twelve years later, at 6 feet 2 inches, the West German captured her second gold with an Olympic record leap of 6-7 1/2.* (ALLSPORT / DUFFY)

ABOVE / *Joan Benoit raises the flag in victory after becoming the first winner of the women's marathon.* (ALLSPORT / DUFFY)

TOP / *After nearly five hours of cycling, Alexi Grewal celebrates his narrow victory in the 190.2-kilometer road race.* (ALLSPORT)

MIDDLE / *Nelson Vails collects himself — and later the silver medal — in cycling's glamour event, the 1,000-meter sprint, won by fellow American Mark Gorski.* (ALLSPORT / BROUILLET)

BOTTOM / *Speed is essential in the long jump and no one has more than American Carl Lewis as he approaches the long jump. His victory in the long jump gave Lewis his second gold as he proceeded to match Jesse Owen's Olympic legacy.* (ALLSPORT)

peter vidmar

No Experience Necessary

He was wearing a satin blue jacket that said D-O-D-G-E-R-S across the front as he walked into the girls gym at the Culver City Junior High School. His mother, Doris, was with him, clutching in her hand a newspaper article that had run two nights previous in the *Santa Monica Evening Outlook*.

"Future Gymnasts Get Aid in Culver," the article was headlined, and it went on to explain that the Culver City Dept. of Parks & Recreation, in cooperation with Coach Makoto Sakomoto, would be holding tryouts that Saturday at the junior high to select five boys, aged 10-13, to participate in an experimental gymnastics program to "develop future Olympic champions ... No experience necessary."

Today was Saturday and Doris Vidmar and her 11-year-old son, Peter, stood in the middle of the gym, wondering if they were in the right place. Coach Sakomoto, barely taller than the 4-foot-9, 69-pound tow-headed youngster he was greeting, told them they were. As the next

dozen years would reveal, he knew what he was talking about.

Mako Sakomoto had been a champion gymnast himself — seven times a U.S. national champion and a three-time Olympian. At 27, he had barely retired from active competition after the 1972 Munich Games. Now he wanted to find a protege, someone he could teach everything he knew, and more; someone who could win an Olympic gold medal.

That Saturday in the gym in the Los Angeles suburbs, he had a crowd of 20 volunteers standing in front of him.

Of the five he chose, Peter was his first selection. The following weekend, the two of them got to work.

For the next dozen years, without exception, they would remain in business — the coach and the athlete, the mentor and the student, the teacher and the pupil. Peter took a 10-day break once and that was as extensive as the time-off went. Day and night they worked, and night and day. Inseparable. Even when Peter went to college, at UCLA, Coach Mako went along with him — as a UCLA assistant coach.

The training was unconventional,

even by gymnastics' unconventional standards. Coach Mako had his own blueprint, and it became Peter's blueprint as well.

Sometimes the coaches' techniques seemed strange to Peter. Such as not entering him in any competitions for the first two years of his training. Instead, the coach told Peter, as well as his other proteges, to imagine that they were *always* in competition. Every time they did a routine they should do it as if there were judges sitting alongside the mat. Without fail they were required to smile after their dismounts and nod and smile at the imaginary panel of judges.

The technique didn't seem nearly as strange when Peter and the rest of the Culver City Gymnastics Club finally did enter competitions, and enjoyed resounding success.

The hardest test for Peter came six years into his training, after the 1978 national championships, when, in only the 11th competition of his life, he finished with the meet's 13th best all-around score. Since the low 14 made the national team, he was now a card-carrying member of the United States Gymnastics Team.

Except for one problem: Coach

Mako told him to decline membership.

The coach said another year sweating it out in the Culver City gym would be more productive than traveling around the world competing against the best gymnasts from other nations. Peter balked, but he told the U. S. Gymnastics Federation no thanks. In the history of the USGF, it was the first time anyone had ever turned down a spot on the team.

With Vidmar, Sakamoto not only knew he had a gymnast with world-class potential on his hands, he also knew just how fragile that kind of potential could be. He didn't want him jumping too early into international competition, only to have his expectations, and his confidence, dashed. The coach wasn't even disappointed when the United States boycotted the 1980 Olympic Games in Moscow. He didn't think the 19-year-old Vidmar was quite ready for an Olympic experience just yet. Four years after Moscow the Olympics would come to Los Angeles, the hometown of the Culver City Gymnastics Club. That would be much better timing.

When those '84 Games finally did arrive, with the gymnastics venue situated in Pauley Pavilion on the UCLA campus, Vidmar and Sakamoto were as ready as they'd ever be. The home-gym advantage was in place, along with a dozen years of getting ready.

Not only were Vidmar and Sakamoto primed, so was the entire U.S. men's gymnastics team. As the team competition opened the meet, the U.S. men were suddenly a factor to be reckoned with.

This was not normal. For almost a century, American men gymnasts had been the doormat for the world. With the exception of the 1904 Olympics in St. Louis, where almost no foreigners entered the meet, U.S. Olympic glory had been limited, to say the least. A grand total of nine medals, with just three gold, had been won in the 88 Olympic years that preceded the Los Angeles Games. Only one U.S. men's team — the 1932 team with a silver — had ever won a team medal.

Japan, on the other hand, had won five of the last six Olympic team gold medals, and no doubt would have made it six for six had it not boycotted the 1980 Games in Moscow.

Japan was back and ready to resume where it left off in Los Angeles. But with Vidmar leading the way, and with Tim Daggett, Mitch Gaylord, Bart Conner and James Hartung following close behind, the team race quickly slipped out of Japan's control. Instead, the teams from the United States and China — a nation with a rich gymnastics history that had rejoined

the Olympic family after a long layoff — raced well to the front. They battled routine for routine until the U.S. clinched the team title when Daggett and Vidmar, best friends and UCLA teammates, came through with scores of 10.0 and 9.95, respectively, on the horizontal bar, the last U.S. routine.

The team triumph quickly thrust Vidmar and the rest of the U.S. men into a national spotlight they'd never before experienced. Everyone, it seemed, wanted to see their gold medals.

But for Vidmar and Coach Mako — by now an assistant coach with the U.S. team — more work remained. Gymnastics, in its truest form, is an individual sport, and, in that way, their 12-year quest was just beginning as the finals for the all-around and the individual apparatus competitions took center stage after the team medals had been distributed.

To say Vidmar came close in the all-around is to do injustice to the razor-thin margin that decided the

1984 competition. He came into his last event needing a score of 9.95 or higher to win the title over Koji Gushiken, a 27-year-old Japanese gymnast who had patiently waited through the Moscow boycott, who had already completed his routines and totaled a score of 118.700, the highest in Olympic history. A 9.95 or a 10 would give Vidmar yet another highest-in-Olympic-history score, not to mention the gold medal. He was well on his way, but on his dismount, with the Olympic championship hanging in the balance, he hit the mat a fraction harder than he wanted to, and hopped forward an inch. The .05 it cost him lowered his bars score to 9.9 and his grand total to 118.675 — twenty-five thousandths of a point from tying Gushiken.

The next night during the individual event finals, Vidmar placed seventh in floor exercise and fourth on rings and the horizontal bar. That he was among the best in the world was now beyond question.

Then came the pommel horse, traditionally his best event — and his last chance for a gold medal. He mounted the horse confidently and proceeded to produce the routine of his life, shifting and swinging from side to side effortlessly, making it look easy, making it look like he was five miles away, in the Culver City Junior High girls gym, going through another interminable workout.

His dismount was without waver. The judges didn't applaud. They did better than that. They gave him 10's across the board — a perfect score for a perfect routine.

When they awarded him his gold medal, Peter Vidmar stood at attention and waited until the national anthem had been played. Then, with the Pauley Pavilion capacity crowd still on its feet and watching his every move, he took it off his neck and walked across the gym — where he gave it to Coach Mako. π

ABOVE / *Bart Conner (left) and coach Mako Sakomoto (right) congratulate Peter Vidmar. Vidmar was so indebted to his coach he later presented him with his gold medal.*
(ALLSPORT)

RIGHT / *The women's 3,000-meter race in Los Angeles will be remembered for reasons other than its Olympic debut. American Mary Decker (far left) was a pre-race favorite; however, after tangling feet with the bare-footed Zola Budd of Great Britain, Decker's hope of Olympic gold ended with a crash.*
(Allsport)

3 , 0 0 0

METERS

1988

September 17 - October 2, 1988
160 Nations
9,421 Athletes
23 Sports
36 USA golds

SEOUL

Peace and unity came to the Olympic movement in a most unexpected place in 1988. The Olympic Games came to the Land of the Morning Calm and found ... calm.

Not that there weren't worries as the first virtually boycott-free Olympics since 1964 approached. Less than 50 miles to the north of Seoul, North Korea was in a boycott stance, and since the two Koreas had been observing an uneasy peace for almost 40 years, the threat of some kind of military intervention was ever-present. Too, there was the threat of riots from within, a potential heightened in the months leading up to the Games by increased student unrest and demonstrations that led to numerous clashes with South Korean police.

But even if history and geography suggested otherwise, the Games of '88 went off without political statements or protests. They wound up being the most secure Games in history, as well as the most "secured." Military strength was ever-present. Spectators and competitors alike were required to enter venues through metal detectors. Security personnel routinely used mirrors to check underneath cars and buses for bombs and/or stowaways; and machine-gun toting policemen, a force numbering 120,000, stood at the ready 24 hours a day. Clearly, the city of Seoul hadn't spent its Olympic budget of $3.1 billion just to have its Games disrupted by party-crashers.

International skeptics who thought the much-publicized $3.1 billion budget was an exaggeration soon became believers once they arrived in the Korean capital and saw firsthand how it's possible to spend more than three thousand million

TOP / *Everyone seemed happy that for the first time in 16 years the Olympics were not boycotted by any group of nations.* (ALLSPORT / VANDYSTADT)

RIGHT / *A star of the Seoul Games, American Florence Griffith-Joyner looks for divine assistance in the 4x400-meter relay.* (ALLSPORT / VANDYSTADT)

REST SECURED

Even if history and geography suggested otherwise, the Games of '88 went off without political statements or protests. They wound up being the most secure Games in history. Clearly, the city of Seoul hadn't spent its budget of $3.1 billion just to have its Games disrupted by party-crashers.

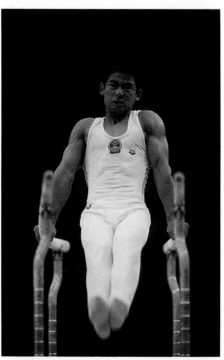

dollars on an Olympics. The South Koreans did not skimp. They built two stunning new sports parks, featuring no less than 11 completely new specialty arenas — fencing, for instance, had a custom-designed hall, as did gymnastics, judo and any number of other sports — and the areas around the parks were transformed into city reconstruction projects. The Yan River, polluted to the point of non-use six years previous, was cleaned up to beautifully handle the rowing and wind-surfing events.

Into this Olympic Taj Mahal came a record 160 nations — 38 more than ever before — to compete in a record 23 sports. Never before, in all of Olympic history, had a more complex, more level, playing field been established. And never before did so many nations split up the

ABOVE / *Tied up in knots: Bronze medalist Michael Swain was one of two American success stories in judo.* (ALLSPORT / M. POWELL)

TOP / *Ben Johnson's world-record run of 9.79 was nullified and he was banned after his post-race test detected steroids.* (ALLSPORT / VANDYSTADT)

MIDDLE / *Olympic Spirit: Gymnast Zhiqiang Xu of China struggles for composure.* (ALLSPORT / RONDEAU)

BOTTOM / *Young Turk: Turkey's 60 kg Niam Suleymangolu set world records in both the clean and jerk and the snatch (pictured).* (ALLSPORT / VANDYSTADT)

spoils.

It wasn't an easy assignment for any one athlete to single-handedly upstage such a massive collection of athletes, but Canada's Ben Johnson proved up to the task. The Jamaican-born sprinter first set the Games buzzing by lowering the world record in the 100-meter dash from 9.83 to 9.79 — a speed so mind-boggling it seemed super human. As urine samples would prove the next day, when traces of performance-enhancing steroids were found in Johnson's specimen, it *was* super human. Johnson was summarily dismissed from the Seoul Games by the IOC and suspended from international competition by the International Amateur Athletic Federation (IAAF) for the next two years.

There was another performance in Seoul equally as stunning. That came from U.S. sprinter Florence Griffith Joyner — Flo-Jo to the world — who raced to three gold medals and one silver medal in a one-woman show not seen since the days of Fanny Blankers-Koen. Besides an-choring the winning 4x100-meter relay team from the United States, Flo-Jo won the women's 100-meter final in 10.54 — not far off the world record 10.49 she'd set at the U.S. trials; and the 200-meter final in a world record 21.34. Her 100 time would have won the men's final in Melbourne in 1956.

Overshadowed by Johnson and Flo-Jo was a track meet that set 29 Olympic records and four world records and featured two more gold medals by Carl Lewis (Johnson's vacated 100 title and the long jump), another two from Flo-Jo's sister-in-law, Jackie Joyner-Kersee, in the heptathlon and long jump, and an eye-popping performance by Kenya in the distance events. Out of six races 3,000 meters and beyond, Kenyan runners won seven medals, with three golds, two silvers and one bronze.

Other Seoul highlights included diver Greg Louganis' springboard/platform double, Soviet gymnasts Vladimir Artemov and Elena Shoushounova, with four gold medals each; outstanding individual swimming performances by East Germany's Kristin Otto (six golds), America's Matt Biondi (five golds, a silver

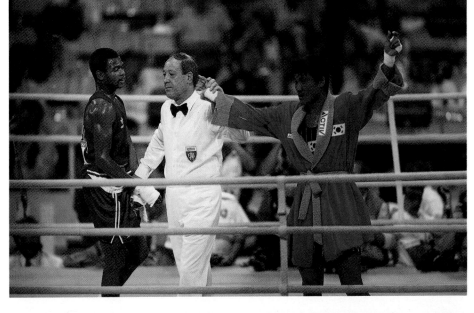

and a bronze) and California teenager Janet Evans (three golds); and, in boxing, a Most Outstanding Boxing award for U.S. light heavyweight Roy Jones, who inexplicably lost the gold medal to Korean Park Si-hun.

Seoul would mark the last grand stand for East Germany, a team that would be absorbed into a united Germany four years hence in Barcelona. The East Germans won 37 gold medals and 102 medals overall in Korea, totals that ranked behind only the Soviet Union's 55 golds out of 132. The United States won 36 gold medals and 94 overall.

The host Koreans wound up sixth in the medals race, with 12 golds and 33 overall. By dominating table tennis (new to the Olympics in 1988), archery and team handball, they easily won the Asian bragging rights, outdistancing China's 28 medals and Japan's 14.

All of the above was broadcast to the world like never before. The National Broadcasting Company paid $300 million alone for the rights to send the Games back to America — prepared to

broadcast anything that happened in Seoul, peaceful or not. As it turned out, NBC sent back just sports — and 120,000 Korean policemen never had it so good.

LEFT / *Power play: Guard Cynthia Cooper of Team USA gave the Soviets a lesson in the game of hoops. Later, Cooper gave her Mom, who was celebrating her birthday in Seoul, the perfect present — her gold medal.* (ALLSPORT / PATRONITE)

TOP / *Disillusioned: Questionable judging, protests, and appeals marred the boxing competition in Seoul. American Roy Jones became the No. 1 victim when Park Si-hun of Korea was awarded the gold in a shocking 3-2 decision.* (ALLSPORT / MORTIMORE)

BOTTOM / *Soviet Adlan Varaev probably never liked Mondays; he likes them less now. American Kevin Monday defeated Varaev for the gold in the 74 kg division of freestyle wrestling.* (ALLSPORT / M. POWELL)

CLOCKWISE (LEFT TO RIGHT) / *Phoebe Mills became the first female gymnast to win a medal in a full-field Olympics for the United States.* (ALLSPORT / STICKLAND)

Janet Evans spits out another gold in Seoul. The American teenager captured golds in all three of her races — the 400-meter and 800-meter freestyle and the 400-meter individual medley. (ALLSPORT / BRUTY)

Americans Matt Cetlinski, Doug Gjertsen and Troy Dalbey celebrate as Matt Biondi comes from behind to post a world-record time of 7:12.51 in the 4x200-meter freestyle relay. (ALLSPORT / DUFFY)

Behind the Iron Curtain: Winner of three gold medals, including the all-around title, Vladimir Artemov would be the last of a dynasty to compete under the USSR flag. (ALLSPORT / RONDEAU)

ABOVE / *Throwing the hammer further than anyone has ever thrown it in Olympic history, Serguei Litvinov led a Soviet sweep of the event in Seoul.* (ALLSPORT / DUFFY)

RIGHT / *Bob Partie kills the ball against rival USSR. The Americans went undefeated for the gold in 1988.* (ALLSPORT / PATRONITE)

LEFT / *With a leap of faith, American high jumper Hollis Conway was able to claim the silver in Seoul.* (ALLSPORT / M. POWELL)

RIGHT / *Pitching ace Jim Abbott demonstrated why baseball is America's favorite pastime. After Seoul, baseball would be raised from a demonstration to a full-medal sport.* (ALLSPORT / PATRONITE)

CARL LEWIS

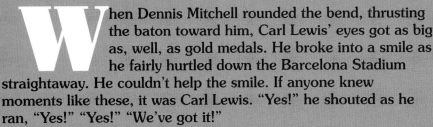

STAYING POWER

When Dennis Mitchell rounded the bend, thrusting the baton toward him, Carl Lewis' eyes got as big as, well, as gold medals. He broke into a smile as he fairly hurtled down the Barcelona Stadium straightaway. He couldn't help the smile. If anyone knew moments like these, it was Carl Lewis. "Yes!" he shouted as he ran, "Yes!" "Yes!" "We've got it!"

He was right of course. No sooner did he finish the anchor leg for the United States team in the men's 4x100-meter relay than the scoreboard revealed a world record of 37.40. Lewis was clocked at 8.8 seconds, unofficially the fastest 100-meter leg ever run. As if to validate the economy of their effort, Lewis, Mitchell, Mike Marsh and Leroy Burrell fairly loped around the track in their synchronized victory lap.

Once again, Carl Lewis had seized an Olympic moment and wrung from it everything possible. Has anyone ever graced the stage so well? Has anyone ever had a better sense of quadrennial timing?

Barcelona was the same as Seoul four years previous, and Los Angeles four years before that. There was always suspense, there was always questioning, and there was always triumph.

In Los Angeles, when he was brash and 23, he drew the wrath of the crowd when he retired early from the long jump, content to win instead of pursuing a world record. The crowd couldn't understand such seeming nonchalance. But five days later, when he joined Jesse Owens as the only men to win four track and field gold medals, they saluted his position in history.

In Seoul, when he was the fastest man in the world, he was suddenly just another bridesmaid after Ben Johnson trounced him in their "race of the century." But again, just days later, it was Lewis who was cheered, not only for winning because Johnson was disqualified for using steroids, but for running clean.

In Barcelona, he was a 31-year-old in decline. The previous year Mike Powell surpassed him to become the world's best long jumper and the month previous he failed to make the U.S. Olympic Team in the individual sprints.

But in a Barcelona showdown with Powell, he prevailed for his third consecutive long jump gold medal, and then, after an injury took Mark Witherspoon off the 4x100-meter team, he joined the gang of four to make a little more history.

Few in the stadium on Montjuic that early August day would forget the sight of Carl Lewis, his head high, his face beaming, running to the tape. He had what it took. They knew it. And so did he. π

LEFT / *After testing positive for an illegal substance by IOC officials, Canadian Ben Johnson was stripped of his 100-meter world record and gold medal, which was awarded to American Carl Lewis.* (ALLSPORT / PATRONITE)

greg barton

Photo Finish

There have been any number of close, exciting finishes in the history of the Olympic Games. Conclusions seemingly too tight to call. Outrageously narrow outcomes.

There was Eddie Tolan's two-inch victory over Ralph Metcalfe in the 100 meter dash in 1932. There was Abebe Bikila's stretch run to beat Rhadi Ben Abdesselem for the 1960 marathon. There was George Rhoden of Jamaica's lunge at the tap for an 18-inch victory over teammate Herb McKenley in the 400 meters in 1952.

Eternities, by comparison.

The closest race in the history of the Olympic Games, or, as Bud Greenspan said in the film documentary he produced on the subject, "the closest race in the history of anything," took place on Oct. 10, 1988 on the Han River outside Seoul, South Korea. The occasion was the finals of the 1,000-meter kayak singles: A race that featured a finish so close, so tight, so narrow, so fine, that the photo-finish camera couldn't tell who won, and it was shooting at 10,000th of a second.

After a furious, back-and-forth, ebb-and-flow, water-churning run down the river, the boats of Greg Barton, an American, and Grant Davies, an Australian, converged at the finish line at seemingly the same mili-second. Those watching from the stands swiveled their heads almost as one to the electronic scoreboard next to the dock. They would need help with this one.

The scoreboard was slow to respond, but almost immediately, on the big-screen video board next to the scoreboard, a live picture was flashed of Barton in his shell, with the caption "Gold Medal" at the bottom of the screen. It seemed a historic moment had arrived. The first-ever Olympic gold medal for the United States in kayaking.

But it was a fleeting historic moment.

As Barton pulled his boat out of the water and got into another shell, this time in the company of his doubles partner Norm Bellingham, the results board came to life. It listed Davies as the official winner and Barton — whose picture was now vanishing from the video board — second. Suddenly the Aussies in the crowd were bursting into cheers as the Americans, by now well into their celebration, grew quiet.

Barton looked at the results board briefly and didn't change expression as he and Bellingham paddled around the finishing area. The 1,000-meter pairs race was to begin shortly and there was no time for standing around or looking back. A year ago, when the singles and pairs were also raced back-to-back at the 1987 world championships in Germany, Barton won the singles, becoming a world champion for the second time, and then spent too much time out of the water before joining Bellingham for the pairs final. They finished fourth and Barton blamed himself. At the Olympics, he was determined not to have a repeat.

As Barton and Bellingham continued to paddle, the scoreboards changed again. This time both screens went blank.

Sufficiently warmed down, and up, Barton left Bellingham and got out of the water to change into his full U.S.A. uniform for the medals' ceremony. By

now he had reconciled himself to the fact that the gold medal that seemed to be his for about seven seconds had turned into silver. That was the worst case scenario and he was prepared to accept it. To be honest, he wasn't sure who won either.

Gold or silver, Barton wasn't about to complain. When you'd been where he'd been and done what he'd done, all because of a 17-foot, 26-pound kayak, being an ingrate wasn't part of the program. Besides, he knew what adversity was, and this didn't qualify. He was born with clubfeet. *That* was adversity. When the doctors tried to correct the situation and fused the bones in both of his feet they didn't do a very good job of it and he never had enjoyed a full range of motion. He had to wear special orthopedic shoes.

It was one of the things that attracted him to kayaking — his feet could more or less come along for the ride. For more than a decade now he had attacked the sport of flatwater kayaking with all his passion. He had integrated it with his schooling at the University of Michigan, where he graduated summa cum laude with a engineering degree, and, after that, with the job he had taken with an engineering firm in Irvine, Calif. His employers at Fluor-Daniel were understanding and gave him enough time off for training, but without pay. Barton was 28 years old by the time Seoul rolled around, and was yet to collect a full year's salary.

Four years before, in the Los Angeles Games of 1984, he had finished third in the 1,000, a second and a half behind Alan Thompson of New Zealand and a half-second behind Milan Janic of Yugoslavia. Upon receiving his bronze medal he proclaimed it "the best day of my life,"

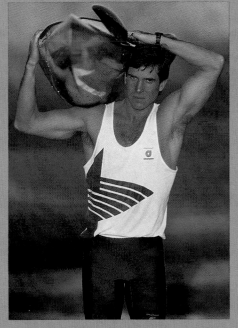

and decided then and there to train another four years with Seoul's Han River in his sights. In 1985, he won his first world championship and in 1987, his second. He had not come to Korea an unknown or unmarked man.

He liked his chances as the nine shells had lined up that morning for the 1,000-meter final. A 15-knot wind was blowing in their faces and Barton, whose forte was endurance more than raw speed, liked headwinds immensely. He settled into third position as the race began, the pace being dictated by Ferenc Csipses of Hungary. Davies, in the far lane across from Bart-on, settled into the second position.

Just past halfway, the Hungarian, a victim of his impatience, started to fade, as did the other shells, if ever so slightly. In a 1,000-meter flatwater kayak race, nothing is done by leaps and bounds.

Now it was just the American and the Australian.

Or, rather, the Australian and the American.

As Barton wondered, the scoreboard suddenly sprang to life for the third time — and reversed itself again.

This time the American was declared the winner ... by five-thousandths of a second. Metric translation: less than one centimeter. English translation: less than a quarter of an inch. Layman's translation: about the width of a credit card.

As Barton walked to the medal stand he still wasn't sure the issue had

been settled. Neither was Davies, coming from the other direction. Only when the American flag was raised to the top of the pole and the Star Spangled Banner was played did reality seem to set in. As Davies turned and said stoically, "If that's the biggest disappointment in my life, I can handle it," there was no question.

For his part, Barton was momentarily speechless. In the past few minutes he had raced the closest race of his life — maybe the closest race of anyone's life — after which he thought he won, thought he lost, and thought he won again.

He presently composed himself and congratulated Davies, telling him it was a shame either of them had to lose a race that close. Winning by five-

In a 1,000-meter flatwater kayak race, nothing is done by leaps and bounds.

thousandths of a second tends to make one humble.

Soon, Barton was back on the river. He and Bellingham forged their way to the starting line, where the wind was still blowing in their face. This time Barton left nothing to doubt. Rowing as if every quarter inch counted, he and Bellingham won by 29-hundredths of a second. The second place boat from New Zealand finished more than a quarter of a length behind. Olympic races had been won by wider margins of victory, it was true, but as Greg Barton knew full well, they had also been won by a lot less.

ABOVE / *Kayaker Greg Barton prepares to take to the water in an early morning practice session. The practice paid off for Barton, who won two gold medals in Seoul.* (ALLSPORT / M. POWELL)

1992

July 25 - August 9, 1992

172 Nations

10,563 Athletes

25 Sports

37 USA golds

BARCELONA

A NEW OLYMPIC ORDER

They will be remembered as the Games of the New World Order, featuring a record 172 nations, many of them officially represented in the Olympics for the first time after years of oppression. They will be remembered as the Games that rebuilt Barcelona, a crumbling city by the shores of the Mediterranean that was revived by a six-year, $8 billion reconstruction effort inspired almost solely by the news that the world's athletes were coming. They will be remembered as the Games of the *paseo*, as Barcelona's natives took their tranquil evening strolls past the Olympic venues overlooking the city on Montjuic, a custom that gave rise to a whole new Olympic phenomenon of more people *outside* the stadium than inside.

But as time goes on, the Games of the XXVth Olympiad held in Barcelona, Spain, will be remembered mostly as the Games that finally and openly welcomed professionals.

Ninety-six years of dogged and principled opposition gave way to the inevitable as most sports on the Barcelona calendar allowed any and all contestants, amateur and otherwise. The Games in Seoul four years previous had started the trend and the Games in Spain made it irreversible, numbering among its official competitors one Michael Jordan, the U.S. basketball player and one of the highest-paid athletes on the face of the earth.

Some sports clung, by their own separate policies, to amateur-only status

TOP / *The Olympics have long been a stage for political voices. In Barcelona, Catalonian independence-seekers were no exception.* (ALLSPORT / MARTIN)

RIGHT / *Linford Christie of Great Britain proved in Barcelona that, at 31, he was the world's fastest human. His time: 9.96.* (ALLSPORT / DUFFY)

SUCCEEDING PAGES / *Winning form: Jackie Joyner-Kersee* (LEFT - ALLSPORT / DUFFY) *and Mark Lenzi* (RIGHT- ALLSPORT / LEAH) *each garner golds for the USA in Barcelona. She in the heptathlon and he in the three-meter springboard.*

Ninety-six years of dogged and principled opposition gave way to the inevitable as most sports on the Barcelona calendar allowed any and all contestants, amateur and otherwise. The Games in Seoul had started the trend and the Games in Spain made it irreversible.

or to other forms of admission control. Boxing barred prize-fighters, as did cycling, and soccer stayed with its 23-and-under policy in an attempt to differentiate the Olympic tournament from the World Cup. But for the most part, play-for-pay was OK and nation after nation openly publicized what used to be top secret information: that their winners would be paid handsomely. In the case of Spain, "handsomely" meant a $1 million stipend for every gold medalist, to begin in monthly installments at the age of 50.

Perhaps that was why Spaniards won no less than 13 gold medals/$1 million annuities. In 96 years of previous Olympic effort, Spanish athletes had won a grand total of four gold medals.

In some ways it was difficult to tell that they were the Games of Spain at all. As the capital of Catalonia, one of Spain's 17 autonomous regions, the port of Barcelona marched more to Catalan than Spanish drums. During the course of the Games, the Catalans, who speak their own language and have their own identity, bombarded visitors and

international TV cameras with "Free Catalonia" placards and Catalonian flags.

But the demonstrations were peaceful enough and the Games — opened by King Juan Carlos of Spain in both Spanish and Catalan — proceeded as tranquilly as any in history. The spirit of freedom was unmistakable as countries previously encumbered by occupied status marched into Barcelona under their own flags. Included was a united Germany — for the first time since 1952 — and many of the former republics of the disbanded Soviet Union and its

TOP/ *Sharpshooter Launi Meili wins the gold for the U.S.* (ALLSPORT / MORTIMORE)

MIDDLE / *Split-second timing: Uneven bars champion Li Lu of China.* (ALLSPORT / VANDYSTADT)

BOTTOM / *The United States trounces Germany, 7-2 , in Barcelona.* (ALLSPORT / BOTTERILL)

TOP / *Gao Min's grace earned her top honors in diving.* (ALLSPORT / MARTIN)

MIDDLE / *A flair for the dramatic: Equestrian team dressage.* (ALLSPORT / CANNON)

BOTTOM / *Whitewater kayaking makes its reappearance in Barcelona.* (ALLSPORT / RONDEAU)

TOP / *Gold medalist Oscar De La Hoya scores on a jab.* (ALLSPORT / VANDYSTADT)

MIDDLE / *In the spotlight: Fencing in Barcelona.* (ALLSPORT / RONDEAU)

BOTTOM / *Americans Gigi Fernandez and Mary Jo Fernandez team up for the gold in tennis.* (ALLSPORT / RONDEAU)

surrounding satellite system. Twelve of those former Soviet republics, unable to organize Olympic teams by themselves in the short year since the USSR's downfall, came together as the Unified Team, although they were hardly that, and by 1993 all 12 were recognized as separate National Olympic Committees by the IOC. South Africa, too, rejoined the Olympic movement in the wake of its denunciation of apartheid policies that had kept its teams from the Olympics for the past 32 years. And both Cuba and North Korea resumed their Olympic participation after 12 years of isolation.

The result was a record number of 10,563 athletes — some 10,252 more than entered the first games of the

Americans enjoyed their most success, as usual, on the track, where Carl Lewis was again the headliner with two gold medals. After failing to make the U.S. sprint team because of illness at the qualifying trials, the 31-year-old three-time Olympian won in his specialty, the long jump, and anchored the U.S. 4x100-meter relay team to a world record.

Cuba and China, with 14 and 16 gold medals, respectively, made their marks in Barcelona. The Cubans dominated the boxing venue, winning seven of the 12 gold medals there. Cuba also outclassed the world in winning the first-ever Olympic baseball gold medal. In the distance races on the track, Africans

hockey team won the gold over Germany, and when Fermin Cacho, a longshot if that, took advantage of a tight and crowded race to break away to a win at 1,500 meters and capture Spain's first-ever gold medal in a running race.

The most decorated athlete of the 16-day run was Russian gymnast Vitaly Scherbo, who claimed six gold medals. His medal haul helped the Unified Team win the overall medal race, 112-108 over the United States. But there was no cohesiveness among the soon-to-be-disbanded Unified Team and when Scherbo was asked where he would live and who he would compete for in the next Olympic Games he answered, "wherever I can make the most money."

TOP / *Triple jumper gold medalist Mike Conley takes time out for the fans.* (ALLSPORT / MARTIN)

ABOVE / *Two legs up: synchronized swimming in Barcelona.* (ALLSPORT / VANDYSTADT)

modern era in Athens in 1896.

From this army of athletes came the most international array of medal winners in the Olympic history. Sixty-four countries, another record, went home with medals. Included among the individual winners was Paraskevi Patoulidou, the winner of the women's 100-meter hurdle race and Greece's first-ever woman track and field champion.

TOP / *The quiet side of rowing.* (ALLSPORT / RONDEAU)

ABOVE / *Gail Devers celebrates her gold in the 100 meters.* (ALLSPORT / CANNON)

came close to sweeping all the medals. But nowhere was the world more outclassed than at the basketball hall in Badalona, where the United States "Dream Team" dominated the opposition by an average of 44 points per game.

Spain's proudest moments came when its national 23-and-under team won the soccer tournament in front of a packed stadium, when its women's field

TOP / *Dara Torres, with teammates Angel Martino and Nicole Haislett, picks up the poolside pace. In the water, anchor Jenny Thompson screams to a world-record win of 3:49.46 in the 4x100-meter medley relay.* (ALLSPORT / BRUTY)

ABOVE / *"Stick together" is the motto of team cyclists.* (ALLSPORT / VANDYSTADT)

A remark that wouldn't have sat well with Pierre de Coubertin, whose vision was of an Olympic movement devoid of the lure of riches, but nonetheless, a remark accurately reflecting the modern-day reality of sport and the Olympic Games.

the dream team

WHAT MONEY CAN'T BUY

Karl Malone was sitting in his mother's house in Louisiana when it happened, all alone unless you count his dog, with whom he was in earnest conversation. The United States of America had just lost its semifinal game in the Olympic basketball tournament of 1988 to the team from the Soviet Union, 82-76. Watching on TV, Malone seethed as the announcers talked about the rest of the world catching up to the United States; about the Soviet Union now being the basketball capital of the world.

"Can you imagine," said Malone to his dog, his voice rising as he got madder, "what would happen if we put our best team on the floor!"

Malone, as it turned out, was not alone with such a sentiment.

Buoyed by that 1988 loss in Seoul to the Soviets — the first-ever Olympic loss accepted by the Americans (the infamous 51-50 loss to the Soviets in 1972 when three seconds were added to the clock not counting) — a groundswell movement began to

change the way America selected its Olympic basketball team. Instead of limiting the roster to college-age amateurs with no professional experience, why not fill it with the best players?

Especially when the best players — Malone, for instance — were ready, able ... and willing.

Malone wasn't the only one who offered his services. So did virtually every other player in the National Basketball Association. They said they'd give up their summer for a cause as important as this. The pride of the nation that invented the sport was at stake.

Thus was the "Dream Team" born — a collection of the finest players America, the NBA, and the world, could dream of.

Malone was soon penciled onto the roster that would go to the next Olympic Games, in Barcelona. So was the name of his teammate on the Utah Jazz, John Stockton. Chicago Bulls teammates Michael Jordan and Scottie Pippen were added, along with Charles Barkley, Clyde Drexler, Patrick Ewing and Chris Mullin. David Robinson was the lone returnee from

the 1988 team, while Christian Laettner, the 1991 college player of the year, was included to appease the traditionalists. To complete the legendary lineup, Larry Bird and Magic Johnson rounded out the squad.

A good case could be made that this team could have beaten any basketball team in the history of the world, let alone the current world. But if such a thought might have produced overconfidence, indifference and lethargy under other circumstances, under the circumstances of 1992 it did not. Through training camp against a group of college all-stars in San Diego, through the Olympic qualifying tournament in Portland, through yet another training camp in Monte Carlo, and right through the Olympic tournament proper in the Barcelona suburb of Badalona, the Dream Team never wavered in its role as Team Possessed. It came, it saw, it settled the score.

Never before, in its 96 years of modern history, had the Olympic Games seen such a phenomenon unfold. The Dream Team brought an element of stardom and celebrity to

Barcelona quite apart from the Olympic norm. Whereas most Olympians — from Jim Thorpe and Jesse Owens onward — achieved their fame *after* their events, the Dream Team was famous before it played a single Olympic minute. When Magic Johnson marched into the Olympic Stadium during the Opening Ceremonies, athletes from all nations broke ranks to get a closer look and snap a picture. To avoid just such a mob scene as the athletes lined up outside the stadium for their traditional parade, Johnson and the Dream Team were purposely kept out of the queue, sequestered in an adjacent building.

They were housed in a hotel in Barcelona just off Las Ramblas, with tight security to keep out the teeming, autograph-seeking masses.

The clamor did not stop when the basketball started. During timeouts, several players from opposing teams handed their cameras to teammates, asking them to snap a photo of them when the game resumed and they were being "dunked on by Jordan." During the qualifying tournament in

BELOW / *Charles Barkley slams home two points against a hapless Angolan team.* (ALLSPORT / M. POWELL)

Portland, a player from Cuba turned in midair as Jordan flew over him and smiled for the camera.

Also traditional were postgame pictures with the team just beaten, suitable for framing, no hard feelings. When the Dream Team played the team from Spain on its homecourt, the group photo was taken *before* the game began.

Given the enviable assignment of "coaching" this collection of all-stars was Chuck Daly, twice an NBA championship coach with the Detroit Pistons. The normally excitable Daly had two stated goals in Barcelona. One was to give every player a fair

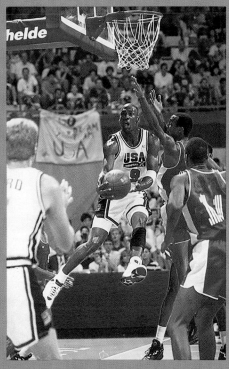

ABOVE / *Michael Jordan sails past the defense.* (ALLSPORT / M. POWELL)

number of minutes. The other was to never get out of his chair. He succeeded on both counts, although he did forget where he was once and rose out of chair to adjust his suit.

The U.S. team handily won all eight of its games in the gym in Badalona, where each of its games was a sellout, no matter the time of day or the opponent. The U.S. team averaged 117.3 points a game and won by an average of 43.8 points. Croatia came

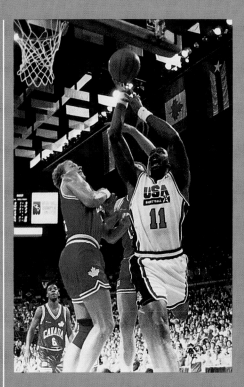

ABOVE / *Karl Malone was too much for the Canadians to handle during the Tournament of the Americas.* (ALLSPORT / LEAH)

The Dream Team never wavered in its role as Team Possessed. It came, it saw, it settled the score.

the closest with a 32-point loss in the gold-medal game.

Since the Soviet Union had disbanded under the weight of civil unrest the previous summer, the Dream Team's only disappointment was that it was unable to truly avenge the 1988 Olympic defeat at the hands of the USSR. In a game against the Lithuanian team that featured the bulk of that 1988 Soviet Union squad — including center Arvidas Sabonis and NBA star Sarunas Marciulionis — the United States was able to get at least

a measure of revenge, however, winning that game handily, 127-76.

After securing the championship against Croatia, the U.S. players mounted the victory peristyle with all the enthusiasm of any first-time Olympians. They waved to the crowd and pumped their fists. Some of them cried. As youngsters, they had their Olympic dreams, too — and now they had been fulfilled. It was true, they were all millionaires, but now, after sacrificing their summer in a united cause, they had something those millions couldn't buy.

As the Dream Team left the arena, they were asked if the experience had been worth it, and would they do it again?

"Yeah, in a heartbeat," answered Malone. "In a heartbeat." ◌

TOP/ *They lost to the Dream Team, 127-76, but the Lithuanians were happy to celebrate their bronze medal.* (ALLSPORT / M. POWELL)

RIGHT / *Clyde Drexler concentrates on a free throw.* (ALLSPORT / LEAH)

OPPOSITE PAGE / *Sweet victory, Magic Johnson.* (ALLSPORT / M. POWELL)

RESULTS

WR = WORLD RECORD		DNQ = DID NOT QUALIFY	
EWR = EQUALS WR		DNC = DID NOT COMPETE	
OR = OLYMPIC RECORD		DNS = DID NOT START	
EOR = EQUALS OR		DNF = DID NOT FINISH	
FOR = FINAL OR		RSC = REFEREE STOPPED CONTEST	

NOTE: USA DID NOT COMPETE IN 1980

ARCHERY

MEN'S INDIVIDUAL

YEAR	RANK	CTRY	ATHLETE	POINTS	
1896-1968	(not held)				
1972	1	USA	John Williams	2528	WR
	2	SWE	Gunnar Jarvil	2481	
	3	FIN	Kyösti Laasonen	2467	
1976	1	USA	Darrell Pace	2571	WR
	2	JPN	Hiroshi Michinaga	2502	
	3	ITA	Giancarlo Ferrari	2495	
1980	1	FIN	Tomi Poikolainen	2455	
	2	URS	Boris Isachenko	2452	
	3	ITA	Giancarlo Ferrari	2449	
1984	1	USA	Darrell Pace	2616	OR
	2	USA	Richard McKinney	2564	
	3	JPN	Hiroshi Yamamoto	2563	
1988	1	USA	Jay Barrs	338	
	2	KOR	Park Sung-soo	336	
	3	URS	Vladimir Echeev	335	
1992	1	FRA	Sebastien Flute		
	2	KOR	Chung Jae-hun		
	3	GBR	Simon Terry		
	5	USA	Jay Barrs		

MEN'S TEAM

YEAR	RANK	CTRY	ATHLETES	POINTS
1896-1984	(not held)			
1988	1	KOR		986
	2	USA	Jay Barrs / Rick McKinney / Darrell Pace	972
	3	GBR		968
1992	1	ESP		
	2	FIN		
	3	GBR		
	6	USA	Jay Barrs / Richard "Butch" Johnson / Rick McKinney	

WOMEN'S INDIVIDUAL

YEAR	RANK	CTRY	ATHLETE	POINTS	
1896-1968	(not held)				
1972	1	USA	Doreen Wilber	2424	WR
	2	POL	Irena Szydlowska	2407	
	3	URS	Emma Gaptchenko	2403	
1976	1	USA	Luann Ryon	2499	WR
	2	URS	Valentina Kovpan	2460	
	3	URS	Zebiniso Rustamova	2407	
1980	1	URS	Keto Losaberidze	2491	
	2	URS	Natalya Butuzova	2477	
	3	FIN	Päivi Meriluoto	2449	
1984	1	KOR	Seo Hyang-soon	2568	OR
	2	CHN	Li Lingjuan	2559	
	3	KOR	Kim Jin-ho	2555	
	6T	USA	Katrina King	2508	
1988	1	KOR	Kim Soo-nyung	344	
	2	KOR	Wang Hee-kyung	332	
	3	KOR	Yun Young-sook	327	
	10	USA	Melanie Skillman		
1992	1	KOR	Cho Youn-jeong		
	2	KOR	Kim Soo-nyung		
	3	EUN	Natalia Valeeva		
	5	USA	Denise Parker		

WOMEN'S TEAM

YEAR	RANK	CTRY	ATHLETES	POINTS	SHOOT OFF
1896-1964	(not held)				
1988	1	KOR		982	
	2	INA		952	72
	3	USA	Debra Ochs / Denise Parker Melanie Skillman	952	67
1992	1	KOR			
	2	CHN			
	3	EUN			
	8	USA	Sherry Block / Jennifer O'Donnell / Denise Parker		

ATHLETICS

MEN'S 100 METERS

YEAR	RANK	CTRY	ATHLETE	TIME	
1896	1	USA	Thomas Burke	12.0	
	2	GER	Fritz Hofmann	12.2e	
	3	HUN	Alajos Szokolyi	12.6e	
1900	1	USA	Frank Jarvis	11.0	
	2	USA	John Walter Tewksbury	11.1	
	3	AUS	Stanley Rowley	11.2	
1904	1	USA	Archibald Hahn	11.0	
	2	USA	Nathaniel Cartmell	11.2	
	3	USA	William Hogenson	11.2	
1906	1	USA	Archibald Hahn	11.2	
	2	USA	Fay Moulton	11.3	
	3	AUS	Nigel Barker	11.3	
1908	1	RSA	Reginald Walker	10.8	EOR
	2	USA	James Rector	10.9	
	3	CAN	Robert Kerr	11.0	
1912	1	USA	Ralph Craig	10.8	
	2	USA	Alvah Meyer	10.9	
	3	USA	Donald Lippincott	10.9	
1920	1	USA	Charles Paddock	10.8	
	2	USA	Morris Kirksey	10.8	
	3	GBR	Harry Edward	11.0	
1924	1	GBR	Harold Abrahams	10.6	EOR
	2	USA	Jackson Scholz	10.7	
	3	NZL	Arthur Porritt	10.8	
1928	1	CAN	Percy Williams	10.8	
	2	GBR	Jack London	10.9	
	3	GER	Georg Lammers	10.9	
	4	USA	Frank Wykoff	11.0	
1932	1	USA	Thomas "Eddie" Tolan	10.3	OR
	2	USA	Ralph Metcalfe	10.3	
	3	GER	Arthur Jonath	10.4	
1936	1	USA	Jesse Owens	10.3	EOR
	2	USA	Ralph Metcalfe	10.4	
	3	HOL	Martinus Osendarp	10.5	
1948	1	USA	Harrison Dillard	10.3	EOR
	2	USA	H. Norwood "Barney" Ewell	10.4	
	3	PAN	Lloyd LaBeach	10.4	
1952	1	USA	Lindy Remigino	10.4	
	2	JAM	Herbert McKenley	10.4	
	3	GBR	Emmanuel McDonald Bailey	10.4	
1956	1	USA	Bobby Joe Morrow	10.5	
	2	USA	W. Thane Baker	10.5	
	3	AUS	Hector Hogan	10.6	
1960	1	GER	Armin Hary	10.2	OR
	2	USA	David Sime	10.2	
	3	GBR	Peter Radford	10.3	
1964	1	USA	Robert Hayes	10.0	EWR
	2	CUB	Enrique Figuerola Camue	10.2	
	3	CAN	Harry Jerome	10.2	
1968	1	USA	James Hines	9.95	WR
	2	JAM	Lennox Miller	10.0	
	3	USA	Charles Greene	10.0	
1972	1	URS	Valery Borzov	10.14	
	2	USA	Robert Taylor	10.24	
	3	JAM	Lennox Miller	10.33	
1976	1	TRI	Hasely Crawford	10.06	
	2	JAM	Donald Quarrie	10.08	
	3	URS	Valery Borzov	10.14	
	4	USA	Harvey Glance	10.19	
1980	1	GBR	Allan Wells	10.25	
	2	CUB	Silvio Leonard Tartabull	10.25	
	3	BUL	Peter Petrov	10.39	
1984	1	USA	Carl Lewis	9.99	
	2	USA	Sam Graddy	10.19	
	3	CAN	Ben Johnson	10.22	
1988	1	USA	Carl Lewis	9.92	OR
	2	GBR	Linford Christie	9.97	
	3	USA	Calvin Smith	9.99	
1992	1	GBR	Linford Christie	9.96	
	2	NAM	Frank Fredericks	10.02	
	3	USA	Dennis Mitchell	10.04	

MEN'S 200 METERS

YEAR	RANK	CTRY	ATHLETE	TIME	
1896	(not held)				
1900	1	USA	John Walter Tewksbury	22.2	
	2	IND	Norman Pritchard	22.8	
	3	AUS	Stanley Rowley	22.9	
1904	1	USA	Archie Hahn	21.6	OR
	2	USA	Nathaniel Cartmell	21.9	
	3	USA	William Hogenson		
1906	(not held)				
1908	1	CAN	Robert Kerr	22.6	
	2	USA	Robert Cloughen	22.6	
	3	USA	Nathaniel Cartmell	22.7	
1912	1	USA	Ralph Craig	21.7	
	2	USA	Donald Lippincott	21.8	
	3	GBR	William Applegarth	22.0	
1920	1	USA	Allen Woodring	22.0	
	2	USA	Charles Paddock	22.1	
	3	GBR	Harry Edward	22.2	
1924	1	USA	Jackson Scholz	21.6	
	2	USA	Charles Paddock	21.7	
	3	GBR	Eric Liddell	21.9	
1928	1	CAN	Percy Williams	21.8	
	2	GBR	Walter Rangeley	21.9	
	3	GER	Helmuth Körnig	21.9	
	4	USA	Jackson Scholz	21.9	
1932	1	USA	Thomas "Eddie" Tolan	21.2	OR
	2	USA	George Simpson	21.4	
	3	USA	Ralph Metcalfe	21.5	
1936	1	USA	Jesse Owens	20.7	OR
	2	USA	Matthew "Mack" Robinson	21.1	
	3	HOL	Martinus Osendarp	21.3	
1948	1	USA	Melvin Patton	21.1	
	2	USA	H. Norwood "Barney" Ewell	21.1	
	3	PAN	Lloyd LaBeach	21.2	
1952	1	USA	Andrew Stanfield	20.7	
	2	USA	W. Thane Baker	20.8	
	3	USA	James Gathers	20.8	
1956	1	USA	Bobby Joe Morrow	20.6	OR
	2	USA	Andrew Stanfield	20.7	
	3	USA	W. Thane Baker	20.9	
1960	1	ITA	Livio Berruti	20.5	EWR
	2	USA	Lester Carney	20.6	
	3	FRA	Abdoulaye Seye	20.7	
1964	1	USA	Henry Carr	20.3	OR
	2	USA	O. Paul Drayton	20.5	
	3	TRI	Edwin Roberts	20.6	
1968	1	USA	Tommie Smith	19.83	WR
	2	AUS	Peter Norman	20.0	
	3	USA	John Carlos	20.0	
1972	1	URS	Valery Borzov	20.00	
	2	USA	Larry Black	20.19	
	3	ITA	Pietro Mennea	20.30	
1976	1	JAM	Donald Quarrie	20.23	
	2	USA	Millard Hampton	20.29	
	3	USA	Dwayne Evans	20.43	
1980	1	ITA	Pietro Mennea	20.19	
	2	GBR	Allan Wells	20.21	
	3	JAM	Donald Quarrie	20.29	
1984	1	USA	Carl Lewis	19.80	OR
	2	USA	Kirk Baptiste	19.96	
	3	USA	Thomas Jefferson	20.26	
1988	1	USA	Joe Deloach	19.75	OR
	2	USA	Carl Lewis	19.79	
	3	BRA	Robson Silva	20.04	
1992	1	USA	Mike Marsh	20.01	
	2	NAM	Frank Fredericks	20.13	
	3	USA	Michael Bates	20.38	

MEN'S 400 METERS

YEAR	RANK	CTRY	ATHLETE	TIME	
1896	1	USA	Thomas Burke	54.2	
	2	USA	Herbert Jamison		
	3	GBR	Charles Gmelin		
1900	1	USA	Maxwell "Maxey" Long	49.4	OR
	2	USA	William Holland	49.6	
	3	DEN	Ernst Schultz		
1904	1	USA	Harry Hillman	49.2	OR
	2	USA	Frank Waller	49.9	
	3	USA	Herman Groman	50.0	
1906	1	USA	Paul Pilgrim	53.2	
	2	GBR	Wyndham Halswelle	53.8	
	3	AUS	Nigel Barker	54.1	
1908	1	GBR	Wyndham Halswelle	50.0	
		USA	William Robbins	DNS	
		USA	John Taylor	DNS	
1912	1	USA	Charles Reidpath	48.2	OR
	2	GER	Hanns Braun	48.3	
	3	USA	Edward Lindberg	48.4	
1920	1	RSA	Bevil Rudd	49.6	
	2	GBR	Guy Butler	49.9	
	3	SWE	Nils Engdahl	50.0	
	4	USA	Frank Shea		
1924	1	GBR	Eric Liddell	47.6	OR
	2	USA	Horatio Fitch	48.4	
	3	GBR	Guy Butler	48.6	
1928	1	USA	Raymond Barbuti	47.8	
	2	CAN	James Ball	48.0	
	3	GER	Joachim Büchner	48.2	
1932	1	USA	William Carr	46.2	WR
	2	USA	Benjamin Eastman	46.4	
	3	CAN	Alexander Wilson	47.4	
1936	1	USA	Archie Williams	46.5	
	2	GBR	Arthur Godfrey Brown	46.7	
	3	USA	James LuValle	46.8	
1948	1	JAM	Arthur Wint	46.2	
	2	JAM	Herbert McKenley	46.4	
	3	USA	Malvin Whitfield	46.9	
1952	1	JAM	V. George Rhoden	45.9	OR
	2	JAM	Herbert McKenley	45.9	
	3	USA	Ollie Matson	46.8	
1956	1	USA	Charles Jenkins	46.7	
	2	GER	Karl-Friedrich Haas	46.8	
	3	FIN	Voitto Hellsten	47.0	
1960	1	USA	Otis Davis	44.9	WR
	2	GER	Carl Kaufmann	44.9	WR
	3	RSA	Malcolm Spence	45.5	
1964	1	USA	Michael Larrabee	45.1	
	2	TRI	Wendell Mottley	45.2	
	3	POL	Andrzej Badenski	45.6	
1968	1	USA	Lee Evans	43.86	WR
	2	USA	Larry James	43.9	
	3	USA	Ronald Freeman	44.4	
1972	1	USA	Vincent Matthews	44.66	
	2	USA	Wayne Collett	44.80	
	3	KEN	Julius Sang	44.92	
1976	1	CUB	Alberto Juantorena	44.26	
	2	USA	Frederick Newhouse	44.40	
	3	USA	Herman Frazier	44.95	
1980	1	URS	Viktor Markin	44.60	
	2	AUS	Richard Mitchell	44.84	
	3	GDR	Frank Schaffer	44.87	
1984	1	USA	Alonzo Babers	44.27	
	2	IVC	Gabriel Tiacoh	44.54	
	3	USA	Antonio McKay	44.71	
1988	1	USA	Steven Lewis	43.87	
	2	USA	Harry "Butch" Reynolds	43.93	
	3	USA	Danny Everett	44.09	
1992	1	USA	Quincy Watts	43.50	OR
	2	USA	Steve Lewis	44.21	
	3	KEN	Samson Kitur	44.24	

MEN'S 800 METERS

YEAR	RANK	CTRY	ATHLETE	TIME	
1896	1	AUS	Edwin Flack	2:11.0	
	2	HUN	Nándor Dáni	2:11.8e	
	3	GRE	Demitrios Golemis		
(no USA entry)					
1900	1	GBR	Alfred Tysoe	2:01.2	
	2	USA	John Cregan	2:03.0	
	3	USA	David Hall		
1904	1	USA	James Lightbody	1:56.0	OR
	2	USA	Howard Valentine	1:56.3	
	3	USA	Emil Breitkreutz	1:56.4	
1906	1	USA	Paul Pilgrim	2:01.5	
	2	USA	James Lightbody	2:01.6	
	3	GBR	Wyndham Halswelle	2:03.0	
1908	1	USA	Melvin Sheppard	1:52.8	WR
	2	ITA	Emilio Lunghi	1:54.2	
	3	GER	Hanns Braun	1:55.2	
1912	1	USA	James "Ted" Meredith	1:51.9	WR
	2	USA	Melvin Sheppard	1:52.0	
	3	USA	Ira Davenport	1:52.0	
1920	1	GBR	Albert Hill	1:53.4	
	2	USA	Earl Eby	1:53.6	
	3	RSA	Bevil Rudd	1:54.0	
1924	1	GBR	Douglas Lowe	1:52.4	
	2	SUI	Paul Martin	1:52.6	
	3	USA	Schuyler Enck	1:53.0	
1928	1	GBR	Douglas Lowe	1:51.8	OR
	2	SWE	Erik Byléhn	1:52.8	
	3	GER	Hermann Engelhard	1:53.2	
	5	USA	Lloyd Hahn	1:54.2	
1932	1	GBR	Thomas Hampson	1:49.7	WR
	2	CAN	Alexander Wilson	1:49.9	
	3	CAN	Philip Edwards	1:51.5	
	4	USA	Edwin Genung	1:51.7	
1936	1	USA	John Woodruff	1:52.9	
	2	ITA	Mario Lanzi	1:53.3	
	3	CAN	Philip Edwards	1:53.6	
1948	1	USA	Malvin Whitfield	1:49.2	OR
	2	JAM	Arthur Wint	1:49.5	
	3	FRA	Marcel Hansenne	1:49.8	
1952	1	USA	Malvin Whitfield	1:49.2	EOR
	2	JAM	Arthur Wint	1:49.4	
	3	GER	Heinz Ulzheimer	1:49.7	
1956	1	USA	Thomas Courtney	1:47.7	OR
	2	GBR	Derek Johnson	1:47.8	
	3	NOR	Audun Boysen	1:48.1	
1960	1	NZL	Peter Snell	1:46.3	OR
	2	BEL	Roger Moens	1:46.5	
	3	JAM	George Kerr	1:47.1	
		USA	T. Murphy (1:48.2) / W. Cunlife (1:50.8)	elim. semis	
1964	1	NZL	Peter Snell	1:45.1	OR
	2	CAN	William Crothers	1:45.6	
	3	KEN	Wilson Kiprugut Chuma	1:45.9	
	5	USA	Thomas Farrell	1:46.6	
1968	1	AUS	Ralph Doubell	1:44.3	EWR
	2	KEN	Wilson Kiprugut Chuma	1:44.5	
	3	USA	Thomas Farrell	1:45.4	

1972	1	USA	David Wottle	1:45.9	
	2	URS	Yevgeny Arzhanov	1:45.9	
	3	KEN	Michael Boit	1:46.0	
1976	1	CUB	Alberto Juantorena	1:43.50	WR
	2	BEL	Ivo van Damme	1:43.86	
	3	USA	Richard Wohlhuter	1:44.12	
1980	1	GBR	Steven Ovett	1:45.4	
	2	GBR	Sebastian Coe	1:45.9	
	3	URS	Nikolai Kirov	1:46.0	
1984	1	BRA	Joaquim Cruz	1:43.00	OR
	2	GBR	Sebastian Coe	1:43.64	
	3	USA	Earl Jones	1:43.83	
1988	1	KEN	Paul Ereng	1:43.45	
	2	BRA	Joaquim Cruz	1:43.90	
	3	MAR	Said Aouita	1:44.06	
	5	USA	Johnny Gray	1:44.80	
1992	1	KEN	William Tanui	1:43.66	
	2	KEN	Nixon Kiprotich	1:43.70	
	3	USA	Johnny Gray	1:43.97	

MEN'S 1,500 METERS

YEAR	RANK	CTRY	ATHLETE	TIME	
1896	1	AUS	Edwin Flack	4:33.2	
	2	USA	Arthur Blake	4:34.0e	
	3	FRA	Albin Lermusiaux	4:36.0e	
1900	1	GBR	Charles Bennett	4:06.2	WR
	2	FRA	Henri Deloge	4:06.6	
	3	USA	John Bray	4:07.2	
1904	1	USA	James Lightbody	4:05.4	WR
	2	USA	William Frank Verner	4:06.8	
	3	USA	Lacey Hearn		
1906	1	USA	James Lightbody	4:12.0	
	2	GBR/IRL	John McGough	4:12.6	
	3	SWE	Kristian Hellström	4:13.4	
1908	1	USA	Melvin Sheppard	4:03.4	OR
	2	GBR	Harold Wilson	4:03.6	
	3	GBR	Norman Hallows	4:04.0	
1912	1	GBR	Arnold Jackson	3:56.8	OR
	2	USA	Abel Kiviat	3:56.9	
	3	USA	Norman Taber	3:56.9	
1920	1	GBR	Albert Hill	4:01.8	
	2	GBR	Philip Baker	4:02.4	
	3	USA	Lawrence Shields	4:03.1	
1924	1	FIN	Paavo Nurmi	3:53.6	OR
	2	SUI	Wilhelm Schärer	3:55.0	
	3	GBR	Henry Stallard	3:55.6	
	5	USA	Raymond Buker	3:58.6	
1928	1	FIN	Harry Larva	3:53.2	OR
	2	FRA	Jules Ladoumègue	3:53.8	
	3	FIN	Eino Purje-Borg	3:56.4	
	10	USA	Ray Conger		
1932	1	ITA	Luigi Beccali	3:51.2	OR
	2	GBR	John Cornes	3:52.6	
	3	CAN	Philip Edwards	3:52.8	
	4	USA	Glenn Cunningham	3:53.4	
1936	1	NZL	John Lovelock	3:47.8	WR
	2	USA	Glenn Cunningham	3:48.4	
	3	ITA	Luigi Beccali	3:49.2	
1948	1	SWE	Henry Eriksson	3:49.8	
	2	SWE	Lennart Strand	3:50.4	
	3	HOL	Willem Slijkhuis	3:50.4	
	8	USA	Donald Gehrmann		
1952	1	LUX	Josef "Josy" Barthel	3:45.1	OR
	2	USA	Robert McMillen	3:45.2	
	3	GER	Werner Lueg	3:45.4	
1956	1	IRL	Ron Delany	3:41.2	OR
	2	GDR	Klaus Richtzenhain	3:42.0	
	3	AUS	John Landy	3:42.0	
		USA	Donald Bowden / Jerome Walter / Theodore Wheeler	elim. trials	
1960	1	AUS	Herbert Elliott	3:35.6	WR
	2	FRA	Michel Jazy	3:38.4	
	3	HUN	István Rózsavölgyi	3:39.2	
	6	USA	Dyrol Burleson	3:40.9	
1964	1	NZL	Peter Snell	3:38.1	
	2	TCH	Josef Odlozil	3:39.6	
	3	NZL	John Davies	3:39.6	
	5	USA	Dyrol Burleson	3:40.0	
1968	1	KEN	H. Kipchoge Keino	3:34.9	OR
	2	USA	James Ryun	3:37.8	
	3	GER	Bodo Tümmler	3:39.0	
1972	1	FIN	Pekkha Vasala	3:36.3	
	2	KEN	H. Kipchoge Keino	3:36.8	
	3	NZL	Rodney Dixon	3:37.5	
		USA	David Wottle (3:41.6) / Robert Wheeler (3:40.4)	elim. 2nd rd	
1976	1	NZL	John Walker	3:39.17	
	2	BEL	Ivo van Damme	3:39.27	
	3	GER	Paul-Heinz Wellmann	3:39.33	
	6	USA	Richard Wohlhuter	3:40.64	
1980	1	GBR	Sebastian Coe	3:38.4	
	2	GDR	Jürgen Straub	3:38.8	
	3	GBR	Steven Ovett	3:39.0	
1984	1	GBR	Sebastian Coe	3:32.53	OR
	2	GBR	Steve Cram	3:33.40	
	3	ESP	José Abascal	3:34.30	
	5	USA	Jim Spivey	3:36.07	
1988	1	KEN	Peter Rono	3:35.96	
	2	GBR	Peter Elliott	3:36.15	
	3	GDR	Jens-Peter Herold	3:36.21	
	5	USA	Steve Scott	3:36.99	
1992	1	ESP	Fermin Cacho Ruiz	3:40.12	
	2	MAR	Rachid El-Basir	3:40.62	
	3	QAT	Mohamed Sulaiman	3:40.69	
	8	USA	Jim Spivey	3:41.74	

MEN'S 5,000 METERS

YEAR	RANK	CTRY	ATHLETE	TIME	
1896-1908			(not held)		
1912	1	FIN	Johannes Kolehmainen	14:36.6	WR
	2	FRA	Jean Bouin	14:36.7	
	3	GBR	George Hutson	15:07.6	
	4	USA	George Bonhag	15:09.8	
1920	1	FRA	Joseph Guillemot	14:55.6	
	2	FIN	Paavo Nurmi	15:00.0	
	3	SWE	Erik Backman	15:13.0	
		USA	Horace Brown / Ivan Dresser / C.C. Furnas	DNF	
1924	1	FIN	Paavo Nurmi	14:31.2	OR
	2	FIN	Vilho "Ville" Ritola	14:31.4	
	3	SWE	Edvin Wide	15:01.8	
	4	USA	John Romig	15:12.4	
1928	1	FIN	Vilho "Ville" Ritola	14:38.0	
	2	FIN	Paavo Nurmi	14:40.0	
	3	SWE	Edvin Wide	14:41.2	
	4	USA	Leo Lermond	14:50.0	
1932	1	FIN	Lauri Lehtinen	14:30.0	OR
	2	USA	Ralph Hill	14:30.0	
	3	FIN	Lauri Virtanen	14:44.0	
1936	1	FIN	Gunnar Höckert	14:22.2	OR
	2	FIN	Lauri Lehtinen	14:25.8	
	3	SWE	Henry Jonsson	14:29.0	
	8	USA	Louis Zamperini	14:46.8	
1948	1	BEL	Gaston Reiff	14:17.6	OR
	2	TCH	Emil Zátopek	14:17.8	
	3	HOL	Willem Slijkhuis	14:26.8	
	6	USA	Curtis Stone	14:39.4	
1952	1	TCH	Emil Zátopek	14:06.6	OR
	2	FRA	Alain Mimoun O'Kacha	14:07.4	
	3	GER	Herbert Schade	14:08.6	
		USA	Charles Capozzoli / David Santee / Curtis Stone	elim. trials	
1956	1	URS	Vladimir Kuts	13:39.6	OR
	2	GBR	Gordon Pirie	13:50.6	
	3	GBR	Derek Ibbotson	13:54.4	
		USA	William Dellinger (DNF)/ Max Truex (withdrew)		
1960	1	NZL	Murray Halberg	13:43.4	
	2	GDR	Hans Grodotzki	13:44.6	
	3	POL	Kazimierz Zimny	13:44.8	
		USA	William Dellinger (14:08.6) / James Beatty (14:43.8) / Robert Soth (14:40.4)	elim. 1st rd	
1964	1	USA	Robert Schul	13:48.8	
	2	GER	Harald Norpoth	13:49.6	
	3	USA	William Dellinger	13:49.8	
1968	1	TUN	Mohamed Gammoudi	14:05.0	
	2	KEN	H. Kipchoge Keino	14:05.2	
	3	KEN	Naftali Temu	14:06.4	
		USA	Jack Bacheler	DNC	
1972	1	FIN	Lasse Viren	13:26.4	OR
	2	GUN	Mohamed Gammoudi	13:27.4	
	3	GBR	Ian Stewart	13:27.6	
	4	USA	Steve Prefontaine	13:28.4	
1976	1	FIN	Lasse Viren	13:24.76	
	2	NZL	Dick Quax	13:25.16	
	3	GER	Klaus-Peter Hildenbrand	13:25.38	
	12	USA	Paul Geis	13:42.51	
1980	1	ETH	Miruts Yifter	13:21.0	
	2	TAN	Suleiman Nyambui	13:21.6	
	3	FIN	Kaarlo Maaninka	13:22.0	
1984	1	MAR	Said Aouita	13:05.59	OR
	2	SUI	Markus Ryffel	13:07.54	
	3	POR	Antonio Leitão	13:09.20	
	7	USA	Doug Padilla	13:23.56	
1988	1	KEN	John Ngugi	13:11.70	
	2	FRG	Dieter Baumann	13:15.72	
	3	GDR	Hansjoerg Kunze	13:15.73	
	5	USA	Sydney Maree	13:23.69	
1992	1	GER	Dieter Baumann	13:12.52	
	2	KEN	Paul Bitok	13:12.71	
	3	ETH	Fita Bayisa	13:13.03	
	12	USA	Robert Owen Kennedy, Jr.	13:39.72	

MEN'S 10,000 METERS

YEAR	RANK	CTRY	ATHLETE	TIME	
1896-1908			(not held)		
1912	1	FIN	Johannes Kolehmainen	31:20.8	
	2	USA	Louis Tewanima	32:06.6	
	3	FIN	Albin Stenroos	32:21.8	
1920	1	FIN	Paavo Nurmi	31:45.8	
	2	FRA	Joseph Guillemot	31:47.2	
	3	GBR	James Wilson	31:50.8	
	8	USA	Frederick Faller	32:38.0	
1924	1	FIN	Vilho "Ville" Ritola	30:23.2	WR
	2	SWE	Edvin Wide	30:55.2	
	3	FIN	Eero Berg	31:43.0	
	8	USA	Earl Johnson	32:17.0	
1928	1	FIN	Paavo Nurmi	30:18.8	OR
	2	FIN	Vilho "Ville" Ritola	30:19.4	
	3	SWE	Edvin Wide	31:00.8	
	14	USA	Joie Ray		
1932	1	POL	Janusz Kusocinski	30:11.4	OR
	2	FIN	Volmari Iso-Hollo	30:12.6	
	3	FIN	Lauri Virtanen	30:35.0	
		USA	Louis Gregory / Thomas Ottey / Eino Pentti	DNF	
1936	1	FIN	Ilmari Salminen	30:15.4	
	2	FIN	Arvo Askola	30:15.6	
	3	FIN	Volmari Iso-Hollo	30:20.2	
	8	USA	Donald Lash	31:39.4	
1948	1	TCH	Emil Zátopek	29:59.6	OR
	2	FRA	Alain Mimoun O'Kacha	30:47.4	
	3	SWE	Bertil Albertsson	30:53.6	
	10	USA	Edward O'Toole		
1952	1	TCH	Emil Zátopek	29:17.0	OR
	2	FRA	Alain Mimoun O'Kacha	29:32.8	
	3	URS	Aleksandr Anufriev	29:28.2	
	20	USA	Curtis Stone	31:02.6	
1956	1	URS	Vladimir Kuts	28:45.6	OR
	2	HUN	József Kovács	28:52.4	
	3	AUS	Allan Lawrence	28:53.6	
	18	USA	Gordon McKenzie		
1960	1	URS	Pyotr Bolotnikov	28:32.2	OR
	2	GDR	Hans Grodotzki	28:37.0	
	3	AUS	David Power	28:38.2	
	6	USA	Max Truex	28:50.2	
1964	1	USA	William Mills	28:24.4	OR
	2	TUN	Mohamed Gammoudi	28:24.8	
	3	AUS	Ronald Clarke	28:25.8	
1968	1	KEN	Naftali Temu	29:27.4	
	2	ETH	Mamo Wolde	29:28.0	
	3	TUN	Mohamed Gammoudi	29:34.2	
	11	USA	Tracy Smith	30:14.6	
1972	1	FIN	Lasse Viren	27:38.4	WR
	2	BEL	Emiel Puttemans	27:39.6	
	3	ETH	Miruts Yifter	27:41.0	
	5	USA	Frank Shorter	27:51.4	
1976	1	FIN	Lasse Viren	27:40.38	
	2	POR	Carlos Lopes	27:45.17	
	3	GBR	Brendan Foster	27:54.92	
	13	USA	Gary Gjorklund	28:38.08	
1980	1	ETH	Miruts Yifter	27:42.7	
	2	FIN	Kaarlo Maaninka	27:44.3	
	3	ETH	Mohammed Kedir	27:44.7	
1984	1	ITA	Alberto Cova	27:47.54	
		FIN	Martti Vainio	27:51.10	
	2	GBR	Michael McLeod	28:06.22	
	3	KEN	Mike Musyoki	28:06.46	
	16	USA	Pat Porter	28:34.59	
1988	1	MAR	Mly. Brahim Boutaib	27:21.46	OR
	2	ITA	Salvatore Antibo	27:23.55	
	3	KEN	Kipkemboi Kimeli	27:25.16	
	18	USA	Bruce Bickford	29:09.74	
1992	1	MAR	Khalid Skah	27:46.70	
	2	KEN	Richard Chelimo	27:47.72	
	3	ETH	Addis Abebe	28:00.07	
	10	USA	Todd Williams	28:29.38	

MEN'S 110-METER HURDLES

YEAR	RANK	CTRY	ATHLETE	TIME	
1896	1	USA	Thomas Curtis	17.6	
	2	GBR	Grantley Goulding	17.7e	
		USA	William Hoyt	DNS	
1900	1	USA	Alvin Kraenzlein	15.4	OR
	2	USA	John McLean	15.5	
	3	USA	Frederick Moloney		
1904	1	USA	Frederick Schule	16.0	
	2	USA	Thaddeus Shideler	16.3	
	3	USA	Lesley Ashburner	16.4	
1906	1	USA	Robert Leavitt	16.2	
	2	GBR	Alfred Healey	16.2	
	3	RSA	Vincent Duncker	16.3	
1908	1	USA	Forrest Smithson	15.0	WR
	2	USA	John Garrels	15.7	
	3	USA	Arthur Shaw		
1912	1	USA	Frederick Kelly	15.1	
	2	USA	James Wendell	15.2	
	3	USA	Martin Hawkins	15.3	
1920	1	CAN	Earl Thomson	14.8	WR
	2	USA	Harold Barron	15.1	
	3	USA	Frederick Murray	15.2	
1924	1	USA	Daniel Kinsey	15.0	
	2	RSA	Sydney Atkinson	15.0	
	3	SWE	Sten Pettersson	15.4	
1928	1	RSA	Sydney Atkinson	14.8	
	2	USA	Stephen Anderson	14.8	
	3	USA	John Collier	14.9	
1932	1	USA	George Saling	14.6	
	2	USA	Percy Beard	14.7	
	3	GBR	Donald Finlay	14.8	
1936	1	USA	Forrest Towns	14.2	
	2	GBR	Donald Finlay	14.4	
	3	USA	Frederick Pollard	14.4	
1948	1	USA	William Porter	13.9	OR
	2	USA	Clyde Scott	14.1	
	3	USA	Craig Dixon	14.1	
1952	1	USA	Harrison Dillard	13.7	OR
	2	USA	Jack Davis	13.7	
	3	USA	Arthur Barnard	14.1	
1956	1	USA	Lee Calhoun	13.5	OR
	2	USA	Jack Davis	13.5	
	3	USA	Joel Shankle	14.1	
1960	1	USA	Lee Calhoun	13.8	
	2	USA	Willie May	13.8	
	3	USA	Hayes Jones	14.0	
1964	1	USA	Hayes Jones	13.6	
	2	USA	H. Blaine Lindgren	13.7	
	3	URS	Anatoly Mikhailov	13.7	
1968	1	USA	Willie Davenport	13.3	OR
	2	USA	Ervin Hall	13.4	
	3	ITA	Eddy Ottoz	13.4	
1972	1	USA	Rodney Milburn	13.24	EWR
	2	FRA	Guy Drut	13.34	
	3	USA	Thomas Hill	13.48	
1976	1	FRA	Guy Drut	13.30	
	2	CUB	Alejandro Casañas Ramirez	13.33	
	3	USA	Willie Davenport	13.38	
1980	1	GDR	Thomas Munkelt	13.39	
	2	CUB	Alejandro Casañas Ramirez	13.40	
	3	URS	Aleksandr Puchkov	13.44	
1984	1	USA	Roger Kingdom	13.20	OR
	2	USA	Gregory Foster	13.23	
	3	FIN	Arto Bryggare	13.40	
1988	1	USA	Roger Kingdom	12.98	OR
	2	GBR	Colin Jackson	13.28	
	3	USA	Anthony Campbell	13.38	
1992	1	CAN	Mark McKoy	13.12	
	2	USA	Tony Dees	13.24	
	3	USA	Jack Pierce	13.26	

MEN'S 400-METER HURDLES

YEAR	RANK	CTRY	ATHLETE	TIME	
1896			(not held)		
1900	1	USA	John Walter Tewksbury	57.6	
	2	FRA	Henri Tauzin	58.3	
	3	CAN/USA	George Orton		
1904	1	USA	Harry Hillman	53.0	
	2	USA	Frank Waller	53.2	
	3	USA	George Poage		
1906			(not held)		
1908	1	USA	Charles Bacon	55.0	WR
	2	USA	Harry Hillman	55.3	
	3	GBR	Leonard Tremeer	57.0	
1912			(not held)		
1920	1	USA	Frank Loomis	54.0	WR
	2	USA	John Norton	54.3	
	3	USA	August Desch	54.5	
1924	1	USA	F. Morgan Taylor	52.6	
	2	FIN	Erik Vilén	53.8	OR
	3	USA	Ivan Riley	54.2	
1928	1	GBR	David Burghley	53.4	OR
	2	USA	Frank Cuhel	53.6	
	3	USA	F. Morgan Taylor	53.6	
1932	1	IRL	Robert Tisdall	51.7	
	2	USA	Glenn Hardin	51.9	WR
	3	USA	F. Morgan Taylor	52.0	
1936	1	USA	Glenn Hardin	52.4	
	2	CAN	John Loaring	52.7	
	3	PHI	Miguel White	52.8	
1948	1	USA	Roy Cochran	51.1	OR
	2	SRI	Duncan White	51.8	
	3	SWE	Rune Larsson	52.2	
1952	1	USA	Charles Moore	50.8	OR
	2	URS	Yuri Lituyev	51.3	
	3	NZL	John Holland	52.2	

1956	1	USA	Glenn Davis	50.1	EOR
	2	USA	Silas "Eddie" Southern	50.8	
	3	USA	Joshua Culbreath	51.6	
1960	1	USA	Glenn Davis	49.3	EOR
	2	USA	Clifton Cushman	49.6	
	3	USA	Richard Howard	49.7	
1964	1	USA	Warren "Rex" Crawley	49.6	
	2	GBR	John Cooper	50.1	
	3	ITA	Salvatore Morale	50.1	
1968	1	GBR	David Hemery	48.12	WR
	2	GER	Gerhard Hennige	49.02	
	3	GBR	John Sherwood	49.03	
	4	USA	Geoffrey Vanderstock	49.06	
1972	1	UGA	John Akii-Bua	47.82	WR
	2	USA	Ralph Mann	48.51	
	3	GBR	David Hemery	48.52	
1976	1	USA	Edwin Moses	47.64	WR
	2	USA	Michael Shine	48.69	
	3	URS	Yevgeny Gavrilenko	49.45	
1980	1	GDR	Volker Beck	48.70	
	2	URS	Vassily Arkhipenko	48.86	
	3	GBR	Gary Oakes	49.11	
1984	1	USA	Edwin Moses	47.75	
	2	USA	Danny Harris	48.13	
	3	GER	Harald Schmid	48.19	
1988	1	USA	Andre Phillips	47.19	OR
	2	SEN	El Hadj Dia Ba	47.23	
	3	USA	Edwin Moses	47.56	
1992	1	USA	Kevin Young	46.78	WR
	2	JAM	Winthrop Graham	47.66	
	3	GBR	Kirss Akabusi	47.82	

MEN'S 3,000-METER STEEPLECHASE

YEAR	RANK	CTRY	ATHLETE	TIME	
1896 (not held)					
1900	1	CAN/USA	George Orton	7:34.4	
	2	GBR	Sidney Robinson	7:38.0	
	3	FRA	Jacques Chastanié		
1904	1	USA	James Lightbody	7:39.6	
	2	IRL	John Daly	7:40.6	
	3	USA	Arthur Newton		
1906 (not held)					
1908	1	GBR	Arthur Russell	10:47.8	
	2	GBR	Archie Robertson	10:48.4	
	3	USA	John Eisele		
1912 (not held)					
1920	1	GBR	Percy Hodge	10:00.4	OR
	2	USA	Patrick Flynn		
	3	ITA	Ernesto Ambrosini		
1924	1	FIN	Vilho "Ville" Ritola	9:33.6	OR
	2	FIN	Elias Katz	9:44.0	
	3	FRA	Paul Bontemps	9:45.2	
	4	USA	E. Marvin Rick	9:56.4	
1928	1	FIN	Toivo Loukola	9:21.8	WR
	2	FIN	Paavo Nurmi	9:31.2	
	3	FIN	Ove Andersen	9:35.6	
	7	USA	Melvin Dalton		
1932	1	FIN	Volmari Iso-Hollo	10:33.4	
	2	GBR	Thomas Evenson	10:46.0	
	3	USA	Joseph McCluskey	10:46.2	
1936	1	FIN	Volmari Iso-Hollo	9:03.8	WR
	2	FIN	Kaarlo Tuominen	9:06.8	
	3	GER	Alfred Dompert	9:07.2	
	5	USA	Harold Manning	9:11.2	
1948	1	SWE	Thore Sjöstrand	9:04.6	
	2	SWE	Erik Elmsäter	9:08.2	
	3	SWE	Göte Hagström	9:11.3	
	7	USA	H. Browning Ross	9:23.2	
1952	1	USA	Horace Ashenfelter	8:45.4	WR
	2	URS	Vladimir Kazantsev	8:51.6	
	3	GBR	John Disley	8:51.8	
1956	1	GBR	Christopher Brasher	8:41.2	OR
	2	HUN	Sándor Rozsnyól	8:43.6	
	3	NOR	Ernst Larsen	8:44.0	
	9	USA	Charles Jones	9:01.4	
1960	1	POL	Zdzislaw Krzyszkowiak	8:34.2	OR
	2	URS	Nikolai Sokolov	8:36.4	
	3	URS	Semyon Rzhischin	8:42.2	
	7	USA	Charles "Deacon" Jones	9:18.2	
1964	1	BEL	Gaston Roelants	8:30.8	OR
	2	GBR	Maurice Herriott	8:32.4	
	3	URS	Yvan Belyayev	8:33.8	
	5	USA	George Young	8:38.2	
1968	1	KEN	Amos Biwott	8:51.0	
	2	KEN	Benjamin Kogo	8:51.6	
	3	USA	George Young	8:51.8	
1972	1	KEN	H. Kipchoge Keino	8:23.6	OR
	2	KEN	Benjamin Jipcho	8:24.6	
	3	FIN	Tapio Kantanen	8:24.8	
	10	USA	Michael Manley	8:50.4	
1976	1	SWE	Anders Gärderud	8:08.2	WR
	2	POL	Bronislaw Malinowski	8:09.2	
	3	GDR	Frank Baumgartl	8:10.4	
	10	USA	Henry Marsh	8:23.99	
1980	1	POL	Bronislaw Malinowski	8:09.7	
	2	TAN	Filbert Bayi	8:12.5	
	3	ETH	Eshetu Tura	8:13.6	
1984	1	KEN	Julius Korir	8:11.80	
	2	FRA	Joseph Mahmoud	8:13.31	
	3	USA	Brian Diemer	8:14.06	
1988	1	KEN	Julius Kariuki	8:05.51	OR
	2	KEN	Peter Koech	8:06.79	
	3	GBR	Mark Rowland	8:07.96	
	6	USA	Henry Marsh	8:14.39	
1992	1	KEN	Mathew Birir	8:08.84	
	2	KEN	Patrick Sang	8:09.55	
	3	KEN	William Mutwol	8:10.74	
	7	USA	Brian Diemer	8:18.77	

MEN'S 20 KM WALK

YEAR	RANK	CTRY	ATHLETE	TIME	
1896-1952	(not held)				
1956	1	URS	Leonid Spirin	1:31:27.4	
	2	URS	Antanas Mikenas	1:32:03.0	
	3	URS	Bruno Junk	1:32:12.0	
	12	USA	Henry Laskau	1:38:46.8	
1960	1	URS	Vladimir Golubnichiy	1:34:07.2	
	2	AUS	Noel Freeman	1:34:16.4	
	3	GDR	Stanley Vickers	1:34:56.4	
	19	USA	Ronald Zinn	1:42:47.0	
1964	1	GBR	Kenneth Matthews	1:29:34.0	OR
	2	GDR	Dieter Lindner	1:31:13.2	
	3	URS	Vladimir Golubnichiy	1:31:59.4	
	6	USA	Ronald Zinn	1:32:43.0	
1968	1	URS	Vladimir Golubnichiy	1:33:58.4	
	2	MEX	José Pedraza Zuniga	1:34:00.0	
	3	URS	Nikolai Smaga	1:34:03.4	
	4	USA	Rudolph Haluza	1:35:00.2	
1972	1	GDR	Peter Frenkel	1:26:42.4	OR
	2	URS	Vladimir Golubnichiy	1:26:55.2	
	3	GDR	Hans Reimann	1:27:16.6	
	10	USA	Larry Young	1:32:53.4	
1976	1	MEX	Daniel Bautista Rocha	1:24:40.6	OR
	2	GDR	Hans-Georg Reimann	1:25:13.8	
	3	GDR	Peter Frenkel	1:25:29.4	
	20	USA	Ronald Laird	1:33:27.6	
1980	1	ITA	Maurizio Damilano	1:23:35.5	OR
	2	URS	Pyotr Pochinchuk	1:24:45.4	
	3	GDR	Roland Wieser	1:25:58.2	
1984	1	MEX	Ernesto Canto	1:23:13.0	OR
	2	MEX	Raúl González	1:23:20.0	
	3	ITA	Maurizio Damilano	1:23:26.0	
	7	USA	Marco Evoniuk	1:25:42.0	
1988	1	TCH	Jozef Pribilinec	1:19.57	OR
	2	GDR	Ronald Weigel	1:20.00	
	3	ITA	Maurizio Damilano	1:20.14	
	37	USA	Gary Morgan	1:27.26	
1992	1	ESP	Daniel Plaza Montero	1:21.45	
	2	CAN	Guillaume LeBlanc	1:22.25	
	3	ITA	Giovanni De Benedictis	1:23.11	
	30	USA	Allen James	1:35.12	

MEN'S 50 KM WALK

YEAR	RANK	CTRY	ATHLETE	TIME	
1896-1928	(not held)				
1932	1	GBR	Thomas Green	4:50:10	
	2	LAT	Jánis Dalinsch	4:57:20	
	3	ITA	Ugo Frigerio	4:59:06	
	8	USA	Ernest Crosbie	5:28:02	
1936	1	GBR	H. Harold Whitlock	4:30:41.4	OR
	2	SUI	Arthur Schwab	4:32:09.2	
	3	LAT	Adalberts Bubenko	4:32:42.2	
	21	USA	Albert Mangan	5:12:00.2	
1948	1	SWE	John Ljunggren	4:41:52	
	2	SUI	Godel Gaston	4:48:17	
	3	GBR	Tebbs Lloyd-Johnson	4:48:31	
	12	USA	Ernie Crosbie	5:15:16	
1952	1	ITA	Giuseppe Dordoni	4:28:07.8	OR
	2	TCH	Josef Dolezal	4:30:17.8	
	3	HUN	Antal Róka	4:31:27.2	
	22	USA	Adolf Weinacker	5:01:00.4	
1956	1	NZL	Norman Read	4:30:42.8	
	2	URS	Yevgeny Maskinskov	4:32:57.0	
	3	SWE	John Ljunggren	4:35:02.0	
	7	USA	Adolf Weinacker	5:00:16.0	
1960	1	GBR	Donald Thompson	4:25:30.0	OR
	2	SWE	John Ljunggren	4:25:47.0	
	3	ITA	Abdon Pamich	4:27:55.4	
	19	USA	Ronald Laird	4:53:21.6	
1964	1	ITA	Abdon Pamich	4:11:12.4	OR
	2	GBR	Paul Nihill	4:11:31.2	
	3	SWE	Ingvar Pettersson	4:14:17.4	
	21	USA	Christopher McCarthy	4:37:31.8	
1968	1	GDR	Christoph Höhne	4:20:13.6	
	2	HUN	Antal Kiss	4:30:17.0	
	3	USA	Larry Young	4:31:55.4	
1972	1	GER	Bernd Kannenberg	3:56:11.6	OR
	2	URS	Veniamin Soldatenko	3:58:24.0	
	3	USA	Larry Young	4:00:46.0	
1976	(not held)				
1980	1	GDR	Hartwig Gauder	3:49:24.0	OR
	2	ESP	Jorge Llopart	3:51:25.0	
	3	URS	Yevgeny Ivchenko	3:56:32.0	
1984	1	MEX	Raúl González	3:47:26	OR
	2	SWE	Bo Gustafsson	3:53:19	
	3	ITA	Alessandro Bellucci	3:53:45	
	6	USA	Carl Schueler	3:59:46	
1988	1	URS	Viacheslav Ivanenko	3:38.29	OR
	2	GDR	Ronald Weigel	3:38.56	
	3	GDR	Hartwig Gauder	3:39.45	
	22	USA	Marco Evoniuk	3:56.55	
1992	1	EUN	Andrey Perlov	3:50.13	
	2	MEX	Carlos Mercenario	3:52.09	
	3	GER	Ronald Weigel	3:53.45	
	23	USA	Carl Schueler	4:13.38	

MEN'S 4x100-METER RELAY

YEAR	RANK	CTRY	ATHLETES	TIME	
1896-1908	(not held)				
1912	1	GBR		42.4	OR
	2	SWE		42.6	
		GER		DISQ	
		USA	J. Ira Courtney / Frank Beloit / Clement Wilson / Carl Cooke *round 2, illegal baton exchange	DQ*	
1920	1	USA	Charles Paddock / Jackson Scholz /Loren Murchison / Morris Kirksey	42.2	WR
	2	FRA		42.6	
	3	SWE		42.9	
1924	1	USA	Francis Hussey / Louis Clarke / Loren Murchison / Alfred Leconey	41.0	EWR
	2	GBR		41.2	
	3	HOL		41.8	
1928	1	USA	Frank Wykoff / James Quinn / Charles Borah / Henry Russell	41.0	EWR
	2	GER		41.2	
	3	GBR		41.8	
1932	1	USA	Robert Kiesel / Emmett Toppino / Hector Dyer / Frank Wykoff	40.0	WR
	2	GER		40.9	
	3	ITA		41.2	
1936	1	USA	Jesse Owens / Ralph Metcalfe / Foy Draper / Frank Wykoff	39.8	WR
	2	ITA		41.1	
	3	GER		41.2	
1948	1	USA	Norwood "Barney" Ewell / Lorenzo Wright /Harrison Dillard / Melvin Patton	40.6	
	2	GBR		41.3	
	3	ITA		41.5	
1952	1	USA	F. Dean Smith / Harrison Dillard / Lindy Remigino / Andrew Stanfield	40.1	
	2	URS		40.3	
	3	HUN		40.5	
1956	1	USA	Ira Murchison / Leamon King / W. Thane Baker / Bobby Joe Morrow	39.5	WR
	2	URS		39.8	
	3	GER		40.3	
1960	1	GER		39.5	EWR
	2	URS		40.1	
	3	GBR		40.2	
		USA	Frank Budd / O. Ray Norton / Stonewall Johnson / David Sime	DQ	
1964	1	USA	O. Paul Drayton / Gerald Ashworth / Richard Stebbins / Robert Hayes	39.0	WR
	2	POL		39.3	
	3	FRA		39.3	
1968	1	USA	Charles Greene / Melvin Pender / Ronnie Ray Smith / James Hines	38.2	WR
	2	CUB		38.3	
	3	FRA		38.4	
1972	1	USA	Larry Black / Robert Taylor / Gerald Tinker / Edward Hart	38.19	EWR
	2	URS		38.50	
	3	GER		38.79	
1976	1	USA	Harvey Glance / John Wesley Jones /Millard Hampton / Steven Riddick	38.33	
	2	GDR		38.66	
	3	URS		38.78	
1980	1	URS		38.26	
	2	POL		38.33	
	3	FRA		38.53	
1984	1	USA	Sam Graddy / Ron Brown / Calvin Smith / Carl Lewis	37.83	WR
	2	JAM		38.62	
	3	CAN		38.70	
1988	1	URS		38.19	
	2	GBR		38.28	
	3	FRA		38.40	
		USA	Dennis Mitchell / Albert Robinson / Calvin Smith / Lee McNeill *round 1, heat 1.	DQ*	
1992	1	USA	Mike Marsh / Leroy Burrell / Dennis Mitchell / Carl Lewis / James Jett	37.40	WR
	2	NIG		37.98	
	3	CUB		38.00	

MEN'S 4x400-METER RELAY

YEAR	RANK	CTRY	ATHLETES	TIME	
1896-1906	(not held)				
1908	1	USA	William Hamilton / Nathaniel Cartmell /John Taylor / Melvin Sheppard	3:29.4	
	2	GER		3:32.4	
	3	HUN		3:32.5	
1912	1	USA	Melvin Sheppard / Edward / Lindberg / James "Ted" Meredith / Charles Reidpath	3:16.6	WR
	2	FRA		3:20.7	
	3	GBR		3:23.2	
1920	1	GBR		3:22.2	
	2	RSA		3:24.2	
	3	FRA		3:24.8	
	4	USA	James "Ted" Meredith / Frank Shea / George Bretnall / George Schiller	3:25.2	
1924	1	USA	Commodore Cochrane / Alan Helffrich /J. Oliver MacDonald / William Stevenson	3:16.0	WR
	2	SWE		3:17.0	
	3	GBR		3:17.4	
1928	1	USA	George Baird / Emerson "Bud" Spencer / Frederick Alderman / Raymond Barbuti	3:14.2	WR
	2	GER		3:14.8	
	3	CAN		3:15.4	
1932	1	USA	Ivan Fuqua / Edgar Ablowich / Karl Warner / William Carr	3:08.2	WR
	2	GBR		3:11.2	
	3	CAN		3:12.8	
1936	1	GBR		3:09.0	
	2	USA	Harold Cagle / Robert Young / Edward O'Brien / Alfred Fitch	3:11.0	
	3	GER		3:11.8	
1948	1	USA	Arthur Harnden / Clifford / Bourland Roy Cochran / Malvin Whitfield	3:10.4	
	2	FRA		3:14.8	
	3	SWE		3:16.0	
1952	1	JAM		3:03.9	WR
	2	USA	Ollie Matson / Gerald Cole / Charles Moore / Malvin Whitfield	3:04.0	
	3	GER		3:06.6	
1956	1	USA	Louis Jones / Jesse Mashburn / Charles Jenkins / Thomas Courtney	3:04.8	
	2	AUS		3:06.2	
	3	GBR		3:07.2	
1960	1	USA	Jack Yerman / Earl Young / Glenn Davis / Otis Davis	3:02.2	WR
	2	GER		3:02.7	
	3	BWI		3:04.0	
1964	1	USA	Ollan Cassell / Michael Larrabee / Ulis Williams / Henry Carr	3:00.7	WR
	2	GBR		3:01.6	
	3	TRI		3:01.7	
1968	1	USA	Vincent Matthews / Ronald Freeman /Larry James / Lee Evans	2:56.16	WR
	2	KEN		2:59.6	
	3	GER		3:00.5	
1972	1	KEN		2:59.8	
	2	GBR		3:00.5	
	3	FRA		3:00.7	
(no USA entry)					
1976	1	USA	Herman Frazier / Benjamin Brown /Frederick Newhouse / Maxie Parks	2:58.65	
	2	POL		3:01.43	
	3	GER		3:01.98	
1980	1	URS		3:01.1	
	2	GDR		3:01.3	
	3	ITA		3:04.3	
1984	1	USA	Sunder Nix / Ray Armstead / Alonzo Babers / Antonio McKay / Walter McCoy / Willie Smith	2:57.91	
	2	GBR		2:59.13	
	3	NGR		2:59.32	
1988	1	USA	Danny Everett / Steven Lewis / Kevin Robinzine / Butch Reynolds / Andrew Valmon / Antonio McKay	2:56.16	EWR
	2	JAM		3:00.30	
	3	FRG		3:00.56	
1992	1	USA	Andrew Valmon / Quincy Watts / Michael Johnson / Steve Lewis / Darnell Hall / Chip Jenkins	2:55.74	WR
	2	CUB		2:59.51	
	3	GBR		2:59.73	

MEN'S MARATHON

YEAR	RANK	CTRY	ATHLETE	TIME	
1896	1	GRE	Spiridon Louis	2:58.50	
	2	GRE	Charilaos Vasilakos	3:06.03	
	3	HUN	Gyula Kellner	3:06.35	
(no USA entry)					
1900	1	FRA	Michel Théato	2:59.45	
	2	FRA	Emile Champion	3:04.17	
	3	SWE	Ernst Fast	3:37.14	
	5	USA	Arthur Newton	4:04.12	
1904	1	USA	Thomas Hicks	3:28.63	
	2	FRA	Albert Corey	3:34.52	
	3	USA	Arthur Newton	3:47.33	
1906	1	CAN	William Sherring	2:51:23.6	
	2	SWE	John Svanberg	2:58:20.8	
	3	USA	William Frank	3:00:46.8	
1908		ITA	Dorando Pietri	2:54:46.4	
	1	USA	John Hayes	2:55:18.4	OR
	2	RSA	Charles Hefferson	2:56:06.0	
	3	USA	Joseph Forshaw	2:57:10.4	
1912	1	RSA	Kenneth McArthur	2:36:54.8	
	2	RSA	Christian Gitsham	2:37:52.0	
	3	USA	Gaston Strobino	2:38:42.4	
1920	1	FIN	Johannes Kolehmainen	2:32:35.8	WR
	2	EST	Jüri Lossmann	2:32:48.6	
	3	ITA	Valerio Arri	2:36:32.8	
	7	USA	Joseph Organ	2:41:30.8	
1924	1	FIN	Albin Stenroos	2:41:22.6	
	2	ITA	Romeo Bertini	2:47:19.6	
	3	USA	Clarence DeMar	2:48:14.0	
1928	1	FRA	Boughèra El Ouafi	2:32:57.0	
	2	CHI	Miguel Plaza Reyes	2:33:23.0	
	3	FIN	Martti Marttelin	2:35:02.0	
	5	USA	Joie Ray	2:36:04.0	
1932	1	ARG	Juan Carlos Zabala	2:31:36.0	OR
	2	GBR	Samuel Ferris	2:31:55.0	
	3	FIN	Armas Toivonen	2:32:12.0	
	7	USA	Albert Michelsen	2:39:38.0	
1936	1	JPN/KOR	Sohn Kee-chung (Kitei Son)	2:29:19.2	OR
	2	GBR	Ernest Harper	2:31:23.2	
	3	JPN/KOR	Nam Seung-yong (Shoryu Nan)	2:31:42.0	
	18	USA	John A. Kelley	2:49:32.4	
1948	1	ARG	Delfo Cabrera	2:34:51.6	
	2	GBR	Thomas Richards	2:35:07.6	
	3	BEL	Etienne Gailly	2:35:33.6	
	14	USA	Theodore J. Vogel	2:45:27.0	
1952	1	TCH	Emil Zátopek	2:23:03.2	OR
	2	ARG	Reinaldo Gorno	2:25:35.0	
	3	SWE	Gustav Jansson	2:26:07.0	
	13	USA	Victor Dyrgall	2:32:52.4	
1956	1	FRA	Alain Mimoun O'Kacha	2:25:00.0	
	2	YUG	Franjo Mihali	2:26:32.0	
	3	FIN	Veikko Karvonen	2:27:47.0	
	20	USA	Nick Costes	2:42:20.0	
1960	1	ETH	Abebe Bikila	2:15:16.2	WB
	2	MAR	Rhadi Ben Abdesselem	2:15:41.6	
	3	NZL	Barry Magee	2:17:18.2	
	19	USA	John Kelley	2:24:58.0	
1964	1	ETH	Abebe Bikila	2:12:11.2	WB
	2	GBR	Basil Heatley	2:16:19.2	
	3	JPN	Kokichi Tsuburaya	2:16:22.8	
	6	USA	Leonard "Buddy" Edelen	2:18:12.4	
1968	1	ETH	Mamo Wolde	2:20:26.4	
	2	JPN	Kenji Kimihara	2:23:31.0	
	3	NZL	Michael Ryan	2:23:45.0	
	14	USA	Kenneth Moore	2:29:49.4	
1972	1	USA	Frank Shorter	2:12:19.8	
	2	BEL	Karel Lismont	2:14:31.8	
	3	ETH	Mamo Wolde	2:15:08.4	
1976	1	GDR	Waldemar Cierpinski	2:09:55.0	OR
	2	USA	Frank Shorter	2:10:45.8	
	3	BEL	Karel Lismont	2:11:12.6	
1980	1	GDR	Waldemar Cierpinski	2:11:03.0	
	2	HOL	Gerald Nijboer	2:11:20.0	
	3	URS	Satymkul Dzhumanazarov	2:11:35.0	
1984	1	POR	Carlos Lopes	2:09:21.0	OR
	2	IRL	John Treacy	2:09:56.0	
	3	GBR	Charles Spedding	2:09:58.0	
	11	USA	Peter Pfitzinger	2:13:53.0	
1988	1	ITA	Gelindo Bordin	2:10.32	
	2	KEN	Douglas Wakiihuri	2:10.47	
	3	DJI	Houssein Ahmed Saleh	2:10.59	
	14	USA	Peter Pfitzinger	2:14.44	
1992	1	KOR	Hwang Young-cho	2:13.23	
	2	JPN	Koichi Morishita	2:13.45	
	3	GER	Stephan Timo Freigang	2:14.00	
	12	USA	Steven Spence	2:15.21	

MEN'S HIGH JUMP

YEAR	RANK	CTRY	ATHLETE	METERS	FT/IN	
1896	1	USA	Ellery Clark	1.81	5-11 1/4	
	2	USA	James Connolly	1.65	5-5	
	3	USA	Robert Garrett	1.65	5-5	
1900	1	USA	Irving Baxter	1.90	6-2 3/4	OR
	2	GBR/IRL	Patrick Leahy	1.78	5-10	
	3	HUN	Lajos Gönczy	1.75	5-8 3/4	
1904	1	USA	Samuel Jones	1.80	5-11	
	2	USA	Garrett Serviss	1.77	5-9 3/4	
	3	GER	Paul Weinstein	1.77	5-9 3/4	
1906	1	GBR/IRL	Cornelius Leahy	1.775	5-10	
	2	HUN	Lajos Gönczy	1.75	5-8 3/4	
	3	GRE	Themistoklis Diakidis	1.725	5-8	
	3	USA	Herbert Kerrigan	1.725	5-8	
1908	1	USA	Harry Porter	1.905	6-3	OR
	2	FRA	Georges "Géo" André	1.88	6-2	
	3	GBR/IRL	Cornelius Leahy	1.88	6-2	
1912	1	USA	Alma Richards	1.93	6-4	OR
	2	GER	Hans Liesche	1.91	6-3 1/4	
	3	USA	George Horine	1.89	6-2 1/4	
1920	1	USA	Richmond Landon	1.935	6-4	EOR
	2	USA	Harold Muller	1.90	6-2 3/4	
	3	SWE	Bo Ekelund	1.90	6-2 3/4	
1924	1	USA	Harold Osborn	1.98	6-6	OR
	2	USA	Leroy Brown	1.95	6-4 3/4	
	3	FRA	Pierre Lewden	1.92	6-3 1/2	
1928	1	USA	Robert King	1.94	6-4 1/2	
	2	USA	Benjamin Hedges	1.91	6-3 1/4	
	3	FRA	Claude Ménard	1.91	6-3 1/4	
1932	1	CAN	Duncan McNaughton	1.97	6-5 1/2	
	2	USA	Robert Van Osdel	1.97	6-5 1/2	
	3	PHI	Simeon Toribio	1.97	6-5 1/2	
1936	1	USA	Cornelius Johnson	2.03	6-8	OR
	2	USA	David Albritton	2.00	6-6 3/4	
	3	USA	Delos Thurber	2.00	6-6 3/4	
1948	1	AUS	John Winter	1.98	6-6	
	2	NOR	Björn Paulson	1.95	6-4 3/4	
	3	USA	George Stanich	1.95	6-4 3/4	
1952	1	USA	Walter Davis	2.04	6-8 1/2	OR
	2	USA	Kenneth Wiesner	2.01	6-7	
	3	BRA	José Telles da Conceição	1.98	6-6	
1956	1	USA	Charles Dumas	2.12	6-11 1/2	OR
	2	AUS	Charles Porter	2.10	6-10 3/4	
	3	URS	Igor Kashkarov	2.08	6-9 3/4	
1960	1	URS	Robert Shavlakadze	2.16	7-1	OR
	2	URS	Valery Brumel	2.16	7-1	
	3	USA	John Thomas	2.14	7-0 1/4	
1964	1	URS	Valery Brumel	2.18	7-1 3/4	OR
	2	USA	John Thomas	2.18	7-1 3/4	OR
	3	USA	John Rambo	2.16	7-1	
1968	1	USA	Richard Fosbury	2.24	7-4 1/4	OR
	2	USA	Edward Caruthers	2.22	7-3 1/4	
	3	URS	Valentin Gavrilov	2.20	7-2 1/2	
1972	1	URS	Yuri Tarmak	2.23	7-3 3/4	
	2	GDR	Stefan Junge	2.21	7-3	
	3	USA	Dwight Stones	2.21	7-3	
1976	1	POL	Jacek Wszola	2.25	7-4 1/2	OR
	2	CAN	Gregory Joy	2.23	7-3 3/4	
	3	USA	Dwight Stones	2.21	7-3	
1980	1	GDR	Gerd Wessig	2.36	7-8 3/4	WR
	2	POL	Jacek Wszola	2.31	7-7	
	3	GDR	Jörg Freimuth	2.31	7-7	
1984	1	GER	Dietmar Mögenburg	2.35	7-8 1/2	
	2	SWE	Patrik Sjöberg	2.33	7-7 3/4	
	3	CHN	Zhu Jianhua	2.31	7-7	
	4	USA	Dwight Stones	2.31	7-7	
1988	1	URS	Guennadi Avdeenko	2.38	7-9 3/4	OR
	2	USA	Hollis Conway	2.36	7-8 3/4	
	3T	URS	Roudolf Povarnitsyne	2.36	7-8 3/4	
	3T	SWE	Patrik Sjöberg	2.36	7-8 3/4	
1992	1	CUB	Javier Sotomayor	2.34	7-8 1/4	
	2	SWE	Patrik Sjöberg	2.34	7-8 1/4	
	3T	POL	Artur Partyka	2.34	7-8 1/4	
	3T	AUS	Timothy Forsythe	2.34	7-8 /14	
	3T	USA	Hollis Conway	2.34	7-8 1/4	

MEN'S LONG JUMP

YEAR	RANK	CTRY	ATHLETE	METERS	FT/IN	
1896	1	USA	Ellery Clark	6.35	20-10	
	2	USA	Robert Garrett	6.18	20-3 1/2	
	3	USA	James Connolly	6.11	20-0 1/2	
1900	1	USA	Alvin Kraenzlein	7.18	23-6 3/4	OR
	2	USA	Meyer Prinstein	7.17	23-6 1/4	
	3	GBR/IRL	Patrick Leahy	6.95	22-9 3/4	
1904	1	USA	Meyer Prinstein	7.34	24-1	OR
	2	USA	Daniel Frank	6.89	22-7 1/4	
	3	USA	Robert Stangland	6.88	22-7	
1906	1	USA	Meyer Prinstein	7.20	23-7 1/2	
	2	GBR/IRL	Peter O'Connor	7.02	23-0 1/2	
	3	USA	Hugo Friend	6.96	22-10	
1908	1	USA	Francis "Frank" Irons	7.48	24-6 1/2	OR
	2	USA	Daniel Kelly	7.09	23-3 1/4	
	3	CAN	Calvin Bricker	7.08	23-3	
1912	1	USA	Albert Gutterson	7.60	24-11 1/4	OR
	2	CAN	Calvin Bricker	7.21	23-8	
	3	SWE	Georg Aberg	7.18	23-6 3/4	
1920	1	SWE	William Petersson (Björneman)	7.15	23-5 1/2	
	2	USA	Carl Johnson	7.09	23-3 1/4	
	3	SWE	Erik Abrahamsson	7.08	23-2 3/4	
1924	1	USA	William De Hart Hubbard	7.44	24-5	
	2	USA	Edward Gourdin	7.27	23-10 1/4	
	3	NOR	Sverre Hansen	7.26	23-10	
1928	1	USA	Edward Hamm	7.73	25-4 1/2	OR
	2	HAI	Silvio Cator	7.58	24-10 1/2	
	3	USA	Alfred Bates	7.40	24-3 1/2	
1932	1	USA	Edward Gordon	7.64	25-0 3/4	
	2	USA	Charles Lambert Redd	7.60	24-11 1/4	
	3	JPN	Chuhei Nambu	7.45	24-5 1/2	
1936	1	USA	Jesse Owens	8.06	26-5 1/2	OR
	2	GER	Luz Long	7.87	25-10	
	3	JPN	Naoto Tajima	7.74	25-4 3/4	
1948	1	USA	Willie Steele	7.82	25-8	
	2	AUS	Thomas Bruce	7.55	24-9 1/4	
	3	USA	Herbert Douglas	7.54	24-9	
1952	1	USA	Jerome Biffle	7.57	24-10	
	2	USA	Meredith Gourdine	7.53	24-8 1/2	
	3	HUN	Ödön Földessy	7.30	23-11 1/2	
1956	1	USA	Gregory Bell	7.83	25-8 1/4	
	2	USA	John Bennett	7.68	25-2 1/2	
	3	FIN	Jorma Valkama	7.48	24-6 1/2	
1960	1	USA	Ralph Boston	8.12	26-7 3/4	OR
	2	USA	Irvin "Bo" Roberson	8.11	26-7 1/4	
	3	URS	Igor Ter-Ovanesyan	8.04	26-4 1/2	
1964	1	GBR	Lynn Davies	8.07	26-5 3/4	
	2	USA	Ralph Boston	8.03	26-4 1/4	
	3	URS	Igor Ter-Ovanesyan	7.99	26-2 3/4	
1968	1	USA	Robert Beamon	8.90	29-2 1/2	WR
	2	GDR	Klaus Beer	8.19	26-10 1/2	
	3	USA	Ralph Boston	8.16	26-9 1/4	
1972	1	USA	Randy Williams	8.24	27-0 1/2	
	2	GER	Hans Baumgartner	8.18	26-10	
	3	USA	Arnie Robinson	8.03	26-4 1/4	
1976	1	USA	Arnie Robinson	8.35	27-4 3/4	
	2	USA	Randy Williams	8.11	26-7 1/4	
	3	GDR	Frank Wartenberg	8.02	26-3 3/4	
1980	1	GDR	Lutz Dombrowski	8.54	28-0 1/4	
	2	GDR	Frank Paschek	8.21	26-11 1/4	
	3	URS	Valery Podluzhniy	8.18	26-10	
1984	1	USA	Carl Lewis	8.54	28-0 1/4	
	2	AUS	Gary Honey	8.24	27-0 1/2	
	3	ITA	Giovanni Evangelisti	8.24	27-0 1/2	
1988	1	USA	Carl Lewis	8.72	28-7 1/2	
	2	USA	Mike Powell	8.49	27-10 1/4	
	3	USA	Larry Myricks	8.27	27-1 3/4	
1992	1	USA	Carl Lewis	8.67	28-5 1/2	
	2	USA	Mike Powell	8.64	28-4 1/4	
	3	USA	Joe Greene	8.34	27-4 1/2	

MEN'S TRIPLE JUMP

YEAR	RANK	CTRY	ATHLETE	METERS	FT/IN	
1896	1	USA	James Connolly	13.71	44-11 3/4	
	2	FRA	Alexandre Tuffère	12.70	41-8	
	3	GRE	Ioannis Persakis	12.52	41-1	
1900	1	USA	Meyer Prinstein	14.47	47-5 3/4	OR
	2	USA	James Connolly	13.97	45-10	
	3	USA	Lewis Sheldon	13.64	44-9	
1904	1	USA	Meyer Prinstein	14.35	47-1	
	2	USA	Fred Englehardt	13.90	45-7 1/4	
	3	USA	Robert Stangland	13.36	43-10	
1906	1	GBR/IRL	Peter O'Connor	14.075	46-2 1/4	
	2	GBR/IRL	Cornelius Leahy	13.98	45-10 1/2	
	3	USA	Thomas Cronan	13.70	44-11 1/2	
1908	1	GBR/IRL	Timothy Ahearne	14.92	48-11 1/4	OR
	2	CAN	J. Garfield MacDonald	14.76	48-5 1/4	
	3	NOR	Edvard Larsen	14.39	47-2 3/4	
	5	USA	Platt Adams	14.07	46-2	
1912	1	SWE	Gustaf Lindblom	14.76	48-5 1/4	
	2	SWE	Georg Åberg	14.51	47-7 1/4	
	3	SWE	Erik Almlöf	14.17	46-6	
	5	USA	Platt Adams	14.09	46-2 3/4	
1920	1	FIN	Vilho Tuulos	14.50	47-7	
	2	SWE	Folke Jansson	14.48	47-6	
	3	SWE	Erik Almlöf	14.27	46-9 3/4	
	5	USA	Sherman Landers	14.17	46-6	
1924	1	AUS	Anthony Winter	15.525	50-11 1/4	WR
	2	ARG	Luis Brunetto	15.42	50-7 1/4	
	3	FIN	Vilho Tuulos	15.37	50-5	
	7	USA	R. Earle Wilson	14.235	46-8	
1928	1	JPN	Mikio Oda	15.21	49-11	
	2	USA	Levi Casey	15.17	49-9 1/4	
	3	FIN	Vilho Tuulos	15.11	49-7	
1932	1	JPN	Chuhei Nambu	15.72	51-7	WR
	2	SWE	Eric Svensson	15.32	50-3 1/4	
	3	JPN	Kenkichi Oshima	15.12	49-7 1/4	
	6	USA	Sol Furth	14.88	48-10	
1936	1	JPN	Naoto Tajima	16.00	52-6	WR
	2	JPN	Masao Harada	15.66	51-4 1/2	
	3	AUS	John Metcalfe	15.50	50-10 1/4	
	5	USA	Rolland Romero	15.08	49-5 3/4	
1948	1	SWE	Arne Åhman	15.40	50-6 1/4	
	2	AUS	George Avery	15.36	50-4 3/4	
	3	TUR	Ruhi Sarialp	15.02	49-3 1/2	
	10	USA	William Albans	14.33	47-0 1/4	
1952	1	BRA	Adhemar Ferreira da Silva	16.22	53-2 3/4	WR
	2	URS	Leonid Sherbakov	15.98	52-5 1/4	
	3	VEN	Arnoldo Devonish	15.52	50-11	
	4	USA	Walter Ashbaugh	15.39	50-6	
1956	1	BRA	Adhemar Ferreira da Silva	16.35	53-7 3/4	OR
	2	ICE	Vilhjálmur Einarsson	16.26	53-4 1/4	
	3	URS	Vitold Kreyer	16.02	52-6 3/4	
	4	USA	William Sharpe	15.88	52-1 1/4	
1960	1	POL	Józef Schmidt	16.81	55-2	
	2	URS	Vladimir Goryayev	16.63	54-6 3/4	
	3	URS	Vitold Kreyer	16.43	53-11	
	4	USA	Ira Davis	16.41	53-10 1/4	
1964	1	POL	Józef Schmidt	16.85	55-3 1/2	OR
	2	URS	Oleg Fyedoseyev	16.58	54-4 3/4	
	3	URS	Viktor Kravchenko	16.57	54-4 1/2	
	9	USA	Ira Davis	16.00	52-5 3/4	
1968	1	URS	Viktor Saneyev	17.39	57-0 3/4	WR
	2	BRA	Nelson Prudencio	17.27	56-8	
	3	ITA	Giuseppe Gentile	17.22	56-6	
	4	USA	Arthur Walker	17.12	56-2	
1972	1	URS	Viktor Saneyev	17.35	56-11 1/4	
	2	GDR	Jörg Drehmel	17.31	56-9 1/2	
	3	BRA	Nelson Prudencio	17.05	55-11 1/4	
	5	USA	John Craft	16.83	55-2 3/4	
1976	1	URS	Viktor Saneyev	17.29	56-8 3/4	
	2	USA	James Butts	17.18	56-4 1/2	
	3	BRA	João Carlos de Oliveira	16.90	55-5 1/2	
1980	1	URS	Jaak Uudmäe	17.35	56-11 1/4	
	2	URS	Viktor Saneyev	17.24	56-6 3/4	
	3	BRA	João Carlos de Oliveira	17.22	56-6	
1984	1	USA	Alfrederick Joyner	17.26	56-7 1/2	
	2	USA	Mike Conley	17.18	56-4 1/2	
	3	GBR	Keith Connor	16.87	55-4 1/4	
1988	1	BUL	Hristo Markov	17.61	57-9 1/2	OR
	2	URS	Igor Lapchine	17.52	57-5 3/4	
	3	URS	Alexandre Kovalenko	17.42	57-2	
	5	USA	Charlie Simpkins	17.29	56-8 3/4	
1992	1	USA	Mike Conley	18.17	59-7 1/2	
	2	USA	Charles Simpkins	17.60	57-9	
	3	BAH	Frank Rutherford	17.36	56-11 1/2	

MEN'S POLE VAULT

YEAR	RANK	CTRY	ATHLETE	METERS	FT/IN	
1896	1	USA	William Welles Hoyt	3.30	10-10	
	2	USA	Albert Tyler	3.25	10-8	
	3	GRE	Evangelos Damaskos	2.85	9-4 1/4	
1900	1	USA	Irving Baxter	3.30	10-10	
	2	USA	Michael Colket	3.25	10-8	
	3	NOR	Carl-Albert Andersen	3.20	10-6	
1904	1	USA	Charles Dvorak	3.50	11-5 3/4	
	2	USA	Leroy Samse	3.43	11-3	
	3	USA	Louis Wilkins	3.43	11-3	
1906	1	FRA	Fernand Gonder	3.50	11-5 3/4	
	2	SWE	Bruno Söderström	3.40	11-1 3/4	
	3	USA	Edward Glover	3.35	10-11 3/4	
1908	1T	USA	Edward Cooke	3.71	12-2	OR
	1T	USA	Alfred Gilbert	3.71	12-2	OR
	3	CAN	Ed Archibald	3.58	11-9	
1912	1	USA	Harry Babcock	3.95	12-11 1/2	OR
	2	USA	Frank Nelson	3.85	12-7 1/2	
	3	USA	Marcus Wright	3.85	12-7 1/2	
1920	1	USA	Frank Foss	4.09	13-5	WR
	2	DEN	Henry Petersen	3.70	12-1 1/2	
	3	USA	Edwin Myers	3.60	11-9 3/4	
1924	1	USA	Lee Barnes	3.95	12-11 1/2	
	2	USA	Glenn Graham	3.95	12-11 1/2	
	3	USA	James Brooker	3.90	12-9 1/2	
1928	1	USA	Sabin Carr	4.20	13-9 1/4	OR
	2	USA	William Droegemuller	4.10	13-5 1/4	
	3	USA	Charles McGinnis	3.95	12-11 1/2	
1932	1	USA	William Miller	4.31	14-1 3/4	OR
	2	JPN	Shuhei Nishida	4.30	14-1 1/4	
	3	USA	George Jefferson	4.20	13-9 1/2	
1936	1	USA	Earle Meadows	4.35	14-3 1/4	OR
	2	JPN	Shuhei Nishida	4.25	13-11 1/4	
	3	JPN	Sueo Oe	4.25	13-11 1/4	
1948	1	USA	O. Guinn Smith	4.30	14-1 1/4	
	2	FIN	Erkki Kataja	4.20	13-9 1/4	
	3	USA	Robert Richards	4.20	13-9 1/4	
1952	1	USA	Robert Richards	4.55	14-11	OR
	2	USA	Donald Laz	4.50	14-9	
	3	SWE	Ragnar Lundberg	4.40	14-5 1/4	
1956	1	USA	Robert Richards	4.56	14-11 1/2	OR
	2	USA	Robert Gutowski	4.53	14-10 1/4	
	3	GRE	Georgios Roubanis	4.50	14-9	

1960	1	USA	Donald Bragg	4.70	15-5	OR
	2	USA	Ronald Morris	4.60	15-1	
	3	FIN	Eeles Landström	4.55	14-11	
1964	1	USA	Frederick Hansen	5.10	16-8 3/4	OR
	2	GER	Wolfgang Reinhardt	5.05	16-6 3/4	
	3	GER	Klaus Lehnertz	5.00	16-4 3/4	
1968	1	USA	Robert Seagren	5.40	17-8 1/2	OR
	2	GER	Claus Schiprowski	5.40	17-8 1/2	OR
	3	GDR	Wolfgang Nordwig	5.40	17-8 1/2	OR
1972	1	GDR	Wolfgang Nordwig	5.50	18-0 1/2	OR
	2	USA	Robert Seagren	5.40	17-8 1/2	
	3	USA	Jan Johnson	5.35	17-6 1/2	
1976	1	POL	Tadeusz lusarski	5.50	18-0 1/2	EOR
	2	FIN	Antti Kalliomäki	5.50	18-0 1/2	EOR
	3	USA	David Roberts	5.50	18-0 1/2	EOR
1980	1	POL	Wladyslaw Kozakiewicz	5.78	18-11 1/2	WR
	2	POL	Tadeusz lusarski	5.65	18-6 1/2	
	3	URS	Konstantin Volkov	5.65	18-6 1/2	
1984	1	FRA	Pierre Quinon	5.75	18-10 1/4	
	2	USA	Mike Tully	5.65	18-6 1/2	
	3	USA	Earl Bell	5.60	18-4 1/2	
1988	1	URS	Sergei Bubka	5.90	19-4 1/4	OR
	2	URS	Radion Gataoulline	5.85	19-2 1/4	
	3	URS	Grigori Egorov	5.80	19-0 1/4	
	4	USA	Earl Bell	5.70	18-8 1/4	
1992	1	EUN	Maxim Tarassov	5.80	19-0 1/4	
	2	EUN	Igor Trandenkov	5.80	19-0 1/4	
	3	ESP	Javier Garcia	5.75	18-10 1/4	
	4	USA	Kory Tarpenning	5.75	18-10 1/4	

MEN'S SHOT PUT

YEAR	RANK	CTRY	ATHLETE	METERS	FT/IN	
1896	1	USA	Robert Garrett	11.22	36-9 3/4	
	2	GRE	Miltiades Gouskos	11.20	36-9	
	3	GRE	Georgios Papasideris	10.36	34-0	
1900	1	USA	Richard Sheldon	14.10	46-3 1/4	OR
	2	USA	Josiah McCracken	12.85	42-2	
	3	USA	Robert Garrett	12.37	40-7	
1904	1	USA	Ralph Rose	14.81	48-7	WR
	2	USA	William Coe	14.40	47-3	
	3	USA	Leon Feuerbach	13.37	43-10 1/2	
1906	1	USA	Martin Sheridan	12.325	40-5 1/4	
	2	HUN	Mihály Dávid	11.83	38-9 3/4	
	3	SWE	Eric Lemming	11.26	36-11 1/2	
1908	1	USA	Ralph Rose	14.21	46-7 1/2	
	2	GBR/IRL	Dennis Horgan	13.62	44-8 1/4	
	3	USA	John Garreis	13.18	43-3	
1912	1	USA	Patrick McDonald	15.34	50-4	OR
	2	USA	Ralph Rose	15.25	50-0 1/2	
	3	USA	Lawrence Whitney	13.93	45-8 1/2	
1920	1	FIN	Frans "Ville" Pörhölä	14.81	48-7 1/4	
	2	FIN	Elmer Niklander	14.155	46-5 1/4	
	3	USA	Harry Liversedge	14.15	46-5 1/4	
1924	1	USA	Clarence "Bud" Houser	14.99	49-2 1/4	
	2	USA	Glenn Hartranft	14.89	48-10 1/4	
	3	USA	Ralph Hills	14.64	48-0 1/2	
1928	1	USA	John Kuck	15.87	52-0 3/4	WR
	2	USA	Herman Brix	15.75	51-8 1/4	
	3	GER	Emil Hirschfeld	15.72	51-7	
1932	1	USA	Leo Sexton	16.00	52-6	OR
	2	USA	Harlow Rothert	15.67	51-5	
	3	TCH	Frantisek Douda	15.61	51-2 3/4	
1936	1	GER	Hans Woellke	16.20	53-1 3/4	OR
	2	FIN	Sulo Bärlund	16.12	52-10 3/4	
	3	GER	Gerhard Stöck	15.66	51-4 1/2	
	4	USA	Samuel Francis	15.45	50-8 1/4	
1948	1	USA	Wilbur Thompson	17.12	56-2	OR
	2	USA	F. James Delaney	16.68	54-8 3/4	
	3	USA	James Fuchs	16.42	53-10 1/2	
1952	1	USA	W. Parry O'Brien	17.41	57-1 1/2	OR
	2	USA	C. Darrow Hooper	17.39	57-0 3/4	
	3	USA	James Fuchs	17.06	55-11 3/4	
1956	1	USA	W. Parry O'Brien	18.57	60-11 1/4	OR
	2	USA	William Nieder	18.18	59-7 3/4	
	3	TCH	Jiri Skobla	17.65	57-11	
1960	1	USA	William Nieder	19.68	64-6 3/4	OR
	2	USA	W. Parry O'Brien	19.11	62-8 1/2	
	3	USA	Dallas Long	19.01	62-4 1/2	
1964	1	USA	Dallas Long	20.33	66-8 1/2	OR
	2	USA	James Randel Matson	20.20	66-3 1/4	
	3	HUN	Vilmos Varju	19.39	63-7 1/2	
1968	1	USA	James Randel Matson	20.54	67-4 3/4	
	2	USA	George Woods	20.12	66-0 1/4	
	3	URS	Eduard Gushchin	20.09	65-11	
1972	1	POL	Wladyslaw Komar	21.18	69-6	OR
	2	USA	George Woods	21.17	69-5 1/2	
	3	GDR	Hartmut Briesenick	21.14	69-4 1/4	
1976	1	GDR	Udo Beyer	21.05	69-0 3/4	
	2	URS	Yevgeny Mironov	21.03	69-0	
	3	URS	Aleksandr Baryshnikov	21.00	68-10 3/4	
	4	USA	Allan Feuerbach	20.55	67-5 1/2	
1980	1	URS	Vladimir Kiselyov	21.35	70-0 1/2	OR
	2	URS	Aleksandr Baryshnikov	21.08	69-2	
	3	GDR	Udo Beyer	21.06	69-1 1/4	
1984	1	ITA	Alessandro Andrei	21.26	69-9	
	2	USA	Michael Carter	21.09	69-2 1/2	
	3	USA	Dave Laut	20.97	68-9 3/4	
1988	1	GDR	Ulf Timmermann	22.47	73-8 3/4	OR
	2	USA	Randy Barnes	22.39	73-5 1/2	
	3	SUI	Werner Guenthoer	21.99	72-1 3/4	
1992	1	USA	Michael Stulce	21.70	71-2 1/2	
	2	USA	James Doehring	20.96	68-9 1/4	
	3	EUN	Viacheslav Lykho	20.94	68-8 1/2	

MEN'S DISCUS

YEAR	RANK	CTRY	ATHLETE	METERS	FT/IN	
1896	1	USA	Robert Garrett	29.15	95-7 1/2	
	2	GRE	Panagiotis Paraskevopoulos	28.955	95-0	
	3	GRE	Sotirios Versis	28.78	94.5	
1900	1	HUN	Rudolf (Rezsö) Bauer	36.04	118-3	OR
	2	TCH	Frantisek Janda-Suk	35.25	115-7	
	3	USA	Richard Sheldon	34.60	113-6	
1904	1	USA	Martin Sheridan	39.28	128-10 1/2	OR
	2	USA	Ralph Rose	39.28	128-10 1/2	
	3	GRE	Nicolaos Georgantas	37.68	123-7 1/2	
1906	1	USA	Martin Sheridan	41.46	136-0	
	2	GRE	Nicolaos Georgantas	38.06	124-10	
	3	FIN	Werner Järvinen	36.82	120-9	
1908	1	USA	Martin Sheridan	40.89	134-2	OR
	2	USA	Merritt Griffin	40.70	133-6	
	3	USA	Marquis Horr	39.44	129-5	
1912	1	FIN	Armas Taipale	45.21	148-3	OR
	2	USA	Richard Byrd	42.32	138-10	
	3	USA	James Duncan	42.28	138-8	
1920	1	FIN	Elmer Niklander	44.685	146-7	
	2	FIN	Armas Taipale	44.19	145-0	
	3	USA	Augustus Pope	42.13	138-2	
1924	1	USA	Clarence "Bud" Houser	46.15	151-4	OR
	2	FIN	Vilho Niittymaa	44.95	147-5	
	3	USA	Thomas Lieb	44.83	147-0	
1928	1	USA	Clarence "Bud" Houser	47.32	155-3	OR
	2	FIN	L. Antero Kivi	47.23	154-11	
	3	USA	James Corson	47.10	154-6	
1932	1	USA	John Anderson	49.49	162-4	OR
	2	USA	Henri Jean Laborde	48.47	159-0	
	3	FRA	Paul Winter	47.85	156-11	
1936	1	USA	W. Kenneth Carpenter	50.48	165-7	OR
	2	USA	Gordon Dunn	49.36	161-11	
	3	ITA	Giorgio Oberweger	49.23	161-6	
1948	1	ITA	Adolfo Consolini	52.78	173-2	OR
	2	ITA	Giuseppe Tosi	51.78	169-10	
	3	USA	Fortune Gordien	50.77	166-6	
1952	1	USA	Sim Iness	55.03	180-6	OR
	2	ITA	Adolfo Consolini	53.78	176-5	
	3	USA	James Dillon	53.28	174-10	
1956	1	USA	Alfred Oerter	56.36	184-11	OR
	2	USA	Fortune Gordien	54.81	179-9	
	3	USA	Desmond Koch	54.40	178-6	
1960	1	USA	Alfred Oerter	59.18	194-2	OR
	2	USA	Richard "Rink" Babka	58.02	190-4	
	3	USA	Richard Cochran	57.16	187-6	
1964	1	USA	Alfred Oerter	61.00	200-1	OR
	2	TCH	Ludvik Danek	60.52	198-7	
	3	USA	David Weill	59.49	195-2	
1968	1	USA	Alfred Oerter	64.78	212-6	OR
	2	GDR	Lothar Milde	63.08	206-11	
	3	TCH	Ludvik Danek	62.92	206-5	
1972	1	TCH	Ludvik Danek	64.40	211-3	
	2	USA	L. Jay Silvester	63.50	208-4	
	3	SWE	Björn Rickard Bruch	63.40	208-0	
1976	1	USA	Mac Wilkins	67.50	221-5	
	2	GDR	Wolfgang Schmidt	66.22	217-3	
	3	USA	John Powell	65.70	215-7	
1980	1	URS	Viktor Rashchupkin	66.64	218-8	
	2	TCH	Imrich Bugár	66.38	217-9	
	3	CUB	Luis Delis Fournier	66.32	217-7	
1984	1	GER	Rolf Danneberg	66.60	218-6	
	2	USA	Mac Wilkins	66.30	217-6	
	3	USA	John Powell	65.46	214-9	
1988	1	GDR	Jurgen Schult	68.82	225-9	OR
	2	URS	Romas Oubartas	67.48	221-5	
	3	FRG	Rolf Danneberg	67.38	221-1	
	5	USA	Mac Wilkins	65.90	216-2	
1992	1	LTU	Romas Ubartas	65.12	213-8	
	2	GER	Jurgen Schult	64.94	213-1	
	3	CUB	Roberto Moya	64.12	210-4	
	12	USA	Anthony Washington	59.96	196-8 3/4	

MEN'S JAVELIN

YEAR	RANK	CTRY	ATHLETE	METERS	FT/IN	
1896-1906		(not held)				
1908	1	SWE	Eric Lemming	54.825	179-10	WR
	2	NOR	Arne Halse	50.57	165-11	
	3	SWE	Otto Nilsson	47.105	154-6	
(no USA entry)						
1912	1	SWE	Eric Lemming	60.64	198-11	WR
	2	FIN	Julius Juho Saaristo	58.66	192-5	
	3	HUN	Mór Kóczán	55.50	182-1	
(no USA entry)						
1920	1	FIN	Jonni Myyrä	65.78	215-10	OR
	2	FIN	Urho Peltonen	63.50	208-4	
	3	FIN	Paavo Jaale-Johansson	63.095	207-0	
	7	USA	Milton Angier	59.26	194-5	
1924	1	FIN	Jonni Myrrä	62.96	206-7	
	2	SWE	Gunnar Lindström	60.92	199-10	
	3	USA	Eugene Oberst	58.35	191-5	
1928	1	SWE	Erik Lundkvist	66.60	218-6	OR
	2	HUN	Béla Szepes	65.26	214-1	
	3	NOR	Olav Sunde	63.97	209-10	
		USA	Charles Harlow / Lee Bartlett / Creth Hines / Arthur Sager		elim. trials	
1932	1	FIN	Matti Järvinen	72.71	238-6	OR
	2	FIN	Matti Sippala	69.80	229-0	
	3	FIN	Eino Penttilä	68.70	225-5	
	5	USA	Lee Bartlett	64.46	211-6	
1936	1	GER	Gerhard Stöck	71.84	235-8	
	2	FIN	Yrjö Nikkanen	70.77	232-2	
	3	FIN	Kaarlo Kalervo Toivonen	70.72	232-0	
	6	USA	Alton Terry	67.15	220-4	
1948	1	FIN	Kai Tapio Rautavaara	69.77	228-10	
	2	USA	Steve Seymour	67.56	221-8	
	3	HUN	József Várszegi	67.03	219-11	
1952	1	USA	Cyrus Young	73.78	242-1	OR
	2	USA	William Miller	72.46	237-9	
	3	FIN	Toivo Hyytiäinen	71.89	235-10	
1956	1	NOR	Egil Danielson	85.71	281-2	WR
	2	POL	Janusz Sidlo	79.98	262-5	
	3	URS	Viktor Tsibulenko	79.50	260-10	
	10	USA	Philip Conley	70.59	228-3 1/2	
1960	1	URS	Viktor Tsibulenko	84.64	277-8	
	2	GDR	Walter Krüger	79.36	260-4	
	3	HUN	Gergely Kulcsár	78.57	257-9	
	10	USA	Albert Cantello	74.70		
1964	1	FIN	Pauli Nevala	82.66	271-2	
	2	HUN	Gergely Kulcsár	82.32	270-1	
	3	URS	Jãnis Lusis	80.57	264-4	
		USA	Walter Red	71.52	234-7 3/4	
1968	1	URS	Jãnis Lusis	90.10	295-7	OR
	2	FIN	Jorma Kinnunen	88.58	290-7	
	3	HUN	Gergely Kulcsár	87.06	285-7	
	9	USA	Mike Murro	80.08	262-8 3/4	
1972	1	GER	Klaus Wolfermann	90.48	296-10	OR
	2	URS	Jãnis Lusis	90.46	296-9	
	3	USA	William Schmidt	84.42	277-0	
1976	1	HUN	Miklos Németh	94.58	310-4	WR
	2	FIN	Hannu Siitonen	87.92	288-5	
	3	ROM	Gheorghe Megelea	87.16	285-11	
	5	USA	Sam Colson	86.16	282-8	
1980	1	URS	Dainis Kula	91.20	299-2	
	2	URS	Aleksandr Makarov	89.64	294-1	
	3	GDR	Wolfgang Hanisch	86.72	284-6	
1984	1	FIN	Arto Härkönen	86.76	284-8	
	2	GBR	David Ottley	85.74	281-3	
	3	SWE	Kenth Eldebrink	83.72	274-8	
	10	USA	Tom Petranoff	78.41	257-3	
1988	1	FIN	Tapio Korjus	84.28	276-6	
	2	TCH	Jan Zelezny	84.12	276	
	3	FIN	Seppo Raty	83.26	273-2	
		USA	David Stephens			
1992	1	TCH	Jan Zelezny	89.66	294-2	OR
	2	FIN	Seppo Raty	86.60	284-1	
	3	GBR	Steve Backley	83.38	273-7	
	7	USA	Mike Barnett	78.64	258-4	

MEN'S HAMMER

YEAR	RANK	CTRY	ATHLETE	METERS	FT/IN	
1896 (not held)						
1900	1	USA	John Flanagan	49.73	163-1	
	2	USA	Thomas Truxtun Hare	49.13	161-2	
	3	USA	Josiah McCracken	42.46	139-4	
1904	1	USA	John Flanagan	51.23	168-1	OR
	2	USA	John DeWitt	50.26	164-11	
	3	USA	Ralph Rose	45.73	150-0	
1906 (not held)						
1908	1	USA	John Flanagan	51.92	170-4	OR
	2	USA	Matthew McGrath	51.18	167-11	
	3	USA	Cornelius Walsh	48.51	159-1	
1912	1	USA	Matthew McGrath	54.74	179-7	OR
	2	CAN	Duncan Gillis	48.39	158-9	
	3	USA	Clarence Childs	48.17	158-0	
1920	1	USA	Patrick Ryan	52.875	173-5	
	2	SWE	Carl Johan Lind	48.43	158-10	
	3	USA	Basil Bennet	48.25	158-3	
1924	1	USA	Frederick Tootell	53.295	174-10	
	2	USA	Matthew McGrath	50.84	166-9	
	3	GBR	Malcolm Nokes	48.875	1604	
1928	1	IRL	Patrick O'Callaghan	51.39	168-7	
	2	SWE	Ossian Skiöld	51.29	168-3	
	3	USA	Edmund Black	49.03	160-10	
1932	1	IRL	Patrick O'Callaghan	53.92	176-11	
	2	FIN	Frans "Ville" Pörhölä	52.27	171-6	
	3	USA	Peter Zaremba	50.33	165.1	
1936	1	GER	Karl Hein	56.49	185-4	OR
	2	GER	Erwin Blask	55.04	180-7	
	3	SWE	O. Fred Warngård	54.83	179-10	
	5	USA	William Rowe	51.66	169-6	
1948	1	HUN	Imre Németh	56.07	183-11	
	2	YUG	Ivan Gubijan	54.27	178-0	
	3	USA	Robert Bennett	53.73	176-3	
1952	1	HUN	József Csérmák	60.34	197-11	WR
	2	GER	Karl Storch	58.86	193-1	
	3	HUN	Imre Németh	57.74	189-5	
	11	USA	Samuel Felton, Jr.	53.32	174-11 1/4	
1956	1	USA	Harold Connolly	63.19	207-3	OR
	2	URS	Mikhail Krivonosov	63.03	206-9	
	3	URS	Anatoly Samotsvetov	62.56	205-3	
1960	1	URS	Vasily Rudenkov	67.10	220-2	OR
	2	HUN	Gyula Zsivótzky	65.79	215-10	
	3	POL	Tadeusz Rut	65.64	215-4	
	8	USA	Harold Connolly	63.58	208-7	
1964	1	URS	Romuald Klim	69.74	228-10	OR
	2	HUN	Gyula Zsivótzky	69.09	226-8	
	3	GER	Uwe Beyer	68.09	223-4	
	6	USA	Harold Connolly	66.65	218-8	
1968	1	HUN	Gyula Zsivótzky	73.36	240-8	OR
	2	URS	Romuald Klim	73.28	240-5	
	3	HUN	Lázár Lovász	69.78	228-11	
	12	USA	Ed Burke	65.72	215-7 1/2	
1972	1	URS	Anatoly Bondarchuk	75.50	247-8	OR
	2	GDR	Jochen Sachse	74.96	245-11	
	3	URS	Vasily Khmelevski	74.04	242-11	
	12	USA	Thomas Gage	69.5	228-0 1/4	
1976	1	URS	Yuri Sedykh	77.52	254-4	OR
	2	URS	Aleksei Spiridonov	76.08	249-7	
	3	URS	Anatoly Bondarchuk	75.48	247-8	
		USA	Lawrence Hart (67.74/222-4)		elim. 3rd rd	
1980	1	URS	Yuri Sedykh	81.80	268-4	WR
	2	URS	Sergei Litvinov	80.64	264-7	
	3	URS	Yuri Tamm	78.96	259-1	
1984	1	FIN	Juha Tiainen	78.08	256-2	
	2	GER	Karl-Hans Riehm	77.98	255-10	
	3	GER	Klaus Ploghaus	76.68	251-7	
	5	USA	Bill Green	75.60	248-0	
1988	1	URS	Serguei Litvinov	84.80	278-2	OR
	2	URS	Yuriy Sedykh	83.76	274-10	
	3	URS	Iouri Tamm	81.16	266-3	
		USA	Lance Deal		elim.	
1992	1	EUN	Andrey Abduvaliyev	82.54	270-9 1/2	
	2	EUN	Igor Astapkovich	81.96	268-10 3/4	
	3	EUN	Igor Nikulin	81.38	267-0	
	7	USA	Lance Deal	76.84	252-1 1/4	

DECATHLON

YEAR	RANK	CTRY	ATHLETE	POINTS	
1896-1900		(not held)			
1904	1	IRL	Thomas Kiely	6036	
	2	USA	Adam Gunn	5907	
	3	USA	Thomas Truxtun Hare	5813	
1906-1908		(not held)			
1912	1	USA	James Thorpe	8412	WR
	2	SWE	Hugo Wieslander	7724	
	3	SWE	Charles Lomberg	7414	
1920	1	NOR	Helge Lövland	6803	
	2	USA	Brutus Hamilton	6771	
	3	SWE	Bertil Ohlson	6580	
1924	1	USA	Harold Osborn	7711	WR
	2	USA	Emerson Norton	7351	
	3	EST	Alexander Klumberg	7329	
1928	1	FIN	Paavo Yrjölä	8053	WR
	2	FIN	Akilles Järvinen	7932	
	3	USA	John Kenneth Doherty	7707	
1932	1	USA	James Bausch	8462	WR
	2	FIN	Akilles Järvinen	8292	
	3	GER	Wolrad Eberle	8031	
1936	1	USA	Glenn Morris	7900	WR
	2	USA	Robert Clark	7601	
	3	USA	Jack Parker	7275	
1948	1	USA	Robert Mathias	7139	
	2	FRA	Ignace Heinrich	6974	
	3	USA	Floyd Simmons	6950	
1952	1	USA	Robert Mathias	7887	WR
	2	USA	Milton Campbell	6975	
	3	USA	Floyd Simmons	6788	
1956	1	USA	Milton Campbell	7937	OR
	2	USA	Rafer Johnson	7587	
	3	URS	Vassily Kuznyetsov	7465	
1960	1	USA	Rafer Johnson	8392	OR
	2	TAI	Yang Chuan-Kwang	8334	
	3	URS	Vassily Kuznyetsov	7809	
1964	1	GER	Willi Holdorf	7887	
	2	URS	Rein Aun	7842	
	3	GER	Hans-Joachim Walde	7809	
	4	USA	Paul Herman	7787	

1968	1	USA	**William Toomey**	**8193**	OR
	2	GER	Hans-Joachim Walde	8111	
	3	GER	Kurt Bendlin	8064	
1972	1	URS	Nikolai Avilov	8454	WR
	2	URS	Leonid Litvinenko	8035	
	3	POL	Ryszard Katus	7984	
	4	USA	**Jefferson Bennett**	**7974**	
1976	1	USA	**Bruce Jenner**	**8617**	WR
	2	GER	Guido Kratschmer	8411	
	3	URS	Nikolai Avilov	8369	
1980	1	GBR	Francis "Daley" Thompson	8495	
	2	URS	Yuri Kutsenko	8331	
	3	URS	Sergei Zhelanov	8315	
1984	1	GBR	Francis "Daley" Thompson	8798	EWR
	2	GER	Jürgen Hingsen	8673	
	3	GER	Siegfried Wentz	8412	
	6	USA	**John Crist**	**8130**	
1988	1	GDR	Christian Schenk	8488	
	2	GDR	Torsten Voss	8399	
	3	CAN	Dave Steen	8328	
	7	USA	**Tim Bright**	**8216**	
1992	1	TCH	Robert Zmelik	8611	
	2	ESP	Antonio Penalver	8412	
	3	USA	**David Johnson**	**8309**	

WOMEN'S 100 METERS

YEAR	RANK	CTRY	ATHLETE	TIME	
1896-1924		(not held)			
1928	1	USA	**Elizabeth Robinson**	**12.2**	EWR
	2	CAN	Fanny Rosenfield	12.3	
	3	CAN	Ethel Smith	12.3	
1932	1	POL	Stanislawa Walasiewicz	11.9	EWR
	2	CAN	Hilde Strike	11.9	
	3	USA	**Wilhelmina Von Bremen**	**12.0**	
1936	1	USA	**Helen Stephens**	**11.5w**	
	2	POL	Stanislawa Walasiewicz	11.7	
	3	GER	Käthe Krauss	11.9	
1948	1	HOL	Francina "Fanny" Blankers-Koen	11.9	
	2	GBR	Dorothy Manley	12.2	
	3	AUS	Shirley Strickland	12.2	
		USA	**Audrey Patterson**	**12.8**	
		USA	**Mabel E. Walker**	**12.8**	
1952	1	AUS	Marjorie Jackson	11.5	EWR
	2	RSA	Daphne Hasenjager (Robb)	11.8	
	3	AUS	Shirley Strickland	11.9	
	6	USA	**Mae Faggs**	**12.1**	
1956	1	AUS	Betty Cuthbert	11.5	
	2	GDR	Christa Stubnick	11.7	
	3	AUS	Marlene Matthews	11.7	
	4	USA	**Isabelle Daniels**	**11.8**	
1960	1	USA	**Wilma Rudolph**	**11.0w**	
	2	GBR	Dorothy Hyman	11.3	
	3	ITA	Giuseppina Leone	11.3	
1964	1	USA	**Wyomia Tyus**	**11.4**	
	2	USA	**Edith McGuire**	**11.6**	
	3	POL	Ewa Klobukowska	11.6	
1968	1	USA	**Wyomia Tyus**	**11.0**	WR
	2	USA	**Barbara Ferrell**	**11.1**	
	3	POL	Irena Szewinska (Kirszenstein)	11.1	
1972	1	GDR	Renate Stecher	11.07	
	2	AUS	Raelene Boyle	11.23	
	3	CUB	Silvia Chibás	11.24	
	4	USA	**Iris Davis**	**11.32**	
1976	1	GER	Annegret Richter	11.08	
	2	GDR	Renate Stecher	11.13	
	3	GER	Inge Helten	11.17	
	5	USA	**Evelyn Ashford**	**11.24**	
1980	1	URS	Lyudmila Kondratyeva	11.06	
	2	GDR	Marlies Göhr (Oelsner)	11.07	
	3	GDR	Ingrid Auerswald	11.14	
1984	1	USA	**Evelyn Ashford**	**10.97**	OR
	2	USA	**Alice Brown**	**11.13**	
	3	JAM	Merlene Ottey-Page	11.16	
1988	1	USA	**Florence Griffith Joyner**	**10.54**	
	2	USA	**Evelyn Ashford**	**10.83**	
	3	GDR	Heike Drechsler	10.85	
1992	1	USA	**Gail Devers**	**10.82**	
	2	JAM	Juliet Cuthbert	10.83	
	3	EUN	Irina Privalova	10.84	

WOMEN'S 200 METERS

YEAR	RANK	CTRY	ATHLETE	TIME	
1896-1936		(not held)			
1948	1	HOL	Francina "Fanny" Blankers-Koen	24.4	
	2	GBR	Audrey Williamson	25.1	
	3	USA	**Audrey Patterson**	**25.2**	
1952	1	AUS	Marjorie Jackson	23.7	
	2	HOL	Bertha Brouwer	24.2	
	3	URS	Nadezhda Khnykina	24.2	
		USA	**Catherine Hardy (24.7)**	**elim. semis**	
1956	1	AUS	Betty Cuthbert	23.4	EOR
	2	GDR	Christa Stubnick	23.7	
	3	AUS	Marlene Matthews	23.8	
		USA	**Heriwentha Faggs (24.8)**	**elim. semis**	
1960	1	USA	**Wilma Rudolph**	**24.0**	
	2	GER	Jutta Heine	24.4	
	3	GBR	Dorothy Hyman	24.7	
1964	1	USA	**Edith McGuire**	**23.0**	OR
	2	POL	Irena Kirszenstein	23.1	
	3	AUS	Marilyn Black	23.1	
1968	1	POL	Irena Szewinska (Kirszenstein)	22.5	WR
	2	AUS	Raelene Boyle	22.7	
	3	AUS	Jennifer Lamy	22.8	
	4	USA	**Barbara Ferrell**	**22.9**	
1972	1	GDR	Renate Stecher	22.40	EWR
	2	AUS	Raelene Boyle	22.45	
	3	POL	Irena Szewinska (Kirszenstein)	22.74	
		USA	**Jackie Thompson (23.18) / Barbara Ferrell (23.39)**	**elim. semis**	
1976	1	GDR	Bärbel Eckert	22.37	OR
	2	GER	Annegret Richter	22.39	
	3	GDR	Renate Stecher	22.47	
	6	USA	**Debra Armstrong (23.16) / Chandra Cheeseborough (23.20)**	**elim. semis**	
1980	1	GDR	Bärbel Wöckel (Eckert)	22.03	OR
	2	URS	Natalya Bochina	22.19	
	3	JAM	Merlene Ottey	22.20	
1984	1	USA	**Valerie Brisco-Hooks**	**21.81**	OR
	2	USA	**Florence Griffith**	**22.04**	
	3	JAM	Merlene Ottey-Page	22.09	
1988	1	USA	**Florence Griffith Joyner**	**21.34**	WR
	2	JAM	Grace Jackson	21.72	
	3	GDR	Heike Drechsler	21.95	
1992	1	USA	**Gwen Torrence**	**21.81**	
	2	JAM	Juliet Cuthbert	22.02	
	3	JAM	Merlene Ottey	22.09	

WOMEN'S 400 METERS

YEAR	RANK	CTRY	ATHLETE	TIME	
1896-1960		(not held)			
1964	1	AUS	Betty Cuthbert	52.0	OR
	2	GBR	Ann Packer	52.2	
	3	AUS	Judith Amoore	53.4	
		USA	**Janell Smith (54.5)**	**elim. semis**	
1968	1	FRA	Colette Besson	52.0	EOR
	2	GBR	Lillian Board	52.1	
	3	URS	Natalya Pechenkina	52.2	
	6	USA	**Jarvis Scott**	**52.7**	
1972	1	GDR	Monika Zehrt	51.08	OR
	2	GER	Rita Wilden	51.21	
	3	USA	**Kathy Hammond**	**51.64**	
1976	1	POL	Irena Szewinska (Kirszenstein)	49.29	WR
	2	GDR	Christina Brehmer	50.51	
	3	GDR	Ellen Streidt	50.55	
	5	USA	**Rosalyn Bryant**	**50.65**	
1980	1	GDR	Marita Koch	48.88	OR
	2	TCH	Jarmila Kratochvílová	49.46	
	3	GDR	Christina Lathan (Brehmer)	49.66	
1984	1	USA	**Valerie Brisco-Hooks**	**48.83**	OR
	2	USA	**Chandra Cheeseborough**	**49.05**	
	3	GBR	Kathryn Cook (Smallwood)	49.42	
1988	1	URS	Olga Bryzguina	48.65	OR
	2	GDR	Petra Mueller	49.45	
	3	URS	Olga Nazarova	49.90	
	4	USA	**Valerie Brisco**	**50:16**	
1992	1	FRA	Marie-Jose Perec	48.83	
	2	EUN	Olga Bryzgina	49.05	
	3	COL	Ximena Restrepo Gaviria	49.64	
	6	USA	**Rochelle Stevens**	**50.11**	

WOMEN'S 800 METERS

YEAR	RANK	CTRY	ATHLETE	TIME	
1896-1924		(not held)			
1928	1	GER	Lina Radke	2:16.8	WR
	2	JPN	Kinue Hitomi	2:17.6	
	3	SWE	Inga Gentzel	2:17.8	
	6	USA	**Florence McDonald**	**2:22.6**	
1932-1956		(not held)			
1960	1	URS	Lyudmila Shevtsova	2:04.3	EWR
	2	AUS	Brenda Jones	2:04.4	
	3	GDR	Ursula Donath	2:05.6	
		USA	**Billie Daniels**	**DQ**	
1964	1	GBR	Ann Packer	2:01.1	OR
	2	FRA	Maryvonne Dupureur	2:01.9	
	3	NZL	M. Ann Chamberlain	2:02.8	
		USA	**Sandra Knott (2:12.2)**	**elim. 1st rd**	
1968	1	USA	**Madeline Manning**	**2:00.9**	OR
	2	ROM	Ileana Silai	2:02.5	
	3	HOL	Maria Gommers	2:02.6	
1972	1	GER	Hildegard Falck	1:58.55	OR
	2	URS	Niole Sabaite	1:58.65	
	3	GDR	Gunhild Hoffmeister	1:59.19	
		USA	**Madeline Manning (2:02.40)**	**elim. semis**	
1976	1	URS	Tatyana Kazankina	1:54.94	WR
	2	BUL	Nikolina Shtereva	1:55.42	
	3	GDR	Elfi Zinn	1:55.60	
		USA	**Wendy Knudson (2:02.31)**	**elim. semis**	
1980	1	URS	Nadezhda Olizarenko	1:53.42	WR
	2	URS	Olga Mineyeva	1:54.9	
	3	URS	Tatyana Providokhina	1:55.5	
1984	1	ROM	Doina Melinte	1:57.60	
	2	USA	**Kim Gallagher**	**1:58.63**	
	3	ROM	Rafira Fita Lovin	1:58.83	
1988	1	GDR	Sigurn Wodars	1:56.10	
	2	GDR	Christine Wachtel	1:56.64	
	3	USA	**Kim Gallagher**	**1:56.91**	
1992	1	NED	Ellen Van Langen	1:55.54	
	2	EUN	Lilia Nurutdinova	1:55.99	
	3	CUB	Ana Fidelia Quirot Moret	1:56.80	
	7	USA	**Joetta Clark**	**1:58.06**	

WOMEN'S 1,500 METERS

YEAR	RANK	CTRY	ATHLETE	TIME	
1896-1968		(not held)			
1972	1	URS	Lyudmila Bragina	4:01.4	WR
	2	GDR	Gunhild Hoffmeister	4:02.8	
	3	ITA	Paola Cacchi	4:02.9	
		USA	**Francie Larrieu (4:15.3) / Francie Kraker (4:12.8)**	**elim. semis**	
1976	1	URS	Tatyana Kazankina	4:05.48	
	2	GDR	Gunhild Hoffmeister	4:06.02	
	3	GDR	Ulrike Klapezynski	4:06.09	
	8	USA	**Janice Merrill**	**4:08.54**	
1980	1	URS	Tatyana Kazankina	3:56.6	OR
	2	GDR	Christiane Wartenberg	3:57.8	
	3	URS	Nadezhda Olizarenko	3:59.6	
1984	1	ITA	Gabriella Dorio	4:03.25	
	2	ROM	Doina Melinte	4:03.76	
	3	ROM	Maricica Puic	4:04.15	
	8	USA	**Ruth Wysocki**	**4:08.92**	
1988	1	ROM	Paula Ivan	3:53.96	OR
	2	URS	Lailoute Baikauskaite	4:00.24	
	3	URS	Tatiana Samolenko	4:00.30	
	8	USA	**Mary Slaney**	**4:02.49**	
1992	1	ALG	Hassiba Boulmerka	3:55.30	
	2	EUN	Lyudmila Rogacheva	3:56.91	
	3	CHN	Qu Yunxia	3:57.08	
	10	USA	**PattiSue Plumer**	**4:03.42**	

WOMEN'S 3,000 METERS

YEAR	RANK	CTRY	ATHLETE	TIME	
1896-1980		(not held)			
1984	1	ROM	Maricica Puic	8:35.96	OR
	2	GBR	Wendy Sly	8:39.47	
	3	CAN	Lynn Williams	8:42.14	
	4	USA	**Cindy Bremser**	**8:42.78**	
1988	1	URS	Tatiana Samolenko	8:26.53	OR
	2	ROM	Paula Ivan	8:27.15	
	3	GBR	Yvonne Murray	8:29.02	
	6	USA	**Vicki Huber**	**8:37.25**	
1992	1	EUN	Elena Romanova	8:46.04	
	2	EUN	Tatiana Dorovskikh	8:46.85	
	3	CAN	Angela Frances Chalmers	8:47.22	
	5	USA	**PattiSue Plumer**	**8:48.29**	

WOMEN'S 10,000 METERS

YEAR	RANK	CTRY	ATHLETE	TIME	
1896-1984		(not held)			
1988	1	URS	Olga Bondarenko	31:05.21	OR
	2	GBR	Elizabeth McColgan	31:08.44	
	3	URS	Elena Joupieva	31:19.82	
	5	USA	**Francie Larrieu-Smith**	**31:35.52**	
1992	1	ETH	Derartu Tulu	31:06.02	
	2	RSA	Elana Meyer	31:11.75	
	3	USA	**Lynn Jennings**	**31:19.89**	

WOMEN'S 100-METER HURDLES

YEAR	RANK	CTRY	ATHLETE	TIME	
1896-1928		(not held)			
1932	1	USA	**Mildred Didriksen**	**11.7**	WR
	2	USA	**Evelyne Hall**	**11.7**	
	3	RSA	Marjorie Clark	11.8	
1936	1	ITA	Trebisonda Valla	11.7	
	2	GER	Anni Steuer	11.7	
	3	CAN	Elizabeth Taylor	11.7	
		USA	**A.V. O'Brien / Tidye Pickett / Simone Schaller**	**elim. semis**	
1948	1	HOL	Francina "Fanny" Blankers-Koen	11.2	OR
	2	GBR	Maureen Gardner	11.2	
	3	AUS	Shirley Strickland	11.4	
		USA	**Jean Walraven**	**elim. semis**	
1952	1	AUS	Shirley Strickland	10.9	WR
	2	URS	Maria Golubnichaya	11.1	
	3	GER	Maria Sander	11.1	
		USA	**Constance Darnowski (12.1)**	**elim. trials**	
1956	1	AUS	Shirley Strickland	10.7	OR
	2	GDR	Gisela Köhler	10.9	
	3	AUS	Norma Thrower	11.0	
		USA	**Constance Darnowski (11.9) / Barbara Ann Mueller (11.6) / Irene Robertson (11.9)**	**elim. trials**	
1960	1	URS	Irina Press	10.8	
	2	GBR	Carole Quinton	10.9	
	3	GDR	Gisela Birkemeyer (Köhler)	11.0	
		USA	**Irene Robertson (11.6) / Jo Ann Terry (14.4) / Shirley Crowder (12.3)**	**elim. 1st rd**	
1964	1	GDR	Karin Balzer	10.5w	
	2	POL	Teresa Ciepla-Wieczorek	10.5	
	3	AUS	Pamela Kilborn	10.5	
	8	USA	**Rosie Bonds**	**10.8**	
1968	1	AUS	Maureen Caird	10.3	OR
	2	AUS	Pamela Kilborn	10.4	
	3	TAI	Chi Cheng	10.4	
	4	USA	**Patricia Van Wolvelaere**	**10.5**	
1972	1	GDR	Annelie Ehrhardt	12.59	WR
	2	ROM	Valeria Bufanu	12.84	
	3	GDR	Karin Balzer	12.90	
		USA	**Patty Johnson (13.26) / Mamie Rallins (13.75) / Lacey O'Neal (13.89)**	**elim. semis**	
1976	1	GDR	Johanna Schaller	12.77	
	2	URS	Tatiana Anisimova	12.78	
	3	URS	Natalya Lebedeva	12.80	
	6	USA	**Debra Laplante (13.36)**	**elim. semis**	
1980	1	URS	Vera Komisova	12.56	OR
	2	GDR	Johanna Klier (Schaller)	12.63	
	3	POL	Lucyna Langer	12.65	
1984	1	USA	**Benita Fitzgerald-Brown**	**12.84**	
	2	GBR	Shirley Strong	12.88	
	3	FRA	Michele Chardonnet	13.06	
1988	1	BUL	Jordanka Donkova	12.38	OR
	2	GDR	Gloria Siebert	12.61	
	3	FRG	Claudia Zackiewicz	12.75	
		USA	**LaVonna Martin**		
1992	1	GRE	Paraskevi Patoulidou	12.64	
	2	USA	**LaVonna Martin**	**12.69**	
	3	BUL	Yordanka Donkova	12.70	

WOMEN'S 400-METER HURDLES

YEAR	RANK	CTRY	ATHLETE	TIME	
1896-1980		(not held)			
1984	1	MAR	Nawal El Moutawakel	54.61	OR
	2	USA	**Judi Brown**	**55.20**	
	3	ROM	Christina Cojocaru	55.41	
1988	1	AUS	Debra Flintoff-King	53.17	OR
	2	URS	Tatiana Ledovskaia	53.18	
	3	GDR	Ellen Fiedler	53.63	
	8	USA	**Latanya Sheffield**	**55.37**	
1992	1	GBR	Sally Gunnell	53.23	
	2	USA	**Sandra Farmer-Patrick**	**53.69**	
	3	USA	**Janeene Vickers**	**54.31**	

WOMEN'S 10 KM WALK

YEAR	RANK	CTRY	ATHLETE	TIME	
1896-1988		(not held)			
1992	1	CHN	Chen Yueling	44:32	
	2	EUN	Elena Nikolaeva	44:33	
	3	CHN	Li Chunxiu	44:41	
	20	USA	**Michelle Rohl**	**46:45**	

WOMEN'S 4x100-METER RELAY

YEAR	RANK	CTRY	ATHLETES	TIME	
1896-1924		(not held)			
1928	1	CAN		48.4	WR
	2	USA	**Mary Washburn / Jessie Cross / Loretta McNeil / Elizabeth Robinson**	**48.8**	
	3	GER		49.0	
1932	1	USA	**Mary Carew / Evelyn Furtsch / Annette Rogers / Wilhelmina Von Bremen**	**46.9**	WR
	2	CAN		47.0	
	3	GBR		47.6	
1936	1	USA	**Harriet Bland / Annette Rogers / Elizabeth Robinson / Helen Stephens**	**46.9**	
	2	GBR		47.6	
	3	CAN		47.8	
1948	1	HOL		47.5	
	2	AUS		47.6	
	3	CAN		47.8	
1952	1	USA	**Mae Faggs / Barbara Jones / Janet Moreau / Catherine Hardy**	**45.9**	WR
	2	GER		45.9	WR
	3	GBR		46.2	
1956	1	AUS		44.5	WR
	2	GBR		44.7	
	3	USA	**Mae Faggs / Margaret Matthews / Wilma Rudolph / Isabelle Daniels**	**44.9**	

1960	**1**	**USA**	**Martha Hudson / Lucinda Williams /Barbara Jones / Wilma Rudolph**	**44.5**	
	2	GER		44.8	
	3	POL		45.0	
1964	1	POL		43.6	
	2	**USA**	**Willye White / Wyomia Tyus / Marilyn White / Edith McGuire**	**43.9**	
	3	GBR		44.0	
1968	**1**	**USA**	**Barbara Ferrell / Margaret Bailes / Mildrette Netter / Wyomia Tyus**	**42.8**	**WR**
	2	CUB		43.3	
	3	URS		43.4	
1972	1	GER		42.81	**EWR**
	2	GDR		42.95	
	3	CUB		43.36	
	4	**USA**	**Martha Watson / Mattline Render / Mildrette Netter / Iris Davis**	**43.39**	
1976	1	GDR		42.55	**OR**
	2	GER		42.59	
	3	URS		43.09	
	7	**USA**	**Martha Watson / Evelyn Ashford / Debra Armstrong / Chandra Cheeseborough**	**43.35**	
1980	1	GDR		41.60	**WR**
	2	URS		42.10	
	3	GBR		42.43	
1984	**1**	**USA**	**Alice Brown / Jeanette Bolden / Chandra Cheeseborough / Evelyn Ashford**	**41.65**	
	2	CAN		42.77	
	3	GBR		43.11	
1988	**1**	**USA**	**Alice Brown / Sheila Echols Florence Griffith Joyner / Evelyn Ashford / Dannette Young**	**41.98**	
	2	GDR		42.09	
	3	URS		42.75	
1992	**1**	**USA**	**Evelyn Ashford / Esther Jones / Carlette Guidry-White / Gwen Torrence / Michelle Finn**	**42.11**	
	2	EUN		42.16	
	3	NIG		42.81	

WOMEN'S 4x400-METER RELAY

YEAR	RANK	CTRY	ATHLETES	TIME	
1896-1968		(not held)			
1972	1	GDR		3:23.0	**WR**
	2	**USA**	**Mable Fergerson / Madeline Manning / Manning / Cheryl Toussaint / Kathy Hammond**	**3:25.2**	
	3	GER		3:26.5	
1976	1	GDR		3:19.23	**WR**
	2	**USA**	**Debra Sapenter / Sheila Ingram / Pamela Jiles / Rosalyn Bryant**	**3:22.81**	
	3	URS		3:24.24	
1980	1	URS		3:20.2	
	2	GDR		3:20.4	
	3	GBR		3:27.5	
1984	**1**	**USA**	**Lillie Leatherwood / Sherri Howard / Valerie Brisco-Hooks / Chandra Cheeseborough / Diane Dixon / Denean Howard**	**3:18.29**	**OR**
	2	CAN		3:21.21	
	3	GER		3:22.98	
1988	1	URS		3:15.18	**WR**
	2	**USA**	**Denean Howard-Hill / Diane Dixon / Valerie Brisco / Florence Griffith Joyner / Sherri Howard / Lillie Leatherwood**	**3:15.51**	
	3	GDR		3:18.29	
1992	1	EUN		3:20.20	
	2	**USA**	**Natasha Kaiser / Gwen Torrence / Jearl Miles / Rochelle Stevens / Denean Hill / Dannette Young**	**3:20.92**	
	3	GBR		3:24.23	

WOMEN'S MARATHON

YEAR	RANK	CTRY	ATHLETE	TIME
1896-1980		(not held)		
1984	**1**	**USA**	**Joan Benoit**	**2:24.52**
	2	NOR	Grete Waitz	2:26.18
	3	POR	Rosa Mota	2:26.57
1988	1	POR	Rosa Mota	2:25.40
	2	AUS	Lisa Martin	2:25.53
	3	GDR	Kathrin Doerre	2:26.21
	17	**USA**	**Nancy Ditz**	**2:33.42**
1992	1	EUN	Valentina Yegorova	2:32.41
	2	JPN	Yuko Arimori	2:32.49
	3	NZL	Lorraine Mary Moller	2:33.59
	10	**USA**	**Cathy O'Brien**	**2:39.42**

WOMEN'S HIGH JUMP

YEAR	RANK	CTRY	ATHLETE	METERS	FT/IN	
1896-1924		(not held)				
1928	1	CAN	Ethel Catherwood	1.59	5-2 1/2	
	2	HOL	Carolina Gisolf	1.56	5-1 1/4	
	3	**USA**	**Mildred Wiley**	**1.56**	**5-1 1/4**	
1932	**1**	**USA**	**Jean Shiley**	**1.657**	**5-5 1/4**	**WR**
	2	**USA**	**Mildred Didriksen**	**1.657**	**5-5 1/4**	**WR**
	3	CAN	Eva Dawes	1.60	5-3	
1936	1	HUN	Ibolya Csák	1.60	5-3	
	2	GBR	Dorothy Odam	1.60	5-3	
	3	GER	Elfriede Kaun	1.60	5-3	
	6	**USA**	**Annette Rogers**	**1.55**	**5-1**	
1948	**1**	**USA**	**Alice Coachman**	**1.68**	**5-6**	**OR**
	2	GBR	Dorothy Tyler (Odam)	1.68	5-6	**OR**
	3	FRA	Micheline Ostermeyer	1.61	5-3 1/4	
1952	1	RSA	Esther Brand	1.67	5-5 3/4	
	2	GBR	Sheila Lerwill	1.65	5-5	
	3	URS	Aleksandra Chudina	1.63	5-4 1/4	
(no USA entry)						
1956	**1**	**USA**	**Mildred McDaniel**	**1.76**	**5-9 1/4**	**WR**
	2	URS	Thelma Hopkins	1.67	5-5 3/4	
	3	URS	Maria Pissaryeva	1.67	5-5 3/4	
1960	1	ROM	Iolanda Bala	1.85	6-0 3/4	**OR**
	2	POL	Jaroslawa Józwiakowska	1.71	5-7 1/4	
	2	GBR	Dorothy Shirley	1.71	5-7 1/4	
	14	**USA**	**Neomia Rogers**	**1.65**	**5-5**	
1964	1	ROM	Iolanda Bala	1.90	6-2 3/4	**OR**
	2	AUS	Michele Brown (Mason)	1.80	5-11	
	3	URS	Taisiya Chenchik	1.78	5-10	
	8	**USA**	**Eleanor Montgomery**	**1.71**	**5-7 1/4**	
1968	1	TCH	Miloslava Rezková	1.82	5-11 1/2	
	2	URS	Antonina Okorokova	1.80	5-10 3/4	
	3	URS	Valentina Kozyr	1.80	5-10 3/4	
		USA	**Eleanor Montgomery / Estelle Baskerville**	**elim. qualif. rd**		
1972	1	GER	Ulrike Meyfarth	1.92	6-3 1/2	**EWR**
	2	BUL	Yordanka Blagoeva	1.88	6-2	
	3	AUT	Ilona Gusenbauer	1.88	6-2	
		USA	**Sandy Goldsberry / Cindy Gilbertt / Deanne Wilson**	**elim. qualif. rd**		
1976	1	GDR	Rosemarie Ackermann (Witschas)	1.93	6-4	**OR**
	2	ITA	Sara Simeoni	1.91	6-3 1/4	
	3	BUL	Yordanka Blagoeva	1.91	6-3 1/4	
	5	**USA**	**Joni Huntley**	**1.89**	**6-2 1/2**	
1980	1	ITA	Sara Simeoni	1.97	6-5 1/2	**OR**
	2	POL	Urszula Kielan	1.94	6-4 1/4	
	3	GDR	Jutta Kirst	1.94	6-4 1/4	
1984	1	GER	Ulrike Meyfarth	2.02	6-7 1/2	**OR**
	2	ITA	Sara Simeoni	2.00	6-6 3/4	
	3	**USA**	**Joni Huntley**	**1.97**	**6-5 1/2**	
1988	**1**	**USA**	**Louise Ritter**	**2.03**	**6-8**	**OR**
	2	BUL	Stefka Kostadinova	2.01	6-7	
	3	URS	Tamara Bykova	1.99	6-6 1/4	
1992	1	GER	Heike Henkel	2.02	6-7 1/2	
	2	ROM	Galina Astafei	2.00	6-6 3/4	
	3	CUB	Ioanat Quintero	1.97	6-5 1/2	
	11T	**USA**	**Tanya Hughes**	**1.88**	**6-2**	

WOMEN'S LONG JUMP

YEAR	RANK	CTRY	ATHLETE	METERS	FT/IN	
1896-1936		(not held)				
1948	1	HUN	Olga Gyarmati	5.695	18-8 1/4	
	2	ARG	Noëmi Simonetto De Portela	5.60	18-4 1/2	
	3	SWE	Ann-Britt Leyman	5.575	18-3 1/4	
	12	**USA**	**Emma Reed**	**4.845**	**15-10 1/4**	
1952	1	NZL	Yvette Williams	6.24	20-5 3/4	**OR**
	2	URS	Aleksandra Chudina	6.14	20-1 3/4	
	3	GBR	Shirley Cawley	5.92	19-5 1/4	
	7	**USA**	**Mabel Landry**	**5.75**	**18-10 1/2**	
1956	1	POL	Elzbieta Krzesinska	6.35	20-10	**EWR**
	2	**USA**	**Willye White**	**6.09**	**19-11 3/4**	
	3	URS	Nadezhda Dvalischvili (Khynkina)	6.07	19-11	
1960	1	URS	Vyera Krepkina	6.37	20-10 3/4	**OR**
	2	POL	Elzbieta Krzesinska	6.27	20-7	
	3	GDR	Hildrun Claus	6.21	20-4 1/2	
	16	**USA**	**Willye White**	**5.77**	**18-11 1/4**	
1964	1	GBR	Mary Rand (Bignal)	6.76	22-2 1/4	**WR**
	2	POL	Irena Kirszenstein	6.60	21-8	
	3	URS	Tatyana Schelkanova	6.42	21-0 3/4	
	12	**USA**	**Willye White**	**6.07**	**19-11**	
1968	1	ROM	Viorica Viscopoleanu	6.82	22-4 1/2	**WR**
	2	GBR	Sheila Sherwood	6.68	21-11	
	3	URS	Tatyana Talisheva	6.66	21-10 1/4	
	10	**USA**	**Martha Watson**	**6.20**	**20-4**	
1972	1	GER	Heidemarie Rosendahl	6.78	22-3	
	2	BUL	Diana Yorgova	6.77	22-2 1/2	
	3	TCH	Eva Suranová	6.67	21-10 3/4	
	11	**USA**	**Willye White**	**6.27**	**20-7**	
1976	1	GDR	Angela Voigt	6.72	22-0 3/4	
	2	**USA**	**Kathy McMillan**	**6.66**	**21-10 1/4**	
	3	URS	Lidia Alfeyeva	6.60	21-8	
1980	1	URS	Tatiana Kolpakova	7.06	23-2	**OR**
	2	GDR	Brigitte Wujak	7.04	23-1 1/4	
	3	URS	Tatiana Skachko	7.01	23-0	
1984	1	ROM	Anisoara Cusmir-Stanciu	6.96	22-10	
	2	ROM	Valeria Ionescu	6.81	22-4 1/4	
	3	GBR	Susan Hearnshaw	6.80	22-3 3/4	
	4	**USA**	**Angela Thacker**	**6.78**	**22-3**	
1988	**1**	**USA**	**Jackie Joyner-Kersee**	**7.40**	**24-3 1/2**	**OR**
	2	GDR	Heike Drechsler	7.22	23-8 1/4	
	3	URS	Galina Tchistiakova	7.11	23-4	
1992	1	GER	Heike Drechsler	7.14	23-5 1/4	
	2	EUN	Inessa Kravets	7.12	23-4 1/2	
	3	**USA**	**Jackie Joyner-Kersee**	**7.07**	**23-2 1/2**	

WOMEN'S SHOT PUT

YEAR	RANK	CTRY	ATHLETE	METERS	FT/IN	
1896-1936		(not held)				
1948	1	FRA	Micheline Ostermeyer	13.75	45-1 1/2	
	2	ITA	Amelia Piccinini	13.09	42-11 1/2	
	3	AUT	Ine Schäffer	13.08	42-11	
		USA	**Dorothy Dodson / Frances Kaszubski**	**DNQ**		
1952	1	URS	Galina Zybina	15.28	50-1 3/4	**WR**
	2	GER	Marianne Werner	14.57	47-9 3/4	
	3	URS	Kaludia Tochenova	14.50	47-7	
		USA	**Janet Dicks**	**DNQ**		
1956	1	URS	Tamara Tyshkevich	16.59	54-5	**OR**
	2	URS	Galina Zybina	16.53	54-2 3/4	
	3	GER	Marianne Werner	15.61	51-2 3/4	
	6	**USA**	**Earlene Brown**	**15.12**	**49-7 1/4**	
1960	1	URS	Tamara Press	17.32	56-10	**OR**
	2	GDR	Johanna Lüttge	16.61	54-6	
	3	**USA**	**Earlene Brown**	**16.42**	**53-10 1/2**	
1964	1	URS	Tamara Press	18.14	59-6 1/4	**OR**
	2	GDR	Renate Garisch-Culmberger	17.61	57-9 1/2	
	3	URS	Galina Zybina	17.45	57-3	
	12	**USA**	**Earlene Brown**	**14.80**	**48-6 1/2**	
1968	1	GDR	Margitta Gummel (Helmboldt)	19.61	64-4	**WR**
	2	GDR	Marita Lange	18.78	61-7 1/2	
	3	URS	Nadezhda Chizhova	18.19	59-8 1/4	
	11	**USA**	**Maren Seidler**	**14.86**	**48-9**	
1972	1	URS	Nadezhda Chizhova	21.03	69-0	**WR**
	2	GDR	Margitta Gummel (Helmboldt)	20.22	66-4 1/4	
	3	BUL	Ivanka Hristova	19.35	63-6	
		USA	**Maren Seidler / Jan Svendsen**		**elim. 1st rd**	
1976	1	BUL	Ivanka Hristova	21.16	69-5 1/4	**OR**
	2	URS	Nadezhda Chizhova	20.96	68-9 1/4	
	3	TCH	Helena Fibingerová	20.67	67-9 3/4	
	12	**USA**	**Maren Seidler**	**15.60**	**51-2 1/4**	
1980	1	GDR	Ilona Slupianek (Schoknecht)	22.41	73-6 1/4	
	2	URS	Svetlana Krachevskaya	21.42	70-3 1/2	
	3	GDR	Margitta Pufe (Droese)	21.20	69-6 3/4	
1984	1	GER	Claudia Losch	20.48	67-2 1/4	
	2	ROM	Mihaela Loghin	20.47	67-2	
	3	AUS	Gael Martin	19.19	62-11 1/2	
	7	**USA**	**Carol Cady**	**17.23**	**56-6 1/2**	
1988	1	URS	Natalia Lisovskaya	22.24	72-11 3/4	
	2	GDR	Kathrin Neimke	21.07	69-1 1/2	
	3	CHN	Li Meisu	21.06	69-1 1/4	
	12	**USA**	**Bonnie Dasse**	**17.60**	**57-9**	
1992	1	EUN	Svetlana Krivaleva	21.06	69-1 1/4	
	2	CHN	Huang Zhihong	20.47	67-2	
	3	GER	Kathrin Neimke	19.78	64-10 3/4	
	11	**USA**	**Ramona Pagel**	**18.24**	**59-10 1/4**	

WOMEN'S DISCUS

YEAR	RANK	CTRY	ATHLETE	METERS	FT/IN	
1896-1924		(not held)				
1928	1	POL	Halina Konopacka	39.62	129-11 3/4	**WR**
	2	**USA**	**Lillian Copeland**	**37.08**	**121-8**	
	3	SWE	Ruth Svedberg	35.92	117-10	
1932	**1**	**USA**	**Lillian Copeland**	**40.58**	**133-2**	**OR**
	2	**USA**	**Ruth Osburn**	**40.12**	**131-7**	
	3	POL	Jadwiga Wajs	38.74	127-1	
1936	1	GER	Gisela Mauermayer	47.63	156-3	**OR**
	2	POL	Jadwiga Wajs	46.22	151-8	
	3	GER	Paula Mollenhauer	39.80	130-7	
	8	**USA**	**Gertrude Wilhemsen**	**34.43**	**112-11 1/2**	
1948	1	FRA	Micheline Ostermeyer	41.92	137-6	
	2	ITA	Edera Cordiale Gentile	41.17	135-0	
	3	FRA	Jacqueline Mazeas	40.47	132-9	
	11	**USA**	**Frances Kaszubski**	**36.49**	**119-8 1/2**	
1952	1	URS	Nina Romaschkova	51.42	168-8	**OR**
	2	URS	Yelisaveta Bagryantseva	47.08	154-5	
	3	URS	Nina Dumbadze	46.29	151-10	
(no USA entry)						
1956	1	TCH	Olga Fikotová	53.69	176-1	**OR**
	2	URS	Irina Beglyakova	52.54	174-4	
	3	URS	Nina Ponomaryeva (Romaschkova)	52.02	170-8	
	4	**USA**	**Earlene Brown**	**51.35**	**168-5**	
1960	1	URS	Nina Ponomaryeva (Romaschkova)	55.10	180-9	**OR**
	2	URS	Tamara Press	52.59	172-4	
	3	ROM	Lia Manoliu	52.36	171-9	
	6	**USA**	**Earlene Brown**	**51.29**	**168-3**	
1964	1	URS	Tamara Press	57.27	187-10	**OR**
	2	GDR	Ingrid Lotz	57.21	187-8	
	3	ROM	Lia Manoliu	56.97	186-10	
	12	**USA**	**Olga Connolly**	**51.58**	**169-2 3/4**	
1968	1	ROM	Lia Manoliu	58.28	191-2	**OR**
	2	GER	Liesel Westermann	57.76	189-6	
	3	HUN	Jolán Kleiber	54.90	180-1	
	6	**USA**	**Olga Connolly**	**52.96**	**173-9**	
1972	1	URS	Faina Melnik	66.62	218-7	**OR**
	2	ROM	Argentina Menis	65.06	213-5	
	3	BUL	Vassilka Stoeva	64.34	211-1	
		USA	**Olga Connolly (51.58/169-2 3/4)**		**elim.**	
1976	1	GDR	Evelin Schlaak	69.00	226-4	**OR**
	2	BUL	Maria Vergova	67.30	220-9	
	3	GDR	Gabriele Hinzmann	66.84	219.3	
	14	**USA**	**M. Lynne Winbigler**	**48.22**	**158-2 1/2**	
1980	1	GDR	Evelin Jahl (Schlaak)	69.96	229.6	**OR**
	2	BUL	Maria Petkova (Vergova)	67.90	222-9	
	3	URS	Tatyana Lesovaya	67.40	221-1	
1984	1	HOL	Ria Stalman	65.36	214-5	
	2	**USA**	**Leslie Deniz**	**64.86**	**212-9**	
	3	ROM	Florenta Craciunescu (Tacu)	63.64	208-9	
1988	1	GDR	Martina Hellmann	72.30	237-2	**OR**
	2	GDR	Diana Gansky	71.88	235-10	
	3	BUL	Tzvetanka Hristova	69.74	228-10	
	11	**USA**	**Carol Cady**	**63.42**	**208-1**	
1992	1	CUB	Maritza Marten	70.06	229-10	
	2	BUL	Tsvetanka Khristova	67.78	222-4	
	3	AUS	Daniela Costian	66.24	217-4	
	20	**USA**	**Connie Price-Smith**	**58.66**	**192-5**	

WOMEN'S JAVELIN

YEAR	RANK	CTRY	ATHLETE	METERS	FT/IN	
1896-1928		(not held)				
1932	**1**	**USA**	**Mildred Didriksen**	**43.68**	**143-4**	**OR**
	2	GER	Ellen Braumüller	43.49	142-8	
	3	GER	Tilly Fleischer	43.00	141-1	
1936	1	GER	Tilly Fleischer	45.18	148-3	**OR**
	2	GER	Luise Krüger	43.29	142-8	
	3	POL	Maria Kwa niewska	41.80	137-2	
	7	**USA**	**Gertrude Wilhelmsen**	**37.35**	**122-6**	
1948	1	AUT	Hermine "Herma" Bauma	45.57	149-6	
	2	FIN	Kaisa Parviainen	43.79	143-8	
	3	DEN	Lily Carlstedt	42.08	138-1	
	4	**USA**	**Dorothy Dodson**	**41.96**	**137-8**	
1952	1	TCH	Dana Zátopková (Ingrova)	50.47	165-7	
	2	URS	Aleksandra Chudina	50.01	164-0	
	3	URS	Yelena Gorchakova	49.76	163-3	
	13	**USA**	**Marjorie Larney**	**40.58**	**133-1 3/4**	
1956	1	URS	Inese Jaunzeme	53.86	176-8	
	2	CHI	Marlene Ahrens	50.38	165-3	
	3	URS	Nadezhda Konyayeva	50.28	164-11 1/2	
	8	**USA**	**Karen Anderson**	**48.00**	**157-5 1/2**	
1960	1	URS	Elvira Ozolina	55.98	183-8	**OR**
	2	TCH	Dana Zátopková (Ingrova)	53.78	176-5	
	3	URS	Birute Kalediene	53.45	175-4	
	13	**USA**	**Karen Oldham**	**46.52**	**152-7 1/2**	
1964	1	ROM	Mihaela Pene	60.54	198-7	
	2	HUN	Márta Rudas	58.27	191-2	
	3	URS	Yelena Gorchakova	57.06	187-2	
		USA	**ReNae Bair (56.89/153-10)**		**elim.**	
1968	1	HUN	Angéla Németh	60.36	198-0	
	2	ROM	Mihaela Pene	59.92	196-7	
	3	AUT	Eva Janko	58.04	190-5	
	9	**USA**	**Barbara Friedrich**	**53.59**	**175-10**	
1972	1	GDR	Ruth Fuchs	63.88	209-7	**OR**
	2	GDR	Jacqueline Todten	62.54	205-2	
	3	**USA**	**Kathryn Schmidt**	**59.94**	**196-8**	
1976	1	GDR	Ruth Fuchs	65.94	216-4	**OR**
	2	GER	Marion Becker	64.70	212-3	
	3	**USA**	**Kathryn Schmidt**	**63.96**	**209-10**	
1980	1	CUB	Maria Colon Rueñes	68.40	22-45	**OR**
	2	URS	Saida Gunba	67.76	222-2	
	3	GDR	Ute Hommola	66.56	218-4	
1984	1	GBR	Theresa "Tessa" Sanderson	69.56	228-2	**OR**
	2	FIN	Ilse "Tiina" Lillak	69.00	226-4	
	3	GBR	Fatima Whitbread	67.14	220-3	
	8	**USA**	**Karin Smith**	**62.06**	**203-7**	
1988	1	GDR	Petra Felke	74.68	245	**OR**
	2	GBR	Fatima Whitbread	70.32	230-8	
	3	GDR	Beate Koch	67.30	220-9	
	7	**USA**	**Donna Mayhew**	**61.78**	**202-8**	
1992	1	GER	Silke Renk	68.34	224	
	2	EUN	Natalia Shikolenko	68.26	223-11	
	3	GER	Karen Forkel	66.86	219-4	
	12	**USA**	**Donna Mayhew**	**55.68**	**182-8**	

HEPTATHLON

YEAR	RANK	CTRY	ATHLETE	POINTS	
1896-1960		(not held)			
1964	1	URS	Irina Press	5246	**WR**
	2	GBR	Mary Rand	5035	
	3	URS	Galina Bystrova	4956	
	7	**USA**	**Patricia Winslow**	**4724**	

1968	1	GER	Ingrid Becker	5098	
	2	AUT	Elisabeth "Liese" Prokop	4966	
	3	HUN	Annamária Tóth	4959	
	6	**USA**	**Patricia Winslow**	**4877**	
1972	1	GBR	Mary Peters	4801	WR
	2	GER	Heidemarie Rosendahl	4791	
	3	GDR	Burglinde Pollak	4768	
	10	**USA**	**Gale Fitzgerald**	**4208**	
1976	1	GDR	Siegrun Siegl	4745	
	2	GDR	Christine Laser (Bodner)	4745	
	3	GDR	Burglinde Pollak	4740	
	7	**USA**	**Jane Frederick**	**4566**	
1980	1	URS	Nadezhda Tkachenko	5083	WR
	2	URS	Olga Rukavishnikova	4937	
	3	URS	Olga Kuragina	4875	
1984	1	AUS	Glynis Nunn	6390	OR
	2	**USA**	**Jackie Joyner**	**6385**	
	3	GER	Sabine Everts	6363	
1988	**1**	**USA**	**Jackie Joyner-Kersee**	**7291**	WR
	2	GDR	Sabine John	6897	
	3	GDR	Anke Behmer	6858	
1992	**1**	**USA**	**Jackie Joyner-Kersee**	**7044**	
	2	EUN	Irina Belova	6845	
	3	GER	Sabine Braun	6649	

BADMINTON

MEN'S SINGLES

YEAR	RANK	CTRY	ATHLETE
1896-1988	(not held)		
1992	1	INA	Alan Budi Kusuma
	2	INA	Ardy Bernardus Wiranata
	3	INA	Hermawan Susanto
	3	DEN	Thomas Stuer-Lauridsen
		USA	**Chris Jogis**

MEN'S DOUBLES

YEAR	RANK	CTRY	ATHLETES
1896-1988	(not held)		
1992	1	KOR	Kim Moon-soo / Park Joo-bong
	2	INA	Eddy Hartono / Gudy Gunawan
	3	CHN	Li Yongbo / Tian Binghi
	3	MAS	Razif Sidek / Jalani Dato Haji Sidek
		USA	**Benny Lee / Thomas Reidy**

WOMEN'S SINGLES

YEAR	RANK	CTRY	ATHLETE
1896-1988	(not held)		
1992	1	INA	Susi Susanti
	2	KOR	Bang Soo-hyun
	3	CHN	Tang Jiuhong
	3	CHN	Huang Hua
		USA	**Linda French / Erika von Heiland / Joy Kitzmiller**

WOMEN'S DOUBLES

YEAR	RANK	CTRY	ATHLETES
1896-1988	(not held)		
1992	1	KOR	Hwang Hye Young / Chung So-yung
	2	CHN	Guan Weizhen / Nong Qunhua
	3	CHN	Lin Yanfen / Yao Fen
	3	KOR	Gil Young-ah / Shim Eun-jung
		USA	**Linda French / Joy Kitzmiller**

BASEBALL

YEAR	RANK	CTRY	RECORD	SCORE	USA GAME SCORES	
1896-1988	(not held)					
1992	1	CUB	9-0	11-1	USA vs. ESP	6-1
	2	TPE	6-3	(Final)	USA vs. TPE	10-9
	3	JPN	6-3	8-3	USA vs. ITA	10-0
	4	**USA**	**5-4**	(3rd-4th)	USA vs. CUB	6-9
	5	PUR	2-5		USA vs. PUR	8-2
	6	DOM	2-5		USA vs. DOM	10-0
	7	ITA	1-6		USA vs. JPN	1-7
	8	ESP	1-6		USA vs. CUB	1-6
					USA vs. JPN	3-8

USA Team: William Adams / Jeff Alkire / Darren Dreifort / Nomar Garciaparra / Jason Giambi / Rick Greene / Jeffrey Hammonds / Rick Helling / Charles Johnson / Daron Kirkreit / Chad McConnell / Jason Moler / Calvin Murray / Phil Nevin / Chris Roberts / Michael Tucker / Jason Varitek / Ron Villone / B.J. Wallace / Craig Wilson / Chris Wimmer

BASKETBALL

MEN

YEAR	RANK	CTRY	RECORD	SCORE	USA GAME SCORES	
1896-1932	(not held)					
1932	**1**	**USA**	**4-0**			
	2	CAN	5-1			
	3	MEX	4-2			
	4	POL	1-4			
	5	PHI	4-1			
	6	URU	2-3			
	7	ITA	3-2			

USA TEAM: Ralph Bishop / Joe Fortenberry / Carl Knowles / Jack Ragland / Carl Shy / William Wheatley / Francis Johnson / Samuel Balter / John Gibbons / Frank Lubin / Arthur Mollner / Duane Swanson / Willard Schmidt

1948	**1**	**USA**	**8-0**			
	2	FRA	5-2			
	3	BRA	7-1			
	4	MEX	5-2			
	5	URU	5-3			
	6	CHI	4-4			
	7	TCH	5-3			
	8	KOR	3-5			

USA Team: Clifford Barker / Donald Barksdale / Ralph Beard / Lewis Beck / Vincent Boryla / Gordon Carpenter / Alexander Groza / Wallace Jones / Robert Kurland / Raymond Lumpp / Robert Pitts / Jesse Renick / Robert Robinson / Kenneth Rollins

1952	**1**	**USA**	**8-0**			
	2	URS	6-2			
	3	URU	5-3			
	4	ARG	5-3			
	5	CHI	4-4			
	6	BRA	4-4			
	7	BUL	4-4			
	8	FRA	4-4			

USA Team: Charles Hoag / William Hougland / Melvin Dean Kelley / Robert Kenney / Clyde Lovellette / Marcus Freiberger / Victor Wayne Glasgow / Frank McCabe / Daniel Pippin / Howard Williams / Ronald Bontemps / Robert Kurland / William Lienhard / John Keller

1956	**1**	**USA**	**8-0**			
	2	URS	5-3			
	3	URU	6-2			
	4	FRA	5-3			
	5	BUL	5-3			
	6	BRA	3-4			
	7	PHI	4-4			
	8	CHI	2-5			

USA Team: Carl Cain / William Hougland / K.C. Jones / William Russell / James Walsh / William Evans / Burdette Haldorson / Ronald Tomsic / Richard Boushka / Gilbert Ford / Robert Jeangerard / Charles Darling

1960	**1**	**USA**	**8-0**			
	2	URS	6-2			
	3	BRA	6-2			
	4	ITA	4-4			
	5	TCH	5-3			
	6	YUG	4-4			
	7	POL	4-4			
	8	URU	2-6			

USA Team: Jay Arnette / Walter Bellamy / Robert Boozer / Terry Dischinger / Jerry Lucas / Oscar Robertson / Adrian Smith / Burdette Haldorson / Darrall Imhoff / Allen Kelley / Lester Lane / Jerry West

1964	**1**	**USA**	**9-0**			
	2	URS	8-1			
	3	BRA	6-3			
	4	PUR	5-4			
	5	ITA	6-3			
	6	POL	5-4			
	7	YUG	6-3			
	8	URU	4-5			

USA Team: James Barnes / William Bradley / Lawrence Brown / Joseph Caldwell / Mel Counts / Richard Davies / Walter Hazzard / Lucius Jackson / John McCaffrey / Jeffrey Mullins / Jerry Shipp / George Wilson

1968	**1**	**USA**	**9-0**			
	2	YUG	7-2			
	3	URS	8-1			
	4	BRA	6-3			
	5	MEX	7-2			
	6	POL	5-4			
	7	ESP	5-4			
	8	ITA	5-4			

USA Team: John Clawson / Kenneth Spain / Joseph "Jo-Jo" White / Michael Barrett / Spencer Haywood / Charles Scott / William Hosket / Calvin Fowler / Michael Silliman / Glynn Saulters / James King / Donald Dee

1972	1	URS	9-0			
	2	**USA**	**8-1**			
	3	CUB	7-2			
	4	ITA	5-4			
	5	YUG	7-2			
	6	PUR	6-3			
	7	BRA	3-5			
	8	TCH	4-5			

USA Team: Kenneth Davis / Douglas Collins / Thomas Henderson / Michael Bantom / Robert Jones / Dwight Jones / James Forbes / James Brewer / Tommy Burleson / Thomas McMillen / Kevin Joyce / Ed Ratleff

1976	**1**	**USA**	**7-0**			
	2	YUG	5-2			
	3	URS	6-1			
	4	CAN	4-3			
	5	ITA	5-2			
	6	TCH	3-4			
	7	CUB	4-3			
	8	AUS	2-5			

USA Team: Phil Ford / Steve Sheppard / Adrian Dantley / Walter Davis / William "Quinn" Buckner / Ernie Grunfield / Kenneth Carr / Scott May / Michel Armstrong / Thomas La Garde / Philip Hubbard / Mitchell Kupchak

1980	1	YUG	9-0			
	2	ITA	5-4			
	3	URS	7-2			
	4	ESP	4-5			
	5	BRA	4-4			
	6	CUB	2-6			
	7	POL	5-3			
	8	AUS	6-2			
1984	**1**	**USA**	**8-0**			
	2	ESP	6-2			
	3	YUG	7-1			
	4	CAN	4-4			
	5	ITA	6-2			
	6	URU	3-5			
	7	AUS	4-4			
	8	GER	2-6			

USA Team: Steve Alford / Leon Wood / Patrick Ewing / Vern Fleming / Alvin Robertson / Michael Jordan / Joseph Kleine / Jon Koncak / Wayman Tisdale / Chris Mullin / Samuel Perkins / Jeffrey Turner

1992	**1**	**USA**	**8-0**	**117-85**	USA vs. CRO	103-70
	2	CRO	6-2	(Final)	USA vs. BRA	127-83
	3	LTU	6-2	82-78	USA vs. GER	111-68
	4	EUN	5-3	(3rd-4th)	USA vs. ANG	116-48
	5	BRA	4-4	90-80	USA vs. ESP	122-81
	6	AUS	4-4	(5th-6th)	USA vs. PUR	115-77
	7	GER	3-5		USA vs. LTU	127-76
	8	PUR	3-5		USA vs. CRO	117-85

USA TEAM: Charles Barkley / Larry Bird / Clyde Drexler / Patrick Ewing / Earvin Johnson / Michael Jordan / Christian Laettner / Karl Malone / Chris Mullin / Scottie Pippen / David Robinson / John Stockton

WOMEN

YEAR	RANK	CTRY	RECORD	SCORE	USA GAME SCORES	
1896-1972	(not held)					
1976	1	URS	5-0			
	2	**USA**	**3-2**			
	3	BUL	3-2			
	4	TCH	2-3			
	5	JPN	2-3			
	6	CAN	0-5			

USA Team: Cindy Brogdon / Susan Rojcewicz / Ann Meyers / Lusia Harris / Nancy Dunkle / Charlotte Lewis / Nancy Lieberman / Gail Marquis / Patricia Roberts / Mary Anne O'Connor / Patricia Head / Julienne Simpson

1980	1	URS	6-0			
	2	BUL	4-2			
	3	YUG	4-2			
	4	HUN	2-4			
	5	CUB	1-4			
	6	ITA	0-5			
1984	**1**	**USA**	**6-0**			
	2	KOR	4-2			
	3	CHN	3-3			
	4	CAN	2-4			
	5	AUS	1-4			
	6	YUG	1-4			

USA Team: Teresa Edwards / Lea Henry / Lynette Woodard / Anne Donovan / Cathy Boswell / Cheryl Miller / Janice Lawrence / Cindy Noble / Kim Mulkey / Denise Curry / Pamela McGee / Carol Menken-Schaudt

1992	1	EUN	4-1	76-66	USA vs. CHN	93-67
	2	CHN	3-2	(Final)	USA vs. ESP	114-59
	3	**USA**	**4-1**	**88-74**	USA vs. TCH	111-55
	4	CUB	3-2	(3rd-4th)	USA vs. EUN	73-79
	5	ESP	3-2		USA vs. CUB	88-74
	6	TCH	1-4			
	7	BRA	2-3			
	8	ITA	0-5			

USA TEAM: Vicky Bullet / Daedra Charles / Cynthia Cooper / Clarissa Davis / Medina Dixon / Teresa Edwards / Tammy Jackson / Carolyn Jones / Katrina McClain / Suzie McConnell / Vickie Orr / Teresa Weatherspoon

BOXING

LIGHT FLYWEIGHT - (46 KG/101 LBS)

YEAR	RANK	CTRY	ATHLETE	DECISION
1896-1964	(not held)			
1968	1	VEN	Francisco Rodriguez	3-2
	2	KOR	Jee Yong-ju	
	3T	**USA**	**Harlan Marbley**	
	3T	POL	Hubert Skrzypczak	
1972	1	HUN	György Gedó	5-0
	2	PRK	Kim U Gil	
	3T	GBR	Ralph Evans	
	3T	ESP	Enrique Rodriguez	
		USA	**Davey Armstrong**	**elim. 2nd rd**
1976	1	CUB	Jorge Hernandez	4-1
	2	PRK	Li Byong Uk	
	3T	PUR	Orlando Maldonado	
	3T	THA	Payao Pooltarat	
		USA	**Louis Curtis**	**elim. 1/16 final**
1980	1	URS	Shamil Sabyrov	3-2
	2	CUB	Hipolito Ramos	
	3T	PRK	Li Byong Uk	
	3T	BUL	Ismail Hijuseinov	
1984	**1**	**USA**	**Paul Gonzales**	**Default**
	2	ITA	Salvatore Todisco	
	3T	VEN	José Marcelino Bolivar	
	3T	ZAM	Keith Mwila	
1988	1	BUL	Ivailo Hristov	5-0
	2	**USA**	**Michael Carbajal**	
	3T	PHI	Leopoldo Serantes	
	3T	HUN	Robert Isaszegi	
1992	1	CUB	Rogelio Marcelo	24-10
	2	BUL	Daniel Bojinov	
	3T	PHI	Roel Velasco	
	3T	GER	Jan Quast	
		USA	**Eric Griffin**	

FLYWEIGHT - (51 KG/112 LBS)

YEAR	RANK	CTRY	ATHLETE	DECISION
1896-1900	(not held)			
1904	**1**	**USA**	**George Finnegan**	**RSC-1**
	2	**USA**	**Miles Burke**	
1906-1912	(not held)			
1920	**1**	**USA**	**Frank Di Gennara**	**Dec**
	2	DEN	Anders Petersen	
	3	GBR	William Cuthbertson	
1924	**1**	**USA**	**Fidel LaBarba**	**Dec**
	2	GBR	James McKenzie	
	3	**USA**	**Raymond Fee**	
1928	1	HUN	Antal Kocsis	Dec
	2	FRA	Armand Appell	
	3	ITA	Carlo Cavagnoli	
		USA	**Hyman Miller**	**elim. 1st rd**
1932	1	HUN	István Énekes	Dec
	2	MEX	Francisco Cabañas	
	3	**USA**	**Louis Salica**	
1936	1	GER	Willi Kaiser	Dec
	2	ITA	Gavino Matta	
	3	**USA**	**Louis Daniel Laurie**	
1948	1	ARG	Pascual Perez	Dec
	2	ITA	Spartaco Bandinelli	
	3	KOR	Han Soo-ann	
	5T	**USA**	**Frank Sodano**	
1952	**1**	**USA**	**Nathan Brooks**	**3-0**
	2	GER	Edgar Basel	
	3T	URS	Anatoly Bulakov	
	3T	RSA	William Toweel	
1956	1	GBR	Terence Spinks	Dec
	2	ROM	Mircea Dobrescu	
	3T	IRL	John Caldwell	
	3T	FRA	Rene Libeer	
		USA	**Ray Perez**	**elim. qtr finals**
1960	1	HUN	Gyula Török	3-2
	2	URS	Sergey Sivko	
	3T	UAR	Abdelmoneim Elguindi	
	3T	JPN	Kiyoshi Tanabe	
	5T	**USA**	**Humberto Barrera**	
1964	1	ITA	Fernando Atzori	
	2	POL	Artur Olech	
	3T	**USA**	**Robert Carmody**	
	3T	URS	Stanislav Sorokin	
1968	1	MEX	Ricardo Delgado	5-0
	2	POL	Artur Olech	
	3T	BRA	Servilio Oliveira	
	3T	UGA	Leo Rwabwogo	
		USA	**David Vasquez**	
1972	1	BUL	Georgi Kostadinov	5-0
	2	UGA	Leo Rwabwogo	
	3T	POL	Leszek Blazynski	
	3T	CUB	Douglas Rodriguez	
		USA	**Timothy Dement**	**elim. 3rd rd**
1976	**1**	**USA**	**Leo Randolph**	**3-2**
	2	CUB	Ramon Duvalon	
	3T	POL	Leslek Blazynski	
	3T	URS	David Torosyan	

YEAR	RANK	CTRY	ATHLETE	DECISION	
1980	1	BUL	Peter Lessov	2:08	RSC-2
	2	URS	Viktor Miroshnichenko		
	3T	IRL	Hugh Russell		
	3T	HUN	János Váradi		
1984	**1**	**USA**	**Steven McCrory**	**4-1**	
	2	YUG	Redzep Redzepovski		
	3T	KEN	Ibrahim Bilali		
	3T	TUR	Eyup Can		
1988	1	KOR	Kim Kwang-sun	4-1	
	2	GDR	Andreas Tews		
	3T	MEX	Mario Gonzalez		
	3T	URS	Timofei Skriabin		
		USA	**Arthur Johnson**		
1992	1	PRK	Choi Choi	12-2	
	2	MEX	Raul Gonzalez		
	3T	**USA**	**Timothy Austin**		
	3T	HUN	Istvan Kovacs		

BANTAMWEIGHT - (54 KG/119 LBS)

YEAR	RANK	CTRY	ATHLETE	DECISION	
1896-1900	(not held)				
1904	**1**	**USA**	**Oliver Kirk**	**RSC-3**	
	2	**USA**	**George Finnegan**		
1906	(not held)				
1908	1	GBR	A. Henry Thomas	Dec	
	2	GBR	John Condon		
	3	GBR	W. Webb		
(no USA entry)					
1912	(not held)				
1920	1	RSA	Clarence Walker	Dec	
	2	CAN	Chris Graham		
	3	GBR	James McKenzie		
		USA	**Edward Hartman / M.N. Herschman**	**elim. 1st rd**	
1924	1	RSA	William Smith	Dec	
	2	**USA**	**Salvatore Tripoli**		
	3	FRA	Jean Ces		
1928	1	ITA	Vittorio Tamagnini	Dec	
	2	**USA**	**John Daley**		
	3	RSA	Harry Isaacs		
1932	1	CAN	Horace Gwynne		
	2	GER	Hans Ziglarski		
	3	PHI	José Villanueva		
	4	**USA**	**Joseph Lang**		
1936	1	ITA	Ulderico Sergo	Dec	
	2	**USA**	**Jack Wilson**		
	3	MEX	Fidel Ortiz		
1948	1	HUN	Tibor Csik	Dec	
	2	ITA	Giovanni Battista Zuddas		
	3	PUR	Juan Venegas		
		USA	**William Bossio**	**elim. 1st rd**	
1952	1	FIN	Pentti Hämäläinen	2-1	
	2	IRL	John McNally		
	3T	URS	Gennady Garbuzov		
	3T	KOR	Kang Joon-ho		
	5T	**USA**	**David Moore**		
1956	1	GDR	Wolfgang Behrendt	Dec	
	2	KOR	Song Soon-chun		
	3T	CHI	Claudio Barrientos		
	3T	IRL	Frederick Gilroy		
		USA	**Choken Maekawa**	**did not make weight**	
1960	1	URS	Oleg Grigoryev	Dec	
	2	ITA	Primo Zamparini		
	3T	POL	Brunon Bendig		
	3T	AUS	Oliver Taylor		
	5T	**USA**	**Jerry Armstrong**		
1964	1	JPN	Takao Sakurai	1:18	RSC-2
	2	KOR	Chung Shin-cho		
	3T	MEX	Juan Fabila Mendoza		
	3T	URU	Washington Rodriguez		
		USA	**Louis Johnson**	**elim. 2nd rd**	
1968	1	URS	Valery Sokolov	2:15	RSC-2
	2	UGA	Eridari Mukwanga		
	3T	KOR	Chang Kyou-chull		
	3T	JPN	Eiji Morioka		
		USA	**Samuel Goss**		
1972	1	CUB	Orlando Martinez	Dec	5-0
	2	MEX	Alfonso Zamora		
	3T	**USA**	**Ricardo Carreras**		
	3T	GBR	George Turpin		
1976	1	PRK	Gu Yong Jo	Dec	5-0
	2	**USA**	**Charles Mooney**		
	3T	GBR	Patrick Cowdell		
	3T	URS	Victor Rybakov		
1980	1	CUB	Juan Hernandez	Dec	5-0
	2	VEN	Bernardo José Pinango		
	3T	GUY	Michael Anthony		
	3T	ROM	Dumitru Cipere		
1984	1	ITA	Maurizio Stecca	Dec	4-1
	2	MEX	Hector Lopez		
	3T	DOM	Pedro Nolasco		
	3T	CAN	Dale Walters		
		USA	**Robert Shannon**	**elim. 1/16 final**	
1988	**1**	**USA**	**Kennedy McKinney**	**5-0**	
	2	BUL	Alexandar Hristov		
	3T	THA	Phajol Moolsan		
	3T	COL	Jorge Julio Rocha		
1992	1	CUB	Joel Casamayor	14-8	
	2	IRL	Wayne McCullough		
	3T	MAR	Mohamed Achik		
	3T	PRK	Li Gwang		
		USA	**Sergio Reyes**		

FEATHERWEIGHT - (57 KG/125 LBS)

YEAR	RANK	CTRY	ATHLETE	DECISION	
1896-1900	(not held)				
1904	**1**	**USA**	**Oliver Kirk**	**Dec**	
	2	**USA**	**Frank Haller**		
	3	**USA**	**Fred Gilmore**		
1906	(not held)				
1908	1	GBR	Richard Gunn	Dec	
	2	GBR	Charles Morris		
	3T	GBR	Hugh Roddin		
	3T	GBR	T. Ringer		
(no USA entry)					
1912	(not held)				
1920	1	FRA	Paul Fritsch	Dec	
	2	FRA	Jean Gachet		
	3	ITA	Edoardo Garzena		
	4	**USA**	**Jack Zivic**		
1924	**1**	**USA**	**John Fields**	**Dec**	
	2	**USA**	**Joseph Salas**		
	3	ARG	Pedro Quartucci		
1928	1	HOL	Lambertus van Klaveren	Dec	
	2	ARG	Victor Peralta		
	3	**USA**	**Harold Devine**		
1932	1	ARG	Carmelo Robledo	Dec	
	2	GER	Josef Schleinkofer		
	3	SWE	Carl Carlsson		
	5T	**USA**	**John Hines**		
1936	1	ARG	Oscar Casanovas	Dec	
	2	RSA	Charles Catterall		
	3T	GER	Josef Miner		
	5T	**USA**	**Theodore Ernst Kara**		
1948	1	ITA	Ernesto Formenti	Dec	
	2	RSA	Dennis Shephard		
	3	POL	Aleksy Antkiewicz		
	5T	**USA**	**Edward Johnson**		
1952	1	TCH	Jan Zachara	Dec	2-1
	2	ITA	Sergio Caprari		
	3T	RSA	Leonard Leisching		
	3T	FRA	Joseph Ventaja		
	5T	**USA**	**Edson Brown**		
1956	1	URS	Vladimir Safronov	Dec	
	2	GBR	Thomas Nicholls		
	3T	FIN	Pentti Hämäläinen		
	3T	POL	Henryk Niedzwiedzki		
		USA	**Harry Smith**	**did not make weight**	
1960	1	ITA	Francesco Musso	Dec	4-1
	2	POL	Jerzy Adamski		
	3T	FIN	Jorma Limmonen		
	3T	RSA	William Meyers		
		USA	**Nicholas Spanakos**	**elim. 1st rd**	
1964	1	URS	Stanislav Stepashkin	Dec	3-2
	2	PHI	Anthony Villanueva		
	3T	**USA**	**Charles Brown**		
	3T	GDR	Heinz Schulz		
1968	1	MEX	Antonio Roldan		DISQ 2
	2	**USA**	**Albert Robinson**		
	3T	BUL	Ivan Mihailov		
	3T	KEN	Philipp Waruinge		
1972	1	URS	Boris Kousnetsov	Dec	3-2
	2	KEN	Philip Waruinge		
	3T	HUN	András Botos		
	3T	COL	Clemente Rojas		
		USA	**Louis Self**	**elim. 3rd rd**	
1976	1	CUB	Angel Herrera	2:18	KO-2
	2	GDR	Richard Nowakowski		
	3T	POL	Leszek Kosedowski		
	3T	MEX	Juan Paredes		
	5	**USA**	**Davey Armstrong**		
1980	1	GDR	Rudi Rink	Dec	4-1
	2	CUB	Adolfo Horta		
	3T	POL	Krzysztof Kosedowski		
	3T	URS	Viktor Rybakov		
1984	**1**	**USA**	**Meldrick Taylor**	**Dec**	**5-0**
	2	NGR	Peter Konyegwachie		
	3T	TUR	Targut Aykac		
	3T	VEN	Omar Catari Peraza		
1988	1	ITA	Giovanni Parisi	1:41	RSC-1
	2	ROM	Daniel Dumitrescu		
	3T	KOR	Lee Jae-hyuk		
	3T	MAR	Abdelhak Achik		
		USA	**Kelcie Banks**		
1992	1	GER	Andreas Tews	16-7	
	2	ESP	Faustino Reyes		
	3T	EUN	Ramazi Paliani		
	3T	ALG	Hocine Soltani		
		USA	**Julian Wheeler**		

LIGHTWEIGHT - (60 KG/132 LBS)

YEAR	RANK	CTRY	ATHLETE	DECISION	
1896-1900	(not held)				
1904	**1**	**USA**	**Harry Spanger**	**Dec**	
	2	**USA**	**James Eagan**		
	3T	**USA**	**Russell Van Horn**		
	3T	**USA**	**Peter Sturholdt**		
1906	(not held)				
1908	1	GBR	Frederick Grace	Dec	
	2	GBR	Frederick Spiller		
	3	GBR	H.H. Johnson		
(no USA entry)					
1912	(not held)				
1920	**1**	**USA**	**Samuel Mosberg**	**Dec**	
	2	DEN	Gotfred Johansen		
	3	CAN	Clarence Newton		
1924	1	DEN	Hans Nielsen	Dec	
	2	ARG	Alfredo Copello		
	3	**USA**	**Frederick Boylstein**		
1928	1	ITA	Carlo Orlandi	Dec	
	2	**USA**	**Stephen Michael Halaiko**		
	3	SWE	Gunnar Berggren		
1932	1	RSA	Lawrence Stevens	Dec	
	2	SWE	Thure Ahlqvist		
	3	**USA**	**Nathan Bor**		
1936	1	HUN	Imre Harangi	Dec	
	2	EST	Nikolai Stepulov		
	3	SWE	Erik Ågren		
		USA	**Andrew Scrivani**	**elim. 3rd rd**	
1948	1	RSA	Gerald Dreyer	Dec	
	2	BEL	Joseph Vissers		
	3	DEN	Svend Wad		
	4	**USA**	**Wallace Smith**		
1952	1	ITA	Aureliano Bolognesi	Dec	2-1
	2	POL	Aleksy Antkiewicz		
	3T	ROM	Gheorghe Fiat		
	3T	FIN	Erkki Pakkanen		
		USA	**Robert Bickle**	**elim. 2nd rd**	
1956	1	GBR	Richard McTaggart	Dec	
	2	GER	Harry Kurschat		
	3T	IRL	Anthony Byrne		
	3T	URS	Anatoly Lagetko		
		USA	**Louis Molina**	**elim. qtr finals**	
1960	1	POL	Kazimierz Pazdzior	Dec	4-1
	2	ITA	Sandro Lopopolo		
	3T	ARG	Abel Laudonio		
	3T	GBR	Richard McTaggart		
	5T	**USA**	**Harry Campbell**		
1964	1	POL	Józef Grudzie	Dec	
	2	URS	Velikton Barannikov		
	3T	**USA**	**Ronald Allan Harris**		
	3T	IRL	James McCourt		
1968	**1**	**USA**	**Ronald W. Harris**	**Dec**	**5-0**
	2	POL	Józef Grudzie		
	3T	ROM	Calistrat Cutov		
	3T	YUG	Zvonimir Vujin		
1972	1	POL	Jan Szczepanski	Dec	5-0
	2	HUN	László Orbán		
	3T	KEN	Samuel Mbugua		
	3T	COL	Alfonso Pérez		
		USA	**James Busceme**	**elim. 2nd rd**	
1976	**1**	**USA**	**Howard Davis**	**Dec**	**5-0**
	2	ROM	Simion Cutov		
	3T	YUG	Ace Rusevski		
	3T	URS	Vasily Solomin		
1980	1	CUB	Angel Herrera	0:13	RSC-3
	2	URS	Viktor Demianenko		
	3T	POL	Kazimierz Adach		
	3T	GDR	Richard Nowakowski		
1984	**1**	**USA**	**Pernell Whitaker**	**2:57**	**RET-2**
	2	PUR	Luis Ortiz		
	3T	KOR	Chun Chil-sung		
	3T	CAM	Martin Ndongo Ebanga		
1988	1	GDR	Andreas Zuelow	5-0	
	2	SWE	George Cramne		
	3T	**USA**	**Romallis Ellis**		
	3T	MGL	Nerguy Enkhbat		
1992	**1**	**USA**	**Oscar De La Hoya**	**7-2**	
	2	GER	Marco Rudolph		
	3T	MGL	Namjil Bayarsaikhan		
	3T	KOR	Sung Hong		

LIGHT WELTERWEIGHT - (63.5 KG/140 LBS)

YEAR	RANK	CTRY	ATHLETE	DECISION	
1896-1948	(not held)				
1952	**1**	**USA**	**Charles Adkins**	**Dec**	**2-1**
	2	URS	Viktor Mednov		
	3T	FIN	Erkki Mallenius		
	3T	ITA	Bruno Visintin		
1956	1	URS	Vladimir Yengibaryan	Dec	
	2	ITA	Franco Nenci		
	3T	ROM	Constantin Dumitrescu		
	3T	RSA	Henry Loubscher		
	5T	**USA**	**Joseph Shaw**		
1960	1	TCH	Bohumil Nemecek	Dec	5-0
	2	GHA	Clement "Ike" Quartey		
	3T	**USA**	**Quincey Daniels**		
	3T	POL	Marian Kasprzyk		
1964	1	POL	Jerzy Kulej	Dec	5-0
	2	URS	Yevgeny Frolov		
	3T	GHA	Eddie Blay		
	3T	TUN	Habib Galhia		
		USA	**Charles Ellis**	**elim. 2nd rd**	
1968	1	POL	Jerzy Kulej	Dec	3-2
	2	CUB	Enrique Regueiferos		
	3T	FIN	Arto Nilsson		
	3T	**USA**	**James Wallington**		
1972	**1**	**USA**	**Ray Seales**	**Dec**	**3-2**
	2	BUL	Angel Angelov		
	3T	NIG	Issaka Daborg		
	3T	YUG	Zvonimir Vujin		
1976	**1**	**USA**	**Ray Leonard**	**Dec**	**5-0**
	2	CUB	Andrés Aldama		
	3T	BUL	Vladimir Kolev		
	3T	POL	Kazimierz Szczerba		
1980	1	ITA	Patrizio Oliva	Dec	4-1
	2	URS	Serik Konakbaev		
	3T	CUB	José Aguilar		
	3T	GBR	Anthony Willis		
1984	**1**	**USA**	**Jerry Page**	**Dec**	**5-0**
	2	THA	Dhawee Umponmaha		
	3T	ROM	Mircea Fulter		
	3T	YUG	Mirko Puzovi		
1988	1	URS	Viatcheslav Janovski	5-0	
	2	AUS	Grahame Cheney		
	3T	FRG	Reiner Gies		
	3T	SWE	Lars Myrbert		
		USA	**Todd Foster**		
1992	1	CUB	Hector Vincent	11-1	
	2	CAN	Mark Leduc		
	3T	ROM	Leonard Doroftei		
	3T	FIN	Jyri Kjall		
		USA	**Vernon Forrest**		

WELTERWEIGHT - (67 KG/147 LBS)

YEAR	RANK	CTRY	ATHLETE	DECISION	
1896-1900	(not held)				
1904	**1**	**USA**	**Albert Young**	**Dec**	
	2	**USA**	**Harry Spanger**		
	3T	**USA**	**Jack Eagan**		
	3T	**USA**	**Joseph Lydon**		
1906-1912	(not held)				
1920	1	CAN	Albert Schneider	Dec	
	2	GBR	Alexander Ireland		
	3	**USA**	**Frederick Colberg**		
1924	1	BEL	Jean Delarge	Dec	
	2	ARG	Héctor Méndez		
	3	CAN	Douglas Lewis		
	5T	**USA**	**Hugh Haggerty**		
1928	1	NZL	Edward Morgan	Dec	
	2	ARG	Raúl Landini		
	3	CAN	Raymond Smillie		
		USA	**Thomas Lown**	**elim. 1st rd**	
1932	**1**	**USA**	**Edward Flynn**	**Dec**	
	2	GER	Erich Campe		
	3	FIN	Bruno Ahlberg		
1936	1	FIN	Sten Suvio	Dec	
	2	GER	Michael Murach		
	3	DEN	Gerhard Petersen		
		USA	**Chester Rutecki**	**elim. 2nd rd**	
1948	1	TCH	Julius Torma	Dec	
	2	**USA**	**Horace Herring**		
	3	ITA	Alessandro D'Ottavio		
1952	1	POL	Zygmunt Chychla	Dec	3-0
	2	URS	Sergei Scherbakov		
	3T	GER	Günther Heidemann		
	3T	DEN	Victor Jörgensen		
		USA	**Louis Gage**	**elim. 2nd rd**	
1956	1	ROM	Nicolae Linca	Dec	3-2
	2	IRL	Frederick Tiedt		
	3T	GBR	Nicholas Gargano		
	3T	AUS	Kevin John Hogarth		
		USA	**Pearce Lane**	**elim. qtr finals**	
1960	1	ITA	Giovanni Benvenuti	Dec	4-1
	2	URS	Yuri Radonyak		
	3T	POL	Leszek Drogosz		
	3T	GBR	James Lloyd		
	5T	**USA**	**A. Phil Baldwin**		
1964	1	POL	Marian Kasprzyk	Dec	4-1
	2	URS	Richardas Tamulis		
	3T	ITA	Silvano Bertini		
	3T	FIN	Pertti Purhonen		
		USA	**Maurice Friloт**	**elim. 1st rd**	
1968	1	GDR	Manfred Wolke	Dec	4-1
	2	CAM	Joseph Bessala		
	3T	ARG	Mario Guilloti		
	3T	URS	Vladimir Mussalimov		
	5T	**USA**	**Armando Muniz**		

1972	1	CUB	Emilio Correa	Dec 5-0
	2	HUN	János Kajdi	
	3T	KEN	Dick Tiger Murunga	
	3T	**USA**	**Jesse Valdez**	
1976	1	GDR	Jochen Bachfeld	Dec 3-2
	2	VEN	Pedro Gamarro	
	3T	GER	Reinhard Skricek	
	3T	ROM	Victor Zilberman	
	5T	**USA**	**Clinton Jackson**	
1980	1	CUB	Andrés Aldama	Dec 4-1
	2	UGA	John Mugabi	
	3T	GDR	Karl-Heinz Krüger	
	3T	POL	Kazimierz Szczerba	
1984	**1**	**USA**	**Mark Breland**	**Dec 5-0**
	2	KOR	An Young-su	
	3T	ITA	Luciano Bruno	
	3T	FIN	Joni Nyman	
1988	1	KEN	Robert Wangila	0:44 RSC-2
	2	FRA	Laurent Boudouani	
	3T	**USA**	**Kenneth Gould**	
	3T	POL	Jan Dydak	
1992	1	IRL	Michael Carruth	13-10
	2	CUB	Juan Hernandez	
	3T	THA	Arkom Chenglai	
	3T	PUR	Anibal Acevedo	
		USA	**Pepe Reilly**	

LIGHT MIDDLEWEIGHT - (71 KG/156 LBS)

YEAR	RANK	CTRY	ATHLETE	DECISION
1896-1948	(not held)			
1952	1	HUN	László Papp	Dec 3-0
	2	RSA	Theunis van Schalkwyk	
	3T	ARG	Eladio Herrera	
	3T	URS	Boris Tischin	
		USA	**Ellsworth Webb**	**elim. 1st rd**
1956	1	HUN	László Papp	Dec
	2	**USA**	**José Torres**	
	3T	GBR	John McCormack	
	3T	POL	Zbigniew Pietrzykowski	
1960	**1**	**USA**	**Wilbert McClure**	**Dec 4-1**
	2	ITA	Carmelo Bossi	
	3T	GBR	William Fisher	
	3T	URS	Boris Lagutin	
1964	1	URS	Boris Lagutin	Dec 4-1
	2	FRA	Joseph Gonzales	
	3T	POL	Józef Grzesiak	
	3T	NGR	Nojim Maiyegun	
		USA	**Tolman Gibson, Jr**	**elim. 2nd rd**
1968	1	URS	Boris Lagutin	Dec 5-0
	2	CUB	Rolando Garbey	
	3T	**USA**	**John Baldwin**	
	3T	GER	Günther Meier	
1972	1	GER	Dieter Kottysch	Dec 3-2
	2	POL	Wiesław Rudkowski	
	3T	GBR	Alan Minter	
	3T	GDR	Peter Tiepold	
		USA	**Reginold Jones**	**elim. 1st rd**
1976	1	POL	Jerzy Rybicki	Dec 5-0
	2	YUG	Tadija Kacar	
	3T	CUB	Rolando Garbey	
	3T	URS	Victor Savchenko	
		USA	**Charles Walker**	**elim. 1/8 final**
1980	1	CUB	Armando Martinez	Dec 4-1
	2	URS	Aleksandr Koshkin	
	3T	TCH	Ján Franek	
	3T	GDR	Detlef Kästner	
1984	**1**	**USA**	**Frank Tate**	**Dec 5-0**
	2	CAN	Shawn O'Sullivan	
	3T	FRA	Christophe Tiozzo	
	3T	GER	Manfred Zielonka	
1988	1	KOR	Park Si-hun	3-2
	2	**USA**	**Roy Jones**	
	3T	CAN	Raymond Downey	
	3T	GBR	Richard Woodhall	
1992	1	CUB	Juan Lemus	6-1
	2	NED	Orhan Delibas	
	3T	HUN	Gyorgy Mizsei	
	3T	GBR	Robin Reed	
		USA	**Raul Marquez**	

MIDDLEWEIGHT - (75 KG/165 LBS)

YEAR	RANK	CTRY	ATHLETE	DECISION
1896-1900	(not held)			
1904	**1**	**USA**	**Charles Mayer**	**1:40 RSC-3**
	2	**USA**	**Benjamin Spradley**	
1906	(not held)			
1908	1	GBR	John Douglas	Dec
	2	AUS	Reginald Baker	
	3T	GBR	W. Philo	
	3T	GBR	Ruben Warnes	
	(no USA entry)			
1912	(not held)			
1920	1	GBR	Harry Mallin	Dec
	2	CAN	Georges Prudhomme	
	3	CAN	Montgomery "Moe" Herscovitch	
	5T	**USA**	**Samuel Lagonia**	
1924	1	GBR	Harry Mallin	Dec
	2	GBR	John Elliott	
	3	BEL	Joseph Beecken	
		USA	**Adolph Lefkowitch / Ben Funk**	**elim. qtr finals**
1928	1	ITA	Piero Toscani	Dec
	2	TCH	Jan Hermánek	
	3	BEL	Leonard Steyaert	
	5T	**USA**	**Harry Henderson**	
1932	**1**	**USA**	**Carmen Barth**	**Dec**
	2	ARG	Amado Azar	
	3	RSA	Ernest Pierce	
1936	1	FRA	Jean Despeaux	Dec
	2	NOR	Henry Tiller	
	3	ARG	Raúl Villareal	
	5T	**USA**	**James Atkinson**	
1948	1	HUN	László Papp	Dec
	2	GBR	John Wright	
	3	ITA	Ivano Fontana	
		USA	**Washington Jones**	**elim. 2nd rd**
1952	**1**	**USA**	**Floyd Patterson**	**1:14 KO-1**
	2	ROM	Vasile Tit	
	3T	BUL	Boris Georgiev	
	3T	SWE	Stig Sjölin	
1956	1	URS	Gennady Schatkov	KO-1
	2	CHI	Rámon Tapia	
	3T	FRA	Gilbert Chapron	
	3T	ARG	Victor Zalazar	
	5T	**USA**	**Roger Rouse**	
1960	**1**	**USA**	**Edward Crook**	**Dec 3-2**
	2	POL	Tadeusz Walasek	
	3T	URS	Evgeny Feofanov	
	3T	ROM	Ion Monea	
1964	1	URS	Valery Popenchenko	2:05 RSC-1
	2	GER	Emil Schulz	
	3T	ITA	Franco Valle	
	3T	POL	Tadeusz Walasek	
		USA	**James Rosette**	**elim. 2nd rd**
1968	1	GBR	Christopher Finnegan	Dec 3-2
	2	URS	Aleksei Kisselyov	
	3T	**USA**	**Alfred Jones**	
	3T	MEX	Agustin Zaragoza	
1972	1	URS	Vyacheslav Lemechev	2:17 KO-1
	2	FIN	Reima Virtanen	
	3T	GHA	Prince Amartey	
	3T	**USA**	**Marvin Johnson**	
1976	**1**	**USA**	**Michael Spinks**	**1:54 RSC-3**
	2	URS	Rufat Riskiev	
	3T	CUB	Luis Martinez	
	3T	ROM	Alec Nastac	
1980	1	CUB	José Gomez	Dec 4-1
	2	URS	Viktor Savchenko	
	3T	POL	Jerzy Rybicki	
	3T	ROM	Valentin Silaghi	
1984	1	KOR	Shin Joon-sup	Dec 3-2
	2	**USA**	**Virgil Hill**	
	3T	PUR	Aristides Gonzalez	
	3T	ALG	Mohamed Zaoui	
1988	1	GDR	Henry Maske	5-0
	2	CAN	Egerton Marcus	
	3T	KEN	Chris Sande	
	3T	PAK	Hussain Shah Syed	
		USA	**Anthony Hembrick**	**walkover**
1992	1	CUB	Ariel Hernandez	12-7
	2	**USA**	**Chris Byrd**	
	3T	CAN	Chris Johnson	
	3T	KOR	Lee Seung	

LIGHT HEAVYWEIGHT - (81 KG/178 LBS)

YEAR	RANK	CTRY	ATHLETE	DECISION
1896-1912	(not held)			
1920	**1**	**USA**	**Edward Eagan**	**Dec**
	2	NOR	Sverre Sörsdal	
	3	GBR	H. Franks	
1924	1	GBR	Harry Mitchell	Dec
	2	DEN	Thyge Petersen	
	3	NOR	Sverre Sörsdal	
	5T	**USA**	**Thomas Kirby**	
1928	1	ARG	Victor Avendaño	Dec
	2	GER	Ernst Pistulla	
	3	HOL	Karl Leendert Miljon	
		USA	**Loen Lucas**	**elim. 1st rd**
1932	1	RSA	David Carstens	Dec
	2	ITA	Gino Rossi	
	3	DEN	Peter Jörgensen	
		USA	**John Miler**	**elim. 1st rd**
1936	1	FRA	Roger Michelot	Dec
	2	GER	Richard Vogt	
	3	ARG	Francisco Risiglione	
		USA	**Carl Vinciauerra**	**elim. 1st rd**
1948	1	RSA	George Hunter	Dec
	2	GBR	Donald Scott	
	3	ARG	Maurio Cia	
		USA	**Charles Speiser**	**elim. 2nd rd**
1952	**1**	**USA**	**Norvel Lee**	**Dec 3-0**
	2	ARG	Antonio Pacenza	
	3T	URS	Anatoly Perov	
	3T	FIN	Harri Siljander	
1956	**1**	**USA**	**James Boyd**	**Dec**
	2	ROM	Gheorghe Negrea	
	3T	CHI	Carlos Lucas	
	3T	URS	Romualdas Murauskas	
1960	**1**	**USA**	**Cassius Clay**	**Dec 5-0**
	2	POL	Zbigniew Pietrzykowski	
	3T	AUS	Anthony Madigan	
	3T	ITA	Giulio Saraudi	
1964	1	ITA	Cosimo Pinto	Dec 3-2
	2	URS	Aleksei Kisselyov	
	3T	BUL	Alexander Nikolov	
	3T	POL	Zbigniew Pietrzykowski	
		USA	**Robert Christopherson**	**elim. 2nd rd**
1968	1	URS	Dan Poznyak	Default
	2	ROM	Ion Monea	
	3T	POL	Stanisław Dragan	
	3T	BUL	Georgi Stankov	
		USA	**Arthur Redden**	
1972	1	YUG	Mate Parlov	2:39 RSC-2
	2	CUB	Gilberto Carrillo	
	3T	POL	Janusz Gortat	
	3T	NGR	Isaac Ikhouria	**USA**
		USA	**Raymond Russell**	**elim. 2nd rd**
1976	**1**	**USA**	**Leon Spinks**	**1:09 RSC-3**
	2	CUB	Sixto Soria	
	3T	ROM	Costica Dafinoiu	
	3T	POL	Janusz Gortat	
1980	1	YUG	Slobodan Kacar	Dec 4-1
	2	POL	Pawel Skrzeck	
	3T	GDR	Herbert Bauch	
	3T	CUB	Ricardo Rojas	
1984	1	YUG	Anton Josipovi	Default
	2	NZL	Kevin Barry	
	3T	**USA**	**Evander Holyfield**	
	3T	ALG	Mustapha Moussa	
1988	**1**	**USA**	**Andrew Maynard**	**5-0**
	2	URS	Nourmagomed Chanavazov	
	3T	YUG	Damir Skaro	
	3T	POL	Henryk Petrich	
1992	1	GER	Torsten May	8-3
	2	EUN	Rostislav Zaoulitchnyi	
	3T	HUN	Zoltan Beres	
	3T	POL	Wojciech Bartnik	
		USA	**Montell Griffin**	

HEAVYWEIGHT - (91 KG/200 LBS)

YEAR	RANK	CTRY	ATHLETE	DECISION
1896-1980	(not held)			
1984	**1**	**USA**	**Henry Tillman**	**Dec 5-0**
	2	CAN	William deWit	
	3T	ITA	Angelo Musone	
	3T	HOL	Arnold van der Lijde	
1988	**1**	**USA**	**Ray Mercer**	**2:16 KO-1**
	2	KOR	Baik Hyun-man	
	3T	HOL	Arnold Vanderlijde	
	3T	POL	Andrzej Golota	
1992	1	CUB	Felix Savon	14-1
	2	NGR	David Izonritei	
	3T	NED	Van Der Lijde	
	3T	NZL	David Tua	
		USA	**Danell Nicholson**	

SUPER HEAVYWEIGHT - (+91 KG/+200 LBS)

YEAR	RANK	CTRY	ATHLETE	DECISION
1896-1900	(not held)			
1904	**1**	**USA**	**Samuel Berger**	**Dec**
	2	**USA**	**Charles Mayer**	
	3	**USA**	**William Michaels**	
1906	(not held)			
1908	1	GBR	Albert Oldham	2:00 KO-1
	2	GBR	S.C.H. Evans	
	3	GBR	Frederick Parks	
	(no USA entry)			
1912	(not held)			
1920	1	GBR	Ronald Rawson	Dec
	2	DEN	Sören Petersen	
	3	FRA	Xavier Eluere	
	4	**USA**	**William Spengler**	
1924	1	NOR	Otto von Porat	Dec
	2	DEN	Sören Petersen	
	3	ARG	Alfredo Porzio	
	5T	**USA**	**H.G. Greathouse**	
1928	1	ARG	Arturo Rodriguez Jurado	RSC-1
	2	SWE	Nils Ramm	
	3T	DEN	M. Jacob Michaelsen	
	5T	**USA**	**Alexander Kaletchetz**	
1932	1	ARG	Santiago Lovell	Dec
	2	ITA	Luigi Rovati	
	3	**USA**	**Frederick Feary**	
	4	CAN	George Maughan	
1936	1	GER	Herbert Runge	Dec
	2	ARG	Guillermo Lovell	
	3	NOR	Erling Nilsen	
		USA	**Arthur Oliver**	**elim. 2nd rd**
1948	1	ARG	Rafael Iglesias	KO-2
	2	SWE	Gunnar Nilsson	
	3	RSA	John Arthur	
	5T	**USA**	**Jay Lambert**	
1952	**1**	**USA**	**H. Edward Sanders**	**DQ-2**
	2	SWE	Ingemar Johansson	
	3T	FIN	Ilkka Koski	
	3T	RSA	Andries Nieman	
1956	**1**	**USA**	**T. Peter Rademacher**	**2:27 RSC-1**
	2	URS	Lev Mukhin	
	3T	RSA	Daniel Bekker	
	3T	ITA	Giacomo Bozzano	
1960	1	ITA	Franco De Piccoli	1:30 KO-1
	2	RSA	Daniel Bekker	
	3T	TCH	Josef Nemec	
	3T	GDR	Günter Siegmund	
	5T	**USA**	**Percy Price**	
1964	**1**	**USA**	**Joseph Frazier**	**Dec 3-2**
	2	GER	Hans Huber	
	3T	ITA	Giuseppe Ros	
	3T	URS	Vadim Yemelyanov	
1968	**1**	**USA**	**George Foreman**	**RSC-2**
	2	URS	Ionas Chepulis	
	3T	ITA	Giorgio Bambini	
	3T	MEX	Joaquin Rocha	
1972	1	CUB	Teófilo Stevenson	Default
	2	ROM	Ion Alexe	
	3T	GER	Peter Hussing	
	3T	SWE	Hasse Thomsén	
	5T	**USA**	**Duane Bobick**	
1976	1	CUB	Teófilo Stevenson	2:35 KO-3
	2	ROM	Mircea Simon	
	3T	BER	Clarence Hill	
	3T	**USA**	**Johnny Tate**	
1980	1	CUB	Teófilo Stevenson	Dec 4-1
	2	URS	Pyotr Zaev	
	3T	GDR	Jürgen Fanghänel	
	3T	HUN	István Levai	
1984	**1**	**USA**	**Tyrell Biggs**	**Dec 4-1**
	2	ITA	Francesco Damiani	
	3T	YUG	Salihu Azis	
	3T	GBR	Robert Wells	
1988	1	CAN	Lennox Lewis	0:43 RSC-2
	2	**USA**	**Riddick Bowe**	
	3T	POL	Janusz Zarenkiewicz	
	3T	URS	Alexandre Mirochnitchenko	
1992	1	CUB	Roberto Balado	13-2
	2	NGR	Richard Igbineghu	
	3T	DEN	Brian Nielsen	
	3T	BUL	Svilen Roussinov	
		USA	**Larry Donald**	

CANOE KAYAK

MEN'S C-1 FLATWATER 500 METERS

YEAR	RANK	CTRY	ATHLETE	TIME
1896-1972	(not held)			
1976	1	URS	Aleksandr Rogov	1:59.23
	2	CAN	John Wood	1:59.58
	3	YUG	Matija Ljubek	1:59.60
		USA	**Angus Morrison (2:12.92)**	**elim. rep.**
1980	1	URS	Sergei Postrekhin	1:53.37
	2	BUL	Lyubomir Lyubenov	1:53.49
	3	GDR	Olaf Heukrodt	1:54.38
1984	1	CAN	Larry Cain	1:57.01
	2	DEN	Henning Jakobsen	1:58.45
	3	ROM	Costica Olaru	1:59.86
		USA	**John Plankenhorn**	**DNQ**
1988	1	GDR	Olaf Heukrodt	1:56.42
	2	URS	Mikhail Slivinskii	1:57.26
	3	BUL	Martin Marinov	1:57.27
		USA	**James Terrell**	
1992	1	BUL	Nikolai Boukhalov	1:51.15
	2	EUN	Mikhail Slivinski	1:51.40
	3	GER	Olaf Heukrodt	1:53.00
		USA	**Fred Spaulding**	**elim. semis**

MEN'S C-1 FLATWATER 1,000 METERS

YEAR	RANK	CTRY	ATHLETE	TIME
1896-1932	(not held)			
1936	1	CAN	Francis Amyot	5:32.1
	2	TCH	Bohuslav Karlik	5:39.9
	3	GER	Erich Koschik	5:39.0
	5	**USA**	**Joseph Hasenfus**	**6:02.6**

MEN'S K-4 FLATWATER 1,000 METERS

YEAR	RANK	CTRY	ATHLETES	TIME
1896-1960			(not held)	
1964	1	URS		3:14.67
	2	GER		3:15.39
	3	ROM		3:15.51
				elim. rep. 1st rd
1968	1	NOR		3:14.38
	2	ROM		3:14.81
	3	HUN		3:15.10
1972	1	URS		3:14.02
	2	ROM		3:15.07
	3	NOR		3:15.27
				elim. 1st rd
1976	1	URS		3:08.69
	2	ESP		3:08.95
	3	GDR		3:10.76
1980	1	GDR		3:13.76
	2	ROM		3:15.35
	3	BUL		3:15.46
1984	1	NZL		3:02.28
	2	SWE		3:02.81
	3	FRA		DQ
1988	1	HUN		3:00.20
	2	GDR		3:01.40
	3	BUL		3:02.37
1992	1	GER		2:54.18
	2	HUN		2:54.82
	3	AUS		2:56.97
	9	USA		3:04.30

MEN'S K-1 WHITEWATER SLALOM

YEAR	RANK	CTRY	ATHLETE	POINTS
1896-1968			(not held)	
1972	1	GER	Siegbert Horn	258.56
	2	AUT	Norbert Sattler	270.76
	3	GDR	Harald Gimpel	277.95
	7	USA	Eric Evans	296.34
1976-1988			(not held)	
1992	1	ITA	Pierpaolo Ferrazzi	106.89
	2	FRA	Sylvain Curinier	107.06
	3	GER	Jochen Lettmann	108.52
	13	USA	Eric Jackson	112.59

WOMEN'S K-1 FLATWATER 500 METERS

YEAR	RANK	CTRY	ATHLETE	TIME
1896-1936			(not held)	
1948	1	DEN	Karen Hoff	2:31.9
	2	HOL	Alida van der Anker-Doedens	2:32.8
	3	AUT	Fritzi Schwingl	2:32.9
			(no USA entry)	
1952	1	FIN	Sylvi Saimo	2:18.4
	2	URS	Gertrude Liebhart	2:18.8
	3	GER	Nina Savina	2:21.6
			(no USA entry)	
1956	1	URS	Yelisaveta Dementyeva	2:18.9
	2	GER	Therese Zenz	2:19.6
	3	DEN	Tove Soby	2:22.3
			(no USA entry)	

MEN'S C-1 WHITEWATER SLALOM

YEAR	RANK	CTRY	ATHLETE	POINTS
1896-1968			(not held)	
1972	1	GDR	Reinhard Eiben	315.84
	2	GER	Reinhold Kauder	327.89
	3	USA	Jamie McEwan	335.95
1976-1988			(not held)	
1992	1	TCH	Lukas Pollert	113.69
	2	GER	Gareth John Marriott	116.48
	3	FRA	Jacky Avril	117.18

MEN'S C-2 WHITEWATER SLALOM

YEAR	RANK	CTRY	ATHLETE	POINTS
1896-1968			(not held)	
1972	1	GDR	Walter Hofmann / Rolf-Dieter Amend	310.68
	2	GER	Hans Otto Schumacher / Wilhelm Baues	311.90
	3	USA	Tom Southworth / John Burton	315.10
1976-1988			(not held)	
1992	1	USA	Scott Strausbaugh / Joe Jacobi	122.41
	2	TCH	Miroslav Simek / Jiri Rohan	124.25
	3	FRA	Franck Adisson / Wilfrid Forgues	124.38

MEN'S K-1 FLATWATER 500 METERS

YEAR	RANK	CTRY	ATHLETE	TIME
1896-1972			(not held)	
1976	1	GDR	Joachim Mattern / Bernd Olbricht	1:35.87
	2	ROM	Sergei Nagorny / Vladimir Romanovsky	1:36.81
	3		Larion Serghei / Policarp Malihin	1:37.43
	4	URS	Michael Johnson / William Leach (1:49.95)	elim. rep.
1980	1	GDR	Vladislav Parfenovich / Sergei Chukhrai	1:32.38
	2	ESP	Herminio Menendez / Guillermo Del Riego	1:33.65
	3	GDR	Rüdiger Helm / Bernd Olbricht	1:34.00
1984	1	NZL	Ian Ferguson	1:34.21
	2	SWE	Per-Inge Bengtsson / Lars-Erik Moberg	1:35.26
	3	CAN	Hugh Fisher / Alwyn Morris	1:35.41
1988	1	NZL	David Halpher / Olney "Terry" Kent	DNQ for final
	2	HUN	Ian Ferguson / Paul MacDonald	1:34.15
	3	URS	Igor Nagaev / Victor Denissov	1:34.32
	8	GER	Olney "Terry" Kent / Carl "Terry" White	1:36.62
1992	1	GER	Kay Bluhm / Torsten Gutsche	1:28.27
	2	POL	Maciej Freimut / Wojciech Kurpiewski	1:29.84
	3	ITA	Antonio Rossi / Bruno Dreossi	1:30.00
	8	USA	Michael Harbold / Peter Newton	1:33.02

MEN'S K-2 FLATWATER 1,000 METERS

YEAR	RANK	CTRY	ATHLETE	TIME
1896-1932			(not held)	
1936	1	AUT	Adolf Kainz / Alfons Dorfner	4:03.8
	2	GER	Ewald Tilker / Fritz Bondroit	4:08.9
	3	HOL	Nicolaas Tates / Willem Frederik	4:12.2
			van der Kroft	
1948	7	USA	William Gehler / William Lofgren (two-seater rigid)	45:15.4
	7	USA	John Lysak / James O'Rourke (two-seater folding)	49:46.0
1952	1	FIN	Kurt Wires / Yrjö Hietanen	4:07.3
	2	SWE	Lars Glasser / Ingemar Hedberg	4:07.5
	3	AUT	Max Raub / Herbert Wiedermann	4:08.7
	13	USA	Raymond Clark / John Eiseman	50:26.6
1956	1	GER	John Anderson / Paul Bochnewich	48:30.7
	2	URS	Michail Kaaleste / Anatoly Demitkov	3:49.6
	3	AUT	Maximilian Raub / Herbert Wiedermann	3:51.4
	14	USA	Edward Houston / Kenneth Wilson	3:55.8
1960	1	SWE	Gert Fredriksson / Sven-Olov Sjödelius	3:34.73
	2	HUN	György Mészáros / András Szente	3:34.91
	3	POL	Stefan Kaplaniak / Wladislaw Zielinski	3:37.34
	12	USA	Kenneth Wilson / John Wolters (4:01.46)	elim. semis
1964	1	SWE	Sven-Olov Sjödelius / Nils Gunnar Utterberg	3:38.54
	2	HOL	Antonius Geurts / Paul Hoekstra	3:39.30
	3	GER	Heinz Büker / Holger Zander	3:40.69
1968	1	URS	Aleksandr Shaparenko / Vladimir Morozov	3:37.54
	2	HUN	Csaba Giczi / István Timár	3:38.44
	3	AUT	Gerhard Seibold / Günther Pfaff	3:40.71

MEN'S K-2 FLATWATER 500 METERS

YEAR	RANK	CTRY	ATHLETE	TIME
1896-1972			(not held)	
1976	1	ROM	Vasile Dîba	1:46.41
	2	GDR	Zoltán Sztanity	1:46.95
	3	NZL	Rüdiger Helm	1:48.30
1980	1	URS	Vladimir Parfenovich	1:43.43
	2	AUS	John Sumegi	1:44.12
	3	ROM	Vasile Dîba	1:44.90
1984	1	NZL	Ian Ferguson	1:47.84
	2	SWE	Lars-Erik Moberg	1:48.18
	3	FRA	Bernard Bregeon	1:48.41
			Terry White	DNQ
1988	1	HUN		1:44.82
	2	GDR		1:46.38
	3	NZL		1:46.46
	7	USA	Michael Herbert	1:46.73
1992	1	FIN	Mikko Kolehmainen	1:40.34
	2	POL	Zsolt Gyulay	1:40.64
	3	NOR	Knut Holmann	1:40.71
	13	USA	Norman Bellingham	1:40.84

MEN'S K-1 FLATWATER 1,000 METERS

YEAR	RANK	CTRY	ATHLETE	TIME
1896-1932			(not held)	
1936	1	AUT	Gregor Hradetzky	4:22.9
	2	GER	Helmut Cämmerer	4:25.6
	3	HOL	Jacob Kraaier	4:35.1
	4	USA	Ernest Riedel	4:38.1
1948	1	SWE	Gert Fredriksson	4:33.2
	2	DEN	Johann Frederik Kobberup	4:39.9
	3	FIN	Henri Eberhardt	4:41.4
	4	USA	Thomas Horton (4:58.0)	elim. trials
1952	1	SWE	Gert Fredriksson	4:07.9
	2	FIN	Thorvald Strömbert	4:09.7
	3	AUT	Louis Gantois	4:20.1
			Michael Budrock (4:39.5) /	elim. trials

MEN'S K-1 FLATWATER 500 METERS

YEAR	RANK	CTRY	ATHLETE	TIME
1896-1972			(not held)	
1976	1			1:46.41
1992	1	AUT	Vladimir Syrovatka / Jan Brzák-Felix	4:50.1
	2	AUT	Rupert Weinstabl / Karl Proisl	4:53.8
	3		Frank Saker / Harvey Charters	4:56.7
	13	USA		5:14.0

MEN'S C-2 FLATWATER 1,000 METERS

YEAR	RANK	CTRY	ATHLETE	TIME
1896-1932			(not held)	
1936	1	TCH	Vladimir Syrovatka / Jan Brzák-Felix	4:50.1
	2	AUT	Rupert Weinstabl / Karl Proisl	4:53.8
	3	CAN	Frank Saker / Harvey Charters	4:56.7
1948	1	TCH	Clarence McNutt / Robert Graf	5:07.1
	2	USA	Stephen Lysak / Stephen Macknowski	5:08.2
	3	FRA	Georges Dransart / Georges Gandil	5:15.2
1952	1	DEN	Bent Peter Rasch / Finn Haunstoft	4:38.3
	2	TCH	Jan Brzák-Felix / Bohumil Kudrna	4:42.9
	3	GER	Egon Drews / Wilfried Soltau	4:48.3
	7	USA	John Haas / Frank Krick	4:59.0
1956	1	ROM	Alexe Dumitru / Simion Ismailciuc	4:47.4
	2	URS	Pavel Kharine / Gratisan Botev	4:48.6
	3	HUN	Károly Wieland / Ferenc Mohácsi	4:54.3
	4	USA	George Byers / Richard Moran (5:16.1)	elim. trials
1960	1	URS	Leonid Geischtor / Sergei Makarenko	4:17.94
	2	ITA	Aldo Dezi / Francesco La Macchia	4:20.77
	3	HUN	Imre Farkas / András Törö	4:20.89
			Richard Moran(4:59.15) / Arnold Demos /	elim. 1st rd
1964	1	URS	Andrey Khimich / Stepan Oschepkov	4:04.64
	2	FRA	Jean Boudehen / Michel Chapuis	4:06.52
	3	DEN	Peer Nørtholm Nielsen / John Sørensen	4:07.48

1960	1	URS	Antonina Seredina	2:08.8
	2	GER	Therese Zenz	2:08.22
	3	POL	Daniela Walkowiak	2:10.46
		USA	**Glorianne Perrier (2:21.29)**	**elim. rep.**
1964	1	URS	Lyudmila Khvedosyuk	2:12.87
	2	ROM	Hilde Lauer	2:15.35
	3	**USA**	**Marcia Jones**	**2:15.68**
1968	1	URS	Lyudmila Pinayeva (Khvedosyuk)	2:11.09
	2	GER	Renate Breuer	2:12.71
	3	ROM	Victoria Dumitru	2:13.22
	4	**USA**	**Marcia Smoke (Jones)**	**2:14.68**
1972	1	URS	Yulia Ryabchinskaya	2:03.17
	2	HOL	Mieke Jappies	2:04.03
	3	HUN	Anna Pfeffer	2:05.50
	9	**USA**	**Marcia Smoke**	**2:07.98**
1976	1	GDR	Carola Zirzow	2:01.05
	2	URS	Tatiana Korshunova	2:03.07
	3	HUN	Klara Rajnai	2:05.01
		USA	**Julie Leach**	**2:06.92**
1980	1	GDR	Birgit Fischer	1:57.96
	2	BUL	Vania Gesheva	1:59.48
	3	URS	Antonina Melnikova	1:59.66
1984	1	SWE	Agneta Andersson	1:58.72
	2	GER	Barbara Scuttpelz	1:59.93
	3	HOL	Annemiek Derckx	2:00.11
	6	**USA**	**Sheila Conover**	**2:02.38**
1988	1	GUL	Vania Guecheva	1:55.19
	2	GDR	Birgit Schmidt	1:55.31
	3	POL	Izabela Dylewska	1:57.38
	6	**USA**	**Traci Phillips**	**2:00.81**
1992	1	GER	Birgit Schmidt	1:51.60
	2	HUN	Rita Koban	1:51.96
	3	POL	Izabella Dylewska	1:52.36
		USA	**Sheila Conover**	

WOMEN'S K-2 FLATWATER 500 METERS

YEAR	RANK	CTRY	ATHLETES	TIME
1896-1980 (not held)				
1960	1	URS	Maria Chubina / Antonina Seredina	1:54.76
	2	GER	Therese Zenz / Ingrid Hartmann	1:56.66
	3	HUN	Klara Fried-Banfalvi / Vilma Egresi	1:58.22
		USA	**Mary Ann Du Chai / Dianne Jerome**	**elim. rep.**
1964	1	GER	Roswitha Esser / Annemarie Zimmerman	1:56.95
	2	**USA**	**Francine Fox / Glorianne Perrier**	**1:59.16**
	3	ROM	Hilde Gruzintseva / Cornelia Sideri	2:00.69
1968	1	GER	Roswitha Esser / Annemarie Zimmerman	1:56.44
	2	HUN	Anna Pfeffer / Katalin Rozsnyoi	1:58.60
	3	URS	Lyudmila Pinayeva / Antonina Seredina	1:58.61
	7	**USA**	**Sperry Rademaker / Marcia Smoke (Jones)**	**2:02.97**
1972	1	URS	Lyudmila Pinayeva / Ekaterina Kuryshko	1:53.50
	2	GDR	Ilse Kaschube / Petra Grabowski	1:54.30
	3	ROM	Maria Nichiforov / Victoria Dumitru	1:55.01
		USA	**Nanch Purvis/Linda Murray**	**elem.2nd Heat**
1976	1	URS	Nina Gopova / Galina Kreft	1:51.15
	2	HUN	Anna Pfeffer / Klara Rajnai	1:51.69
	3	GDR	Barbel Koster / Carola Zirzow	1:51.81
	4	**USA**	**Ann Turner/Linda Dragan**	**elem semis**
1980	1	GDR	Carsta Genauss / Martina Bischor	1:43.88
	2	URS	Galina Alexeyeva / Nina Trofimova	1:46.91
	3	HUN	Eva Rakusz / Maria Zakarias	1:47.95
1984	1	SWE	Agneta Andersson / Anna Olsson	1:45.25
	2	CAN	Alexandra Barre / Sue Holloway	1:47.13
	3	GER	Josefa Idem / Barbara Schuttpelz	1:47.32
	5	**USA**	**Shirley Dery / Leslie Klein**	**1:49.51**
1988	1	GDR	Birgit Schmidt / Anke Nothnagel	1:43.46
	2	BUL	Vania Guecheva / Diana Paliiska	1:44.06
	3	HOL	Annemiek Derckx / Annemarie Cox	1:46.00
	7	**USA**	**Sheila Conover / Cathy Marino Geers**	**1:50.33**
1992	1	GER	Ramona Portwich / Anke Von Seck	1:40.29
	2	SWE	Susanne Gunnarsson / Agneta Andersson	1:40.41
	3	HUN	Rita Koban / Evan Donusz	1:40.81
		USA	**Traci Phillips / Cathy Marino**	**elim.semis**

WOMEN'S K-4 FLATWATER 500 METERS

YEAR	RANK	CTRY	ATHLETES	TIME
1896-1980 (not held)				
1984	1	ROM		1:38.34
	2	SWE		1:38.87
	3	CAN		1:39.40
	4	**USA**	**Sheila Conover / Shirley Dery Leslie Klein / Ann Turner**	**1:40.49**
1988	1	GDR		1:40.78
	2	HUN		1:41.88
	3	BUL		1:42.63
	9	**USA**	**Traci Phillips / Sheila Conover / Cathy Marino Geers / Shirley Dery-Batlik**	**1:47.94**
1992	1	HUN		1:38.32
	2	GER		1:38.47
	3	SWE		1:39.79
	7	**USA**	**Traci Phillips / Sheila Conover / Cathy Marino / Alexandra B. Harbold**	**1:43.00**

WOMEN'S K-1 WHITEWATER SLALOM

YEAR	RANK	CTRY	ATHLETE	POINTS
1896-1968 (not held)				
1972	1	GDR	Angelika Bahmann	364.50
	2	GER	Gisela Grothaus	398.15
	3	GER	Magdalena Wunderlich	400.50
	9	**USA**	**Carrie (Lynn) Ashton**	**476.41**
1992	1	GER	Elisabeth Micheler	126.41
	2	AUS	Danielle Woodward	128.27
	3	**USA**	**Dana Chladek**	**131.75**

CYCLING

MEN'S ONE KM TIME TRIAL

YEAR	RANK	CTRY	ATHLETE	TIME	
1896-1924 (not held)					
1928	1	DEN	Willy Flack Hansen	1:14.4	
	2	HOL	Gerard Bosch van Drakestein	1:15.2	
	3	AUS	Edgar Gray	1:15.6	
(no USA entry)					
1932	1	AUS	Edgar Gray	1:13.0	**OR**
	2	HOL	Jacobus van Egmond	1:13.3	
	3	FRA	Charles Rampelberg	1:13.4	
	8	**USA**	**Bernard Mammes**	**1:18.0**	
1936	1	HOL	Arie van Vilet	1:12.0	**OR**
	2	FRA	Pierre Georget	1:12.8	
	3	GER	Rudolf Karsch	1:13.2	
	10	**USA**	**Albert Sellinger**	**1:15.2**	
1948	1	FRA	Jacques Dupont	1:13.5	
	2	BEL	Pierre Nihant	1:14.5	
	3	GBR	Thomas Godwin	1:15.0	
	6	**USA**	**John Heid**	**1:16.2**	
1952	1	AUS	Russell Mockridge	1:11.1	**OR**
	2	ITA	Marino Morettini	1:12.7	
	3	RSA	Raymond Robinson	1:13.0	
	23	**USA**	**Frank Brilando**	**1:17.8**	
1956	1	ITA	Leandro Faggin	1:09.8	**OR**
	2	TCH	Ladislav Fou ek	1:11.4	
	3	RSA	Alfred Swift	1:11.6	
	10	**USA**	**Allen Bell**	**1:16.1**	
1960	1	ITA	Sante Gaiardoni	1:07.27	**WR**
	2	GER	Dieter Gieseler	1:08.75	
	3	URS	Rostislav Vargashkin	1:08.86	
	13	**USA**	**Allen Bell**	**1:11.33**	
1964	1	BEL	Patrick Sercu	1:09.59	
	2	ITA	Giovanni Pettenella	1:10.09	
	3	FRA	Pierre Trentin	1:10.42	
	14	**USA**	**William Kund**	**1:12.89**	
1968	1	FRA	Pierre Trentin	1:03.91	**WR**
	2	DEN	Niels Fredborg	1:04.61	
	3	POL	Janusz Kierzkowski	1:04.63	
	12	**USA**	**Jack Simes**	**1:05.67**	
1972	1	DEN	Niels Fredborg	1:06.44	
	2	AUS	Daniel Clark	1:06.87	
	3	GDR	Jürgen Schütze	1:07.02	
	12	**USA**	**Steven Woznick**	**1:08.56**	
1976	1	GDR	Klaus-Jürgen Grünke	1:05.927	
	2	BEL	Michel Vaarten	1:07.516	
	3	DEN	Niels Fredborg	1:07.617	
	15	**USA**	**Robert Vehe**	**1:09.057**	
1980	1	GDR	Lothar Thoms	1:02.955	**WR**
	2	URS	Aleksandr Panfilov	1:04.845	
	3	JAM	David Weller	1:05.241	
1984	1	GER	Fredy Schmidtke	1:06.10	
	2	CAN	Curtis Harnett	1:06.44	
	3	FRA	Fabrice Colas	1:06.65	
	8	**USA**	**Rory O'Reilly**	**1:07.39**	
1988	1	URS	Alexandre Kiritchenko	1:40.499	
	2	AUS	Martin Vinnicombe	1:04.784	
	3	FRG	Robert Lechner	1:05.114	
	14	**USA**	**Bobby Livingston**	**1:06.926**	
1992	1	ESP	Jose Moreno	1:03.342	
	2	AUS	Shane Kelly	1:04.288	
	3	**USA**	**Erin Hartwell**	**1:04.753**	

MEN'S MATCH SPRINT

YEAR	RANK	CTRY	ATHLETE	TIME
1896	1	FRA	Paul Masson	4:58.2
	2	GRE	Stamatios Nikolopoulos	5:00.2
	3	FRA	Léon Flameng	
(no USA entry)				
1900	1	FRA	George Taillandier	2:52.0
	2	FRA	Fernand Sanz	
	3	**USA**	**John Henry Lake**	
1904 (not held)				
1906	1	ITA	Francesco Verri	1:42.2
	2	GBR	H.C. Bouffler	
	3	BEL	Eugène Debongnie	
(no USA entry)				
1908 (final declared void because the time limit of 1:45 was exceeded)				
1912 (not held)				
1920	1	HOL	Maurice Peeters	1:38.3
	2	GBR	Thomas Johnson	
	3	GBR	Harry Ryan	
(no USA entry)				
1924	1	FRA	Lucien Michard	12.8
	2	HOL	Jacob Meijer	
	3	FRA	Jean Cugnot	
		USA	**William Fenn**	**elim. semis**
1928	1	FRA	Roger Beaufrand	13.2
	2	HOL	Antoine Mazairac	
	3	DEN	Willy Falck-Hansen	
(no USA entry)				
1932	1	HOL	Jacobus van Egmond	
	2	FRA	Louis Chaillot	
	3	ITA	Bruno Pellizzari	
		USA	**Eddie Testa**	**elim. trials**
1936	1	GER	Toni Merkens	
	2	HOL	Arie van Vliet	
	3	FRA	Louis Chaillot	
		USA	**Albert Sellinger**	**elim. 2nd rd**
1948	1	ITA	Mario Ghella	
	2	GBR	Reginald Harris	
	3	DEN	Axel Schandorff	
		USA	**John Heid**	**elim. semis**
1952	1	ITA	Enzo Sacchi	12.0
	2	AUS	Lionel Cox	
	3	GER	Werner Potzernheim	
		USA	**Steve Hromjak**	**elim. rep.**
1956	1	FRA	Michel Rousseau	11.4
	2	ITA	Guglielmo Presenti	
	3	AUS	Richard Ploog	
		USA	**Jack Disney**	**elim. qtr finals**
1960	1	ITA	Sante Gaiardoni	
	2	BEL	Leo Sterckx	
	3	ITA	Valentino Gasparella	
		USA	**Herbert Francis**	**elim. rep.**
1964	1	ITA	Giovanni Pettenella	
	2	ITA	Sergio Bianchetto	
	3	FRA	Daniel Morelon	
		USA	**Alan Grieco / Jackie Simes**	**elim. 1st rd**
1968	1	FRA	Daniel Morelon	
	2	ITA	Giordano Turrini	
	3	FRA	Pierre Trentin	
		USA	**Jack Simes / Tim Mountford**	**elim. 2nd rd rep.**
1972	1	FRA	Daniel Morelon	
	2	AUS	John Nicholson	
	3	URS	Omari Phakadze	
		USA	**Roger Young / Jeffrey Spencer**	**elim. 2nd rd**
1976	1	TCH	Anton Tkác	
	2	FRA	Daniel Morelon	
	3	GDR	Hans-Jürgen Geschke	
		USA	**Leigh Barczewski**	**DQ 1st rep.**
1980	1	GDR	Lutz Hesslich	12.01
	2	FRA	Yave Cahard	
	3	URS	Sergei Kopylov	
1984	**1**	**USA**	**Mark Gorski**	**10.95**
	2	**USA**	**Nelson Vails**	
	3	JPN	Tsutomu Sakamoto	
1988	1	GDR	Lutz Hesslich	
	2	URS	Nikolai Kovche	
	3	AUS	Gary Neiwand	
		USA	**Ken Carpenter**	
1992	1	GER	Jens Fiedler	
	2	AUS	Gary Neiwand	
	3	CAN	Curtis Harnett	
	5	**USA**	**Ken Carpenter**	

MEN'S 4,000-METER INDIVIDUAL PURSUIT

YEAR	RANK	CTRY	ATHLETE	TIME
1896-1960 (not held)				
1964	1	TCH	Ji i Daler	5:04.75
	2	ITA	Giorgio Ursi	5:05.96
	3	DEN	Preben Isaksson	5:01.90
		USA	**Harry Cutting**	**elim. 1st rd**
1968	1	FRA	Daniel Rebillard	4:41.71
	2	DEN	Mogens Frey Jensen	4:42.43
	3	SUI	Xaver Kurmann	4:39.42
	18	**USA**	**David Brink**	
1972	1	NOR	Knut Knudsen	4:45.74
	2	SUI	Xaver Kurmann	4:51.96
	3	GER	Hans Lutz	4:50.80
	12	**USA**	**John Vande Velde**	**5:01.75**
1976	1	GER	Gregor Braun	4:47.61
	2	HOL	Herman Ponsteen	4:49.72
	3	GDR	Thomas Huschke	4:52.71
	19	**USA**	**Leonard Nitz**	**5:01.54**
1980	1	SUI	Robert Dill-Bundi	4:35.66
	2	FRA	Alain Bondue	4:42.96
	3	DEN	Hans-Henrik Örsted	4:36.54
1984	**1**	**USA**	**Steve Hegg**	**4:39.35**
	2	GER	Rolf Gölz	4:43.82
	3	**USA**	**Leonard Nitz**	**4:44.03**
1988	1	URS	Gintaoutas Umaras	4:32.00
	2	AUS	Dean Woods	4:35.00
	3	GDR	Bernd Dittert	4:34.17
		USA	**David Brinton**	
1992	1	GBR	Chris Boardman	3:21.649
	2	GER	Jens Lehmann	3:27.357
	3	NZL	Gary Anderson	3:31.061
	12	**USA**	**Carl Sundquist**	

MEN'S 4,000-METER TEAM PURSUIT

YEAR	RANK	CTRY	ATHLETES	TIME
1896-1906 (not held)				
1908	1	GBR		2:18.6
	2	GER		2:28.6
	3	CAN		2:29.6
(no USA entry)				
1912 (not held)				
1920	1	ITA		5:20.0
	2	GBR		
	3	RSA		
(no USA entry)				
1924	1	ITA		5:15.0
	2	POL		
	3	BEL		
(no USA entry)				
1928	1	ITA		5:01.8
	2	HOL		5:06.2
	3	GBR		
(no USA entry)				
1932	1	ITA		4:53.0
	2	FRA		4:55.7
	3	GBR		4:56.0
		USA	**Harold Ade / Russell Allen / Ruggero Berti /John Sinibaldi**	**elim. trials**
1936	1	FRA		4:45.0
	2	ITA		4:51.0
	3	GBR		4:53.6
		USA	**Albert Byrd / William Logan / Charles Morton / John Sinbaldi**	**elim. trials**
1948	1	FRA		4:57.8
	2	ITA		5:36.7
	3	GBR		4:55.8
(no USA entry)				
1952	1	ITA		4:46.1
	2	RSA		4:53.6
	3	GBR		4:51.5
		USA	**Steve Hromjak / James Lauf / T.R. Montemage / Don Sheldon (5:11.6)**	**elim. trials**
1956	1	ITA		4:37.4
	2	FRA		4:39.4
	3	GBR		4:42.4
(no USA entry)				
1960	1	ITA		4:30.90
	2	GDR		4:35.78
	3	URS		4:34.05
		USA	**Richard Cortright / Charles Hewitt / Robert Praff / James Rossi**	**elim. 1st rd**
1964	1	GER		4:35.67
	2	ITA		4:35.74
	3	HOL		4:38.99
(no USA entry)				
1968	1	DEN		4:22.44
	2	GER		4:18.94
	3	ITA		4:18.35
	16	**USA**	**David Chauner / Harry Cuttin / Steven Maaranen / John Vande Velde**	**4:32.87**
1972	1	GER		4:22.14
	2	GDR		4:25.25
	3	GBR		4:23.78
	17	**USA**	**David Chauner / John Vande Velde / David Mulica / James Ochowicz**	**4:38.19**
1976	1	GER		4:21.06
	2	URS		4:27.15
	3	GBR		4:22.41
	10	**USA**	**Paul Deem / Leonard Nitz / Ronald Skarin / Talph Therrio**	**4:31.25**
1980	1	URS		4:15.70
	2	GDR		4:19.67
	3	TCH		Overtook
1984	1	AUS		4:25.99
	2	**USA**	**David Grylls / Steve Hegg / R. Patrick McDonough / Leonard Nitz**	**4:29.85**
	3	GER		4:25.60
1988	1	URS		4:13.31
	2	GDR		4:14.09
	3	AUS		4:16.02
		USA	**Dave Lettieri / Michael McCarthy / Leonard Harvey Nitz / Carl Sundquist**	**elim.**
1992	1	GER		4:08.791
	2	AUS		4:10.218
	3	DEN		4:15.860
	9	**USA**	**Dirk Copeland / Matt Hamon / Jim Pollak / Chris Coletta**	

MEN'S 50 KM POINT RACE

YEAR	RANK	CTRY	ATHLETE	POINTS
1896-1980 (not held)				
1984	1	BEL	Roger Ilegems	37
	2	GER	Uwe Messerschmidt	15
	3	MEX	José Manuel Youshimatz	29
		USA	**Danny Van Haute / Mark Whitehead**	**DNQ**

YEAR	RANK	CTRY	ATHLETE	TIME
1988	1	DEN	Dan Frost	38
	2	HOL	Leo Peelen	26
	3	URS	Marat Ganeev	46
	8	**USA**	**Frankie Andreu**	**21**
1992	1	ITA	Giovanni Lombardi	44
	2	NED	Leon Van Bon	43
	3	BEL	Cedric Mathy	41
		USA	**James Carney**	**DNS**

MEN'S TEAM TIME TRIAL

YEAR	RANK	CTRY	ATHLETES	TIME
1896-1908	(not held)			
1912	1	SWE		44:35:33.6
	2	GBR		44:44:39.2
	3	**USA**	**Carl Schutte / Alvin Loftes / Albert Krushel / Walter Martin**	**44:47:55.5**
1920	1	FRA		19:16:43.2
	2	SWE		19:23:10.0
	3	BEL		19:28:44.4
	7	**USA**	**James Freeman / Ernest / Kockler August Nogara / John Otto**	**21:32:36.6**
1924	1	FRA		19:30:14.0
	2	BEL		19:46:55.4
	3	SWE		19:59:41.6
(no USA entry)				
1928	1	DEN		15:09:14.0
	2	GBR		15:14:49.0
	3	SWE		15:27:49.0
(no USA entry)				
1932	1	ITA		7:27:15.2
	2	DEN		7:38:50.2
	3	SWE		7:39:12.6
	6	**USA**	**Henry O'Brien / Frank Connell / Otto Luedeke**	**7:51:55.6**
1936	1	FRA		7:39:16.2
	2	SUI		7:39:20.4
	3	BEL		7:39:21.0
(no USA entry)				
1948	1	BEL		15:58:17.4
	2	GBR		16:03:31.6
	3	FRA		16:08:19.4
(no USA entry)				
1952	1	BEL		15:20:46.6
	2	ITA		15:33:27.3
	3	FRA		15:38:58.1
(no USA entry)				
1956	1	FRA		22
	2	GBR		23
	3	GDR/GER		27
(no USA entry)				
1960	1	ITA		2:14:33.53
	2	GDR		2:16:56.31
	3	URS		2:18:41.67
	11	**USA**	**William Freund / Michael Hiltner / Wesley Chowen / Robert Tetzaff**	
1964	1	HOL		2:26:31.19
	2	ITA		2:26:55.39
	3	SWE		2:27:11.52
		USA	**Michael Hiltner / John Allis / Michael Allen / Wesley Chowen**	**2:40:30.13**
1968	1	HOL		2:07:49.06
	2	SWE		2:09:26.60
	3	ITA		2:10:18.74
	20	**USA**	**Jack Howard / Oliver Martin / John Allis / James Van Boven**	**2:24:13.50**
1972	1	URS		2:11:17.8
	2	POL		2:11:47.5
		HOL		2:12:27.1
	3	BEL		2:12:36.7
	15	**USA**	**Richard Ball / John Howard / Ronald Skarin / Wayne Stetina**	**2:17:06.4**
1976	1	URS		2:08:53.0
	2	POL		2:09:13.0
	3	DEN		2:12:20.0
	19	**USA**	**John Howard / Wayne Stetina / Marc Thompson / Alan Kingsbery**	**2:18:53.0**
1980	1	URS		2:01:21.7
	2	GDR		2:02:53.2
	3	TCH		2:02:53.9
1984	1	ITA		1:58:28
	2	SUI		2:02:38
	3	**USA**	**Ronald Kiefel / Roy Knickman / Davis Phinney / Andrew Weaver**	**2:02:46**
1988	1	GDR		1:57:47.7
	2	POL		1:57:54.2
	3	SWE		1:59:47.3
	10	**USA**	**Norm Alvis / James Copeland / Tony Palmer / Andy Paulin**	**2:02:35.7**
1992	1	GER		2:01.39
	2	ITA		2:02.39
	3	FRA		2:05.25
	16	**USA**	**George Hincapie / Nathan Sheafor / Scott Mercier / John Stenner / Dave Nicholson (INJ)**	**2:13.35**

MEN'S ROAD RACE

YEAR	RANK	CTRY	ATHLETE	TIME
1896	1	GRE	Aristidis Konstantinidis	3:32:31.0
	2	GER	August Goedrich	3:42:18.0
	3	GBR	F. Battel	
(no USA entry)				
1900-1904	(not held)			
1906	1	FRA	Fernand Vast	2:41:28.0
	2	FRA	Maurice Bardonneau	2:41:28.4
	3	FRA	Edmond Luguet	2:41:28.6
(no USA entry)				
1908	(not held)			
1912	1	RSA	Rudolf "Okey" Lewis	10:42:39.0
	2	GBR	Frederick Grubb	10:51:24.2
	3	**USA**	**Carl Schutte**	**10:52:38.8**
1920	1	SWE	Harry Stenqvist	4:40:01.8
	2	RSA	Henry Kaltenbrun	4:41:26.6
	3	FRA	Fernand Canteloube	4:42:54.4
	13	**USA**	**Ernest P. Kockler**	
1924	1	FRA	Armand Blanchonnet	6:20:48.0
	2	BEL	Henri Hoevenaers	6:30:27.0
	3	FRA	René Hamel	6:30:51.6
	33	**USA**	**John Bonlicault**	**7:15:51.6**
1928	1	DEN	Henry Hansen	4:47:18.0
	2	GBR	Frank Southall	4:55:06.0
	3	SWE	Gösta Carlsson	5:00:17.0
	51	**USA**	**Chester Nelson**	**5:42:57.0**
1932	1	ITA	Attilio Pavesi	2:28:05.6
	2	ITA	Guglielmo Segato	2:29:21.4
	3	SWE	Bernhard Britz	2:29:45.2
1936	1	FRA	Robert Charpentier	2:33:05.0
	2	FRA	Guy Lapébie	2:33:05.2
	3	SUI	Ernst Nievergelt	2:33:05.8
	44	**USA**	**Albert Byrd**	
1948	1	FRA	José Beyaert	5:18:12.6
	2	HOL	Gerardus Petrus Voorting	5:18:16.2
	3	BEL	Lode Wouters	5:18:16.2
		USA	**Frank Brilando / Edward Lynch / Chester Nelson, Jr. / Wendell Rollins**	**DNF**
1952	1	BEL	André Noyelle	5:06:03.4
	2	BEL	Robert Grondelaers	5:06:51.2
	3	GER	Edi Ziegler	5:07:47.5
	32	**USA**	**Donald T. Sheldon**	**5:22:33.3**
1956	1	ITA	Ercole Baldini	5:21:17.0
	2	FRA	Arnaud Geyre	5:23:16.0
	3	GBR	Alan Jackson	5:23:16.0
	44	**USA**	**Joseph H. Becker**	**5:47:02.0**
1960	1	URS	Viktor Kapitonov	4:20:37.0
	2	ITA	Livio Trapè	4:20:37.0
	3	BEL	Willy van den Berghen	4:20:57.0
	23	**USA**	**Michael Hiltner**	**4:20:57.0**
1964	1	ITA	Mario Zanin	4:39:51.63
	2	DEN	Kjell Åkerström Rodian	4:39:51.65
	3	BEL	Walter Godefroot	4:39:51.74
	75	**USA**	**John Allis**	**4:39:51.83**
1968	1	ITA	Pierfranco Vianelli	4:41:25.24
	2	DEN	Leif Mortensen	4:42:49.71
	3	SWE	Gösta Pettersson	4:43:15.24
	44	**USA**	**John Howard**	**4:52:45.8**
1972	1	HOL	Hennie Kuiper	4:14:37.0
	2	AUS	Keven Clyde Sefton	4:15:04.0
		ESP	Jaime Huelamo	4:15:04.0
	3	NZL	Bruce Biddle	4:15:04.0
	61	**USA**	**John Howard**	**4:17:13.0**
1976	1	SWE	Bernt Johansson	4:46:52.0
	2	ITA	Giuseppe Martinelli	4:47:23.0
	3	POL	Mieczysław Nowicki	4:47:23.0
	6	**USA**	**George Mount**	**4:47:23.0**
1980	1	URS	Sergei Sukhoruchenkov	4:48:28.9
	2	POL	Czeslaw Lang	4:51:26.9
	3	URS	Yuri Barinov	4:51:29.9
1984	**1**	**USA**	**Alexi Grewal**	**4:59:57.0**
	2	CAN	Steve Bauer	4:59:57.0
	3	NOR	Dag Otto Lauritzen	5:00:18.0
1988	1	GDR	Olaf Ludwig	4:32.22
	2	FRG	Bernd Groene	4:32.25
	3	FRG	Christian Henn	4:32.46
	4	**USA**	**Robert Mionske**	**same time**
1992	1	ITA	Fabio Casatelli	4:35.21
	2	NED	Hendrik Dekker	4:35.22
	3	LAT	Dainis Ozols	4:35.24
	14	**USA**	**Lance Armstrong**	**4:35.56**

WOMEN'S MATCH SPRINT

YEAR	RANK	CTRY	ATHLETE	TIME
1896-1984	(not held)			
1988	1	URS	Erika Salumae	
	2	GDR	Christa Rothenburger-Luding	
	3	**USA**	**Connie Paraskevin-Young**	
1992	1	EST	Erika Salumae	
	2	GER	Annette Neumann	
	3	NED	Ingrid Haringa	
		USA	**Connie Paraskevin-Young**	

WOMEN'S 3,000-METER INDIVIDUAL PURSUIT

YEAR	RANK	CTRY	ATHLETE	TIME
1992	1	GER	Petra Rossner	3:41.753
	2	AUS	Kathryn Watt	3:43.438
	3	**USA**	**Rebecca Twigg**	**3:52.429**

WOMEN'S INDIVIDUAL ROAD RACE

YEAR	RANK	CTRY	ATHLETE	TIME
1984	**1**	**USA**	**Connie Carpenter-Phinney**	**2:11:14.0**
	2	**USA**	**Rebecca Twigg**	**2:11:14.0**
	3	GER	Sandra Schumacher	2:11:14.0
1988	1	HOL	Monique Knol	2:00.52
	2	FRG	Jutta Niehaus	same time
	3	URS	Laima Zilporitee	same time
	8	**USA**	**Inga Thompson-Benedict**	**same time**
1992	1	AUS	Kathryn Watt	2:04.42
	2	FRA	Jeannie Longo-Ciprelli	2:05.02
	3	NED	Monique Knol	2:05.03
	6	**USA**	**Jeanne Golay**	**2:05.03**

DIVING

MEN'S PLATFORM

YEAR	RANK	CTRY	ATHLETE	TOTAL
1896-1900	(not held)			
1904	**1**	**USA**	**George Sheldon**	**12.66**
	2	GER	Georg Hoffmann	11.66
	3	GER	Alfred Braunschweiger	11.33
1906	1	GER	Gottlob Walz	156.0
	2	GER	Georg Hoffmann	150.2
	3	AUT	Otto Satzinger	147.4
		USA	**F.A. Bornemann**	
1908	1	SWE	Hjalmar Johansson	83.75
	2	SWE	Karl Malmström	78.73
	3	SWE	Arvid Spångberg	74.00
	5	**USA**	**George Gaidzik**	**56.30**
1912	1	SWE	Erik Adlerz	73.94
	2	GER	Albert Zürner	72.60
	3	SWE	Gustaf Blomgren	69.56
		USA	**George Gaidzik / Arthur McAleenan**	**elim. 1st rd**
1920	**1**	**USA**	**Clarence Pinkston**	**100.67**
	2	SWE	Erik Adlerz	99.08
	3	**USA**	**Harry Prieste**	**93.73**
1924	**1**	**USA**	**Albert White**	**97.46**
	2	**USA**	**David Fall**	**97.30**
	3	**USA**	**Clarence Pinkston**	**94.60**
1928	**1**	**USA**	**Ulise "Pete" DesJardins**	**98.74**
	2	EGY	Farid Simaika	99.58
	3	**USA**	**Michael Galitzen (Mickey Riley)**	**92.34**
1932	**1**	**USA**	**Harold Smith**	**124.80**
	2	**USA**	**Michael Galitzen (Mickey Riley)**	**124.28**
	3	**USA**	**Frank Kurtz**	**121.98**
1936	**1**	**USA**	**Marshall Wayne**	**113.58**
	2	**USA**	**Elbert Root**	**110.60**
	3	GER	Hermann Stork	110.31
1948	**1**	**USA**	**Samuel Lee**	**130.05**
	2	**USA**	**Bruce Harlan**	**122.30**
	3	MEX	Joaquin Capilla Pérez	113.52
1952	**1**	**USA**	**Samuel Lee**	**156.28**
	2	MEX	Joaquin Capilla Pérez	145.21
	3	GER	Günther Haase	141.31
1956	1	MEX	Joaquin Capilla Pérez	152.44
	2	**USA**	**Gary Tobian**	**152.41**
	3	**USA**	**Richard Connor**	**149.79**
1960	**1**	**USA**	**Robert Webster**	**165.56**
	2	**USA**	**Gary Tobian**	**165.25**
	3	GBR	Brian Phelps	157.13
1964	**1**	**USA**	**Robert Webster**	**148.58**
	2	ITA	Klaus Dibiasi	147.54
	3	**USA**	**Thomas Gompf**	**146.57**
1968	1	ITA	Klaus Dibiasi	164.18
	2	MEX	Alvaro Gaxiola	154.49
	3	**USA**	**Edwin Young**	**153.93**
1972	1	ITA	Klaus Dibiasi	504.12
	2	**USA**	**Richard Rydze**	**480.75**
	3	ITA	Franco Giorgio Cagnotto	475.83
1976	1	ITA	Klaus Dibiasi	600.51
	2	**USA**	**Gregory Louganis**	**576.99**
	3	URS	Vladimir Aleynik	548.61
1980	1	GDR	Falk Hoffmann	835.650
	2	URS	Vladimir Aleynik	819.705
	3	URS	David Ambartsumyan	817.440
1984	**1**	**USA**	**Gregory Louganis**	**710.91**
	2	**USA**	**Bruce Kimball**	**643.50**
	3	CHN	Li Kongzheng	638.28
1988	**1**	**USA**	**Gregory Louganis**	**638.61**
	2	CHN	Ni Xiong	637.47
	3	MEX	Jesus Mena	594.39
1992	1	CHN	Sun Shuwei	677.31
	2	**USA**	**Scott Donie**	**633.63**
	3	CHN	Ni Xiong	600.15

MEN'S SPRINGBOARD

YEAR	RANK	CTRY	ATHLETE	TOTAL
1896-1906	(not held)			
1908	1	GER	Albert Zürner	85.5
	2	GER	Kurt Behrens	85.3
	3	**USA**	**George Gaidzik**	**80.8**
1912	1	GER	Paul Günther	79.23
	2	GER	Hans Luber	76.78
	3	GER	Kurt Behrens	73.73
	8	**USA**	**George Gaidzik**	**68.01**
1920	**1**	**USA**	**Louis Kuehn**	**675.4**
	2	**USA**	**Clarence Pinkston**	**655.3**
	3	**USA**	**Louis Balbach**	**649.5**
1924	**1**	**USA**	**Albert White**	**696.4**
	2	**USA**	**Ulise "Pete" DesJardins**	**693.2**
	3	**USA**	**Clarence Pinkston**	**653.0**
1928	**1**	**USA**	**Ulise "Pete" DesJardins**	**185.04**
	2	**USA**	**Michael Galitzen (Mickey Riley)**	**174.06**
	3	EGY	Farid Simaika	172.46
1932	**1**	**USA**	**Michael Galitzen (Mickey Riley)**	**161.38**
	2	**USA**	**Harold Smith**	**158.54**
	3	**USA**	**Richard Degener**	**151.82**
1936	**1**	**USA**	**Richard Degener**	**163.57**
	2	**USA**	**Marshall Wayne**	**159.56**
	3	**USA**	**Albert Greene**	**146.29**
1948	**1**	**USA**	**Bruce Harlan**	**163.64**
	2	**USA**	**Miller Anderson**	**157.29**
	3	**USA**	**Samuel Lee**	**145.52**
1952	**1**	**USA**	**David Browning**	**205.29**
	2	**USA**	**Miller Anderson**	**199.84**
	3	**USA**	**Robert Clotworthy**	**184.92**
1956	**1**	**USA**	**Robert Clotworthy**	**159.56**
	2	**USA**	**Donald Harper**	**156.23**
	3	MEX	Joaquin Capilla Pérez	150.69
1960	**1**	**USA**	**Gary Tobian**	**170.00**
	2	**USA**	**Samuel Hall**	**167.08**
	3	MEX	Juan Botella	162.30
1964	**1**	**USA**	**Kenneth Sitzberger**	**159.90**
	2	**USA**	**Francis Gorman**	**157.63**
	3	**USA**	**Larry Andreasen**	**143.77**
1968	**1**	**USA**	**Bernard Wrightson**	**170.15**
	2	ITA	Klaus Dibiasi	159.74
	3	**USA**	**James Henry**	**158.09**
1972	1	URS	Vladimir Vasin	594.09
	2	ITA	Franco Giorgio Cagnotto	591.63
	3	**USA**	**Craig Lincoln**	**577.29**
1976	**1**	**USA**	**Philip Boggs**	**619.05**
	2	ITA	Franco Giorgio Cagnotto	570.48
	3	URS	Aleksandr Kosenkov	567.24
1980	1	URS	Aleksandr Portnov	905.025
	2	MEX	Carlos Giron	892.140
	3	ITA	Franco Giorgio Cagnotto	871.500
1984	**1**	**USA**	**Gregory Louganis**	**754.41**
	2	CHN	Tan Liangde	662.31
	3	**USA**	**Ronald Merriott**	**661.32**
1988	**1**	**USA**	**Gregory Louganis**	**730.80**
	2	CHN	Tan Liangde	704.88
	3	CHN	Li Deliang	665.28
1992	**1**	**USA**	**Mark Lenzi**	**676.53**
	2	CHN	Tan Liangde	645.57
	3	EUN	Dmitri Saoutine	627.78

WOMEN'S PLATFORM

YEAR	RANK	CTRY	ATHLETE	TOTAL
1896-1908	(not held)			
1912	1	SWE	Greta Johansson	39.9
	2	SWE	Lisa Regnell	36.0
	3	GBR	Isabelle White	34.0
(no USA entry)				
1920	1	DEN	Stefani Fryland-Clausen	34.6
	2	GBR	Eileen Armstrong	33.3
	3	SWE	Eva Ollivier	33.3
	5	**USA**	**Aileen Riggin**	**31.4**
1924	**1**	**USA**	**Caroline Smith**	**33.2**
	2	**USA**	**Elizabeth Becker**	**33.4**
	3	SWE	Hjördis Töpel	32.8
1928	**1**	**USA**	**Elizabeth Becker Pinkston**	**31.6**
	2	**USA**	**Georgia Coleman**	**30.6**
	3	SWE	Lela Sjöquist	29.2
1932	**1**	**USA**	**Dorothy Poynton**	**40.26**
	2	**USA**	**Georgia Coleman**	**35.56**
	3	**USA**	**Marion Roper**	**35.22**
1936	**1**	**USA**	**Dorothy Poynton Hill**	**33.93**
	2	**USA**	**Velma Dunn**	**33.63**
	3	GER	Käthe Köhler	33.43
1948	**1**	**USA**	**Victoria Draves**	**68.87**
	2	**USA**	**Patricia Elsener**	**66.28**
	3	DEN	Birte Christoffersen	66.04
1952	**1**	**USA**	**Patricia McCormick**	**79.37**
	2	**USA**	**Paula Jean Myers**	**71.63**
	3	**USA**	**Juno Irwin (Stover)**	**70.49**
1956	**1**	**USA**	**Patricia McCormick**	**84.85**
	2	**USA**	**Juno Irwin (Stover)**	**81.64**
	3	**USA**	**Paula Jean Myers**	**81.58**

1960	1	GDR	Ingrid Krämer	91.28
	2	**USA**	**Paula Jean Pope (Myers)**	**88.94**
	3	URS	Ninel Krutova	86.99
1964	**1**	**USA**	**Lesley Bush**	**99.80**
	2	GDR	Ingrid Engel-Krämer	98.45
	3	URS	Galina Alekseyeva	97.60
1968	1	TCH	Milena Duchková	109.59
	2	URS	Natalya Lobanova (Kuznetsova)	105.14
	3	**USA**	**Ann Peterson**	**101.11**
1972	1	SWE	Ulrika Knape	390.00
	2	TCH	Milena Duchková	370.92
	3	GDR	Marina Janicke	360.54
	4	**USA**	**Janet Ely**	**352.68**
1976	1	URS	Elena Vaytsekhovskaya	406.59
	2	SWE	Ulrika Knape	402.60
	3	**USA**	**Deborah Wilson**	**401.00**
1980	1	GDR	Martina Jäschke	596.250
	2	URS	Servard Emirzyan	576.465
	3	URS	Liana Tsotadze	575.925
1984	1	CHN	Zhou Jihong	435.51
	2	**USA**	**Michele Mitchell**	**431.19**
	3	**USA**	**Wendy Wyland**	**422.07**
1988	1	CHN	Xu Yanmei	445.20
	2	**USA**	**Michele Mitchell**	**436.95**
	3	**USA**	**Wendy Williams**	**400.44**
1992	1	CHN	Fu Mingxia	461.43
	2	EUN	Elena Mirochina	411.63
	3	**USA**	**Mary Ellen Clark**	**401.91**

WOMEN'S SPRINGBOARD

YEAR	RANK	CTRY	ATHLETE	TOTAL
1896-1912	(not held)			
1920	**1**	**USA**	**Aileen Riggin**	**539.9**
	2	**USA**	**Helen Wainwright**	**534.8**
	3	**USA**	**Thelma Payne**	**534.1**
1924	**1**	**USA**	**Elizabeth Becker**	**474.5**
	2	**USA**	**Aileen Riggin**	**460.4**
	3	**USA**	**Caroline Fletcher**	**436.4**
1928	**1**	**USA**	**Helen Meany**	**78.62**
	2	**USA**	**Dorothy Poynton**	**75.62**
	3	**USA**	**Georgia Coleman**	**73.38**
1932	**1**	**USA**	**Georgia Coleman**	**87.52**
	2	**USA**	**Katherine Rawls**	**82.56**
	3	**USA**	**Jane Fauntz**	**82.12**
1936	**1**	**USA**	**Marjorie Gestring**	**89.27**
	2	**USA**	**Katherine Rawls**	**88.35**
	3	**USA**	**Dorothy Poynton Hill**	**82.36**
1948	**1**	**USA**	**Victoria Draves**	**108.74**
	2	**USA**	**Zoe Ann Olsen**	**108.23**
	3	**USA**	**Patricia Elsener**	**101.30**
1952	**1**	**USA**	**Patricia McCormick**	**147.30**
	2	FRA	Madeleine Moreau	139.34
	3	**USA**	**Zoe Ann Jensen-Olsen**	**127.57**
1956	**1**	**USA**	**Patricia McCormick**	**142.36**
	2	**USA**	**Jeanne Stunyo**	**125.89**
	3	CAN	Irene McDonald	121.40
1960	1	GDR	Ingrid Krämer	155.81
	2	**USA**	**Paula Jean Pope (Myers)**	**141.24**
	3	GBR	Elizabeth Ferris	139.09
1964	1	GDR	Ingrid Engle-Krämer	145.00
	2	**USA**	**Jeanne Collier**	**138.36**
	3	**USA**	**Mary "Patsy" Willard**	**138.18**
1968	**1**	**USA**	**Sue Gossick**	**150.77**
	2	URS	Tamara Pogoscheva (Fyedosova)	145.30
	3	**USA**	**Keala O'Sullivan**	**145.23**
1972	**1**	**USA**	**Maxine "Micki" King**	**450.03**
	2	SWE	Ulrika Knape	434.19
	3	GDR	Marina Janicke	430.92
1976	**1**	**USA**	**Jennifer Chandler**	**506.19**
	2	GDR	Christa Köhler	469.41
	3	**USA**	**Cynthia Potter**	**466.83**
1980	1	URS	Irina Kalinina	725.910
	2	GDR	Martina Proeber	698.895
	3	GDR	Karin Guthke	685.245
1984	1	CAN	Sylvie Bernier	530.70
	2	**USA**	**Kelly McCormick**	**527.46**
	3	**USA**	**Christina Seufert**	**517.62**
1988	1	CHN	Gao Min	580.23
	2	CHN	Li Qing	534.33
	3	**USA**	**Kelly McCormick**	**533.19**
1992	1	CHN	Gao Min	572.40
	2	EUN	Irina Lachko	514.14
	3	GER	Brita Pia Baldus	503.07
	5	**USA**	**Julie Ovenhouse**	**477.84**

EQUESTRIAN

INDIVIDUAL JUMPING

YEAR	RANK	CTRY	ATHLETE / HORSE	TOTAL
1896	(not held)			
1900	1	BEL	Aimé Haegeman / Benton II	2:16.0
	2	BEL	Georges van de Poele / Windsor Squire	2:17.6
	3	FRA	M. de Champsavin / Terpsichore	2:26.0
(no USA entry)				
1904-1908	(not held)			
1912	1	FRA	Jean Cariou / Mignon	5
	2	GER	Rabod Wilhelm von Kröcher / Dohna	7
	3	BEL	Emanuel de Blommaert de Soye / Clonmore	
(no USA entry)				
1920	1	ITA	Tommaso Lequio / Trebecco	
	2	ITA	Alessandro Valerio / Cento	
	3	SWE	Carl-Gustaf Lewenhaupt / Mon Coeur	
	7	**USA**	**Henry Allen / Don**	
1924	1	SUI	Alphonse Gemuseus / Lucette	
	2	ITA	Tommaso Lequio / Trebecco	
	3	POL	Adam Królikiewicz / Picador	
		USA	**Maj. J.A. Barry / Lt. F. H. Bontecau / Maj. Sloan Doak / Capt V.L. Padgett**	**unplaced**
1928	1	TCH	František Ventura / Eliot	
	2	FRA	Pierre Bertran de Balanda / Papillon	
	3	SWE	Charley Kuhn / Pepita	
	17	**USA**	**Maj. H. Chamberlin**	
1932	1	JPN	Takeichi Nishi / Uranus	
	2	**USA**	**Harry Chamberlin / Show Girl**	
	3	SWE	Clarence von Rosen, Jr. / Empire	
1936	1	GER	Kurt Hasse / Tora	
	2	ROM	Henri Rang / Delfis	
	3	HUN	József Platthy / Sello	
	5	**USA**	**Carl Raguse / Dakota**	
1948	1	MEX	Humberto Mariles Cortés / Arete	
	2	MEX	Rubén Uriza / Harvey	
	3	FRA	Jean François d'Orgeix / Sucre de Pomme	
	4	**USA**	**Franklin Wing / Democrat**	
1952	1	FRA	Pierre Jonquères d'Oriola / Ali Baba	
	2	CHI	Oscar Cristi / Bambi	
	3	GER	Fritz Thiedemann / Meteor	
	11	**USA**	**William Steinkraus**	
1956	1	GER	Hans-Günter Winkler / Haila	
	2	ITA	Raimondo D'Inzeo / Merano	
	3	ITA	Piero D'Inzeo / Uruguay	
	11	**USA**	**Hugh Wiley**	
1960	1	ITA	Raimondo D'Inzeo / Posillipo	
	2	ITA	Piero D'Inzeo / The Rock	
	3	GBR	David Broome / Sunslave	
	4	**USA**	**George Morris / Simjon**	
1964	1	FRA	Pierre Jonquères d'Oriola / Lutteur	
	2	GER	Hermann Schridde / Dozent	
	3	GBR	Peter Robeson / Firecrest	
	7	**USA**	**Frank Chapot / San Lucas**	
1968	**1**	**USA**	**William Steinkraus / Snowbound**	
	2	GBR	Marion Coakes / Stroller	
	3	GBR	David Broome / Mister Softee	
1972	1	ITA	Graziano Mancinelli / Ambassador	
	2	GBR	Ann Moore / Psalm	
	3	**USA**	**Neal Shapiro / Sloopy**	
1976	1	GER	Alwin Schockemöhle / Warwick Rex	
	2	CAN	Michel Vaillancourt / Branch County	
	3	BEL	François Mathy / Gai Luron	
	5	**USA**	**Frank Chapot / Viscount**	
1980	1	POL	Jan Kowalczyk / Artemor	
	2	URS	Nikolai Korolkov / Espardron	
	3	MEX	Joaquin Perez Heras / Alymony	
1984	**1**	**USA**	**Joe Fargis / Touch of Class**	
	2	**USA**	**Conrad Homfeld / Abdullah**	
	3	SUI	Heidi Robbiana / Jessica V	
1988	1	FRA	Pierre Durand / Jappeloup	1.25
	2	**USA**	**Greg Best / Gem Twist**	**4.00**
	3	FRG	Karsten Huck / Nepomuk 8	4.00
1992	1	GER	Ludger Beerbaum / Classic Touch	0.00
	2	NED	Piet Raymakers/ Ratina Z	0.25
	3	**USA**	**Norman Dello Joio / Irish**	**4.75**

TEAM JUMPING

YEAR	RANK	CTRY	ATHLETE / HORSE	TOTAL
1896-1908	(not held)			
1912	1	SWE		25
	2	FRA		32
	3	GER		40
	4	**USA**	**John Montgomery / Deceive** **Guy Henry / Chiswell** **Benjamin Lear / Poppy**	**43**
1920	1	SWE		14.00
	2	BEL		16.25
	3	ITA		18.75
	5	**USA**	**Harry Chamberlin / Nigra** **Karl Greenwald / Moses** **Vincent Erwin / Joffre**	**42.00**
1924	1	SWE		42.25
	2	SUI		50.00
	3	POR		53.00
		USA	**Maj. J.A. Barry / Lt. F.H. Bontecau / Maj. Sloan Doak / Capt. V.L. Padgett**	**unplaced**
1928	1	ESP		4
	2	POL		8
	3	SWE		10
	9	**USA**	**Capt. Frank L. Carr / Maj. H. Chamberlin / Capt A. W. Roffe**	
1932	(no nation completed the course)			
1936	1	GER		44.00
	2	HOL		51.50
	3	POR		56.00
	4	**USA**	**Carl Raguse / Dakota** **William Bradford / Don** **Cornelius Jadwin / Ugly**	**72.50**
1948	1	MEX		34.25
	2	ESP		56.50
	3	GBR		67.00
1952	1	GBR		40.75
	2	CHI		45.75
	3	**USA**	**William Steinkraus / Hollandia** **Arthur John McCashin / Miss Budweiser** **John Russell / Democrat**	**52.25**
1956	1	GER		40.00
	2	ITA		66.00
	3	GBR		69.00
	5	**USA**	**Hugh Wiley / Trail Guide** **William Steinkraus / Night Owl** **Frank Chapot / Belair**	**104.50**
1960	1	GER		46.50
	2	**USA**	**Frank Chapot / Trail Guide** **William Steinkraus / Ksar d'Esprit** **George Morris / Sinjon**	**66.00**
	3	ITA		80.50
1964	1	GER		68.50
	2	FRA		77.75
	3	ITA		88.50
	6	**USA**	**Frank Chapot / San Lucas** **Kathryn Kusner / Untouchable** **Mary Mairs / Tomboy**	**107.00**
1968	1	CAN		102.75
	2	FRA		110.50
	3	GER		117.25
	4	**USA**	**Frank Chapot / San Lucas** **Kathryn Kusner / Untouchable** **Mary Chapot / White Lightning**	**117.50**
1972	1	GER		32.00
	2	**USA**	**William Steinkraus / Main Spring** **Neal Shapiro / Sloopy** **Kathryn Kusner / Fleet Apple** **Frank Chapot / White Lightning**	**32.25**
	3	ITA		48.00
1976	1	FRA		40.00
	2	GER		44.00
	3	BEL		63.00
	4	**USA**	**Frank Chapot / Viscount** **Robert Ridland / South Side** **William Brown / Sandsablaze** **Michael Matz / Grande**	**64.00**
1980	1	URS		20.25
	2	POL		56.00
	3	MEX		59.75
1984	**1**	**USA**	**Joe Fargis / Touch of Class** **Conrad Homfeld / Abdullah** **Leslie Burr / Albany** **Melanie Smith / Calypso**	**12.00**
	2	GBR		36.75
	3	GER		39.25
1988	1	FRG		17.25
	2	**USA**	**Greg Best / Gem Twist** **Lisa Jacquin / For The Moment** **Anne Kursinski / Starman** **Joe Fargis / Mill Pearl**	**20.50**
	3	FRA		27.50
1992	1	NED		12.00
	2	AUT		16.75
	3	FRA		24.75
	5	**USA**	**Anne Kursinski / Cannonball** **Norman Dello Joio / Irish** **Lisa Jacquin / For The Moment** **Michael Matz / Heisman**	**28.00**

INDIVIDUAL DRESSAGE

YEAR	RANK	CTRY	ATHLETE / HORSE	TOTAL
1896-1908	(not held)			
1912	1	SWE	Carl Bonde / Emperor	15
	2	SWE	Gustaf-Adolf Boltenstern, Sr. / Neptun	21
	3	SWE	Hans von Blixen-Finecke, Sr. / Maggie	32
(no USA entry)				
1920	1	SWE	Janne Lundblad / Uno	27.937
	2	SWE	Bertil Sandström / Sabel	26.312
		SWE	Gustaf-Adolf Boltenstern, Sr. / Iron	26.187
	3	SWE	Hans von Rosen / Running Sister	25.125
(no USA entry)				
1924	1	SWE	Ernst Linder / Piccolomini	276.4
	2	SWE	Bertil Sandström / Sabel	275.8
	3	FRA	Xavier Lesage / Plumard	265.8
(no USA entry)				
1928	1	GER	Carl Friedrich Freiherr von Langen-Parow / Draufganger	237.42
	2	FRA	Charles Marion / Linon	231.00
	3	SWE	Ragnar Ohlson / Gunstling	229.78
(no USA entry)				
1932	1	FRA	Xavier Lesage / Taine	343.75
	2	FRA	Charles Marion / Linon	305.42
	3	**USA**	**Hiram Tuttle / Olympic**	**300.50**
1936	1	GER	Heinz Pollay / Kronos	1760.0
	2	GER	Friedrich Gerhard / Absinth	1745.5
	3	AUT	Alois Podhajsky / Nero	1721.5
	23	**USA**	**Capt. C.S. Babcock**	**109**
1948	1	SUI	Hans Moser / Hummer	492.5
	2	FRA	André Jousseaume / Harpagon	480.0
	3	SWE	Gustaf-Adolf Boltenstern, Jr. / Trumf	477.5
	4	**USA**	**Robert Borg / Klingson**	**473.5**
1952	1	SWE	Henri Saint Cyr / Master Rufus	561.0
	2	DEN	Lis Hartel / Jubilee	541.5
	3	FRA	André Jousseaume / Harpagon	541.0
	11	**USA**	**Maj. Robert Borg**	**498.0**
1956	1	SWE	Henri Saint Cyr / Juli	860
	2	DEN	Lis Hartel / Jubilee	850
	3	GER	Liselott Linsenhoff / Adular	832
	17	**USA**	**Maj. Robert Borg**	**720**
1960	1	URS	Sergei Filatov / Absent	2144
	2	SUI	Gustav Fischer / Wald	2087
	3	GER	Josef Neckermann / Asbach	2082
	6	**USA**	**Patricia Galvin / Rath Patrick**	**995**
1964	1	SUI	Henri Chammartin / Woermann	1504
	2	GER	Harry Boldt / Remus	1503
	3	URS	Sergei Filatov / Absent	1486
	8	**USA**	**Patricia Galvin de la Tour d'Auvergne / Rath Patrick**	**783**
1968	1	URS	Ivan Kizimov / Ikhor	1572
	2	GER	Josef Neckermann / Mariano	1546
	3	GER	Reiner Klimke / Dux	1537
	21	**USA**	**Mrs. Kyra Downton / Kadett**	
1972	1	GER	Liselott Linsenhoff / Piaff	1229
	2	URS	Yelena Petushkova / Pepel	1185
	3	GER	Josef Neckertmann / Venetia	1177
	19	**USA**	**Edith Master**	**1480**
1976	1	SUI	Christine Stückelberger / Granat	1486
	2	GER	Harry Boldt / Woycek	1435
	3	GER	Reiner Klimke / Mehmed	1395
	5	**USA**	**Dorothy Morkis / Monaco**	**1249**
1980	1	AUT	Elisabeth Theurer / Mon Cherie	1370
	2	URS	Yuri Kovshov / Igrok	1300
	3	URS	Viktor Ugryumov / Shkval	1234
1984	1	GER	Reiner Klimke / Ahlerich	1504
	2	DEN	Anne Grethe Jensen / Marzog	1442
	3	SUI	Otto Hofer / Limandus	1364
(no USA entry)				
1988	1	FRG	Nicole Uphoff / Rembrandt 24	1521
	2	FRA	Margitt Otto-Crepin / Corlandus	1462
	3	SUI	Chris Stueckelberger / Gauguin de Lully Ch.	1417
	13	**USA**	**Robert Dover / Federleicht**	**1320**
1992	1	GER	Nicole Uphoff / Rembrandt	1626
	2	GER	Isabelle Werth / Gigolo	1551
	3	GER	Klaus Balkenhol / Goldsterm	1515
	6	**USA**	**Carol Lavell / Gifted**	**1408**

TEAM DRESSAGE

YEAR	RANK	CTRY	ATHLETE / HORSE	TOTAL
1896-1924	(not held)			
1928	1	GER		669.72
	2	SWE		650.86
	3	HOL		642.96
(no USA entry)				
1932	1	FRA		2818.75
	2	SWE		2678.00
	3	**USA**	**Hiram Tuttle / Olympic** **Isaac Kitts / American Lady** **Alvin Moore / Water Pat**	**2576.75**
1936	1	GER		5074.0
	2	FRA		4846.0
	3	SWE		4660.5
	9	**USA**	**Capt. C.S. Babcock / Capt. Isaac Kitts / Maj. Hiram Tuttle**	
1948		SWE		1366.0
	1	FRA		1269.0
	2	**USA**	**Robert Borg / Klingson** **Earl Thomson / Pancraft** **Frank Henry / Reno Overdo**	**1256.0**
	3	POR		1182.0
1952	1	SWE		1597.5
	2	SUI		1579.0
	3	GER		1501.0
	6	**USA**	**Robert Borg / Bill Biddle** **Marjorie Haines / The Flying Dutchman** **Hartmann Pauly / Reno Overdo**	**1253.5**
1956	1	SWE		2475.0
	2	GER		2346.0
	3	SUI		2346.0
(no USA entry)				
1960	(not held)			
1964	1	GER		2558.0
	2	SUI		2526.0
	3	URS		2311.0
	4	**USA**	**Patricia Galvin de la Tour d'Auvergne / Rath Patrick** **Anne Newberry / Forstrat** **Karen McIntosh / Malteser**	**2130.0**

1968	1	GER		2699.0
	2	URS		2657.0
	3	SUI		2547.0
	8	**USA**	**Kyra Downton / Cadet Edith Master / Helios Donnan Plumb / Attache**	**1919.0**
1972	1	URS		5095.0
	2	GER		5083.0
	3	SWE		4849.0
	9	**USA**	**Edith Master / John Winnett / Lois Stephens**	**4283.0**
1976	1	GER		5155.0
	2	SUI		4684.0
	3	**USA**	**Hilda Gurney / Keen Dorothy Morkis / Monaco Edith Master / Dahlwitz**	**4647.0**
1980	1	URS		4383.0
	2	BUL		3580.0
	3	ROM		3346.0
1984	1	GER		4955
	2	SUI		4673
	3	SWE		4630
	6	**USA**	**Hilda Gurney / Keen Sandy Pflueger-Clarke / Marco Polo Robert Dover / Romantico**	**4559**
1988	1	FRG		4302
	2	SUI		4164
	3	CAN		3969
	6	**USA**	**Belinda Baudin / Christopher Robert Dover / Federleicht Lendon Gray / Later On Jessica Ransehousen / Orpheus**	**3883**
1992	1	GER		5224
	2	NED		4742
	3	**USA**	**Charlotte Bredahl / Monsieur Michael Poulin / Graf George Robert Dover / Lectron Carol Lavell / Gifted**	**4643**

INDIVIDUAL THREE-DAY EVENT

YEAR	RANK	CTRY	ATHLETE / HORSE	TOTAL
1896-1908	(not held)			
1912	1	SWE	Axel Nordlander / Lady Artis	46.59
	2	GER	Friedrich von Rochow / Idealist	46.42
	3	FRA	Jean Cariou / Cocotte	46.32
	8	**USA**	**John Montgomery / Deceive**	**45.88**
1920	1	SWE	Helmer Mörner / Germania	1775.00
	2	SWE	Åge Lundström / Ysra	1738.75
	3	ITA	Ettore Caffaratti / Caniche	1733.75
	6	**USA**	**Harry Chamberlin / Nigra**	**1568.75**
1924	1	HOL	Adolph van der Voort van Zijp / Silver Piece	1976.0
	2	DEN	Frode Kirkebjerg / Meteor	1853.5
	3	**USA**	**Sloan Doak / Pathfinder**	**1845.5**
1928	1	HOL	Charles Pahud de Mortanges / Marcroix	1969.82
	2	HOL	Gerard de Kruyff / Va-t-en	1967.26
	3	GER	Bruno Neumann / Ilja	1944.42
	17	**USA**	**Major Sloan Doak / Misty Morn**	**1841.68**
1932	1	HOL	Charles Pahud de Mortanges / Marcroix	1813.83
	2	**USA**	**Earl Thomson / Jenny Camp**	**1811.00**
	3	SWE	Clarence von Rosen / Sunnyside Maid	1809.42
1936	1	GER	Ludwig Stubbendorff / Nurmi	-37.7
	2	**USA**	**Earl Thomson / Jenny Camp**	**-99.9**
	3	DEN	Hans Mathiesen-Lunding / Jason	-102.2
1948	1	FRA	Bernard Chevallier / Aiglonne	4
	2	**USA**	**Frank Henry / Swing Low**	**-21**
	3	SWE	Robert Selfelt / Claque	-25
1952	1	SWE	Hans von Blixen-Finecke, Jr / Jubal	-28.33
	2	FRA	Guy Lefrant / Verdun	-54.50
	3	GER	Wilhelm Büsing / Hutbertus	-55.50
	9	**USA**	**Charles Hough, Jr. / Cassavellanus**	**70.66**
1956	1	SWE	Petrus Kastenman / Iluster	-66.53
	2	GER	August Lütke-Westhues / Trux von Kamax	-84.87
	3	GBR	Francis Weldon / Kilbarry	-85.48
		USA	**Maj. Jonathan Burton (inj./withdrew) / Frank Duffy (elim. jumps) / Walter Staley, Jr. (horse inj.)**	
1960	1	AUS	Lawrence Morgan / Salad Days	7.15
	2	AUS	Neale Lavis / Mirrabooka	-16.50
	3	SUI	Anton Bühler / Gay Spark	-51.21
	15	**USA**	**Michael Plumb / Markham**	**153.46**
1964	1	ITA	Mauro Checcoli / Surbean	64.40
	2	ARG	Carlos Moratorio / Chalan	56.40
	3	GER	Fritz Ligges / Donkosak	49.20
	4	**USA**	**Michael Page / Grasshopper**	**47.40**
1968	1	FRA	Jean-Jacques Guyon / Pitou	-38.86
	2	GBR	Derek Allhusen / Lochinvar	-41.61
	3	**USA**	**Michael Page / Foster**	**-52.31**
1972	1	GBR	Richard Meade / Laurieston	-57.73
	2	ITA	Alessandro Argenton / Woodland	-43.33
	3	SWE	Jan Jönsson / Sarajevo	-39.67
	5	**USA**	**Kevin Freeman / Good Mixture**	**-29.87**
1976	**1**	**USA**	**Edmund Coffin / Bally-Cor**	**-114.99**
	2	**USA**	**J. Michael Plumb / Better & Better**	**-125.85**
	3	GER	Karl Schultz / Madrigal	-129.45
1980	1	ITA	Euro Federico Roman / Rossinan	-108.6
	2	URS	Aleksandr Blinov / Galzun	-120.8
	3	URS	Yuri Salnikov / Pintset	-151.6
1984	1	NZL	Mark Todd / Charisma	-51.6
	2	**USA**	**Karen Stives / Ben Arthur**	**-54.2**
	3	GBR	Virginia Holgate / Priceless	-56.8
1988	1	NZL	Mark Todd / Charisma	42.60
	2	GBR	Ian Stark / Sir Wattie	52.80
	3	GBR	Virginia Leng / Master Craftsman	62.00
	10	**USA**	**Phyllis Dawson / Albany II**	**99.60**
1992	1	AUS	Mathew Ryan / Kibah Tic Toc	70.00
	2	GER	Herman Blocker / Feine Dame	81.30
	3	NZL	Blyth Tait / Messiah	87.60
	17	**USA**	**Jil Walton / Patrona**	**116.80**

TEAM THREE-DAY EVENT

YEAR	RANK	CTRY	ATHLETE / HORSE	TOTAL
1896-1908	(not held)			
1912	1	SWE		139.06
	2	GER		138.48
	3	**USA**	**Benjamin Lear / Poppy John Montgomery / Deceive Guy Henry / Chiswell**	**137.33**
1920	1	SWE		5057.50
	2	ITA		4735.00
	3	BEL		4560.00
	4	**USA**	**Harry Chamberlin / Nigra William West / Black Boy John Barry / Raven**	**4477.50**
1924	1	HOL		5297.5
	2	SWE		4743.5
	3	ITA		4512.5
		USA	**Lt. F.L. Carr / Maj. Sloan Doak / Capt. V.L. Padgett**	**(withdrew)**
1928	1	HOL		5865.68
	2	NOR		5395.68
	3	POL		5067.92
	7	**USA**	**Capt. Frank L. Carr / Maj. H. Chamberlin / Capt. A.W. Roffe**	
1932	**1**	**USA**	**Earl Thomson / Jenny Champ Harry Chamberlin / Pleasant Smiles Edwin Argo / Honolulu Tomboy**	**5038.083**
	2	HOL		4689.083
1936	1	GER		-676.65
	2	POL		-991.70
	3	GBR		-9195.50
		USA	**Capt. C.W.A. Raguse / Capt. Earl Thomson / Capt. J.M. Williams**	
1948	**1**	**USA**	**Frank Henry / Swing Low Charles Anderson / Reno Palisade Earl Thomson / Reno Rhythm**	**-161.5**
	2	SWE		-165.00
	3	MEX		-305.25
1952	1	SWE		-221.94
	2	GER		-235.49
	3	**USA**	**Charles Hough / Cassivellannus Walter Staley / Craigwood Park John Wofford / Benny Grimes**	**-587.16**
1956	1	GBR		-355.48
	2	GER		-475.91
	3	CAN		-572.72
		USA	**Maj. Jonathan Burton (inj./withdrew) / Frank Duffy (elim. jumps) / Walter Staley, Jr. (horse inj.)**	
1960	1	AUS		-128.18
	2	SUI		-386.02
	3	FRA		-515.71
		USA	**John Plumb / Michael Page / David Lurie**	**elim.**
1964	1	ITA		85.80
	2	**USA**	**Michael Page / Grasshopper Kevin Freeman / Gallopade J. Michael Plumb / Bold Minstrel**	**65.86**
	3	GER/GDR		56.73
1968	1	GBR		-175.93
	2	**USA**	**Michael Page / Foster James Wofford / Kilkenny J. Michael Plumb / Plain Sailing**	**-245.87**
	3	AUS		-331.26
1972	1	GBR		95.53
	2	**USA**	**Kevin Freeman / Good Mixture Bruce Davidson / Plain Sailing J. Michael Plumb / Free and Easy**	**10.81**
	3	GER		-18.00
1976	**1**	**USA**	**Edmund Coffin / Bally-Cor J. Michael Plumb / Better & Better Bruce Davidson / Irish-Cap**	**-441.00**
	2	GER		-584.60
	3	AUS		-599.54
1980	1	URS		-457.00
	2	ITA		-656.20
	3	MEX		-1172.85
1984	**1**	**USA**	**Karen Stives / Ben Arthur Torrance Watkins Fleischmann / Finvarra J. Michael Plumb / Blue Stone**	**-186.00**
	2	GBR		-189.20
	3	GER		-234.00
1988	1	FRG		225.95
	2	GBR		271.20
	3	NZL		256.80
		USA	**Phyllis Dawson / Albany II Bruce Davidson / Dr. Peaches Ann Sutton / Tarzan Karen Lende / The Optimist**	
1992	1	AUS		288.60
	2	NZL		290.80
	3	GER		300.30
	10	**USA**	**Jil Walton / Patrona J. Michael Plumb / Adonis Stephen Bradley / Sassy Reason Todd Trewin / Sandscript**	**515.20**

FENCING

MEN'S INDIVIDUAL FOIL

YEAR	RANK	CTRY	ATHLETE	
1896	1	FRA	Eugene-Henri Gravelotte	
	2	FRA	Henri Callot	
	3	GRE	Perikles Pierrakos-Mavromichalis	
(no USA entry)				
1900	1	FRA	Emile Coste	
	2	FRA	Henri Masson	
	3	FRA	Marcel Jacques Boulenger	
(no USA entry)				
1904	1	CUB	Ramón Fonst	
	2	**USA**	**Albertson Van Zo Post**	
	3	**USA**	**Charles Tatham**	
1906	1	FRA	Georges Dillon-Cavanagh	
	2	GER	Gustav Casmir	
	3	FRA	Pierre d'Hugues	
(no USA entry)				
1908	(not held)			
1912	1	ITA	Nedo Nadi	
	2	ITA	Pietro Speciale	
	3	AUT	Richard Verderber	
		USA	**Sherman Hall**	**elim. 3rd rd**
1920	1	ITA	Nedo Nadi	
	2	FRA	Philippe Cattiau	
	3	FRA	Roger Ducret	
		USA	**Maj. F.W. Honeycutt**	**elim. semis**
1924	1	FRA	Roger Ducret	
	2	FRA	Philippe Cattiau	
	3	BEL	Maurice van Damme	
		USA	**George Calnan**	**elim. semis**
1928	1	FRA	Lucien Gaudin	
	2	GER	Erwin Casmir	
	3	ITA	Giulio Gaudini	
	11	**USA**	**Joseph Levis**	
1932	1	ITA	Gustavo Marzi	
	2	**USA**	**Joseph Levis**	
	3	ITA	Giulio Gaudini	
1936	1	ITA	Giulio Gaudini	
	2	FRA	Edward Gardère	
	3	ITA	Giorgio Bocchino	
		USA	**Joseph Levis**	**elim. semis**
1948	1	FRA	Jehan Buhan	
	2	FRA	Christian d'Oriola	
	3	HUN	Lajos Maszlay	
		USA	**Dean Cetrulo / Silvio Giolito**	**elim. semis**
1952	1	FRA	Christian d'Oriola	
	2	ITA	Edoardo Mangiarotti	
	3	ITA	Manlio Di Rosa	
		USA	**Albert Axelrod / Nathaniel Lubell**	**elim. semis**
1956	1	FRA	Christian d'Oriola	
	2	ITA	Giancarlo Bergamini	
	3	ITA	Antonio Spallino	
		USA	**Albert Axelrod**	**elim. semis**
1960	1	URS	Viktor Zhdanovich	
	2	URS	Yuri Sissikin	
	3	**USA**	**Albert Axelrod**	
1964	1	POL	Egon Franke	
	2	FRA	Jean-Claude Magnan	
	3	FRA	Daniel Revenu	
		USA	**Albert Axelrod**	**elim. 4th rd**
1968	1	ROM	Ionel Drimb	
	2	HUN	Jenö Kamuti	
	3	FRA	Daniel Revenu	
		USA	**Larry Anastasi / Jeffrey Checkes / Herbert Cohen**	**elim. 2nd rd**
1972	1	POL	Witold Woyda	
	2	HUN	Jenö Kamuti	
	3	FRA	Christian Noël	
		USA	**Joseph Freeman**	**elim. 2nd rd**
1976	1	ITA	Fabio Dal Zotto	
	2	URS	Aleksandr Romankov	
	3	FRA	Bernard Talvard	
	13	**USA**	**Edward Donofrio**	
1980	1	URS	Vladimir Smirnov	
	2	FRA	Paskal Jolyot	
	3	URS	Aleksandr Romankov	
1984	1	ITA	Mauro Numa	
	2	GER	Matthias Behr	
	3	ITA	Stefano Cerioni	
	11	**USA**	**Peter Lewison**	
1988	1	ITA	Stefano Cerioni	
	2	GDR	Udo Wagner	
	3	URS	Alexandre Romankov	
	12	**USA**	**Peter Lewison**	
1992	1	FRA	Philippe Omnes	
	2	EUN	Serguei Goloubitski	
	3	CUB	Elvis Gregory Gil	
	36	**USA**	**Michael Marx**	

MEN'S TEAM FOIL

YEAR	RANK	CTRY	ATHLETES
1896-1900	(not held)		
1904	**1**	**CUB/USA**	**Ramón Fonst / Manuel Diaz / Albertson Van Zo Post**
	2	**USA**	**Charles Tatham / Fitzhugh Townsend / Arthur Fox**
1906-1912	(not held)		
1920	1	ITA	
	2	FRA	
	3	**USA**	**Henry Breckinridge / Francis Honeycutt / Arthur Lyon / Harold Rayner / Robert Sears**
1924	1	FRA	
	2	BEL	
	3	HUN	
1928	1	ITA	
	2	FRA	
	3	ARG	
	5T	**USA**	**George Calnan / René Peroy / Joseph Levis / Harold Rayner / Henry Breckinridge / Dernell Every**
1932	1	FRA	
	2	ITA	
	3	**USA**	**George Calnan / Joseph Levis / Hugh Allesandroni / Dernell Every / Richard Steere / Frank Righeimer**
1936	1	ITA	
	2	FRA	
	3	GER	
	5T	**USA**	**Joseph Levis / Hugh Alessandroni / John Potter / John Hurd / Warren Dow / William Pecora**
1948	1	FRA	
	2	ITA	
	3	BEL	
	4	**USA**	**Daniel Bukantz / Dean Cetrulo / Dernell Every / Silvio Giolito / Nathaniel Lubell / Austin Prokop**
1952	1	FRA	
	2	ITA	
	3	HUN	
	8	**USA**	**Daniel Bukantz / Nathaniel Lubell / Albert Axelrod / Silvio Giolito / Bryon Krieger / Harold D. Goldsmith**
1956	1	ITA	
	2	FRA	
	3	HUN	
	4	**USA**	**Albert Axelrod / Daniel Bukantz / Harold Goldsmith / Byron Kreiger / Nathaniel Lubell / Sewall Shurtz**
1960	1	URS	
	2	ITA	
	3	GER	
	5T	**USA**	**Gene Glazer / Harold Goldsmith / Joseph Paletta / Albert Axelrod / Daniel Bukantz**
1964	1	URS	
	2	POL	
	3	FRA	
		USA	**Lawrence Anastasi / Albert Axelrod / Herbert Cohen / Eugene Glazer / Edwin Richards**
1968	1	FRA	
	2	URS	
	3	POL	
		USA	**Albert Axelrod / Lawrence Anastasi / Herbert Cohen / Uriah Jones**
1972	1	POL	
	2	URS	
	3	FRA	
		USA	**Martin Davis / Tyrone Simmonds / Lt. Joseph Freeman / Carl Borack / Seaman John Nonna**
1976	1	GER	
	2	ITA	
	3	FRA	
	7T	**USA**	**Martin Lang / Edward Ballinger / Edward Wright / Edward Donofrio / Brooke Mackler**
1980	1	FRA	
	2	URS	
	3	POL	
1984	1	ITA	
	2	GER	
	3	FRA	
	5	**USA**	**Michael Marx / Gregory Massialas / Peter Lewison / Mark Smith / Michael McCahey**
1988	1	URS	
	2	FRG	
	3	HUN	
	14	**USA**	**Peter Lewison / David Littell / Michael Marx / Gregory Massialas / George Nomomura**

1980	1	FRA		
	2	POL		
	3	URS		
1984	1	GER		
	2	FRA		
	3	ITA		
	10	**USA**	**Robert Marx / John Moreau / Peter Schifrin / C. Lee Shelley / Stephen Trevor**	
1988	1	FRA		
	2	FRG		
	3	URS		
	11	**USA**	**Robert Marx / John Moreau / Lee Shelley / Robert Stull / Stephen Trevor**	
1992	1	GER		
	2	HUN		
	3	EUN		
		USA	**DNQ**	

WOMEN'S INDIVIDUAL FOIL

YEAR	RANK	CTRY	ATHLETE	
1896-1920	(not held)			
1924	1	DEN	Ellen Osiier	
	2	GBR	Gladys Davis	
	3	DEN	Grete Heckscher	
		USA	**Adeline Gehrig / Irma Hopper**	**elim. 1st rd**
1928	1	GER	Helene Mayer	
	2	GBR	Muriel Freeman	
	3	GER	Olga Oelkers	
		USA	**Marion Lloyd**	**elim. semis**
1932	1	AUT	Ellen Preis	
	2	GBR	J. Heather Guinness	
	3	HUN	Erna Bogáthy Bogen	
	8T	**USA**	**Marion Lloyd**	
1936	1	HUN	Ilona Schacherer-Elek	
	2	GER	Helene Mayer	
	3	AUT	Ellen Preis	
		USA	**Dorothy Locke / Marion Lloyd**	**elim. semis**
1948	1	HUN	Ilona Elek	
	2	DEN	Karen Lachmann	
	3	AUT	Ellen Müller-Preis	
	4	**USA**	**Maria Cerra**	
1952	1	ITA	Irene Camber	
	2	HUN	Ilona Elek	
	3	DEN	Karen Lachmann	
	4	**USA**	**Janice-Lee York**	
1956	1	GBR	Gillian Sheen	
	2	ROM	Olga Orban	
	3	FRA	Renée Garilhe	
	4	**USA**	**Janice-Lee Romary (York)**	
1960	1	GER	Heidi Schmid	
	2	URS	Valentina Rastvorova	
	3	ROM	Maria Vicol	
		USA	**Janice-Lee Romary**	**elim. 1st rd**
1964	1	HUN	Ildikó Ujlaki-Rejtö	
	2	GER	Helga Mees	
	3	ITA	Antonella Ragno	
		USA	**Harriet King**	**elim. 3rd rd**
1968	1	URS	Yelena Novikova	
	2	MEX	Maria del Pilar Roldan	
	3	HUN	Ildikó Ujlaki-Rejtö	
		USA	**Janice-Lee Romary / Harriet King**	
1972	1	ITA	Antonella Ragno-Lonzi	
	2	HUN	Ildikó Bóbis	
	3	URS	Galina Gorokhova	
		USA	**Ruth White**	**elim. qtr. final**
1976	1	HUN	Ildikó Schwarczenberger	
	2	ITA	Maria Consolata Collino	
	3	URS	Yelena Belova (Novikova)	
	38	**USA**	**Nikki Franke**	
1980	1	FRA	Pascale Trinquet	
	2	HUN	Magda Maros	
	3	POL	Barbara Wysoczanska	
1984	1	CHN	Luan Jujie	
	2	GER	Cornelia Hanisch	
	3	ITA	Dorina Vaccaroni	
	20	**USA**	**Debra Waples**	
1988	1	FRG	Anja Fichtel	
	2	FRG	Sabine Bau	
	3	FRG	Zita Funkenhauser	
	11	**USA**	**Caitlin Bilodeaux**	
1992	1	ITA	Giovanna Trillini	
	2	CHN	Wang Huifeng	
	3	EUN	Tatiana Sadovskaia	
	29	**USA**	**Caitlin Bilodeaux-Banos**	

WOMEN'S TEAM FOIL

YEAR	RANK	CTRY	ATHLETES
1896-1956	(not held)		
1960	1	URS	
	2	HUN	
	3	ITA	
	10	**USA**	**Janice-Lee Romary / Maxine Mitchell / Judy Goodrich / Evelyn Terhune / Harriet King**
1964	1	HUN	
	2	URS	
	3	GER	
		USA	**Janice-Lee Romary / Denise O'Connor / Ann Drungis / Tommy Angell / Harriet King**
1968	1	URS	
	2	HUN	
	3	ROM	
		USA	**Janice-Lee Romary / Maxine Mitchell / Sally Pechinsky / Harriet King / Veronica Smith**
1972	1	URS	
	2	HUN	
	3	ITA	
	7	**USA**	**Ruth White / Natalia Clovis / Tanya Adamovich / Harriet King / Ann O'Donnell**
1976	1	URS	
	2	FRA	
	3	HUN	
		USA	**Denise O'Connor / Nikke Franke / Gay D'Asaro / Ann O'Donnell / Dorothy Armstrong**
1980	1	FRA	
	2	URS	
	3	HUN	
1984	1	GER	
	2	ROM	
	3	FRA	
	6	**USA**	**Vincent Bradford / Sharon Monplaisir / Susan Badders / Debra Waples / Jana Angelakis**
1988	1	FRG	
	2	ITA	
	3	HUN	
	6	**USA**	**Caitlin Bilodeaux / Elaine Cheris / Sharon Monplaisir / Mary Jane O'Neill / Molly Sullivan**
1992	1	ITA	
	2	GER	
	3	ROM	
	9	**USA**	**Caitlin Bilodeaux-Banos / Ann Marsh / Sharon Monplaisir / Mary Jane O'Neill / Molly Sullivan**

FIELD HOCKEY

MEN

YEAR	RANK	CTRY	SCORE		
1896-1908	(not held)				
1908	1	GBR	3-0		
	2	IRL	1-1		
	3	GBR	1-1		
	3T	GBR	0-1		
(no USA entry)					
1912	(not held)				
1920	1	GBR	3-0		
	2	DEN	2-1		
	3	BEL	1-2		
	4	FRA	0-3		
(no USA entry)					
1924	(not held)				
1928	1	IND	5-0		
	2	HOL	3-1		
	3	GER	3-1		
	4	BEL	3-2		
(no USA entry)					
1932	1	IND	2-0		
	2	JPN	1-1		
	3	**USA**	**0-2**		
USA Team: William Boddington / Harold Brewster / Lanphear Buck / Roy Coffin / Amos Deacon / Horace Disston / Sam Ewing / James Gentle / Henry Greer / Wilson Hobson / Warren Ingersoll / Lawrence Knapp / David McMillin / Leonard O'Brien / Robert Pyle / Charles Sheaffer / Fred Wolters					
1936	1	IND	5-0		
	2	GER	3-1		
	3	HOL	3-1-1		
	4	FRA	2-3		
		USA	0-3-0		
USA Team: William Ahlemeyer / Walter Bowden / Charles Dauner / Edward John Hagen / Joseph Kaylor / Fred Leinweber / Henry Oehler / Otto Oehler / Herbert C. Oehmichen / Willy K. Renz / Alfred Roseco / Edmund Schallenberg / Philip Schupp / Gerard Yantz / Dietrich Wortmann / Walter Mangel / Fred Brenner					
1948	1	IND	5-0		
	2	GBR	3-1-1		
	3	HOL	4-2-1		
	4	PAK	4-2-1		
		USA	0-3-0		
USA Team: Donald Buck / David Cauffman / Claus Gerson / Henry Goode / Frederic Hewitt / William Kurtz / Henrik Lubbers / Harry Marcoplos / Kurt Orban / John Renwick, Jr / Philip Schoettle / Sanders Sims / John Slade / Walter Stude / Felix Ucko / William Wilson					
1952	1	IND	3-0		
	2	HOL	2-1		
	3	GBR	2-1		
	4	PAK	1-2		
(no USA entry)					
1956	1	IND	5-0		
	2	PAK	3-1-1		
	3	GER	2-1-2		
	3	GBR	2-2-2		
	5	AUS	2-2		
	6	NZL	1-2		
	11	USA	0-3-1		
USA Team: E. Newbold Black / Henry Clifford / John Kirk Greer / Stanley Harris / James Jongeneel / Gerrit Kruize / Tjerk Hidde Leegstra / Harry Marcoplos / Kurt Orban / John Rote / Charles Shanks / Walter Stude / Felix Ucko / H. Van Nouhuys / R.C. Wittelsberger /John Kirk Greer					
1960	1	PAK	6-0		
	2	IND	5-1		
	3	ESP	4-1-1		
	4	GBR	3-2-1		
	5	NZL	4-3-1		
	6	AUS	4-3-2		
	7	GER	2-3		
	7	KEN	2-2-2		
(no USA entry - DNQ)					
1964	1	IND	7-0-2		
	2	PAK	7-1		
	3	AUS	5-3		
	4	ESP	4-2-3		
	5	GDR	4-0-5		
	6	KEN	4-3-1		
	7	HOL	4-3-1		
	7	JPN	3-4		
(no USA entry - DNQ)					
1968	1	PAK	9-0		
	2	AUS	5-3-1		
	3	IND	7-2		
	4	GER	5-3-1		
	5	HOL	6-3		
	6	ESP	3-3-3		
	7	NZL	3-1-4		
	8	KEN	4-3-1		
(no USA entry - DNQ)					
1972	1	GER	8-1		
	2	PAK	6-2-1		
	3	IND	6-1-2		
	4	HOL	5-3-1		
	5	AUS	5-2-2		
	6	GBR	5-3-1		
	7	ESP	3-2-4		
	8	MAL	4-4-1		
(no USA entry - DNQ)					
1976	1	NZL	3-1-2		
	2	AUS	4-3		
	3	PAK	4-1-1		
	4	HOL	5-2		
	5	GER	3-2-1		
	6	ESP	2-2-2		
	7	IND	4-3		
	8	MAL	2-5		
(no USA entry - DNQ)					
1980	1	IND	4-0-2		
	2	ESP	4-1-1		
	3	URS	4-2		
	4	POL	2-3-1		
	5	CUB	2-4		
	6	TAN	0-6		
1984	1	PAK	4-0-3		
	2	GER	4-2-1		
	3	GBR	5-1-1		
	4	AUS	5-2		
	5	IND	5-1-1		
	6	HOL	4-2-1		
	7	NZL	2-3-2		
	8	ESP	2-5		
	12	**USA**			
USA Team: Mohammed Barakat / Ken Barrett / Rawle Cox / Trevor Fernandes / Scott Gregg / Manzar Iqbal / Michael Krause / Randy Lipscher / Dave McMichael / Gary Newton / Mike Newton / Brian Spencer / Morgan Stebbins / Bob Stiles / Drew Stone / Nigel Traverso					
1988	1	GBR	3-1		(Final)
	2	FRG			
	3	HOL	2-1		(3rd-4th)
	4	AUS			
	5	PAK	2-1		(5th-6th)
	6	IND			
(no USA entry)					
1992	1	GER	GER vs. AUS	2-1	(Final)
	2	AUS	PAK vs. NED	4-3	(3rd-4th)
	3	PAK	ESP vs. GBR	2-1	(5th-6th)
	4	NED	IND vs. NZL	3-2	(7th-8th)
	5	ESP	MAS vs. EUN	4-3	(9th-10th)
	6	GBR	ARG vs. EGY	7-3	(11th-12th)
	7	IND			
	8	NZL			
	9	MAS			
	10	EUN			
	11	ARG			
	12	EGY			
(no USA entry - DNQ)					

WOMEN

YEAR	RANK	CTRY	SCORE		
1896-1976	(not held)				
1980	1	ZIM	3-0-2		
	2	TCH	3-1-1		
	3	URS	3-2		
	4	IND	2-2-1		
	5	AUT	2-3		
	6	POL	0-5		
1984	1	HOL	4-0-1		
	2	GER	2-1-2		
	3	**USA**	**2-2-1**		
	4	AUS	2-2-1		
	5	CAN	2-2-1		
	6	NZL	0-5		
USA Team: Gwen Cheeseman / Beth Anders / Kathleen McGahey / Anita Miller / Regina Buggy / Christine Larson-Mason / Beth Beglin / Marcella Place / Julie Stazer / Diane Moyer / Sheryl Johnson / Charlene Morett / Karen Shelton / Brenda Stauffler / Leslie Milne / Judy Strong					
1988	1	AUS	USA vs. HOL 1-3	2-0	(Final)
	2	KOR	USA vs. ARG 1-2		
	3	HOL	USA vs. GBR 2-2	3-1	(3rd-4th)
	4	GBR	USA vs. FRG 1-2		
	5	FRG	USA vs. ARG 1-3	4-2	(5th-6th)
	6	CAN			
	7	ARG		3-1	(7th-8th)
	8	**USA**			
USA Team: Patricia Shea / Yolanda Hightower / Mary Koboldt / Marcia Pankratz / Cheryl Van Kuren / Diane Bracalente / Beth Beglin / Marcel Von Schottenstein / Sandra Vander-Heyden / Tracey Fuchs / Sheryl Johnson / Sandra Costigan / Christy Morgan / Barbara Marois / Megan Donnelly / Donna Lee					
1992	1	ESP	ESP vs. GER	2-1 a.e.t.	(Final)
	2	GER	GBR vs. KOR	4-3 a.e.t	(3rd-4th)
	3	GBR	AUS vs. NED	2-0	(5th-6th)
	4	KOR	CAN vs. NZL	2-0	(7th-8th)
	5	AUS			
	6	NED		a.e.t.=after extra time	
	7	CAN			
	8	NZL			
		USA	**DNQ**		

GYMNASTICS

MEN'S TEAM COMPETITION

YEAR	RANK	CTRY	ATHLETES	TOTAL
1896-1900	(not held)			
1904*	**1**	**USA**	**Julius Lenhart / Philipp Kassel / Anton Heida / Max Hess / Ernst Reckeweg / John Grieb (Club: Turngemeinde Philadelphia)**	**374.43**
	2	**USA**	**Otto Steffen / John Bissinger / Emil Beyer / Max Wolf / Julian Schmitz / Arthur Rosenkampf (Club: New York Turnverein)**	**356.37**
	3	**USA**	**George Mayer / John Duha / Edward Siegler / Philipp Schuster / Robert Mayack / Charles Krause (Club: Central Turnverein Chicago)**	**349.69**
*Only USA teams competed.				
1906	1	NOR		19.00
	2	DEN		18.00
	3	ITA		16.71
(no USA entry)				
1908	1	SWE		438
	2	NOR		425
	3	FIN		405
(no USA entry)				
1912	1	ITA		265.75
	2	HUN		227.25
	3	GBR		184.5
(no USA entry)				
1920	1	ITA		359.855
	2	BEL		346.785
	3	FRA		340.100
(no USA entry)				
1924	1	ITA		839.058
	2	FRA		820.528
	3	SUI		816.661
	5	**USA**	**Frank Kriz / Alfred Jochim / John Pearson / Frank Safanda / Curtis Rottman / Rudolph Novak / Max Wandrer / John Mais**	**715.117**
1928	1	SUI		1718.625
	2	TCH		1712.25
	3	YUG		1648.75
	7	**USA**	**Alfred Jochim / Glenn Berry / Frank Kriz / Frank Haubold / Harold Newhart / John Pearson / Herman Witzig / Paul Krempel**	**1519.125**
1932	1	ITA		541.850
	2	**USA**	**Frank Haubold / Frederick Meyer / Alfred Joachim / Frank Cumiskey**	**522.275**
	3	FIN		509.995

MEN'S TEAM

(Continuation — pommel horse combined results)

> (this event combined the results above with the results of pommel horse)

YEAR	RANK	CTRY	ATHLETE(S)	TOTAL
1936	1	GER	Frank Cumiskey / Frederick H. Meyer / George E. Wheeler / Chester W. Phillips / Arthur Pitt / Frank O. Haubold / Alfred Jochim / Kenneth Griffin	657.430
	2	SUI		654.802
	3	FIN		638.468
	10	**USA**	**Frank Cumiskey / Frederick H. Meyer / George E. Wheeler / Chester W. Phillips / Arthur Pitt / Frank O. Haubold / Alfred Jochim / Kenneth Griffin**	**551.301**
1948	1	FIN		1358.30
	2	SUI		1356.70
	3	HUN		1330.85
	7	**USA**	**Edward Scrobe / Vincent D'Antorio / William Roetzheim / Joseph Kotys / Frank Cumiskey / Raymond Sorensen**	**1252.50**
1952	1	URS		574.40
	2	SUI		567.50
	3	FIN		564.20
	8	**USA**	**Edward Scrobe / Robert Stout / William Roetzheim / Donald Holder / John Beckner / Charles Simms / Walter Blattmann / Vincent D'Antorio**	**543.15**
1956	1	URS		568.25
	2	JPN		566.40
	3	FIN		555.95
	10	**USA**	**John Beckner / Jose Armando Vega / Charles Simms / Richard Beckner / Abraham Grossfeld / William Tom**	**547.50**
1960	1	JPN		575.20
	2	URS		572.70
	3	ITA		559.05
	5	**USA**	**Larry Banner / John Beckner / Donald Tonry / Abraham Grossfeld / Fred Orlofsky / Garland O'Quinn**	**555.20**
1964	1	JPN		577.95
	2	GER/GDR		575.45
	3			565.10
	7	**USA**	**Makoto Sakamoto / Russell Mitchell / Ronald Barak / Larry Banner / Gregor Weiss / Arthur Shurlock**	**556.95**
1968	1	JPN		575.90
	2	URS		571.10
	3	GDR		557.15
	7	**USA**	**David Thor / Fred Roethlisberger / Steve Hug / Stephen Cohen / Sidney Freudenstein / Kanati Allen**	**548.90**
1972	1	JPN		571.25
	2	URS		564.05
	3	GDR		559.70
	10	**USA**	**Marshall Avener / John Crosby, Jr. / James Culhane, Jr. / George Greenfield / Steven Hug / Makoto Sakamoto**	**533.85**
1976	1	JPN		576.85
	2	URS		576.45
	3	GDR		564.65
	7	**USA**	**Wayne Young / Kurt Thomas / Peter Kormann / Thomas Beach / Marshall Avener / Bart Conner**	**556.10**
1980	1	URS		598.60
	2	GDR		581.15
	3	HUN		575.00
	(no USA entry)			
1984	1	USA	Peter Vidmar / Bart Conner / Mitchell Gaylord / Timothy Daggett / James Hartung / Scott Johnson	591.40
1988	1	URS		593.350
	2	GDR		588.450
	3	JPN		585.600
	11	**USA**	**Charles Lakes / Scott Johnson / Kenneth "Wes" Suter / Kevin Davis / Lance Ringnald / Dominick Minicucci**	**576.850**
1992	1	EUN		585.450
	2	CHN		580.375
	3	JPN		578.250
	6	**USA**	**Trent Dimas / Scott Keswick / Jair Lynch / Dominick Minicucci / John Roethlisberger / Chris Waller**	**571.725**

MEN'S INDIVIDUAL ALL-AROUND

YEAR	RANK	CTRY	ATHLETE	TOTAL
1896	(not held)			
1900	1	FRA	Gustave Sandras	302
	2	FRA	Noël Bas	295
	3	FRA	Lucien Démanet	293
1904	1	AUT	Julius Lenhart	69.80
	2	GER	Wilhelm Weber	69.10
	3	SUI	Adolf Spinnler	67.99
	6	**USA**	**Otto Steffen**	**67.03**

MEN'S VAULT

YEAR	RANK	CTRY	ATHLETE	TOTAL
1896	1	GER	Karl Schumann	
	2	SUI	Jules Zutter	
	3	GER	Hermann Weingärtner	
1900	(not held)			
1904	1T	USA	George Eyser	36
	1T	USA	Anton Heida	36
	3	USA	William Merz	31
1908–1920	(not held)			
1924	1	USA	Frank Kriz	9.98
	2	TCH	Jan Koutny	9.97
	3	TCH	Bohumil Morkovsky	9.93
1928	1	SUI	Eugen Mack	9.58
	2	SUI	Emanuel Löffler	9.50
	3	YUG	Stane Derganc	9.46
	7	USA	Herman Witzig	9.28
1932	1	ITA	Savino Guglielmetti	18.03
	2	USA	Alfred Jochim	17.77
	3	USA	Edward Carmichael	17.53
1936	1	GER	Alfred Schwarzmann	19.20
	2	SUI	Eugen Mack	18.967
	3	GER	Matthias Volz	18.467
	24	USA	George Wheeler	17.433
1948	1	FIN	Paavo Aaltonen	19.55
	2	FIN	Olavi Rove	19.50
	3	HUN	János Mogyorósi-Klencs	19.25
	23	USA	William Bonsall	37.50
1952	1	URS	Viktor Chukarin	19.20
	2	JPN	Masao Takemoto	19.15
	3	JPN	Takashi Ono	19.10
	40	USA	Charles Simms	18.45
1956	1	GER	Helmut Bantz	18.85
	1	URS	Valentin Muratov	18.85
	3	URS	Yuri Titov	18.75
	7	USA	John Beckner	18.60
1960	1	JPN	Takashi Ono	19.35
	1	URS	Boris Shakhlin	19.35
	3	URS	Vladimir Portnoi	19.225
	17	USA	Fred Orofino	18.55
1964	1	JPN	Haruhiro Yamashita	19.60
	2	URS	Viktor Lisitsky	19.325
	3	FIN	Hannu Rantakari	19.30
	31	USA	Makoto Sakamoto	18.95
1968	1	JPN	Mikhail Voronin	19.00
	2	JPN	Yukio Endo	18.95
	3	URS	Sergei Diomidov	18.925
1972	1	URS	Klaus Köste	18.85
	2	URS	Viktor Klimenko	18.825
	3	JPN	Nikolai Andrianov	18.80
	(USA best finish N/A - DNQ for finals)			
1976	1	URS	Nikolai Andrianov	19.45
	2	JPN	Mitsuo Tsukahara	19.375
	3	JPN	Hiroshi Kajiyama	19.275
	(USA best finish N/A - DNQ for finals)			
1980	1	URS	Nikolai Andrianov	19.825
	2	GDR	Roland Brückner	19.775
	3	URS	Aleksandr Dityatin	19.775
1984	1	CHN	Lou Yun	19.95
	2	USA	Mitchell Gaylord	19.825
	3	JPN	Koji Gushiken	19.825
1988	1	CHN	Lou Yun	19.875
	2	URS	Sylvio Kroll	19.862
	3	KOR	Park Jong-hoon	19.775
	(USA best finish N/A - DNQ for finals)			

MEN'S HORIZONTAL BAR

YEAR	RANK	CTRY	ATHLETE	TOTAL
1896	1	GER	Hermann Weingärtner	
	2	GER	Alfred Flatow	
	3	GRE	Petmezas	
1900	(no USA entry)			
1904	1T	USA	Anton Heida	40
	1T	USA	Edward Hennig	40
	3	USA	George Eyser	39
1908–1920	(not held)			
1924	1	YUG	Leon Štukelj	19.73
	2	SUI	Jean Gutweniger	19.236
	3	FRA	André Higelin	19.163
	18	USA	Frank Kriz	
1928	1	SUI	Georges Miez	19.17
	2	ITA	Romeo Neri	19.00
	3	SUI	Eugen Mack	18.92
	27	USA	Frank Kriz	53.00
1932	1	USA	Dallas Bixler	18.33
	2	FIN	Heikki Savolainen	18.07
	3	FIN	Einari Teräsvirta	18.07
1936	1	FIN	Aleksanteri Saarvala	19.367
	2	GER	Konrad Frey	19.267
	3	GER	Alfred Schwarzmann	19.233
	15	USA	Frank Cumiskey	18.600
1948	1	SUI	Josef Stalder	19.85
	2	SUI	Walter Lehmann	19.70
	3	FIN	Veikko Huhtanen	19.60
	25	USA	Frank Cumiskey	37.30
1952	1	SUI	Jack Günthard	19.55
	2T	GER	Alfred Schwarzmann	19.50
	2T	SUI	Josef Stalder	19.50
	16	USA	Charles Simms	19.00
1956	1	JPN	Takashi Ono	19.60
	2	URS	Yuri Titov	19.40
	3	JPN	Masao Takemoto	19.30
	7	USA	John Beckner	19.00
1960	1	JPN	Takashi Ono	19.60
	2	JPN	Masao Takemoto	19.525
	3	URS	Boris Shakhlin	19.475
	15	USA	Abraham Grossfeld	18.95
1964	1	URS	Boris Shakhlin	19.625
	2	URS	Yuri Titov	19.550
	3	YUG	Miroslav Cerar	19.50
	28	USA	Makoto Sakamoto	18.75

MEN'S FLOOR EXERCISE

YEAR	RANK	CTRY	ATHLETE	TOTAL
1896–1928	(not held)			
1932	1	HUN	István Pelle	9.60
	2	SUI	Georges Miez	9.47
	3	ITA	Mario Lertora	9.23
	4	USA	Frank Haubold	9.00
1936	1	SUI	Georges Miez	18.666
	2	SUI	Josef Walter	18.50
	3	GER	Konrad Frey	18.466
	23	USA	George Wheeler	17.367

YEAR	RANK	CTRY	ATHLETE	TOTAL
1992	1	EUN	Vitali Scherbo	9.856
	2	EUN	Grigori Misioutine	9.781
	3	KOR	Ryul Yoo Ok	9.762
	31T	**USA**	**Scott Keswick**	**9.525**

MEN'S PARALLEL BARS

YEAR	RANK	CTRY	ATHLETE	TOTAL
1896	1	GER	Alfred Flatow	
	2	SUI	Jules Zutter	
	3	GER	Hermann Weingärtner	
(no USA entry)				
1900 (not held)				
1904	**1**	**USA**	**George Eyser**	**44**
	2	**USA**	**Anton Heida**	**43**
	3	**USA**	**John Duha**	**40**
1908-1920	(not held)			
1924	1	SUI	August Güttiner	21.63
	2	TCH	Robert Praak	21.61
	3	ITA	Giorgio Zampori	21.45
	32	**USA**	**Frank Kriz**	
1928	1	TCH	Ladislav Vácha	18.83
	2	YUG	Josip Primoi	18.50
	3	SUI	Hermann Hnggi	18.08
	25	**USA**	**Alfred Jochim**	**50.25**
1932	1	ITA	Romeo Neri	18.97
	2	HUN	István Pelle	18.60
	3	FIN	Heikki Savolainen	18.27
	6	**USA**	**Alfred Jochim**	**17.47**
1936	1	GER	Konrad Frey	19.067
	2	SUI	Michael Reusch	19.034
	3	GER	Alfred Schwarzmann	18.967
	30	**USA**	**Chester Phillips**	**17.400**
1948	1	SUI	Michael Reusch	19.75
	2	FIN	Veikko Huhtanen	19.65
	3	SUI	Christian Kipfer	19.55
	21	**USA**	**Edward Scrobe**	**37.80**
1952	1	SUI	Hans Eugster	19.65
	2	URS	Viktor Chukarin	19.60
	3	SUI	Josef Stalder	19.50
	21	**USA**	**Edward Scrobe**	**18.80**
1956	1	URS	Viktor Chukarin	19.20
	2	JPN	Masami Kubota	19.15
	3	JPN	Takashi Ono	19.10
	15	**USA**	**John Beckner**	**18.75**
1960	1	URS	Boris Shakhlin	19.40
	2	ITA	Giovanni Carminucci	19.375
	3	JPN	Takashi Ono	19.35
	26	**USA**	**John Beckner**	**18.70**
1964	1	JPN	Yukio Endo	19.675
	2	JPN	Shuji Tsurumi	19.45
	3	ITA	Franco Menichelli	19.35
	25	**USA**	**Makoto Sakamoto**	**18.90**
1968	1	JPN	Akinori Nakayama	19.475
	2	URS	Mikhail Voronin	19.425
	3	URS	Vladimir Klimenko	19.225
(USA best finish N/A - DNQ for finals)				
1972	1	JPN	Sawao Kato	19.475
	2	JPN	Shigeru Kasamatsu	19.375
	3	JPN	Eizo Kenmotsu	19.25
(USA best finish N/A - DNQ for finals)				
1976	1	JPN	Sawao Kato	19.675
	2	URS	Nikolai Andrianov	19.50
	3	JPN	Mitsuo Tsukahara	19.475
(USA best finish N/A - DNQ for finals)				
1980	1	URS	Aleksandr Tkachyov	19.775
	2	URS	Aleksandr Dityatin	19.75
	3	GDR	Roland Brückner	19.65
1984	**1**	**USA**	**Bart Conner**	**19.95**
	2	JPN	Nobuyuki Kajitani	19.925
	3	**USA**	**Mitchell Gaylord**	**19.85**
1988	1	URS	Vladimir Artemov	19.925
	2	URS	Valeri Lioukine	19.900
	3	GDR	Sven Tippelt	19.750
(USA best finish N/A - DNQ for finals)				
1992	1	EUN	Vitali Scherbo	9.900
	2	CHN	Li Jing	9.812
	3	CHN	Guo Linyao	9.800
	6	**USA**	**Jair Lynch**	**9.712**

MEN'S POMMEL HORSE

YEAR	RANK	CTRY	ATHLETE	TOTAL
1896	1	SUI	Jules Zutter	
	2	GER	Hermann Weingärtner	
	3	HUN	Gyula Kakas	
(no USA entry)				
1900 (not held)				
1904	**1**	**USA**	**Anton Heida**	**42**
	2	**USA**	**George Eyser**	**33**
	3	**USA**	**William Merz**	**29**
1908-1920	(not held)			
1924	1	SUI	Josef Wilhelm	21.23
	2	SUI	Jean Gutweniger	21.13
	3	SUI	Antoine Rebetez	20.73
	8	**USA**	**Frank Kriz**	
1928	1	SUI	Hermann Hänggi	19.75
	2	SUI	Georges Miez	19.25
	3	FIN	Heikki Savolainen	18.83
	7	**USA**	**Herman Witzie, Jr.**	**27.75**
1932	1	HUN	István Pelle	19.07
	2	ITA	Omero Bonoli	18.87
	3	**USA**	**Frank Haubold**	**18.57**
1936	1	GER	Konrad Frey	19.333
	2	SUI	Eugen Mack	19.167
	3	SUI	Albert Bachmann	19.067
	18	**USA**	**Frederick Meyer**	**18.166**
1948	1T	FIN	Paavo Aaltonen	19.35
	1T	FIN	Veikko Huhtanen	19.35
	1T	FIN	Heikki Savolainen	19.35
	6	**USA**	**Frank Cumiskey**	**18.95**
1952	1	URS	Viktor Chukarin	19.50
	2T	URS	Evgeny Korolkov	19.40
	2T	URS	Grant Shaginyan	19.40
	22	**USA**	**William Roetzheim**	**18.60**
1956	1	URS	Boris Shakhlin	19.25
	2	JPN	Takashi Ono	19.20
	3	URS	Viktor Chukarin	19.10
	25	**USA**	**John Beckner**	**18.40**
1960	1T	FIN	Eugen Ekman	19.375
	1T	URS	Boris Shakhlin	19.375
	3	JPN	Shuji Tsurumi	19.15
	8	**USA**	**Larry Banner**	**19.00**
1964	1	YUG	Miroslav Cerar	19.525
	2	JPN	Shuji Tsurumi	19.325
	3	URS	Yuri Tsapenko	19.20
	28	**USA**	**Arthur Shurlock**	**18.55**
1968	1	YUG	Miroslav Cerar	19.325
	2	FIN	Olli Eino Laiho	19.225
	3	URS	Mikhail Voronin	19.20
(USA best finish N/A - DNQ for finals)				
1972	1	URS	Viktor Klimenko	19.125
	2	JPN	Sawao Kato	19.00
	3	JPN	Eizo Kenmotsu	18.95
(USA best finish N/A - DNQ for finals)				
1976	1	HUN	Zoltán Magyar	19.70
	2	JPN	Eizo Kenmotsu	19.575
	3	URS	Nikolai Andrianov	19.525
(USA best finish N/A - DNQ for finals)				
1980	1	HUN	Zoltán Magyar	19.925
	2	URS	Aleksandr Dityatin	19.80
	3	GDR	Michael Nikolay	19.775
1984	1T	CHN	Li Ning	19.95
	1T	**USA**	**Peter Vidmar**	**19.95**
	3	**USA**	**Timothy Daggett**	**19.825**
1988	1T	BUL	Lyubomir Gueraskov	19.950
	1T	HUN	Zsolt Borkai	19.950
	1T	URS	Dmitri Bilozertchev	19.950
(USA best finish N/A - DNQ for finals)				
1992	1T	EUN	Vitali Scherbo	9.925
	1T	PRK	Pae Gil Su	9.925
	3	GER	Andreas Wecker	9.887
	5	**USA**	**Chris Waller**	**9.825**

MEN'S RINGS

YEAR	RANK	CTRY	ATHLETE	TOTAL
1896	1	GRE	Ioannis Mitropoulos	
	2	GER	Hermann Weingärtner	
	3	GRE	Petros Persakis	
(no USA entry)				
1900 (not held)				
1904	**1**	**USA**	**Hermann Glass**	**45**
	2	**USA**	**William Merz**	**35**
	3	**USA**	**Emil Voigt**	**32**
1908-1920	(not held)			
1924	1	ITA	Francesco Martino	21.553
	2	TCH	Robert Prazak	21.483
	3	TCH	Ladislav Vácha	21.43
	35	**USA**	**Frank Safanda**	
1928	1	YUG	Leon Stukelj	19.25
	2	TCH	Ladislav Vácha	19.17
	3	TCH	Emanuel Löffler	18.83
	7	**USA**	**Paul Krempel**	**18.17**
1932	**1**	**USA**	**George Gulack**	**18.97**
	2	**USA**	**William Denton**	**18.60**
	3	ITA	Giovanni Lattuada	18.50
1936	1	TCH	Alois Hudec	19.433
	2	YUG	Leon Stukelj	18.867
	3	GER	Matthias Volz	18.667
	52	**USA**	**Alfred Jochim**	**16.334**
1948	1	SUI	Karl Frei	19.80
	2	SUI	Michael Reusch	19.55
	3	TCH	Zdenek Ruzicka	19.25
	19	**USA**	**Raymond Sorenson**	**37.00**
1952	1	URS	Grant Shaginyan	19.75
	2	URS	Viktor Chukarin	19.55
	3	SUI	Hans Eugster	19.40
	45T	**USA**	**Edward Scrobe / Robert Stout**	**18.40**
1956	1	URS	Albert Azaryan	19.35
	2	URS	Valentin Muratov	19.15
	3	JPN	Masami Kubota	19.10
	17	**USA**	**Richard Beckner**	**18.65**
1960	1	URS	Albert Azaryan	19.725
	2	URS	Boris Shakhlin	19.50
	3	BUL	Velik Kapsazov	19.425
	21	**USA**	**Larry Banner**	**18.8**
1964	1	JPN	Takuji Haytta	19.475
	2	ITA	Franco Menichelli	19.425
	3	URS	Boris Shakhlin	19.40
	19	**USA**	**Makoto Sakamoto**	**18.80**
1968	1	JPN	Akinori Nakayama	19.45
	2	URS	Mikhail Voronin	19.325
	3	JPN	Sawao Kato	19.225
(USA best finish N/A - DNQ for finals)				
1972	1	JPN	Akinori Nakayama	19.35
	2	URS	Mikhail Voronin	19.275
	3	JPN	Mitsuo Tsukahara	19.225
(USA best finish N/A - DNQ for finals)				
1976	1	URS	Nikolai Andrianov	19.65
	2	URS	Aleksandr Dityatin	19.55
	3	ROM	D nut Grecu	19.50
(USA best finish N/A - DNQ for finals)				
1980	1	URS	Aleksandr Dityatin	19.875
	2	URS	Aleksandr Tkachyov	19.725
	3	TCH	Jiri Tabak	19.60
1984	1	JPN	Koji Gushiken	19.85
	2	CHN	Li Ning	19.85
	3	**USA**	**Mitchell Gaylord**	**19.825**
1988	1T	GDR	Holger Behrendt	19.925
	1T	URS	Dmitri Bilozertchev	19.925
	3	GDR	Sven Tippelt	19.875
(USA best finish N/A - DNQ for finals)				
1992	1	EUN	Vitali Scherbo	9.937
	2	CHN	Li Jing	9.875
	3	CHN	Li Xiaosahuang	9.862
	15T	**USA**	**Scott Keswick**	**9.775**

WOMEN'S TEAM COMPETITION

YEAR	RANK	CTRY	ATHLETES	TOTAL
1896-1924	(not held)			
1928	1	HOL		316.75
	2	ITA		289.00
	3	GBR		258.25
(no USA entry)				
1932 (not held)				
1936	1	GER		506.50
	2	TCH		503.60
	3	HUN		499.0
	5	**USA**	**Consetta Caruccio / Jennie Caputo / Irma Haubold / Margaret Duff / Ada Lunardoni / Adelaide Meyer / Mary Wright / Marie Kibler**	**471.60**
1948	1	TCH		445.45
	2	HUN		440.55
	3	**USA**	**Helen Schifano / Clara Schroth / Meta Elste / Marian Barone / Ladislava Bakanic / Consetta Lenz / Anita Simonis / Dorothy Dalton**	**422.63**
1952	1	URS		527.03
	2	HUN		520.96
	3	TCH		503.32
	15	**USA**	**Clara S. Lomady / Meta Elste / Marian Barone / Ruth Grulkowski / Dorothy Dalton / Ruth Topalian / Doris Kirkman / Marie Hoesly**	**471.41**
1956	1	URS		444.80
	2	HUN		443.500
	3	ROM		438.200
	9	**USA**	**Muriel Davis / Jacquelyn Klein / Judith Howe / Sandra Ruddick / Joyce Racek / Doris Fuchs**	**413.20**
1960	1	URS		382.320
	2	TCH		373.323
	3	ROM		372.053
	9	**USA**	**Doris Fuchs / Muriel Grossfeld / Betty Maycock / Theresa Montefusco / Sharon Richardson / Gail Sontgerath**	**363.053**
1964	1	URS		380.890
	2	TCH		379.989
	3	JPN		377.889
	9	**USA**	**Kathleen Corrigan / Muriel Grossfeld / Dale McClements / Linda Metheny / Janie Speaks / Marie Walther**	**367.321**
1968	1	URS		382.85
	2	TCH		382.20
	3	GDR		379.10
	6	**USA**	**Cathy Rigby / Linda Metheny / Joyce Tanac / Kathy Gleason / Colleen Mulvihill / Wendy Cluff**	**369.75**
1972	1	URS		380.50
	2	GDR		376.55
	3	HUN		368.25
	4	**USA**	**Cathy Rigby / Kimberly Chace / Roxanne Pierce / Linda Metheny / Joan Moore / Nancy Thies**	**365.90**
1976	1	URS		466.00
	2	ROM		462.35
	3	GDR		459.30
	6	**USA**	**Kimberly Chace / Debra Willcox / Leslie Wolfsberger / Colleen Casey / Carrie Englert / Doris Howard**	**448.20**
1980	1	URS		394.90
	2	ROM		393.50
	3	GDR		392.55
1984	1	ROM		392.02
	2	**USA**	**Mary Lou Retton / Julianne McNamara / Kathy Johnson / Michelle Dusserre / Tracee Talavera / Pamela Bileck**	**391.20**
	3	CHN		388.60
1988	1	URS		395.475
	2	ROM		394.125
	3	GDR		390.875
	4	**USA**	**Melissa Marlowe / Chelle Stack / Kelly Garrison-Steves / Theresa "Hope" Spivey / Brandy Johnson / Phoebe Mills**	**390.575**
1992	1	EUN		395.666
	2	ROM		395.079
	3	**USA**	**Wendy Bruce / Dominique Dawes / Shannon Miller / Betty Okino / Kerri Strug / Kim Zmeskal**	**394.704**

WOMEN'S INDIVIDUAL ALL-AROUND

YEAR	RANK	CTRY	ATHLETE	TOTAL
1896-1948	(not held)			
1952	1	URS	Maria Gorokhovskaya	76.78
	2	URS	Nina Bocharova	75.94
	3	HUN	Margit Korondi	75.82
	64	**USA**	**Marion Barone**	**69.30**
1956	1	URS	Larissa Latynina	74.933
	2	HUN	Ágnes Keleti	74.633
	3	URS	Sofia Muratova	74.466
	51	**USA**	**S.M. Ruddick**	**69.133**
1960	1	URS	Larissa Latynina	77.031
	2	URS	Sofia Muratova	76.696
	3	URS	Polina Astakhova	76.164
	28	**USA**	**Gail Sontegrath**	**73.097**
1964	1	TCH	Vera Cáslavská	77.564
	2	URS	Larissa Latynina	76.998
	3	URS	Polina Astakhova	76.965
	34	**USA**	**Dale McClements**	**74.065**
1968	1	TCH	Vera Cáslavská	78.25
	2	URS	Zinaida Voronina	76.85
	3	URS	Natalya Kuchinskaya	76.75
	16	**USA**	**Cathy Rigby**	**74.95**
1972	1	URS	Lyudmila Tourischeva	77.025
	2	GDR	Karin Janz	76.875
	3	URS	Tamara Lazakovitch	76.85
	10	**USA**	**Cathy Rigby**	**37.125**
1976	1	ROM	Nadia Comaneci	79.275
	2	URS	Nelli Kim	78.675
	3	URS	Lyudmila Tourischeva	78.625
	14	**USA**	**Kimberly Chace**	**75.875**
1980	1	URS	Yelena Davydova	79.15
	2	ROM	Nadia Comaneci	79.075
	2	GDR	Maxi Gnauck	79.075
1984	**1**	**USA**	**Mary Lou Retton**	**79.175**
	2	ROM	Ecaterina Szabó	79.125
	3	ROM	Simona Pauca	78.675
1988	1	URS	Elena Shoushounova	79.662
	2	ROM	Daniela Silivas	79.637
	3	URS	Svetlana Boguinskaia	79.40
	10	**USA**	**Brandy Johnson**	**78.525**
1992	1	EUN	Tatiana Goutsou	39.737
	2	**USA**	**Shannon Miller**	**39.725**
	3	ROM	Lavinia Milosovici	39.687

WOMEN'S BALANCE BEAM

YEAR	RANK	CTRY	ATHLETE	TOTAL
1896-1948	(not held)			
1952	1	URS	Nina Bocharova	19.22
	2	URS	Maria Gorokhovskaya	19.13
	3	HUN	Margit Korondi	19.02
	48	**USA**	**Ruth Grulkowski**	**17.46**
1956	1	HUN	Ágnes Keleti	18.80
	2	TCH	Eva Bosáková	18.633
	3	URS	Tamara Manina	18.633
	32	**USA**	**Muriel Davis**	**17.60**
1960	1	TCH	Eva Bosáková	19.283
	2	URS	Larissa Latynina	19.233
	3	URS	Sofia Muratova	19.232
	21	**USA**	**Gail Sontegrath**	**18.33**
1964	1	TCH	Vera Cáslavská	19.449
	2	URS	Tamara Manina	19.399
	3	URS	Larissa Latynina	19.382
	24	**USA**	**Linda Jo Metheny**	**18.699**

1968	1	URS	Natalya Kuchinskaya	19.65
	2	TCH	Vera Cáslavská	19.575
	3	URS	Larissa Petrik	19.25
	4	**USA**	**Linda Metheny**	**19.225**
1972	1	URS	Olga Korbut	19.40
	2	URS	Tamara Lazakovitch	19.375
	3	GDR	Karin Janz	18.975
(USA best finish N/A - DNQ for finals)				
1976	1	ROM	Nadia Comaneci	19.95
	2	URS	Olga Korbut	19.725
	3	ROM	Teodora Ungureanu	19.70
(USA best finish N/A - DNQ for finals)				
1980	1	ROM	Nadia Comaneci	19.80
	2	URS	Yelena Davydova	19.75
	3	URS	Natalya Shaposhnikova	19.725
1984	1	ROM	Simona Pauca	19.80
	2	ROM	Ecaterina Szabó	19.80
	3	**USA**	**Kathy Johnson**	**19.65**
1988	1	ROM	Daniela Silivas	19.924
	2	URS	Elena Shoushounova	19.875
	3T	**USA**	**Phoebe Mills**	**19.837**
	3T	ROM	Gabriela Potorac	19.837
1992	1	EUN	Tatiana Lyssenko	9.975
	2T	CHN	Li Lu	9.912
	2T	**USA**	**Shannon Miller**	**9.912**

WOMEN'S FLOOR EXERCISE

YEAR	RANK	CTRY	ATHLETE	TOTAL
1896-1948	(not held)			
1952	1	HUN	Ágnes Keleti	19.36
	2	URS	Maria Gorokhovskaya	19.20
	3	HUN	Margit Korondi	19.00
	28	**USA**	**Clara Lomady**	**18.06**
1956	1T	HUN	Ágnes Keleti	18.733
	1T	URS	Larissa Latynina	18.733
	3	ROM	Elena Leustean	18.70
	25	**USA**	**Muriel Davis**	**18.133**
1960	1	URS	Larissa Latynina	19.583
	2	URS	Polina Astakhova	19.532
	3	URS	Tamara Lyukhina	19.449
	19	**USA**	**Muriel Grossfeld**	**18.86**
1964	1	URS	Larissa Latynina	19.599
	2	URS	Polina Astakhova	19.50
	3	HUN	Anikó Jánosi-Ducza	19.30
	17	**USA**	**Muriel Grossfeld**	**18.866**
1968	1T	TCH	Vera Cáslavská	19.675
	1T	URS	Larissa Petrik	19.675
	3	URS	Natalya Kuchinskaya	19.6
(USA best finish N/A - DNQ for finals)				
1972	1	URS	Olga Korbut	19.575
	2	URS	Lyudmila Tourischeva	19.55
	3	URS	Tamara Lazakovitch	19.45
(USA best finish N/A - DNQ for finals)				
1976	1	URS	Nelli Kim	19.85
	2	URS	Lyudmila Tourischeva	19.825
	3	ROM	Nadia Comaneci	19.75
(USA best finish N/A - DNQ for finals)				
1980	1	ROM	Nadia Comaneci	19.875
	1	URS	Nelli Kim	19.875
	3	GDR	Maxi Gnauck	19.825
1984	1	ROM	Ecaterina Szabó	19.975
	2	**USA**	**Julianne McNamara**	**19.95**
	3	**USA**	**Mary Lou Retton**	**19.775**
1988	1	ROM	Daniela Silivas	19.937
	2	URS	Svetlana Boguinskaia	19.887
	3	BUL	Diana Doudeva	19.850
	6	**USA**	**Phoebe Mills**	**19.662**
1992	1	ROM	Lavinia Corina Milosovici	10.00
	2	HUN	Henrietta Onodi	9.950
	3T	EUN	Tatiana Goutsou	9.912
	3T	ROM	Christina Bontas	9.912
	3T	**USA**	**Shannon Miller**	**9.912**

WOMEN'S UNEVEN BARS

YEAR	RANK	CTRY	ATHLETE	TOTAL
1896-1948	(not held)			
1952	1	HUN	Margit Korondi	19.40
	2	URS	Maria Gorokhovskaya	19.26
	3	HUN	Ágnes Keleti	19.16
	43	**USA**	**Marian Barone**	**17.69**
1956	1	HUN	Ágnes Keleti	18.966
	2	URS	Larissa Latynina	18.833
	3	URS	Sofia Muratova	18.80
	46	**USA**	**S.M. Ruddick**	**17.33**
1960	1	URS	Polina Astakhova	19.616
	2	URS	Larissa Latynina	19.416
	3	URS	Tamara Lyukhina	19.399
	8	**USA**	**Doris Fuchs**	**19.0**
1964	1	URS	Polina Astakhova	19.332
	2	HUN	Katalin Makray	19.216
	3	URS	Larissa Latynina	19.199
	19	**USA**	**Linda Jo Metheny**	**18.70**

1968	1	TCH	Vera Cáslavská	19.65
	2	GDR	Karin Janz	19.50
	3	URS	Zinaida Voronina	19.425
	12	**USA**	**Cathy Rigby**	**18.90**
1972	1	GDR	Karin Janz	19.675
	2T	URS	Olga Korbut	19.45
	2T	GDR	Erika Zuchold	19.45
(USA best finish N/A - DNQ for finals)				
1976	1	ROM	Nadia Comaneci	20.00
	2	ROM	Teodora Ungureanu	19.80
	3	HUN	Márta Egervári	19.775
(USA best finish N/A - DNQ for finals)				
1980	1	GDR	Maxi Gnauck	19.875
	2	ROM	Emilia Eberle	19.85
	3	URS	Maria Filatova	19.775
1984	1T	CHN	Ma Yanhong	19.95
	1T	**USA**	**Julianne McNamara**	**19.95**
	3	**USA**	**Mary Lou Retton**	**19.80**
1988	1	ROM	Daniela Silivas	20.000
	2	GDR	Dagmar Kersten	19.987
	3	URS	Elena Shoushounova	19.962
	8	**USA**	**Phoebe Mills**	**19.787**
1992	1	CHN	Li Lu	10.00
	2	EUN	Tatiana Goutsou	9.975
	3	**USA**	**Shannon Miller**	**9.962**

WOMEN'S VAULT

YEAR	RANK	CTRY	ATHLETE	TOTAL
1896-1948	(not held)			
1952	1	URS	Yekaterina Kalinchuk	19.20
	2	URS	Maria Gorokhovskaya	19.19
	3	URS	Galina Minaicheva	19.16
	58	**USA**	**Ruth Topalian**	**17.92**
1956	1	URS	Larissa Latynina	18.833
	2	URS	Tamara Manina	18.80
	3	SWE	Ann-Sofi Colling-Pettersson	18.733
	32	**USA**	**Joyce Racek**	**18.033**
1960	1	URS	Margarita Nikolayeva	19.316
	2	URS	Sofia Muratova	19.049
	3	URS	Larissa Latynina	19.016
	9	**USA**	**Sharon Richardson**	**18.53**
1964	1	TCH	Vera Cáslavská	19.483
	2T	URS	Larissa Latynina	19.283
	2T	GDR	Birgit Radochla	19.283
	18	**USA**	**Dale McClements**	**18.867**
1968	1	TCH	Vera Cáslavská	19.775
	2	GDR	Erika Zuchold	19.625
	3	URS	Zinaida Voronina	19.50
	28	**USA**	**Kathy Gleason**	**18.60**
1972	1	GDR	Karin Janz	19.525
	2	GDR	Erika Zuchold	19.275
	3	URS	Lyudmila Tourischeva	19.25
(USA best finish N/A - DNQ for finals)				
1976	1	URS	Nelli Kim	19.80
	2T	GDR	Carola Dombeck	19.65
	2T	URS	Lyudmila Tourischeva	19.65
(USA best finish N/A - DNQ for finals)				
1980	1	URS	Natalya Shaposhnikova	19.725
	2	GDR	Steffi Kräker	19.675
	3	ROM	Melita Rühn	19.65
1984	1	ROM	Ecaterina Szabó	19.875
	2	**USA**	**Mary Lou Retton**	**19.85**
	3	ROM	Lavinia Agache	19.75
1988	1	URS	Svetlana Boguinskaia	19.905
	2	ROM	Gabriela Potorac	19.830
	3	ROM	Daniela Silivas	19.818
	5	**USA**	**Brandy Johnson**	**19.774**
1992	1T	HUN	Henrietta Onodi	9.925
	1T	ROM	Lavinia Milosovici	9.925
	3	EUN	Tatiana Lyssenko	9.912
	6	**USA**	**Shannon Miller**	**9.837**

RHYTHMIC ALL-AROUND

YEAR	RANK	CTRY	ATHLETE	TOTAL
1896-1980	(not held)			
1984	1	CAN	Lori Fung	57.950
	2	ROM	Doina Staiculescu	57.900
	3	GER	Regina Weber	57.700
	11	**USA**	**Valerie Zimring**	**56.250**
1988	1	URS	Marina Lobatch	60.000
	2	BUL	Adriana Dounavska	59.950
	3	URS	Alexandra Timochenko	59.875
		USA	**Michelle Berube**	
1992	1	EUN	Alexandra Timoshenko	59.037
	2	ESP	Carolina Pascual	58.100
	3	EUN	Oksan Skaldina	57.912
	23	**USA**	**Jenifer Lovell**	**18.062**

JUDO

MEN'S EXTRA LIGHTWEIGHT (60 KG/132 LBS)

YEAR	RANK	CTRY	ATHLETE	
1896-1976	(not held)			
1980	1	FRA	Thierry Rey	
	2	CUB	Rafael Rodriguez Carbenell	
	3T	URS	Aramby Emizh	
	3T	HUN	Tibor Kincses	
1984	1	JPN	Shinji Hosokawa	
	2	KOR	Kim Jae-yup	
	3T	GBR	Neil Eckersley	
	3T	**USA**	**Edward Liddie**	
1988	1	KOR	Kim Jae-yup	
	2	**USA**	**Kevin Asano**	
	3T	JPN	Shinji Hosokawa	
	3T	URS	Amiran Totikachvili	
1992	1	EUN	Nazim Gousseinov	
	2	KOR	Hyun Yoon	
	3	JPN	Tadanori Koshino	
		USA	**Tony Okada**	

MEN'S HALF LIGHTWEIGHT (65 KG/143 LBS)

YEAR	RANK	CTRY	ATHLETE	
1896-1976	(not held)			
1980	1	URS	Nikolai Solodukhin	
	2	MON	Tsendying Damdin	
	3T	BUL	Iliyan Nedkov	
	3T	POL	Janusz Pawlowski	
1984	1	JPN	Yoshiyuki Matsuoka	
	2	KOR	Hwang Jung-oh	
	3T	FRA	Marc Alexandre	
	3T	AUT	Josef Reiter	
		USA	**Craig Agina**	**elim. 1st rd**
1988	1	KOR	Lee Kyung-keun	
	2	POL	Janusz Pawlowski	
	3T	FRA	Bruno Carabetta	
	3T	JPN	Yosuke Yamamoto	
		USA	**Joe Marchal**	
1992	1	BRA	Rogerio Sampaio Cardoso	
	2	HUN	Jozsef Csak	
	3T	GER	Udo Gunter Quellmalz	
	3T	CUB	Israel Hernandez Planas	
		USA	**James Pedro**	

MEN'S LIGHTWEIGHT (71 KG/156 LBS)

YEAR	RANK	CTRY	ATHLETE	
1896-1960	(not held)			
1964	1	JPN	Takehide Nakatani	
	2	SUI	Eric Hänni	
	3T	URS	Aron Bogolyubov	
	3T	URS	Oleg Stepanov	
		USA	**Paul Maruyama**	**elim. 1st rd**
1968	(not held)			
1972	1	JPN	Takao Kawaguchi	
		MON	Bakhaavaa Buidaa	
	3T	PRK	Kim Yong Ik	
	3T	FRA	Jean-Jacques Mounier	
		USA	**Kenneth Okada**	**elim. 1st rd**
1976	1	CUB	Hector Rodriguez Torres	
	2	KOR	Chang Eun-kyung	
	3T	ITA	Felice Mariani	
	3T	HUN	József Tuncsik	
		USA	**Joseph Bost**	**elim. 1st rd**
1980	1	ITA	Ezio Gamba	
	2	GBR	Neil Adams	
	3T	MON	Ravdan Davaadalai	
	3T	GDR	Karl-Heinz Lehmann	
1984	1	KOR	Ahn Byeong-keun	
	2	ITA	Ezio Gamba	
	3T	GBR	Kerrith Brown	
	3T	BRA	Luis Onmura	
		USA	**Michael Swain**	**elim. 3rd rd**
1988	1	FRA	Marc Alexandre	
	2	GDR	Sven Loll	
	3T*	**USA**	**Michael Swain**	
	3T	URS	Gueogui Tenadze	

*Kerrith Brown (GBR), original bronze medalist, tested positive for use of a banned substance

1992	1	JPN	Toshihiko Koga	
	2	HUN	Bertalan Hajtos	
	3	ISR	Shay Oren Smadga	
		USA	**Mike Swain**	

MEN'S HALF MIDDLEWEIGHT (78 KG/172 LBS)

YEAR	RANK	CTRY	ATHLETE	
1896-1968	(not held)			
1972	1	JPN	Toyokazu Nomura	
	2	POL	Antoni Zajkowski	
	3T	GDR	Dietmar Hötger	
	3T	URS	Anatoli Novikov	
		USA	**Patrick Burris**	**elim. 1st rd**
1976	1	URS	Vladimir Nevzorov	
	2	JPN	Koji Kuramoto	
	3T	POL	Marian Talaj	
	3T	FRA	Patrick Vial	
		USA	**Patrick Burris**	**elim. 2nd rd**
1980	1	URS	Shota Khabareli	
	2	CUB	Juan Ferrer La Hera	
	3	GDR	Harald Heinke	
	3	FRA	Bernard Tchoullouyan	
1984	1	GER	Frank Wieneke	
	2	GBR	Neil Adams	
	3T	ROM	Mircea Fratiç	
	3T	FRA	Michel Nowak	
		USA	**Brett Barron**	**elim. 1st rd**
1988	1	POL	Waldemar Legien	
	2	FRG	Frank Wieneke	
	3T	GDR	Torsten Brechot	
	3T	URS	Bachir Varaev	
		USA	**Jason Morris**	
1992	1	JPN	Hidehiko Yoshida	
	2	**USA**	**Jason Morris**	
	3	FRA	Bertrand Damaisin	

MEN'S MIDDLEWEIGHT (86 KG/189 LBS)

YEAR	RANK	CTRY	ATHLETE	
1896-1960	(not held)			
1964	1	JPN	Isao Okano	
	2	GER	Wolfgang Hofmann	
	3T	**USA**	**James Bregman**	
	3T	KOR	Kim Eui-tae	
1968	(not held)			
1972	1	JPN	Shinobu Sekine	
	2	KOR	Oh Seung-jip	
	3T	FRA	Jean-Paul Coché	
	3T	GBR	Brian Jacks	
		USA	**Irwin Cohen**	**elim. 1st rd**
1976	1	JPN	Isamu Sonoda	
	2	URS	Valery Dvoinikov	
	3T	YUG	Slavko Obadov	
	3T	KOR	Park Young-chul	
(no USA entry)				
1980	1	SUI	Jürg Röthlisberger	
	2	CUB	Isaac Azcuy Oliva	
	3T	URS	Aleksandr Iatskevich	
	3T	GDR	Detlef Ultsch	
1984	1	AUT	Peter Seisenbacher	
	2	**USA**	**Robert Berland**	
	3T	BRA	Walter Carmona	
	3T	JPN	Seiki Nose	
1988	1	AUT	Peter Seisenbacher	
	2	URS	Vladmir Chestakov	
	3T	HOL	Ben Spijkers	
	3T	JPN	Akinobu Osaka	
		USA	**Rene Capo**	
1992	1	POL	Waldemar Legien	
	2	FRA	Pascal Tayot	
	3T	JPN	Hirotaka Okada	
	3T	CAN	Nicolas Gill	
		USA	**Joey Wanag**	

MEN'S HALF HEAVYWEIGHT (95 KG/209 LBS)

YEAR	RANK	CTRY	ATHLETE	
1896-1968	(not held)			
1972	1	URS	Shota Chochoshvili	
	2	GBR	David Starbrook	
	3T	GER	Paul Barth	
	3T	BRA	Chiaki Ishii	
	5	**USA**	**James Wooley**	
1976	1	JPN	Kazuhiro Ninomiya	
	2	URS	Ramaz Harshiladze	
	3T	SUI	Jürg Röthlisberger	
	3T	GBR	David Starbrook	
		USA	**Tommy Martin**	**elim. 3rd rd**
1980	1	BEL	Robert van de Walle	
	2	URS	Tengiz Khubuluri	
	3T	GDR	Dietmar Lorenz	
	3T	HOL	Henk Numan	
1984	1	KOR	Ha Hyoung-zoo	
	2	BRA	Douglas Vieira	
	3T	ICE	Bjarni Fridriksson	
	3T	GER	Günter Neureuther	
		USA	**Leo White**	**elim. 3rd rd**

1988	1	BRA	Aurelio Miguel	
	2	FRG	Marc Meiling	
	3T	BEL	Robert Van De Walle	
	3T	GBR	Dennis Stewart	
		USA	**Bob Berland**	
1992	1	HUN	Antal Kovacs	
	2	GBR	Raymond Stevens	
	3T	EUN	Dmitri Sergeev	
	3T	NED	Theo Meijer	
		USA	**Leo White**	

MEN'S HEAVYWEIGHT (+95 KG/+209 LBS)

YEAR	RANK	CTRY	ATHLETE	
1896-1960	(not held)			
1964	1	JPN	Isao Inokuma	
	2	CAN	Alfred Douglas Rogers	
	3T	URS	Anzor Kiknadze	
	3T	URS	Parnaoz Chikviladze	
		USA	**George L. Harris**	
1968	(not held)			
1972	1	HOL	Willem Ruska	
	2	GER	Klaus Glahn	
	3T	JPN	Motoki Nishimura	
	3T	URS	Givi Onashvili	
	5	**USA**	**Douglas Nelson**	
1976	1	URS	Sergei Novikov	
	2	GER	Günther Neureuther	
	3T	**USA**	**Allen Coage**	
	3T	JPN	Sumio Endo	
1980	1	FRA	Angelo Parisi	
	2	BUL	Dimitur Zapryanov	
	3T	YUG	Radomir Kovacevic	
	3T	TCH	Vladimir Kocman	
1984	1	JPN	Hitoshi Saito	
	2	FRA	Angelo Parisi	
	3T	CAN	Mark Berger	
	3T	KOR	Cho Yong-chul	
	5	**USA**	**Doug Nelson**	
1988	1	JPN	Hitoshi Saito	
	2	GDR	Henry Stoehr	
	3T	KOR	Cho Yong-chul	
	3T	URS	Grigori Veritchev	
		USA	**Steve Cohen**	
1992	1	EUN	David Khakhaleichvili	
	2	JPN	Naoya Ogawa	
	3T	FRA	David Douillet	
	3T	HUN	Imre Csosz	
	7T	**USA**	**Damon Keeve**	

OPEN

YEAR	RANK	CTRY	ATHLETE	
1896-1960	(not held)			
1964	1	HOL	Antonius Geesink	
	2	JPN	Akio Kaminaga	
	3T	AUS	Theodore Boronovskis	
	3T	GER	Klaus Glahn	
		USA	**Ben Campbell**	**inj. - elim. 2nd rd**
1968	(not held)			
1972	1	HOL	Willem Ruska	
	2	URS	Vitali Kusnezov	
	3T	FRA	Jean-Claude Brondani	
	3T	GBR	Angelo Parisi	
		USA	**Johnny Watts**	**elim. 3rd rd**
1976	1	JPN	Haruki Uemura	
	2	GBR	Keith Remfry	
	3T	KOR	Jeaki Cho	
	3T	URS	Shota Chochoshvilli	
		USA	**James Wooley**	**elim. 2nd rd**
1980	1	GDR	Dietmar Lorenz	
	2	FRA	Angelo Parisi	
	3T	GBR	Arthur Mapp	
	3T	HUN	András Ozsvár	
1984	1	JPN	Yasuhiro Yamashita	
	2	EGY	Mohamed Ali Rashwan	
	3T	ROM	Mihai Cioc	
	3T	GER	Arthur Schnabel	
		USA	**Dewey Mitchell**	**elim. 1st rd**

WOMEN'S EXTRA LIGHTWEIGHT (48 KG/106 LBS)

YEAR	RANK	CTRY	ATHLETE	
1896-1988	(not held)			
1992	1	FRA	Cecile Nowak	
	2	JPN	Ryoko Tamura	
	3T	TUR	Huya Senyurt	
	3T	CUB	Amarilis Savon Carmenaty	
		USA	**Valerie Lafon**	**DNC**

WOMEN'S HALF LIGHTWEIGHT (52 KG/114 LBS)

YEAR	RANK	CTRY	ATHLETE
1896-1988	(not held)		
1992	1	ESP	Almudena Munoz Martinez
	2	JPN	Noriko Mizoguchi
	3T	CHN	Li Zhongyun
	3T	GBR	Sharon Rendle
		USA	**Jo Quiring**

WOMEN'S LIGHTWEIGHT (56 KG/123 LBS)

YEAR	RANK	CTRY	ATHLETE
1896-1988	(not held)		
1992	1	ESP	Miriam Blasco Soto
	2	GBR	Nicola Kim Fairbrother
	3T	JPN	Chiyori Tateno
	3T	CUB	Driulis Gonzalez Morales
	5T	**USA**	**Kate Marie Donahoo**

WOMEN'S HALF MIDDLEWEIGHT (61 KG/134 LBS)

YEAR	RANK	CTRY	ATHLETE
1896-1988	(not held)		
1992	1	FRA	Catherine Fleury
	2	ISR	Yael Arad
	3T	CHN	Di Zhang
	3T	EUN	Elena Petrova
		USA	**Lynn Roethke**

WOMEN'S MIDDLEWEIGHT (66 KG/145 LBS)

YEAR	RANK	CTRY	ATHLETE
1896-1988	(not held)		
1992	1	CUB	Odalis Reve Jimenez
	2	ITA	Emanuela Pierantozzi
	3T	BEL	Heidi Rakels
	3T	GBR	Kate Howey
	7T	**USA**	**Grace L. Jividen**

WOMEN'S HALF HEAVYWEIGHT (72 KG/158 LBS)

YEAR	RANK	CTRY	ATHLETE
1896-1988	(not held)		
1992	1	KOR	Kim Mi-jung
	2	JPN	Yoko Tanabe
	3T	NED	Irene de Kok
	3T	FRA	Laetitia Meignan
		USA	**Sandra Bacher**

WOMEN'S HEAVYWEIGHT (+72 KG/+158 LBS)

YEAR	RANK	CTRY	ATHLETE
1896-1988	(not held)		
1992	1	CHN	Zhuang Xiaoyan
	2	CUB	Este Rodriguez
	3T	FRA	Natalia Lupino
	3T	JPN	Yoko Sakaue
		USA	**Colleen Rosensteel**

MODERN PENTATHLON

INDIVIDUAL

YEAR	RANK	CTRY	ATHLETE	TOTAL
1896-1908	(not held)			
1912	1	SWE	Gösta Lilliehöök	27
	2	SWE	Gösta Åsbrink	28
	3	SWE	George de Laval	30
	5	**USA**	**George Patton**	**41**
1920	1	SWE	Gustaf Dryssen	18
	2	SWE	Erik de Laval	23
	3	SWE	Gösta Runö	27
	6	**USA**	**Harold Rayner**	**48**
1924	1	SWE	Bo Lindman	18
	2	SWE	Gustaf Dryssen	39.5
	3	SWE	Bertil Uggla	45
	10	**USA**	**Lt. George Bane**	**52**
1928	1	SWE	Sven Thofelt	47
	2	SWE	Bo Lindman	50
	3	GER	Helmuth Kahl	52
	15	**USA**	**Lt. A.S. Newmann**	**83**
1932	1	SWE	Johan Oxenstierna	32
	2	SWE	Bo Lindman	35.5
	3	**USA**	**Richard Mayo**	**38.5**
1936	1	GER	Gothardt Handrick	31.5
	2	**USA**	**Charles Leonard**	**39.5**
	3	ITA	Silvano Abba	45.5
1948	1	SWE	William "Willie" Grut	16
	2	**USA**	**George Moore**	**47**
	3	SWE	Gösta Gärdin	49
1952	1	SWE	Lars Hall	32
	2	HUN	Gábor Benedek	39
	3	HUN	István Szondy	41
	5T	**USA**	**Frederick Denman**	**62**
1956	1	SWE	Lars Hall	4833
	2	FIN	Olavi Mannonen	4774
	3	FIN	Väinö Korhonen	4750
	5	**USA**	**George Lambert**	**4693**
1960	1	HUN	Férenc Németh	5024
	2	HUN	Imre Nagy	4988
	3	**USA**	**Robert Beck**	**4981**
1964	1	HUN	Ferenc Török	5116
	2	URS	Igor Novikov	5067
	3	URS	Albert Mokeyev	5039
	6	**USA**	**James Moore**	**4891**
1968	1	SWE	Björn Ferm	4964
	2	HUN	András Balczó	4953
	3	URS	Pavel Lednev	4795
	11	**USA**	**James Moore**	
1972	1	HUN	András Baclzó	5412
	2	URS	Boris Onischenko	5335
	3	URS	Pavel Lednev	5328
	9	**USA**	**Charles Richards**	**5074**
1976	1	POL	Janusz Pyciak-Peciak	5520
	2	URS	Pavel Lednev	5485
	3	TCH	Jan Bártu	5466
	6	**USA**	**John Fitzgerald**	**5286**
1980	1	URS	Anatoly Starostin	5568
	2	HUN	Tamás Szombathelyi	5502
	3	URS	Pavel Lednev	5382
1984	1	ITA	Daniele Masala	5469
	2	SWE	Svante Rasmuson	5456
	3	ITA	Carlo Massullo	5406
	5	**USA**	**Michael Storm**	**5325**
1988	1	HUN	Janos Martinek	5404
	2	ITA	Carlo Massullo	5379
	3	URS	Vakhtang Iagorachvili	5367
	18	**USA**	**Robert Nieman**	**5034**
1992	1	POL	Arkadiusz Skrzypaszek	5559
	2	HUN	Attila Mizser	5446
	3	EUN	Edouard Zenovka	5361
	9	**USA**	**J. Mike Gostigian**	**5275**

TEAM

YEAR	RANK	CTRY	ATHLETES	POINTS
1896-1948	(not held)			
1952	1	HUN		166
	2	SWE		182
	3	FIN		213
	4	**USA**	**Frederick Denman / W. Thad McArthur / Guy Troy**	**215**
1956	1	URS		13690.5
	2	**USA**	**George Lambert / William André / Jack Daniels**	**13482**
	3	FIN		13185.5
1960	1	HUN		14863
	2	URS		14309
	3	**USA**	**Robert Beck / Jack Daniels / George Lambert**	**14192**
1964	1	URS		14961
	2	**USA**	**James Moore / David Kirkwood / Paul Pesthy**	**14189**
	3	HUN		14173
1968	1	HUN		14325
	2	URS		14248
		SWE		14188
	3	FRA		13289
	4	**USA**	**James Moore / Robert Beck / M. Thomas Lough**	**13280**
1972	1	URS		15968
	2	HUN		15348
	3	FIN		14812
	4	**USA**	**Charles Richards / John Fitzgerald / Scott Taylor**	**14802**
1976	1	GBR		15559
	2	TCH		15451
	3	HUN		15395
	5	**USA**	**John Fitzgerald / Michael Burley / Robert Nieman**	**15285**
1980	1	URS		16126
	2	HUN		15912
	3	SWE		15845
1984	1	ITA		16066
	2	**USA**	**Michael Storm / Robert Gregory Losey / Dean Glenesk**	**15568**
	3	FRA		15565
1988	1	HUN		15886
	2	ITA		15571
	3	GBR		15276
	16	**USA**	**Robert Nieman / Robert Stull / Michael Gostigian**	**13645**
1992	1	POL		16018
	2	EUN		15924
	3	ITA		15760
	4	**USA**	**Mike Gostigian / Jim Haley / Rob Stull**	**15649**

ROWING

MEN'S SINGLE SCULLS

YEAR	RANK	CTRY	ATHLETE	TIME
1896	(not held)			
1900	1	FRA	Henri Barrelet	7:35.6
	2	FRA	André Gaudin	7:41.6
	3	GBR	George Saint Ashe	8:15.6
(no USA entry)				
1904	**1**	**USA**	**Frank Greer**	**10:08.5**
	2	**USA**	**James Juvenal**	
	3	**USA**	**Constance Titus**	
1906	(not held)			
1908	1	GBR	Harry Blackstaffe	9:26.0
	2	GBR	Alexander McCulloch	
	3	GER	Bernhard von Gaza	
(no USA entry)				
1912	1	GBR	William Kinnear	7:47.6
	2	BEL	Polydore Veirman	7:56.0
	3T	CAN	Everard Butler	
	3T	RUS	Mikhail Kusik	
(no USA entry)				
1920	**1**	**USA**	**John Kelly, Sr.**	**7:35.0**
	2	GBR	Jack Beresford	7:36.0
	3	NZL	D. Clarence Hadfield d'Arcy	7:48.0
1924	1	GBR	Jack Beresford	7:49.2
	2	**USA**	**William Garrett Gilmore**	**7:54.0**
	3	SUI	Josef Schneider	8:01.1
1928	1	AUS	Henry Pearce	7:11.0
	2	**USA**	**Kenneth Myers**	**7:20.8**
	3	GBR	Theodore Collet	7:29.8
1932	1	AUS	Henry Pearce	7:44.4
	2	**USA**	**William Miller**	**7:45.2**
	3	URU	Guillermo Douglas	8:13.6
1936	1	GER	Gustav Schäfer	8:21.5
	2	AUT	Josef Hasenöhrl	8:25.8
	3	**USA**	**Daniel Barrow**	**8:28.0**
1948	1	AUS	Mervyn Wood	7:24.4
	2	URU	Eduardo Risso	7:38.2
	3	ITA	Romolo Catasta	7:51.4
	4T	**USA**	**John Kelly, Jr.**	
1952	1	URS	Yuri Tyukalov	8:12.8
	2	AUS	Mervyn Wood	8:14.5
	3	POL	Teodor Kocerka	8:19.4
		USA	**John Kelly, Jr (7:42.0)**	**elim. semis**
1956	1	URS	Vyacheslav Ivanov	8:02.5
	2	AUS	Stuart Mackenzie	8:07.7
	3	**USA**	**John Kelly, Jr.**	**8:11.8**
1960	1	URS	Vyacheslav Ivanov	7:13.96
	2	GDR	Achim Hill	7:20.21
	3	POL	Teodor Kocerka	7:21.26
	5	**USA**	**Harry Parker**	**7:29.26**
1964	1	URS	Vyacheslav Ivanov	8:22.51
	2	GDR	Achim Hill	8:26.24
	3	SUI	Gottfried Kottmann	8:29.68
	6	**USA**	**Donald Spero**	**8:37.53**
1968	1	HOL	Henri Jan Wienese	7:47.80
	2	GER	Jochen Meissner	7:52.00
	3	ARG	Alberto Demiddi	7:57.19
	4	**USA**	**John Van Blom**	**8:00.51**
1972	1	URS	Yuri Malishev	7:10.12
	2	ARG	Alberto Demiddi	7:11.53
	3	GDR	Wolfgang Güldenpfennig	7:14.45
	5	**USA**	**James Dietz**	**7:24.81**
1976	1	FIN	Pertti Karppinen	7:29.03
	2	GER	Peter-Michael Kolbe	7:31.67
	3	GDR	Joachim Dreifke	7:38.03
	7	**USA**	**James Dietz**	
1980	1	FIN	Pertti Karppinen	7:09.61
	2	URS	Vassily Yakusha	7:11.6
	3	GDR	Peter Kersten	7:14.88
1984	1	FIN	Pertti Karppinen	7:00.24
	2	GER	Peter-Michael Kolbe	7:02.19
	3	CAN	Robert Mills	7:10.38
	4	**USA**	**John Biglow**	**7:12.00**
1988	1	GDR	Thomas Lange	6:49.86
	2	FRG	Peter Michael Kolbe	6:54.77
	3	NZL	Eric Verdonk	6:58.66
	6	**USA**	**Andrew Sudduth**	**7:11.45**
1992	1	GER	Thomas Lange	6:51.40
	2	TCH	Vaclav Chalupa	6:52.93
	3	POL	Kajetan Broniewski	6:56.82
	19	**USA**	**Greg Walker**	**7:12.32**

MEN'S DOUBLE SCULLS

YEAR	RANK	CTRY	ATHLETES	TIME
1896-1900	(not held)			
1904	1	USA	John Mulcahy / William Varley	10.03.2
	2	USA	John Hoben / James McLoughlin	
	3	USA	John Wells / Joseph Ravanack	
1906-1912	(not held)			
1920	1	USA	John Kelly, Sr. / Paul Costello	7:09.0
	2	ITA	Erminio Donex / Pietro Annoni	7:19.0
	3	FRA	Alfred Pié / Gaston Giran	7:21.0
1924	1	USA	Paul Costello / John Kelly, Sr.	6:34.0
	2	FRA	Marc Detton / Jean-Pierre Stock	6:38.0
	3	SUI	Rudolf Bosshard / Heinrich Thoma	
1928	1	USA	Paul Costello / Charles McIlvaine	6:41.4
	2	CAN	Joseph Wright / Jack Guest	6:51.0
	3	AUT	Leo Losert / Viktor Flessl	6:48.8
1932	1	USA	Kenneth Myers / William Gilmore	7:17.4
	2	GER	Herbert Buhtz / Gerhard Boetzelen	7:22.8
	3	CAN	Charles Pratt / Noël de Mille	7:27.6
1936	1	GER	Jack Beresford / Leslie Southwood	7:20.8
	2	GER	Willy Kaidel / Joachim Pirsch	7:26.2
	3	POL	Roger Verey / Jersy Ustupski	7:36.2
	5	USA	John Houser / William Dugan	7:44.8
1948	1	GBR	Richard Burnell / Bertram Bushnell	6:51.3
	2	DEN	Ebbe Parsner / Aage Larsen	6:55.3
	3	URU	William Jones / Juan Rodriguez	7:12.4
		USA	Arthur Gallagher / Joseph Angyal	
1952	1	ARG	Tranquilo Cappozzo / Eduardo Guerrero	7:32.2
	2	URS	Georgi Zhilin / Igor Yemchuk	7:38.3
	3	URU	Miguel Seijas / Juan Rodriguez	7:43.7
		USA	W. McCall Hoover, Jr. / Bernard Costello	elim. semi rep.
1956	1	URS	Aleksandr Berkutov / Yuri Tyukalov	7:24.0
	2	USA	Bernard Costello / James Gardiner	7:32.2
	3	AUS	Murray Riley / Mervyn Wood	7:37.4
1960	1	TCH	Václav Kozák / Pavel Schmidt	6:47.50
	2	URS	Aleksandr Berkutov / Yuri Tyukalov	6:50.49
	3	SUI	Ernst Hürlimann / Rolf Larcher	6:50.59
		USA	John Kelly, Jr. / William Knecht (6:55.25)	elim. rep.
1964	1	URS	Oleg Tyurin / Boris Dubrovsky	7:10.66
	2	USA	Seymour Cromwell / James Storm	7:13.16
	3	TCH	Vladimir Andrs / Pavel Hofmann	7:14.23
1968	1	URS	Anatoly Sass / Aleksandr Timoshinin	6:51.82
	2	HOL	Leendert Frans van Dis / Henricus Droog	6:52.80
	3	USA	William Maher / John Nunn	6:54.21
1972	1	URS	Aleksandr Timoshinin / Gennady Korshikov	7:01.77
	2	NOR	Frank Hansen / Svein Thögersen	7:02.58
	3	GDR	Joachim Böhmer / Hans-Ulrich Schmied	7:05.55
		USA	Thomas McKibbon / John Van Blom	elim. 2nd rd
1976	1	NOR	Frank Hansen / Alf Hansen	7:13.20
	2	GBR	Chris Baillieu / Michael Hart	7:15.26
	3	GDR	Hans-Ulrich Schmied / Jürgen Bertow	7:17.45
	8	USA	William Belden / Lawrence Klecatsky	
1980	1	GDR	Joachim Dreifke / Klaus Kröppelien	6:24.33
	2	YUG	Zoran Pancic / Milorad Stanulov	6:26.34
	3	TCH	Zdenek Pecka / Václav Vochoska	6:29.07
1984	1	USA	Bradley Lewis / Paul Enquist	6:36.87
	2	BEL	Pierre-Marie Deloof / Dirk Crois	6:38.19
	3	YUG	Zoran Pancic / Milorad Stanulov	6:39.59
1988	1	HOL	Ronald Florijn / Nicolas Rienks	6:21.13
	2	SUI	Beat Schwerzmann / Ueli Bodenmann	6:22.59
	3	URS	Alexandre Martchenko / Vassily Iakoucha	6:22.87
		USA	Glen Florio / Kevin Still	
1992	1	AUS	Stephen Mark Hawkins / Peter Antonie	6:17.32
	2	AUT	Arnold Jonke / Christoph Zerbst	6:18.42
	3	NED	Henk-Jan Zwolle / Nico Rienks	6:22.82
	9	USA	Greg Springer / Jonathan Smith	6:26.67

MEN'S QUADRUPLE SCULLS

YEAR	RANK	CTRY	ATHLETES	TIME
1896-1972	(not held)			
1976	1	GDR		6:18.65
	2	URS		6:19.89
	3	TCH		6:21.77
	6	USA	Peter Cortes / Kenneth Foote / Neil Halleen / John Van Blom	6:34.33
1980	1	GDR		5:49.81
	2	URS		5:51.47
	3	BUL		5:52.38
1984	1	GER		5:57.55
	2	AUS		5:57.98
	3	CAN		5:59.07
	7	USA	Curtis Fleming / Gregg Montesi / Ridgely Johnson / Bruce Beall	
1988	1	ITA		5:53.37
	2	NOR		5:55.08
	3	GDR		5:56.13
		USA	Charles Altekruese / John Frackelton / Greg Montesi / John Strotbeck	
1992	1	GER		5:45.17
	2	NOR		5:47.09
	3	ITA		5:47.33
	8	USA	Chip McKibben / Robert Kaehler / John Riley / Keir Pearson	5:52.48

MEN'S PAIRS W/O COXSWAIN

YEAR	RANK	CTRY	ATHLETES	TIME
1896-1900	(not held)			
1904	1	USA	Robert Farnam / Joseph Ryan	10:57.0
	2	USA	John Mulcahy / William Varley	
	3	USA	John Joachim / Joseph Buerger	
1906	(not held)			
1908	1	GBR	John Fenning / Gordon Thomson	9:41.0
	2	GBR	George Fairbairn / Philip Verdon	
(no USA entry)				
1912-1920	(not held)			
1924	1	HOL	Antonie Beijnen / Wilhelm Rösingh	8:19.4
	2	FRA	Maurice Bouton / Georges Piot	8:21.6
(no USA entry)				
1928	1	GER	Bruno Müller / Kurt Moschter	7:06.4
	2	GBR	Terence O'Brien / R. Archibald Nisbet	7:08.6
	3	USA	Paul McDowell / John Schmitt	7:20.4
1932	1	GBR	Hugh Arthur Edwards / Lewis Clive	8:00.0
	2	NZL	Cyril Stiles / Frederick Thompson	8:02.4
	3	POL	Henryk Budzinski / Janusz Mikolajczak	8:08.2
		USA	Eugene Clark / Thomas Clark	
1936	1	GER	Willi Eichhorn / Hugo Strauss	8:16.1
	2	DEN	Richard Olsen / Harry Larsen	8:19.2
	3	ARG	Horacio Podestá / Julio Curatella	8:23.0
		USA	Harry Shrakey / George Dahm, Jr.	elim. rep.
1948	1	GBR	John Wilson / William Laurie	7:21.1
	2	SUI	Hans Kalt / Josef Kalt	7:23.9
	3	ITA	Felice Fanetti / Bruno Boni	7:31.5
1952	1	USA	Charles Logg / Thomas Price	8:20.7
	2	BEL	Michel Knuysen / Robert Baetens	8:23.5
	3	SUI	Kurt Schmid / Hans Kalt	8:32.7
1956	1	USA	James Fifer / Duvall Hecht	7:55.4
	2	URS	Igor Buldakov / Viktor Ivanov	8:03.9
	3	AUT	Alfred Sageder / Josef Kloimstein	8:11.8
1960	1	URS	Valentin Boreyko / Oleg Golovanov	7:02.01
	2	AUT	Alfred Sageder / Josef Kloimstein	7:03.69
	3	FIN	Veli Lehtelä / Toimi Pitkänen	7:03.80
	5	USA	Ted Frost / Robert Rogers	7:17.08
1964	1	CAN	George Hungerford / Roger Jackson	7:32.94
	2	HOL	Steven Blaisse / Ernst Venemans	7:33.40
	3	GER	Michael Schwan / Wolfgang Hottenrott	7:38.63
		USA		elim.1st rep.
1968	1	GDR	Jörg Lucke / Hans-Jürgen Bothe	7:26.56
	2	USA	Lawrence Hough / Philip "Tony" Johnson	7:26.71
	3	DEN	Peter Christiansen / Ib Ivan Larsen	7:31.84
1972	1	GDR	Siegfried Brietzke / Wolfgang Mager	6:53.16
	2	SUI	Heinrich Fischer / Alfred Bachmann	6:57.06
	3	HOL	Roelof Luynenburg / Rudolf Stokvis	6:58.70
	9	USA	Richard Lyon / Lawrence Hough	
1976	1	GDR	Jörg Landvoigt / Bernd Landvoigt	7:23.31
	2	USA	Calvin Coffey / Michael Staines	7:26.73
	3	GER	Peter Vanroye / Thomas Strauss	7:30.03
1980	1	GDR	Bernd Landvoigt / Jörg Landvoigt	6:48.01
	2	URS	Yuri Pimenov / Nikolai Pimenov	6:50.50
	3	GBR	Charles Wiggin / Malcolm Carmichael	6:51.47
1984	1	ROM	Petru Iosub / Valer Toma	6:45.39
	2	ESP	Fernando Climent / Luis Lasurtegui	6:48.47
	3	NOR	Hans Magnus Grepperud / Sverre Loken	6:51.81
	6	USA	David De Ruff / John Strotbeck	6:58.46
1988	1	GBR	Andrew Holmes / Steven Redgrave	6:36.84
	2	ROM	Dragos Neagu / Danut Dobre	6:38.06
	3	YUG	Bojan Presern / Sadik Mujkic	6:41.01
		USA	Kurt Bausback / Edward Ives	
1992	1	GBR	Steven Redgrave / Matthew Clive Pinsent	6:27.72
	2	GER	Peter J. Hoeltzenbein / Colin Von Ettinghausen	6:32.68
	3	SLO	Iztok Cop / Denis Zvegelj	6:33.43
	6	USA	Peter Sharis / John Pescatore	6:39.23

MEN'S PAIRS W/COXSWAIN

YEAR	RANK	CTRY	ATHLETES	TIME
1896	(not held)			
1900	1	HOL		7:34.2
	2	FRA		7:34.4
	3	FRA		7:57.2
(no USA entry)				
1904	(not held)			
(1000 meters)				
1906	1	ITA		4:23.0
	2	ITA		4:30.0
	3	FRA		
(no USA entry)				
(1609 meters)				
	1	ITA		7:32.4
	2	BEL		8:00.0
	3	FRA		8:08.6
(no USA entry)				
1908-1912	(not held)			
1920	1	ITA		7:56.0
	2	FRA		7:57.0
	3	SUI		
(no USA entry)				
1924	1	SUI		8:39.0
	2	ITA		8:39.1
	3	USA	Leon Butler / Harold Wilson / Edward Jennings	
1928	1	SUI		7:42.6
	2	FRA		7:48.4
	3	BEL		
		USA	Joseph Dougherty / John Schmitt / Thomas Mack	elim. rep.
1932	1	USA	Joseph Schauers / Charles Kieffer / Edward Jennings	8:25.8
	2	POL		8:31.2
	3	FRA		8:41.2
1936	1	GER		8:36.9
	2	ITA		8:49.7
	3	FRA		8:54.0
		USA	Thomas Curran / Joseph Dougherty / George Loveless	elim. rep.
1948	1	DEN		8:00.5
	2	ITA		8:12.2
	3	HUN		8:25.2
		USA	Joseph Toland / J. Vincent Deeney / John McIntyre	
1952	1	FRA		8:28.6
	2	GER		8:32.1
	3	DEN		8:34.9
		USA	James Fifer / Duvall Hecht / James Beggs	elim. semis rep.
1956	1	USA	Arthur Ayrault / Conn Findlay / A. Kurt Seiffert	8:26.1
	2	GER		8:29.2
	3	URS		8:31.0
1960	1	GER		7:29.14
	2	URS		7:30.17
	3	USA	Richard Draeger / Conn Findlay / H. Kent Mitchell	7:34.58
1964	1	USA	Edward Ferry / Conn Findlay / H. Kent Mitchell	8:21.23
	2	FRA		8:23.15
	3	HOL		8:23.42
1968	1	ITA		8:04.81
	2	HOL		8:06.80
	3	DEN		8:08.07
	5	USA	William Hobbs / Richard Edmunds / Stewart MacDonald	8:12.60
1972	1	GDR		7:17.25
	2	TCH		7:19.57
	3	ROM		7:21.36
	11	USA	Luther Jones / Michael Staines / Aaron Herman	
1976	1	GDR		7:58.99
	2	URS		8:01.82
	3	TCH		8:03.82
		USA	John Mathews / Darrell Vreugdenhil / Kenneth Dreyfuss	elim. semis
1980	1	GDR		7:02.54
	2	URS		7:03.35
	3	YUG		7:04.92
1984	1	ITA		7:05.99
	2	ROM		7:11.21
	3	USA	Kevin Still / Robert Espeseth / Douglas Herland	7:12.81
1988	1	ITA		6:58.79
	2	GDR		7:00.63
	3	GBR		7:01.95
		USA	Robert Espeseth / Jonathan Fish / Daniel Lyons	
1992	1	GBR		6:49.83
	2	ITA		6:50.98
	3	ROM		6:51.58
	8	USA	John Moore / Aaron Pollock / Stephen Shellans	6:54.78

MEN'S FOUR OARS W/COXSWAIN

YEAR	RANK	CTRY	ATHLETES	TIME
1896	(not held)			
1900	1	FRA		7:11.0
	2	FRA		7:18.0
	3	GER		7:18.2
(no USA entry)				
2nd final				
	1	GER		5:59.0
	2	HOL		6:33.0
	3	GER		6:35.0
(no USA entry)				
1904	(not held)			
1906	1	ITA		8:13.0
	2	FRA		
	3	FRA		
		USA		
1908	(not held)			
1912	1	GER		6:59.4
	2	GBR		
	3	DEN		
(no USA entry)				
1920	1	SUI		6:54.0
	2	USA	Kenneth Myers / Carl Otto Klose / Franz Federschmidt / Erich Federschmidt / Sherman Clark	6:58.0
	3	NOR		7:02.0
1924	1	SUI		7:18.4
	2	FRA		7:21.6
	3	USA	Robert Gerhardt / Sidney Jelinek / Edward Mitchell / Henry Welsford / John Kennedy	7:23.0
1928	1	ITA		6:47.8
	2	SUI		7:03.4
	3	POL		7:12.8
		USA	Allerton Cushman / Charles Mason, Jr. / J. Dewolf Hubbard / F.A. Clarke, Jr. / Eugene Belisle	elim. 2nd rd
1932	1	GER		7:19.0
	2	ITA		7:19.2
	3	POL		7:26.8
		USA	Edward Marshall / Francis English / Harry Grossmiller / Charles Drueding / Thomas Mack	
1936	1	GER		7:16.2
	2	SUI		7:24.3
	3	FRA		7:33.3
		USA	William Haskins / Rogert Cutler Jr / John Austin /Robert Cutler Jr / Edward Bennett	elim. rep.
1948	1	USA	Warren Westlund / Robert Martin / Robert Will / Gordon Giovanelli / Allen Morgan	6:50.3
	2	SUI		6:53.3
	3	DEN		6:58.6
1952	1	TCH		7:33.4
	2	SUI		7:36.5
	3	USA	Carl Lovested / Alvin Ulbrickson / Richard Wahlström / Matthew Leanderson / Albert Rossi	7:37.0
1956	1	ITA		7:19.4
	2	SWE		7:22.4
	3	FIN		7:30.9
		USA	J.M. Wynne / D.L. Turner / J.A. McMullen / R.E. Cardwell / E.A. Masterson	elim. 2nd rd
1960	1	GER		6:39.12
	2	FRA		6:41.62
	3	ITA		6:43.72
		USA	C. Alm / R. Rubin / A. Stocker / M. Yonker Cos / K. Seiffert (7:06.25)	elim. semis
1964	1	GER		7:00.44
	2	ITA		7:02.84
	3	HOL		7:06.46
	7	USA	Paul Gunderson / Harry Pollock / Thomas Pollock / James Tew / Edward Washburn	
1968	1	NZL		6:45.62
	2	GDR		6:48.20
	3	SUI		6:49.04
	5	USA	Luther Jones / William Purdy / Anthony Martin / Aspinwall Gardner Cadwalader / John Hartigan	6:51.41
1972	1	GER		6:31.85
	2	GDR		6:33.30
	3	TCH		6:35.64
	5	USA	David Sawyer / Charles Ruthford / Chad Rudolph / Michael Vespoli / Stewart MacDonald	6:41.86
1976	1	URS		6:40.22
	2	GDR		6:42.70
	3	GER		6:46.96
	11	USA	Robert Zagunis / Patrick Hayes / Michael Plumb /Earl Borchelt / John Hartigan	6:54.92
1980	1	GDR		6:14.51
	2	URS		6:19.05
	3	POL		6:22.52
1984	1	GBR		6:18.64
	2	USA	Thomas Kiefer / Gregory Springer / Michael Bach / Edward Ives / John Stillings	6:20.28
	3	NZL		6:23.68
1988	1	GDR		6:10.74
	2	ROM		6:13.58
	3	NZL		6:15.78
	5	USA	John Terwilliger / Christopher Huntington / Tom Darling / John Walters / Mark Zembsch	6:18.47
1992	1	ROM		5:59.37
	2	GER		6:00.34
	3	POL		6:03.27
	4	USA	James Neil / Teo Bielefeld / Sean Hall / Jack Rusher / Tim Evans	6:06.03

MEN'S FOUR OARS W/O COXSWAIN

YEAR	RANK	CTRY	ATHLETES	TIME
1896-1900	(not held)			
1904	**1**	**USA**	**George Dietz / August Erker / Albert Nasse / Arthur Stockhoff**	**9:05.8**
	2	**USA**	**Charles Aman / Michael Begley / Martin Fromanack / Frederick Seurig**	
	3	**USA**	**Gustav Voerg / John Freitag / Louis Helm / Frank Dummerth**	
1906	(not held)			
1908	1	GBR		8:34.0
	2	GBR		
(no USA entry)				
1912-1920	(not held)			
1924	1	GBR		7:08.6
	2	CAN		7:18.0
	3	SUI		
(no USA entry)				
1928	1	GBR		6:36.0
	2	**USA**	**Charles Karle / William Miller / George Heales / Ernest Bayer**	**6:37.0**
	3	ITA		6:37.6
1932	1	GBR		6:58.2
	2	GER		7:03.0
	3	ITA		7:04.0
	4	**USA**	**John McCosker / George Mattson / Thomas Pierie / Edgar Johnson**	**7:14.2**
1936	1	GER		7:01.8
	2	GBR		7:06.5
	3	SUI		7:10.6
		USA	**James Thompson / George Hague / Charles Fries / Alfred Sapecky**	**elim. rep.**
1948	1	ITA		6:39.0
	2	DEN		6:43.5
	3	**USA**	**Frederick John Kingsbury / Stuart Griffing / Gregory Gates / Robert Perew**	**6:47.7**
1952	1	YUG		7:16.0
	2	FRA		7:18.9
	3	FIN		7:23.3
		USA	**Louis McMillan / D. McKee Jackson / John Davis / James Welsh**	**elim. semis rep.**
1956	1	CAN		7:08.8
	2	**USA**	**John Welchli / John McKinlay / Arthur McKinlay / James McIntosh**	**7:18.4**
	3	FRA		7:20.9
1960	**1**	**USA**	**Arthur Ayrault / Ted Nash / John Sayre / Richard Wailes**	**6:26.26**
	2	ITA		6:28.78
	3	URS		6:29.62
1964	1	DEN		6:59.30
	2	GBR		7:00.47
	3	**USA**	**Geoffrey Picard / Richard Lyon / Theodore Mittet / Theodore Nash**	**7:01.37**
1968	1	GDR		6:39.18
	2	HUN		6:41.64
	3	ITA		6:44.01
	5	**USA**	**Peter Raymond / Raymond Wright / Charles Hamlin / Lawrence Terry**	**6:47.70**
1972	1	GDR		6:24.27
	2	NZL		6:25.64
	3	GER		6:28.41
		USA	**Charles Hewitt / William Miller / Richard Dreissigacker / James Moroney**	**elim. 1st rd**
1976	1	GDR		6:37.42
	2	NOR		6:41.22
	3	URS		6:42.52
	8	**USA**	**Tony Brooks / James Moroney / Gary Piantedosi / Hugh Stevenson**	
1980	1	GDR		6:08.17
	2	URS		6:11.81
	3	GBR		6:16.58
1984	1	NZL		6:03.48
	2	**USA**	**David Clark / Jonathan Smith / Philip Stekl / Alan Forney**	**6:06.10**
	3	DEN		6:07.72
1988	1	GDR		6:03.11
	2	**USA**	**Raoul Rodriguez / Thomas Bohrer / David Krmpotich / Richard Kennelly**	**6:05.53**
	3	FRG		6:06.22
1992	1	AUS		5:55.04
	2	**USA**	**Doug Burden / Jeff McLaughlin / Thomas Bohrer / Patrick Manning**	**5:56.68**
	3	SLO		5:58.24

MEN'S EIGHT OARS W/COXSWAIN

YEAR	RANK	CTRY	ATHLETES	TIME
1896	(not held)			
1900	**1**	**USA**	**Louis Abell / Harry Debaecke / William Carr / John Exley / John Geiger / Edward Hedley / James Juvenal / Roscoe Lockwood / Edward Marsh**	**6:09.8**
	2	BEL		6:13.8
	3	HOL		6:23.0
1904	**1**	**USA**	**Louis Abell / Joseph Dempsey / Michael Gleason / Frank Schell / James Flanigan / Charles Armstrong / Harry Lott / Frederick Cresser / John Exley**	**7:50.0**
	2	CAN		
1906	(not held)			
1908	1	GBR		7:52.0
	2	BEL		
	3T	CAN		
	3T	GBR		
(no USA entry)				
1912	1	GBR		6:15.0
	2	GBR		6:19.0
	3	GER		
(no USA entry)				
1920	**1**	**USA**	**Virgil Jacomini / Edwin Graves / William Jordan / Edward Moore / Allen Sanborn / Donald Johnston / Vincent Gallagher / Clyde King / Sherman Clark**	**6:02.6**
	2	GBR		6:05.0
	3	NOR		6:36.0
1924	**1**	**USA**	**Leonard Carpenter / Howard Kingsbury / Daniel Lindley / John Miller / James Rockefeller / Frederick Sheffield / Benjamin Spock / Alfred Wilson / Laurence Stoddard**	**6:33.4**
	2	CAN		6:49.0
	3	ITA		
1928	**1**	**USA**	**Marvin Stalder / John Brinck / Francis Frederick / William Thompson / William Dally / James Workman / Hubert Caldwell / Peter Donlon / Donald Blessing**	**6:03.2**
	2	GBR		6:05.6
	3	CAN		
1932	**1**	**USA**	**Edwin Salisbury / James Blair / Duncan Gregg / David Dunlap / Burton Jastram / Charles Chandler / Harold Tower / Winslow Hall / Norris Graham**	**6:37.6**
	2	ITA		6:37.8
	3	CAN		6:40.4
1936	**1**	**USA**	**Herbert Morris / Charles Day / Gordon Adam / John White / James McMillin / George Hunt / Joseph Rantz / Donald Hume / Robert Moch**	**6:25.4**
	2	ITA		6:26.0
	3	GER		6:26.4
1948	**1**	**USA**	**Ian Turner / David Turner / James Hardy / George Ahlgren / Lloyd Butler / David Brown / Justus Smith / John Stack / Ralph Purchase**	**5:56.7**
	2	GBR		6:06.9
	3	NOR		6:10.3
1952	**1**	**USA**	**Franklin Shakespeare / William Fields / James Dunbar / Richard Murphy / Robert Detweiler / Henry Proctor / Wayne Frye / Edward Stevens / Charles Manring**	**6:25.9**
	2	URS		6:31.2
	3	AUS		6:33.1
1956	**1**	**USA**	**Thomas Charlton / David Wight / John Cooke / Donald Beer / Caldwell Esselstyn / Charles Grimes / Richard Wailes / Robert Morey / William Becklean**	**6:35.2**
	2	CAN		6:37.1
	3	AUS		6:39.2
1960	1	GER		5:57.18
	2	CAN		6:01.52
	3	TCH		6:04.84
	5	**USA**	**Joseph Baldwin / Peter Bos / Mark Moore / Lyman Perry / Warren Sweetser / Gayle Thompson / Robert Wilson / Howard Winfree / William Long**	**6:08.06**
1964	**1**	**USA**	**Joseph Amlong / Thomas Amlong / Harold Budd / Emory Clark / Stanley Cwiklinski / Hugh Foley / William Knecht / William Stowe / Robert Zimonyi**	**6:18.23**
	2	GER		6:239.29
	3	TCH		6:25.11
1968	1	GER		6:07.00
	2	AUS		6:07.98
	3	URS		6:09.11
	6	**USA**	**Stephen Brooks / Curtis Canning / Andrew Larkin / Scott Steketee/ Franklin Hobbs / Jacques Fiechter / Cleve Livingston / David Higgins / Paul Hoffman**	**6:14.34**
1972	1	NZL		6:08.94
	2	**USA**	**Lawrence Terry / Fritz Hobbs / Peter Raymond / Timothy Mickelson / Eugene Clapp / William Hobbs / Cleve Livingston / Michael Livingston / Paul Hoffman**	**6:11.61**
	3	GDR		6:11.67
1976	1	GDR		5:58.29
	2	GBR		6:00.82
	3	NZL		6:03.51
1980	1	GDR		5:49.05
	2	GBR		5:51.92
	3	URS		5:52.66
1984	1	CAN		5:41.32
	2	**USA**	**Walter Lubsen / Andrew Sudduth / John Terwilliger / Christopher Penny / Thomas Darling / Earl Borchelt / Charles Clapp / Bruce Ibbetson / Robert Jaugstetter**	**5:41.74**
	3	AUS		5:43.40
1988	1	FRG		5:46.05
	2	URS		5:48.01
	3	**USA**	**Mike Teti / John Smith / Ted Patton / John Rusher / Peter Nordell / Jeff McLaughlin / Doug Burden / John Pescatore / Seth Bauer**	**5:48.26**
1992	1	CAN		5:29.53
	2	ROM		5:29.67
	3	GER		5:31.00
	4	**USA**	**Michael Francis Teti / James Scott Munn / Christian Sahs / Jeff Gerard Klepacki / Robert Tharp Shepherd / Malcolm Baker / Richard Kennelly / John MacDougall Parker / Michael James Moore**	**5:33.18**

WOMEN'S SINGLE SCULLS

YEAR	RANK	CTRY	ATHLETE	TIME
1896-1972	(not held)			
1976	1	GDR	Christine Scheiblich	4:05.56
	2	**USA**	**Joan Lind**	**4:06.21**
	3	URS	Elena Antonova	4:10.24
1980	1	ROM	Sanda Toma	3:40.69
	2	URS	Antonina Makhina	3:41.65
	3	GDR	Martina Schröter	3:43.54
1984	1	ROM	Valeria Racila	3:40.68
	2	**USA**	**Charlotte Geer**	**3:43.89**
	3	BEL	Ann Haesebrouck	3:45.72
1988	1	GDR	Jutta Behrendt	7:47.19
	2	**USA**	**Anne Marden**	**7:50.28**
	3	BUL	Magdalena Gueorguieva	7:53.65
1992	1	ROM	Elisabeta Lipa	7:25.54
	2	BEL	Annelies Bredael	7:26.64
	3	CAN	Silken Suzette Laumann	7:28.85
	4	**USA**	**Anne Marden**	**7:29.84**

WOMEN'S DOUBLE SCULLS

YEAR	RANK	CTRY	ATHLETES	TIME
1896-1972	(not held)			
1976	1	BUL	Svetla Otsetova / Zdravka Yordanova	3:44.36
	2	GDR	Sabine Jahn / Petra Boesler	3:47.86
	3	URS	Leonora Kaminskaite / Genovate Ramoshkene	3:49.93
	5	**USA**	**Jan Palchikoff / Diane Braceland**	**3:58.25**
1980	1	URS	Yelena Khloptseva / Larissa Popova	3:16.27
	2	GDR	Cornelia Linse / Heidi Westphal	3:17.63
	3	ROM	Olga Homeghi / Valeria Racila-Rosca	3:18.91
1984	1	ROM	Marioara Popescu / Elisabeta Oleniuc	3:26.75
	2	HOL	Greet Hellemans / Nicolette Hellemans	3:29.13
	3	CAN	Daniele Laumann / Silken Laumann	3:29.82
	6	**USA**	**Cathleen Thaxton / Julia Geer**	**3:32.33**
1988	1	GDR	Birgit Peter / Martina Schroeter	7:00.48
	2	ROM	Veronica Cogeanu / Elisabeta Lipa	7:04.36
	3	BUL	Violeta Ninova / Stefka Madina	7:06.03
	6	**USA**	**Monica Havelka / Cathy Tippett**	**7:21.28**
1992	1	GER	Kerstin Koeppen / Kathrin Boron	6:49.00
	2	ROM	Veronica Cochelea / Elisabeta Lipa	6:51.47
	3	CHN	Gu Xiaoli / Lu Huali	6:55.16
	11	**USA**	**Cynthia Ryder / Mary Mazzio**	**7:12.24**

WOMEN'S QUADRUPLE SCULLS

YEAR	RANK	CTRY	ATHLETES	TIME
1896-1972	(not held)			
1976	1	GDR		3:29.99
	2	URS		3:32.49
	3	ROM		3:32.76
	7	**USA**	**Karen McCloskey / Lisa Hansen / Elizabet Hills / Claudia Schneider / Irene Moreno**	
1980	1	GDR		3:15.32
	2	URS		3:15.73
	3	BUL		3:16.10
1984	1	ROM		3:14.11
	2	**USA**	**Anne Marden / Lisa Rohde / Joan Lind / Virginia Gilder / Kelly Rickon**	**3:15.57**
	3	DEN		3:16.02
1988	1	GDR		6:21.06
	2	URS		6:23.47
	3	ROM		6:23.81
		USA	**Sherry Cassuto / Angie Herron / Jennis Marshall / Ann Martin**	
1992	1	GER		6:20.18
	2	ROM		6:24.34
	3	EUN		6:25.07
	5	**USA**	**Kristine Karlson / Alison Townley / Serena Eddy-Moulton / Michelle Knox-Zaloom**	**6:32.65**

WOMEN'S PAIRS W/O COXSWAIN

YEAR	RANK	CTRY	ATHLETES	TIME
1896-1972	(not held)			
1976	1	BUL		4:01.22
	2	GDR		4:01.64
	3	GER		4:02.35
	7	**USA**	**Susan Morgan / Laura Staines**	
1980	1	GDR		3:30.49
	2	POL		3:30.95
	3	BUL		3:32.39
1984	1	ROM		3:32.60
	2	CAN		3:36.06
	3	GER		3:40.50
	5	**USA**	**Barbara Kirch / Chari Towne**	**3:44.35**
1988	1	ROM	Rodica Arba / Olga Homeghi	7:28.13
	2	BUL	Radka Stoyanova / Lalka Berberova	7:31.95
	3	NZL	Nicola Payne / Lynley Hannen	7:35.68
	6	**USA**	**Barbara Kirch / Mara Keggi**	**7:56.27**
1992	1	CAN	Marnie Elizabeth McBean / Kathleen Heddle	7:06.22
	2	GER	Stefani Werremeier / Ingeburg Schwerzmann	7:07.96
	3	**USA**	**Stephanie Maxwell-Pierson / Anna B. Seaton**	**7:08.11**

WOMEN'S FOUR OARS W/O COXSWAIN

YEAR	RANK	CTRY	ATHLETES	TIME
1896-1988	(not held)			
1992	1	CAN		6:30.85
	2	**USA**	**Shelagh Donohoe / Cindy Eckert / Amy Fuller / Carol Feeney**	**6:31.86**
	3	GER		6:32.34

WOMEN'S FOUR OARS W/COXSWAIN

YEAR	RANK	CTRY	ATHLETES	TIME
1896-1972	(not held)			
1976	1	GDR		3:45.08
	2	BUL		3:48.24
	3	URS		3:49.38
	6	**USA**	**Pamela Behrens / Catherine Menges / Nancy Storrs / Julia Geer / Mary Kellogg**	**3:56.50**
1980	1	GDR		3:19.27
	2	BUL		3:20.75
	3	URS		3:20.92
1984	1	ROM		3:19.30
	2	CAN		3:21.55
	3	AUS		3:23.29
	4	**USA**	**Abigail Peck / Patricia Spratlen / Janet Harville / Elizabeth Miles / Valerie McClain-Ward**	**3:23.58**
1988	1	GDR		6:56.00
	2	CHN		6:58.78
	3	ROM		7:01.13
	5	**USA**	**Jennifer Corbet / Sarah Gengler / Elizabeth Bradley / Cynthia Eckert / Kimberly Santiago**	**7:09.12**

WOMEN'S EIGHT OARS W/COXSWAIN

YEAR	RANK	CTRY	ATHLETES	TIME
1896-1972	(not held)			
1976	1	GDR		3:33.32
	2	URS		3:36.17
	3	USA	**Jacqueli Zoch / Anita DeFrantz / Carie Graves / Marion Greig / Anne Warner / Peggy McCarthy / Carol Brown / Gail Ricketson / Lynn Silliman**	**3:38.68**
1980	1	GDR		3:03.32
	2	URS		3:04.29
	3	ROM		3:05.63
1984	**1**	**USA**	**Shyril O'Steen / Harriet Metcalf / Carol Bower / Carie Graves / Jeanne Flanagan/ Kristine Norelius / Kristen Thorsness / Kathryn Keeler / Betsy Beard**	**2:59.80**
	2	ROM		3:00.87
	3	HOL		3:02.92
1988	1	GDR		6:15.17
	2	ROM		6:17.44
	3	CHN		6:21.83
	6	**USA**	**Juliet Thompson / Christine Campbell / Abigail Peck / Margaret Mallery / Susan Broome / Stephanie Maxwell / Anna Seaton / Alison Townley / Elizabeth "Betsy" Beard**	**6:26.66**
1992	1	CAN		6:02.62
	2	ROM		6:06.26
	3	GER		6:07.80
	6	**USA**	**Tina Brown / Shannon Day / Betsy McCagg / Mary McCagg / Sarah Gengler / Tracy Rude / Kelley Jones / Diana Olson / Yasmin Farooq**	**6:12.25**

SHOOTING

MEN'S AIR PISTOL

YEAR	RANK	CTRY	ATHLETE	SCORE	TOTAL
1896-1972	(not held)				
1988	1	BUL	Taniou Kiriakov	585	687.9
	2	**USA**	**Erich Buljung**	**590 EWR**	**687.9**
	3	CHN	Xu Haifeng	584	684.5
1992	1	CHN	Wang Yifu	585 684.8	FOR
	2	EUN	Sergei Pyjianov	584	684.1
	3	ROM	Sorin Babii	586	684.1
	14T	**USA**	**Ben Amonette**	**577**	

MEN'S FREE PISTOL

YEAR	RANK	CTRY	ATHLETE	SCORE	TOTAL/SHOOT-OFF
1896	**1**	**USA**	**Sumner Paine**		**442**
	2	DEN	Holger Nielsen		285
1900	1	SUI	Conrad Karl Röderer		503
	2	FRA	Achille Paroche		466
	3	SUI	Konrad Stäheli		453
(no USA entry)					
1904 (not held)					
1906	1	GRE	Georgios Orphanidis		221
	2	FRA	Jean Fouconnier		219
	3	GRE	Aristides Rangavis		218
(no USA entry)					
1908 (not held)					
1912	**1**	**USA**	**Alfred Lane**		**499**
	2	**USA**	**Peter Dolfen**		**474**
	3	GBR	Charles Stewart		470
1920	**1**	**USA**	**Karl Frederick**		**496**
	2	BRA	Afranio da Costa		489
	3	**USA**	**Alfred Lane**		**481**
1924-1932	(not held)				
1936	1	SWE	Torsten Ullman		559 WR
	2	GER	Erich Krempel		544
	3	FRA	Charles des Jammonières		540
	6	**USA**	**Elliott Jones**		**536**
1948	1	PER	Edwin Vasquez Cam		545
	2	SUI	Rudolf Schnyder		539/60/21
	3	SWE	Torsten Ullman		539/60/16
	4	**USA**	**Huelet Benner**		**539/58**
1952	**1**	**USA**	**Huelet Benner**		**553 OR**
	2	ESP	Angel León de Gozalo		550
	3	HUN	Ambrus Balogh		549
1956	1	FIN	Pentti Linnosvuo		556/26 **OR**
	2	URS	Makhmud Umarov		556/24 OR
	3	**USA**	**Offutt Pinion**		**551**
1960	1	URS	Aleksei Gustchin		560 **OR**
	2	URS	Makhmud Umarov		552/26
	3	JPN	Yoshihisa Yoshikawa		552/20
	9	**USA**	**N. Lincoln**		
1964	1	FIN	Väinö Markkanen		560 **EOR**
	2	**USA**	**Franklin Green**		**557**
	3	JPN	Yoshihisa Yoshikawa		554/26
1968	1	URS	Grigory Kossykh		562/30 **OR**
	2	GER	Heinz Mertel		562/26 **OR**
	3	GDR	Harald Vollmar		560
	4	**USA**	**Arnold Vitarbo**		**559**
1972	1	SWE	Ragnar Shanåker		567 **OR**
	2	ROM	Dan Iuga		562
	3	AUT	Rudolf Dollinger		560
	28	**USA**	**Jimmie Dorsey**		
1976	1	GDR	Uwe Potteck		573 **WR**
	2	GDR	Harald Vollmar		567
	3	AUT	Rudolf Dollinger		562
	10	**USA**	**Hershel Anderson**		
1980	1	URS	Aleksandr Melentev		581 **WR**
	2	GDR	Harald Vollmar		568
	3	BUL	Ljubcho Diakov		565
1984	1	CHN	Xu Haifeng		566
	2	SWE	Ragnar Skanåker		565
	3	CHN	Wang Yifu		564
	9	**USA**	**Erich Buljung**		
1988	1	ROM	Sorin Babii	566	660
	2	SWE	Ragnar Skanaker	564	657
	3	URS	Igor Bassinski	570	657
	11	**USA**	**Donald Nygord**	**559**	
1992	1	EUN	K. Loukachik	567	658
	2	CHN	Wang Yifu	565	657
	3	SWE	Ragnar Skanaker	566	657
	4	**USA**	**Darius Young**	**566**	**655**

MEN'S RAPID-FIRE PISTOL

YEAR	RANK	CTRY	ATHLETE	SCORE	TOTAL/SHOOT-OFF
1896	1	GRE	Ioannis Phrangoudis		344
	2	GRE	Georgios Orphanidis		249
	3	DEN	Holger Nielsen		
(no USA entry)					
1900	1	FRA	Maurice Larrouy		58
	2	FRA	Léon Moreaux		57
	3	FRA	Eugène Balme		57
(no USA entry)					
1904 (not held)					
1906	1	FRA	Maurice Lecoq		258
	2	FRA	Léon Moreaux		249
	3	GRE	Aristides Rangavis		244
(no USA entry)					
1908	1	BEL	Paul van Asbroeck		490
	2	BEL	Réginald Storms		487
	3	**USA**	**James Gorman**		**485**
1912	**1**	**USA**	**Alfred Lane**		**287**
	2	SWE	Paul Palén		286
	3	SWE	Johan Hübner von Holst		283
1920	1	BRA	Guilherme Paraense		274
	2	**USA**	**Raymond Bracken**		**272**
	3	SUI	Fritz Zulauf		269
1924	**1**	**USA**	**Henry Bailey**		**18**
	2	SWE	Wilhelm Carlberg		18
	3	FIN	Lennart Hannelius		18
1928 (not held)					
1932	1	ITA	Renzo Morigi		36
	2	GER	Heinz Hax		36
	3	ITA	Domenico Matteucci		36
		USA	**Luther Roberts**	**elim. 4 sec.**	
1936	1	GER	Cornelius van Oynn		30/6
	2	GER	Heinz Hax		30/5
	3	SWE	Torsten Ullman		30/4/4
	15	**USA**	**Clarence Fisher**	**elim. 4 sec.**	
1948	1	HUN	Károly Takács		580 **WR**
	2	ARG	Carlos Enrique Diaz Sáenz Valiente		571
	3	SWE	Sven Lundqvist		569
	13	**USA**	**Frank Chow**		
1952	1	HUN	Károly Takács		579
	2	HUN	Szilárd Kun		578
	3	ROM	Gheorghe Lichiardopol		578
	7	**USA**	**William McMillan**		**575**
1956	1	ROM	Stefan Petrescu		587 **OR**
	2	URS	Yevgeny Cherkassov		585
	3	ROM	Gheorghe Lichiardopol		581
	9	**USA**	**John Beaumont, Jr.**		
1960	**1**	**USA**	**William McMillan**		**587/147 EOR**
	2	FIN	Pentti Linnosvuo		587/139 **EOR**
	3	URS	Aleksandr Zabelin		587/135 **EOR**
1964	1	FIN	Pentti Linnosvuo		592 **OR**
	2	ROM	Ion Tripsa		591
	3	TCH	Lubomir Nacovsky		590
	12	**USA**	**William McMillan**		
1968	1	POL	Józef Zapedzki		593 **OR**
	2	ROM	Marcel Rosca		591/147
	3	URS	Renart Suleimanov		591/146/148
	17	**USA**	**Lt. Col. William McMillan**		
1972	1	POL	Józef Zapedzki		595 **OR**
	2	TCH	Ladislav Falta		594
	3	URS	Victor Torshin		593
	10	**USA**	**James McNally**		
1976	1	GDR	Norbert Klaar		597 **OR**
	2	GDR	Jürgen Wiefel		596
	3	ITA	Roberto Ferraris		595
	20	**USA**	**William McMillan**		
1980	1	ROM	Corneliu Ion		596/148/147/148
	2	GDR	Jürgen Wiefel		596/148/147/147
	3	AUT	Gerhard Petritsch		596/146
1984	1	JPN	Takeo Kamachi		595
	2	ROM	Corneliu Ion		593
	3	RIN	Rauno Bies		591/146
	20	**USA**	**Allyn Johnson**		
1988	1	URS	Afanasi Kouzmine	598 **OR**	698 **FWR**
	2	GDR	Ralf Schumann	597	696
	3	HUN	Zoltan Kovacs	594	693
	7	**USA**	**John McNally**	**597**	**690.0**
1992	1	GER	Ralf Schumann	789	885 **FOR**
	2	LAT	A. Kuzmins	785	882
	3	EUN	V. Vokmianine	786	882
	5	**USA**	**John McNally**	**781**	

MEN'S RUNNING GAME TARGET

YEAR	RANK	CTRY	ATHLETE	SCORE	TOTAL
1896 (not held)					
1900	1	FRA	Louis Debray		20
	2	FRA	P. Nivet		20
	3	FRA	Comte de Lambert		19
(no USA entry)					
1904-1968	(not held)				
1972	1	URS	Lakov Zhelezniak		569 **WR**
	2	COL	Helmut Bellingrodt		565
	3	GBR	John Kynoch		562
	9	**USA**	**Edmund Moeller**		
1976	1	URS	Aleksandr Gazov		579 **WR**
	2	URS	Aleksandr Kedyarov		576
	3	POL	Jerzy Greszkiewicz		571
	8	**USA**	**Louis Theimer**		**564**
1980	1	URS	Igor Sokolov		589 **WR**
	2	GDR	Thomas Pfeffer		589
	3	URS	Aleksandr Gazov		587
1984	1	CHN	Li Yuwei		587
	2	COL	Helmut Bellingrodt		584
	3	CHN	Huang Shiping		581
	9	**USA**	**Randy Stewart**		
1988	1	NOR	Tor Heiestad	591 **OR**	689.0
	2	CHN	Huang Shiping	589	687.0
	3	URS	Guennadi Avramenko	591 **OR**	686.0
	17	**USA**	**Todd Bensley**	**581**	
1992	1	GER	Michael Jakosits	580	673 **FOR**
	2	EUN	Anatolij Asrabaev	579	672
	3	TCH	Lubos Racansky	576	670
	11	**USA**	**Rusty Hill**	**570**	

MEN'S AIR RIFLE

YEAR	RANK	CTRY	ATHLETE	SCORE	TOTAL
1896-1980	(not held)				
1984	1	FRA	Philippe Heberle		589
	2	AUT	Andreas Kronthaler		587
	3	GBR	Barry Dagger		587
	5	**USA**	**John Rost**		**583**
1988	1	YUG	Goran Maksimovic	594 **OR**	695.6
	2	FRA	Nicolas Berthelot	593	694.2
	3	FRG	Johann Riederer	592	694.0
	4	**USA**	**Robert Foth**	**591**	**692.5**
1992	1	EUN	Iouri Fedkine	593	695.3 **FOR**
	2	FRA	Franck Badiou	591	691.9
	3	GER	Johann Riederer	590	691.7
	7	**USA**	**Robert Foth**	**590**	**689.4**

MEN'S SMALLBORE RIFLE, ENGLISH MATCH

YEAR	RANK	CTRY	ATHLETE	SCORE	TOTAL
1896-1984	(not held)				
1988	1	TCH	Miroslav Varga	600 **WR**	703.9
	2	KOR	Cha Young-chul	598	702.8
	3	HUN	Attila Zahonyl	597	701.9
	15T	**USA**	**Glenn Dubis**	**595**	

MEN'S SMALLBORE RIFLE, THREE POSITIONS

YEAR	RANK	CTRY	ATHLETE	SCORE	TOTAL/SHOOT-OFF
1896-1948	(not held)				
1952	1	NOR	Erling Kongshaug		1164/53
	2	FIN	Vilho Ylönen		1164/53
	3	URS	Boris Andreyev		1163
	12	**USA**	**Arthur Jackson**		
1956	1	URS	Anatoly Bogdanov		1172 **OR**
	2	TCH	Otakar Horinek		1172 **OR**
	3	SWE	Nils Johan Sundberg		1167
	12	**USA**	**Arthur Jackson**		
1960	1	URS	Viktor Shamburkin		1149 **EWR**
	2	URS	Marat Niyasov		1145
	3	GER	Klaus Zähringer		1139
	7	**USA**	**Daniel Puckel**		**1137**
1964	**1**	**USA**	**Lones Wigger**		**1164 WR**
	2	BUL	Velichko Velichkov		1152
	3	HUN	László Hammerl		1151
	6	**USA**	**Tommy Pool**		**1147**
1968	1	GER	Bernd Klingner		1157
	2	**USA**	**John Writer**		**1156**
	3	URS	Viktor Parkhimovich		1154
1972	**1**	**USA**	**John Writer**		**1166 WR**
	2	**USA**	**Lanny Bassham**		**1157**
	3	GDR	Werner Lippoldt		1153
1976	**1**	**USA**	**Lanny Bassham**		**1162**
	2	**USA**	**Margaret Murdock**		**1162**
	3	GER	Werner Seibold		1160
1980	1	URS	Viktor Vlasov		1173 **WR**
	2	GDR	Bernd Hartstein		1166
	3	SWE	Sven Johansson		1165
1984	1	GBR	Malcolm Cooper		1173 **EWR**
	2	SUI	Daniel Nipkow		1163
	3	GBR	Alister Allan		1162
	6	**USA**	**Glenn Dubis**		**1151**
1988	1	GBR	Malcolm Cooper	1180	1279.3
	2	GBR	Alister Allan	1181 **OR**	1275.6
	3	URS	Kirill Ivanov	1173	1275.0
	5	**USA**	**Glenn Dubis**	**1174**	**1273.5**
1992	1	EUN	Gracha Petikian	1169	1267.4 **FOR**
	2	**USA**	**Robert Foth**	**1169**	**1266.6**
	3	JPN	Ryohei Koba	1171	1265.9

MEN'S SMALLBORE RIFLE, PRONE

YEAR	RANK	CTRY	ATHLETE	SCORE	TOTAL
1896-1906	(not held)				
1908	1	GBR	A.A. Carnell		387
	2	GBR	Harry Humby		386
	3	GBR	George Barnes		385
(no USA entry)					
1912	**1**	**USA**	**Frederick Hird**		**194**
	2	GBR	William Milne		193
	3	GBR	Harry Burt		192
1920	**1**	**USA**	**Lawrence Nuesslein**		**391**
	2	**USA**	**Arthur Rothrock**		**386**
	3	**USA**	**Dennis Fenton**		**385**
1924	1	FRA	Pierre Coquelin de Lisle		398
	2	**USA**	**Marcus Dinwiddie**		**396**
	3	SUI	Josias Hartmann		394
1928 (not held)					
1932	1	SWE	Bertil Rönnmark		294/296
	2	MEX	Gustavo Huet		294/290
	3	HUN	Zoltán Hradetzky-Soós		293
	5	**USA**	**William Harding**		**292**
1936	1	NOR	Willy Rögeberg		300 **WR**
	2	HUN	Ralph Berzsenyi		296
	3	POL	Wladyslaw Kara		296
(no USA entry)					
1948	**1**	**USA**	**Arthur Cook**		**599/43 WR**
	2	**USA**	**Walter Tomsen**		**599/42 WR**
	3	SWE	Jonas Jonsson		597/44
1952	1	ROM	Josif Sârbu		400/33 **EWR**
	2	URS	Boris Andreyev		400/28 **EWR**
	3	**USA**	**Arthur Jackson**		**399/28**
1956	1	CAN	Gerald Ouellette		600
	2	URS	Vassily Borissov		599
	3	CAN	Gilmour Boa		598
	31	**USA**	**A.C. Jackson**		
1960	1	GER	Peter Kohnke		590
	2	**USA**	**James Hill**		**589**
	3	VEN	Enrico Forcella Pelliccioni		587
1964	1	HUN	László Hammerl		597 **WR**
	2	**USA**	**Lones Wigger**		**597 WR**
	3	USA	Tommy Pool		596
1968	1	TCH	Jan Kurka		598 **EWR**
	2	HUN	László Hammerl		598 **EWR**
	3	NZL	Ian Ballinger		597
	8	**USA**	**Gary Anderson**		
1972	1	PRK	Li Ho Jun		599 **WR**
	2	**USA**	**Victor Auer**		**598**
	3	ROM	Nicolae Rotaru		598
1976	1	GER	Karlheinz Smieszek		599 **EWR**
	2	GER	Ulrich Lind		597
	3	URS	Gennady Lushchikov		595
	20	**USA**	**David Ross**		
1980	1	HUN	Károly Varga		599 **EWR**
	2	GDR	Hellfried Heilfort		599 **EWR**
	3	BUL	Petur Zapianov		598
1984	**1**	**USA**	**Edward Etzel**		**599 EOR**
	2	FRA	Michel Bury		596
	3	GBR	Michael Sullivan		596
1992	1	KOR	Lee Eun-chul	597	702.5 **FOR**
	2	NOR	Harald Stenvaag	597	701.4
	3	IOP	S. Pletikosic	597	701.1
	9	**USA**	**Bill Meek**	**596**	

SKEET MIXED

YEAR	RANK	CTRY	ATHLETE	SCORE	TOTAL/SHOOT-OFF
1896-1964	(not held)				
1968	1	URS	Yevgeny Petrov		198/25 **EWR**
	2	ITA	Romano Garagnani		198/24/25 **EWR**
	3	GER	Konrad Wirnhier		198/24/23 **EWR**
	16	**USA**	**Earl Herring**		
1972	1	GER	Konrad Wirnhier		195/25
	2	URS	Yevgeny Petrov		195/24
	3	GDR	Michael Buchheim		195/23
	9	**USA**	**Jack Johnson**		
1976	1	TCH	Josef Panacek		198 **EOR**
	2	HOL	Eric Swinkels		198 **EOR**
	3	POL	Wieslaw Gawlikowski		196
	14	**USA**	**John Satterwhite**		
1980	1	DEN	Hans Kjeld Rasmussen		196/25/25
	2	SWE	Lars-Göran Carlsson		196/25/24
	3	CUB	Roberto Castrillo Garcia		196/25/23
1984	**1**	**USA**	**Matthew Dryke**		**198 EOR**
	2	DEN	Ole Riber Rasmussen		196/25
	3	ITA	Luca Scribani Rossi		196/23
1988	1	GDR	Azel Wegner	198 **EOR**	222
	2	CHI	Alfonso De Iruarrizaga	198 **EOR**	221
	3	ESP	Jorge Guardiola	196	220
	4	**USA**	**Daniel Carlisle**	**197**	**220**
1992	1	CHN	Zhang Shan	200	223 **FOR**
	2	PER	Juan Jorge Giha	198	222
	3	ITA	Bruno Mario Rossetti	198	222
	6	**USA**	**Matthew Dryke**	**198**	**221**

TRAP MIXED

YEAR	RANK	CTRY	ATHLETE	SCORE	TOTAL/SHOOT-OFF
1896 (not held)					
1900	1	FRA	Roger de Barbarin		17
	2	FRA	René Guyot		17
	3	FRA	Justinien de Clary		17
(no USA entry)					
1904 (not held)					

(Single shot)

WOMEN'S AIR RIFLE

YEAR	RANK	CRY	ATHLETE	SCORE	TOTAL
1896-1980			(not held)		
1984	1	USA	**Pat Spurgin**		**393**
	2	ITA	Edith Gufler		391
	3	CHN	Wu Xiaoxuan		389
1988	1	URS	Irina Chilova	395 OR	498.5
	2	FRG	Silvia Sperber	393	497.5
	3	URS	Anna Maloukhina	394	495.8
	6	USA	**Launi Meili**	395 OR	**493.3**
1992	1	KOR	Yeo Kab-soon	396	498.2
	2	BUL	Vessela Letcheva	396	495.3
	3	IOP	Aka Binder	393	495.1
	11T	USA	**Launi Meili**	391	

WOMEN'S SMALLBORE RIFLE, 3-POS.

YEAR	RANK	CRY	ATHLETE	SCORE	TOTAL
1896-1980			(not held)		
1984	1	CHN	Wu Xiaoxuan		581
	2	GER	Ulrike Holmer		578
	3	USA	**Wanda Jewell**		**578**
1988	1	FRG	Silvia Sperber		685.6
	2	BUL	Vessela Letcheva		683.2
	3	URS	Valentina Tcherkassova		681.4
	7	USA	**Launi Meili**	582	**676.5**
1992	1	USA	**Launi Meili**	587	**684.3 FOR**
	2	BUL	Nonka Matova	584	682.7
	3	POL	M. Ksiazkiewicz	585	681.5

SOCCER (FOOTBALL)

YEAR	RANK	CRY	SCORE
1896			(not held)
1900	1	GBR	1-0
	2	FRA	1-1
	3	BEL	0-1
			(no USA entry)
1904	1	CAN	2-0
	2	**USA**	**1-1-1**
	3	**USA**	**0-2-1**
1906	1	DEN	2-0
	2	INT	1-1
	3	GRE	0-2
			(no USA entry)
1908	1	GBR	3-0
	2	DEN	2-1
	3	HOL	1-1
	4	SWE	0-2
			(no USA entry)
1912	1	GBR	3-0
	2	DEN	2-1
	3	HOL	2-1
	4	FIN	2-2
	5	HUN	2-2
	5	AUT	3-2
	7	GER	1-2
	7	ITA	1-2
			(no USA entry)
1920	1	BEL	3-0
	2	ESP	4-1
	3	HOL	2-2
	4	ITA	2-1
	4	NOR	2-1
	5	SWE	1-2
			(no USA entry)
1924	1	URU	5-0
	2	SUI	4-1-1
	3	SWE	3-1-1
	4	HOL	2-2-1
	4	EGY	1-1
	5	FRA	1-1
	5	IRL	2-1
	5	ITA	2-1
	5	ESP	1-1-1
		USA	elim. 2nd rd

USA Team: Dr. Aage Brix / S.H. Dalrymple / Irving Davis / W.J. Demko / James Douglas / Carl Johnson / F. Burke Jones / Henry Charles Farrell / Ed Hart / R.A. O'Connor / James Rhody / Arthur George Rudd / Andrew John Straduan / Herb Wells

	1928			

(Far left column — continuation)

YEAR	RANK	CRY	ATHLETE		TOTAL
1906	1	GBR	Gerald Merlin		24
	2	GRE	Ioannis Peridis		24
	3	GBR	Sidney Merlin		23
			(no USA entry)		
(Double shot)					
1906	1	USA	Sidney Merlin		15
	2	GRE	Anastasios Metaxas		13
	3	GBR	Gerald Merlin		12
			(no USA entry)		
1908	1	CAN	Walter Ewing		72
	2	CAN	George Beattie		60
	3	CAN	Alexander Maunder		57
			(no USA entry)		
1912	**1**	**USA**	**James Graham**		**96**
	2	GER	Alfred Goldel		94
	3	RUS	Harry Blau		91
1920	**1**	**USA**	**Mark Arie**		**95**
	2	USA	Frank Troeh		93
	3	USA	Frank Wright		87
1924	1	HUN	Gyula Halasy		98/8 OR
	2	FIN	Konrad Huber		98/7 OR
	3	**USA**	**Frank Hughes**		**97**
1928-1948			(not held)		
1952	1	CAN	George Généreux		192
	2	SWE	Knut Holmqvist		191
	3	SWE	Hans Liljedahl		190
1956	1	ITA	Galliano Rossini		195 OR
	2	POL	Adam Smelczynski		190
	3	ITA	Alessandro Ciceri		188/24
1960	1	ROM	Ion Dumitrescu		192
	2	ITA	Galliano Rossini		191
	3	URS	Sergei Kalinin		190
	4	**USA**	**James Clark**		**188**
1964	1	ITA	Ennio Mattarelli		198 OR
	2	URS	Pavel Senichev		194/25
	3	**USA**	**William Morris**		**194/24**
1968	1	GBR	John Braithwaite		198 EWR
	2	**USA**	**Thomas Garrigus**		**196/25/25**
	3	GDR	Kurt Czekalla		196/25/23
1972	1	ITA	Angelo Scalzone		199 WR
	2	FRA	Michel Carrega		198
	3	ITA	Silvano Basagni		195
	6	**USA**	**James Poindexter**		**192**
1976	**1**	**USA**	**Donald Haldeman**		**190**
	2	POR	Armando Silva Marques	189	
	3	ITA	Ubaldesco Baldi		
1980	1	URS	Luciano Giovannetti		198
	2	URS	Rustam Yambulatov		196/24/25
	3	GDR	Jorg Damme		196/24/24
1984	1	ITA	Luciano Giovannetti		192/24
	2	PER	Francisco Boza		192/23
	3	**USA**	**Daniel Carlisle**		**192/22**
1988	1	URS	Dmitri Monakov		222
	2	TCH	Miloslav Bednarik		222
	3	BEL	Frans Peeters		219
	4	**USA**	**Daniel Carlisle**		**194**
1992	1	TCH	Petr Hrdlicka		219 FOR
	2	JPN	Kazumi Watanabe		219
	3	ITA	Marco Venturini		218
	6	**USA**	**Jay Waldron**		**217**

WOMEN'S AIR PISTOL

YEAR	RANK	CRY	ATHLETE	SCORE	TOTAL
1896-1984			(not held)		
1988	1	YUG	Jasna Sekaric	389	489.5 FWR
	2	URS	Nino Saloukvadze	390 WR	487.9
	3	URS	Marina Dobrantcheva	385	485.2
	16T	USA	**Kimberly Dyer**	377	
1992	1	EUN	Marina Logvinenko	387	486.4 FOR
	2	IOP	Jasna Sekaric	389	486.4
	3	BUL	Maria Grousdeva	383	481.6
	24T	USA	**Connie Petracek**	375	

WOMEN'S SPORT PISTOL

YEAR	RANK	CRY	ATHLETE	SCORE	TOTAL/SHOOT-OFF
1896-1980			(not held)		
1984	1	CAN	Linda Thom		585/198
	2	**USA**	**Ruby Fox**		**585/197**
	3	AUS	Patricia Dench		583/196
1988	1	URS	Nino Saloukvadze	690.0	
	2	JPN	Tomoko Hasegawa	587 OR	686.0
	3	YUG	Jasna Sekaric	591	686.0
	24T	USA	**Kim Dyer**	578	
1992	1	EUN	M. Logvinenko	587	684 FOR
	2	CHN	Li Duihong	586	680
	3	MGL	D. Munkhbayar	584	679
	24T	USA	**Roxane Thompson**	572	

(Center column — continuation, team results and rosters)

YEAR	RANK	CRY	SCORE
1932			(not held)
1936	1	ITA	4-0
	2	AUT	2-1
	3	NOR	2-2
	4	POL	1-1
	5	GER	1-1
	5	PER	1-0
		USA	elim. 1st rd

USA Team: Charles Altemose / Francis Barikus / Edward Leo Begley / James Crockett / J.W. Chimielewski / Robert Denton / William John Fiedler / Andrew Gajda / Frank Greinert / Peter Pietras / Francis Ryan / George Nemchik / John Joseph Olthuans / Fred Stoll / F.J. Zidkowski / John Zwan

1948	1	SWE	4-0
	2	YUG	3-1
	3	DEN	2-2
	4	GBR	2-1
	5	FRA	1-1
	5	KOR	3-1
	5	TUR	1-1
		USA	elim. 1st rd

USA Team: Robert Annis / Walter Bahr / Raymond Beckman / William Bertani / Charles Columbo / Joseph Costa / Joseph Ferreira / Stephen Grivnow / Manuel Martin / Bernard McLaughlin / Gino Pariani / Edward Souza / John Souza / Archie Strimel / Rolf Valtin

1952	1	HUN	5-0
	2	YUG	4-1-1
	3	SWE	3-1
	4	GER	2-2
	5	AUT	2-1
	5	BRA	2-1
	5	DEN	1-1
	5	TUR	1-1
		USA	elim. prelim. rd

USA Team: Robert Burkhard / Charles Columbo / William Conterio / Elwood Cook / John Dunn / Andrew Keir / Harry Keough / Martin Krumm / Ruben Mendoza / E.J. McHugh Jr / Lloyd Monsen / Willy Schaller / William Sheppell / John Souza / Lawrence Surock

1956	1	URS	4-0-1
	2	YUG	3-0
	3	BUL	1-1
	4	IND	0-1-2
	5	AUS	1-1
	5	JPN	0-1
		USA	elim. qtr. finals

USA Team: John Carden / Ronald Coder / William Conterio / James Patrick Dorrian / Svend Engedal / Harry Keough / William Looby / Alfonso Marina / Ruben Mendoza / Lloyd Monsen / Edward John Murphy / Richard Rice Packer / Zenon Snylyk / Herman Wecke / Siegbert Wirth / Albert Zerhusen

1960	1	YUG	3-0-2
	2	DEN	4-1
	3	HUN	4-1
	4	ITA	2-1-2
		(no USA entry - DNQ)	
1964	1	HUN	5-0
	2	TCH	5-1
	3	GER	4-1
	4	UAR	2-3-1
	5	GHA	1-1-1
	5	JPN	1-2
	5	ROM	2-1
	5	YUG	1-2
		(no USA entry - DNQ)	
1968	1	HUN	5-0-1
	2	BUL	3-1-2
	3	JPN	3-3
	4	MEX	2-2-1
	5	FRA	2-2
	5	GUA	2-1
	5	ISR	2-1
	5	ESP	2-1-1
		(no USA entry - DNQ)	
1972	1	POL	6-0-1
	2	HUN	5-0-1
	3	GDR	4-2-1
	3	URS	5-1
	5	DEN	3-2-1
	5	GER	3-2-1
	5	MEX	2-3-1
	5	MAR	1-4-1
		USA	elim. 1st rd

USA Team: Michael Ivanow / Walter Behr / John Bocwinski / John Carenza / Arthur Demling / Manuel Hernandez / Archie Roboostoff / Hugo Salcedo / Michael Seerey / Neil Stam / Horst Stemke / Joseph Hamm / Steve Gay

			(no USA entry)

(Far right column — water polo / soccer continuation and rosters)

YEAR	RANK	CRY	SCORE
1976			(no USA entry - DNQ)
	1	GDR	4-0-1
	2	POL	3-1-1
	3	URS	4-1
	4	BRA	2-2-1
	5	FRA	2-2-1
	5	IRN	1-2
	5	ISR	1-2
	5	PRK	1-2
1980			(no USA entry - DNQ)
	1	TCH	4-0-2
	2	GDR	4-1-1
	3	URS	5-1
	4	YUG	3-2-1
	5	ALG	1-2-1
	5	JPN	1-1
	5	CUB	2-2
	5	IRQ	1-1-2
	5	KUW	1-1-2
1984	1	FRA	4-0-2
	2	BRA	5-1
	3	YUG	5-1
	4	ITA	3-3
	5	CAN	1-2-1
	5	CHI	1-1-2
	5	EGY	1-1-2
	5	GER	2-2
		USA	elim. prelim. rd

USA Team: Ami Aly / Hernan Borja / David Brcic / Kevin Crow / Richard Davis / Angel Dibernardo / Jeff Durgan / Michael Fox / Jeff Hooker / Erhardt Kapp / Steve Moyers / Hugo Perez / William Savage / Jamie Swanner / Kazbek Tambi / Gregg Thompson / Jean Willrich

1988	1	URS	3-2	(Final)
	2	BRA	3-0	(3rd-4th)
	3	FRG		
		ITA		
		USA	elim. 1st rd	

USA TEAM: C. Borja/ M. Kydes/ F. Klopas/ M. Fall/ J. Banks / J. Stollmeyer/ P. Krumpe/ J. Harkes/ M. Windischmann/ A. Aly/ T. Snyder / S. Trittschuh/ T. Kain/ S. Fuchs/ T. Hantak/ D. Vanole/ J. Doyle/ K. Crow

1992	1	ESP	3-2	(Final)
	2	POL	1-0	(3rd-4th)
	3	GHA		ESP vs. GHA 2-0 (semi)
	4	AUS		POL vs. AUS 6-1 (semi)
		USA	prelim. rd	

USA TEAM: Yari Allnutt / Dario Brose / Michael Burns / Troy Dayak / Anthony Feuer / Brad Friedel / Rhett Hardy / Chris Henderson / Michael Hutuller / Zak Ibsen / Erik Imler / Cobi Jones / Manuel Lagos / Alexi Lalas / Michael Lapper / Joe Moore / Curtis Onalfo / Cameron Rast / Claudio Reyna / Steve Snow / Dante Washington

SWIMMING

MEN'S 50-METER FREESTYLE

YEAR	RANK	CRY	ATHLETE	TIME
1896-1900			(not held)	
1904	1	HUN	Zoltan Halmay	28.0
	2	**USA**	**J. Scott Leary**	**28.6**
	3	USA	**Charles Daniels**	
1906-1984			(not held)	
1988	**1**	**USA**	**Matt Biondi**	**22.14 WR**
	2	**USA**	**Tom Jager**	**22.36**
	3	URS	Gennadi Prigoda	22.71
1992	1	EUN	Alexander Popov	21.91 OR
	2	**USA**	**Matt Biondi**	**22.09**
	3	**USA**	**Tom Jager**	**22.30**

MEN'S 100-METER FREESTYLE

YEAR	RANK	CRY	ATHLETE	TIME
1896	1	HUN	Alfred Hajós	1:22.2
	2	GRE	Efstathios Choraphas	1:23.0
	3	AUT	Otto Herschmann	
	5	**USA**	**Gardner Williams**	
1900			(not held)	
1904	1	HUN	Zoltan Halmay	1:02.8
	2	**USA**	**Charles Daniels**	
	3	**USA**	**J. Scott Leary**	
1906	1	HUN	**Charles Daniels**	1:13.4
	2	HUN	Zoltan Halmay	1:14.2
	3	AUS	Cecil Healy	
1908	**1**	**USA**	**Charles Daniels**	**1:05.6 WR**
	2	HUN	Zoltan Halmay	1:06.2
	3	SWE	Harald Julin	1:08.0
1912	**1**	**USA**	**Duke Paoa Kahanamoku**	**1:03.4**
	2	AUS	Cecil Healy	1:04.6
	3	**USA**	**Kenneth Huszagh**	**1:05.6**
(first final)				
1920	**1**	**USA**	**Duke Paoa Kahanamoku**	**1:00.4 WR**

O'Carroll / John Rudge / Francis Ryan / Harry Smith

YEAR	RANK	CTRY	ATHLETE	TIME	
	2	USA	**Pua Kela Kealoha**	**1:02.2**	
	3	USA	**William Harris**	**1:03.2**	
(second final)	1	USA	**Duke Paoa Kahanamoku**	**1:01.4**	
	2	USA	**Pua Kela Kealoha**	**1:02.6**	
	3	USA	**William Harris**	**1:03.0**	
1924	1	USA	**Johnny Weissmuller**	**59.0**	OR
	2	USA	**Duke Paoa Kahanamoku**	**1:01.4**	
	3	USA	**Samuel Kahanamoku**	**1:01.8**	
1928	1	USA	**Johnny Weissmuller**	**58.6**	OR
	2	HUN	István Bárány	59.8	
	3	JPN	Katsuo Takaishi	1:00.0	
1932	1	JPN	Yasuji Miyazaki	58.2	
	2	JPN	Tatsugo Kawaishi	58.6	
	3	USA	**Albert Schwartz**	**58.8**	
1936	1	HUN	Ferenc Csik	57.6	
	2	JPN	Masanori Yusa	57.9	
	3	JPN	Shigeo Arai	58.0	
	6	USA	**Peter Fick**	**59.7**	
1948	1	USA	**Walter Ris**	**57.3**	OR
	2	USA	**Alan Ford**	**57.8**	
	3	HUN	Géza Kádas	58.1	
1952	1	USA	**Clarke Scholes**	**57.4**	
	2	JPN	Hiroshi Suzuki	57.4	
	3	SWE	Göran Larsson	58.2	
1956	1	AUS	John Henricks	55.4	OR
	2	AUS	John Devitt	55.8	
	3	AUS	Gary Chapman	56.7	
	4	USA	**Logan Reid Patterson**	**57.2**	
1960	1	AUS	John Devitt	55.2	OR
	2	USA	**Lance Larson**	**55.2**	OR
	3	BRA	Manuel Dos Santos	55.4	
1964	1	USA	**Donald Schollander**	**53.4**	OR
	2	GBR	Robert McGregor	53.5	
	3	GER	Hans-Joachim Klein	54.0	
1968	1	AUS	Michael Wenden	52.2	WR
	2	USA	**Kenneth Walsh**	**52.8**	
	3	USA	**Mark Spitz**	**53.0**	
1972	1	USA	**Mark Spitz**	**51.22**	WR
	2	USA	Jerry Heidenreich	51.65	
	3	URS	Vladimir Bure	51.77	
1976	1	USA	**Jim Montgomery**	**49.99**	WR
	2	USA	**Jim Babashoff**	**50.81**	
	3	GER	Peter Nocke	51.31	
1980	1	GDR	Jörg Woithe	50.40	
	2	SWE	Per Holmertz	50.91	
	3	SWE	Per Johansson	51.29	
1984	1	USA	**Ambrose "Rowdy" Gaines**	**49.80**	OR
	2	AUS	Mark Stockwell	50.24	
	3	SWE	Per Johansson	50.31	
1988	1	USA	**Matthew Biondi**	**48.63**	OR
	2	USA	**Christopher Jacobs**	**49.08**	
	3	FRA	Stephan Caron	49.62	
1992	1	EUN	Alexander Popov	49.02	
	2	BRA	Gustavo Borges	49.43	
	3	FRA	Stephen Caron	49.50	
	4	USA	**Jon Olsen**	**49.51**	

MEN'S 200-METER FREESTYLE

YEAR	RANK	CTRY	ATHLETE	TIME	
1896	(not held)				
1900	1	AUS	Frederick Lane	2:25.2	OR
	2	HUN	Zoltán Halmay	2:31.4	
	3	AUT	Karl Ruberl	2:32.0	
(no USA entry)					
1904	1	USA	**Charles Daniels**	**2:44.2**	
	2	USA	**Francis Gailey**	**2:46.0**	
	3	GER	Emil Rausch	2:56.0	
1906-1964	(not held)				
1968	1	AUS	Michael Wenden	1:55.2	OR
	2	USA	**Donald Schollander**	**1:55.8**	
	3	USA	**John Nelson**	**1:58.1**	
1972	1	USA	**Mark Spitz**	**1:52.78**	WR
	2	USA	**Steven Genter**	**1:53.73**	
	3	GER	Werner Lampe	1:53.99	
1976	1	USA	**Bruce Furniss**	**1:50.29**	WR
	2	USA	**John Naber**	**1:50.50**	
	3	USA	**Jim Montgomery**	**1:50.58**	
1980	1	URS	Sergei Kopliakov	1:49.81	OR
	2	URS	Andrei Krylov	1:50.76	
	3	AUS	Graeme Brewer	1:51.60	
1984	1	GER	Michael Gross	1:47.44	WR
	2	USA	**Michael Heath**	**1:49.10**	
	3	GER	Thomas Fahrner	1:49.69	
1988	1	AUS	Duncan Armstrong	1:47.25	WR
	2	SWE	Anders Holmertz	1:47.89	
	3	USA	**Matt Biondi**	**1:47.99**	
1992	1	EUN	Evgueni Sadovyi	1:46.70	OR
	2	SWE	Anders Holmertz	1:46.86	

YEAR	RANK	CTRY	ATHLETE	TIME	
	3	FIN	Alexander Kasvio	1:47.63	
	6	USA	**Joe Hudepohl**	**1:48.36**	

MEN'S 400-METER FREESTYLE

YEAR	RANK	CTRY	ATHLETE	TIME	
1896	1	AUT	Paul Neumann	8:12.6	
	2	GRE	Antonios Pepanos		
	3	GRE	Efstathios Choraphas		
(no USA entry)					
1900	(not held)				
1904	1	USA	**Charles Daniels**	**6:16.2**	
	2	USA	**Francis Gailey**	**6:22.0**	
	3	AUT	Otto Wahle	6:39.0	
1906	1	AUT	Otto Scheff	6:23.8	
	2	GBR	Henry Taylor	6:24.4	
	3	GBR	John Arthur Jarvis	6:27.2	
(no USA entry)					
1908	1	GBR	Henry Taylor	5:36.8	
	2	AUS	Frank Beaurepaire	5:44.2	
	3	AUT	Otto Scheff	5:46.0	
		USA	**L.B. Goodwin / C.W. Trubenbach**	**elim. 1st rd**	
1912	1	CAN	George Hodgson	5:24.4	
	2	GBR	John Hatfield	5:25.8	
	3	AUS	Harold Hardwick	5:31.2	
		USA	**James Reilly**	**elim. 1st rd**	
1920	1	USA	**Norman Ross**		
	2	USA	**Ludy Langer**		
	3	CAN	George Vernot		
1924	1	USA	**Johnny Weissmuller**	**5:04.2**	OR
	2	SWE	Arne Borg	5:05.6	
	3	AUS	Andrew "Boy" Charlton	5:06.6	
1928	1	ARG	Alberto Zorilla	5:01.6	OR
	2	AUS	Andrew "Boy" Charlton	5:03.6	
	3	SWE	Arne Borg	5:04.6	
	4	USA	**Clarence "Buster" Crabbe**	**5:05.4**	
1932	1	USA	**Clarence "Buster" Crabbe**	**4:48.4**	OR
	2	FRA	Jean Taris	4:48.5	
	3	JPN	Tsutomu Oyokota	4:52.3	
1936	1	USA	**Jack Medica**	**4:44.5**	OR
	2	JPN	Shumpei Uto	4:45.6	
	3	JPN	Shozo Makino	4:48.1	
1948	1	USA	**William Smith**	**4:41.0**	OR
	2	USA	**James McLane**	**4:43.4**	
	3	AUS	John Marshall	4:47.4	
1952	1	FRA	Jean Boiteux	4:30.7	OR
	2	USA	**Ford Konno**	**4:31.3**	
	3	SWE	Per-Olof Ostrand	4:35.2	
1956	1	AUS	Murray Rose	4:27.3	OR
	2	JPN	Tsuyoshi Yamanaka	4:30.4	
	3	USA	**George Breen**	**4:32.5**	
1960	1	AUS	Murray Rose	4:18.3	OR
	2	JPN	Tsuyoshi Yamanaka	4:21.4	
	3	AUS	John Konrads	4:21.8	
	5	USA	**Alan Somers**	**4:22.0**	
1964	1	USA	**Donald Schollander**	**4:12.2**	WR
	2	GDR	Frank Wiegand	4:14.9	
	3	AUS	Allan Wood	4:15.1	
1968	1	USA	**Michael Burton**	**4:09.0**	OR
	2	CAN	Ralph Hutton	4:11.7	
	3	FRA	Alain Mosconi	4:13.3	
1972	*	USA	**Rick DeMont**	**4:00.26**	
	1	AUS	Bradford Cooper	4:00.27	OR
	2	USA	**Steven Genter**	**4:01.94**	
	3	USA	**Tom McBreen**	**4:02.64**	

*Failed drug test—Unwittedly took a banned substance contained in his asthma medication.

YEAR	RANK	CTRY	ATHLETE	TIME	
1976	1	USA	**Brian Goodell**	**3:51.93**	WR
	2	USA	**Tim Shaw**	**3:52.54**	
	3	URS	Vladimir Raskatov	3:55.76	
1980	1	URS	Vladimir Salnikov	3:51.31	OR
	2	URS	Andrei Krylov	3:53.24	
	3	URS	Ivar Stukolkin	3:53.95	
1984	1	USA	**George DiCarlo**	**3:51.23**	OR
	2	USA	**John Mykkanen**	**3:51.49**	
	3	AUS	Justin Lemberg	3:51.79	
1988	1	GDR	Uwe Dassler	3:46.95	WR
	2	AUS	Duncan Armstrong	3:47.15	
	3	POL	Artur Wojdat	3:47.34	
	4	USA	**Matthew Cetlinski**	**3:48.09**	
1992	1	EUN	Evgueni Sadovyi	3:45.00	WR
	2	AUS	Kieren Perkins	3:45.16	
	3	SWE	Anders Holmertz	3:46.77	
	11	USA	**Sean Killion**	**3:52.76**	

MEN'S 1500-METER FREESTYLE

YEAR	RANK	CTRY	ATHLETE	TIME	
1896	1	HUN	Alfréd Hajós	18:22.2	OR
	2	GRE	Jean Andreou	21:03.4	
	3	GRE	Efstathios Choraphas		
	4	USA	**Gardner Williams**		
1900	1	GBR	John Arthur Jarvis	13:40.2	
	2	AUT	Otto Wahle	14:53.6	
	3	HUN	Zoltán Halmay	15:16.4	
(no USA entry)					
1904	1	GER	Emil Rausch	27:18.2	
	2	HUN	Géza Kiss	28:28.2	
	3	USA	**Francis Gailey**	**28:54.0**	
1906	1	GBR	Henry Taylor	28:28.0	
	2	GBR	John Arthur Jarvis	30:07.6	
	3	AUT	Otto Scheff	30:53.4	
(no USA entry)					
1908	1	GBR	Henry Taylor	22:48.4	WR
	2	GBR	Thomas Battersby	22:51.2	
	3	AUS	Frank Beaurepaire	22:56.2	
		USA	**J.B. Green**	**elim. 1st rd**	
1912	1	CAN	George Hodgson	22:00.0	WR
	2	GBR	John Hatfield	22:39.0	
	3	AUS	Harold Hardwick	23:15.4	
(no USA entry)					
1920	1	USA	**Norman Ross**	**22:23.2**	
	2	CAN	George Vernot	22:36.4	
	3	AUS	Frank Beaurepaire	23:04.0	
1924	1	AUS	Andrew "Boy" Charlton	20:06.6	WR
	2	SWE	Arne Borg	20:41.4	
	3	AUS	Frank Beaurepaire	21:48.4	
		USA	**Adam Smith**	**elim. semis**	
1928	1	SWE	Arne Borg	19:51.8	OR
	2	AUS	Andrew "Boy" Charlton	20:02.6	
	3	USA	**Clarence "Buster" Crabbe**	**20:28.8**	
1932	1	JPN	Kusuo Kitamura	19:12.4	OR
	2	JPN	Shozo Makino	19:14.1	
	3	USA	**James Cristy**	**19:39.5**	
1936	1	JPN	Noboru Terada	19:13.7	
	2	USA	**Jack Medica**	**19:34.0**	
	3	JPN	Shumpei Uto	19:34.5	
1948	1	USA	**James McLane**	**19:18.5**	
	2	AUS	John Marshall	19:31.3	
	3	HUN	György Mitró	19:43.2	
1952	1	USA	**Ford Konno**	**18:30.3**	OR
	2	JPN	Shiro Hashizume	18:41.4	
	3	BRA	Tetsuo Okamoto	18:51.3	
1956	1	AUS	Murray Rose	17:58.9	
	2	JPN	Tsuyoshi Yamanaka	18:00.3	
	3	USA	**George Breen**	**18:08.2**	
1960	1	AUS	John Konrads	17:19.6	OR
	2	AUS	Murray Rose	17:21.7	
	3	USA	**George Breen**	**17:30.6**	
1964	1	AUS	Robert Windle	17:01.7	OR
	2	USA	**John Nelson**	**17:03.0**	
	3	AUS	Allan Wood	17:07.7	
1968	1	USA	**Michael Burton**	**16:38.9**	OR
	2	USA	**John Kinsella**	**16:57.3**	
	3	AUS	Gregory Brough	17:04.7	
1972	1	USA	**Michael Burton**	**15:52.58**	WR
	2	AUS	Graham Windeatt	15:58.48	
	3	USA	**Douglas Northway**	**16:09.25**	
1976	1	USA	**Brian Goodell**	**15:02.40**	WR
	2	USA	**Bobby Hackett**	**15:03.91**	
	3	AUS	Stephen Holland	15:04.66	
1980	1	URS	Vladimir Salnikov	14:58.27	WR
	2	URS	Aleksandr Chaev	15:14.30	
	3	AUS	Max Metzker	15:14.49	
1984	1	USA	**Michael O'Brien**	**15:05.20**	
	2	USA	**George DiCarlo**	**15:10.59**	
	3	GER	Stefan Pfeiffer	15:12.11	
1988	1	URS	Vladimir Salnikov	15:00.40	
	2	FRG	Stefan Pfeiffer	15:02.69	
	3	GDR	Uwe Dassler	15:06.15	
	4	USA	**Matthew Cetlinski**	**15:06.42**	
1992	1	AUS	Kieren John Perkins	14:43.48	WR
	2	AUS	Glen Housman	14:55.29	
	3	GER	Joerg Hoffman	15:02.29	
	7	USA	**Lawrence Frostad**	**15:19.41**	

MEN'S 100-METER BACKSTROKE

YEAR	RANK	CTRY	ATHLETE	TIME	
1896-1900	(not held)				
1904	1	GER	Walter Brack	1:16.8	
	2	GER	Georg Hoffmann		
	3	GER	Georg Zacharias		
	4	USA	**William Orthwein**		
1906	(not held)				
1908	1	GER	Arno Bieberstein	1:24.6	WR
	2	DEN	Ludvig Dam	1:26.6	
	3	GBR	Herbert Haresnape	1:27.0	
		USA	**A.M. Goessling**	**elim. 1st rd**	
1912	1	USA	**Harry Hebner**	**1:21.2**	
	2	GER	Otto Fahr	1:22.4	
	3	GER	Paul Kellner	1:24.0	
1920	1	USA	**Warren Paoa Kealoha**	**1:15.2**	
	2	USA	**Ray Kegeris**	**1:16.2**	
	3	BEL	Gérard Blitz	1:19.0	
1924	1	USA	**Warren Paoa Kealoha**	**1:13.2**	OR
	2	USA	**Paul Wyatt**	**1:15.4**	
	3	HUN	Károly Bartha	1:17.8	
1928	1	USA	**George Kojac**	**1:08.2**	WR
	2	USA	**Walter Laufer**	**1:10.0**	
	3	USA	**Paul Wyatt**	**1:12.0**	
1932	1	JPN	Masaji Kiyokawa	1:08.6	
	2	JPN	Toshio Irie	1:09.8	
	3	JPN	Kentaro Kawatsu	1:10.0	
	4	USA	**Robert Zehr**	**1:10.9**	
1936	1	USA	**Adolf Kiefer**	**1:05.9**	OR
	2	USA	**Albert Vandeweghe**	**1:07.7**	
	3	JPN	Masaji Kiyokawa	1:08.4	
1948	1	USA	**Allen Stack**	**1:06.4**	
	2	USA	**Robert Cowell**	**1:06.5**	
	3	FRA	Georges Vallerey	1:07.8	
1952	1	USA	**Yoshinobu Oyakawa**	**1:05.4**	OR
	2	FRA	Gilbert Bozon	1:06.2	
	3	USA	**Jack Taylor**	**1:06.4**	
1956	1	AUS	Davie Thiele	1:02.2	OR
	2	AUS	John Monckton	1:03.2	
	3	USA	**Frank McKinney**	**1:04.5**	
1960	1	AUS	David Theile	1:01.9	OR
	2	USA	**Frank McKinney**	**1:02.1**	
	3	USA	**Robert Bennett**	**1:02.3**	
1964	(not held)				
1968	1	GDR	Roland Matthes	58.7	OR
	2	USA	**Charles Hickcox**	**1:00.2**	
	3	USA	**Ronald Mills**	**1:00.5**	
1972	1	GDR	Roland Matthes	56.58	OR
	2	USA	**Michael Stamm**	**57.70**	
	3	USA	**John Murphy**	**58.35**	
1976	1	USA	**John Naber**	**55.49**	WR
	2	USA	**Peter Rocca**	**56.34**	
	3	GDR	Ronald Matthes	57.22	
1980	1	SWE	Bengt Baron	56.33	
	2	URS	Viktor Kuznetsov	56.99	
	3	URS	Vladimir Dolgov	57.63	
1984	1	USA	**Richard Carey**	**55.79**	
	2	USA	**David Wilson**	**56.35**	
	3	CAN	Mike West	56.49	
1988	1	JPN	Daichi Suzuki	55.05	
	2	USA	**David Berkoff**	**55.18**	
	3	URS	Igor Polianski	55.20	
1992	1	CAN	Mark Tewksburg	53.98	OR
	2	USA	**Jeff Rouse**	**54.04**	
	3	USA	**David Berkoff**	**54.78**	

MEN'S 200-METER BACKSTROKE

YEAR	RANK	CTRY	ATHLETE	TIME	
1896	(not held)				
1900	1	GER	Ernst Hoppenberg	2:47.0	
	2	AUT	Karl Ruberl	2:56.0	
	3	HOL	Johannes Drost	3:01.0	
(no USA entry)					
1904-1960	(not held)				
1964	1	USA	**Jed Graef**	**2:10.3**	WR
	2	USA	**Gary Dilley**	**2:10.5**	
	3	USA	**Robert Bennett**	**2:13.1**	
1968	1	GDR	Roland Matthes	2:09.6	OR
	2	USA	**Mitchell Ivey**	**2:10.6**	
	3	USA	**Jack Horsley**	**2:10.9**	
1972	1	GDR	Roland Matthes	2:02.82	EWR
	2	USA	**Michael Stamm**	**2:04.09**	
	3	USA	**Mitchell Ivey**	**2:04.33**	
1976	1	USA	**John Naber**	**1:59.19**	WR
	2	USA	**Peter Rocca**	**2:00.55**	
	3	USA	**Dan Harrigan**	**2:01.35**	
1980	1	HUN	Sándor Wladár	2:01.93	
	2	HUN	Zoltán Verrasztó	2:02.40	
	3	AUS	Mark Kerry	2:03.14	
1984	1	USA	**Richard Carey**	**2:00.23**	
	2	FRA	Frédéric Delcourt	2:01.75	
	3	CAN	Cameron Henning	2:02.37	
1988	1	URS	Igor Polianski	1:59.37	
	2	GDR	Frank Baltrusch	1:59.60	
	3	NZL	Paul Kingsman	2:00.48	
	7	USA	**Daniel Veatch**	**2:02.26**	
1992	1	ESP	Martin Lopez-Zubero	1:58.47	OR
	2	EUN	Vladimir Selkov	1:58.87	
	3	ITA	Stefano Battistelli	1:59.40	
	5	USA	**Tripp Schwenk**	**1:59.73**	

MEN'S 100-METER BREASTSTROKE

YEAR	RANK	CTRY	ATHLETE	TIME	
1896-1964	(not held)				
1968	1	USA	**Donald McKenzie**	**1:07.7**	OR
	2	USR	Vladimir Kossinsky	1:08.0	
	3	USR	Nikolai Pankin	1:08.0	
1972	1	JPN	Nobutaka Taguchi	1:04.94	WR
	2	USA	**Thomas Bruce**	**1:05.43**	
	3	USA	**John Hencken**	**1:05.61**	
1976	1	USA	**John Hencken**	**1:03.11**	WR
	2	GBR	David Wilkie	1:03.43	
	3	USR	Arvidas Iuozaytis	1:04.23	
1980	1	GBR	Duncan Goodhew	1:03.44	
	2	USR	Arsen Miskarov	1:03.82	
	3	AUS	Peter Evans	1:03.96	
1984	1	USA	**Steve Lundquist**	**1:01.65**	WR
	2	CAN	Victor Davis	1:01.99	
	3	AUS	Peter Evans	1:02.97	

1988	1	GBR	Adrian Moorhouse	1:02.04	
	2	HUN	Karolyn Guttler	1:02.05	
	3	URS	Dmitri Volkov	1:02.20	
	6	USA	**Richard Schroeder**	**1:02.55**	
1992	1	USA	**Nelson Diebel**	**1:01.50**	OR
	2	HUN	Norbert Rozsa	1:01.68	
	3	AUS	Philip Rogers	1:01.76	

MEN'S 200-METER BREASTSTROKE

YEAR	RANK	CTRY	ATHLETE	TIME	
1896-1906		(not held)			
1908	1	GBR	Frederick Holman	3:09.2	WR
	2	GBR	William Robinson	3:12.8	
	3	SWE	Pontus Hanson	3:14.6	
		USA	**A.M. Goessling**	**elim. 1st rd**	
1912	1	GER	Walter Bathe	3:01.8	OR
	2	GER	Wilhelm Lützow	3:05.0	
	3	GER	Kurt Mahlisch	3:08.0	
		USA	**Michal McDermott**	**elim. 1st rd**	
1920	1	SWE	Håkan Malmroth	3:04.4	
	2	SWE	Thor Henning	3:09.2	
	3	FIN	Arvo Aaltonen	3:12.2	
	4	USA	**Jack Howell**		
1924	1	USA	**Robert Skelton**	**2:56.6**	
	2	BEL	Joseph de Combe	2:59.2	
	3	USA	**William Kirschbaum**	**3:01.0**	
1928	1	JPN	Yoshiyuki Tsuruta	2:48.8	OR
	2	GER	Erich Rademacher	2:50.6	
	3	PHI	Teofilo Yldefonzo	2:56.4	
		USA	**T. Blankenburg**	**elim. semis**	
1932	1	JPN	Yoshiyuki Tsuruta	2:45.4	
	2	JPN	Reizo Koike	2:46.6	
	3	PHI	Teofilo Yldefonzo	2:47.1	
		USA	**Basil Francis**	**elim. trials**	
1936	1	JPN	Tetsuo Hamuro	2:41.5	OR
	2	GER	Erwin Sietas	2:42.9	
	3	JPN	Reizo Koike	2:44.2	
	4	USA	**John Herbert Higgins**	**2:45.2**	
1948	1	USA	**Joseph Verdeur**	**2:39.3**	OR
	2	USA	**Keith Carter**	**2:40.2**	
	3	USA	**Robert Sohl**	**2:43.9**	
1952	1	AUS	John Davies	2:34.4	OR
	2	USA	**Bowen Stassforth**	**2:34.7**	
	3	GER	Herbert Klein	2:35.9	
1956	1	JPN	Masaru Furukawa	2:34.7	OR
	2	JPN	Masahiro Yoshimura	2:36.7	
	3	USR	Charis Yunichev	2:36.8	
		USA	**R. Hughes**	**elim. 1st rd**	
1960	1	USA	**William Mulliken**	**2:37.4**	
	3	JPN	Yoshihiko Osaki	2:38.0	
	3	HOL	Wieger Mensonides	2:39.7	
1964	1	AUS	Ian O'Brien	2:27.8	WR
	2	USR	Georgy Prokopenko	2:28.2	
	3	USA	**Chester Jastremski**	**2:29.6**	
1968	1	MEX	Felipe Muñoz	2:28.7	
	2	USR	Vladimir Kosinsky	2:29.2	
	3	USA	**Brian Job**	**2:29.9**	
1972	1	USA	**John Hencken**	**2:21.55**	WR
	2	GBR	David Wilkie	2:23.67	
	3	JPN	Nobutaka Taguchi	2:23.88	
1976	1	GBR	David Wilkie	2:15.11	WR
	2	USA	**John Hencken**	**2:17.26**	
	3	USA	**Richard Colella**	**2:19.20**	
1980	1	USR	Robertas Zhulpa	2:15.85	
	2	HUN	Albán Vermes	2:16.93	
	3	USR	Arsen Miskarov	2:17.28	
1984	1	CAN	Victor Davis	2:13.34	WR
	2	AUS	Glenn Beringen	2:15.79	
	3	SUI	Etienne Dagon	2:17.41	
	4	USA	**Richard Schroeder**	**2:18.03**	
1988	1	HUN	Jozsef Szabo	2:13.52	
	2	GBR	Nick Gillingham	2:14.12	
	3	ESP	Sergio Lopez	2:15.21	
	4	USA	**Mike Barrowman**	**2:15.45**	
1992	1	USA	**Mike Barrowman**	**2:10.16**	WR
	2	HUN	Norbert Rozsa	2:11.23	
	3	GBR	Nick Gillingham	2:11.29	

MEN'S 100-METER BUTTERFLY

YEAR	RANK	CTRY	ATHLETE	TIME	
1896-1964		(not held)			
1968	1	USA	**Douglas Russell**	**55.9**	OR
	2	USA	**Mark Spitz**	**56.4**	
	3	USA	**Ross Wales**	**57.2**	
1972	1	USA	**Mark Spitz**	**54.27**	WR
	2	CAN	Bruce Robertson	55.56	
	3	USA	**Jerry Heidenreich**	**55.74**	
1976	1	USA	**Matt Vogel**	**54.35**	
	2	USA	**Joe Bottom**	**54.50**	
	3	USA	**Gary Hall**	**54.65**	
1980	1	SWE	Pär Arvidsson	54.92	
	2	GDR	Roger Pyttel	54.94	
	3	ESP	David Lopez	55.13	
1984	1	GER	Michael Gross	53.08	WR
	2	USA	**Pablo Morales**	**53.23**	
	3	AUS	Glenn Buchanan	53.85	
1988	1	SUR	Anthony Nesty	53.00	OR
	2	USA	**Matt Biondi**	**53.01**	
	3	GBR	Andy Jameson	53.30	
1992	1	USA	**Pablo Morales**	**53.32**	
	2	POL	Rafal Szukala	53.35	
	3	SUR	Anthony Nesty	53.41	

MEN'S 200-METER BUTTERFLY

YEAR	RANK	CTRY	ATHLETE	TIME	
1896-1952		(not held)			
1956	1	USA	**William Yorzyk**	**2:19.3**	OR
	2	JPN	Takashi Ishimoto	2:23.8	
	3	HUN	György Tumpek	2:23.9	
1960	1	USA	**Michael Troy**	**2:12.8**	WR
	2	AUS	Neville Hayes	2:14.6	
	3	USA	**J. David Gillanders**	**2:15.3**	
1964	1	AUS	Kevin Berry	2:06.6	WR
	2	USA	**Carl Robie**	**2:07.5**	
	3	USA	**Fred Schmidt**	**2:09.3**	
1968	1	USA	**Carl Robie**	**2:08.7**	
	2	GBR	Martin Woodroffe	2:09.0	
	3	USA	**John Ferris**	**2:09.3**	
1972	1	USA	**Mark Spitz**	**2:00.70**	WR
	2	USA	**Gary Hall**	**2:02.86**	
	3	USA	**Robin Backhaus**	**2:03.23**	
1976	1	USA	**Mike Bruner**	**1:59.23**	WR
	2	USA	**Steven Gregg**	**1:59.54**	
	3	USA	**Bill Forrester**	**1:59.96**	
1980	1	USR	Sergei Fesenko	1:59.76	
	2	GBR	Philip Hubble	2:01.20	
	3	GDR	Roger Pyttel	2:01.39	
1984	1	AUS	Jon Sieben	1:57.04	WR
	2	GER	Michael Gross	1:57.40	
	3	VEN	Rafael Vidal Castro	1:57.51	
	4	USA	**Pablo Morales**	**1:57.75**	
1988	1	FRG	Michael Gross	1:56.94	OR
	2	DEN	Benny Nielsen	1:58.24	
	3	NZL	Anthony Mosse	1:58.28	
	5	USA	**Melvin Stewart**	**1:59.19**	
1992	1	USA	**Melvin Stewart**	**1:56.26**	OR
	2	NZL	Danyon Loader	1:57.93	
	3	FRA	Franck Esposito	1:58.51	

MEN'S 200-METER IND. MEDLEY

YEAR	RANK	CTRY	ATHLETE	TIME	
1896-1964		(not held)			
1968	1	USA	**Charles Hickcox**	**2:12.0**	OR
	2	USA	**Gregory Buckingham**	**2:13.0**	
	3	USA	**John Ferris**	**2:13.3**	
1972	1	SWE	Gunnar Larsson	2:07.17	WR
	2	USA	**Alexander "Tim" McKee**	**2:08.37**	
	3	USA	**Steven Furniss**	**2:08.45**	
1976-1980		(not held)			
1984	1	CAN	Alex Baumann	2:01.42	WR
	2	USA	**Pablo Morales**	**2:03.05**	
	3	GBR	Neil Cochran	2:04.38	
1988	1	HUN	Tamas Darnyi	2:00.17	WR
	2	GDR	Patrick Kuehl	2:01.61	
	3	URS	Vadim Iarochtchouk	2:02.40	
	9	USA	**David Wharton**	**2:03.05**	#
# - Final B					
1992	1	HUN	Tamas Darnyi	2:00.76	
	2	USA	**Greg Burgess**	**2:00.97**	
	3	HUN	Attila Czene	2:01.00	

MEN'S 400-METER IND. MEDLEY

YEAR	RANK	CTRY	ATHLETE	TIME	
1896-1960		(not held)			
1964	1	USA	**Richard Roth**	**4:45.4**	WR
	2	USA	**Roy Saari**	**4:47.1**	
	3	GER	Gerhard Hetz	4:51.0	
1968	1	USA	**Charles Hickcox**	**4:48.4**	
	2	USA	**Gary Hall**	**4:48.7**	
	3	GER	Michael Holthaus	4:51.4	
1972	1	SWE	Gunnar Larsson	4:31.98	OR
	2	USA	**Alexander "Tim" McKee**	**4:31.98**	OR
	3	HUN	András Hargitay	4:32.70	
1976	1	USA	**Rod Strachan**	**4:23.68**	WR
	2	USA	**Alexander "Tim" McKee**	**4:24.62**	
	3	USR	Andrei Smirnov	4:26.90	
1980	1	USR	Aleksandr Sidorenko	4:22.89	OR
	2	USR	Sergei Fesenko	4:23.43	
	3	HUN	Zoltán Verrasztó	4:24.24	
1984	1	CAN	Alex Baumann	4:17.41	WR
	2	BRA	Ricardo Prado	4:18.45	
	3	AUS	Robert Woodhouse	4:20.50	
	4	USA	**Jesus Vassallo**	**4:21.46**	
1988	1	HUN	Tamas Darnyi	4:14.75	WR
	2	USA	**David Wharton**	**4:17.36**	
	3	ITA	Stefano Battistelli	4:18.01	
1992	1	HUN	Tamas Darnyi	4:14.23	OR
	2	USA	**Eric Namesnik**	**4:15.57**	
	3	ITA	Luca Sacchi	4:16.34	

MEN'S 4X100-METER FREESTYLE RELAY

YEAR	RANK	CTRY	ATHLETES	TIME	
1896-1960		(not held)			
1964	1	USA	**Stephen Clark / Michael Austin / Gary Ilman / Donald Schollander**	**3:32.2**	WR
	2	GER/GDR		3:37.2	
	3	AUS		3:39.1	
1968	1	USA	**Zachary Zorn / Stephen Rerych / Mark Spitz / Kenneth Walsh**	**3:31.7**	WR
	2	USR		3:34.2	
	3	AUS		3:34.7	
1972	1	USA	**David Edgar / John Murphy / Jerry Heidenreich / Mark Spitz**	**3:26.42**	WR
	2	USR		3:29.72	
	3	GDR		3:32.42	
1976-1980		(not held)			
1984	1	USA	**Christopher Cavanaugh / Michael Heath / Matt Biondi / Ambrose "Rowdy" Gaines / Tom Jager**	**3:19.03**	WR
	2	AUS		3:19.68	
	3	SWE		3:22.69	
1988	1	USA	**Christopher Jacobs / Troy Dalbey / Tom Jager / Matt Biondi / Brent Lang / Doug Gjertsen / Shaun Jordan**	**3:16.53**	WR
	2	URS		3:18.33	
	3	GDR		3:19.82	
1992	1	USA	**Joe Hudepohl / Matt Biondi / Tom Jager / Jon Olsen / Shaun Jordan**	**3:16.74**	
	2	EUN		3:17.56	
	3	GER		3:17.90	

MEN'S 4X200-METER FREESTYLE RELAY

YEAR	RANK	CTRY	ATHLETES	TIME	
1896-1904		(not held)			
1906	1	HUN		16:52.4	
	2	GER		17:16.2	
	3	GBR			
	4	USA	**Frank Bornamann / Joseph Spencer / Maquard Schwartz / Charles Daniels**		
1908	1	GBR		10:55.6	WR
	2	HUN		10:59.0	
	3	USA	**Harry Hebner / Leo Goodwin / Charles Daniels / Leslie Rich**	**11:02.8**	
1912	1	AUS/NZL		10:11.6	WR
	2	USA	**Kenneth Huszagh / Harry Hebner / Perry McGillivray / Duke Paoa Kahanamoku**	**10:20.0**	
	3	GBR		10:28.2	
1920	1	USA	**Perry McGillivray / Pua Kela Kealoha / Norman Ross / Duke Paoa Kahanamoku**	**10:04.4**	WR
	2	AUS		10:25.4	
	3	GBR		10:37.2	
1924	1	USA	**Wallace O'Connor / Harry Glancy / Ralph Breyer / Johnny Weissmuller**	**9:53.4**	WR
	2	AUS		10:02.2	
	3	SWE		10:06.8	
1928	1	USA	**Austin Clapp / Walter Laufer / George Kojac / Johnny Weissmuller**	**9:36.2**	WR
	2	JPN		9:41.4	
	3	CAN		9:47.8	
1932	1	JPN		8:58.4	WR
	2	USA	**Frank Booth / George Fissler / Marola Kalili / Manuella Kalili**	**9:10.5**	
	3	HUN		9:31.4	
1936	1	JPN		8:51.5	WR
	2	USA	**Ralph Flanagan / John Macionis / Paul Wolf / Jack Medica**	**9:03.0**	
	3	HUN		9:12.3	
1948	1	USA	**Walter Ris / James McLane / Wallace Wolf / William Smith**	**8:46.0**	WR
	2	HUN		8:48.4	
	3	FRA		9:08.0	
1952	1	USA	**Wayne Moore / William Woolsey / Ford Konno / James McLane**	**8:31.1**	OR
	2	JPN		8:33.5	
	3	FRA		8:45.9	
1956	1	AUS		8:23.6	WR
	2	USA	**Richard Hanley / George Breen / William Woolsey / Ford Konno**	**8:31.5**	
	3	USR		8:34.7	
1960	1	USA	**George Harrison / Richard Blick / Michael Troy / F. Jeffrey Farrell**	**8:10.2**	WR
	2	JPN		8:13.2	
	3	AUS		8:13.8	
1964	1	USA	**Stephen Clark / Roy Saari / Gary Ilman / Donald Schollander**	**7:52.1**	WR
	2	GDR/GER		7:59.3	
	3	JPN		8:03.8	
1968	1	USA	**John Nelson / Stephen Rerych / Mark Spitz / Donald Schollander**	**7:52.33**	
	2	AUS		7:53.77	
	3	USR		8:01.66	
1972	1	USA	**John Kinsella / Frederick Tyler / Steven Genter / Mark Spitz**	**7:35.78**	WR
	2	GER		7:41.69	
	3	USR		7:45.76	
1976	1	USA	**Mike Bruner / Bruce Furniss / John Naber / Jim Montgomery**	**7:23.22**	WR
	2	USR		7:27.97	
	3	GBR		7:32.11	
1980	1	USR		7:23.50	
	2	GDR		7:28.60	
	3	BRA		7:29.30	
1984	1	USA	**Michael Heath / David Larson / Jeffrey Float / Lawrence Bruce Hayes / Geoff Gaberino / Rich Saeger**	**7:15.69**	WR
	2	GER		7:15.73	
	3	GBR		7:24.78	
1988	1	USA	**Troy Dalbey / Matthew Cetlinski / Douglas Gjertsen / Matt Biondi / Craig Oppel / Dan Jorgensen**	**7:12.51**	WR
	2	GER		7:13.68	
	3	FRG		7:14.35	
1992	1	EUN		7:11.95	WR
	2	SWE		7:15.51	
	3	USA	**Joe Hudepohl / Melvin Stewart / Joe Olsen / Doug Gjertsen / Scott Jaffe / Dan Jorgensen**	**7:16.23**	

MEN'S 4X100-METER MEDLEY RELAY

YEAR	RANK	CTRY	ATHLETES	TIME	
1896-1956		(not held)			
1960	1	USA	**Frank McKinney / Paul Hait / Lance Larson / F. Jeffrey Farrell**	**4:05.4**	WR
	2	AUS		4:12.0	
	3	JPN		4:12.2	
1964	1	USA	**Harold Mann / William Craig / Fred Schmidt / Stephen Clark**	**3:58.4**	WR
	2	GDR/GER		4:01.6	
	3	AUS		4:02.3	
1968	1	USA	**Charles Hickcox / Donald McKenzie / Douglas Russell / Kenneth Walsh**	**3:54.9**	WR
	2	GDR		3:57.5	
	3	USR		4:00.7	
1972	1	USA	**Michael Stamm / Thomas Bruce / Mark Spitz / Jerry Heidenreich**	**3:48.16**	WR
	2	GDR		3:52.12	
	3	CAN		3:52.26	
1976	1	USA	**John Naber / John Hencken / Matt Voegl / Jim Montgomery**	**3:42.22**	WR
	2	CAN		3:45.94	
	3	GER		3:47.29	
1980	1	AUS		3:45.70	
	2	USR		3:45.92	
	3	GBR		3:47.71	
1984	1	USA	**Richard Carey / Steve Lundquist / Pablo Morales / Ambrose "Rowdy" Gaines / Tom Jager / Dave Wilson / Mike Heath /Richard Schroeder**	**3:39.30**	WR
	2	CAN		3:43.23	
	3	AUS		3:43.25	
1988	1	USA	**David Berkoff / Richard Schroeder / Matt Biondi / Christopher Jacobs / Jay Mortenson / Tom Jager**	**3:36.93**	WR
	2	CAN		3:39.28	
	3	URS		3:39.96	
1992	1	USA	**Jeff Rouse / Nelson Diebel / Pablo Morales / Jon Olsen / Matt Biondi / Hans Dersch / Melvin Stewart / David Berkoff**	**3:36.93**	EWR
	2	EUN		3:38.56	
	3	CAN		3:39.66	

WOMEN'S 50-METER FREESTYLE

YEAR	RANK	CTRY	ATHLETE	TIME	
1896-1984		(not held)			
1988	1	GDR	Kristin Otto	25.49	OR
	2	CHN	Yang Wenyi	25.64	
	3	GDR	Katrin Meissner	25.71	
	3	USA	**Jill Sterkel**	**25.71**	
1992	1	CHN	Yang Wenyi	24.79	WR
	2	CHN	Zhuang Yong	25.08	
	3	USA	**Angel Martino**	**25.23**	

WOMEN'S 100-METER FREESTYLE

YEAR	RANK	CTRY	ATHLETE	TIME	
1896-1908		(not held)			
1912	1	AUS	Fanny Durack	1:22.2	
	2	AUS	Wilhelmina Wylie	1:25.4	
	3	GBR	Jennie Fletcher	1:27.0	
(no USA entry)					

1920	1	USA	Ethelda Bleibtrey	1:13.6	WR
	2	USA	Irene Guest	1:17.0	
	3	USA	Frances Schroth	1:17.2	
1924	1	USA	Ethel Lackie	1:12.4	
	2	USA	Mariechen Wehselau	1:12.8	
	3	USA	Gertrude Ederle	1:14.2	
1928	1	USA	Albina Osipowich	1:11.0	OR
	2	USA	Eleanor Garatti	1:11.4	
	3	GBR	Margaret Joyce Cooper	1:13.6	
1932	1	USA	Helene Madison	1:06.8	OR
	2	HOL	Willemijntje den Ouden	1:07.8	
	3	USA	Eleanor Saville (Garatti)	1:09.3	
1936	1	HOL	Hendrika "Rie" Mastenbroek	1:05.9	OR
	2	ARG	Jeannette Campbell	1:06.4	
	3	GER	Gisela Arendt	1:06.6	
	6	USA	Olive McKean	1:08.4	
1948	1	DEN	Greta Andersen	1:06.3	
	2	USA	Ann Curtis	1:06.5	
	3	HOL	Marie-Louise Vaessen	1:07.6	
1952	1	HUN	Katalin Szöke	1:06.8	
	2	HOL	Johanna Termeulen	1:07.0	
	3	HUN	Judit Temes	1:07.1	
	5	USA	Joan Alderson	1:07.1	
1956	1	AUS	Dawn Fraser	1:02.0	WR
	2	AUS	Lorraine Crapp	1:02.3	
	3	AUS	Faith Leech	1:05.1	
	4	USA	Joan Rosazza	1:05.2	
1960	1	AUS	Dawn Fraser	1:01.2	OR
	2	USA	S. Christine Von Saltza	1:02.8	
	3	GBR	Natalie Steward	1:03.1	
1964	1	AUS	Dawn Fraser	59.5	OR
	2	USA	Sharon Stouder	59.9	
	3	USA	Kathleen Ellis	1:00.8	
1968	1	USA	Jan Henne	1:00.0	
	2	USA	Susan Pedersen	1:00.3	
	3	USA	Linda Gustavson	1:00.3	
1972	1	USA	Sandra Neilson	58.59	OR
	2	USA	Shirley Babashoff	59.02	
	3	AUS	Shane Gould	59.06	
1976	1	GDR	Kornelia Ender	55.65	WR
	2	GDR	Petra Priemer	56.49	
	3	HOL	Enith Brigitha	56.65	
	4	USA	Kim Peyton	56.81	
1980	1	GDR	Barbara Krause	54.79	WR
	2	GDR	Caren Metschuck	55.16	
	3	GDR	Ines Diers	55.65	
1984	1T	USA	Nancy Hogshead	55.92	
	1T	USA	Carrie Steinseifer	55.92	
	3	HOL	Annemarie Verstappen	56.08	
1988	1	GDR	Kristin Otto	54.93	
	2	CHN	Zhuang Yong	55.47	
	3	FRA	Catherine Plewinski	55.49	
	7	USA	Dara Torres	56.25	
1992	1	CHN	Zhuang Yong	54.65	OR
	2	USA	Jenny Thompson	54.84	
	3	GER	Franziska Van Almsick	54.94	

WOMEN'S 200-METER FREESTYLE

YEAR	RANK	CTRY	ATHLETE	TIME	
1896-1964	(not held)				
1968	1	USA	Deborah Meyer	2:10.5	OR
	2	USA	Jan Henne	2:11.0	
	3	USA	Jane Barkman	2:11.2	
1972	1	AUS	Shane Gould	2:03.56	WR
	2	USA	Shirley Babashoff	2:04.33	
	3	USA	Keena Rothhammer	2:04.92	
1976	1	GDR	Kornelia Ender	1:59.26	WR
	2	USA	Shirley Babashoff	2:01.22	
	3	HOL	Enith Brigitha	2:01.40	
1980	1	GDR	Barbara Krause	1:58.33	OR
	2	GDR	Ines Diers	1:59.64	
	3	GDR	Carmela Schmidt	2:01.44	
1988	1	GDR	Heike Friedrich	1:57.65	OR
	2	CRC	Silvia Poll	1:58.67	
	3	GDR	Manuela Stelmach	1:59.01	
	4	USA	Mary Wayte	1:59.04	
1992	1	USA	Nicole Haislett	1:57.90	
	2	GER	Franziska Van Almsick	1:58.00	
	3	GER	Kerstin Kielgass	1:59.67	

WOMEN'S 400-METER FREESTYLE

YEAR	RANK	CTRY	ATHLETE	TIME	
1896-1912	(not held)				
1920	1	USA	Ethelda Bleibtrey	4:34.0	WR
	2	USA	Margaret Woodbridge	4:42.8	
	3	USA	Frances Schroth	4:52.0	
1924	1	USA	Martha Norelius	6:02.2	OR
	2	USA	Helen Wainwright	6:03.8	
	3	USA	Gertrude Ederle	6:04.8	
1928	1	USA	Martha Norelius	5:42.8	WR
	2	HOL	Maria Braun	5:57.8	
	3	USA	Josephine McKim	6:00.2	
1932	1	USA	Helene Madison	5:28.5	WR
	2	USA	Lenore Kight	5:28.6	
	3	RSA	Jennie Maakal	5:47.3	
1936	1	HOL	Hendrika "Rie" Mastenbroek	5:26.4	OR
	2	DEN	Ragnhild Hveger	5:27.5	
	3	USA	Lenore Wingard (Kight)	5:29.0	
1948	1	USA	Ann Curtis	5:17.8	OR
	2	DEN	Karen-Margrete Harup	5:21.2	
	3	GBR	Catherine Gibson	5:22.5	
1952	1	HUN	Valéria Gyenge	5:12.1	OR
	2	HUN	Éva Novák	5:13.7	
	3	USA	Evelyn Kawamoto	5:14.6	
1956	1	AUS	Lorraine Crapp	4:54.6	OR
	2	AUS	Dawn Fraser	5:02.5	
	3	USA	Sylvia Ruuska	5:07.1	
1960	1	USA	S. Christine Von Saltza	4:50.6	OR
	2	SWE	Jane Cederqvist	4:53.9	
	3	HOL	Catharina Lagerberg	4:56.9	
1964	1	USA	Virginia Duenkel	4:43.3	OR
	2	USA	Marilyn RaMENofsky	4:44.6	
	3	USA	Terri Stickles	4:47.2	
1968	1	USA	Debbie Meyer	4:31.8	OR
	2	USA	Linda Gustavson	4:35.5	
	3	AUS	Karen Moras	4:37.0	
1972	1	AUS	Shane Gould	4:19.44	WR
	2	ITA	Novella Calligaris	4:22.44	
	3	GDR	Gudrun Wagner	4:23.11	
	4	USA	Shirley Babashoff	4:23.59	
1976	1	GDR	Petra Thümer	4:09.89	WR
	2	USA	Shirley Babashoff	4:10.46	
	3	CAN	Shannon Smith	4:14.60	
1980	1	GDR	Ines Diers	4:08.76	OR
	2	GDR	Petra Schneider	4:09.16	
	3	GDR	Carmela Schmidt	4:10.86	
1984	1	USA	Tiffany Cohen	4:07.10	OR
	2	GBR	Sarah Hardcastle	4:10.27	
	3	GBR	June Croft	4:11.49	
1988	1	USA	Janet Evans	4:03.85	WR
	2	GDR	Heike Friedrich	4:05.94	
	3	GDR	Anke Moehring	4:06.62	
1992	1	GER	Dagmar Hase	4:07.18	
	2	USA	Janet Evans	4:07.37	
	3	AUS	Hayley Jane Lewis	4:11.22	

WOMEN'S 800-METER FREESTYLE

YEAR	RANK	CTRY	ATHLETE	TIME	
1896-1964	(not held)				
1968	1	USA	Deborah Meyer	9:24.0	OR
	2	USA	Pamela Kruse	9:35.7	
	3	MEX	Maria Teresa Ramirez	9:38.5	
1972	1	USA	Keena Rothhammer	8:53.68	WR
	2	AUS	Shane Gould	8:56.39	
	3	ITA	Novella Calligaris	8:57.46	
1976	1	GDR	Petra Thümer	8:37.14	WR
	2	USA	Shirley Babashoff	8:37.59	
	3	USA	Wendy Weinberg	8:42.60	
1980	1	AUS	Michelle Ford	8:28.90	OR
	2	GDR	Ines Diers	8:32.55	
	3	GDR	Heike Dähne	8:33.48	
1984	1	USA	Tiffany Cohen	8:24.95	OR
	2	USA	Michele Richardson	8:30.73	
	3	GBR	Sarah Hardcastle	8:32.60	
1988	1	USA	Janet Evans	8:20.20	OR
	2	AUS	Astrid Strauss	8:22.09	
	3	AUS	Julie McDonald	8:22.93	
1992	1	USA	Janet Evans	8:25.52	
	2	AUS	Hayley Lewis	8:30.34	
	3	GER	Jana Henke	8:30.99	

WOMEN'S 100-METER BACKSTROKE

YEAR	RANK	CTRY	ATHLETE	TIME	
1896-1920	(not held)				
1924	1	USA	Sybil Bauer	1:23.2	OR
	2	GBR	Phyllis Harding	1:27.4	
	3	USA	Aileen Riggin	1:28.2	
1928	1	HOL	Maria Braun	1:22.0	
	2	GBR	Ellen King	1:22.2	
	3	GBR	Margaret Joyce Cooper	1:22.8	
	4	USA	Marion Gilman	1:24.2	
1932	1	USA	Eleanor Holm	1:19.4	
	2	AUS	Philomena "Bonny" Mealing	1:21.3	
	3	GBR	Elizabeth Valerie Davies	1:22.5	
1936	1	HOL	Dina "Nida" Senff	1:18.9	
	2	HOL	Hendrika "Rie" Mastenbroek	1:19.2	
	3	USA	Alice Bridges	1:19.4	
1948	1	DEN	Karen-Margrete Harup	1:14.4	OR
	2	USA	Suzanne Zimmerman	1:16.0	
	3	AUS	Judith Davies	1:16.7	
1952	1	RSA	Joan Harrison	1:14.3	
	2	HOL	Geertje Wielema	1:14.5	
	3	NZL	Jean Stewart	1:15.8	
	5	USA	Barbara Stark	1:16.2	
1956	1	GBR	Judith Grinham	1:12.9	OR
	2	USA	Carin Cone	1:12.9	
	3	GBR	Margaret Edwards	1:13.1	
1960	1	USA	Lynn Burke	1:09.3	OR
	2	GBR	Natalie Steward	1:10.8	
	3	JPN	Satoko Tanaka	1:11.4	
1964	1	USA	Cathy Ferguson	1:07.7	WR
	2	FRA	Christine Caron	1:07.9	
	3	USA	Virginia Duenkel	1:08.0	
1968	1	USA	Kaye Hall	1:06.2	WR
	2	CAN	Elaine Tanner	1:06.7	
	3	USA	Jane Swagerty	1:08.1	
1972	1	USA	Melissa Belote	1:05.78	OR
	2	HUN	Andrea Gyarmati	1:06.26	
	3	USA	Susie Atwood	1:06.34	
1976	1	GDR	Ulrike Richter	1:01.83	OR
	2	GDR	Birgit Treiber	1:03.41	
	3	CAN	Nancy Garapick	1:03.71	
		USA	Linda Jezek (1:06.01)	elim. semis	
1980	1	GDR	Rica Reinisch	1:00.86	WR
	2	GDR	Ina Kleber	1:02.07	
	3	GDR	Petra Riedel	1:02.64	
1984	1	USA	Theresa Andrews	1:02.55	
	2	USA	Betsy Mitchell	1:02.63	
	3	HOL	Jolanda de Rover	1:02.91	
1988	1	GDR	Kristin Otto	1:00.89	
	2	HUN	Krisztina Egerszegi	1:01.56	
	3	GDR	Cornelia Sirch	1:01.57	
	4	USA	Betsy Mitchell	1:02.71	
1992	1	HUN	Krisztina Egerszegi	1:00.68	OR
	2	HUN	Tunde Szabo	1:01.14	
	3	USA	Lea Loveless	1:01.43	

WOMEN'S 200-METER BACKSTROKE

YEAR	RANK	CTRY	ATHLETE	TIME	
1896-1964	(not held)				
1968	1	USA	Lillian "Pokey" Watson	2:24.8	OR
	2	CAN	Elaine Tanner	2:27.4	
	3	USA	Kaye Hall	2:28.9	
1972	1	USA	Melissa Belote	2:19.19	WR
	2	USA	Susie Atwood	2:20.38	
	3	CAN	Donna Gurr	2:23.22	
1976	1	GDR	Ulrike Richter	2:13.43	OR
	2	GDR	Birgit Treiber	2:14.97	
	3	CAN	Nancy Garapick	2:15.60	
	5	USA	Melissa Belote	2:17.27	
1980	1	GDR	Rica Reinisch	2:11.77	WR
	2	GDR	Cornelia Polit	2:13.75	
	3	GDR	Birgit Treiber	2:14.14	
1984	1	HOL	Jolanda de Rover	2:12.38	
	2	USA	Amy White	2:13.04	
	3	ROM	Aneta Patrascoiu	2:13.29	
1988	1	HUN	Krisztina Egerszegi	2:09.29	OR
	2	GDR	Kathrin Zimmermann	2:10.61	
	3	GDR	Cornelia Sirch	2:11.45	
	4	USA	Beth Barr	2:12.39	
1992	1	HUN	Krisztina Egerszegi	2:07.06	OR
	2	GER	Dagmar Hase	2:09.46	
	3	AUS	Nicole Stevenson	2:10.20	
	4	USA	Lea Loveless	2:11.54	

WOMEN'S 100-METER BREASTSTROKE

YEAR	RANK	CTRY	ATHLETE	TIME	
1896-1964	(not held)				
1968	1	YUG	Djurdjica Bjedov	1:15.8	OR
	2	USR	Galina Prozumenshikova	1:15.9	
	3	USA	Sharon Wichman	1:16.1	
1972	1	USA	Catherine Carr	1:13.58	WR
	2	USR	Galina Stepanova (Prozumenshikova)	1:14.99	
	3	AUS	Beverley Whitfield	1:15.73	
1976	1	GDR	Hannelore Anke	1:11.16	
	2	USR	Lyubov Rusanova	1:13.04	
	3	USR	Marina Koshevaia	1:13.30	
		USA	Laurie Siering (1:14.84)	elim. semis	
1980	1	GDR	Ute Geweniger	1:10.22	
	2	USR	Elvira Vasilkova	1:10.41	
	3	DEN	Susanne Nielsson	1:11.16	
1984	1	HOL	Petra van Staveren	1:09.88	OR
	2	CAN	Anne Ottenbrite	1:10.69	
	3	FRA	Cathérine Poirot	1:10.70	
	4	USA	Tracy Caulkins	1:10.88	
1988	1	BUL	Tania Dangalakova	1:07.95	OR
	2	BUL	Antoaneta Frenkeva	1:08.74	
	3	GDR	Silke Hoerner	1:08.83	
	6	USA	Tracey McFarlane	1:09.60	
1992	1	EUN	Elena Roudkovskaia	1:08.00	
	2	USA	Anita Nall	1:08.17	
	3	AUS	Samantha Riley	1:09.25	

WOMEN'S 200-METER BREASTSTROKE

YEAR	RANK	CTRY	ATHLETE	TIME	
1896-1920	(not held)				
1924	1	GBR	Lucy Morton	3:33.2	OR
	2	USA	Agnes Geraghty	3:34.0	
	3	GBR	Gladys Carson	3:35.4	
1928	1	GER	Hildegard Schrader	3:12.6	
	2	HOL	Mietje "Marie" Baron	3:15.2	
	3	GER	Lotte Mühe	3:17.6	
	5	USA	Margaret Hoffman	3:19.2	
1932	1	AUS	Clare Dennis	3:06.3	OR
	2	JPN	Hideko Maehata	3:06.4	
	3	DEN	Else Jacobsen	3:07.1	
	5	USA	Margaret Hoffman	3:11.8	
1936	1	JPN	Hideko Maehata	3:03.6	
	2	GER	Martha Geneger	3:04.2	
	3	DEN	Inge Sörensen	3:07.8	
		USA	Dorothy Schiller (3:18.5)	elim. semis	
1948	1	HOL	Petronella van Vliet	2:57.2	
	2	AUS	Beatrice Lyons	2:57.7	
	3	HUN	Eva Novák	3:00.2	
		USA	Clara LaMore (3:23) / Carol Pence (3:28.1) / Jeanne Wilson (3:18.3)	elim. 1st rd	
1952	1	HUN	Éva Székely	2:51.7	OR
	2	HUN	Éva Novák	2:54.4	
	3	GBR	Helen "Elenor" Gordon	2:57.6	
		USA	Julia Cornell (3:17.7) / Gail Peters (3:13.3) / Idella Sehorn (3:13.7)	elim. trials	
1956	1	GER	Ursula Happe	2:53.1	OR
	2	HUN	Éva Székely	2:54.8	
	3	GDR	Eva-Maria ten Elsen	2:55.1	
	7	USA	Mary Sears	2:57.2	
1960	1	GBR	Anita Lonsbrough	2:49.5	WR
	2	GER	Wiltrud Urselmann	2:50.0	
	3	GDR	Barbara Göbel	2:53.6	
	6	USA	Anne Warner	2:55.4	
1964	1	USR	Galina Prozumenshikova	2:46.4	OR
	2	USA	Claudia Kolb	2:47.6	
	3	USR	Svetlana Babanina	2:48.6	
1968	1	USA	Sharon Wichman	2:44.4	OR
	2	YUG	Djurdjica Bjedov	2:46.4	
	3	USR	Galina Prozumenshikova	2:47.0	
1972	1	AUS	Beverley Whitfield	2:41.71	OR
	2	USA	Dana Schoenfield	2:42.05	
	3	USR	Galina Stepanova (Prozumenshikova)	2:42.36	
1976	1	USR	Marina Koshevaia	2:33.35	WR
	2	USR	Marina Iurchenia	2:36.08	
	3	USR	Lyubov Rusanova	2:36.22	
		USA	Janis Hape (2:45.57)	elim. semis	
1980	1	USR	Lina Kaciusyté	2:29.54	OR
	2	USR	Svetlana Varganova	2:29.61	
	3	USR	Yulia Bogdanova	2:32.39	
1984	1	CAN	Anne Ottenbrite	2:30.38	
	2	USA	Susan Rapp	2:31.15	
	3	BEL	Ingrid Lempereur	2:31.40	
1988	1	GDR	Silke Hoerner	2:26.71	WR
	2	CHN	Huang Xiaomin	2:27.49	
	3	BUL	Antoaneta Frenkeva	2:28.34	
	13	USA	Susan Rapp	2:32.90	#
1992	1	JPN	Kyoko Iwasaki	2:26.65	OR
	2	CHN	Li Lin	2:26.85	
	3	USA	Anita Nall	2:26.88	

- Final B

WOMEN'S 100-METER BUTTERFLY

YEAR	RANK	CTRY	ATHLETE	TIME	
1896-1952	(not held)				
1956	1	USA	Shelly Mann	1:11.0	OR
	2	USA	Nancy Ramey	1:11.9	
	3	USA	Mary Sears	1:14.4	
1960	1	USA	Carolyn Schuler	1:09.5	OR
	2	HOL	Marianne Heemskerk	1:10.4	
	3	AUS	Janice Andrew	1:12.2	
1964	1	USA	Sharon Stouder	1:04.7	WR
	2	HOL	Ada Kok	1:05.6	
	3	USA	Kathleen Ellis	1:06.0	
1968	1	AUS	Lynette McClements	1:05.5	
	2	USA	Ellie Daniel	1:05.8	
	3	USA	Susan Shields	1:06.2	
1972	1	JPN	Mayumi Aoki	1:03.34	WR
	2	GDR	Roswitha Beier	1:03.61	
	3	HUN	Andréa Gyarmati	1:03.73	
	4	USA	Deena Deardurff	1:03.95	
1976	1	GDR	Kornelia Ender	1:00.13	EWR
	2	GDR	Andrea Pollack	1:00.98	
	3	USA	Wendy Boglioli	1:01.17	
1980	1	GDR	Caren Metschuck	1:00.42	
	2	GDR	Andrea Pollack	1:00.90	
	3	GDR	Christiane Knacke	1:01.44	
1984	1	USA	Mary T. Meagher	59.26	
	2	USA	Jenna Johnson	1:00.19	
	3	GER	Karin Seick	1:01.36	

1988	1	GDR	Kristin Otto	59.00	OR
	2	GDR	Birte Weigang	59.45	
	3	CHN	Hong Qian	59.52	
	5	**USA**	**Janel Jorgensen**	**1:00.48**	
1992	1	CHN	Hong Qian	58.62	OR
	2	**USA**	**Crissy Ahmann-Leighton**	**58.74**	
	3	FRA	Catherine Plewinski	59.01	

WOMEN'S 200-METER BUTTERFLY

YEAR	RANK	CTRY	ATHLETE	TIME	
1896-1964	(not held)				
1968	1	HOL	Ada Kok	2:24.7	OR
	2	GDR	Helga Lindner	2:24.8	
	3	**USA**	**Ellie Daniel**	**2:25.9**	
1972	**1**	**USA**	**Karen Moe**	**2:15.57**	WR
	2	**USA**	**Lynn Colella**	**2:16.34**	
	3	**USA**	**Ellie Daniel**	**2:16.74**	
1976	1	GDR	Andrea Pollack	2:11.41	OR
	2	GDR	Ulrike Tauber	2:12.50	
	3	GDR	Rosemarie Gabriel (Kother)	2:12.86	
	4	**USA**	**Karen Thornton (Moe)**	**2:12.90**	
1980	1	GDR	Ines Geissler	2:10.44	OR
	2	GDR	Sybille Schönrock	2:10.45	
	3	AUS	Michelle Ford	2:11.66	
1984	**1**	**USA**	**Mary T. Meagher**	**2:06.90**	OR
	2	AUS	Karen Phillips	2:10.56	
	3	GER	Ina Beyermann	2:11.91	
1988	1	GDR	Kathleen Nord	2:09.51	
	2	GDR	Birte Weigang	2:09.91	
	3	**USA**	**Mary T. Meagher**	**2:10.80**	
1992	**1**	**USA**	**Summer Sanders**	**2:08.67**	
	2	CHN	Wang Xiaohang	2:09.01	
	3	AUS	Susan O'Neill	2:09.03	

WOMEN'S 200-METER IND. MEDLEY

YEAR	RANK	CTRY	ATHLETE	TIME	
1896-1964	(not held)				
1968	**1**	**USA**	**Claudia Kolb**	**2:24.7**	OR
	2	**USA**	**Susan Pedersen**	**2:28.8**	
	3	**USA**	**Jan Henne**	**2:31.4**	
1972	1	AUS	Shane Gould	2:23.07	WR
	2	GDR	Kornelia Ender	2:23.59	
	3	**USA**	**Lynn Vidali**	**2:24.06**	
1976-1980	(not held)				
1984	**1**	**USA**	**Tracy Caulkins**	**2:12.64**	OR
	2	USA	Nancy Hogshead	2:15.17	
	3	AUS	Michele Pearson	2:15.92	
1988	1	GDR	Daniela Hunger	2:12.59	OR
	2	URS	Elena Dendeberova	2:13.31	
	3	ROM	Noemi Ildiko Lung	2:14.85	
	8	**USA**	**Whitney Hedgepeth**	**2:17.99**	
1992	1	CHN	Li Lin	2:11.65	WR
	2	**USA**	**Summer Sanders**	**2:11.91**	
	3	GER	Daniela Hunger	2:13.92	

WOMEN'S 400-METER IND. MEDLEY

YEAR	RANK	CTRY	ATHLETE	TIME	
1896-1960	(not held)				
1964	**1**	**USA**	**Donna De Varona**	**5:18.7**	OR
	2	**USA**	**Sharon Finneran**	**5:24.1**	
	3	**USA**	**Martha Randall**	**5:24.2**	
1968	**1**	**USA**	**Claudia Kolb**	**5:08.5**	OR
	2	**USA**	**Lynn Vidali**	**5:22.2**	
	3	GDR	Sabine Steinbach	5:25.3	
1972	1	AUS	Gail Neall	5:02.97	WR
	2	CAN	Leslie Cliff	5:03.57	
	3	ITA	Novella Calligaris	5:03.99	
	4	**USA**	**Jennifer Bartz**	**5:05.56**	
1976	1	GDR	Ulrike Tauber	4:42.77	WR
	2	CAN	Cheryl Gibson	4:48.10	
	3	CAN	Becky Smith	4:50.48	
	6	**USA**	**Donnalee Wennerstrom**	**4:55.34**	
1980	1	GDR	Petra Schneider	4:36.29	WR
	2	GBR	Sharron Davies	4:46.83	
	3	POL	Agnieszka Czopek	4:48.17	
1984	**1**	**USA**	**Tracy Caulkins**	**4:39.24**	
	2	AUS	Suzanne Landells	4:48.30	
	3	GER	Petra Zindler	4:48.57	
1988	**1**	**USA**	**Janet Evans**	**4:37.76**	
	2	ROM	Noemi Ildiko Lung	4:39.46	
	3	GDR	Daniela Hunger	4:39.76	
1992	1	HUN	Krisztina Egerszegi	4:36.54	
	2	CHN	Li Lin	4:36.73	
	3	**USA**	**Summer Sanders**	**4:37.58**	

WOMEN'S 4X100-METER FREESTYLE RELAY

YEAR	RANK	CTRY	ATHLETES	TIME	
1896-1908	(not held)				
1912	1	GBR		5:52.8	WR
	2	GER		6:04.6	
	3	AUT		6:17.0	
(no USA entry)					
1920	**1**	**USA**	**Margaret Woodbridge / Frances Schroth /Irene Guest / Ethelda Bleibtrey**	**5:11.6**	WR
	2	GBR		5:40.6	
	3	SWE		5:43.6	
1924	**1**	**USA**	**Gertrude Ederle / Euphrasia Donnelly / Ethel Lackie / Mariechen Wehselau**	**4:58.8**	WR
	2	GBR		5:17.0	
	3	SWE		5:35.6	
1928	**1**	**USA**	**Adelaide Lambert / Eleanor Garatti / Albina Osipowich / Martha Norelius**	**4:47.6**	WR
	2	GBR		5:02.8	
	3	RSA		5:13.4	
1932	**1**	**USA**	**Josephine McKim / Helen Johns / Eleanor Saville (Garatti) / Helene Madison**	**4:38.0**	WR
	2	HOL		4:47.5	
	3	GBR		4:52.4	
1936	1	HOL		4:36.0	OR
	2	GER		4:36.8	
	3	**USA**	**Katherine Rawls / Bernice Lapp / Mavis Freeman / Olive McKean**	**4:40.2**	
1948	**1**	**USA**	**Marie Corridon / Thelma Kalama / Brenda Helser / Ann Curtis**	**4:29.2**	OR
	2	DEN		4:29.6	
	3	HOL		4:31.6	
1952	1	HUN		4:24.4	WR
	2	HOL		4:29.0	
	3	**USA**	**Jacqueline La Vine / Marilee Stepan /Joan Alderson / Evelyn Kawamoto**	**4:30.1**	
1956	1	AUS		4:17.1	WR
	2	**USA**	**Sylvia Russka / Shelly Mann / Nancy Simons / Joan Rosazza**	**4:19.2**	
	3	RSA		4:25.7	
1960	**1**	**USA**	**Joan Spillane / Shirley Stobs / Carolyn Wood / S. Christine Von Saltza**	**4:08.9**	WR
	2	AUS		4:11.3	
	3	GDR/GER		4:19.7	
1964	**1**	**USA**	**Sharon Stouder / Donna De Varona / Lillian "Pokey" Watson / Kathleen Ellis**	**4:03.8**	WR
	2	AUS		4:06.9	
	3	HOL		4:12.0	
1968	**1**	**USA**	**Jane Barkman / Linda Gustavson / Susan Pedersen / Jan Henne**	**4:02.5**	OR
	2	GDR		4:05.7	
	3	CAN		4:07.2	
1972	**1**	**USA**	**Sandra Neilson / Jennifer Kemp / Jane Barkman / Shirley Babashoff**	**3:55.19**	WR
	2	GDR		3:55.55	
	3	GER		3:57.93	
1976	**1**	**USA**	**Kim Peyton / Wendy Boglioli / Jill Sterkel / Shirley Babashoff**	**3:44.82**	WR
	2	GDR		3:45.50	
	3	CAN		3:48.81	
1980	1	GDR		3:42.71	WR
	2	SWE		3:48.93	
	3	HOL		3:49.51	
1984	**1**	**USA**	**Jenna Johnson / Carrie Steinseifer / Dara Torres / Nancy Hogshead / Mary Wayte / Jill Sterkel / Robin Leamy**	**3:43.43**	
	2	HOL		3:44.40	
	3	GER		3:45.56	
1988	1	GDR		3:40.63	OR
	2	HOL		3:43.39	
	3	**USA**	**Mary Wayte / Mitzi Kremer / Laura Walker / Dara Torres / Paige Zemina / Jill Sterkel**	**3:44.25**	
1992	**1**	**USA**	**Nicole Haislett / Dara Torres / Angel Martino / Jenny Thompson / Crissy Ahmann-Leighton / Ashley Tappin**	**3:39.46**	WR
	2	CHN		3:40.12	
	3	GER		3:41.60	

WOMEN'S 4X100 METER MEDLEY RELAY

YEAR	RANK	CTRY	ATHLETES	TIME	
1896-1956	(not held)				
1960	**1**	**USA**	**Lynn Burke / Patty Kempner / CarolynSchuler / S. Christine Von Saltza**	**4:41.1**	WR
	2	AUS		4:45.9	
	3	GDR/GER		4:47.6	
1964	**1**	**USA**	**Cathy Ferguson / Cynthia Goyette / Sharon Stouder / Kathleen Ellis**	**4:33.9**	WR
	2	HOL		4:37.0	
	3	USR		4:39.2	
1968	**1**	**USA**	**Kaye Hall / Catie Ball / Ellie Daniel / Susan Pedersn**	**4:28.3**	OR
	2	AUS		4:30.0	
	3	GER		4:36.4	
1972	**1**	**USA**	**Melissa Belote / Catherine Carr / Deena Deardurff / Sandra Neilson**	**4:20.75**	WR
	2	GDR		4:24.91	
	3	GER		4:26.46	
1976	1	GDR		4:07.95	WR
	2	**USA**	**Linda Jezek / Lauri Siering / Camille Wright / Shirley Babashoff**	**4:14.55**	
	3	CAN		4:15.22	
1980	1	GDR		4:06.67	WR
	2	GBR		4:12.24	
	3	USR		4:13.61	
1984	**1**	**USA**	**Theresa Andrews / Tracy Caulkins / Mary T. Meagher / Nancy Hogshead / Susan Rapp / Carrie Steinseifer / Jenna Johnson / Betsy Mitchell**	**4:08.34**	
	2	GER		4:11.97	
	3	CAN		4:12.98	
1988	1	GDR		4:03.74	OR
	2	**USA**	**Beth Barr / Tracey McFarlane / Janel Jorgensen / Mary Wayte / Betsy Mitchell / Mary T. Meagher / Darra Torres**	**4:07.90**	
	3	CAN		4:10.49	
1992	**1**	**USA**	**Lea Loveless / Anita Nall / Crissy Ahmann-Leighton / Jenny Thompson / Nicole Haislett / Megan Kleine / Summer Sanders / Janie Wagstaff**	**4:02.54**	WR
	2	GER		4:05.19	
	3	EUN		4:06.44	

SYNCHRONIZED SUIMMING

SOLO

YEAR	RANK	CTRY	ATHLETE	POINTS
1896-1980	(not held)			
1984	**1**	**USA**	**Tracie Ruiz**	**198.467**
	2	CAN	Carolyn Waldo	195.300
	3	JPN	Miwako Motoyoshi	187.050
1988	1	CAN	Carolyn Waldo	200.150
	2	**USA**	**Tracie Ruiz-Conforto**	**197.633**
	3	JPN	Mikako Kotani	191.850
1992	**1**	**USA**	**Kristen Babb-Sprague**	**191.848**
	2	CAN	Sylvie Frechette	191.717
	3	JPN	Fumiko Okuno	187.056

DUET

YEAR	RANK	CTRY	ATHLETES	POINTS
1896-1980	(not held)			
1984	**1**	**USA**	**Candy Costie / Tracie Ruiz**	**195.584**
	2	CAN	Sharon Hambrook / Kelly Kryczka	194.234
	3	JPN	Saeko Simura / Miwako Motoyoshi	187.992
1988	1	CAN	Carolyn Waldo / Michelle Cameron	197.717
	2	**USA**	**Sarah Josephson / Karen Josephson**	**197.284**
	3	JPN	Miyako Tanaka / Mikako Kotani	190.159
1992	**1**	**USA**	**Karen Josephson / Sarah Josephson**	**192.175**
	2	CAN	Penny Vilagos / Vicky Vilagos	189.394
	3	JPN	Fumiko Okuno / Aki Takayama	186.868

TABLE TENNIS

MEN'S SINGLES

YEAR	RANK	CTRY	ATHLETE
1896-1984	(not held)		
1988	1	KOR	Yoo Nam-kyu
	2	KOR	Kim Ki-taik
	3	SWE	Erik Lindh
		USA	**Sean O'Neill**
1992	1	SWE	Jan Ove Waldner
	2	FRA	Jean Philippe Gatien
	3	CHN	Ma Wenge
	3	KOR	Kim Taek-soo
		USA	**Jim Butler**

MEN'S DOUBLES

YEAR	RANK	CTRY	ATHLETES
1896-1984	(not held)		
1988	1	CHN	Chen Longcan / Wei Qingguang
	2	YUG	Ilija Lupuleski / Zoran Primorac
	3	KOR	Ahn Jae-hyung / Yoo Nam-kyu
(no USA entry)			
1992	1	CHN	Lu Lin / Wang Tao
	2	GER	Steffen Fetzner / Jorg Rosskopf
	3	KOR	Kang Hee-chan / Lee Chul-seung
	3	KOR	Kim Taek-soo / Yoo Nam-kyu
		USA	**Jim Butler / Sean O'Neill**

WOMEN'S SINGLES

YEAR	RANK	CTRY	ATHLETE
1896-1984	(not held)		
1988	1	CHN	Chen Jing
	2	CHN	Li Huifen
	3	CHN	Jiao Zhimin
		USA	**Insook Brushan**
1992	1	CHN	Deng Yaping
	2	CHN	Qiao Hong
	3	KOR	Hwa Hyun-jung
	3	PRK	Li Bun Hui
		USA	**Insook Bhushan**

WOMEN'S DOUBLES

YEAR	RANK	CTRY	ATHLETES
1896-1984	(not held)		
1988	1	KOR	Hyun Jung-hwa / Yang Young-ja
	2	CHN	Chen Jing / Jiano Zhimin
	3	YUG	Jasna Fazlic / Gordana Perkucin
		USA	**Insook Bhushan / Diana Gee**
1992	1	CHN	Deng Yaping / Qiao Hong
	2	CHN	Chen Zihe / Gao Jun
	3	PRK	Li Bun Hui / Yu Sun Bok
	3	KOR	Hong Cha Ok / Hwa Hyun-jung
		USA	**Diana Gee / Lily Hugh**

TEAM HANDBALL

MEN

YEAR	RANK	CTRY	SCORE
1896-1932	(not held)		
1936	1	GER	5-0
	2	AUT	4-1
	3	SUI	2-3
	4	HUN	1-4
	5	ROM	1-2
	6	**USA**	**0-3**

USA Team: Henry Oehler / Charles Dauner / Alfred Roseco / Herbert Carl Oehmichen / Edmund Schallenberg / William Ahlemeyer / Gerald Yantz / Joe Kaylor / Willy Renz / Walter Bowden / Fred Leinweber / Edward John Hagen / Otto Oehler / Philip Schupp

YEAR	RANK	CTRY	SCORE
1948-1968	(not held)		
1972	1	YUG	7-0
	2	TCH	3-3-1
	3	ROM	6-1
	4	GDR	5-2
	5	USR	3-1-3
	6	GER	2-4-1
	14	USA	

USA Team: Dennis Berkholtz / Abe Abrahams / Bob Sparks / Harry Winkler / Jim Rogers / Roger Baker / Joel Voelkert / Sandor Rivynak / Elmer Edes / Rick Abrahamson / Larry Caton / Brad Schlesinger / Tom Hardiman / Matt Matthews / Vinnie De Calergero

YEAR	RANK	CTRY	SCORE
1976	1	USR	5-1
	2	ROM	3-1-1
	3	POL	4-1
	4	GER	4-2
	5	YUG	5-1
	6	HUN	2-3
	10	USA	

USA Team: Jerry Glenz / Sandor Rivynak / Vinnie De Calcergero / Harry Winkler / Bob Sparks / Kevin Serrepede / Jim Rogers / Willie Bourda / Rob Dean / Randy Dean / Rick Abrahamson / Roger Baker / Bill Johnson / Peter Buehning, Jr / Pat O'Neill

YEAR	RANK	CTRY	SCORE
1980	1	GDR	5-0-1
	2	USR	4-2
	3	ROM	5-1
	4	HUN	3-1-2
	5	ESP	3-2-1
	6	YUG	4-2
	7	POL	3-2-1
	8	SUI	2-4
1984	1	YUG	5-0-1
	2	GER	5-1
	3	ROM	5-1
	4	DEN	4-2
	5	SWE	4-2
	6	ICE	3-2-1
	7	SUI	3-3
	8	ESP	2-4
	9	USA	

USA Team: James Buehning / Robert Djokovich / Tim Dykstra / Tim Funk / Craig Gilbert / Steven Goss / William Kessler / Stephen Kirk / Peter Lash, Jr. / Michael Lenard / Joseph McVein / Gregory Morava / Rod Oshita / Thomas Schneeberger / Joe Story

YEAR	RANK	CTRY		SCORE
1988	1	URS	USA vs. ISL	15-22
	2	KOR	USA vs. YUG	23-31
	3	YUG	USA vs. URS	14-26
	4	HUN	USA vs. SWE	12-26
	5	SWE	USA vs. ALG	17-20
	6	TCH	USA vs. JPN	20-24
	12	**USA**		

USA Team: Scott Driggers / Bryant Johnson / Rod Oshita / Stephen Kirk / Brian Bennett / Steven Goss / M. Sullivan / C. Fitschen / Joseph McVein / Michael Lenard / Joe Story / James Buehning / R. Hillary / Peter Lash, Jr. / William Kessler / B. Janny

YEAR	RANK	CTRY	SCORE
1992	1	EUN	
	2	SWE	
	3	FRA	
	4	ISL	

(no USA entry)

TENNIS

MEN'S SINGLES

YEAR	RANK	CTRY	ATHLETE
1896	1	GBR/IRL	John Pius Boland
	2	GRE	Demis Kasdaglis
(no USA entry)			
1900	1	GBR	Hugh Doherty
	2	GBR/IRL	Harold Mahony
	3T	GBR	Reginald Doherty
	3T	GBR	A.B.J. Norris
1904	1	USA	Beals Wright
	2	USA	Robert LeRoy
	3T	USA	Alonzo Bell
	3T	USA	Edgar Leonard
1906	1	FRA	Max Decugis
	2	FRA	Maurice Germot
	3	BOH	Zdenek "Jánský" Zemla
(no USA entry)			
1908	1	GBR	Josiah Ritchie
	2	GER	Otto Froitzheim
	3	GBR	Wilberforce Vaughan Eaves
(indoor courts) (no USA entry)			
1908	1	GBR	Arthur Gore
	2	GBR	George Caridia
	3	GBR	Josiah Ritchie
(no USA entry)			
1912	1	RSA	Charles Winslow
	2	RSA	Harold Kitson
	3	GER	Oscar Kreuzer
	3T	USA	Theodore Pell
(indoor courts)			
1912	1	FRA	André Gobert
	2	GBR	Charles Dixon
	3	NZL	Anthony Wilding
(no USA entry)			
1920	1	RSA	Louis Raymond
	2	JPN	Ichiya Kumagae
	3	RSA	Charles Winslow
		USA	Theodore Pell

1924	1	USA	Vincent Richards
	2	FRA	Henri Cochet
	3	ITA	Umberto Luigi de Morpurgo
1928-1984 (not held)			
1988	1	TCH	Miloslav Mecir
	2	USA	Tim Mayotte
	3T	USA	Brad Gilbert
	3T	SWE	Stefan Edberg
1992	1	SUI	Marc Rosset
	2	ESP	Jordi Arrese
	3T	CRO	Goran Ivanisevic
	3T	EUN	Andrei Cherkasov
		USA	Pete Sampras / Jim Courier

MEN'S DOUBLES

YEAR	RANK	CTRY	ATHLETES
1896	1	IRL/GER	John Boland / Fritz Traun
	2	GRE	Demis Kasdaglis / Demetrios Petrokokkinos
(no USA entry)			
1900	1	GBR	Reginald Doherty / Hugh Doherty
	2	USA/FRA	Basil Spalding de Garmendia / Max Decugis
	3T	FRA	André Prévost / G. de la Chapelle
	3T	IRL/GBR	Harold Mahony / A.B.J. Norris
1904	1	USA	Edgar Leonard / Beals Wright
	2	USA	Alonzo Bell / Robert LeRoy
	3T	USA	Joseph Wear / Allen West
	3T	USA	Clarence Gamble / Arthur Wear
1906	1	FRA	Max Decugis / Maurice Germot
	2	GRE	Xenophon Kasdaglis / Ioannis Ballis
	3	BOH	Zdenek "Jánský" Zemla / Ladislav "Rázny" Zemla
(no USA entry)			
1908	1	GBR	George Hillyard / Reginald Doherty
	2	GBR	Josiah Ritchie / James Parke
	3	GBR/IRL	Charles Cazalet / Charles Dixon
(indoor courts)			
1908	1	GBR	Arthur Gore / Herbert Roper Barrett
	2	GBR	George Simond / George Caridia
	3	SWE	Gunnar Setterwall / Wollmar Boström
(no USA entry)			
1912	1	RSA	Charles Winslow / Harold Kitson
	2	AUT	Felix Pipes / Arthur Zborzil
	3	FRA	Albert Canet / Marc Meny de Marangue
(no USA entry)			
1912	1	FRA	André Gobert / Maurice Germot
	2	SWE	Gunnar Setterwall / Carl Kempe
	3	GBR	Charles Percy Dixon / Arthur Ernest Beamish
(indoor courts)			
1920	1	GBR	Oswald Noel Turnbull / Max Woosnam
	2	JPN	Ichiya Kumagae / Seiichiro Kashio
	3	FRA	Max Decugis / Pierre Albarran
1924	1	USA	Vincent Richards / Frank Hunter
	2	FRA	Jacques Brugnon / Henri Cochet
	3	FRA	Jean Borotra / René Lacoste
1928-1984 (not held)			
1988	1	USA	Ken Flach / Robert Seguso
	2	ESP	Emilio Sanchez / Sergio Casal
	3T	TCH	Miloslav Mecir / Milan Srejber
	3T	SWE	Stefan Edberg / Anders Jarryd
1992	1	GER	Boris Becker / Michael Stich
	2	RSA	Wayne Ferreira / Piet Norval
	3T	CRO	Goran Ivanisevic / Goran Prpic
	3T	ARG	Javier Frana / Christian Miniussi
		USA	Jim Courier / Pete Sampras

WOMEN'S SINGLES

YEAR	RANK	CTRY	ATHLETE
1896 (not held)			
1900	1	GBR	Charlotte Cooper
	2	FRA	Hélène Prévost
	3	USA	Marion Jones
1904 (not held)			
1906	1	GRE	Esmée Simiriotou
	2	GRE	Sophia Marinou
	3	GRE	Euphrosine Paspati
(no USA entry)			
1908	1	GBR	Dorothy Chambers
	2	GBR	Dorothy Boothby
	3	GBR	Joan Winch
(no USA entry) (indoor courts)			
1908	1	GBR	Gwendoline Eastlake-Smith
	2	GBR	Angela Greene
	3	GBR	Martha Adlerstrahe
(indoor courts)			
1912	1	FRA	Marguerite Broquedis
	2	GER	Dora Köring
	3	NOR	Molla Bjurstedt
(no USA entry) (indoor courts)			

1912	1	GBR	Edith Hannam
	2	DEN	Thora Gerda Sophy Castenschiold
	3	GBR	Mabel Parton
(no USA entry)			
1920	1	FRA	Suzanne Lenglen
	2	GBR	E. Dorothy Holman
	3	GBR	Kathleen "Kitty" McKane
(no USA entry)			
1924	1	USA	Helen Wills
	2	FRA	Julie Vlasto
	3	GBR	Kathleen "Kitty" McKane
1928-1984 (not held)			
1988	1	FRG	Steffi Graf
	2	ARG	Gabriela Sabatini
	3T	USA	Zina Garrison
	3T	BUL	Manuela Maleeva
1992	1	USA	Jennifer Capriati
	2	GER	Steffi Graf
	3T	USA	Mary Joe Fernandez
	3T	ESP	Arantxa Sanchez-Vicario

WOMEN'S DOUBLES

YEAR	RANK	CTRY	ATHLETES
1896-1912 (not held)			
1920	1	GBR	Winifred Margaret McNair / Kathleen "Kitty" McKane
	2	GBR	Geraldine Beamish / E. Dorothy Holman
	3	FRA	Suzanne Lenglen / Elisabeth d'Ayen
1924	1	USA	Hazel Wightman / Helen Wills
	2	GBR	P. Edith Covell / Kathleen "Kitty" McKane
	3	GBR	Dorothy Shepherd-Barron / Evelyn Colyer
1928-1984 (not held)			
1988	1	USA	Pam Shriver / Zina Garrison
	2	TCH	Jana Novotna / Helena Sukova
	3	AUS	Elizabeth Smylie / Wendy Turnbull
	3	FRG	Steffi Graf / Claudia Kohde-Kilsch
1992	1	USA	Gigi Fernandez / Mary Joe Fernandez
	2	ESP	Conchita Martinez / Arantxa Sanchez-Vicario
	3	AUS	Rachel McQuillan / Nicole Provis

VOLLEYBALL

MEN

YEAR	RANK	CTRY	RECORD	USA MATCH SCORES
1896-1960 (not held)				
1964	1	URS	8-1	
	2	TCH	8-1	
	3	JPN	7-2	
	9	USA	2-7	
USA Team: Mike Bright / Barry Brown / Keith Erickson / Bill Grebenow / Richard Hammer / Jacob Highland / Ron Lang / Charles Nelson / Mike O'Hara / Bill Olsson / Ernie Suwara / Pedro Velasco				
1968	1	URS	8-1	
	2	JPN	7-2	
	3	TCH	7-2	
	7	USA	4-5	
USA Team: Daniel Patterson / Pedro Velasco / John Henn / Robert May / Larry Rundle / David Bright / Smitty Duke / John Alstrom / Jon Stanley / Thomas Haine / Rudy Suwara / Winthrop Davenport				
1972	1	JPN	7-0	
	2	GDR	5-2	
	3	URS	6-1	
(no USA entry - DNQ)				
1976	1	POL	6-0	
	2	URS	4-1	
	3	CUB	4-2	
(no USA entry - DNQ)				
1980	1	URS	6-0	
	2	BUL	4-2	
	3	ROM	4-2	
1984	1	USA	5-1	
	2	BRA	4-2	
	3	ITA	4-2	
USA Team: Dusty Dvorak / Dave Saunders / Steve Salmons / Paul Sunderland / Rich Duwelius / Steve Timmons / Craig Buck / Marc Waldie / Chris Marlowe / Aldis Berzins / Pat Powers / Karch Kiraly				
1988	1	USA	7-0	USA vs. JPN 3-0
	2	URS	5-2	USA vs. HOL 3-1
	3	ARG	4-3	USA vs. ARG 3-2
				USA vs. FRA 3-0
				USA vs. TUN 3-0
				USA vs. BRA 3-0
				USA vs. URS 3-1 (13-15, 15-10, 15-11, 15-8 - final)
USA Team: Craig Buck / Bob Ctvrtlik / Scott Fortune / Karch Kiraly / Ricci Luyties / Doug Partie / Jon Root / Eric Sato / Dave Saunders / Jeff Stork / Steve Timmons / Troy Tanner				

1992	1	BRA	8-0	USA vs. JPN 3-2*
	2	NED	4-4	USA vs. CAN 3-2
	3	USA	6-2	USA vs. ESP 3-2
				USA vs. FRA 3-0
				USA vs. ITA 3-1
				USA vs. BRA 1-3
				USA vs. CUB 3-1
USA TEAM: Nick Becker / Carlos Briceno / Bob Ctvrtlik / Scott Fortune / Dan Greenbaum / Brent Hilliard / Bryan Ivie / Doug Partie / Bob Samuelson / Eric Sato / Jeff Stork / Steve Timmons				
*Result overturned on appeal giving Japan a 3-1 victory.				

WOMEN

YEAR	RANK	CTRY	RECORD	USA MATCH SCORES
1896-1960 (not held)				
1964	1	JPN	5-0	
	2	USR	4-1	
	3	POL	3-2	
	5	USA	1-4	
USA Team: Jean Gaertner / Gail O'Rourke / Linda Murphy / Lou Galloway / Verneda Thomas / Mary Perry / Mary Peppler / Nancy Owen / Patricia Bright / Jane Ward / Sharon Peterson / Barbara Harwerth				
1968	1	USR	7-0	
	2	JPN	6-1	
	3	POL	5-2	
	8	USA	0-7	
USA Team: Jane Ward / Nancy Owen / Fanny Hopeau / Barbara Perry / Ninja Jorgensen / Miki McFadden / Sharon Peterson / Patti Bright / Laurie Lewis / Marilyn McReavy / Mary Perry / Kathryn Heck				
1972	1	USR	5-0	
	2	JPN	4-1	
	3	PRK	3-2	
(no USA entry - DNQ)				
1976	1	JPN	5-0	
	2	USR	4-1	
	3	KOR	3-2	
(no USA entry - DNQ)				
1980	1	USR	5-0	
	2	GDR	3-2	
	3	BUL	3-2	
1984	1	CHN	4-1	
	2	USA	4-1	
	3	JPN	4-1	
USA Team: Paula Weishoff / Susan Woodstra / Rita Crockett / Laurie Flachmeier / Carolyn Becker / Flora Hyman / Rose Magers / Julie Vollertsen / Debbie Green / Kimberly Ruddins / Jeanne Beauprey / Linda Chisholm				
1988	1	URS	4-1	USA vs. CHN 0-3
	2	PER	4-1	USA vs. BRA 2-3
	3	CHN	3-2	USA vs. PER 2-3
	7	USA	2-3	USA vs. GDR 3-1
				USA vs. KOR 3-0
USA Team: Deitre Collins / Caren Kemner / Laurel Kessel / Liz Masakayan / Jayne McHugh / Melissa McLinden / Kim Oden / Keba Phipps / Angela Rock / Kim Ruddins / Liane Sato / Tammy Webb				
1992	1	CUB	5-0	USA vs. JPN 2-3
	2	EUN	3-2	USA vs. EUN 3-2
	3	USA	4-2	USA vs. ESP 3-0
				USA vs. NED 3-1
				USA vs. CUB 2-3
				USA vs. BRA 3-0
USA TEAM: Janet Cobbs / Tara Cross-Battle / Lori Endicott / Caren Kemner / Ruth Lawanson / Tammy Liley / Elaina Oden / Kim Oden / Tecce Sanders / Liane Sato / Paula Weishoff / Yoko Zetterlund				

WATER POLO

MEN

YEAR	RANK	CTRY	RECORD	USA GAMES SCORES
1896 (not held)				
1900	1	GBR	2-0	
	2	BEL	1-1	
	3	FRA	0-1	
	4	FRA	0-1	
1904	1	USA		2-0
David Bratton / George Van Cleef / Leo Goodwin / Louis Handley / David Hesser / Joseph Ruddy / James Steen / Rex Beach / Jerome Steever / Edwin Swatek / Charles Healy / Frank Kehoe				
	2	USA		0-1
David Hammond / William Tuttle				
	3	USA		0-1
John Meyers / Manfred Toeppen / Gwynne Evans / Amadee Reyburn / Fred Schreiner / Augustus Goessling / William Orthwein				
1906 (not held)				

1908	1	GBR	1-0
	2	BEL	2-1
	3	SWE	0-1
	4	HOL	0-1
(no USA entry)			
1912	1	GBR	3-0
	2	SWE	3-1
	3	BEL	3-2
	4	AUT	1-3
	5	HUN	0-2
	6	FRA	0-2
(no USA entry)			
1920	1	GBR/IRL	3-0
	2	BEL	4-1
	3	SWE	4-1
	4	**USA**	**2-3**

USA TEAM: Preston Steiger / Sophus Jensen / Michael McDermott / CleMENt Browne / Herbert Vollmer / Harry Hebner / James Cardson / William Vosburgh / G. Albert Taylor / Duke Paoa Kahanamoku / Perry McGillvray

1924	1	FRA	4-0
	2	BEL	5-1
	3	**USA**	**3-3**
	4	SWE	3-3

USA TEAM: Frederick Lauer / Oliver Horn / Clarence Mitchell / George Schroth / Herbert Vollmer / Johnny Weissmuller / Arthur Austin / John Norton / Wallace O'Connor

1928	1	GER	3-0
	2	HUN	3-1
	3	FRA	5-1
	4	GBR	2-2
		USA	**elim. 2nd rd**

USA TEAM: Harry Daniels / Ogden Driggs / Joseph Farrel / R. J. Greenberg / Samuel Greller / Reginald Harrison / Fred Lauer / G. Mitchell / Wallace O'Connor / George Schroth / Hewrbert Topp / David Young / Perry McGillvary

1932	1	HUN	3-0
	2	GER	2-1-1
	3	**USA**	**2-1-1**
	4	JPN	0-3

USA TEAM: Herbert Wildman / F. Calvert Strong / Charles Finn / Harold McAlister / Philip Daubenspeck / Austin Clapp / Wallace O'Connor

1936	1	HUN	8-0-1
	2	GER	8-0-1
	3	BEL	4-3-2
	4	FRA	4-5
	5	HOL	3-1-5
	6	AUT	5-3-1
	7	SWE	3-6
	8	GBR	2-4-3
	9	USA	1-2

USA TEAM: Kenneth Beck / P.B. Dabuenspeck / Charles Finn / Dixon Fiske / Frank Graham / William Kelly / Fred Lauer / C.H. McCallister / James O'Connor / Ray Ruddy / Herbert Wildman

1948	1	ITA	8-0-2
	2	HUN	6-3-1
	3	HOL	6-1-3
	4	BEL	2-2-6
	5	SWE	6-3-1
	6	FRA	4-2-4
	7	EGY	1-4-5
	8	ESP	2-8
1952	1	HUN	7-0-3
	2	YUG	7-0-3
	3	ITA	8-2
	4	**USA**	**5-6**

USA TEAM: Harry Bisbey / James Norris / Edward Jaworski / Norman Lake / William Kooistra / Peter Stange / Norman Dornblaser / John Spargo / Robert Hughes / Maroni Burns

1956	1	HUN	7-0
	2	YUG	6-1-1
	3	URS	5-3
	5	**USA**	**2-5-1**

USA TEAM: Robert Horn / William Ross / Robert Frojen / Wallace Wolf / Ronald Severa / James Gaughran / William Kooistra / Kenneth Hahn / Robert Hughes / Sam Kooistra

1960	1	ITA	8-0-1
	2	URS	6-2-1
	3	HUN	5-2-2
	4	YUG	7-2
	5	ROM	4-3-2
	6	GER	4-5
	7	**USA**	**4-5**
	8	HOL	1-7-1

USA TEAM: Robert Horn / Marvin Burns / Ronald Severa / Ronald Crawford / Fred Tisue / Wallace Wolf / Robert Volmer / Gordon Hall / Charles Bittick / Charles McIlroy

1964	1	HUN	6-0-2
	2	YUG	7-0-2
	3	URS	5-2-1
	4	ITA	4-4
	5	ROM	4-3-1
	6	GDR	3-5
	7	BEL	2-6
	8	HOL	4-5
(no USA entry)			
1968	1	YUG	7-1-1
	2	URS	6-2
	3	HUN	6-2
	4	ITA	6-2-1
	5	**USA**	**5-2-1**
	6	GDR	6-2-1
	7	HOL	5-3-1
	8	CUB	3-4-1

USA TEAM: Anton Van Dorp / David Ashleigh / Russell Webb / Ronald Crawford / Stanley Cole / Bruce Bradley / L. Dean Willeford / Barry Weitzenberg / Gary Sheerer / John Parker / Steven Barnett

1972	1	URS	7-0-2
	2	HUN	6-0-3
	3	**USA**	**7-1-2**
	4	GER	2-2-5
	5	YUG	5-4-1
	6	ITA	3-4-2
	7	HOL	6-1-2
	8	ROM	5-4-1

USA TEAM: James Slatton / Stanley Cole / Russell Webb / Barry Weitzenberg / Gary Sheerer / Bruce Bradley / Peter Asch / James Ferguson / Steven Barnett / John Parker / Eric Lindroth

1976	1	HUN	7-0-1
	2	ITA	4-1-3
	3	HOL	5-1-2
	4	ROM	2-2-4
	5	YUG	1-2-5
	6	GER	2-5-1
	7	CUB	5-1-2
	8	URS	4-2-2
(no USA entry - DNQ)			
1980	1	URS	8-0
	2	YUG	5-1-2
	3	HUN	5-2-1
	4	ESP	4-4
	5	CUB	2-3-3
	6	HOL	2-5-1
	7	AUS	5-2-1
	8	ITA	4-3-1
1984	1	YUG	6-0-1
	2	**USA**	**6-0-1**
	3	GER	4-2-1
	4	ESP	3-2-2
	5	AUS	2-3-2
	6	HOL	2-5-0
	7	ITA	4-1-2
	8	GRE	3-2-2

USA TEAM: Craig Wilson / Kevin Robertson / Gary Figueroa / Peter Campbell / Douglas Burke / Joseph Vargas / Jon Svendsen / John Siman / Andrew McDonald / Terry Schroeder / Jody Campbell / Timothy Shaw

1988	1	YUG	6-1	USA vs. YUG	7-6
	2	**USA**	**5-2**	USA vs. ESP	7-9
	3	URS	4-2-1	USA vs. CHN	14-7
	4	FRG	5-2	USA vs. GRE	18-9
	5	HUN	3-2-3	USA vs. HUN	10-9
	6	ESP	4-2-2	USA vs. URS	8-7
				USA vs. YUG	7-9

USA TEAM: Craig Wilson / Kevin Robertson / James Bergeson / George Campbell / Douglas Kimball / Edward Klass / Alan Mouchawar / Jeffrey Campbell / Gregory Boyer / Terry Schroeder / Jody Campbell / Christopher Duplanty / Michael Evans

1992	1	ITA	5-0	USA vs. AUS	8-4
	2	ESP	5-1	USA vs. TCH	9-3
	3	EUN	6-1	USA vs. FRA	11-7
	4	**USA**	**4-3**	USA vs. EUN	5-8
	5	AUS	4-2	USA vs. GER	7-2
	6	HUN	4-2	USA vs. ESP	4-6
	7	GER	2-3-3		
	8	CUB	2-6		

USA TEAM: Jeff Campbell / Chris Duplanty / Mike Evans / Kirk Everist / Erich Fischer / Charles Harris / Chris Humbert / Doug Kimbell / Craig Klass / Alex Rousseau / Terry Schroeder / John Vargas / Craig Wilson

WEIGHTLIFTING

52 KG (114 LBS)

YEAR	RANK	CTRY	ATHLETE	SNATCH	C & JERK	TOTAL KG
1896-1968	(not held)					
1972	1	POL	Zygmunt Smalcerz			337.5
	2	HUN	Lajos Szûcs			330.0
	3	HUN	Sándor Holczreiter			327.5
(no USA entry)						
1976	1	URS	Aleksandr Voronin	105.0	137.5	242.5 **EWR**
	2	HUN	György Köszegi	107.5	130.0	237.5
	3	IRN	Mohammad Nassiri	100.0	135.0	235.0
(no USA entry)						
1980	1	URS	Kanybek Osmanoliev	107.5	137.5	245.0 **OR**
	2	PRK	Ho Bong Choi	110.0	135.0	245.0
	3	PRK	Han Gyong Si	110.0 **OR**	135.0	245.0
1984	1	CHN	Zeng Guoqiang	105.0	130.0	235.0
	2	CHN	Zhou Peishun	107.5	127.5	235.0
	3	JPN	Kazushito Manabe	102.5	130.0	232.5
(no USA entry)						
1988	1	BUL	Sevdalin Marinov	120.0 **WR**	150.0**OR**	270.0 **WR**
	2	KOR	Chun Byung-kwan	112.5	147.5	260.0
	3#	CHN	He Zhuoqiang	112.5	145.0	257.5
(no USA entry)						

#awarded bronze based on lower body weight)

1992	1	BUL	Ivan Ivanov	115.0	150.0	265.0
	2	CHN	Lin Qisheng	115.0	147.5	262.5
	3	ROM	Traian Ciharean	112.5	140.0	252.5
(no USA entry)						

56 KG (123 LBS)

YEAR	RANK	CTRY	ATHLETE	SNATCH	C & JERK	TOTAL KG
1896-1936	(not held)					
1948	**1**	**USA**	**Joseph Di Pietro**			**307.5 WR**
	2	GBR	Julian Creus			297.5
	3	**USA**	**Richard Tom**			**295.0**
1952	1	URS	Ivan Udodov			315.0 **OR**
	2	IRN	Mahmoud Namjou			307.5
	3	IRN	Ali Mirzai			300.0
		USA	**Richard Tom**			**DNC**
1956	**1**	**USA**	**Charles Vinci**			**342.5 WR**
	2	URS	Vladimir Stogov			337.5
	3	IRN	Mahmoud Namjou			332.5
1960	**1**	**USA**	**Charles Vinci**			**345.0 EWR**
	2	JPN	Yoshinobu Miyake			337.5
	3	IRN	Esmaiil Elmkhan			330.0
1964	1	URS	Aleksei Vakhonin			357.5 **WR**
	2	HUN	Imre Földi			355.0
	3	JPN	Shiro Ichinoseki			347.5
(no USA entry)						
1968	1	IRN	Mohammad Nassiri			367.5 **EWR**
	2	HUN	Imre Földi			367.5 **EWR**
	3	POL	Henryk Trebicki			357.5
(no USA entry)						
1972	1	HUN	Imre Földi			377.5 **WR**
	2	IRN	Mohammad Nassiri			370.0
	3	URS	Gennady Chetin			367.5
(no USA entry)						
1976	1	BUL	Norair Nurikian	117.5 **OR**	145.0	262.5 **WR**
	2	POL	Grzegorz Cziura	115.0	137.5	252.5
	3	JPN	Kenkichi Ando	107.5	142.5	250.0
(no USA entry)						
1980	1	CUB	Daniel Nuñez Aguiar	125.0 **WR**	150.0	275.0 **WR**
	2	URS	Yurik Sarkisian	112.5	157.5 **WR**	270.0
	3	POL	Tadeusz Dembonczyk	120.0	145.0	265.0
1984	1	CHN	Wu Shude	120.0	147.5	267.5
	2	CHN	Lai Runming	125.0 **EOR**	140.0	265.0
	3	JPN	Masahiro Kotaka	112.5	140.0	252.5
	8	**USA**	**Albert Hood**	**112.5**	**130.0**	**242.5**
1988	1*	URS	Oxen Mirzoian	127.5 **OR**	165.0 **OR**	292.5 **OR**
	2	CHN	He Yingqiang	125.0	162.5	287.5
	3	CHN	Liu Shoubin	127.5	140.0	267.5
(no USA entry)						

*Mitko Grablev (BUL), original gold medalist, tested positive for use of a banned substance.

1992	1	KOR	Chun Byung-kwan	132.5 **NOR**	155.0	287.5
	2	CHN	Liu Shoubin	130.0	147.5	277.5
	3	CHN	Luo Jianming	125.0	152.5	277.5
(no USA entry)						

60 KG (132 LBS)

YEAR	RANK	CTRY	ATHLETE	SNATCH	C & JERK	TOTAL KG
1896-1912	(not held)					
1920	1	BEL	Frans de Haes			220.0
	2	EST	Alfred Schmidt			212.5
	3	SUI	Eugène Ryther			210.0
(no USA entry)						
1924	1	ITA	Pierino Gabetti			402.5
	2	AUT	Andreas Stadler			385.0
	3	SUI	Arthur Reinmann			382.5
(no USA entry)						
1928	1	AUT	Franz Andrysek			287.5 **OR**
	2	ITA	Pierno Gabetti			282.5
	3	GER	Hans Wölpert			282.5
(no USA entry)						
1932	1	FRA	Raymond Suvigny			287.5 **EOR**
	2	GER	Hans Wölpert			282.5
	3	**USA**	**Anthony Terlazzo**			**280.0**
1936	**1**	**USA**	**Anthony Terlazzo**			**312.5 WR**
	2	EGY	Saleh Mohammed Soliman			305.0
	3	EGY	Ibrahim Hassan Shams			300.0
1948	1	EGY	Mahmoud Fayad			332.5 **WR**
	2	TRI	Rodney Wilkes			317.5
	3	IRN	Jaafar Salmasi			312.5
	6	**USA**	**Kotaro Ishikawa**			**307.5**
1952	1	URS	Rafael Chimishkyan			337.5 **WR**
	2	URS	Nikolai Saksonov			332.5
	3	TRI	Rodney Wilkes			322.5
		USA	**Richard Tomtai**			**DNC**
1956	**1**	**USA**	**Isaac Berger**			**352.5 WR**
	2	URS	Yevgeny Minayev			342.5
	3	POL	Marian Zielinski			335.0
1960	1	URS	Yevgeny Minayev			372.5 **EWR**
	2	**USA**	**Isaac Berger**			**362.5**
	3	ITA	Sebastiano Mannironi			352.5
1964	1	JPN	Yoshinobu Miyake			397.5 **WR**
	2	**USA**	**Isaac Berger**			**382.5**
	3	POL	Mieczyslaw Nowak			377.5
1968	1	JPN	Yoshinobu Miyake			392.5
	2	URS	Dito Shanidze			387.5
	3	JPN	Yoshiyuki Miyake			385.0
(no USA entry)						
1972	1	BUL	Norair Nurikian			402.5 **EWR**
	2	URS	Dito Shanidze			400.0
	3	HUN	János Benedek			390.0
(no USA entry)						
1976	1	URS	Nikolai Kolesnikov	125.0 **OR**	160.0 **OR**	285.0 **EWR**
	2	BUL	Georgi Todorov	122.5	157.5	280.0
	3	JPN	Kazumasa Hirai	125.0 **OR**	150.0	275.0
(no USA entry)						
1980	1	URS	Viktor Mazin	130.0 **OR**	160.0 **EOR**	290.0 **OR**
	2	BUL	Stefan Dimitrov	127.5	160.0 **EOR**	287.0
	3	POL	Marek Seweryn	127.5	155.0	282.5
1984	1	CHN	Chen Weiqiang	125.0	157.5	282.5
	2	ROM	Gelu Radu	125.0	155.0	280.0
	3	TAI	Wen-Yee Tsai	125.0	147.5	272.5
(no USA entry)						
1988	1	TUR	Naim Suleymanoglu	152.5 **WR**	190.0 **WR**	342.5 **WR**
	2	BUL	Stefan Topourov	137.5	175.0	312.5
	3	CHN	Ye Huanming	127.5	160.0	287.5
(no USA entry)						
1992	1	TUR	Naim Suleymanoglu	142.5	177.5	320.0
	2	BUL	Nikolai Peshalov	137.5	167.5	305.0
	3	CHN	He Yingqiang	130.0	165.0	295.0
	18	**USA**	**Bryan Jacob**	**117.5**	**145.0**	**262.5**

67.5 KG (148.5 LBS)

YEAR	RANK	CTRY	ATHLETE	SNATCH	C & JERK	TOTAL KG
1896-1912	(not held)					
1920	1	EST	Alfred Neuland			257.5
	2	BEL	Louis Williquet			240.0
	3	BEL	Florimond Rooms			230.0
(no USA entry)						
1924	1	FRA	Edmond Décottignies			440.0
	2	AUT	Anton Zwerina			427.5
	3	TCH	Bohumil Durdis			425.0
(no USA entry)						
1928	1	GER	Hans Haas			322.5
	2	AUT	Kurt Helbig			322.5
	3	FRA	Fernand Arnout			302.5
(no USA entry)						
1932	1	FRA	René Duverger			325.0 **EWR**
	2	AUT	Hans Haas			307.5
	3	ITA	Gastone Pierini			302.5
	5	**USA**	**Arnie Sundberg**			**285.0**
1936	1	AUT	Robert Fein			342.5 **WR**
	2	EGY	Anwar Mohammed Mesbah			342.5 **WR**
	3	GER	Karl Jansen			327.5
	5	**USA**	**John Terpak**			**322.5**
1948	1	EGY	Ibrahim Hassan Shams			360.0 **OR**
	2	EGY	Appia Hamouda			360.0 **OR**
	3	GBR	James Halliday			340.0
	4	**USA**	**John Terpak**			**340.0**
1952	**1**	**USA**	**Tamio "Tommy" Kono**			**362.5 OR**
	2	URS	Yevgeny Lopatin			350.0
	3	AUS	Verne Barberis			350.0
1956	1	URS	Igor Rybak			380.0 **OR**
	2	URS	Rafael Khabutdinov			372.5
	3	KOR	Kim Chang-hee			370.0
(no USA entry)						
1960	1	URS	Viktor Buschuyev			397.5 **WR**
	2	SIN	Howe-Liang Tan			380.0
	3	IRQ	Abdul Wahid Aziz			380.0
		USA	**Anthony Gorcy**			**DNC**
1964	1	POL	Waldemar Baszanowski			432.5 **WR**
	2	URS	Vladimir Kaplunov			432.5 **WR**
	3	POL	Marian Zielinski			420.0
	4	**USA**	**Anthony Garcy**			**412.5**
1968	1	POL	Waldemar Baszanowski			437.5 **OR**
	2	IRN	Parviz Jalayer			422.5
	3	POL	Marian Zielinski			420.0
(no USA entry)						
1972	1	URS	Mukharbi Kirzhinov			460.0 **WR**
	2	BUL	Mladen Kuchev			450.0
	3	POL	Zbigniew Kaczmarek			437.5
	9	**USA**	**Daniel Cantore**			
1976		POL	Zbigniew Kaczmarek	135.0	172.5	307.5
	1	URS	Piotr Korol	135.0 **EOR**	170.0	305.0 **OR**
	2	FRA	Daniel Senet	135.0 **EOR**	165.0	300.0
	3	POL	Kazimierz Czarnecki	130.0	165.0	295.0
		USA	**Dan Cantore**			**420.0**
1980	1	BUL	Yanko Roussev	147.5 **OR**	195.0 **WR**	342.5 **WR**
	2	GDR	Joachim Kunz	145.0	190.0	335.0
	3	BUL	Mincho Pachov	142.5	182.5	325.0
1984	1	CHN	Yao Jingyuan	142.5	177.5	320.0
	2	ROM	Andrei Socaci	142.5	170.0	312.5
	2T	FIN	Jouni Grönman	140.0	172.5	312.5
	13	**USA**	**Donald Abrahamson**			**277.5**
1988	1*	GDR	Joachim Kunz	150.0	190.0	340.0
	2	URS	Israel Militossian	155.0 **OR**	182.5	337.5
	3	CHN	Li Jinhe	147.5	177.5	325.0
	13	**USA**	**Michael Jacques**	**125.0**	**157.5**	**282.5**

*Angel Guenchev (BUL), original gold medalist, tested positive for use of a banned

substance.

YEAR	RANK	CTRY	ATHLETE	SNATCH	C & JERK	TOTAL KG
1992	1	EUN	Israel Militossian	155.0	182.5	337.5
	2	BUL	Yoto Yotov	150.0	177.5	327.5
	3	GER	Andreas Behm	145.0	175.0	320.0
	8	**USA**	**Tim McRae**	**135.0**	**162.5**	**297.5**

75 KG (165 LBS)

YEAR	RANK	CTRY	ATHLETE	SNATCH	C & JERK	TOTAL KG
1896-1912	(not held)					
1920	1	FRA	Henri Gance			245.0
	2	ITA	Pietro Bianchi			237.5
	3	SWE	Albert Pettersson			237.5
(no USA entry)						
1924	1	ITA	Carlo Galimberti			492.5
	2	EST	Alfred Neuland			455.0
	3	EST	Jaan Kikkas			450.0
(no USA entry)						
1928	1	FRA	Roger François			335.0 WR
	2	ITA	Carlo Galimberti			332.5
	3	HOL	August Scheffer			327.5
(no USA entry)						
1932	1	GER	Rudolf Ismayr			345.0 WR
	2	ITA	Carlo Galimberti			340.0
	3	AUT	Karl Hipfinger			337.5
	5	**USA**	**Stanley Kratkowski**			**305.0**
1936	1	EGY	Khadr Sayed El Touni			387.5 WR
	2	GER	Rudolf Ismayr			352.5
	3	GER	Adolf Wagner			352.5
	5	**USA**	**Stanley Kratkowski**			**337.5**
1948	**1**	**USA**	**Frank Spellman**			**390.0 OR**
	2	**USA**	**Peter George**			**382.5**
	3	KOR	Kim Sung-jip			380.0
1952	**1**	**USA**	**Peter George**			**400.0 OR**
	2	CAN	Gérard Gratton			390.0
	3	KOR	Kim Sung-jip			382.5
1956	1	URS	Fyodor Bogdanovsky			420.0 WR
	2	**USA**	**Peter George**			**412.5**
	3	ITA	Ermanno Pignatti			302.5
1960	1	URS	Aleksandr Kurynov			437.5 WR
	2	**USA**	**Tamio "Tommy" Kono**			**427.5**
	3	HUN	Gyözö Veres			405.0
1964	1	TCH	Hans Zdrazila			445.0 EWR
	2	URS	Viktor Kurentsov			440.0
	3	JPN	Massashi Ouchi			437.5
(no USA entry)						
1968	1	URS	Viktor Kurentsov			475.0 OR
	2	JPN	Masashi Ouchi			455.0
	3	HUN	Károly Bakos			440.0
	4	**USA**	**Russell Knipp**			**437.5**
1972	1	BUL	Yordan Bikov			485.0 WR
	2	LEB	Mohamed Trabulsi			472.5
	3	ITA	Anselmo Silvino			470.0
	8	**USA**	**Russell Knipp**			**457.5**
1976	1	BUL	Yordan Mitkov	145.0 OR	190.0 OR	335.0 OR
	2	URS	Vartan Militosyan	145.0 OR	185.0	330.0
	3	GDR	Peter Wenzel	145.0 OR	182.5	327.5
		USA	**Frederick Lowe**			**205.0**
1980	1	BUL	Assen Zlatev	160.0 OR	200.0 OR	360.0 WR
	2	URS	Alexandr Pervy	157.5	200.0 OR	357.5
	3	BUL	Nedelcho Kolev	157.5	187.5	345.0
1984	1	GER	Karl-Heinz Radschinsky	150.0	190.0	340.0
	2	CAN	Jacques Demers	147.5	187.5	335.0
	3	ROM	Dragomir Cioroslan	147.5	185.0	332.5
(no USA entry)						
1988	1	BUL	Borislav Guidikov	167.5 OR	207.5 OR	375.0 OR
	2	GDR	Ingo Steinhoefel	165.0	195.0	360.0
	3	BUL	Alexander Varbanov	157.5	200.0	357.5
	8	**USA**	**Roberto Urrutia**	**150.0**	**177.5**	**327.5**
1992	1	EUN	Fedor Kassapu	155.0	202.5	357.5
	2	CUB	Pablo Lara	155.0	202.5	357.5
	3	PRK	Kim Myong Nam	162.5	190.0	352.5
(no USA entry)						

82.5 KG (181.5 LBS)

YEAR	RANK	CTRY	ATHLETE	SNATCH	C & JERK	TOTAL KG
1896-1912	(not held)					
1920	1	FRA	Ernest Cadine			290.0
	2	SWE	Fritz Hünenberger			275.0
	3	SWE	Erik Pettersson			272.5
(no USA entry)						
1924	1	FRA	Charles Rigoulot			502.5
	2	SUI	Fritz Hünenberger			490.0
	3	AUT	Leopold Friedrich			490.0
(no USA entry)						
1928	1	EGY	El Sayed Nosseir			335.0 WR
	2	FRA	Louis Hostin			352.5
	3	HOL	Johannes Verheijen			337.5
(no USA entry)						
1932	1	FRA	Louis Hostin			365.0 EWR
	2	DEN	Svend Olsen			360.0
	3	**USA**	**Henry Duey**			**330.0**
1936	1	FRA	Louis Hostin			372.5 OR
	2	GER	Eugen Deutsch			365.0
	3	EGY	Ibrahim Wasif			360.0
	7	**USA**	**William Good**			**350.0**
1948	**1**	**USA**	**Stanley Stanczyk**			**417.5 OR**
	2	**USA**	**Harold Sakata**			**380.0**
	3	SWE	Gösta Magnusson			375.0
1952	1	URS	Trofim Lomakin			417.5 EOR
	2	**USA**	**Stanley Stanczyk**			**415.0**
	3	URS	Arkady Vorobyev			407.5
1956	**1**	**USA**	**Tamio "Tommy" Kono**			**447.5 WR**
	2	URS	Vassily Stepanov			427.5
	3	**USA**	**James George**			**417.5**
1960	1	POL	Ireneusz Palinski			442.5
	2	**USA**	**James George**			**430.0**
	3	POL	Jan Bochenek			420.0
1964	1	URS	Rudolf Plukfelder			475.0 OR
	2	HUN	Géza Tóth			467.5
	3	HUN	Gyözö Veres			467.5
	5	**USA**	**Gary Cleveland**			**455.0**
1968	1	URS	Boris Selitsky			485.0 EWR
	2	URS	Vladimir Belyayev			485.0 EWR
	3	POL	Norbert Ozimek			472.5
		USA	**Joseph Puleo**			**DQ**
1972	1	NOR	Leif Jenssen			507.5 OR
	2	POL	Norbert Ozimek			497.5
	3	HUN	György Horváth			495.0
		USA	**Michael Karchut**			
1976	1	URS	Valery Shary	162.5 OR	202.5 OR	365.0 OR
		BUL	Blagoi Blagoev	162.5 OR	200.0	362.5
	2	BUL	Trendafil Stoichev	162.5 OR	197.5	360.0
	3	HUN	Péter Baczako	157.5	187.5	345.0
		USA	**Samuel Bigler**			**307.5**
1980	1	URS	Yurik Vardanyan	177.5 WR	222.5 WR	400.0 WR
	2	BUL	Blagoi Blagoev	175.0	197.5	372.5
	3	TCH	Dusan Poliacik	160.0	207.5	367.5
1984	1	ROM	Petre Becheru	155.0	200.0	355.0
	2	AUS	Robert Kabbas	150.0	192.5	342.5
	3	JPN	Ryoji Isaoka	150.0	190.0	340.0
	9	**USA**	**Arn Krinsky**			**315.0**
1988	1	URS	Israil Arsamakov	167.5	210.0	377.5
	2	HUN	Istvan Messzi	170.0	200.0	370.0
	3	KOR	Lee Hyung-kun	160.0	207.5	367.5
	11	**USA**	**Derrick Crass**	**140.0**	**175.0**	**315.0**
1992	1	GRE	Pyrros Dimas	167.5	202.5	370.0
	2	POL	Krzysztof Siemion	165.0	205.0	370.0
	3	EUN	Ibragim Samadov	167.5	202.5	370.0
	17	**USA**	**Roberto "Tony" Urrutia**	**150.0**	**190.0**	**340.0**

90 KG (198 LBS)

YEAR	RANK	CTRY	ATHLETE	SNATCH	C & JERK	TOTAL KG
1896-1948	(not held)					
1952	**1**	**USA**	**Norbert Schemansky**			**445.0 WR**
	2	URS	Grigory Novak			410.0
	3	TRI	Lennox Kilgour			402.5
1956	1	URS	Arkady Vorobyov			462.5 WR
	2	**USA**	**David Sheppard**			**442.5**
	3	FRA	Jean Debuf			425.0
1960	1	URS	Arkady Vorobyov			472.5 WR
	2	URS	Trofim Lomakin			457.5
	3	GBR	Louis Martin			445.0
	4	**USA**	**John Pulskamp**			**432.5**
1964	1	URS	Vladimir Golovanov			487.5 WR
	2	GBR	Louis Martin			475.0
	3	POL	Ireneusz Palinski			467.5
	4	**USA**	**William March**			**467.5**
1968	1	FIN	Kaarlo Kangasniemi			517.5 OR
	2	URS	Jaan Talts			507.5
	3	POL	Marěk Golab			495.0
	7	**USA**	**Philip Grippaldi**			**477.5**
1972	1	BUL	Andon Nikolov			525.0 OR
	2	BUL	Atanas Shopov			517.5
	3	SWE	Hans Bettembourg			512.5
	4	**USA**	**Philip Grippaldi**			**505.0**
1976	1	URS	David Rigert	170.0 OR	212.5 OR	382.5 OR
	2	**USA**	**Lee James**	**165.0**	**197.5**	**362.5**
	3	BUL	Atanas Shopov	155.0	205.0	360.0
1980	1	HUN	Péter Baczakó	170.0 EOR	207.5	377.5
	2	BUL	Rouen Aleksandrov	170.0 EOR	205.0	375.0
	3	GDR	Frank Mantek	165.0	205.0	370.0
1984	1	ROM	Nicu Vlad	172.5 OR	220.0 OR	392.5 OR
	2	ROM	Dumitru Petre	165.0	195.0	360.0
	3	GBR	David Mercer	157.5	195.0	352.5
	21	**USA**	**Thomas Calandro**			**315.0**
1988	1	URS	Anatoli Khrapatyi	187.5 OR	225.0 OR	412.5 OR
	2#	URS	Nail Moukhamediarov	177.5	222.5	400.0
	3	POL	Slawomir Zawada	180.0	220.0	400.0
	11	**USA**	**Arn Kritsky**	**147.5**	**185.0**	**332.5**
#awarded silver based on lower body weight.						
1992	1	EUN	Kakhi Kakhiachvili	177.5	235.0 EWR	412.5 EOR
	2	EUN	Serguei Syrtsov	190.0 OR	222.5	412.5 EOR
	3	POL	Sergiusz Wolcaniecki	172.5	220.0	392.5
	13	**USA**	**Bret Brian**	**150.0**	**187.5**	**337.5**

100 KG (200 LBS)

YEAR	RANK	CTRY	ATHLETE	SNATCH	C & JERK	TOTAL KG
1896-1976	(not held)					
1980	1	TCH	Ota Zaremba	180.0 OR	215.0	395.0 OR
	2	URS	Igor Nikitin	177.5	215.0	392.5
	3	CUB	Alberto Blanco Fernandez	172.5	212.5	385.0
1984	1	GER	Rolf Milser	167.5	217.5 EOR	385.0
	2	ROM	Vasile Groap	165.0	217.5 EOR	382.5
	3	FIN	Pekka Niemi	160.0	207.5	367.5
	5	**USA**	**Ken Clark**	**155.0**	**197.5**	**352.5**
1988	1*	URS	Pavel Kouznetsov	190.0 OR	235.0 OR	425.0 OR
	2	ROM	Nicu Vlad	185.0	217.5	402.5
	3	FRG	Peter Immesberger	175.0	220.0	395.0
(no USA entry)						
1992	1	EUN	Victor Tregoubov	190.0 EOR	220.0	410.0
	2	EUN	Timour Taimazov	185.0	217.5	402.5
	3	POL	Waldemar Malak	185.0	215.0	400.0
	15	**USA**	**Wesley Barnett**	**157.5**	**195.0**	**352.5**

110 KG (243 LBS)

YEAR	RANK	CTRY	ATHLETE	SNATCH	C & JERK	TOTAL KG
1896-1968	(not held)					
1972	1	URS	Jaan Talts			580.0 OR
	2	BUL	Alexander Kraichev			562.5
	3	GDR	Stefan Grützner			555.0
		USA	**Ken Patera**			**DQ**
1976		BUL	Valentin Hristov	175.0	225.0	400.0
	1	URS	Yuri Zaitsev	165.0	220.0 OR	385.0
	2	BUL	Krustiu Semerdzhiev	170.0 OR	215.0	385.0
	3	POL	Tadeusz Rutkowski	167.5	210.0	377.5
		USA	**Mark Cameron**	**162.5**	**212.5**	**375.0**
1980	1	URS	Leonid Taranenko	182.5	240.0 WR	422.5 WR
	2	BUL	Valentin Hristov	185.0 OR	220.0	405.0
	3	HUN	György Szalai	172.5	217.5	390.0
1984	1	ITA	Norberto Oberburger	175.0	215.0	390.0
	2	ROM	Stefan Tasnadi	167.5	212.5	380.0
	3	**USA**	**Guy Carlton**	**167.5**	**210.0**	**377.5**
1988	1	URS	Yuri Zakharevitch	210.0 WR	245.0 OR	455.0 WR
	2	HUN	Jozsef Jacso	190.0	237.5	427.5
	3#	GDR	Ronny Weller	190.0	235.0	425.0
	11#	**USA**	**Rich Schutz**	**160.0**	**200.0**	**360.0**
#awarded placement(s) based on lower body weight.						
1992	1	GER	Ronny Weller	192.5	240.0	432.5
	2	EUN	Artour Akoev	195.0	235.0	430.0
	3	BUL	Stefan Botev	190.0	227.5	417.5
	18	**USA**	**Rich Schutz**	**155.0**	**192.5**	**347.5**

+110 KG (+ 243 LBS)

YEAR	RANK	CTRY	ATHLETE	SNATCH	C & JERK	TOTAL KG
(one-hand lift)						
1896	1	GBR	Launceston Elliot			71.0
	2	DEN	Viggo Jensen			57.2
	3	GRE	Alexandros Nitolopoulos			57.2
(no USA entry)						
(two-hand lift)						
1896	1	DEN	Viggo Jensen			111.5
	2	GBR	Launceston Elliot			111.5
	3T	GER	Carl Schuhmann			100.0
	3T	GRE	Sotirios Versis			100.0
(no USA entry)						
1900 (not held)						
(two-hand lift)						
1904	1	GRE	Perikles Kakousis			111.70
	2	**USA**	**Oscar Osthoff**			**84.37**
	3	**USA**	**Frank Kungler**			**79.61**
(all-around dumbell contest)						
1904	**1**	**USA**	**Oscar Osthoff**			**48 pts.**
	2	**USA**	**Frederick Winters**			**45 pts.**
	3	**USA**	**Frank Kungler**			**10 pts.**
(one-hand lift)						
1906	1	AUT	Josef Steinbach			76.55
	2	ITA	Tullio Camilotti			73.75
	3	GER	Heinrich Schneidereit			70.75
(no USA entry)						
(two-hand lift)						
1906	1	GRE	Dimitrios Tofalos			142.5
	2	AUT	Josef Steinbach			136.5
	3	FRA	Alexandre Maspoli			129.5
(no USA entry)						
1908-1912	(not held)					
1920	1	ITA	Filippo Bottino			270.0
	2	LUX	Joseph Alzin			255.0
	3	FRA	Louis Bernot			250.0
(no USA entry)						
1924	1	ITA	Giuseppe Tonani			517.5
	2	AUT	Franz Aigner			515.0
	3	EST	Harold Tammer			497.5
(no USA entry)						
1928	1	GER	Josef Strassberger			372.5 WR
	2	EST	Arnold Luhäär			360.0
	3	TCH	Jaroslav Skobla			357.5
(no USA entry)						
1932	1	TCH	Jaroslav Skobla			380.0 OR
	2	TCH	Václav Psenicka			377.5
	3	GER	Josef Strassberger			377.5
	5	**USA**	**Albert Manger**			**315.0**
1936	1	GER	Josef Manger			410.0 WR
	2	TCH	Václav Psenicka			402.5
	3	EST	Arnold Luhäär			400.0
	12	**USA**	**David Mayor**			
1948	**1**	**USA**	**John Davis**			**452.5 OR**
	2	**USA**	**Norbert Schemansky**			**425.0**
	3	HOL	Abraham Charité			412.5
1952	**1**	**USA**	**John Davis**			**460.0 OR**
	2	**USA**	**James Bradford**			**437.5**
	3	ARG	Humberto Selvetti			432.5
1956	**1**	**USA**	**Paul Anderson**			**500.0 OR**
	2	ARG	Humberto Selvetti			500.0 OR
	3	ITA	Alberto Pigaiani			452.5
1960	1	URS	Yuri Vlassov			537.5 WR
	2	**USA**	**James Bradford**			**512.5**
	3	**USA**	**Norbert Schemansky**			**500.0**
1964	1	URS	Leonid Zhabotinsky			572.5 OR
	2	URS	Yuri Vlassov			570.0
	3	**USA**	**Norbert Schemansky**			**537.5**
1968	1	URS	Leonid Zhabotinsky			572.5 EOR
	2	BEL	Serge Reding			555.0
	3	**USA**	**Joseph Dube**			**555.0**
1972	1	URS	Vassily Alexeyev			640.0 OR
	2	GER	Rudolf Mang			610.0
	3	GDR	Gerd Bonk			572.5
		USA	**Kenneth Patera**			
1976	1	URS	Vassily Alexeyev	185.0 OR	255.0 WR	440.0
	2	GDR	Gerd Bonk	170.0	235.0	405.0
	3	GDR	Helmut Losch	165.0	222.5	387.5
	5	**USA**	**Bruce Wilhelm**	**172.5**	**215.0**	**387.5**
1980	1	URS	Sultan Rakhmanov	195.0 OR	245.0	440.0 EOR
	2	GDR	Jürgen Heuser	182.5	227.5	410.0
	3	POL	Tadeusz Rutkowski	180.0	227.5	407.5
1984	1	AUS	Dean "Dinko" Lukin	172.5	240.0	412.5
	2	**USA**	**Mario Martinez**	**185.0**	**225.0**	**410.0**
	3	GER	Manfred Nerlinger	177.5	220.0	397.5
1988	1	URS	Alexandre Kourlovitch	212.5 OR	250.0	462.5 OR
	2	FRG	Manfred Nerlinger	190.0	240.0	430.0
	3	FRG	Martin Zawieja	182.5	232.5	415.0
	4	**USA**	**Mario Martinez**	**175.0**	**232.5**	**407.5**
1992	1	EUN	Alexandre Kourlovitch	205.0	245.0	450.0
	2	EUN	Leonid Taranenko	187.5	237.5	425.0
	3	GER	Manfred Nerlinger	180.0	232.5	412.5
	8	**USA**	**Mario Martinez**	**170.0**	**215.0**	**385.0**

WRESTLING

48 KG (106 LBS) FREESTYLE

YEAR	RANK	CTRY	ATHLETE
1896-1900	(not held)		
1904	**1**	**USA**	**Robert Curry**
	2	**USA**	**John Hein**
	3	**USA**	**Gustav Thiefenthaler**
1906-1968	(not held)		
1972	1	URS	Roman Dmitriev
	2	BUL	Ognyan Nikolov
	3	IRN	Ebrahim Javadi
	7	**USA**	**Sergio Gonzalez**
1976	1	BUL	Hasan Isaev
	2	URS	Roman Dmitriev
	3	JPN	Akira Kudo
		USA	**William Rosado**
1980	1	ITA	Claudio Pollio
	2	PRK	Jan Se Hong
	3	URS	Sergei Kornilaev
1984	**1**	**USA**	**Robert Weaver**
	2	JPN	Takashi Irie
	3	KOR	Son Gab-do
1988	1	JPN	Takashi Kobayashi
	2	BUL	Ivan Tzonov
	3	URS	Serguei Karamtchakov
	4	**USA**	**Tim Vanni**
1992	1	PRK	Il Park
	2	KOR	Kim Jong
	3	EUN	Vougar Oroudjov
	5	**USA**	**Tim Vanni**

52 KG (114 LBS) FREESTYLE

YEAR	RANK	CTRY	ATHLETE
1896-1900	(not held)		
1904	**1**	**USA**	**George Mehnert**
	2	**USA**	**Gustav Bauer**
	3	**USA**	**William Nelson**
1906-1936	(not held)		
1948	1	FIN	Lennart Viitala
	2	TUR	Halit Balamir
	3	SWE	Thure Johansson
	7	**USA**	**William Jernigan**

1952	1	TUR	Hasan Gemici
	2	JPN	Yushu Kitano
	3	IRN	Mahmoud Mollaghasemi
	7	**USA**	**Robert Peery**
1956	1	URS	Mirian Tsalkalamanidze
	2	IRN	Mohammad Ali Khojastépour
	3	TUR	Hüseyin Akba
	5	**USA**	**Richard Delgado**
1960	1	TUR	Ahmet Bilek
	2	JPN	Masayuki Matsubara
	3	IRN	Mohammad Ebrahim Seifpour
	5	**USA**	**Elliott Gray Simons**
1964	1	JPN	Yoshikatsu Yoshida
	2	KOR	Chang Chang-sun
	3	IRN	Ali Akbar Heidari
	7	**USA**	**Elliott Gray Simons**
1968	1	JPN	Shigeo Nakata
	2	**USA**	**Richard Sanders**
	3	MON	Surenjav Sukhbaatar
1972	1	JPN	Kiyomi Kato
	2	URS	Arsen Alkhverdiev
	3	PRK	Kim Gwong Hyong
		USA	**James Carr**
1976	1	JPN	Yuji Takada
	2	URS	Aleksandr Ivanov
	3	KOR	Jeon Hae-sup
		USA	**James Haines**
1980	1	URS	Anatoly Beloglazov
	2	POL	Wladyslaw Stecyk
	3	BUL	Nermedin Selimov
1984	1	YUG	Saban Trstena
	2	KOR	Kim Jong-kyu
	3	JPN	Yuji Takada
		USA	**Joe Gonzales**
1988	1	JPN	Mitsuru Sato
	2	YUG	Saban Trstena
	3	URS	Vladimir Togouzov
		USA	**Ken Chertow**
1992	1	PRK	Li Hak
	2	**USA**	**Zeke Jones**
	3	BUL	V. Jordanov

57 KG (125 LBS) FREESTYLE

YEAR	RANK	CTRY	ATHLETE
1896-1900	(not held)		
1904	**1**	**USA**	**Isidor Niflot**
	2	**USA**	**August Wester**
	3	**USA**	**Z.B. Strebler**
1906	(not held)		
1908	**1**	**USA**	**George Mehnert**
	2	GBR	William Press
	3	CAN	Aubert Côté
1912-1920	(not held)		
1924	1	FIN	Kustaa Pihlajamäki
	2	FIN	Kaarlo Mäkinen
	3	**USA**	**Bryant Hines**
1928	1	FIN	Kaarlo Mäkinen
	2	BEL	Edmond Spapen
	3	CAN	James Trifunov
	5	**USA**	**Robert Hewitt**
1932	**1**	**USA**	**Robert Pearce**
	2	HUN	Ödön Zombori
	3	FIN	Aatos Jaskari
1936	1	HUN	Ödön Zombori
	2	**USA**	**Ross Flood**
	3	GER	Johannes Herbert
1948	1	TUR	Nasuh Akar
	2	**USA**	**Gerald Leeman**
	3	FRA	Charles Kouyos
1952	1	JPN	Shohachi Ishii
	2	URS	Rashid Mamedbekov
	3	IND	Kha-Shaba Jadav
		USA	**Bill Borders**
1956	1	TUR	Mustafa Dagistanli
	2	IRN	Mehdi Yaghoubi
	3	URS	Mikhail Chakhov
		USA	**L. Allen**
1960	**1**	**USA**	**Terrence McCann**
	2	BUL	Nezhdet Zalev
	3	POL	Tadeusz Trojanowski
1964	1	JPN	Yojiro Uetake
	2	TUR	Hüseyin Akba
	3	URS	Aydyn Ibragimov
	4	**USA**	**David Auble**
1968	1	JPN	Yojiro Uetake
	2	**USA**	**Donald Behm**
	3	IRN	Abutaleb Talebi
1972	1	JPN	Hideaki Yanagida
	2	**USA**	**Richard Sanders**
	3	HUN	László Klinga
1976	1	URS	Vladimir Umin
	2	GDR	Hans-Dieter Brüchert
	3	JPN	Masao Arai
		USA	**Joe Corso**
1980	1	URS	Sergei Beloglazov
	2	PRK	Li Ho Pyong
	3	MON	Dugarsuren Ouinbold
1984	1	JPN	Hideaki Tomiyama
	2	**USA**	**Barry Davis**
	3	KOR	Kim Eui-kon
1988	1	URS	Serguei Beloglazov
	2	IRN	Askari Mohammadian
	3	KOR	Noh Kyung-sun
		USA	**Barry Davis**
1992	1	CUB	Alejandro Puerto
	2	EUN	Serquei Smal
	3	PRK	Kim Yong Sik
	6	**USA**	**Kendall Cross**

62 KG (136 LBS) FREESTYLE

YEAR	RANK	CTRY	ATHLETE
1896-1900	(not held)		
1904	**1**	**USA**	**Benjamin Bradshaw**
	2	**USA**	**Theodore McLear**
	3	**USA**	**Charles Clapper**
1906	(not held)		
1908	**1**	**USA**	**George Dole**
	2	GBR	James Slim
	3	GBR	William McKie
1912	(not held)		
1920	**1**	**USA**	**Charles Ackerly**
	2	**USA**	**Samuel Gerson**
	3	GBR	P.W. Bernard
1924	**1**	**USA**	**Robin Reed**
	2	**USA**	**Chester Newton**
	3	JPN	Katsutoshi Naito
1928	**1**	**USA**	**Allie Morrison**
	2	FIN	Kustaa Pihlajamäki
	3	SUI	Hans Minder
1932	1	FIN	Hermanni Pihlajamäki
	2	**USA**	**Edgar Nemir**
	3	SWE	Einar Karlsson
1936	1	FIN	Kustaa Pihlajamäki
	2	**USA**	**Francis Millard**
	2	SWE	Gösta Jönsson
1948	1	TUR	Gazanfer Bilge
	2	SWE	Ivar Sjölin
	3	SUI	Adolf Müller
	6	**USA**	**Harold "Hal" Moore**
1952	1	TUR	Bayram Sit
	2	IRN	Nasser Givèchi
	3	**USA**	**Josiah Henson**
1956	1	JPN	Shozo Sasahara
	2	BEL	Joseph Mewis
	3	FIN	Erkki Penttilä
	4	**USA**	**Myron Roderick**
1960	1	TUR	Mustafa Dagistanli
	2	BUL	Stancho Kolev
	3	URS	Vladimir Rubashvili
	9	**USA**	**Louis Giani**
1964	1	JPN	Osamu Watanabe
	2	BUL	Stancho Kolev
	3	URS	Nodar Khokhashvili
	4	**USA**	**Robert "Bobby" Douglas**
1968	1	JPN	Masaaki Kaneko
	2	BUL	Enyu Todorov
	3	IRN	Shamseddin Seyyedabbasi
	4	**USA**	**Wayne Wells**
1972	1	URS	Zagalav Abdulbekov
	2	TUR	Vehbi Akdag
	3	BUL	Ivan Krustev
		USA	**Gene Davis**
1976	1	KOR	Yang Jung-mo
	2	MON	Zeveg Oidov
	3	**USA**	**Gene Davis**
1980	1	URS	Magomedgasan Abushev
	2	BUL	Miho Doukov
	3	GRE	Georges Hadjiioannidis
1984	**1**	**USA**	**Randy Lewis**
	2	JPN	Kosei Akaishi
	3	KOR	Lee Jung-keun
1988	**1**	**USA**	**John Smith**
	2	URS	Stepan Sarkissian
	3	BUL	Simeon Chterev
1992	**1**	**USA**	**John Smith**
	2	IRI	Agari Mohammadian
	3	CUB	Lazaro Reinoso

68 KG (150 LBS) FREESTYLE

YEAR	RANK	CTRY	ATHLETE
1896-1900	(not held)		
1904	**1**	**USA**	**Otto Roehm**
	2	**USA**	**Rudolph Tesing**
	3	**USA**	**Albert Zirkel**
1906	(not held)		
1908	1	GBR	George de Relwyskow
	2	GBR	William Wood
	3	GBR	Albert Gingell
	5	**USA**	**John Krug**
1912	(not held)		
1920	1	FIN	Kaarlo "Kalle" Anttila
	2	SWE	Gottfrid Svensson
	3	GBR	Peter Wright
	(USA best finish N/A)		
1924	**1**	**USA**	**Russell Vis**
	2	FIN	Volmari Vikström
	3	FIN	Arvo Haavisto
1928	1	EST	Osvald Käpp
	2	FRA	Charles Pacôme
	3	FIN	Eino Leino
	6	**USA**	**Clarence Berryman**
1932	1	FRA	Charles Pacôme
	2	HUN	Károly Kárpáti
	3	SWE	Gustaf Klarén
	4	**USA**	**Melvin Clodfelter**
1936	1	HUN	Károly Kárpáti
	2	GER	Wolfgang Ehrl
	3	FIN	Hermanni Pihlajamäki
	5	**USA**	**Harley De Witt Strong**
1948	1	TUR	Celal Atik
	2	SWE	Gösta Frändfors
	3	SUI	Hermann Baumann
	5	**USA**	**William Koll**
1952	1	SWE	Olle Anderberg
	2	**USA**	**Jay Thomas Evans**
	3	IRN	Jahanbakte Towfigh
1956	1	IRN	Emamali Habibi
	2	JPN	Shigeru Kasahara
	3	URS	Alimbeg Bestayev
	5	**USA**	**Jay Thomas Evans**
1960	**1**	**USA**	**Shelby Wilson**
	2	URS	Vladimir Sinyavsky
	3	BUL	Enyu Dimov
1964	1	BUL	Enyu Vulchev (Dimov)
	2	GER	Klaus-Jürgen Rost
	3	JPN	Iwao Horiuchi
	6	**USA**	**Gregory Ruth**
1968	1	IRN	Abdollah Movahhed
	2	BUL	Enyu Vulchev (Dimov)
	3	MON	Sereeter Danzandarjaa
	4	**USA**	**Wayne Wells**
1972	**1**	**USA**	**Dan Gable**
	2	JPN	Kikuo Wada
	3	URS	Ruslan Ashuraliev
1976	1	URS	Pavel Pinigin
	2	**USA**	**Lloyd Keaser**
	3	JPN	Yasaburo Sugawara
1980	1	URS	Saipulla Absaidov
	2	BUL	Ivan Yankov
	3	YUG	Saban Sejdi
1984	1	KOR	You In-tak
	2	**USA**	**Andrew Rein**
	3	FIN	Jukka Rauhala
1988	1	URS	Arsen Fadzaev
	2	KOR	Park Jang-soon
	3	**USA**	**Nate Carr**
1992	1	EUN	Arsen Fadzaev
	2	BUL	Valentin Getzov
	3	JPN	Kosei Akaishi
	7	**USA**	**Townsend Saunders**

74 KG (163 LBS) FREESTYLE

YEAR	RANK	CTRY	ATHLETE
1896-1900	(not held)		
1904	**1**	**USA**	**Charles Erickson**
	2	**USA**	**William Beckmann**
	3	**USA**	**Jerry Winholtz**
1906-1920	(not held)		
1924	1	SUI	Hermann Gehri
	2	FIN	Eino Leino
	3	SUI	Otto Müller
	4	**USA**	**Guy Lookabough**
1928	1	FIN	Arvo Haavisto
	2	**USA**	**Lloyd Appelton**
	3	CAN	Maurice Letchford
1932	**1**	**USA**	**Jack Van Bebber**
	2	CAN	Daniel MacDonald
	3	FIN	Eino Leino
1936	**1**	**USA**	**Frank Lewis**
	2	SWE	Ture Andersson
	3	CAN	Joseph Schleimer
1948	1	TUR	Yasar Dogu
	2	AUS	Richard Garrard
	3	**USA**	**Leland Merrill**
1952	**1**	**USA**	**William Smith**
	2	SWE	Per Berlin
	3	IRN	Abdullah Modjtabavi
1956	1	JPN	Mitsuo Ikeda
	2	TUR	Ibrahim Zengin
	3	URS	Vakhtang Balavadze
	8	**USA**	**Ernest Fischer**
1960	**1**	**USA**	**Douglas Blubaugh**
	2	TUR	Ismail Ogan
	3	PAK	Muhammed Bashir
1964	1	TUR	Ismail Ogan
	2	URS	Guliko Sagaradze
	3	IRN	Mohammad Ali Sanatkaran
		USA	**Charles Tribble**
1968	1	TUR	Mahmut Atalay
	2	FRA	Daniel Robin
	3	MON	Dagvasuren Purev
	7	**USA**	**Stephen Combs**
1972	**1**	**USA**	**Wayne Wells**
	2	SWE	Jan Karlsson
	3	GER	Adolf Seger
1976	1	JPN	Jiichiro Date
	2	IRN	Mansour Barzegar
	3	**USA**	**Stanley Dziedzic**
1980	1	BUL	Valentin Angelov
	2	MON	Jamtsying Davaajav
	3	TCH	Dan Karabin
1984	**1**	**USA**	**David Schultz**
	2	GER	Martin Knosp
	3	YUG	Saban Sejdi
1988	**1**	**USA**	**Kenny Monday**
	2	URS	Adlan Varaev
	3	BUL	Rakhmad Sofiadi
1992	1	KOR	Park Jang
	2	**USA**	**Kenny Monday**
	3	IRI	Amir Khadem

82 KG (180 LBS) FREESTYLE

YEAR	RANK	CTRY	ATHLETE
1896-1906	(not held)		
1908	1	GBR	Stanley Bacon
	2	GBR	George de Relwyskow
	3	GBR	Frederick Beck
		USA	**F. Narganes**
1912	(not held)		
1920	1	FIN	Eino Leino
	2	FIN	Väinö Penttala
	3	**USA**	**Charles Johnson**
1924	1	SUI	Fritz Hagmann
	2	BEL	Pierre Ollivier
	3	FIN	Viho Pekkala
		USA	**H.A. Smith**
1928	1	SUI	Ernst Kyburz
	2	CAN	Donald Stockton
	3	GBR	Samuel Rabin
	4	**USA**	**Ralph Hammond**
1932	1	SWE	Ivar Johansson
	2	FIN	Kyösti Luukko
	3	HUN	József Tunyogi
	4	**USA**	**Robert Hess**
1936	1	FRA	Emile Poilvé
	2	**USA**	**Richard Voliva**
	3	TUR	Ahmet Kireççi
1948	**1**	**USA**	**Glen Brand**
	2	TUR	Adil Candemir
	3	SWE	Erik Lindén
1952	1	URS	David Tsimakuridze
	2	IRN	Gholam Reza Takhti
	3	HUN	György Gurics
1956	1	BUL	Nikola Stanchev
	2	**USA**	**Daniel Hodge**
	3	URS	Georgy Skhirtladze
1960	1	TUR	Hasan Güngör
	2	URS	Georgy Skhirtladze
	3	SWE	Hans Yngve Antonsson
	4	**USA**	**Edward De Witt**
1964	1	BUL	Prodan Gardzhev
	2	TUR	Hasan Güngör
	3	**USA**	**Daniel Brand**
1968	1	URS	Boris Gurevitch
	2	MON	Munkbat Jigjid
	3	BUL	Prodan Gardzhev
	4	**USA**	**Thomas Peckham**
1972	1	URS	Levan Tediashvili
	2	**USA**	**John Peterson**
	3	ROM	Vasile Iorga
1976	**1**	**USA**	**John Peterson**
	2	URS	Viktor Novoyilov
	3	GER	Adolf Seger
1980	1	BUL	Ismail Abilov
	2	URS	Magomedhan Aratsilov
	3	HUN	István Kovács
1984	**1**	**USA**	**Mark Schultz**
	2	JPN	Hideyuki Nagashima
	3	CAN	Chris Rinke
1988	1	KOR	Han Myung-woo
	2	TUR	Necmi Gencalp
	3	TCH	Josef Lohyna
	6	**USA**	**Mark Schultz**

1992	**1**	**USA**	**Kevin Jackson**
	2	EUN	Elmadi Jabraijlov
	3	IRI	Rasul Khadem

90 KG (198 LBS) FREESTYLE

YEAR	RANK	CTRY	ATHLETE
1896-1912	(not held)		
1920	1	SWE	Anders Larsson
	2	SUI	Charles Courant
	3	**USA**	**Walter Maurer**
1924	**1**	**USA**	**John Spellman**
	2	SWE	Rudolf Svensson
	3	SUI	Charles Courant
1928	1	SWE	Thure Sjöstedt
	2	SUI	Arnold Bögli
	3	FRA	Henri Lefèbre
	4	**USA**	**Heywood Edwards**
1932	**1**	**USA**	**Peter Mehringer**
	2	SWE	Thure Sjöstedt
	3	AUS	Eddie Scarf
1936	1	SWE	Knut Fridell
	2	EST	August Neo
	3	GER	Erich Siebert
	5	**USA**	**Ray Clemons**
1948	**1**	**USA**	**Henry Wittenberg**
	2	SUI	Fritz Stöckli
	3	SWE	Bengt Fahlkvist
1952	1	SWE	Wiking Palm
	2	**USA**	**Henry Wittenberg**
	3	TUR	Adil Atan
1956	1	IRN	Gholam Reza Takhti
	2	URS	Boris Kulayev
	3	**USA**	**Peter Blair**
1960	1	TUR	Ismet Atli
	2	IRN	Gholam Reza Takhti
	3	URS	Anatoly Albul
	5	**USA**	**Daniel Brand**
1964	1	URS	Aleksandr Medved
	2	TUR	Ahmet Ayik
	3	BUL	Said Mustafov
	6	**USA**	**Gerald Conine**
1968	1	TUR	Ahmet Ayik
	2	URS	Schota Lomidze
	3	HUN	József Csatári
	6	**USA**	**Jess Lewis**
1972	**1**	**USA**	**Benjamin Peterson**
	2	URS	Gennady Strakhov
	3	HUN	Károly Bajkó
1976	1	URS	Levan Tediashvili
	2	**USA**	**Benjamin Peterson**
	3	ROM	Stelica Morcov
1980	1	URS	Sanasar Oganesyan
	2	GDR	Uwe Neupert
	3	POL	Aleksander Cicho
1984	**1**	**USA**	**Ed Banach**
	2	JPN	Akira Ohta
	3	GBR	Noel Loban
1988	1	URS	Makharbek Khadartsev
	2	JPN	Akira Ota
	3	KOR	Kim Tae-woo
	5	**USA**	**Jim Scherr**
1992	1	EUN	Makharbek Khadartsev
	2	TUR	Kenan Kimsek
	3	**USA**	**Chris Campbell**

100 KG (220 LBS) FREESTYLE

YEAR	RANK	CTRY	ATHLETE
1896-1968	(not held)		
1972	1	URS	Ivan Yarygin
	2	MON	Khorloo Baianmunkh
	3	HUN	József Csatári
		USA	**Hank Schenk**
1976	1	URS	Ivan Yarygin
	2	**USA**	**Russell Hellickson**
	3	BUL	Dimo Kostov
1980	1	URS	Ilya Mate
	2	BUL	Slavcho Chervenkov
	3	TCH	Július Strnisko
1984	**1**	**USA**	**Lou Banach**
	2	SYR	Joseph Atiyeh
	3	ROM	Vasile Puscasu
1988	1	ROM	Vasile Puscasu
	2	URS	Leri Khabelov
	3	**USA**	**William Scherr**
1992	1	EUN	Leri Khabelov
	2	GER	Heiko Balz
	3	TUR	Ali Kayali
	7	**USA**	**Mark Coleman**

130 KG (286 LBS) FREESTYLE

YEAR	RANK	CTRY	ATHLETE
1896-1900	(not held)		
1904	**1**	**USA**	**Bernhuff Hansen**
	2	**USA**	**Frank Kungler**
	3	**USA**	**Fred Warmbold**
1906	(not held)		
1908	1	GBR/IRL	George Con O'Kelly
	2	NOR	Jacob Gundersen
	3	GBR/IRL	Edmond Barrett
		USA	**L.J. Talbot**
1912	(not held)		
1920	1	SUI	Robert Roth
	2	**USA**	**Nathan Pendleton**
	3	**USA**	**Frederick Meyer**
1924	**1**	**USA**	**Harry Steel**
	2	SUI	Henri Wernli
	3	GBR	Andrew McDonald
1928	1	SWE	Johan Richthoff
	2	FIN	Aukusti Sihvola
	3	FRA	Edmond Dame
	4	**USA**	**Edward George**
1932	1	SWE	Johan Richthoff
	2	**USA**	**John Riley**
	3	AUT	Nikolaus Hirschi
1936	1	EST	Kristjan Palusalu
	2	TCH	Josef Klapuch
	3	FIN	Hjalmar Nyström
		USA	**Roy Dunn**
1948	1	HUN	Gyula Bóbis
	2	SWE	Bertil Antonsson
	3	AUS	Joseph Armstrong
	7	**USA**	**Richard Hutton**
1952	1	URS	Arsen Mekokishvili
	2	SWE	Bertil Antonsson
	3	GBR	Kenneth Richmond
	5	**USA**	**William Kerslake**
1956	1	TUR	Hamit Kaplan
	2	BUL	Yusein Mehmedov
	3	FIN	Taisto Kangasniemi
	7	**USA**	**William Kerslake**
1960	1	GER	Wilfried Dietrich
	2	TUR	Hamit Kaplan
	3	URS	Savkus Dzarassov
	8	**USA**	**William Kerslake**
1964	1	URS	Aleksandr Ivanitsky
	2	BUL	Lyutvi Ahmedov
	3	TUR	Hamit Kaplan
	7	**USA**	**Larry Kristoff**
1968	1	URS	Aleksandr Medved
	2	BUL	Osman Duraliev
	3	GER	Wilfried Dietrich
	5	**USA**	**Larry Kristoff**
1972	1	URS	Aleksandr Medved
	2	BUL	Osman Duraliev
	3	**USA**	**Chris Taylor**
1976	1	URS	Soslan Andiev
	2	HUN	József Balla
	3	ROM	Ladislau Simon
		USA	**Jimmy Jackson**
1980	1	URS	Soslan Andiev
	2	HUN	József Balla
	3	POL	Adam Sandurski
1984	**1**	**USA**	**Bruce Baumgartner**
	2	CAN	Bob Molle
	3	TUR	Ayhan Taskin
1988	1	URS	David Gobedjichvili
	2	**USA**	**Bruce Baumgartner**
	3	GDR	Andreas Schroeder
1992	**1**	**USA**	**Bruce Baumgartner**
	2	CAN	Jeffrey Thue
	3	EUN	David Gobedjichvili

48 KG (106 LBS) GRECO-ROMAN

YEAR	RANK	CTRY	ATHLETE
1896-1968	(not held)		
1972	1	ROM	Gheorghe Berceanu
	2	IRN	Rahim Aliabadi
	3	BUL	Stefan Angelov
		USA	**Wayne Holmes**
1976	1	URS	Alexei Shumakov
	2	ROM	Gheorghe Berceanu
	3	BUL	Stefan Angelov
	8	**USA**	**Michael Farina**
1980	1	URS	Zaksylik Ushkempirov
	2	ROM	Constantin Alexandru
	3	HUN	Ferenc Seres
1984	1	ITA	Vincenzo Maenza
	2	GER	Markus Scherer
	3	JPN	Ikuzo Saito
		USA	**Mark Fuller**
1988	1	ITA	Vincenzo Maenza
	2	POL	Andrzej Glab
	3	BUL	Bratan Tzenov
		USA	**Mark Fuller**
1992	1	EUN	Oleg Koutcherenko
	2	ITA	Vincenzo Maenza
	3	CUB	Wilber Sanchez
		USA	**Mark Fuller**

52 KG (114 LBS) GRECO-ROMAN

YEAR	RANK	CTRY	ATHLETE
1896-1936	(not held)		
1948	1	ITA	Pietro Lombardi
	2	TUR	Kenan Olcay
	3	FIN	Reino Kangasmaki
(no USA entry)			
1952	1	URS	Boris Gurevitch
	2	ITA	Ignazio Fabra
	3	FIN	Leo Honkala
(no USA entry)			
1956	1	URS	Nikolai Solovyov
	2	ITA	Ignazio Fabra
	3	TUR	Durum Ali Egriba
		USA	**J. Richard Wilson**
1960	1	ROM	Dumitru Pirvulescu
	2	UAR	Osman Sayed
	3	IRN	Mohammad Paziraii
		USA	**J. Richard Wilson**
1964	1	JPN	Tsutomu Hanahara
	2	BUL	Angel Kerezov
	3	ROM	Dumitru Pirvulescu
	4	**USA**	**J. Richard Wilson**
1968	1	BUL	Peter Kirov
	2	URS	Vladimir Bakulin
	3	TCH	Miroslav Zeman
		USA	**Richard Tamble**
1972	1	BUL	Peter Kirov
	2	JPN	Koichiro Hirayama
	3	ITA	Giuseppe Bognanni
		USA	**James Steiger**
1976	1	URS	Vitaly Konstantinov
	2	ROM	Nicu Ginga
	3	JPN	Koichiro Hirayama
		USA	**Bruce Thompson**
1980	1	URS	Vakhtang Blagidze
	2	HUN	Lajos Rácz
	3	BUL	Mladen Mladenov
1984	1	JPN	Atsuji Miyahara
	2	MEX	Daniel Aceves
	3	KOR	Bang Dae-du
(no USA entry)			
1988	1	NOR	Jon Ronningen
	2	JPN	Atsuji Miyahara
	3	KOR	Lee Jae-suk
		USA	**Shawn Sheldon**
1992	1	NOR	Jon Ronningen
	2	EUN	Alfred Ter-Mkrttchian
	3	KOR	Min Kyung-kap
	4	**USA**	**Shawn Sheldon**

57 KG (125 LBS) GRECO-ROMAN

YEAR	RANK	CTRY	ATHLETE
1896-1920	(not held)		
1924	1	EST	Eduard Pütsep
	2	FIN	Anselm Ahlfors
	3	FIN	Väinö Ikonen
(no USA entry)			
1928	1	GER	Kurt Leucht
	2	TCH	Jindrich Maudr
	3	ITA	Giovanni Gozzi
	5	**USA**	**Robert Hewitt**
1932	1	GER	Jakob Brendel
	2	ITA	Marcello Nizzola
	3	FRA	Louis François
(no USA entry)			
1936	1	HUN	Márton Lörincz
	2	SWE	Egon Svensson
	3	GER	Jakob Brendel
(no USA entry)			
1948	1	SWE	Kurt Pettersén
	2	EGY	Ali Mahmoud Hassan
	3	TUR	Halil Kaya
(no USA entry)			
1952	1	HUN	Imre Hódos
	2	LEB	Zakaria Chihab
	3	URS	Artem Teryan
(no USA entry)			
1956	1	URS	Konstantin Vyrupayev
	2	SWE	Edvin Westerby
	3	ROM	Francisc Horvath
		USA	**K.H. Townley**
1960	1	URS	Oleg Karavayev
	2	ROM	Ion Cernea
	3	BUL	Dinko Petrov
		USA	**Larry Lauchle**
1964	1	JPN	Masamitsu Ichiguchi
	2	URS	Vladlen Trostyansky
	3	ROM	Ion Cernea
		USA	**Andrew Fitch**
1968	1	HUN	János Varga
	2	ROM	Ion Baciu
	3	URS	Ivan Kochergin
		USA	**David Hazewinkel**
1972	1	URS	Rustem Kazakov
	2	GER	Hans-Jürgen Veil
	3	FIN	Risto Björlin
		USa	**David Hazewinkel**
1976	1	FIN	Pertti Ukkola
	2	YUG	Ivan Frgi
	3	URS	Farhat Mustafin
		USA	**Joseph Sade**
1980	1	URS	Shamil Serikov
	2	POL	Józef Lipie
	3	SWE	Benni Ljungbeck
1984	1	GER	Pasquale Passarelli
	2	JPN	Masaki Eto
	3	GRE	Haralambos Holidis
	5	**USA**	**Frank Famiano**
1988	1	HUN	Andras Sike
	2	BUL	Stoyan Balov
	3	GRE	Charalambos Holidis
		USA	**Anthony Amado**
1992	1	KOR	An Han-bonguerto
	2	GER	Rifat Yildiz
	3	CHN	Sheng Zetian
	8	**USA**	**Dennis Hall**

62 KG (136 LBS) GRECO-ROMAN

YEAR	RANK	CTRY	ATHLETE	
1896-1908	(not held)			
1912	1	FIN	Kaarlo Koskelo	
	2	GER	Georg Gerstäcker	
	3	FIN	Otto Lasanen	
		USA	**William Jones Lyshon / George St. Retzer**	
1920	1	FIN	Oskar Friman	
	2	FIN	Heikki Kähkönen	
	3	SWE	Fritiof Svensson	
(USA best finish N/A)				
1924	1	FIN	Kaarlo "Kalle" Anttila	
	2	FIN	Aleksanteri Toivola	
	3	SWE	Erik Malmberg	
		USA	**S.H. Brown**	**DNC**
1928	1	EST	Voldemar Väli	
	2	SWE	Erik Malmberg	
	3	ITA	Giacomo Quaglia	
		USA	**Allie Morrison**	
1932	1	ITA	Giovanni Gozzi	
	2	GER	Wolfgang Ehrl	
	3	FIN	Lauri Koskela	
(no USA entry)				
1936	1	TUR	Yasar Erkan	
	2	FIN	Aarne Reini	
	3	SWE	Einar Karlsson	
(no USA entry)				
1948	1	TUR	Mehmet Oktav	
	2	SWE	Olle Anderberg	
	3	HUN	Ferenc Tóth	
(no USA entry)				
1952	1	URS	Yakov Punkin	
	2	HUN	Imre Polyák	
	3	EGY	Abdel Rashed	
(no USA entry)				
1956	1	FIN	Rauno Mäkinen	
	2	HUN	Imre Polyák	
	3	URS	Roman Dzneladze	
		USA	**Alan Rice**	
1960	1	TUR	Müzahir Sille	
	2	HUN	Imre Polyák	
	3	URS	Konstantin Vyrupayev	
	8	**USA**	**Lee Allen**	
1964	1	HUN	Imre Polyák	
	2	URS	Roman Rurua	
	3	YUG	Branislav Martinovi	
	4	**USA**	**Ronald Finley**	
1968	1	URS	Roman Rurua	
	2	JPN	Hideo Fujimoto	
	3	ROM	Simeon Popescu	
	7	**USA**	**James Hazewinkel**	
1972	1	BUL	Georgi Markov	
	2	GDR	Heinz-Helmut Wehling	
	3	POL	Kazimierz Lipie	
		USA	**James Hazewinkel**	
1976	1	POL	Kazimierz Lipie	
	2	URS	Nelson Davidian	
	3	HUN	László Réczi	
		USA	**Gary Alexander**	
1980	1	GRE	Stylianos Mygiakis	
	2	HUN	István Tóth	
	3	URS	Boris Kramorenko	
1984	1	KOR	Kim Weon-kee	
	2	SWE	Kent-Olle Johansson	
	3	SUI	Hugo Dietsche	
	4	**USA**	**Abdurrahim Kuzu**	
1988	1	URS	Kamandar Madjidov	
	2	BUL	Jivko Vanguelov	
	3	KOR	An Dae-hyun	
	6	**USA**	**Isaac Anderson**	

1992	1	TUR	Akif Pirim
	2	EUN	Serguei Martynov
	3	CUB	Juan Luis Maren
	6	**USA**	**Buddy Lee**

68 KG (150 LBS) GRECO-ROMAN

YEAR	RANK	CTRY	ATHLETE
1896-1904	(not held)		
1906	1	AUT	Rudolf Watzl
	2	DEN	Karl Karlsen
	3	HUN	Ferenc Holuban
(no USA entry)			
1908	1	ITA	Enrico Porro
	2	RUS	Nikolai Orlov
	3	FIN	Arvid Lindén
(no USA entry)			
1912	1	FIN	Eemil Wäre
	2	SWE	Gustaf Malmström
	3	SWE	Edvin Matiasson
(no USA entry)			
1920	1	FIN	Eemil Wäre
	2	FIN	Taavi Tamminen
	3	NOR	Frithjof Andersen
(USA best finish N/A)			
1924	1	FIN	Oskar Friman
	2	HUN	Lajos Keresztes
	3	FIN	Kalle Westerlund
(no USA entry)			
1928	1	HUN	Lajos Keresztes
	2	GER	Eduard Sperling
	3	FIN	Edvard Westerlund
	6	**USA**	**Clarence Berryman**
1932	1	SWE	Erik Malmberg
	2	DEN	Abraham Kurland
	3	GER	Eduard Sperling
(no USA entry)			
1936	1	FIN	Lauri Koskela
	2	TCH	Josef Herda
	3	EST	Voldemar Väli
(no USA entry)			
1948	1	SWE	Gustav Freij
	2	NOR	Aage Eriksen
	3	HUN	Károly Ferencz
(no USA entry)			
1952	1	URS	Schazam Safin
	2	SWE	Gustav Freij
	3	TCH	Mikuls Athanasov
(no USA entry)			
1956	1	FIN	Kyösti Lehtonen
	2	TUR	Riza Dogan
	3	HUN	Gyula Tóth
		USA	**Jay Evans**
1960	1	URS	Avtandil Koridze
	2	YUG	Branislav Martinovi
	3	SWE	Gustav Freij
		USA	**Ben Northrup**
1964	1	TUR	Kazim Ayvaz
	2	ROM	Valeriu Bularc
	3	URS	David Gvantseladze
		USA	**James Burke**
1968	1	JPN	Munji Mumemura
	2	YUG	Stevan Horvat
	3	GRE	Petros Galaktopoulos
	6	**USA**	**Werner Holzer**
1972	1	URS	Shamil Khisamutdinov
	2	BUL	Stoyan Apostolov
	3	ITA	Gian-Matteo Ranzi
		USA	**Robert Buzzard**
1976	1	URS	Suren Nalbandyan
	2	ROM	Stefan Rusu
	3	GDR	Heinz-Helmut Wehling
		USA	**Patrick Marcy**
1980	1	ROM	Stefan Rusu
	2	POL	Andrzej Supron
	3	SWE	Lars-Erik Skiöld
1984	1	YUG	Vlado Lisjak
	2	FIN	Tapio Sipilä
	3	**USA**	**James Martinez**
1988	1	URS	Levon Djoulfalakian
	2	KOR	Kim Sung-moon
	3	FIN	Tapio Sipila
		USA	**Andrew Seras**
1992	1	HUN	Attila Repka
	2	EUN	Islam Dougoutchiev
	3	**USA**	**Rodney Smith**

74 KG (163 LBS) GRECO-ROMAN

YEAR	RANK	CTRY	ATHLETE
1896-1928	(not held)		
1932	1	SWE	Ivar Johansson
	2	FIN	Väinö Kajander-Kajukorpi
	3	ITA	Ercole Gallegati
(no USA entry)			
1936	1	SWE	Rudolf Svedberg
	2	GER	Fritz Schäfer
	3	FIN	Eino Virtanen
(no USA entry)			
1948	1	SWE	Gösta Andersson
	2	HUN	Miklós Szilvási
	3	DEN	Henrik Hansen
(no USA entry)			
1952	1	HUN	Miklós Szilvási
	2	SWE	Gösta Andersson
	3	LEB	Khalil Taha
(no USA entry)			
1956	1	TUR	Mithat Bayrak
	2	URS	Vladimir Maneyev
	3	SWE	Per Berlin
	5	**USA**	**James Holt**
1960	1	TUR	Mithat Bayrak
	2	GER	Günter Maritschnigg
	3	FRA	René Schiermeyer
		USA	**Fritz Fivian**
1964	1	URS	Anatoly Kolesov
	2	BUL	Kiril Petkov
	3	SWE	Bertil Nyström
	7	**USA**	**Russell Camilleri**
1968	1	GDR	Rudolf Vesper
	2	FRA	Daniel Robin
	3	HUN	Károly Bajkó
		USA	**Larry Lyden**
1972	1	TCH	Vit zslav Mácha
	2	GRE	Petros Galaktopoulos
	3	SWE	Jan Karlsson
		USA	**Gary Weist**
1976	1	URS	Anatoly Bykov
	2	TCH	Vitezslav Mácha
	3	GER	Karlheinz Helbing
		USA	**John Matthews**
1980	1	HUN	Ferenc Kocsis
	2	URS	Anatoly Bykov
	3	FIN	Mikko Huhtala
1984	1	FIN	Jouko Salomäki
	2	SWE	Roger Tallroth
	3	ROM	Stefan Rusu
	7	**USA**	**Christopher Catalfo**
1988	1	KOR	Kim Young-nam
	2	URS	Daoulet Tourlykhanov
	3	POL	Jozef Tracz
		USA	**David Butler**
1992	1	EUN	Mnatsakan Iskandarian
	2	POL	Jozef Tracz
	3	SWE	Torgjoern Kornbakk
		USA	**Travis West**

82 KG (180 LBS) GRECO-ROMAN

YEAR	RANK	CTRY	ATHLETE
1896-1904	(not held)		
1906	1	FIN	Verner Weckman
	2	AUT	Rudolf Lindmayer
	3	DEN	Robert Behrens
(no USA entry)			
1908	1	SWE	Frithiof Mårtensson
	2	SWE	Mauritz Andersson
	3	DEN	Anders Andersen
(no USA entry)			
1912	1	SWE	Claes Johanson
	2	RUS/EST	Martin Klein
	3	FIN	Alfred Asikainen
(no USA entry)			
1920	1	SWE	Carl Westergren
	2	FIN	Artur Lindfors
	3	FIN	Matti Perttilä
(USA best finish N/A)			
1924	1	FIN	Edvard Westerlund
	2	FIN	Artur Lindfors
	3	EST	Roman Steinberg
(no USA entry)			
1928	1	FIN	Väinö Kokkinen
	2	HUN	László Papp
	3	EST	Albert Kusnets
	4T	**USA**	**Ralph Hammond**
1932	1	FIN	Väinö Kokkinen
	2	GER	Jean Földeak
	3	SWE	Axel Cadier
(no USA entry)			
1936	1	SWE	Ivar Johansson
	2	GER	Ludwig Schweikert
	3	HUN	József Palotás
(no USA entry)			
1948	1	SWE	Axel Grönberg
	2	TUR	Muhlis Tayfur
	3	ITA	Ercole Gallegati
(no USA entry)			
1952	1	SWE	Axel Grönberg
	2	FIN	Kalervo Rauhala
	3	URS	Nikolai Byelov
(no USA entry)			
1956	1	URS	Givy Kartoziya
	2	BUL	Dimiter Dobrev
	3	SWE	Karl-Axel Rune Jansson
	7	**USA**	**James Peckham**
1960	1	BUL	Dimiter Dobrev
	2	GDR	Lothar Metz
	3	ROM	Ion Tarvanu
	8	**USA**	**Russell Camilleri**
1964	1	YUG	Branislav Simi
	2	TCH	Jiri Kormanik
	3	GDR	Lothar Metz
	7	**USA**	**Richard Wayne Baughman**
1968	1	GDR	Lothar Metz
	2	URS	Valentin Olenik
	3	YUG	Branislav Simi
	5	**USA**	**Richard Wayne Baughman**
1972	1	HUN	Csaba Hegedüs
	2	URS	Anatoly Nazarenko
	3	YUG	Milan Nenadi
		USA	**Jay Robinson**
1976	1	YUG	Momir Petkovi
	2	URS	Vladimir Cheboksarov
	3	BUL	Ivan Kolev
		USA	**Daniel Chandler**
1980	1	URS	Gennady Korban
	2	POL	Jan Dolgowicz
	3	BUL	Pavel Pavlov
1984	1	ROM	Ion Draica
	2	GRE	Dimitrios Thanopoulos
	3	SWE	Sören Claesson
		USA	**Daniel Chandler** **did not place**
1988	1	URS	Mikhail Mamiachvili
	2	HUN	Tibor Komaromi
	3	KOR	Kim Sang-kyu
	7	**USA**	**John Morgan**
1992	1	HUN	Peter Farkas
	2	POL	Piotr Stepien
	3	EUN	Daoulet Tourlykhanov
	10	**USA**	**Dan Henderson**

90 KG (198 LBS) GRECO-ROMAN

YEAR	RANK	CTRY	ATHLETE
1896-1906	(not held)		
1908	1	FIN	Verner Weckman
	2	FIN	Yrjö Saarela
	3	DEN	Carl Jensen
(no USA entry)			
1912	1		
	2T	SWE	Anders Ahlgren
	2T	FIN	Ivar Böhling
	3	HUN	Béla Varga
(no USA entry)			
1920	1	SWE	Claes Johanson
	2	FIN	Edil Rosenqvist
	3	DEN	Johannes Eriksen
(no USA entry)			
1924	1	SWE	Carl Westergren
	2	SWE	Rudolf Svensson
	3	FIN	Onni Pellinen
(no USA entry)			
1928	1	EGY	Ibrahim Moustafa
	2	GER	Adolf Rieger
	3	FIN	Onni Pellinen
(no USA entry)			
1932	1	SWE	Rudolf Svensson
	2	FIN	Onni Pellinen
	3	ITA	Mario Gruppioni
(no USA entry)			
1936	1	SWE	Axel Cardier
	2	LAT	Edwins Bietags
	3	EST	August Neo
(no USA entry)			
1948	1	SWE	Karl-Erik Nilsson
	2	FIN	Kaelpo Gröndahl
	3	EGY	Ibrahim Orabi
(no USA entry)			
1952	1	FIN	Kaelpo Gröndahl
	2	URS	Chalva Chikhladze
	3	SWE	Karl-Erik Nilsson
(no USA entry)			
1956	1	URS	Valentin Nikolayev
	2	BUL	Petko Sirakov
	3	SWE	Karl-Erik Nilsson
	5	**USA**	**Dale Thomas**
1960	1	TUR	Tevfik Kis
	2	BUL	Kralyu Bimbalov
	3	URS	Givy Kartozlya
	14	**USA**	**Howard George**
1964	1	BUL	Boyan Radev
	2	SWE	Per Svensson
	3	GER	Heinz Kiehl
		USA	**William Lovell**
1968	1	BUL	Boyan Radev
	2	URS	Nikolai Yakovenko
	3	ROM	Nicolae Martinescu
		USA	**Henk Schenk**
1972	1	URS	Valery Rezantsev
	2	YUG	Josip Corak
	3	POL	Czeslaw Kwiencinski
		USA	**Capt. Wayne Baughman**
1976	1	URS	Valery Rezantsev
	2	BUL	Stoyan Ivanov
	3	POL	Czeslaw Kwiecinski
	7	**USA**	**James Johnson**
1980	1	HUN	Norbert Növényi
	2	URS	Igor Kanygin
	3	ROM	Petre Dicu
1984	**1**	**USA**	**Steven Fraser**
	2	ROM	Ilie Matei
	3	SWE	Frank Andersson
1988	1	BUL	Atanas Komchev
	2	FIN	Harri Koskela
	3	URS	Vladimir Popov
		USA	**Michial Foy**
1992	1	GER	Maik Bullmann
	2	TUR	Hakki Basar
	3	EUN	Gogui Kogouachvili
	6	**USA**	**Michial Foy**

100 KG (220 LBS) FREESTYLE

YEAR	RANK	CTRY	ATHLETE
1896-1968	(not held)		
1972	1	ROM	Nicolae Martinescu
	2	URS	Nikolai Iakovenko
	3	HUN	Ferenc Kiss
		USA	**Buck Deadrich**
1976	1	URS	Nikolai Balboshin
	2	BUL	Kamen Goranov
	3	POL	Andrzej Skrzydlewski
	4	**USA**	**Brad Rheingans**
1980	1	BUL	Georgi Raikov
	2	POL	Roman Bierla
	3	ROM	Vasile Andrei
1984	1	ROM	Vasile Andrei
	2	**USA**	**Greg Gibson**
	3	YUG	Jozef Tertelje
1988	1	POL	Andrzej Wronski
	2	FRG	Gerhard Himmel
	3	**USA**	**Dennis Koslowski**
1992	1	CUB	Hector Milian
	2	**USA**	**Dennis Koslowski**
	3	EUN	Serguei Demiachkievitch

130 KG (286 LBS) FREESTYLE

YEAR	RANK	CTRY	ATHLETE
1896	1	GER	Karl Schumann
	2	GRE	Georgios Tsitas
	3	GRE	Stephanos Christopoulos
(no USA entry)			
1900-1904	(not held)		
1906	1	DEN	Soren Marius Jensen
	2	AUT	Henri Baur
	3	BEL	Marcel Dubois
(no USA entry)			
1908	1	HUN	Richárd Weisz
	2	RUS	Aleksandr Petrov
	3	DEN	Soren Marius Jensen
(no USA entry)			
1912	1	FIN	Yrjö Saarela
	2	FIN	Johan Olin
	3	DEN	Sören Marius Jensen
(no USA entry)			
1920	1	FIN	Adolf Lindfors
	2	DEN	Poul Hansen
	3	FIN	Martti Nieminen
	4	**USA**	**Alexander Weyand**
1924	1	FRA	Henri Deglane
	2	FIN	Edil Rosenqvist
	3	HUN	Rajmund Badó
(no USA entry)			
1928	1	SWE	Rudolf Svensson
	2	FIN	Hjalmar Eemil Nyström
	3	GER	Georg Gehring
	4	**USA**	**Ed George**
1932	1	SWE	Carl Westergren
	2	TCH	Josef Urban
	3	AUT	Nikolaus Hirschi
(no USA entry)			
1936	1	EST	Kristjan Palusalu
	2	SWE	John Nyman
	3	GER	Kurt Hornfischer
(no USA entry)			
1948	1	TUR	Ahmet Kirecci
	2	SWE	Tor Nilsson
	3	ITA	Guido Fantoni
(no USA entry)			
1952	1	URS	Johannes Kotkas
	2	TCH	Josef Ruzicka
	3	FIN	Tauno Kovanen
(no USA entry)			

1956	1	URS	Anatoly Parfenov	
	2	GER	Wilfried Dietrich	
	3	ITA	Adelmo Bulgarelli	
		USA	**Dale Lewis**	
1960	1	URS	Ivan Bogdan	
	2	GER	Wilfried Dietrich	
	3	TCH	Bohumil Kubát	
		USA	**Lewis Dale**	
1964	1	HUN	István Kozma	
	2	URS	Anatoly Roshin	
	3	GER	Wilfried Dietrich	
	6	**USA**	**Robert Pickens**	
1968	1	HUN	István Kozma	
	2	URS	Anatoly Roshin	
	3	TCH	Petr Kment	
		USA	**Robert Roop**	
1972	1	URS	Anatoly Roshin	
	2	BUL	Alexander Tomov	
	3	ROM	Victor Dolipschi	
		USA	**Chris Taylor**	
1976	1	URS	Aleksandr Kolchinsky	
	2	BUL	Alexander Tomov	
	3	ROM	Roman Codreanu	
	5	**USA**	**William "Pete" Lee**	
1980	1	URS	Aleksandr Kolchinsky	
	2	BUL	Alexander Tomov	
	3	LEB	Hassan Bchara	
1984	**1**	**USA**	**Jeffrey Blatnick**	
		SWE	Thomas Johansson	
	2	YUG	Refik Memiševi	
	3	ROM	Victor Dolipschi	
1988	1	URS	Alexandre Kareline	
	2	BUL	Ranguel Guerovski	
	3	SWE	Tomas Johansson	
	8	**USA**	**Duane Koslowski**	
1992	1	EUN	Alexandre Kareline	
	2	SWE	Tomas Johansson	
	3	ROM	Ioan Grigoras	
		USA	**Matt Ghaffari**	

YACHTING

MEN'S 470

YEAR	RANK	CTRY	ATHLETES	NET PTS.
1896-1972 (not held)				
1976	1	GER	Frank Hübner / Harro Bode	42.4
	2	ESP	Antonio Gorostegui / Pedro Millet	49.7
	3	AUS	Ian Brown / Ian Ruff	57.0
	9	**USA**	**Robert Whitehurst / David Whitehurst**	**123.0**
1980	1	BRA	Marcos Rizzo Soares / Eduardo Penido	36.4
	2	GDR	Jörn Borowski / Egbert Swensson	38.7
	3	FIN	Jouko Lindgren / George Tallberg	39.7
1984	1	ESP	Luis Doreste / Roberto Molina	33.7
	2	**USA**	**Stephan Benjamin / Christopher Steinfeld**	**43.0**
	3	FRA	Thierry Peponnet / Luc Pillot	49.4
1988	1	FRA	Thierry Peponnet / Luc Pillot	34.70
	2	URS	Tynou Tyniste / Toomas Tyniste	46.00
	3	**USA**	**John Shadden / Charlie McKee**	**51.00**
1992	1	ESP	Jordi Calafat / Francisco Sanchez	50.00
	2	**USA**	**Morgan Reeser / Kevin Burnham**	**66.70**
	3	EST	Tonu Toniste / Toomas Toniste	68.70

MEN'S LECHNER

YEAR	RANK	CTRY	ATHLETE	NET PTS.
1896-1988 (not held)				
1992	1	FRA	Franck David	70.70
	2	**USA**	**Michael Gebhardt**	**71.10**
	3	AUS	Lars Kleppich	98.70

DIVISION II SAILBOARD

YEAR	RANK	CTRY	ATHLETE	NET PTS.
1896-1980 (not held)				
1984	1	HOL	Stephan van den Berg	27.7
	2	**USA**	**Randall Scott Steele**	**46.0**
	3	NZL	Bruce Kendall	46.4
1988	1	NZL	Bruce Kendall	35.40
	2	AHO	Jan Boersma	42.70
	3	**USA**	**Michael Gebhardt**	**48.00**

FINN

YEAR	RANK	CTRY	ATHLETE	NET PTS.
1896-1912 (not held)				
(12-foot dinghy)				
1920	1	HOL	Johannes Hin / Franciscus Hin	
	2	HOL	Arnoud Eugène van der Biesen / Petrus Beukers	
(no USA entry)				
(18-foot dinghy)				
1920	1	GBR	Francis Richards / T. Hedberg	
(no USA entry)				
1924	1	BEL	Léon Huybrechts	2
	2	NOR	Henrik Robert	7
	3	FIN	Hans Dittmar	8
(no USA entry)				
1928	1	SWE	Sven Thorell	
	2	NOR	Henrik Robert	
	3	FIN	Bertil Broman	
	10	**USA**	**Dr. Manfred Curry**	
1932	1	FRA	Jacques Lebrun	87
	2	HOL	Adriaan Maas	85
	3	ESP	Santiago Amat Cansino	76
	7	**USA**	**Charles Lyon**	**66**
1936	1	HOL	Daniel Kagchelland	163
	2	GER	Werner Krogmann	150
	3	GBR	Peter Scott	131
	9	**USA**	**Frank Jewett, Jr.**	
1948	1	DEN	Paul Elvström	5543
	2	**USA**	**Ralph Evans**	**5408**
	3	HOL	Jacobus de Jong	5204
1952	1	DEN	Paul Elvström	8209
	2	GBR	Charles Currey	5449
	3	SWE	Richard Sarby	5051
	28	**USA**	**Edward Melaika**	
1956	1	DEN	Paul Elvström	7509
	2	BEL	André Nelis	6254
	3	**USA**	**John Marvin**	**5953**
1960	1	DEN	Paul Elvström	8171
	2	URS	Aleksandr Chuchelov	6520
	3	BEL	André Nelis	5934
	11	**USA**	**Peter Barrett**	**3976**
1964	1	GER	Wilhelm Kuhweide	7638
	2	**USA**	**Peter Barrett**	**6373**
	3	DEN	Henning Wind	6190
1968	1	URS	Valentin Mankin	11.7
	2	AUT	Hubert Raudaschl	53.4
	3	ITA	Fabio Albarelli	55.1
	13	**USA**	**Carl Van Duyne**	**117.7**
1972	1	FRA	Serge Maury	58.0
	2	GRE	Ilias Hatzipavlis	71.0
	3	URS	Victor Potapov	74.7
	21	**USA**	**Edward Bennett**	**148.0**
1976	1	GDR	Jochen Schümann	35.4
	2	URS	Andrei Balashov	39.7
	3	AUS	John Bertrand	46.4
	11	**USA**	**Peter Commette**	**115.7**
1980	1	FIN	Esko Rechardt	36.7
	2	AUT	Wolfgang Mayrhofer	46.7
	3	URS	Andrei Balashov	47.4
1984	1	NZL	Russell Coutts	34.7
	2	**USA**	**John Bertrand**	**37.0**
	3	CAN	Terry Neilson	37.7
1988	1	ESP	Jose Luis Doreste	38.10
	2	ISV	Peter Holmberg	40.40
	3	NZL	John Cutler	45.00
	10	**USA**	**Brian Ledbetter**	**91.00**
1992	1	ESP	Jose Van Der Ploeg	33.40
	2	**USA**	**Brian Ledbetter**	**54.70**
	3	NZL	Craig Monk	64.70

FLYING DUTCHMAN

YEAR	RANK	CTRY	ATHLETES	NET PTS.
1896-1956 (not held)				
1960	1	NOR	Peder Lunde, Jr. / Björn Bergvall	6774
	2	DEN	Hans Fogh / Ole Erik Petersen	5991
	3	GER	Rolf Mulka / Ingo von Bredow / Achim Kadelbach	5882
	19	**USA**	**Harry Sindle / Robert Wood**	**2682**
1964	1	NZL	Helmer Pedersen / Earle Wells	6255
	2	GBR	Franklyn Musto / Arthur Morgan	5556
	3	**USA**	**Harry Melges / William Bentsen**	**5158**
1968	1	GBR	Rodney Pattison / Iain Macdonald-Smith	3.0
	2	GER	Ullrich Libor / Peter Naumann	43.7
	3	BRA	Reinaldo Conrad / Burkhard Cordes	48.4
	10	**USA**	**Robert James, Jr. / David James**	**97.4**
1972	1	GBR	Rodney Pattison / Christopher Davies	22.7
	2	FRA	Yves Pajot / Marc Pajot	40.7
	3	GER	Ullrich Libor / Peter Naumann	51.1
	23	**USA**	**Scott Alan / Tim Stearn**	**140.0**
1976	1	GER	Jörg Diesch / Eckart Diesch	34.7
	2	GBR	Rodney Pattison / Julian Brooke Houghton	51.7
	2T	BRA	Reinaldo Conrad / Peter Eicker	52.1
	6	**USA**	**Norman Freeman / John Mathias**	**65.70**
1980	1	ESP	Alesandro Abascal / Miguel Noguer	19.0
	2	IRL	David Wilkins / James Wilkinson	30.0
	3	HUN	Szabolcs Detre / Zsolt Detre	45.7
1984	**1**	**USA**	**Jonathan McKee / William Carl Buchan**	**19.7**
	2	CAN	Terry McLaughlin / Evert Bastet	22.7
	3	GBR	Jonathan Richards / Peter Allam	48.7
1988	1	DEN	Jorgen Bojsen-Moller / Christian Gronborg	31.40
	2	NOR	Olepetter Pollen / Erik Bjorkum	37.40
	3	CAN	Frank McLaughlin / John Millen	48.40
	11	**USA**	**Paul Foerster / Andrew Goldman**	**85.70**
1992	1	ESP	Luis Doreste / Domingo Manrique	29.70
	2	**USA**	**Paul Foerster / Stephen Bourdow**	**32.70**
	3	DEN	Jorgen Bojsen / Jens Bojsen	37.70

TORNADO

YEAR	RANK	CTRY	ATHLETES	NET PTS.
1896-1972		(not held)		
1976	1	GBR	Reginald White / John Osborn	18.0
	2	**USA**	**David McFaull / Michael Rothwell**	**36.0**
	3	GER	Jörg Spengler / Jörg Schmall	37.7
1980	1	BRA	Alexandre Welter / Lars Sigurd Björkström	21.4
	2	DEN	Peter Due / Per Kjergard	30.4
	3	SWE	Göran Marström / Jörgen Ragnarsson	33.7
1984	1	NZL	Rex Sellers / Christopher Timms	14.7
	2	**USA**	**Randy Smyth / Jay Glaser**	**37.0**
	3	AUS	Chris Cairns / John Anderson	50.4
1988	1	FRA	Jean-Yves Le Deroff / Nicolas Henard	16.00
	2	NZL	Christopher Timms / Rex Sellers	35.40
	3	BRA	Lars Grael / Clinio Freitas	40.10
	14	**USA**	**James Melvin / Patrick Muglia**	**110.70**
1992	1	FRA	Yves Loday / Nichlas Henard	40.40
	2	**USA**	**Randy Smyth / Keith Notary**	**42.00**
	3	AUS	Mitch Booth / John Forbes	44.40

STAR

YEAR	RANK	CTRY	ATHLETES	NET PTS.
1896-1928		(not held)		
1932	**1**	**USA**	**Gilbert Gray / Andrew Libano**	**46**
	2	GBR	Colin Ratsey / Peter Jaffe	35
	3	SWE	Gunnar Asther / Daniel Sundén-Cullberg	28
1936	1	GER	Peter Bischoff / Hans-Joachim Weise	80
	2	SWE	Arvid Laurin / Uno Wallentin	64
	3	HOL	Willem de Vries-Lentsch / Adriaan Maas	63
	5	**USA**	**William Waterhouse / Woodbridge Metcalf**	**51**
1948	**1**	**USA**	**Hilary Smart / Paul Smart**	**5828**
	2	CUB	Carlos De Cárdenas Culmell / Carlos De Cárdenas, Jr.	4949
	3	HOL	Adriaan Maas / Edward Stutterheim	4731
1952	1	ITA	Agostino Straulino / Nicolo Rode	7635
	2	**USA**	**John Reid / John Price**	**7126**
	3	POR	Joaquim De Mascarenhas Fiuza / Francisco Rebelo De Andrade	4903
1956	**1**	**USA**	**Herbert Williams / Lawrence Low**	**5876**
	2	ITA	Agostino Straulino / Nicolo Rode	5649
	3	BAH	Durward Knowles / Sloan Farrington	5223
1960	1	URS	Timir Pinegin / Fyodor Shutkov	7619
	2	POR	José Quina / Mário Quina	6665
	3	**USA**	**William Parks / Robert Halperin**	**6269**
1964	1	BAH	Durward Knowles / C. Cecil Cooke	5664
	2	**USA**	**Richard Stearns / Lynn Williams**	**5585**
	3	SWE	Pelle Pettersson / Holger Sundström	5527
1968	**1**	**USA**	**Lowell North / Peter Barrett**	**14.4**
	2	NOR	Peder Lunde / Per Olav Wiken	43.7
	3	ITA	Franco Cavallo / Camilo Gargano	44.7
1972	1	AUS	David Forbes / John Anderson	28.1
	2	SWE	Pelle Pettersson / Stellan Westerdahl	44.0
	3	GER	Wilhelm Kuhweide / Karsten Meyer	44.4
	10	**USA**	**Alan Holt / Richard Gates**	**89.0**
1976 (not held)				
1980	1	URS	Valentin Mankin / Aleksandr Muzychenko	24.7
	2	AUT	Hubert Raudaschi / Karl Ferstl	31.7
	3	ITA	Giorgio Gorla / Alfio Peraboni	36.1
1984	**1**	**USA**	**William E. Buchan / Stephen Erickson**	**29.7**
	2	GER	Joachim Griese / Michael Marcour	41.4
	3	ITA	Giorgio Gorla / Alfio Peraboni	43.5
1988	1	GBR	Michael McIntyre / Philip Bryn Vaile	45.70
	2	**USA**	**Mark Reynolds / Hal Haenel**	**48.00**
	3	BRA	Torben Grael / Nelson Falcao	50.00
1992	**1**	**USA**	**Mark Reynolds / Hal Haenel**	**31.40**
	2	NZL	Roderick Davis / Donald John Cowie	58.40
	3	CAN	D. MacDonald / Eric Jespersen	62.70

SOLING

YEAR	RANK	CTRY	ATHLETES	NET PTS.
1896-1968		(not held)		
1972	**1**	**USA**	**Harry Melges / William Bentsen / William Allen**	**8.7**
	2	SWE		31.7
	3	CAN		47.1
1976	1	DEN		46.7
	2	**USA**	**John Kolius / Walter Glasgow / Richard Hoepfner**	**47.4**
	3	GDR		47.4
1980	1	DEN		23.0
	2	URS		30.4
	3	GRE		31.1
1984	**1**	**USA**	**Robert Haines / Edward Trevelyan / Roderick Davis**	**33.7**
	2	BRA		43.4
	3	CAN		49.7
1988	1	GDR		11.70
	2	**USA**	**John Kostecki / William Baylis / Robert Billingham**	**14.00**
	3	DEN		52.70
1992	1	DEN		
	2	**USA**	**Kevin Mahaney / Jim Brady / Doug Kern**	
	3	GBR		

WOMEN'S 470

YEAR	RANK	CTRY	ATHLETES	NET PTS.
1896-1984		(not held)		
1988	**1**	**USA**	**Allison Jolly / Lynne Jewell**	**26.70**
	2	SWE	Marit Soderstrom / Birgitta Bengtsson	40.00
	3	URS	Larissa Moskalenko / Irina Tchounikhovskai	45.40
1992	1	ESP	Theresa Zabell / Patricia Guerra	29.70
	3	NZL	Leslie Jean Egnot / Janet Shearer	36.70
	3	**USA**	**Jennifer Isler / Pamela Healy**	**40.70**

WOMEN'S LECHNER

YEAR	RANK	CTRY	ATHLETE	NET PTS.
1896-1988		(not held)		
1992	1	NZL	Barbara Anne Kendall	47.80
	2	CHN	Zhang Xiaodong	65.80
	3	NED	Dorien De Vries	68.70
	5	**USA**	**Lanee Butler**	**95.70**

WOMEN'S EUROPE

YEAR	RANK	CTRY	ATHLETE	NET PTS.
1896-1988		(not held)		
1992	1	NOR	Linda Andersen	48.70
	2	ESP	Natalia Via Dufresne	57.40
	3	**USA**	**Julia Trotman**	**62.70**

BIBLIOGRAPHY

The Complete Book of the Olympics. David Wallechinsky, New York: Penguin Books, 1988.

The Olympic Games 1980. Lord Killanin and John Rodda, eds., New York: Collier Books, 1979.

An Illustrated History of the Olympics. Dick Schaap, New York: Knopf, 1975.

The Olympic Story. Associated Press, New York: Grolier, 1979.

The Olympic Challenge 1984. Bill Toomey and Barry King, Costa Mesa, CA: HDL Publishing, 1984.

The Olympic Challenge 1988. Bill Toomey and Barry King, Costa Mesa, CA: HDL Publishing, 1988.

Trials & Triumphs. Lee Benson and Doug Robinson, Salt Lake City: Deseret Book Co, 1992.

100 Years of the Olympic Games of Modern Times. International Olympic Committee, Lausanne, 1992.

Guinness Book of Olympic Records. Greenberg, Stan, ed., New York: Bantam Books, 1992.

The Guinness Book of Olympic Facts & Feats. Greenberg, Stan, ed., Middlesex, England: Guinness Superlatives Limited, 1983.

King Wally's Olympic Fun Fact Book. Michael Walczewski, New York: Dell Publishing, 1988.

Shooting for the Gold. Walter Iooss, Jr. and Dave Anderson, Ottawa, IL: Jameson Books, 1984.

XXVth Olympic Games IAAF handbook. Butler, Mark, ed., IAAF Press and Information Dept, London, 1992.

The Olympics 1960. John V. Brombach, New York: Ballantine Books, 1960.

U.S. Olympic Team Media Guide. U.S. Olympic Committee, Colorado Springs, 1988.

The Olympics, A History of the Games. William Oscar Johnson, The Time Inc. Magazine Company, 1992.

The Olympic Games B.C. 776-A.D. 1896. Published with the sanction and under the patronage of the Central Committee in Athens, presided over by His Royal Highness the Crown Prince Constantine/Les Jeux Olympiques de 1896.

Concours Internationaux d'Exercices Physiques et de Sport: Rapports publies sous la Direction de M.D. Merillon, Delegue General. 2 vols. Paris: Imprimerie National, 1901 (Vol. 1) and 1902 (Vol. 2).

Spalding's Official Athletic Almanac for 1905: Special Olympic Number, Containing the Official Report of the Olympic Games of 1904. Spalding's Athletic Library, James Edward Sullivan, ed., New York: American Sports Publishing, 1905.

Leukoma ton en Athenais B' Diethnon Olympiakon Agonon 1906/Jeux Olympiques Internationaux 1906. Album. Athenes. Pan. S. Savvidis, ed., Athens: Estia K. Maisner and N. Kargadouris, 1907. GREEK/FRENCH

The Fourth Olympiad: Being the Official Report of the Olympic Games of 1908 Celebrated in London under the Patronage of His Most Gracious King Edward VII and By the Sanction of the International Olympic Committee. British OC, Theodore Andrea Cook, ed., London: author, 1909.

The Official Report of the Olympic Games of Stockholm 1912. COJO Stockholm 1912, Erik Vergvall, ed., Trans. Evart Adams Ray, Stockholm: Wahlstrom & Wilstrand, 1913. ENGLISH

Rapport officiel des Jeux de la VIIeme Olympiade, Anvers 1920. COJO Antwerp 1920, Alfred Verdyck, ed., Brussels: author, 19___.

Les Jeux de la VIIIeme Olympiade Paris 1924, Rapport officiel du Comite Olympique Francais. French OC, M.A. Ave, ed., Paris: Librairie de France, nd. FRENCH

The Ninth Olympiad: Being the Official Report of the Olympic Games of 1928 Celebrated at Amsterdam issued by the Netherlands Olympic Committee. Netherlands OC, George van Rossem, ed., Trans. Sydney W. Fleming, Amsterdam: J.H. de Bussy, 1930. ENGLISH

The Games of the Xth Olympiad, Los Angeles, 1932: Official Report. COJO Los Angeles 1932, Frederick Granger Browne, ed., Los Angeles: author, 1933. ENGLISH

The XIth Olympic Games, Berlin, 1936: Official Report. 2 vols. COJO Berlin 1936, Berlin: W. Limpert, 1937.

The Official Report of the Organizing Committee for the XIV Olympiad. COJO London 1948, Lord Burghley, ed., London: Corquodale & Co., Ltd., 1951.

The Official Report of the Organizing Committee for the Games of the XV Olympiad Helsinki 1952. COJO Helsinki, 1952, Sulo Lolkka, eds., Trans. Alex Matson, Porvoo, FIN: Werner Soderstrom Osakeyhtio, 1955. ENGLISH

The Official Report of the Organizing Committee for the Games of the XVI Olympiad, Melbourne, 1956. COJO Melbourne 1956, E.A. Doyle, ed., Melbourne: W. M. Houston, Govt. Printer, 1958. ENGLISH

Ryttarolympiaden Stockholm 1956. The Equestrian Games of the XVIth Olympiad. A Retrospective Survey in Text and Pictures. COJO Stockholm 1956, Stockholm: author, 1959. SWEDISH/ENGLISH

The Games of the XVII Olympiad, Rome, 1960: Official Report. 2 vols. COJO Rome 1960, Romolo Giacomini, eds., Trans. Edwin Byatt. Rome: author, 1960. ENGLISH

The Games of the XVIII Olympiad, Tokyo, 1964: The Official Report of the Organizing Committee. COJO Tokyo 1964, Tokyo: author, 1964. ENGLISH

Mexico 1968. (Memoire Officiel des Jeux de la XIX Olympiade. Commemorative volumes of the Games of the XIX Olympiad). 4 vols, COJO Mexico 1968, Beatrice Trueblood, ed. Vol. 1 - Le Pays. The Country. Vol. 2 - L'organisation. The organization. Vol. 3 - Les jeux sportifs. The Games. Vol. 4 - L'Olympiade culturelle. The Cultural Olympiade.

The Games: The Official Report of the Organizing Committee for the Games of the XXth Olympiad Munich 1972. 3 vols, COJO Munich 1972, Liselott Diem and Ernst Kooesel, eds. Vol. 1 - The Organization. Vol. 2 - The Construction. Vol. 3 - Die Wettkampfe. ENGLISH

Games of the XXI Olympiad, Montreal, 1976: Official Report. 3 vols, COJO Montreal 1976, Roger Rousseau, ed., Montreal: author, c1978. ENGLISH

Games of the XXIInd Olympiad. 3 vols. COJO Moscow 1980, Moscow: Fizkul'tura i sport, 1981. ENGLISH

Official report of the Games of the XXIIIrd Olympiad, Los Angeles, 1984. Los Angeles Olympic Organizing Committee, c1985.

Official report: Games of the XXIVth Olympiad, Seoul 1988. Seoul Olympic Organizing Committee, Seoul: Korea Textbook Co., 1989.

INDEX

NATIONAL OLYMPIC COMMITTEES

AS OF NOVEMBER 1993, THE 194 RECOG-NIZED NOCs AND THEIR RESPECTIVE IOC COUNTRY/TERRITORY ABBREVIATIONS ARE:

AFG	AFGHANISTAN
AHO	NETHERLANDS ANTILLES (DUTCH WEST INDIES)
ALB	ALBANIA
ALG	ALGERIA
AND	ANDORRA
ANG	ANGOLA
ANT	ANTIGUA
ARG	ARGENTINA
ARM	ARMENIA
ARU	ARUBA
ASA	AMERICAN SAMOA
AUS	AUSTRALIA
AUT	AUSTRIA
AZE	AZERBAIJAN
BAH	BAHAMAS
BAN	BANGLADESH
BAR	BARBADOS
BEL	BELGIUM
BEN	BENIN
BER	BERMUDA
BHU	BHUTAN
BIZ	BELIZE
BLS	BELARUS
BOL	BOLIVIA
BOT	BOTSWANA
BRA	BRAZIL
BRN	BAHRAIN
BRU	BRUNEI
BSH	BOSNIA-HERZEGOVINA
BUL	BULGARIA
BUR	BURKINA FASO
CAF	CENTRAL AFRICAN REPUBLIC
CAN	CANADA
CAY	CAYMAN ISLANDS
CGO	PEOPLE'S REPUBLIC OF CONGO
CHA	CHAD
CHI	CHILE
CHN	PEOPLE'S REPUBLIC OF CHINA
CIV	IVORY COAST
CMR	CAMEROON
COK	COOK ISLANDS
COL	COLOMBIA
CRC	COSTA RICA
CRO	CROATIA
CUB	CUBA
CYP	CYPRUS
DEN	DENMARK
DJI	DJIBOUTI
DOM	DOMINICAN REPUBLIC
ECU	ECUADOR
EGY	ARAB REPUBLIC OF EGYPT
ESA	EL SALVADOR
ESP	SPAIN
EST	ESTONIA
ETH	ETHIOPIA
FIJ	FIJI
FIN	FINLAND
FRA	FRANCE
GAB	GABON
GAM	GAMBIA
GBR	GREAT BRITAIN
GEO	GEORGIA
GEQ	EQUATORIAL GUINEA
GER	GERMANY
GHA	GHANA
GRE	GREECE
GRN	GRENADA

GUA	GUATEMALA
GUI	GUINEA
GUM	GUAM
GUY	GUYANA
HAI	HAITI
HKG	HONG KONG
HON	HONDURAS
HUN	HUNGARY
INA	INDONESIA
IND	INDIA
IRL	IRELAND
IRI	ISLAMIC REPUBLIC OF IRAN
IRQ	IRAQ
ISL	ICELAND
ISR	ISRAEL
ISV	VIRGIN ISLANDS
ITA	ITALY
IVB	BRITISH VIRGIN ISLANDS
JAM	JAMAICA
JOR	JORDAN
JPN	JAPAN
KEN	KENYA
KGZ	KYRGHYZSTAN
KOR	KOREA (SOUTH)
KSA	KINGDOM OF SAUDI ARABIA
KUW	KUWAIT
KZK	KAZAKHSTAN
LAO	LAOS
LAT	LATVIA
LBA	LIBYA
LBR	LIBERIA
LES	LESOTHO
LIB	LEBANON
LIE	LIECHTENSTEIN
LIT	LITHUANIA
LUX	LUXEMBOURG
MAD	MADAGASCAR
MAR	MOROCCO
MAS	MALAYSIA
MAW	MALAWI
MDV	MALDIVES
MEX	MEXICO
MGL	MONGOLIA
MLD	MOLDOVA
MLI	MALI
MLT	MALTA
MON	MONACO
MOZ	MOZAMBIQUE
MRI	MAURITIUS
MTN	MAURITANIA
MYA	UNION OF MYANMAR (FORMERLY BURMA)
NAM	NAMIBIA
NCA	NICARAGUA
NED	THE NETHERLANDS
NEP	NEPAL
NIG	NIGER
NGR	NIGERIA
NOR	NORWAY
NZL	NEW ZEALAND
OMA	OMAN
PAK	PAKISTAN
PAN	PANAMA
PAR	PARAGUAY
PER	PERU
PHI	PHILIPPINES
PNG	PAPUA-NEW GUINEA
POL	POLAND
POR	PORTUGAL
PRK	DEMOCRATIC PEOPLE'S REPUBLIC OF KOREA
PUR	PUERTO RICO
QAT	QATAR
ROM	ROMANIA
RSA	SOUTH AFRICA
RUS	RUSSIA

RWA	RWANDA
SAM	WESTERN SAMOA
SEN	SENEGAL
SEY	SEYCHELLES
SIN	SINGAPORE
SLE	SIERRA LEONE
SLO	SLOVENIA
SMR	SAN MARINO
SOL	SOLOMON ISLANDS
SOM	SOMALIA
SRI	SRI LANKA
SUD	SUDAN
SUI	SWITZERLAND
SUR	SURINAM
SVK	SLOVAKIA
SWE	SWEDEN
SWZ	SWAZILAND
SYR	SYRIA
TAN	TANZANIA
TCH	CZECH REPUBLIC
TGA	TONGA
THA	THAILAND
TJK	TADJIKISTAN
TKM	TURKMENISTAN
TOG	TOGO
TPE	CHINESE TAIPEI
TRI	TRINIDAD & TOBAGO
TUN	TUNISIA
TUR	TURKEY
UAE	UNITED ARAB EMIRATES
UGA	UGANDA
UKR	UKRAINE
URU	URUGUAY
USA	UNITED STATES OF AMERICA
UZB	UZBEKISTAN
VAN	VANUATU
VEN	VENEZUELA
VIE	VIETNAM
VIN	ST. VINCENT AND THE GRENADINES
YEM	YEMEN
YUG	YUGOSLAVIA
ZAI	ZAIRE
ZAM	ZAMBIA
ZIM	ZIMBABWE

NATIONAL OLYMPIC COMMITTEES WITH NO IOC COUNTRY ABBREVIATION (AS OF NOVEMBER 1993):

BURUNDI
CAPE VERDE
COMOROS ISLANDS
DOMINICA
MACEDONIA
PALESTINE
ST. KITTS AND NEVIS
ST. LUCIA
SAO TOME

NOTE:	
EUN	UNIFIED TEAM (1992)
IOP	INDEPENDENT OLYMPIC PARTICIPANTS (1992)
GDR	FORMER GERMAN DEMOCRATIC REPUBLIC (1952-1988)
URS	FORMER UNION OF SOVIET SOCIALIST REPUBLICS (1952-1988)